Edited by Jacqueline Levitin,
Judith Plessis, and Valerie Raoul

Women Filmmakers: Refocusing

Routledge
New York and London

Published in 2003 by
Routledge
29 West 35th Street
New York, NY 10001
www.routledge-ny.com

Published in Great Britain by
Routledge
11 New Fetter Lane
London EC4P 4EE
www.routledge.co.uk

Published by arrangement with UBC Press.

Routledge is an imprint of the Taylor & Francis Group.

10 9 8 7 6 5 4 3 2 1

Cataloging-in-Publication Data is available from the Library of Congress

Contents

Part 8: Revisioning Gender and Diversity in Canada

Illustrations

Acknowledgments

The editors of *Women Filmmakers: Refocusing* would like to thank all the contributors who have made this book a unique collection. Our collaborative project has been published with financial help from the Aid to Scholarly Publications Programme. We are grateful to the *Georgia Straight* and *Kinesis* for permission to use previously published articles. This volume would not have been possible without the generous support of the UBC Centre for Research in Women's Studies and Gender Relations, the UBC Writing Centre, UBC Continuing Studies, and Simon Fraser University. We are especially grateful to Vera Lowe of the UBC Writing Centre for her invaluable organizational and editing skills. In addition, we wish to thank UBC students Tannis Morgan, who helped us compile the initial version of the manuscript, and Leah Szabo, who assisted during the early stages of the project, as well as several other UBC and SFU Work Study students who transcribed interviews, panel discussions, and master classes. We would also like to acknowledge Alison McIlwaine and Gaik Cheng Khoo for their excellent work on the extensive bibliography and filmography. Finally, we thank Jean Wilson of UBC Press for her wise counsel and Darcy Cullen for her efficiency in keeping things on track, as well as Joanne Richardson for her expert copyediting.

Women Filmmakers

Introduction

Refocusing:
Talking about (and with) Women Filmmakers

Jacqueline Levitin, Judith Plessis, and Valerie Raoul

The Origins of This Book

When we first came together in 1998, we realized that we shared a desire to refocus on women's filmmaking – to take stock of what has occurred, what has been gained, and what directions feminist film theory has taken since the early 1970s. At that time, a lost history of women's filmmaking resurfaced in film festivals and the first feminist film journals appeared, provoking excitement and debate. We wanted to recreate that initial excitement by organizing an international women's film conference, along with a women's film festival. This book is the final stage in a series of projects that arose from our first meeting, including the events entitled "Women Filmmakers: Refocusing," held in Vancouver in March 1999.[1] We designed the conference-festival to cross several boundaries – between disciplines, between countries, between theory and practice, between universities and the community, and between those who make films and those who see and write about them. Our own backgrounds have been conducive to achieving this dialogue: Jacqueline Levitin is a filmmaker and scholar attached to the School for the Contemporary Arts and the Women's Studies Department at Simon Fraser University (SFU) in Vancouver; Judith Plessis is the Director of Language Programs in Continuing Studies at the University of British Columbia (UBC) in Vancouver, and her doctorate in Comparative Literature focused on women filmmakers; Valerie Raoul is in French and Women's Studies at UBC, and she has an interest in feminist film theory and francophone filmmakers. We saw this as a unique opportunity to pool the resources of our two local universities in order to bring together both local and international filmmakers and academics. We were delighted by the interest our initial call for papers aroused and the quality of the many proposals we received – any fears we had beforehand that the enthusiasm might no longer be there were soon allayed.

The papers accepted ranged over time and space, covering various issues related to women making films and films by women in many parts of the world. With the support of local consulates and cultural associations, such as the Goethe Institute,[2] and from local filmmakers through Women in Film and Video Vancouver, the original idea for a conference expanded into two weekends of presentations, one weekend at each university. Thanks to government and university funding,[3] we were able to invite several well-known directors to attend and also some prominent academic specialists in women and film from the United States, France, and the United Kingdom as well as Canada. Collaboration and support from the Pacific Cinémathèque in downtown Vancouver allowed us, over a two-week period before and between the two weekends of presentations, to screen films by women not readily available in Vancouver. The result was a series of events that attracted many film enthusiasts and feminists from all walks of life. However, the division of the conference into two parts, while enabling more people to participate, also posed the problem of how to divide the topics.

Women Filmmakers: A Dual Focus

Our solution was to focus on Europe, film history, and feature films for the first weekend (at SFU's downtown campus) and on postcolonial contexts and documentaries for the second (at UBC). Although this distinction enabled us to separate the papers, panels, interviews, and master classes into two programs, there was still considerable overlap between the two weekends. For example, the importance of immigrant, or second-generation, filmmakers in Europe is as much an aspect of the postcolonial context as is the expansion of filmmaking in countries that were formerly colonies. Several of the directors who agreed to attend and to be interviewed, including Deepa Mehta and Pratibha Parmar, have roots in both the East and the West. Furthermore, issues related to technology, funding, and distribution sprang up in all the sessions. The presence of Ann Kaplan, a specialist in film history, theory, and postcolonial contexts, was invaluable in enabling us to connect the two weekends. Patricia Plattner, who represented Switzerland at the first weekend, also contributed to the second weekend through the screening of her film *Made in India*.

The fact that the events took place in British Columbia added a further dimension to the discussion, since our province has a multi-ethnic population, including a rich First Nations culture. "Central Canada" sometimes still seems to treat British Columbia like a colonial outpost. While predominantly Western, Vancouver is located between North America and Asia, both geographically and culturally, and the city has a strong Asian presence. Canada's other official language and culture, French, seems less relevant here. However, since all three of us have connections to Quebec or France, we wanted to emphasize the significance of the fact that Canada produces films in both languages. The conference revealed some fruitful connections between British Columbia and Quebec, and the Canada Council provided a subsidy that enabled us to benefit from the presence of Quebec documentary filmmaker Nicole Giguère. Swiss filmmaker Patricia Plattner and French academic and film critic Caroline Eades provided a European francophone perspective, and several papers were presented in French and translated for this volume.[4] Cultural diversity was broadened much further by representation from British Columbia's First Nations community, which has a number of strong emerging women filmmakers, and by filmmakers of Asian origin who make films both here and abroad.

Being involved in the North American Free Trade Agreement with the United States and Mexico, Canadians are as aware as anyone of the worldwide domination exercised by the American commercial film industry. Vancouver is sometimes referred to as "Hollywood North" because of the number of American movies filmed here. The relative absence of material on American filmmakers in this volume reflects an initial decision to prioritize women directors working elsewhere in the world. This focus is introduced through Ann Kaplan's chapter on the history of women in film, which provides background on developments in Europe and Hollywood. Kaplan also comments on filmmaking by minority women in the United States, reminding us that the United States is itself a "postcolonial" context. Her chapter reflects the shift in emphasis from the centre to the margins in her own extensive work on women in film, which is symptomatic of the evolution of women's participation in filmmaking. Our focus on Canada rather than the United States also enables us to maintain a balance between makers of feature films and makers of documentaries. Again, while the second weekend included more discussion of documentary filmmaking than did the first, it must be remembered that many of the directors featured in this book make both types of film, and, in many cases, their choices are governed by practical considerations rather than personal preferences.

The conference incorporated eye-opening discussions of funding for film production, commercial distribution, and technical advice to fellow filmmakers, as well as theoretical debates about the role of women filmmakers in relation to feminism, politics, and mainstream culture. When the time came to solicit submissions for this book, we realized that our original dual focus did not do justice to the crosscutting debates that continued well after the conference. Consequently, we have regrouped topics, while attempting to maintain the combination of academic discourse and practical experience that enlivened the presentations. Papers were selected and, for the most part, have been extensively reworked to focus upon the themes chosen for the various parts of this book. Material has also been added to complement those papers we have chosen to include. Ann Kaplan provided an expanded version of her Vancouver Institute presentation on the evolution of women's participation in film production. This overview leads into a collection of material grouped around issues rather than geographical areas or time frames. In keeping with our original objectives, a unique feature of this collection is the inclusion of informal accounts of personal experiences from several remarkable filmmakers who participated in public interviews and gave master classes. The result reflects the level of excitement generated, while producing a coherent synthesis of the main debates that emerged over two weeks of animated discussions among people from across the world.

Conversations with Directors, Analysis of Films, and Theoretical Frameworks

The book is divided into eight parts, each representing a transition from one focus to the next. In Part 1, Kaplan's historical survey and the chapters by Angela Martin, Donia Mounsef, and Catherine Fowler provide a historical and theoretical basis for the discussion that follows in subsequent parts. Kaplan's insights here, based on her work on film and the "imperial gaze," illuminate later sections on minority filmmakers. Angela Martin dissects the terms "auteur" and "authorship" and questions how they have been employed in discussions of women filmmakers. Mounsef focuses on film history in France, looking at the relation of women filmmakers to experimental, avant-garde movements that go beyond film. Fowler discusses the work of several prominent directors and the changes that have occurred in their films, in relation to the evolution of feminist film theory.

Part 2 looks more closely at several European filmmakers who may be considered to be auteures.[5] German director Helma Sanders Brahms (introduced by Steven Taubeneck) made an exceptional contribution to the first weekend, not only answering questions at film screenings, but also generously sharing her personal experience as a filmmaker in Europe. We have juxtaposed her contributions with an interview given by Margarethe von Trotta a year before at the University of Victoria, along with Siew Jin Ooi's detailed analysis of one of von Trotta's earlier films. The careers of these two well-known writer-directors traverse the contemporary history of women's filmmaking. Sanders Brahms talks about the obstacles she has faced (and still faces), not only due to her gender in the male-dominated world of film production, but also due to the type of films she chooses to make. Von Trotta lucidly discusses the interaction of politics and aesthetics in her films. The chapters by B. Amarillis Lugo de Fabritz and Corinn Columpar analyze continuity and change in the work of two other major directors who are both auteures, Agnieszka Holland and Sally Potter. The work of the filmmakers discussed in Part 2 relates to the issues of continuity and change raised by Catherine Fowler in Part 1.

Part 3 turns away from filmmaking careers and authorship to concentrate on the ways in which the filmmakers' choice of film genre affects the production and reception of their films. Retaining a focus on Europe, four chapters address the work of some women filmmakers who have gained access to commercial markets by using popular film genres. Kathryn Barnwell and Marni Stanley focus on how Doris Dörrie uses comedy to convey a somewhat ambivalent critical message in *Nobody Loves Me,* a film that raises issues of sexual orientation and race relations. Brigitte Rollet and Caroline Eades survey how a younger generation of women filmmakers in France has successfully appropriated male models such as the road movie. Josette Déléas concludes this part with a discussion of Lina Wertmüller's original use of the grotesque, discerning the gender critique beneath Wertmüller's seemingly misogynist veneer. Today, few would condemn women filmmakers' attempts to succeed in the mainstream. The question for the feminist critic now is rather: *How* can success be achieved? And what is the balance sheet of gains and losses in achieving popularity? The examples here demonstrate that women are finding creative ways of succeeding – and transforming cinema in the process. In their discussion of women's contributions to the mainstream, all the papers in this section highlight the particularities of the gender-race-class dynamic in their corner of Europe, bringing out the diversity of locations in relation to mainstream culture in general, as well as to commercial cinema.

The choice of whether or not to join the mainstream is frequently governed by the need for access to resources to make films at all, a constant preoccupation of both the filmmakers interviewed and the film students who participated in the conference. Part 4 concentrates on issues related to the conditions of production, including training, funding, and distribution. These have changed radically for filmmakers from Eastern Europe, many of whom have moved to the West and now make films in English, as is illustrated in the case of Agnieszka Holland. Janina Falkowska and Ute Lischke both provide information on the effects of political upheaval on filmmaking in Poland and in the former East Germany. Elsewhere, the possibilities of filmmaking are limited by having to work in a small country, such as Switzerland, with a limited public that is itself divided into several language groups. Suzanne Buchan and Swiss filmmaker Patricia Plattner discuss government funding and its limits, the problems associated with working in the shadow of a dominant culture, and the need to gain experience through associating with filmmakers from and in other countries.

Part 4 concludes with excerpts from two lively panel discussions, each with four participants. In the first, which deals with feature films, Canadian filmmaker Anne Wheeler and Helma Sanders Brahms share their experiences of mentoring younger women filmmakers, while Patricia Plattner and Caroline Eades comment on the problems faced by emerging young directors in a francophone context. The second panel conveys the animated debate that took place among several Canadian documentary filmmakers: Nicole Giguère from Quebec, Brenda Longfellow from Ontario, Loretta Todd, a First Nations filmmaker living in British Columbia, and Aerlyn Weissman, now of British Columbia, who has made documentaries with a lesbian focus. These sessions provided filmmakers with some practical and personal lessons, and it gave others an unusual opportunity to eavesdrop on conversations that revealed the daunting but exhilarating situations women filmmakers constantly encounter.

Border Crossings

The next three parts of the book focus on filmmaking by women in non-Western contexts and the representation of minority women in countries with a dominant culture. Part 5 looks beyond Europe and North America to discuss women filmmakers in Kenya (Beatrice Wanjiku Mikora), Malaysia (Gaik Cheng Khoo), Argentina (Rita de Grandis and three graduate students from UBC and SFU), Cuba (Susan Lord), and China (Yue-Qing Yang). While film cultures are still barely emerging in some of these contexts, in others they are already well established. As was the case for some of the European filmmakers, the choice of what language to use in a film is often a central issue. The audience to be addressed affects both resources for production and the distribution and reception of the films. Representation of women in these films by women draws attention to the differences as well as to the commonalities of women's experiences around the world. In many cases, the filmmaker's perspective is informed by training or living abroad, as in the case of director Yue-Qing Yang, who lives in Vancouver but continues to make films in her native China. Her films deal with topics that she would probably not address if she made them in Vancouver. The chapter on her experience of making *Nu Shu: A Hidden Language of Women in China* is reprinted from the Vancouver-based feminist newspaper *Kinesis*.

Yue-Qing Yang was not the only filmmaker to participate in the conference whose life and work cross continental divides. Part 6 brings together the experiences of four filmmakers, all present at the conference, who have different connections to India. Deepa Mehta resides in Canada and makes feature films in India, where her work has provoked violent controversy. Pratibha Parmar is of Indian/East African background but has spent most of her life in England. She has made controversial documentary and experimental films dealing with topics such as lesbianism in India and racism in Britain. Raman Mann and Patricia Plattner have both made documentaries about women's struggles for empowerment in India, but with very different resources and results. Raman Mann lives in Delhi and, primarily with government funding, makes educational films. She has travelled to Europe and Canada to receive awards and to search for financing for projects that are addressed primarily to Indian women and that have an immediate impact in India. Patricia Plattner, in contrast, went to India with an all-woman European crew to make a feature-length film of great beauty. Her aim was to raise awareness of Indian women workers' successful organizng by address-ing women in the West and other parts of the world.

Pratibha Parmar's films address issues related to minority women in Eng-land. Patricia Plattner's film *Piano Panier* deals with communication between "majority" and "minority" women: a Swiss woman living in Geneva visits the family of her Portuguese immigrant friend only to discover cultural alienation in reverse. These issues of border-crossings and cross-cultural communication are central in films by minority women filmmakers and are a major focus throughout these discussions. Increasingly, gender can-not be considered apart from race and class. For this reason, in Part 7 we have grouped together chapters by Carrie Tarr (on the representation of women of North African origin in French films), Lesley Marx (on the work of White South African filmmaker Katinka Heyns), and Elena Feder (on films by Latina women in Canada). We have also included an interview with Jewish Mexican filmmaker Guita Schyfter (raised in Costa Rica), who dis-cusses the depiction of divisions within the Jewish community in Mexico in her film *Like a Bride*.

Changing Perspectives in Canada

While several Canadian filmmakers are already represented in the earlier sections, Part 8 takes a closer look at various dimensions of women's filmmaking in this country. Tribute is paid to the enormous contribution of documentary and feature filmmakers in Quebec in complementary overviews by Nicole Giguère and Jocelyne Denault. Another francophone filmmaker, Carole Ducharme (originally from Quebec and now living in British Co-lumbia) contributes an interview about making *Straight from the Suburbs*, a short and highly original film that demonstrates the effective use of parody to challenge homophobia. The introduction to First Nations women film-makers in British Columbia that follows begins with an article by journalist Ken Eisner (reprinted from the Vancouver cultural newspaper the *Georgia Straight*). It deals, in part, with the work of Loretta Todd, who also contrib-uted to the panel discussion in Part 4. Michelle La Flamme's chapter situ-ates the work of some emerging Aboriginal women filmmakers in British Columbia in the context of postcolonial theory and the struggle for recog-nition of First Nations' identities. Such topics were among those treated in many National Film Board films made at Studio D, the women's studio in Montreal that no longer exists, to the regret of many. Diane Burgess ad-dresses the issues raised by its demise in terms of (1) how best to support feminist filmmaking and (2) how gender frequently disappears as a cat-egory. Whether or not the disappearance of gender is desirable is one of the central questions raised by Ann Kaplan at the beginning of this book. In the concluding chapter camerawoman Zoe Dirse tackles tough issues when she asks, Does it still make any difference when it is a woman wielding the camera? How does the feminist critique of the male "gaze" hold up, when examined by a practising camerawoman?

Refocusing the Kaleidoscope

The answers to these questions connect concerns about representation and appropriation, voice and gaze, ideas and their realization. The panorama that emerges from this book reveals different trends, either towards or away from the mainstream, and varying levels of commitment to or rejection of the label "feminist." Whatever their position in this regard, none of the directors included here denies that being a woman has made a difference to her career as a filmmaker. While there are far more women making films today than there were before, the numbers can be deceiving. The battle-fields of the film industry are still strewn with the stifled ambitions of women directors who only manage to produce one film. Ideological issues around what and how to film are still all too frequently eclipsed by material questions of funding and survival. Initiatives that, two decades ago, targeted women in order to enable them to compete with men, have largely disappeared. Today's multichannel universe can seem both rich in opportunity and poor in realization. Both female and male filmmakers find themselves scaling down the scope and vision of their projects when presented with the alternative of making no film at all.

Whether a feminist message, or even a "woman's point of view," can still be conveyed without falling into stereotypes is debatable. Technological developments may again favour women filmmakers, as they did in the 1970s, now that new advances make digital equipment more portable and less expensive. Women still enjoy the possibilities of the margins and experimental filmmaking. Problems of distribution remain, however, as we discovered – literally to our cost – when it came to organizing screenings. Many of the films by filmmakers represented in this volume are difficult to obtain, and the small number of viewers able to see them contributes to the lack of attention given to them in film criticism.

For that reason alone we are delighted to present this book, which will provide many more people with the opportunity to hear directly the stories of women who are actually making films and have a wealth of professional expertise in various aspects of film production. This focus on the perspectives of women directors departs from most studies, where the films are the main object of analysis. The directors remind us that theorists and critics must not forget that practical issues and technical innovations determine aesthetic effects and are also behind the successful delivery of a political message. The range of films that women are making across the world is extraordinary. As recently as the 1970s it seemed possible for a film festival to cover all aspects of women's filmmaking. That is certainly no longer the case, even for one category of films. Similarly, in the 1970s the books devoted to women in film could be counted on one hand, whereas today they fill many library shelves. The chapters presented here provide a rich sampling of the wealth of thought and experience that is now available on this topic; however, they also demonstrate that women filmmakers still have difficulty making their work known.

With this in mind, we have, wherever possible, included information on how to gain access to materials on both film and video. In some instances, two dates are given for a particular film. The earlier of the two usually refers to the year production ended while the other refers to the year the film was released. However, discrepancies can also result from the fact that films are often released in different countries at different times. The bibliography collects references of general interest from all the chapters and includes works published since they were written. This book will, we believe, be useful in both Women's Studies and Film Studies courses; it will also be of interest to theorists, practitioners, and film enthusiasts of both sexes. We hope it will introduce lesser known filmmakers to a wider public as well as help in reassessing the work of some well established women directors. Our aim is to break down the barriers between women who make films and those who see them, between Film Studies and Women's Studies, and between theory and practice. But above all, we believe these essays and interviews demonstrate the excitement generated by an amazing wealth and variety of films by women and are a tribute to their achievements.

Notes

1 Sneja Gunew (Women's Studies and English, UBC) was also part of the original conference organizing committee, and its practical success was largely due to the efforts of Jo Hinchliffe, the administrative assistant at the UBC Centre for Research in Women's Studies and Gender Relations. The production of this book also owes much to the generous support of UBC Continuing Studies through the UBC Writing Centre.
2 The French and Mexican Consulates both paid for visiting speakers to attend, as did the Goethe Institute and the Swiss organization Pro Helvetia. The French Consulate and Alliance française also contributed.
3 The conference was funded by the Social Science and Humanities Research Council of Canada, and we also received grants from UBC and SFU. Ann Kaplan was at UBC for ten days, funded through the Cecil and Ida Green Visiting Professor Programme; she returned under the same program to give a course at UBC in January 2001. Students from both UBC and SFU were funded through a provincial work-study program to assist with transcribing audio- and videotapes, as well as to help prepare the manuscript.
4 The chapters by Déléas, Eades, Mounsef, and Rollet were originally written and presented in French and were translated for this book. The section by Denault was added after the conference.
5 "Auteure" with an "e" is used in Quebec. We are adopting this spelling as a way of differentiating women's output, bearing in mind Angela Martin's discussion of "auteurship."

Women Filmmakers:
Refocusing History and Theory

Part 1 begins with an overview by Ann Kaplan of the history of women in filmmaking – a topic her work has addressed from several perspectives over a number of years. She begins with the first phase (1906-30) and with pioneers like Alice Guy Blaché in Paris and Lois Weber in Hollywood. It is in the second "classical" phase (1930-60) that American cinema becomes dominant and women are largely silenced, apart from exceptions like Dorothy Arzner and Ida Lupino. The third phase (1960-90) saw the emergence of a number of successful women directors in both North America and Europe, accompanied by an increasingly impressive body of feminist film criticism and theory. The fourth phase, which began in 1990, has been characterized by a variety of films made by minority women in Europe and North America, as well as by women in other parts of the world. The films of this latter phase place a new focus on old questions, such as what difference it may make if a woman is behind the camera, and whether gender has now become eclipsed by concerns about race, class, and other hierarchies. This issue becomes central in later parts of this book.

Angela Martin approaches the history of women in film from a different angle as she examines the reasons why prominent women filmmakers may not be considered "auteur(e)s." In addition to problems of recognition dependent on distribution, the individual genius model associated with the term "auteur" is conflated with virility and excludes by its definition some aspects of women's films that may be ascribed to the author's being a woman, or to her feminism. It also runs counter to postmodern concepts of the "death of the author." Many women filmmakers are very conscious of how their films diverge from both mainstream male models and politically engaged feminist ones. Using Kathryn Bigelow as an example, Martin discusses how the concept of "auteur" would need to be modified in order to account for and include such great women filmmakers as Weber, Arzner, and Germaine Dulac. Reclaiming the term, some other women directors who may be considered to be auteures are interviewed in Part 2.

Dulac is central to the chapter by Donia Mounsef, which is devoted to the French tradition of avant-garde, experimental film. Women have been significantly present in this field, from Dulac in the 1920s to Duras in the 1970s. Their work raises questions about film in relation to wider artistic and literary movements, as well how issues of gender affect the reception of controversial films by women. Mounsef asks if the controversy surrounding Dulac has not been misunderstood. Are these directors' contributions and originality underestimated because of their sex? Duras, for example, drew on the transgressive possibilities of film to create aesthetic effects that challenge the conventions of filmic representation. How does her experimentation in film relate to her writing and to her ideas about femininity?

The last chapter in Part 1 concentrates on Potter, Akerman, and Rainer as three prominent women directors, often the focus of early feminist film theory, who have now reached a certain point in their lives and in their films. Catherine Fowler reflects on how their current work corresponds to the evolution of a body of theory that is also in its "middle ages." Looking at their treatment of the female body, Fowler emphasizes a shift to a "visual pleasure" that is directed by a female rather than a male gaze. Potter's autobiographical presence in *The Tango Lesson* is a notable example of this, and it led to accusations of "female narcissism" – a topic treated in more detail by Corinn Columpar in Part 2.

1 Women, Film, Resistance: Changing Paradigms
E. Ann Kaplan

This chapter reflects the recent evolution of my research on women and film, which is moving away from North American hegemony and White filmmakers and towards the presence and work of minority filmmakers in the United States and other parts of the world. The conference "Women Filmmakers: Refocusing" provided an opportunity for me to share my perspectives with a wide range of filmmakers from diverse nations and, especially, for me to find out more about the work of contemporary Canadian women directors.

One of the aims of this book is to celebrate the achievements of women filmmakers, and there is, indeed, a lot to celebrate. In fact, the changes in the relation of women to film over the past three decades are such that many no longer consider it necessary to single out female artists for special consideration. One of our tasks is, therefore, to ponder how we can justify maintaining a focus on *women* filmmakers, and, even more provocatively, whether we still need to single out minority film directors for special attention. In addressing these questions I will review four main phases in the relation of women to film from 1900 to the present, primarily in the United States but in later sections in other contexts. I will look at the specific constraints confronting women and minorities in these four phases and then return to two phenomena. The first concerns the ideological stance in the films women direct; the second concerns issues pertaining to women's relation to technology. The latter is crucial since gendered and raced constructions of technology present it as White and masculine, thus inhibiting women's involvement in directing films.

With regard to feminist ideology, what "feminism" can mean in any historical period depends upon the specific constraints within which women lived and worked. Varying constraints require different strategies of resistance, and later generations are able to build on challenges made by those preceding them. Like a kaleidoscope, the ideological landscape changes with each feminist intervention as new ways of seeing open up in the wake of prior resistances. While the feminine has been cut off from technology in the past, I will argue that our future may well lie in accommodating ourselves to its challenges. Over the four stages, themes in women directors' films have changed: first, topics were chosen for them, but it slowly became possible for them to choose their own. Consideration of how these topics are treated raises the final question: is the gender of the filmmaker more significant than the values or political perspectives a film espouses?

Phase One: Women Pioneers in America, 1906-30

The Victorian era was a period during which major technological explosions reinforced the middle-class Victorian separation of male and female spheres, with women confined to the home as private objects of desire and males free to dominate the world outside the home, which was linked to science and technology. It also produced distinct class differences.[1] Since a culture's myths and fantasies follow closely upon its social organization (and interact within it in a circular fashion), we would expect, in early cinema, to find women in front of the camera being made into objects and represented in traditional roles. Indeed, many early male filmmakers enjoyed photographing women dancing, laying the groundwork for what feminist film critics in the 1980s called "the male gaze."[2] In early as well as classic cinema (1906-60), we mainly find women imaged as wives and mothers, or, before marriage, as virgins and whores. A little later, male filmmakers produced the vamp genre: von Stroheim's famous film, *A Fool There Was* (1914), established the female prototype that would become the notorious femme fatale. We find few working women in silent film narratives before the 1920s, and even in the so-called Jazz Age, when many more women entered the workforce,[3] working women on the screen were always single so that they could be married off at the end.

Despite Victorian stances towards women, and cultural fantasies that included a cultural prohibition regarding women and technology, scholars have unearthed a large number of women working in film studios from as early as 1906 (when Alice Guy Blaché started directing in Paris) up until the mid 1920s (when Hollywood became fully institutionalized). These early women filmmakers evidently adapted quite easily to the new technology and were skilled at mastering its mysteries. Yet Blaché and Lois Weber, the two early women directors whom I will briefly discuss, still worked within very specific historical and institutional constraints. Given the continuing severe separation of male and female spheres, it was an achievement simply to get oneself behind the camera, let alone produce films that resisted the dominant ideology. Often, until very recently, the women who managed to wield the camera did so with the aid of men already active in Hollywood. Hollywood was at the time still a scorned and fledgling industry, so having women directors did not offend anyone. By 1915 the heady atmosphere of the suffragette movement gave women the courage and confidence to be active within the film industry.

However, did the filmmaker's female gender produce a different genre of film, or a different perspective on film genre? The answer is yes and no, and this is too large an issue to address fully here.[4] Suffice it to say that by 1914 Blaché had directed hundreds of pictures and owned her own studio, the Solax Company, an astounding and solitary achievement at that time.[5] What

evidence we have of Blaché's ideas about women in film shows her acceptance of Victorian ideas of the female as emotional, religious, and well versed
in "matters of the heart," although her heroines often have pluck and creativity. For instance, in Blaché's 1913 short film *Matrimony*, the heroine is
clearly in charge of things and finds an ingenious way to bring about the
marriage she wants. Blaché's labour relations films supported management
rather than labour, yet feminist awareness emerges in her plea for more
women to participate in making films: "There is nothing connected with
the staging of a motion picture that a woman cannot do as easily as a man,
and there is no reason why she cannot completely master every technicality of the art."[6]

Lois Weber at first worked by helping her husband, Philip Smiley, but it
soon became clear that she was the smarter and more talented of the two.
She too made hundreds of films, most of them lost, but enough remain to
indicate that Weber also made films with strong heroines. In her 1913 *How
Men Propose*, in the service of "research" the heroine plays a joke on three
men. Weber pioneered a brave 1914 film about abortion, called *Where Are
My Children?* Although it seems to be a plea from the husband's point of
view (which opposes the wife having an abortion), Weber nevertheless intended to make the case for access to legal abortion. This plea emerges when
a young working-class girl dies from an abortion. Meanwhile, the film also
condemns the middle-class married woman for trying to avoid being a wife
and mother. In another acclaimed film, *The Blot* (1921), Weber is very much
concerned with presenting the narrative in terms of her heroine's feelings,
anxieties, and suffering, while clearly depicting the frustrations of her social role as a mother and as the wife of a poor professor. Such ambivalence
is typical of this first period.

Phase Two: The Classical Hollywood Years and the Silencing of Women, 1930-60

For complex socio-political reasons (having to do with the Depression, the
Second World War, the growth of Hollywood studios into powerful male
bastions, and post-Second World War gender conservatism) women were rarely
able to direct films during the classical period, when famous male auteurs
such as Alfred Hitchcock, John Ford, Fritz Lang, and Nicholas Ray accomplished some of their most brilliant work. Only two women, Dorothy Arzner
and Ida Lupino, managed to make a significant body of films in the US at that
time, and then each only for short periods. Arzner, a complicated director,
became an icon for 1980s feminist film theorists, who viewed films such
as *Christopher Strong* (1932), *Craig's Wife* (1936), and *Dance, Girl, Dance* (1940)
as undercutting standard Hollywood images of women. Nevertheless, as
Judith Mayne eventually pointed out, no one examined her fascination for

feminist critics and her possible lesbianism, or followed up Claire Johnston's early research on Arzner as a unique female director until Mayne did so herself.[7]

Ida Lupino, the second extraordinary Hollywood woman in the classical period, grew up in an English theatrical family. Her ambition to act in important, fulfilling roles led her into difficulties in Hollywood, but she became a superb film noir actress, famous for her powerful portrayals of glittering femmes fatales in the 1940s. Tired of such roles and seeking larger socio-political themes in Hollywood films, in 1950 Lupino set up her own production company with her then husband, Colin Collier. The company made five strong films with powerful social messages, including one about rape and another about abortion, both topics rarely if ever fully treated in Hollywood.

As for the women pioneers, the "feminist" aspects of these 1940s and 1950s Hollywood female directors lie mainly in the very fact that they managed to get behind a camera at all. In the case of Arzner and Lupino, however, the "resistance" is both in the breaking of a professional barrier and in the specific forward-looking and controversial woman-linked themes of some of their films.

Phase Three: Mid-Century White Women, Film, and Resistance, 1960-90

It sometimes appears as if fierce resistance on the part of White women in the mid-1960s sprang from nowhere. Women seemed suddenly to react violently to their prior silencing as artists and intellectuals, their lack of power and presence in public life, their subjugation to unjust social laws, their objectification in science, technology, and medicine, and so on. Yet, as we began to resist our varied oppressions, or even as part of that resistance, we were discovering traces of women in prior generations in literature, theatre, painting, photography, scholarship, and film. This phase may be sharply differentiated from both prior phases in that, in this era, an increasing number of women entered academia, contributing to an ideological critique of established (White male) intellectual traditions. Nineteenth-century feminists had been able to address socio-political injustices and inequalities experienced by women, but they had not been in a position to articulate theoretical positions or to shape an aesthetic criticism informed by feminist concepts. The period from the late 1960s through to the 1990s saw an unprecedented rise of new work related to the emergence of women's studies. Cine-feminist scholars were among the first to elaborate feminist theoretical positions.

Since many have written extensively on this period, only a brief summary is required. Part of the power of the post-1960s films by independent women directors like Julia Reichert, Barbara Kopple, Barbara Hammer, Ariel Dougherty, and Jan Oxenberg (from the United States); Patricia Gruben,

Jacqueline Levitin, and Cynthia Scott from Canada; and Laura Mulvey and Sally Potter from Britain (to name just a few) lay in strong personal statements combined with socio-political documentation of all aspects of women's lives and oppressions, from lesbian sexualities to trade unions, from education to advertising, and much more. Styles were as varied as themes, ranging from poetic and lyrical works to experimental avant-garde theory films, from narrative films to documentaries. White European women in the 1960s, 1970s, and 1980s in Germany, France, and Eastern Europe (directors like Márta Mészáros, Mai Zetterling, Marguerite Duras, Margarethe von Trotta, and Helma Sanders Brahms) made exceptional fictional films dealing with women's issues. These all gained power from the 1970s/1980s sense of embattlement, of challenging an unjust patriarchal order and claiming what was due to women. But filmmakers were in fact building on the few women who, while not able to work in Hollywood during its classical period, managed to find a space on the edge of the well known European male avant-garde of the 1920s and 1940s. Germaine Dulac (see Chapter 3) stands out in Europe, and in American film Maya Deren emerged as an artist who, until her untimely death, kept feminist fires burning during the dark times of the late 1940s and early 1950s.

Women filmmakers of the 1970s and 1980s were able to draw strength from their avant-garde foremothers, who influenced the theories and practices of films made by White women. Feminist academics also began to produce a formidable amount of scholarship, working in tandem with activists and practising artists. Our thesis and belief was, in Teresa de Lauretis's words, that film could "intervene in the symbolic order through practices of reappropriation or re-signification which ... affect and alter the imaginary."[8] In hindsight, I would say that, for White women at least, the North American imaginary *has* been altered, partly through the work of independent and foreign filmmakers. In this period, women are again seen to take to film technology with zest and to combine being behind the camera with deliberately anti-mainstream themes that found a space because of the general oppositional discursive moment that emerged in the 1970s in North America and Europe.

In Canada, the filmmakers noted above were an essential part of developments in the 1970s and continue to contribute original and pioneering films to this day.

Phase Four: A Decade of Multicultural Women's Films in European and North American Contexts (1990-2000)

One of the strange aspects of 1960s and 1970s feminist rhetoric was its assumption that "we" were unified. Perhaps such an assumption was born of the sheer need to obtain public and political attention. In fact, it soon became clear, there was not one "we" but many. Especially absent in this rhetoric were women of colour, since it has been much harder for them to construct a mythical "we" than it has been for White women. While White women began to insist, in the 1960s, on a place in film for their imaginary worlds, and while they developed theories about the oppressive images of White women in mainstream film, it is only recently that women of colour have managed to mount their own resistance to the ways they have been imaged. The emergence of minority women in film theories, practices, and filmmaking characterizes, for me, the decade of the 1990s. Looking back, painful challenges to White mainstream institutions and socio-political practices have led to remarkable results. These challenges slowly gathered steam in the 1970s and 1980s, finally coming into their own in visual culture in the 1990s. Minority women have, against all odds, produced a wealth of independent films of many kinds; they have adopted a plurality of themes, styles, and ideological perspectives, as befits their actual diversity. Yet the 1990s was a very different socio-political context than was the 1970s. Multicultural women did benefit from the general oppositional atmosphere of the 1960s, in which White women first claimed the right to produce films and then produced them. However, by the 1990s it was that much harder to obtain funding, to be heard, to get behind the camera, and to produce films that challenged the status quo.

Through the scholarship and films/videos of minority theorists and film-makers such as Trinh T. Minh-ha and Pratibha Parmar, White feminist critics and filmmakers began to understand their blindness about issues of race in Hollywood film, as well as their neglect of independent films by women of colour. As part of this re-evaluation, I undertook the writing of a second book about women and film, this time focusing specifically upon multicultural women and their films. Complementary to my 1983 volume, *Looking for the Other: Feminism, Film, and the Imperial Gaze* (1997)[9] first deals with White feminists' neglect of race in the 1970s and early 1980s. It then goes on to explore Hollywood racial stereotypes, such as those in *Blonde Venus* and many other 1930s films, in addition to the more obviously offensive *Tarzan* or *King Kong* series. From there it moves on to examine issues of the inter-racial gaze, as it can be studied in multicultural women's films, and its relevance to changing White spectators' imaginary constructions about race.

"Looking" relations are never innocent. They are always determined by the cultural systems that people travelling from or to new places bring with them. They are also determined by the visual systems a particular stage or type of technology makes possible. Hollywood films dealing with people travelling reveal how American culture mobilizes inter-racial and intercultural looking relations, usually to the detriment of people of colour (as in *Congo, Raiders of the Lost Ark,* etc.). Meanwhile, independent women's films by people of colour, and some by White women, offer a study of resistance to

dominant looking relations and to stereotypical bodily figurations. Spectator identification with screen images may offer new experiences in racial
looking, outside the dominant scopic regime, and present bodies whose
forms challenge the stereotypes, thus raising many questions. How far is
film limited by its particular spectatorial technology? How far may its anx-
ious gazes be turned back on itself? How do Western films contest the relation of women of colour to the mythical construct of the American "nation"
that Hollywood so easily conjures up from a White patriarchal position?
How do White critics and filmmakers position themselves in regard to multicultural themes?

In North America today a new historical context is producing new images, many by women from ethnic minorities, some by White women. These
images necessarily function in relation to prior images and stereotypes as
well as in relation to the history of imaging minorities, rather than aiming
to produce any new "truth" about minority groups. Women filmmakers are
producing new ways of seeing, new readings of the past, as well as new
images of inter-racial looking relations. They seek to intervene in the imaginary, to change how images are produced, rather than to present minorities
"as they really are." While North American social realities regarding minorities have indeed changed dramatically in the wake of 1960s liberation
movements, the advances are uneven, some groups gaining access to the
mainstream while others are even more marginalized. Class, economics,
and age are all elements that determine what advances are open to minorities in the 1990s. The films and writings of Vietnamese-American filmmaker
and theorist Trinh T. Minh-ha have shown that any aim to represent the
"truth" about minorities would, in any case, be doomed to failure. Her work
highlights the importance of asking who can speak for whom, under what
conditions, and for what purposes. White filmmakers and critics have learned
the necessity of positioning themselves in relation to their representations
of the "Other," and to attempt to see from the Other place, as part of a
reconciliation process.

The worlds imagined in films by independent North American multicultural filmmakers vary greatly, depending on the specific concerns the
filmmaker has, her particular location (geographical, cultural, political, ethnic, historical), and the context of the film's making. In one sense or another, all these films deal with questions of hybrid subjects, subjectivities in
between, the impacts of colonialism, and the diaspora. They also show the
varying positions minority groups construct according to communities they
live in vis-à-vis a dominant "nation" or "culture," as well as their relationships to the idea of "community."

What all the films have in common is an attempt to see differently – to
see, as far as possible, outside of the constraints of prior Western modes. In
what follows, I have chosen to look at a few multicultural women's films

dealing with themes of literal and metaphorical travel, as developed by women of colour, because these also address the "body politics" to which I referred earlier.[10] These films offer opportunities to examine how looking is conceived, what looking is possible, what boundaries there are to looking relations, and how White body stereotypes are contested yet cause inter- as well as intrapersonal conflict. Second, these films allow me to examine the linked nature of inter-racial and intergender looking relations, as these are developed by women filmmakers through concepts of travel as metaphor or trope.[11] All of the films challenge normative spectator-screen relations: these films confront the spectator with unfamiliar worlds as well as with unfamiliar perspectives on these worlds.

Out of the plethora of strategies I could have chosen, since multicultural directors are making films of very different kinds, I will focus on three main devices: (1) reversing the gaze, (2) what I (following Toni Cade Bambara) call "healing imperialized eyes," and (3) body politics (figuring hybrid subjects or challenging racial stereotypes in mainstream culture). Often films adopt more than one of these strategies at the same time.

Reversing the Gaze

In 1990, British filmmaker Pratibha Parmar celebrated the strategy of reversing the gaze in her deliberately polemical essay, "Black Feminism: The Politics of Articulation." At that time, Parmar was optimistic about the possibility for Black oppositional artistic practice in photography and film: "Historically, photographic images of black people all over the world have been captured by the intrepid white photographers, looking for the 'exotic,' the 'different,' the anthropological native types for local colour," all of which created myths, fictions, and fantasies that have "shaped the actual nature of encounters between contemporary black and migrant settlers in the mainly white metropolis."[12] She argues that "it is in representing elements of the self which are considered 'other' by dominant systems of representation that an act of reclamation, empowerment and self-definition occurs."[13] Her poignant early video, *Sari Red* (1987), made (as Parmar says in an interview in this volume) almost on the spur of the moment in response to a tragic racist killing in London, shows such an act of empowerment and self-definition. The video remains powerful and effective over a decade later. It is Parmar's ability to combine documentary footage with poetic, lyrical motifs that enables the video to make its point. The soundtrack, too, destabilizes traditional voice-over by using repeated phrases, much in the manner of a Greek Chorus, emphasizing how the cruel racist murder violated human civility, human decency.

Australian Tracey Moffatt was one of the first women filmmakers to use the strategy of reversing the gaze. Made in 1986, her powerful *Nice Coloured Girls* makes into visual images what postcolonial critics have theorized since

Edward Said's path-breaking 1978 *Orientalism,* followed by Mary Louise Pratt's exhaustive 1992 *Imperial Eyes: Travel Writing and Transculturation.*[14] Moffatt builds on the trope of the explorer penetrating the virgin land, which reflects the White male unconscious. By juxtaposing her three contemporary Aboriginal heroines with images representing early nineteenth-century British explorers arriving on the Sydney shore and trying to take Aboriginal women as playthings, Moffatt explodes the European male colonizer's use of the Native woman's body to restore himself. She positions these women somewhat threateningly, facing the camera, speaking directly to it in their own language, looking fierce and confident. Far from being passive objects existing solely for the colonizers' pleasure, they are seen managing to grab from the explorers the money proffered for sex. The women in the present – named "unruly," like their foremothers – are seen taking revenge for their own and their mothers' exploitation by seducing, then fleeing, White males in a Sydney bar. White spectators are challenged to see differently: the bodily filiation between the strong nineteenth-century Aboriginal women and those in the present, who are confident and having fun, critiques old racist body stereotypes. Asking us to listen to an Aboriginal language we do not understand puts us in the position of many Aborigines when the White men arrived on their shores.

Fatimah Tobing Rony reverses the gaze in her short film *On Cannibalism,* and her critique of colonial film and photography (i.e., of the imperial gaze) is even more direct than Moffatt's. Her strategy is to take the early ethnographic films of physician Félix-Louis Regnault and to expose how he constructs different anatomies of so-called "civilized" and "savage" peoples in what became a traditional Western racial hierarchy. Viewers of Regnault's films, as of classical Hollywood films, are shown "specimens of race and culture, specimens that provide the viewer with a visualization of the evolutionary past."[15]

Interestingly, Rony uses her own body to confront the spectator with an image that looks back at the Whites who have locked her into oppressive, one-dimensional positions. This strategy involves producing new meanings from old degrading signifiers. The juxtaposition of clips of Regnault films and Rony's own strong image, staring out of the frame, together with the words of racist colonizers and anthropologists travelling across the screen, reverses the gaze. It insists that White spectators see from the position of their own constructed "Other," while also revealing Rony's difference from this Other.

Toni Cade Bambara describes an early shot in Julie Dash's *Daughters of the Dust,* which begins conventionally enough with what looks like a colonial image (or at least a Hollywood version of one – think of *African Queen*): a boat is gliding down a river, a woman in a White dress and hat is standing in it. Then we realize this is an African-American woman, Yellow Mary, standing "hipshot, chin cocked, one arm akimbo," adopting a stance that is far from the submissive European female one of colonial cinema. Bambara reads the shot as an emblem for Dash's entire film, claiming that Dash "intends to heal our imperialized eyes."[16]

Western spectators' eyes have been "imperialized" throughout the history of Hollywood cinema. It is a cinema that has set the tone for other cinemas, and it has often been blindly imitated. Bambara's phrase aptly catches how spectators have been visually affected by the ways in which African Americans, and other ethnic minorities, have been imaged. In one long sequence in Dash's film, the Gullah women prepare a ritual evening meal when several of their group are leaving for North America to seek a new, more modern mode of life. Dash's powerful photography and her actors' magnificent performances allow the audience to experience the beauty of Gullah women, the majesty of their men, and to learn about their deeply held values and conflicts, their historical suffering and pain. This process "heals" our eyes, which have been damaged by the way they have hitherto been forced to see African Americans.

The intense needs of many women to please and to belong often make internal identity conflict inevitable. These needs may render diasporic women especially vulnerable to the desire to modify their appearance to conform to a dominant norm – a desire that also affects older (and, increasingly, even younger) White women.[17] In both cases, issues linked to "passing" (which usually refers to Black women trying to "pass" as White) emerge. Cosmetic surgery to "correct" eyelids or other parts of the face or body, or to "eliminate" wrinkles, lines, and sagging skin, may be seen as trying to pass for a Caucasian woman or for a younger woman. It is this kind of body politics that some multicultural women's films, like those by Pam Tom or Ngozie Onwurah, often address.

Hybrid subjectivities are often central in films by transnational filmmakers like Trinh T. Minh-ha and Pratibha Parmar, who are both also theorists and writers. For example, regarding new strategies for imaging the Other, Trinh T. Minh-ha has struggled (in her film, writing, photography, and music) to work outwards from a level of subjectivity rather than to work inwards from broad abstractions. Perhaps more than anyone else, Trinh focuses on "how to make oneself a 'subject' within struggles against the State and make women's concerns central; how to link the specificity of one's particular context and struggles with those of women in different national, cultural and geographical locations, etc."[18] Her 1983 *Reassemblage* already showed how Trinh offers a different way of thinking through problems of "nation," global relations, and imperialism. In "Outside In/Inside Out," written in 1989, Trinh explores the strategies of White ethnographic filmmakers before noting the different strategies of the "insider" in her filmmaking and questioning the concepts of verisimilitude and authenticity.

Towards the Future

To return to my initial questions, in light of all these developments, do we still need to focus on women (as a biological sex) and film? Do we need to single out minority filmmakers as a distinct entity? Should these categories take precedence over more general socio-political perspectives/ideologies? And finally, what about the importance of women being familiar with technology?

Whereas in the 1970s we needed an embattled stance, and searched for female directors who obviously challenged and resisted dominant male cultures, now it is clear that being "female" or "male" does not signify any *necessary* social stance vis-à-vis dominant cultural attitudes. We have learned that biological women are not necessarily more progressive or forward-looking than are biological men, and the terms "male" and "female" do not automatically link biological sex to masculine or feminine behaviours or to certain film genres. We are now wary of essentializing gender in this fashion. Male directors have produced empathetic melodramas about female suffering, working from women's fiction. Some male directors are able to penetrate deeply into the female point of view, as is illustrated in my *Motherhood and Representation* (1992) volume. In a new book exploring the messy topic of women's rights, Linda Kerber shows that challenges to women's inequality were also initiated by men. Meanwhile, female directors may make male action films or films about the military. The point is that Western culture has constructed active and passive "positions" for "male" and "female." But people can take up cultural/psychic places that differ from the ones officially assigned to their sex, and it is this fact that makes it possible to envision progressive social change where gender is concerned.

We can also see now that previous categories of "Black" and "White" are equally dichotomous and essentializing. The one term obviously depends for its meaning on the other, as Homi Bhabha and Trinh, among others, have shown. Trinh envisages a figure, "not quite the Same, not quite the Other, [that] stands in that undetermined threshold place where she constantly drifts in and out," and undercuts the inside/outside opposition. The figure at once affirms, "'I am like you,' while persisting in her difference; and reminds herself 'I am different' while unsettling every definition of otherness arrived at."[19] It is because of this that Trinh's "Inappropriate Other/Same" is so threatening to dominant White culture.

Nevertheless, since the traditional symbolic "male/female" and "Black/White" positions are so hard to escape or to move beyond, a focus on women filmmakers and films by women of all colours is still warranted. Although now, as a result of generations of feminist theorizing and practices, women have so many new positions to occupy, some kind of "feminist" stance –

however hard to define – is still essential. As noted above, different generations of women may understand "feminism" differently, both because the
constraints women endure are different and because prior generations of
feminists provided new perspectives that enabled women to see differently.[20]
We need to better understand each other's positions, while agreeing that
there is still much to achieve in terms of gender and racial parity. The emergence of queer studies has complicated what feminism used to mean, and
that is all for the good. Some women filmmakers who speak in this book are
challenging heteronormative ways of being women, resisting prevailing discourses, institutions, and socio-political practices that continue to oppress
women of all colours.

A focus on women in film is also warranted because of how hard it still is
for women artists to break into mainstream art institutions and to gain the
attention that male directors achieve. Yet, set against the situation when I
wrote *Women in Film* in 1983, things really have advanced. Then, I mainly
had to turn to European women's films for feature film analysis (Cuban
Sara Gómez was a delightful exception). By 1983, American women had
produced an exciting collection of mainly documentary and experimental
films but had barely broken into the feature film business. The intervening
years have certainly made a difference, and not only in North America: we
now have well known White filmmakers like Kathryn Bigelow, Susan
Seidelman, Donna Deitch, Joyce Chopra, and Allison Anders, as well as African American filmmakers like Julie Dash, Cheryl Dunye, and Leslie Harris,
all of whom have made feature films that have had fairly wide distribution
and attracted attention. The themes of many of their films push the envelope: independently made *Go Fish* dealt with young inter-racial lesbians,
challenging Black/White and student/teacher boundaries; Hollywood's *Two
Girls in Love* included an inter-racial lesbian couple, as did *When Night Falls*
and *Chutney Popcorn*.

Globally, women are now producing more films. Within a few years, Kathryn
Bigelow made her sci-fi film *Strange Days*; Yvonne Rainer, another White
American independent director, made *Murder*; Deepa Mehta (an Indo-
Canadian director interviewed in this book) made her astounding *Fire*;
Pratibha Parmar created a brilliant documentary, *Warrior Marks*; and Gurinder
Chadha (an Indian/British filmmaker) made *Bhaji on the Beach*. More recently,
Iranian director Samira Makhmalbaf made her stunning debut with *The
Apple*, a remarkable film critiquing (in a careful way) Iranian repression of
women by recreating a true story about two young girls locked into their
house until they were twelve years old. These films with a message are as
visually and technically impressive as any films by men.

Yet we need to avoid falsely believing that everything is equal. There are
relatively few women's films on controversial themes that meet with success
and gain attention. On the surface it may seem that suddenly there has

been an international expansion of women involved in filmmaking of all kinds, but the struggles many of these women have endured to produce their films is recorded in the essays and interviews that follow in this volume. Compared to how male directors – even minority directors – have fared, women still lag behind in terms of access to funding and resources as well as in terms of distribution. One major problem in attempting to break into the big time, for both men and women, is how to combine the commercial success that draws critical attention with presenting an imaginary world that is original, even counter-cultural (or that at least resists prevailing cultural norms, perhaps by critiquing racial and gender stereotypes). Funding for minority perspectives on the world remains a serious problem. Our foremothers certainly struggled with this barrier, and it remains with us today, though to a lesser extent and in different ways in different places. Nonetheless, the fact that independent women filmmakers and scholars dealing with their efforts to question gender and racial identities are thriving is cause for hope.[21]

There has also been progress in women's access to technology. Digital cameras do not intimidate those who have grown up with the computer. Two films, *Artemisia* and *The Governess,* show how far women have come in challenging the domination of the male gaze and masculine fantasies of women's "natural" divorce from technology. These films show the fascination already felt by women in the sixteenth and nineteenth centuries when exposed to the technologies of painting and photography. The heroines have to challenge the system in order to gain access to the equipment reserved for males, and they destroy their possibilities for love as a result. The women are also shown as succumbing to the (perhaps inevitable) voyeurism of the technological apparatus – the erotic framing of the subject in both painting and photography.[22] At the start of this new millennium, at a moment of unprecedented change, we still carry with us into the new digital universe many entrenched symbolic gendered and racial discourses and assumptions. Technology alone cannot challenge the symbolic. Women need to create new "feminist" positions appropriate for the present and the future, building on the struggles of prior generations: the story of women, resistance, and filmmaking is far from over.

Notes

1 Women's subjugation naturally varied in style and content from class to class.

2 Women may also take pleasure in watching other women, and women spectators always have an opportunity to read films against the grain.

3 See Sumiko Higashi, *Virgins, Vamps, and Flappers: The American Silent Movie Heroine* (St. Albans, VT: Eden Press Women's Publications, 1978), 110.

4 See the increasing amount of criticism on early cinema, including my own book on motherhood in film (E. Ann Kaplan, *Motherhood and Representation: The Mother in Popular Culture and Melodrama* [London: Routledge, 1992]); and Judith Mayne's *Cinema and Spectatorship* (London: Routledge, 1993).

5   However, for fear of offending likely customers, it was only in 1912 that she allowed her name to be used in Solax advertisements.

6   Karen Kay and Gerald Peary, eds., *Women and the Cinema: A Critical Anthology* (New York: Dutton, 1977), 337.

7   Judith Mayne, *The Woman at the Keyhole: Feminism and Women's Cinema* (Bloomington: Indiana University Press, 1990).

8   Teresa de Lauretis, *The Practice of Love: Lesbian Sexuality and Perverse Desire* (Bloomington: Indiana University Press, 1994), 297.

9   E. Ann Kaplan, *Looking for the Other: Feminism, Film, and the Imperial Gaze* (London: Routledge, 1997).

10 See, for instance, E. Ann Kaplan, *Women and Film: Both Sides of the Camera* (New York: Methuen, 1983); Annette Kuhn, *Women's Pictures*, 2nd ed. (London: Verso, 1994); and E. Ann Kaplan's introduction to the critical anthology *Feminism and Film*, ed. Kaplan (Oxford: Oxford University Press, 1999).

11 Trinh T. Minh-ha talks about the symbiosis of "travelling" and "dwelling": travelling can be akin to staying "home," when "home" is not a fixed place. Michele Wallace has also conceptualized writing as travelling from one position to another, and Yvonne Rainer talked about her camera in a similar way when I interviewed her. Maria Lugones has termed the production of "micro-subjectivities" a kind of "'world'-travelling, a process of simultaneous displacement and placement that acknowledges multiple locations" (quoted in Caren Kaplan, "The Politics of Location as Transnational Feminist Critical Practice," in *Scattered Hegemonies: Postmodernity and Transnational Feminist Practices*, ed. Inderpal Grewal and Caren Kaplan [Minneapolis, MN: University of Minnesota Press, 1994], 150).

12 Pratibha Parmar, "Black Feminism: The Politics of Articulation," in *Identity: Community, Culture, Difference*, ed. Jonathan Rutherford (London: Lawrence and Wishart, 1990), 115.

13 Ibid., 116.

14 Edward Said, *Orientalism* (New York: Vintage, 1994); Mary Louise Pratt, *Imperial Eyes: Travel Writing and Transculturation* (London: Routledge, 1992).

15 Fatimah Tobing Rony, *The Third Eye: Race, Cinema and Ethnographic Spectacle* (Durham: Duke University Press, 1996), 265.

16 Julie Dash, with Toni Cade Bambara and bell hooks, *Daughters of the Dust: The Making of an African Woman's Film* (New York: New Press, 1992), xii.

17 Recent North American news stories illustrate how younger and younger women are demanding cosmetic surgery of all kinds. As Anne Marie Balsamo, *Technologies of the Gendered Body: Reading Cyborg Women* (Durham: Duke University Press, 1996), points out, Kathryn Pauly Morgan sees cosmetic surgery as "one of the deepest of original sins, the choice of the apparent over the real." I do not, however, agree with the claim that there is a certain "real" that is being chosen over an "apparent."

18 Trinh T. Minh-ha, *Woman, Native, Other: Writing Postcoloniality and Feminism* (Bloomington: Indiana University Press, 1989), 145.

19 See Trinh T. Minh-ha's "Outside In/Inside Out," reprinted in *Woman, Native, Other.*

20 For more discussion of this point, see my co-edited volume, *Generations: Academic Feminists in Dialogue*, ed. Devoney Looser and E. Ann Kaplan (Minneapolis: University of Minnesota Press, 1997).

21 To give just two examples, an Asian-American NYU film student recently won an award for a film about North American people in an old people's community, and Pratibha Parmar's *Righteous Babes* deals with the members of predominantly White female rock groups, who argue that they are at the forefront of feminism.

22 I can only allude here to the complexities of the relationships between women and technology. As I tried to show in my MTV book and my work on the rock star Madonna, women in our own period have taken to the complicated technologies of popular music with gusto.

2 Refocusing Authorship in Women's Filmmaking
Angela Martin

This chapter has two points of departure. The first is my teaching of film theory and practice; the second is the availability of women's films – specifically within the educational context but also within the wider context of distribution and exhibition. It seems to me that we are experiencing two new kinds of omission of women filmmakers:

1   In addition to the many lost films by women from the earliest period of the cinema, we have also lost a disturbing number from the 1970s. For example, when I was putting a festival program strand together on pioneer women documentary filmmakers,[1] I could not get hold of the prints of films by the London Women's Film Group[2] or of Heiny Srour's *The Hour of Liberation* (Lebanon 1974). The filmmakers themselves were not entirely aware that their films were no longer in distribution.[3] Many more recent films are often available only during brief cinema runs, and only a few of these find their way onto video; even fewer will be widely available on video.

2   This loss of important films by women reflects and is reflected in the discipline of film studies, which tends to ignore or omit women's films – not consciously, but because the theory that informs the discipline is still largely only concerned with male filmmakers. This applies to film history, genre studies, authorship, narrative, film language, and so on. Furthermore, while feminist film theory has, rightly, had a great impact on film theory in general, its attention, too, has tended to focus on the work of male filmmakers. As a teacher and as a film worker, I find this extremely worrying and would suggest that we need to look at film theory in general from this point of view. But I wish here to address the issue only in two related ways: by looking at the notion of authorship and by suggesting a different angle on women's filmmaking.

Authorship is the main aspect of film theory that directly affects women filmmakers; however, for historical reasons, it actually contributes to the omission of women's films from circulation and from film theory. I want to argue, therefore, that unless we talk about women's films in a different way, we will not be able to address that omission. And although I am not going to talk here about Kathryn Bigelow, her work as a woman filmmaker makes the need for this argument very clear; so I will start and end with references to her.

I originally intended to produce a paper on Bigelow's work and the possibility of talking about a gendered authorship, with particular reference to her film *Point Break,* but I found the proposal of "authorship" increasingly problematic. At the same time, excellent publications have appeared in English on the work of Agnès Varda, Diane Kurys, Marguerite Duras, and Dorothy Arzner;[4] and Christina Lane has published an important article on Bigelow.[5] All these texts point to the uneasy relationship between theoretical notions of authorship and women's filmmaking:

> I will not claim that Arzner's films are unqualified successes from beginning to end; I am far too suspicious of such a "great genius" theory of authorship.[6]

> Within the specific context of French cinema and French culture ... the concept of the *auteur,* if ostensibly ungendered, remains resolutely masculine.[7]

> It is ... hard to deny to Varda's work that rather over-used title of *cinéma d'auteur.*[8]

However, as Carrie Tarr points out: "feminist critics and historians have argued the political necessity for defending female authorship as a useful and necessary category."[9] Otherwise the theory of authorship continues its tendency towards a "league table" of "great genius" (read male), and: "female-authored films may be more open to representations of women reworked to feminist or woman-identified ends."[10]

At the same time, several women filmmakers (Kurys and Coline Serreau amongst them)[11] do not identify themselves or their work with a feminist (or even specifically female) project; on the other hand, the theory of authorship has become something of a tangled web, and I want now to look briefly at a few of the signposts along the way of film theory and of film studies as I pursue my argument that "auteurism," as we call it in English, has nothing to do with women's filmmaking.[12]

The original suggestion that the filmmaker should be an auteur was a matter of policy, not of theory: it was about the desire for a cinema of self-expression, a generational revolt on the part of the young *Cahiers du cinéma* critics, who were demanding a break with the persistently traditional mainstream French cinema, which they saw as heavy, entrenched, and tied to the wordiness of the theatre-inspired script. They spoke about auteurs because they desperately wanted to claw the creative centre away from the writers of these scripts. Everything, they said, should be geared towards, shaped, and even produced by the "true brilliance"[13] of the director, the film auteur's "self-expression"[14] of "primary emotion."[15] In his attempt "to make a personal work,"[16] the auteur transforms, "as if by magic, a screenplay written by someone else."[17] And they saw the epitome of the *politique* in the work of a number of hitherto little thought of commercial Hollywood directors. One example illustrates the gender-bound nature of their enthusiasm. In his announcement of the arrival of "the age of the *auteurs,*" Jacques Rivette names four filmmakers: Nicholas Ray, Richard Brooks, Anthony Mann, and Robert Aldrich, who, if one accepted nothing else about them, he wrote, share the common trait of youth. But of the virtues of youth that they share, violence is the primary one:

> not that easy brutality which constituted the success of a Dmytryk or a Benedek, but a virile anger, which comes from the heart, and lies less in the scenario or the choice of events, than in the tone of the narrative and the very technique of the *mise en scène.* Violence is never an end, but a means of approach ... to drill an opening: in short, to open the shortest routes. And the frequent resort to a technique which is discontinuous, halting, which refuses the conventions of cutting and continuity, is a form of that "superior madness" which Cocteau speaks about, born out of the need for an immediate expression which accounts for and shares in the primary emotions of the *auteur* ... trying to make a personal work ... In short, violence is the external sign of rupture.[18]

Actually, this male-centredness notwithstanding, the demands of the *Cahiers* critics were understandable within their own historical and political context – being part of the first new post- Second World War generation, implicated in the French colonial war against the Algerian struggle for independence, and disillusioned by the state, the Church, and bourgeois culture. But virility is, by definition, masculine,[19] which is easily attached to notions of violence, anger, and "the need for an immediate expression"; and the *Nouvelle Vague*'s call for a personal self-expression is very different from the later feminist call for the personal to be political rather than ego-centric.

The inevitable male-centredness of the *politique des auteurs* was compounded by Andrew Sarris's theory that the source of value was *the director.* At the same time, the British film journal *Movie* published "The talent histogram" in its first issue in June 1962,[20] categorizing directors according to "Great, Brilliant, Very Talented, Talented, Competent or Ambitious, and The Rest." Two women appear in it, in the last two categories – Shirley Clarke was in the longest (American) "Competent or Ambitious" column, while Muriel Box was one of "The [almost as many British] Rest."[21] Victor Perkins summarized the theory and critical practice of auteurism as looking for "the achievement within the single film of values like economy, unity, eloquence, subtlety, depth and *vigour* [on the one hand; and on the other] recurrent themes in a director's films considered as a series ... themes, viewpoints and methods of sufficient personal significance to carry over from film to film" (emphasis mine).[22]

We have now moved on a long way from this position, but it is apparently still alive and well. Just a cursory keyword computer reference check produced a dozen or so journal articles between 1981 and 1993 that defend the greatness of, for example, Fassbinder, Kazan, John Ford (revisited), Jacques Doillon, Louis Malle, Sirk, and the Marx Brothers but not a single woman filmmaker. However, if we attempted to apply the theory to women filmmakers, as Claire Johnston understandably suggested in 1973,[23] we could then have applied it only to the work of Arzner or Lupino because only those filmmakers had produced a body of work within a single production context. Bigelow would be one of the few current women filmmakers who would be eligible, if one wanted to make the claim.

Later, as auteur analysis, the theory looked to *the text* as the source of a meaning of which the filmmaker himself may not have been aware. This involves

> tracing a structure (not a message) within the work, which can *then post factum* be assigned to an individual, the director ... [However,] there can be no doubt that the presence of a structure in the text can often be connected with the presence of a director on the set, but the situation in the cinema, where the director's primary task is often one of co-ordination and rationalisation, is very different from that in the other arts, where there is a much more direct relationship between artist and work. It is in this sense that it is possible to speak of a film *auteur* as an *unconscious catalyst*.[24] (my emphasis)

The problem here, as far as women filmmakers are concerned, is that they are not unconscious industry hacks or jobbing directors, churning out one film after another within recognizable commercial cinema genres. Most women filmmakers we would be interested in are thinking filmmakers, usually working within an independent cinema framework, and many have been to film school, even if, like Chantal Akerman, they didn't stay very long. Kathryn Bigelow, for example, attended classes with Milos Forman and Peter Wollen, among others. She was, therefore, engaged in dialogue about film theory almost as soon as she picked up a camera. It seems reasonable to assume, therefore, that when she approaches the making of a film, she does so with knowledge of the issues of representation, ideology, film history, and aesthetics. In other words, she – like Wollen himself – is a very conscious filmmaker.

Between the publication of *Movie's* "Talent Histogram" and Wollen's distancing the filmmaker's person from his function, Roland Barthes published "The Death of the Author" (1968), which made it clear that meaning was produced by *the reader*: "As soon as a fact is *narrated* ... the voice loses its origins, the author enters into his own death ... a text's unity lies not in its origin but in its destination. Yet this destination cannot any longer be personal: the reader ... is simply that *someone* who holds together in a single field all the traces by which the written text is constituted ... [and] the birth of the reader must be at the cost of the death of the Author."[25]

One cannot claim a filmmaker as auteur if, effectively, the author is dead. Of course, the debate about authorship – in its proper, unabridged context – has developed into extremely important work on language, signification, and enunciation. But the work of women filmmakers remains of marginal interest to it;[26] and it seems to me that the title of Audre Lorde's text, *The Master's Tools Will Never Dismantle the Master's House,* has a useful resonance here, as does a recent comment I understood Germaine Greer to be making[27] – that the way poetry is lauded is actually as male display and, therefore, there is no point in arguing that any woman poet could be better than Shakespeare because, clearly, she is unlikely to be engaging in that kind of poetry. By the same token, the kind of poetry women do write is not accounted for in the "league tables" of poet-names.

Both film theory and film studies have, thank goodness, acknowledged the work of feminist film theorists; however, largely for the reasons already outlined, they only pay lip service to the presence and contribution of women filmmakers – with the possible exception of those filmmakers who are, as Dudley Andrew puts it, "serious and progressive critics themselves," like Duras, Mulvey with Wollen, and Huillet with Straub.[28] Looking at what film studies uses as course literature, this is abundantly clear. I'll give just a couple of recent examples. In his overview of authorship in the important *Oxford Guide to Film Studies,*[29] Stephen Crofts outlines ten modes. The "author as gendered" mode is the *shortest* section, despite the fact that it begins: "The most influential theoretical discourse affecting film theory in the last two decades, feminism has necessarily impinged [sic] on Authorship."[30]

Arzner alone is mentioned here, and only briefly. Otherwise, the *Oxford Guide* effectively mentions female directors only in its chapters dealing with "otherness" – feminism and film; gay, lesbian, and queer cinema; the avant-garde; and non-American cinemas. Chantal Akerman is the only woman director to be given one of the "special mention" boxes. In *The Oxford History of World Cinema* there appears to be no mention whatever of Lois Weber (nor is there any mention of her in Thompson and Bordwell's *Film History*) and only passing mention of Alice Guy Blaché (within the contexts of Gaumont, her husband, and Louis Feuillade, whom she taught). Yet these important texts form part of the material that informs much of the practice of film studies.

Unfortunately, though for very good reasons, feminist film theory has also paid most attention to male-directed mainstream cinema, often with a view to at least understanding, if not "dismantling[,] the master's house," and to those avant-garde women filmmakers mentioned by Dudley Andrew, who can be said to be working within the same theoretical framework; that is, on questions of "the gaze," representations of the body, desire, subjectivity, and so on. For the most part, this work takes place within (or near) the academy. Meanwhile, women have been working in more and more sections of the industry, no longer just in theory-based (or campaign) filmmaking. The associations representing women in production are now more industry-based and, rightly and inevitably, are about women being recognized by, and getting on in, the industry. As a result, while we used to talk in terms of whether there was a feminist aesthetic or a woman's voice that informed women's filmmaking, such questions are now less productive, and, though necessary and very important at the time, they have, in some ways, become as limiting as the auteur theory. It is not surprising that several women filmmakers who became known as feature directors were reluctant to be tied by such a tight framework. Consequently, from the mid-1980s or so there was a divergence of interests. Kathryn Bigelow, for example, has, on the whole, been on the industry side of the divide, and she has not attracted the volume of theory-informed articles that Sally Potter or Jane Campion have (though, admittedly, this is changing).[31] Within authorship theory, what feminist film criticism/theory has done is talk about *female* or *feminist* authorship. Interestingly, however, Kathryn Bigelow's work seems to me to raise considerable problems for this approach, largely *because* of her mainstream position. But I believe the problem is wider than this and that it emanates from the question of definition.

Strictly speaking, there are two definitions of the word "authorship": one concerns the (legal) ownership of an idea or its mode of expression, the other concerns the act and the occupation of writing. But female or feminist authorship tends to be sought in what can be identifiably linked to the filmmaker (as woman):

- a film's autobiographical reference
- a filmmaker's actual presence in the film
- the evidence of a female voice within the narrative (however located).[32]

But none of these, as factors in a film, guarantees authorship. And if a woman filmmaker's film does not produce evidence of a female voice, this does not preclude her from being the film's author (in either of the strict senses). Bigelow's films, for example, do not show easy evidence of her presence or even of a clear female or feminist voice. How to talk about her films, then, from a feminist authorship point of view?

Bigelow's films are produced within Hollywood's mainstream film *industry* context, with a crew. This, of course, is one of the arguments against the theory of "author-name" authorship, and her work confounds this argument. Obviously she works with other people on her films, but she appears to have managed to work with and for empathetic people (and I don't mean in a cosy sense). Although *Point Break* was not, to begin with, a personally initiated project, she was the director the producers kept returning to when they were setting up the film's production. She herself asked for James Cameron to be brought onto the project. Editor Howard Smith had already worked with her on *Near Dark*. Bigelow says she rewrote the script, originally written by Peter Illiff (who scripted *Patriot Games*). Also, having been a painter before becoming a filmmaker, she knows, sooner than she knows anything else about the shoot, how she wants a film to look. Don Peterman, the DOP on *Point Break*, is quite categorical when he says that the look his team produced was the look Bigelow wanted. She also works with storyboards, which she has said was particularly important because several second units were involved in the shooting of *Point Break* and it was essential for their different images to cohere with the rest of the material. It would seem ridiculous, therefore, to suggest that she did not have considerable aesthetic and conceptual control of the film. I would certainly argue for a reading of the film that is informed by feminism, but this does not seem to fit the definition of female or feminist authorship summarized above.

Much more helpful, it seems to me, is the sense of a film being produced in a context of dialogue within which the filmmaker, the context, and the reader/spectator all participate and from which they all produce meanings that will at least overlap if not actually agree. We need to find a way of recognizing this kind of conceptual and aesthetic work around the production of a film. We particularly need to do this for women filmmakers, and we need to do it for exactly the same reasons as we need to claim women filmmakers as auteurs or to define and defend notions of female authorship. One useful way forward would be to take the concept Agnès Varda uses for her work: *cinécriture*[33] (which translates, rather less happily, as "filmic writing"):

> A well-written film is also well-filmed, the actors are well chosen, so are the locations. The cutting, the movement, the points-of-view, the rhythm of filming and editing have been felt and considered in the way a writer chooses the depth and meaning of sentences, the type of words, number of adverbs, paragraphs, asides, chapters which advance the story or break its flow, etc. In writing it's called style. In the cinema, style is *cinécriture*.[34]

I see this as a starting point rather than as an ending point because questions of style are also problematic. However, as a starting point, it would allow us to avoid having to go through and be marginalized by the arguments about the authorship theory, or having to find the filmmaker or her female voice in the text in order to give it authorial credence. It also allows us to move away from the legal definition of "authorship" and towards the definition dealing with the practice of writing, which may or may not emerge from a single person but, in terms of film production, will certainly be organized around the director. It also allows us to talk about women auteur filmmakers[35] and to make a different historical link – a link made through filmmakers like Lois Weber, Germaine Dulac, Arzner, and many others who would never be seen as auteurs but who, like a number of male directors, are filmmakers who produced eloquent filmic writing.

Notes

1 Sheffield International Documentary Festival (England) 1995.
2 The LWFG was active between 1972 and 1977, and amongst the films produced by members of the group (which included Claire Johnston) were the very moving *Women of the Rhondda* (1972); a feature-length "political burlesque," *The Amazing Equal Pay Show* (1974); and the campaign documentary with fictional elements, *Whose Choice?* (1976).
3 As the rights on shorts and documentaries came to the end of their term, Metro (formerly The Other Cinema [TOC]) sadly but necessarily moved away from this area, not renewing the rights but, rather, concentrating on feature film distribution. For material on the excellent work of TOC, see Sylvia Harvey, in "The Other Cinema: A History, 1970-77," *Screen* 26, 6 (November/December 1985): 40-57; and *Screen* 27, 2 (March/April 1986): 80-96.
4 Alison Smith, *Agnès Varda* (Manchester: Manchester University Press, 1998); Carrie Tarr, *Diane Kurys* (Manchester: Manchester University Press, 1999); Judith Mayne, *Directed by Dorothy Arzner* (Bloomington and Indianapolis: Indiana University Press, 1994); Leslie Hill, *Marguerite Duras: Apocalyptic Desires* (London: Routledge, 1993).
5 Christina Lane, "From *The Loveless* to *Point Break*: Kathryn Bigelow's Trajectory in Action," *Cinema Journal* 37, 4 (1998): 59-81.
6 Mayne, *Directed by Dorothy Arzner*, 1.
7 Tarr, *Diane Kurys*, 3.
8 Smith, *Agnès Varda*, 17.
9 Tarr, *Diane Kurys*, 4.
10 Ibid., 5.
11 See Brigitte Rollet's book, *Coline Serreau* (Manchester/New York: Manchester University Press/ St. Martin's Press, 1998).
12 An excellent reader on the subject is John Caughie's *Theories of Authorship* (London: RKP/ BFI, 1981).
13 Eric Rohmer (Maurice Schérer), "Renoir Américain," *Cahiers du cinéma*, 8 (January 1952): 33-40, extracted and translated in Caughie, *Theories of Authorship*, 38-9. My quotations here all come from extracts chosen by John Caughie (1981) to represent the *Cahiers* position (although obviously not with the slant I am now giving them).
14 Pierre Kast, "Des confitures pour un gendarme," *Cahiers du cinéma* 2 (January 1951): 40, extracted and translated in Caughie, *Theories of Authorship*, 38.
15 Jacques Rivette, "Notes sur une révolution," *Cahiers du cinéma* (special issue on American cinema), 54 (Christmas 1955): 12-21, extracted and translated in Caughie, *Theories of Authorship*, 41-2.
16 Ibid.
17 Fereydoun Hoveyda, "La réponse de Nicholas Ray," *Cahiers du cinéma* 107 (May 1960): 41-6, extracted and translated in Caughie, *Theories of Authorship*, 42-3.
18 Rivette, "Notes sur une révolution," 41.
19 The dictionary definition of "virile" is: relating to, or having, the characteristics of an adult male; strong, forceful, vigorous. It surfaced in the fifteenth century and is probably based on a combination of the Latin words "vir," meaning man, and "vis," meaning strength.

20 The concern of the histogram was actually to show "British cinema's lack of what we would consider as talent."

21 Shirley Clarke had recently made *A Scary Time* (1960) and had possibly not long before completed *The Connection* (1961); Muriel Box had recently made *Too Young to Love* and *The Piper's Tune* (both 1960).

22 V.F. Perkins, "Film Authorship: The Premature Burial," *CineAction* 21/22 (1990). Edward Buscombe talks about "the notion of the 'divine spark,' which separates off the artist from ordinary mortals, which divides the genius from the journeyman." This idea seems particularly indebted to Romantic artistic theory. See "Ideas of Authorship," in Caughie, *Theories of Authorship*, 24; see also Michel Foucault, "What Is an Author?" in *Language, Counter-Memory, Practice* (Oxford: Basil Blackwell, 1977), 121-38, and in *Screen* 20, 1 (1979): 13-29; originally published in *Bulletin de la Société Française de Philosophie* 63, 3 (1969): 73-104 . Janet Staiger gives a useful (feminist) critique of this "Romantic auteurism" in "The Politics of Film Cannons," in *Multiple Voices in Feminist Film Criticism*, ed. D. Carson, L. Dittmar, and J.R. Welsch (Minneapolis: University of Minnesota Press, 1994), 197-200.

23 Claire Johnston, "Women's Cinema as Counter Cinema," in *Notes on Women's Cinema* (London: Society for Education in Film and Television, 1973), 26-7.

24 Peter Wollen, "Conclusion," in *Signs and Meaning in the Cinema*, 2nd ed. (London: Martin Seeker and Warburg, 1972), 168. See also Foucault, "What Is an Author."

25 Roland Barthes, "The Death of the Author?" *Image-Music-Text* (London: Fontana, 1977 [1968]), 20.

26 One can wonder how far the texts mentioned earlier (i.e., those on Arzner, Bigelow, Kurys, Serreau, and Varda) will impinge upon the agenda of the wider debate about authorship.

27 On a BBC Radio discussion program, March 1999.

28 Dudley Andrew, *Concepts in Film Theory* (Oxford: Oxford University Press, 1984), 126.

29 John Hill and Pamela Church Gibson, eds., *The Oxford Guide to Film Studies* (Oxford/New York: Oxford University Press, 1998).

30 Ibid., 320.

31 See, for example, Colleen Keane, "Director as 'Adrenaline Junkie,'" in *Metro* 109 (1997): 22-7; Laura Rascaroli, "Steel in the Gaze: On POV and the Discourse of Vision in Kathryn Bigelow's Cinema," *Screen* 38, 3 (Autumn 1997): 232-46; Lane, "From *The Loveless* to *Point Break*"; Yvonne Tasker, "Bigger than life," *Sight and Sound* 9, 5 (May 1999): 12-15; and the forthcoming collection on Bigelow, edited by Deborah Jermyn and Sean Redmond.

32 Extremely important in this context is Kaja Silverman's *The Acoustic Mirror: The Female Voice in Psychoanalysis and Cinema* (Bloomington and Indianapolis: Indiana University Press, 1988), especially the chapter entitled "The Female Authorial Voice." Interestingly, Leslie Hill's book on Duras does not problematize the notion of authorship, and in his chapter entitled "Images of Authorship," he goes right into talking about Duras's work in terms of, for example, authorial persona and performativity, authorial commentary and self-commentary, and authority.

33 See Smith, *Agnès Varda*, 13-5.

34 Varda, "Varda par Agnès," *Cahiers du cinéma* (1994): 14, translated in Alison Smith, *Agnès Varda*, 14.

35 As Ginette Vincendeau indicated in Hill and Church Gibson, *Oxford Guide*, 444.

3 Women Filmmakers and the Avant-Garde: From Dulac to Duras

Donia Mounsef

> Le terrain de cette histoire, c'est cette contradiction, ce déchirement.
> — Marguerite Duras

The first avant-garde of this century (surrealism, dadaism, and futurism) is commonly viewed as diametrically opposed to the second avant-garde of the 1960s and 1970s. Many critics, such as Krysinski, consider the former to be more violently hostile towards artistic tradition, whose language it seeks to destroy, while the latter is more preoccupied with aesthetics, offers new forms and expressions of the existing tradition, and attempts to re-shape its language instead of rejecting it.[1] The difference, according to Peter Wollen, lies in the treatment and privileging of signifier over signified: "One tendency reflects a preoccupation with the specificity of the signifier, holding the signified in suspense or striving to eliminate it. The other has tried to develop new types of relation between signifier and signified through the montage of heterogeneous elements."[2]

In this tug-of-war between content and form, women avant-garde filmmakers, as Teresa de Lauretis noted, "were caught between the movement's demands that women's art portray women's activities, document demonstrations, and such, and the formal demands of 'artistic activity'" essential to the articulation of a radical aesthetic stance.[3] However women avant-garde filmmakers interpret the problematics of form and content, one constant characteristic of avant-garde criticism is to locate the debate on the level of genre and to ignore the problems inherent in the gendered relationship between women filmmakers and de facto male domination over the experimental film industry.[4] This chapter proposes that we not only look at the politics of genre in order to understand women's roles in avant-garde film, but also, and more importantly, that we problematize visual knowledge making and visual knowledge sharing in terms of the politics of gender or, as Donna Haraway suggests, the "politics of visual culture."

In the first instance this discussion will focus on the now (in)famous "bagarre coquille" (seashell battle) surrounding the first surrealist film, *La Coquille et le Clergyman* (1927), which, on its release in 1928, opposed dramatist Antonin Artaud and France's first lesbian filmmaker, Germaine Dulac. Within the context of this controversy, I wish to examine the discrepancy between the rhetoric of radical politics exhibited by the first avant-garde and the exclusionary tactics wielded by some of its most influential members. The second instance involves the 1970s French New Wave, and I will look at Marguerite Duras's *India Song* (1975), where the use of avant-garde visual techniques deconstructs the exercise of power based on gender hierarchies. Here, I will consider the collision of discourses on gender identities as itself an act of resistance to the constructedness of gender hierarchical claims. Without juxtaposing the two experiences by simply spanning five decades, the parallel drawn will predicate the ways in which women, operating in neglected areas, subsume and explore radical aesthetic and political avant-garde principles.

Defying/Defining the Avant-Gardes

In use since the end of the nineteenth century to designate revolutionary groups, the term "avant-garde"[5] made its entry into the language of the visual arts in the 1890s. Then, at the turn of the century, theatre critics borrowed the expression to designate small theatres opposed to conventional and established dramatic tradition. Despite Georges Sadoul's assertion that "avant-garde appeared in cinema around 1925, ten or twenty years behind painting and poetry"[6] it was at the end of the First World War, in 1918, that the critical vocabulary of cinema first employed the term. It appeared that year in a text penned by the mysterious "woman from nowhere" *(la femme de nulle part)*. This pseudonym was first attributed to Eve Francis, who was known as the lover and fiancée of Louis Delluc, and then to Delluc himself, who later (1922) directed a film with the same title. In a text of the same period entitled "Insinuation," this woman from nowhere calls on her fellow filmmakers of the avant-garde to take advantage of a beautiful summer and shoot authentic French landscapes: "Your scripts," she writes, "will benefit in style, elegance and homogeneity."[7] Such a nationalist summons to please by showing the beauty of France seems peculiar in the context of avant-garde discourse, especially since "homogeneity" is prescribed, against the principles of innovation and originality familiar in the critical language of that movement. This appeal to be palatable may be related to the financial crisis of French cinema, which caused the transfer, in the early 1920s, of film production out of Paris to other European capitals as well as to the United States.

Dissident and visionary women filmmakers like Eve Francis foresaw the crisis that, in the late 1920s, put an end to the experimental movement in cinema. This was due, in part, to the entry of sound into film, but also, more importantly, to the recruitment and cooption of the most prominent experimental filmmakers into the mainstream. However, this crisis in financing and producing experimental film would have different effects on women and men filmmakers of the first avant-garde. Backed by well

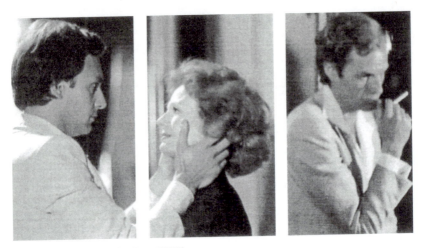

Marguerite Duras's *India Song* (1975)

established promoters in the film industry, male filmmakers were soon recruited to produce conventional films and, thus, were able to survive the crisis of the end of the silent era; examples of such cases include l'Herbier, Cavalcanti, Epstein, and Grémillon. However, their survival came at the price, as noted by André Bazin, of "more or less full[y] accept[ing] ... the rules of the commercial game."[8] For their female counterparts the story is quite different. Women filmmakers who refused to enter the commercial enterprise were denied access to means of production while, at the same time, their achievements were threatened by historical neglect and lack of recognition. The best example is Alice Guy Blaché, who, after fifteen years working in the United States, returned to France to find her career sabotaged by the politics of commercial film in the 1920s. Not only did these women find their efforts bogged down by the economic circumstances of the end of the 1920s, but they also found that their life's work was liable to fall by the wayside.

Dulac

Germaine Dulac is one of those women whose work was hampered by what she calls "slavery to economic vice."[9] After making twenty-six films over thirteen years between 1916 and 1929, Dulac saw her career come to a halt, in part because of her refusal to play the commercial game and to jump on the sound bandwagon. Having had to produce mainstream and serial films, Dulac consistently complained of being subjugated to the yoke of economic constraints. In her view, if the director remains enslaved to these constraints it is because "he or she will not receive the necessary money for the elaboration of his or her work except in exchange for a profession of faith in his or

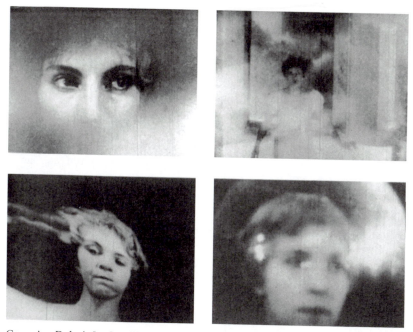

Germaine Dulac's *La Coquille et le Clergyman/The Seashell and the Clergyman* (1928), courtesy of MOMA

her adherence to the spectator's taste."[10] Furthermore, commercial exigency not only made it difficult for Dulac to produce and distribute experimental film, it also condemned her work to the *oubliettes* of history. As Susan Hayward observed:

> Apart from a first, external, economic reason for her being silenced – the reality that sound technology was beyond her financial scope – she had a second, internal aesthetic one which obliged her silence. She believed that too much emphasis would be placed on the talking voice and not enough on the orchestration of meaning through movement and image – an eventuality that, effectively, would marginalize her praxis.[11]

Despite modest attempts by Noël Burch and Jean-André Fieschi in the 1960s to restore to Dulac her rightful place in the history of cinema, they dismissed her work by claiming it to be much too complex to be satisfied by a "brief summary."[12] This pretext, according to Catherine Silberschmidt, is the reason for the silence that surrounds Dulac's work in French academic and critical circles. Other accomplices in this silencing are the women historians who, in 1992, published a five-volume *History of Women in the West*. The volume concerned with the twentieth century contains a long chapter on the work and creative contributions of women in the cultural sector without a single mention of Germaine Dulac.[13] In fact, it was in the United States in the 1960s that feminist analysis of cinema brought Dulac's work to the forefront, locating it within a feminist framework and lineage. E. Ann Kaplan explains the importance of Dulac's work to feminist historians:

> Dulac's work serves the important function of *exposing* the positioning of women in patriarchy, even if she has no sense of alternatives. Equally important is the model she offers as a historical woman, who struggled to overcome prejudices against her, and who, as a woman in a male-dominated field, managed successfully to assert herself, to be visible, even if later her role was neglected by historians.[14]

However, beyond Dulac's contributions to surrealism, her major role in defining the very principles of avant-garde cinema still remains understudied and begs for attention. In fact, it would be underestimating her to see her work as simply another experiment in surrealism. As I will demonstrate, her films and theoretical work contradict many surrealist principles, while helping to define the avant-garde movement and allowing it to adopt a clearly political stance – a stance different from, and sometimes contradictory to, that displayed by anarchic surrealism.

Dulac's first and foremost contribution to the avant-garde is the definition of the term, through a series of articles and theoretical works published over two decades in renowned French cinema journals and magazines such as *Cinémagazine, Photo-Ciné,* and *Cinéa-Ciné pour tous*. Acknowledging the complexities of the term "avant-garde," she preferred the expression "cinema of evolution," which signified not only daring on-screen experimental innovation with the visual scope of film, but also an investigation into film research and a theoretical framework with which to do it. By employing a term oriented towards the future and favouring theory, she not only denied conventional cinema's obsession with the past, but also challenged her colleagues within surrealism to question the ideological assumptions of their work, inviting them to look to progressive models and to assume the distance necessary for critical thinking. She then proceeds to do away with all the terminological qualifiers and categories in use at the time, such as "exceptional cinema," or "special cinema," falsely referred to as "avant-garde cinema," suggesting as a substitute the simple word "cinema."[15] In doing this, Dulac achieves two objectives: first, she calls for a total break with the narrative cinema traditionally sustained by the commercial film industry, a rupture that can be attained by emphasizing the visual aspect of cinema over narrative: "A real film," she wrote, "must not tell its own story since it must draw its active and emotional principle from images made of unique visual vibrations."[16] Second, she rejects the exclusionary practices underlined by

the term "exception" and calls for a unification of the two schools domi-
nating the twenties: "the school of pure movement," where the flow of
pictures is more important than the fragment, and the "anecdotal school,"
where films are accompanied by some form of narration or inter-titles.
Through this double disclaimer Dulac criticizes traditional cinema while
also questioning the exclusionary and elitist practices of the avant-garde
"boys' club."

This struggle on two fronts continued well into the late 1920s, at times
taking on much more violent and controversial overtones. An example of
this process is found in her 1927 quarrel with Antonin Artaud, a controversy known as the "bagarre coquille." It is alleged that Dulac misinterpreted Artaud's screenplay for *La Coquille et le Clergyman* and refused to cast
him in the main role of the priest. While the accounts of the incident are
often contradictory, the most revealing one is provided by Alain Virmaux
in his book *Artaud, un bilan critique:* "Germaine Dulac kept Artaud at bay
during the shooting and the editing; unhappy with this process and unsat-
isfied with the film, [Artaud] obtained from Paulhan the publication of the
original screenplay, in the *Nouvelle Revue Française,* with the intention of
preserving his copyright as the author of *La Coquille;* undoubtedly unhappy
with the *NRF* operation, [Dulac] caused the delay of the release of the film
... however some members of the press had already seen it in private screenings."[17] As a result of this little war, a tract was published assembling a series
of articles and press cuttings, a guerrilla style publication prepared by the
so-called "friends of Artaud." Short of directly attacking Dulac, many articles accused her of mishandling the screenplay and distorting the initial
intention of the author ("the image was often incapable of rendering the
thought of Antonin Artaud"[18]) as well as insisting that the film was the
property of Artaud.

Aside from two seemingly benign accusations of having kept Artaud uninformed during the shooting and delaying the release of the film, there
appears to be no significant proof that Dulac gravely mishandled Artaud's
text, certainly not enough to deserve all the publicity and assaults. In fact,
on taking a closer look, Dulac may have been victim of the inner wars rag-
ing within the surrealist group, which, in 1928, led to the expulsion of
Artaud from the movement led by Breton, Eluard, and Aragon during a
now legendary incident at a performance of Strindberg's *Le Songe* at the
Alfred Jarry Theatre (June 1928). Thus, the events surrounding *La Coquille,*
which took place at the Ursulines Studio a few months before on 9 February
1928, may have prepared the way for Artaud's marginalization from the
surrealist cohort. In fact, the most detailed account demonstrates that Artaud,
as much as Dulac, was the target of surrealist manoeuvres. The following is
how Rousseleau reported the incident:

The audience was watching this curious production with great interest, when we heard a loud voice in the theatre asking the question: "Who made this film?" to which another voice answered: "It is Madame Germaine Dulac." The first voice: "What's Madame Dulac?" Second voice: "It's a cow." Upon hearing the crudeness of the term, Armand Tallier, the sympathetic director of the Ursulines Studios, spotted the agitators ... It was Antonin Artaud, a surrealist, a bit crazy and rather a maniac, the author of the screenplay, who was demonstrating his discontent with Madame Dulac, whom he accused of having deformed his "idea" (a crazy idea anyway).[19]

Despite this seemingly accurate account, Rousseleau's story betrays many uncertainties, including its speculative undertone regarding the identity of the "agitators." In fact, some even question the very presence of Artaud at the first screening of this film, or whether he even had any quarrel with Dulac at all. Sandy Flitterman-Lewis observes judiciously that most of the troublemakers present in the audience were actually protesting against Artaud.[20] Given these inconsistencies, one can conclude that the incident was totally blown out of proportion and that the apparent altercation between Dulac and Artaud has been exaggerated. In fact, there are numerous affinities, aesthetic and otherwise, between the author and the filmmaker, as described in Naomi Greene's article "Artaud and Film: a Reconsideration."[21] These affinities question the foundation of the claim of conflict between Dulac and Artaud and support the theory that this conflict was manufactured by some surrealists who were taking a position against avant-garde aestheticism and using Dulac as a scapegoat to settle their dispute with Artaud.

In fact, surrealism and dadaism never meant or claimed to be avant-garde movements. While they shared with the avant-garde a preoccupation with film language, neither surrealists nor dadaists attempted to articulate a profound "meditation on the formal nature of cinematic language."[22] As Gianni Rondolino noted:

Attentive above all to the formal aspect of the work, and to the rules of an expressive and drastic freeing of the cinema from its literary, theoretical and narrative encrustations, Dadaist cinema, and later Surrealist cinema, ranged themselves against this cinematographic avant-garde concept for a very simple reason: that neither Dadaism nor Surrealism had ever intended to be avant-garde movements. They were, or at least wanted to be, a new conception of the world.[23]

Dulac's concerns with rhythm, structure, and movement contradicted surrealism's notion of a primitive and violent cinema in search of an excessive and magical image *(le primitif et le merveilleux)*, and they also did not serve the main surrealist purpose, which, according to Breton, was to unsettle the spectator: "What we placed at the highest level in cinema, to the point of being disinterested in all the rest, was its power of estrangement."[24] While estrangement may have been explored in avant-garde cinema, it remained a secondary interest, particularly to Dulac, whose main concern was to materialize a pure and visual cinema where structure resembles a musical partition rather than the dreamlike fantasy of disjointed horror pictures familiar in surrealist films. The purpose of film, for Dulac, is to explore rhythm and movement, acceleration and slow-motion, as a way to express through visual harmony what the human eye cannot conceive. She writes: "I repeat these words, incessantly, 'visual, visually, view, eye.'"[25] She echoes Artaud's concern with the visual aspects of cinema, which he expressed when he wrote *La Coquille et le Clergyman* as a process of transgression of traditional narrative and as an example of "psychology ... devoured by acts."[26] Like Artaud, Dulac questioned the very foundation of a narrative cinema based on discursive and psychological exploration of character, thereby rejecting the main focus of surrealist cinema, which was to create a parallel world of dreams and the subconscious. Thus, in both Dulac's and Artaud's vision, cinema should not be considered a "hybrid" art that draws its sources from literature and the visual arts, and it must not be filled with characters in search of the dark secrets of the psyche; rather, it must have its own visual language and forms stemming from non-verbal sources, and it must explore characters as situated subjects.

It becomes clear that all the details of the controversy around *La Coquille* point in the direction of a conspiracy orchestrated by the surrealists, who were unhappy with Artaud and wanted to discredit Dulac's work. Using Dulac to settle the score with Artaud is at the heart of the gendered politics involved in marginalizing women from the first avant-garde. Beyond that, *La Coquille et le Clergyman* remains one of the most experimental works of the silent era because of, and despite, the controversy surrounding it.

Duras

In the same manner as Dulac's, but more subtly and forty years later, Duras's cinematic ventures take place within a movement dominated by men. For Duras as for Dulac, cinema must move towards abstraction; however, in Duras's case, abstraction is total, to the point of denying the very necessity of cinema. Duras's film work, like her literary work, takes a radical turn within an established experimental tradition. Her film career in the 1960s put her in contact with the movers and shakers of the New Wave.[27] Her relationship with the New Wave is complex. It could be summed up in the story that appears in Jean-Luc Godard's 1981 *Sauve qui peut (la vie)*. While giving a university lecture on film sound and picture, the main character (Paul Godard) explains to the audience that his guest, Marguerite Duras, is waiting in the adjacent room but refuses to appear. This is a reminder of the complex relationship Duras maintained with her avant-garde colleagues. Duras abstains from appearing on Godard's screen; the audience can only hear her voice, which comes from the soundtrack of her film *Le Camion*. Madeleine Cottenet-Hage explains that this marked presence of the absence of Duras's image on the screen of the most celebrated filmmaker of the New Wave is a radical sign of transgression of the cinematographic code: "Duras as absence, Duras as refusal; Duras as an aggressive transgressor of the image, denying the viewer's desire for representation, removing the expected relationship of image and sound."[28] In fact, by this clever trick, Godard underlines Duras's preoccupation, even obsession, with the dislocation of the sound/image unity and reminds his audience of her much celebrated 1975 work, *India Song*, a film solely devoted to examining the tropes and forms of this dislocation.

"I am in a relationship of murder with cinema," Duras often said.[29] For her the reality of filmic image is in itself cause for disruption. Exploiting this disruption is at the heart of her filmic experimentation and is what distinguishes her from the *Nouvelle Vague*. In fact, the New Wave, like other avant-garde movements, was an acceleration of events, as Jean Clair explains: "Instead of imagining the Golden Age in the past, we project it into the future ... without considering that the very idea of progress was the secular answer to paradise lost. Avant-garde theory was nothing but a reversed nostalgia, a projection into the future of an inaccessible perfection in time."[30] The New Wave follows this projection, while postulating a subversive political position conveyed by violent language.[31] Like surrealism and dadaism the New Wave aims to dislocate the language of film by pluralizing it. Philippe Sollers summarizes this position when he writes that "avant-garde brings out the clearly contradictory status of the written text, which *is not a language*, but always a destruction of a given language, which, within a given *tongue* transgresses it and gives it the function of multiple *tongues*."[32]

Nevertheless, Duras is one of the few avant-garde filmmakers of the 1960s and 1970s for whom it is not enough, in order to achieve this radical rupture with realist representation, to simply split up language by pluralizing its modes of expression. In other words, on the level of conceptualization, avant-garde processes must be coupled with a critical apparatus that will prevent the spectator from constructing her own seductive illusion. *India Song* shows how to achieve this brutal interruption of the "realness" of the filmic image by expressing simultaneously the present and the past of narrative. By multiplying narrative voices, Duras offers her spectator two coexisting forms of temporality: the present, which is the film projection itself, and a simultaneous critical reflection upon it. This reflection is provided by the various voices hijacking the image and moving it towards a sensory and auditory domain. Duras wrote in the introduction to the screenplay: "*India*

Song will be built first through sound then through light."[33] An example of this construct occurs in the twenty-third take, where Duras writes: "lying down in a fetal position, as if she was clinging to the floor, reduced to a black puddle, her face is invisible, Anne-Marie Stretter. *Voices* (speaking of her)";[34] as the camera captures her body in a lingering pan across the floor, the voices have already started debating her death and evanescent desire.

Thus, the decomposition of sound and image in *India Song* to a series of voices and frames questions the primacy of the filmic image. The various frames of Anne-Marie Stretter superimposed through special effects and camera tricks (travelling, focalization, enlargement and reduction of the field, etc.) and a multiplicity of mirrors and reflections are a confirmation that the story cannot and will not be reproduced in its entirety. This reluctance is not due to a difficulty with the cinematic process itself but, rather, to the fact that the process should not "represent" anything but its own failure. In constant search of the forms and extent of this failure, Duras pushes to the extreme the lack of synchronicity between image and sound, rendering impossible any intended or coincidental harmony between what is seen and what is heard. If, according to Godard, the New Wave is "to listen to what you see, and look at what you're hearing,"[35] then Duras's cinema is, in a way, a materialization and realization of the most radical aspect of the New Wave aesthetic.

What is more, anticipating many postmodern preoccupations, the Durassian camera exceeds this endeavour by inserting, even within the dissociated sound and image binary, a number of processes that favour discontinuity over linear narrative, polyphony over one omniscient voice, and ephemeral vision over continuity. These many experiments with discontinuity set Duras apart from the *Nouvelle Vague*, which, according to Robbe-Grillet, was supposed to be preoccupied with form over content, as he writes in the introduction to *L'Année dernière à Marienbad* (1961): "What makes cinema an art: it creates reality with forms. It is in the form that we must look for its real content."[36]

India Song transcends this very division. In fact, for Duras, in order to reject conventional cinema's ideological assumptions it may not suffice to suggest the disjunction of the form/content duo; rather, it is necessary to block out the rational process that posits them oppositionally in the first place, thereby redefining the parameters of the two in a new relationship of complicit absence of harmony. The Durassian screen is invaded by failing subjects, located in the interstices of subjectivity and objectivity, constantly threatened with being engulfed in the darkness looming around the frame, harassed in their sketchy representation by the narrow space of narration. At any moment during the articulation of the discourse of subjectivity, they appear haunted by the solipsistic end of representation, where apocalyptic and cryptic voices clamour their inevitable death.

Thus, Anne-Marie Stretter's photo of death is there to remind us, through the negation of her subjectivity, of the angst of dispersion of the subject in a sort of nihilistic incarnation of the power of the final gaze. She is parading before our eyes not to fill the screen and confirm that she exists but, rather, to empty the frame and act out her absence. The New Wave theorized this non-representational relationship between a dying subject and a cinematic need to create an object of vision dissociated from its representational counterpart, but it remained caught in what Wheeler Winston Dixon called the "exhaustion of narrative."[37] For Duras, beyond exhausting narrative with visual tricks, the camera must disturb the spectator's usual voyeuristic inclination by forcing him or her into revising his or her position as a passive consumer of images. By making us witness the dying agony of Anne-Marie Stretter, Duras makes us accomplices in the bankruptcy of a filmic language that cannot articulate a unified story. Hence, if we were to follow the director's advice, as she suggested to her friends on the release of the film, we would "go to see it with [our] eyes closed."[38] Duras's cinema instructs us in its own reception, while proposing a praxis of resistance to the tricks of visual illusionism, which are an expression of ideological hegemony. For her, she says, the most important process is based on "a hiatus between a theoretical intelligence and a practical intelligence."[39]

For Duras, all visual referents must disappear, leaving only traces of a world (dis)located somewhere between reality and illusion. Nothing is clearly true nor clearly false, images are not confirmed before our eyes with some realist or phantasmagoric tactic. We are presented with a seedling of an image; as soon as it is sketched out it disappears, vanishing into the empty field that looms around the frame at all times. We cannot find an escape somewhere outside the frame where we can locate our sight because, unlike Godard's spatialization, Duras's "outside" is not located in space and thus does not oppose an "inside." The spatial movements of *India Song* do not take us to India (since the film was shot in France) but through a maze of voices created from a non-visual matrix. Such a geography of the senses, evoked through the various smells and sounds of Calcutta, opens the space of the film to synesthesia, as Sylvie Blum-Reid noted in her article "The Voice-Over in *India Song*."[40]

This synesthetic poetry sets Duras apart from the *Nouvelle Vague*, for Duras's constant quest for a revolutionary visual aesthetic does not stop on the screen but invades the viewer's sense of comfort. At the same time, as the spectator is introduced to the image, the process of signifying is taken away; if the spectator succeeds at anything, it is, as Duras writes, at the very act of failing.[41] Realizing the inherently transgressive process of cinema, Duras epitomizes the relationship of the dying subject vis-à-vis the camera, for cinema must not be constructive of reality, even in its most rudimentary forms, but, rather, destructive of both reality and of its possible interpretations. "Duras's cinema," Cottenet-Hage writes, "is a cinema of denial – of meaning, of the immediate, of existence. It constitutes a system of signs pointing to an absence that threatens everything that we look at."[42]

"We must learn to speak Miró,"[43] Queneau used to say about Juan Miró's paintings, and the same applies to the work of avant-garde women. Such works as *La Coquille* or *India Song* remain unintelligible if we do not deconstruct their codes and if we continue to enclose them in a tradition that they seem to renounce. As Ann Kaplan confirms, although the desire to innovate attracts women filmmakers to avant-garde movements dominated by men, they do not fit easily into the tradition of the avant-garde because they reject the elitist foundation underlying the very concept of "tradition": "for the most part, these traditions were initiated and developed by white men; and when women were involved, ... they were not feminists in our contemporary sense. This very exclusion has enabled women filmmakers to become especially sensitive to issues of form and style, and has prevented any blind following of previous conventions."[44]

Whether by working, like Dulac, within complex aesthetic and political codes while thematizing "woman as a force of desire within the production of the filmic writing itself,"[45] or, like Duras, by consciously eliminating visual pleasure and casting a shadow of silence on the illusionary presumptions of cinema, women filmmakers of the avant-garde stand on the outside of aesthetic schisms by creating a truly experimental cinema – one that destroys the very desire for realist cinema, illustrating Duras's famous title, "Destroy, she said."

Notes

1 Wladimir Krysinski in Christian Berg, Frank Durieux, and Geert Lernout, eds., *The Turn of the Century: Modernism and Modernity in Literature and the Arts* (Berlin: Walter de Gruyter and Co., 1995), 17.

2 Peter Wollen, *Signs and Meaning in the Cinema* (London: Secker and Warburg, 1974), 16.

3 Teresa de Lauretis, "Rethinking Women's Cinema: Aesthetics and Feminist Theory," in *Multiple Voices in Feminist Film Criticism*, ed. Diane Carson, Linda Dittmar, and Janice R. Welsch (Minneapolis: University of Minnesota Press, 1994), 141.

4 I use "avant-garde" and "experimental film" interchangeably, knowing that the expression "experimental film" was not used in France in the 1920s. However, according to Jacques-Bernard Brunius it was in use in Anglo-Saxon countries: "'Cinéma expérimental,' utilisé plus spécialement en Angleterre et aux Etats-Unis, est évidemment le terme qui semble englober le plus de significations. On entend par là tout ce qui ne se fait pas d'ordinaire à une époque donnée dans les films de production courante, qu'il s'agisse d'un film dans son ensemble, ou seulement d'un simple effet isolé." See Jacques-Bernard Brunius, *En marge du cinéma français* (Paris: Arcanes, 1954), 26.

5 The military reference comes from Bakunin who, in 1878, borrowed the military expression "Avant-garde" as a title for his anarchist journal published in Switzerland.

6 "L'Avant-Garde apparut au cinéma, vers 1925, avec dix ou vingt ans de retard sur la peinture ou la poésie." Georges Sadoul, *Histoire du cinéma mondial des origines à nos jours* (Paris: Flammarion, 1972), 194. All translations are mine.

7   "Metteurs en scène d'avant-garde, profitez de ce bel été pour vous attacher aux paysages vraiment français. Vos scénarios y gagneront en style, en élégance et en homogénéité." La *Femme de nulle part*, "Insinuation," *Le Film* 5, 125 (August 1918): 7b.

8   "Ils ont pu survivre à cette crise au prix d'une acceptation plus ou moins totale de la règle du jeu commerciale." André Bazin, "Opinions sur l'avant-garde: 2. l'avant-garde nouvelle," *Cahiers du cinéma* 2, 10 (March 1952): 16-7.

9   "Le secret de cet esclavage: L'étau économique." See Germaine Dulac, "Films visuels et anti-visuels," *Le Rouge et le noir*, "Cinéma," special issue, (July 1928): 32.

10 "Esclave, le réalisateur cinégraphique l'est. On ne lui donne l'argent nécessaire à l'élaboration de son travail que contre une profession de foi de dépendance au goût du public." Dulac, *Le Rouge et le noir*, 31.

11 Susan Hayward, "A History of French Cinema: 1895-1991. Pioneering Film-makers (Guy, Dulac, Varda) and their Heritage," *Paragraph* 15, 1 (March 1992): 29.

12 In Catherine Silberschmidt, "La femme visible: Germaine Dulac," *Etudes de lettres* 12 (avril-juin, 1993): 141.

13 "Un silence dont sont complices aussi les historiennes françaises qui ont publié [en 1992] une *Histoire des Femmes en Occident en cinq volumes* ... et qui, dans le volume concernant le XXème siècle, consacrant un long chapitre au travail et à la création des femmes dans le secteur culturel, ainsi qu'à la représentation féminine, sans mentionner Germaine Dulac." Silberschmidt, *Etudes de lettres*, 141.

14 E. Ann Kaplan, *Women and Film: Both Sides of the Camera* (London: Routledge, 1988), 88.

15 "Ne pourrait-on pas supprimer ces deux termes: 'Cinéma d'exception' (dit improprement 'cinéma d'avant-garde') et 'Cinéma commercial' pour ne laisser subsister que celui plus bref de Cinéma?" Germaine Dulac, "Dans son cadre visuel le cinéma n'a point de limites" *Paris nouvelles*, 9 May 1931.

16 "Un vrai film ne doit pas se raconter puisqu'il doit puiser son principe actif et émotif dans des images faites d'uniques vibrations visuelles." Dulac, *Le Rouge et le noir*, 39.

17 "Germaine Dulac avait tenu Artaud à l'écart du tournage puis du montage; ... celui-ci, mécontent du procédé et peu satisfait du film, obtint de Paulhan la publication, dans la *NRF*, de son scénario original, en vue de préserver ses droits d'auteur de *La Coquille*; ... la réalisatrice, sans doute mécontente à son tour de l'opération NRF, fit en sorte de différer la sortie publique du film; ... une partie de la presse avait néanmoins pu le voir lors de projections privées." Alain et Odette Virmaux, *Artaud, un bilan critique* (Paris: Pierre Belfond, 1979), 46.

18 In Virmaux, *Artaud, un bilan critique*.

19 "Le public suivait avec intérêt cette curieuse production, quand dans la salle on entendit une voix forte poser cette question: 'Qui a fait ce film?' A quoi une autre voix répond: 'C'est Mme Germaine Dulac.' Première voix: 'Qu'est-ce que Mme Dulac?' Deuxième voix: 'C'est une vache.' Devant la grossièreté du terme, Armand Tallier, le sympathique directeur des Ursulines, accourt, fait donner la lumière et repère les deux perturbateurs ... C'était Antonin Artaud, un surréaliste, un peu fou et un peu maniaque, auteur du scénario du film et qui manifestait ainsi son mécontentement contre Mme Dulac, qu'il accusait d'avoir déformé son 'idée' (une idée un peu folle)." In Virmaux, *Artaud, un bilan critique*, 47.

20 Sandy Flitterman-Lewis, "The Image and the Spark: Dulac and Artaud Reviewed," in *Dada and Surrealist Film*, Rudolf E. Kuenzli, ed. (New York: Willis Locker and Owens, 1987), 110.

21 Naomi Greene, "Artaud and Film: a Reconsideration," *Cinema Journal* 23, 4 (Summer 1984): 28-40.

22 Ibid., 32.

23 Gianni Rondolino in Greene, "Artaud and Film," 32.

24 "Ce que nous mettions au plus haut en lui, au point de nous désintéresser de tout le reste, c'était son pouvoir de dépaysement." See André Breton, "Comme dans un bois," *l'âge du cinéma* 4-5 (August-November 1951): 27.

25 "Je répète à tout instant ces mots: 'visuel, visuellement, vue, oeil.'" See Dulac, *Le Rouge et le noir*, 37.

26 "J'ai cherché dans le scénario qui suit à réaliser cette idée de cinéma visuel où la psychologie est dévorée par les actes." See Antonin Artaud, *Oeuvres complètes* III (Paris: Gallimard, 1978), 19.

27 Although I place Duras within the New Wave movement, it should be pointed out that her cinematic work was produced in the late 1960s and 1970s after the end of the New Wave of the 1950s.

28 Madeleine Cottenet-Hage and Robert P. Koller, "The Cinema of Duras in Search of an Ideal Image," *French Review* 63, 1 (October 1989): 88.

29 "Je suis dans un rapport de meurtre avec le cinéma." Marguerite Duras, "Les yeux verts," *Cahiers du cinéma* 312-3 (June 1980): 9.

30 "Au lieu d'imaginer l'Âge d'or dans le passé, écrit, on le projeta dans le futur ... sans se rendre compte que l'idée de progrès n'était pas la réplique sécularisée du paradis perdu. La théorie de l'avant-garde n'était ainsi qu'une nostalgie inversée, la projection dans le futur d'une perfection inaccessible dans le temps." See Jean Clair, *Considérations sur l'état des Beaux-Arts* (Paris: Gallimard, 1983), 35.

31 Charles Russel, *The Avant-Garde Today* (Urbana: University of Illinois Press, 1981), 3.

32 "L'avant-garde met en évidence le statut définitivement contradictoire de l'écriture textuelle *qui n'est pas un langage*, mais, à chaque fois, *destruction d'un langage;* qui, à l'intérieur d'une langue, transgresse cette langue et lui donne une fonction de *langues.*" See Philippe Sollers, *L'ecriture et l'expérience des limites* (Paris: Seuil, 1968), 12 (emphasis in original).

33 Marguerite Duras, *India Song* (Paris: Albatros, 1979), 21.

34 Duras, *India Song*, 30.

35 In Wheeler Winston Dixon, *The Films of Jean-Luc Godard* (New York: SUNY Press, 1997), 205.

36 "Ce qui fait que le cinéma est un art: il crée une réalité avec des formes. C'est dans sa forme qu'il faut chercher son véritable contenu." Alain Robbe-Grillet, *L'Année dernière à Marienbad* (Paris: Minuit, 1961), 8.

37 Dixon, *The Films of Jean-Luc Godard*, 41.

38 In Laure Adler, *Marguerite Duras* (Paris: Gallimard, 1998), 445.

39 Duras, *India Song*, 89.

40 Sylvie Blum-Reid, "The Voice-Over in *India Song* by Marguerite Duras," *Journal of Durassian Studies* 1 (Fall 1989): 39.

41 "S'il y a réussite d'*India Song* il ne peut s'agir que de la mise en oeuvre d'un projet d'échec." See Duras, *India Song*, 22.

42 Cottenet-Hage and Koller, "Cinema of Duras," 96.

43 "Il faut apprendre le miró." See Raymond Queneau, *Bâtons, chiffres et lettres* (Paris: Gallimard, 1950), 127.

44 Kaplan, *Women and Film*, 87.

45 Sandy Flitterman-Lewis, "Theorizing the 'Feminine': Women as the Figure of Desire in *The Seashell and the Clergyman*," *Wide Angle* 6, 3 (1984): 33.

4 Cinefeminism in Its Middle Ages, or "Please, Please, Please Give Me Back My Pleasure": The 1990s Work of Sally Potter, Chantal Akerman, and Yvonne Rainer
Catherine Fowler

Thanks to the centenary of cinema much time has been spent reflecting upon past achievements and subsequent development. In the field of feminist film theory this impulse has produced such books as Sue Thornham's *Passionate Detachment*[1] and Maggie Humm's *Feminism and Film*,[2] both of which attempt to provide textbook studies of the development of cinefeminism (which I use to encompass both theory and practice), and more personal works such as Patricia Mellencamp's *A Fine Romance: Five Ages of Film Feminism*[3] and B. Ruby Rich's *Chick Flicks*.[4]

Despite this evident meditation on how feminism has inflected twenty years of film theory and film practice, I would argue that few of these studies are truly interested in the ways in which cinefeminism has aged. For example, Humm introduces her collection with the assertion that her purpose "in interrelating feminism with film is to look differently, with different visual pleasures than ... has been possible to date."[5] She then goes on to examine a variety of different "visual pleasures," covering subjects ranging from pornography and the gaze to Cronenberg, Black feminism, and postmodernism. While she herself asserts from the beginning that "to present the sequences of these chapters as the evolution of contemporary feminist theory ... would be inaccurate" and, instead, wants to "utilize, in a provisional way, some themes and techniques from contemporary feminism ... in film analysis,"[6] I would argue that her method actually makes it very difficult to talk about different visual pleasures. What this chapter addresses, and what is witnessed by Humm's approach, is the lack of critical attention to feminist film theory's "hoariness."

Too many of the recent studies have focused upon the ways in which feminist film theory has moved on from its origins. Here I wish to emphasize continuity and change by considering how themes from the 1970s have been developed in the work of three filmmakers who have continued making films into the 1990s: Yvonne Rainer, Chantal Akerman, and Sally Potter.[7] My choice of these three filmmakers has largely been influenced by the fact that their early films, *Thriller* (Potter 1979), *Jeanne Dielman, 23 quai du commerce, 1080 Bruxelles* (Akerman 1975), and *Film about a Woman Who ...* (Rainer 1974) were the ur-texts of an adolescent feminist film theory, while their 1980s and 1990s work has rarely been discussed. I will focus here on *The Tango Lesson* (Potter 1997), *Nuit et jour* (Akerman 1991), and *Privilege* (Rainer 1990). I will also restrict my study to the phrase raised by Humm, "visual pleasure," not only because this was the crux of Mulvey's founding feminist text, but also because, as the term "hoariness" suggests, I am interested in the use of the female body in the cinema and in examining the visible effects of twenty-five years of feminist film theory and practice on its surface.

Cinefeminism and (In)visibility

From its initiation in the late 1960s and early 1970s, feminist film theory's battle with the cinema began at the level of the visual and visible. In terms

Yvonne Rainer and Shirley Soffer in Rainer's *Film About a Woman Who ...* (1975), courtesy of Yvonne Rainer

of film history, the problem was one of *invisibility,* as female personnel from scriptwriters to directors had never been written into either the canons or the critical histories of world cinema. By contrast, in terms of film practice and the image of the woman on screen, the problem was one of *over-visibility* brought about by the over-signification of the female body. The path to this conclusion is well worn, so I will simply reiterate those points that are relevant for this present study. The sociological studies of Molly Haskell[8] and Marjorie Rosen[9] pointed out how women were stereotyped into specific roles that constantly subordinated them to male characters. Laura Mulvey[10] then took this to another level. Mulvey suggested that the symbolic order that Metz had used to describe the workings of the cinematic apparatus was dependent upon the representation of the female form, which represents the threat of castration and the male's "other." In order to prevent the threat of castration that the image of the woman signifies, the man (whether director, screen character, or spectator) exerts over the woman the power of his gaze. Through this gaze woman is relegated, in the cinematic process, to the position of image, where she becomes an erotic object for both the character and the spectator.

The strategies adopted by Potter, Akerman, Rainer, and other women filmmakers of this time should all be seen as trying to avoid the overdetermined use of the woman described above. Some went further than others; thus, B. Ruby Rich notes that the experimental filmmaker Peter Gidal "pledge[d] never to show a woman's body in one of his films again, because he'd realized the impossibility of doing so without inherent objectification and subjugation."[11]

Chantal Akerman's *Jeanne Dielman, 23 quai du commerce, 1080 Bruxelles* (1975), courtesy of Paradise Films

However, for most feminist filmmakers this evacuation of the woman from their frames was unacceptable; instead, they wanted to free her from her position as seductive presence or source of visual pleasure and allow her to be seen anew.

In order to signal an alternative representation, Potter, Akerman, and Rainer were united in their denial of illusionism. If the suspension of disbelief so crucial to most narrative cinema also triggered the unconscious processes discussed by Mulvey, then this had to be avoided. Instead of seamless narratives, all three directors disrupted their fictional worlds through strategies of distanciation. Potter and Rainer shared a liking for the use of dance, inter-titles, voice-over, and a division of the film's structure into discrete parts. Akerman's approach was slightly different. *Jeanne Dielman* was clearly more of a linear narrative than were the "collages" of Potter and Rainer, yet in the film Akerman pushed at the seams of illusionism through her use of very long takes and a static camera. These techniques were combined to produce a refusal to seduce the spectator with the normal registers used to inflect meaning (close-ups, camera angles, different shot sizes).

While each director used an alternative film form to overcome the oversignification of the female body, in narrative terms they examined more familiar situations. All three films could be said to touch in some way upon the woman's place in the melodramatic scenario. Rainer suggests one reason for this: "Feminist theorists like Mulvey and Kaplan have pointed out that melodrama ... is a place where women's dilemmas are played out in a very visible way. So this offers the avant-garde filmmaker a formal arena in which to make the tensions and dilemmas of women living in a patriarchy accessible and visible."[12] *Thriller* is the most specific about this reference to melodrama, as it invokes the opera *La Bohème* and examines the position of Mimi the seamstress, who is forced to play the tragic figure in a tale of doomed romance. However, *Thriller* questions Mimi's fate without changing or challenging it. In *Film about a Woman Who ...* the figures provide characters who "act out" certain melodramatic scenarios, thereby allowing Rainer to investigate the structures of feeling associated with this genre. The film takes human relationships as its subject, yet promotes dry analysis over emotion, particularly through the disjunction between image and sound. *Jeanne Dielman* takes the melodrama's focus on the suffering mother into new territory in that, as in Rainer's film, surface emotion is denied and we are forced to engage in the rituals that sustain Jeanne's desperate existence. Although they deconstructed melodramatic scenarios, all three films were also pessimistic in their conclusions. Thus, at the end of *Thriller*, Mimi, the hero, is still caught in a narrative web of victimization, just as Jeanne Dielman is trapped in her repressive regime and the female characters in *Film about a Woman Who ...* find little fulfilment in their relationships.

Conventional engagement with an illusionist narrative and identification with a male protagonist were denied in these films. However, freed from the constraints of the standard seductive gaze at the woman, the cameras of these three filmmakers seemed keen to explore other things. Akerman's camera was "exhibitionist" in its framing; its long lingering shots dissected time and space, indices to Jeanne Dielman's psyche. With Rainer the use of dance, inter-texts, slow-motion action, and inter-titles dislodged the hold of dialogue upon the meaning-making process, forcing us again to pay attention to space and the bodies within it. Potter's approach was similar to Rainer's as she mixed media – dance, photographic stills, and, in particular, musical interludes – to again shatter illusionism and to force the spectator to seek alternative ways of making meaning.

These first films of Potter, Akerman, and Rainer deconstructed the mainstream representation of woman, countering the visual pleasure typically located through an eroticized gaze by using narratives and images that denied all access to such an aesthetic. For feminist film theory these films offered evidence of a female aesthetic so lacking in patriarchal mainstream cinema. Perhaps the full impact of these films can be felt upon reading the quotations below:

> [*Jeanne Dielman*] invents a new language capable of transmitting truths previously unspoken.[13]

> *Thriller* ... and *Jeanne Dielman* ... these films share a discourse which sets up the possibility of sexual difference in spectator-text relations by privileging

a "feminine voice." They pose the possibility of a feminine writing which would construct new forms of pleasure in cinema.[14]

[*Film about a Woman Who* ... is] concerned not only with the juncture between the rituals of everyday life and female subjectivity, but also with an examination of the cinematic and cultural codes through which such a juncture can be examined.[15]

Annette Kuhn's words, in particular, raise the notion of pleasure first introduced here by Humm. Kuhn continues her exploration of *Thriller,* also introducing Rainer's *Lives of Performers* (1972) into her discussion, and suggests that these films offer "the possibility of pleasures other than those of completion [due to a lack of closure]. First, in moments of accretion ... the spectator has the option of pleasurable and open-ended contemplation of an image which constructs no particularly privileged viewpoint. The ellipses offer the possibility of a rather different pleasure, that of piecing together fragments of a story – the active pleasure, that is, of working on a puzzle."[16]

Kuhn's analysis of the pleasures of Rainer's film can easily apply to *Thriller* and *Jeanne Dielman.* We might also note here that Kuhn seems to pinpoint exactly what Maggie Humm claimed as her subject – "looking differently, with different visual pleasures"; here they are those of an "open-ended contemplation."

The coincidence of Potter, Akerman, and Rainer's work with a developing feminist film theory was short-lived. It would be easy to suggest that feminist film theory went one way and practice another as certainly, on reaching the 1980s, they seemed to part. Yet their separate ways actually followed quite similar paths. The difference between the paths taken by theory and practice is that, whereas Potter, Akerman, and Rainer retained their focus on alternative visual pleasures, feminist film theory seemed to want to return to the mainstream. It must be admitted that some critics suggested an essentialist female pleasure, and others suggested that feminism should recognize its feminisms and address its questions to the diversity of women and, hence, of pleasures. However, the majority of feminist film theorists led theory away from Potter, Akerman, and Rainer by suggesting that female spectators could find pleasure in less radical changes (e.g., the use of positive, independent heroines; the subversion of "male" genres; the reappropriation of "female" genres; and/or a reading against the grain that recovers pleasures from places that Laura Mulvey and others had assumed were closed to women).

The parting of theory and practice towards the 1980s is ably expressed in Sally Potter's second film, *Gold Diggers* (1983). Over images of a barren icy landscape through which a woman is slowly making her way we hear the following song:

Sally Potter's *Gold Diggers,* courtesy of BFI Stills, Posters and Designs

Went to the pictures for a break
thought I'd put my feet up
have a bit of intake
but then a man with a gun came through the door
and when he kissed her, I couldn't take it any more.

Please, please, please give me back my pleasure,
please, please, please give me back my good night out,
please give me back my leisure time, I've got the pleasure time blues,
I'm seeing red.

Having set out on a path of denial from which there was no way back, Potter, Akerman, and Rainer found themselves, in the 1980s, on the road described above in the opening image of *Gold Diggers.* While the image track suggests the continuing journey the female characters of these film-makers were to take, the soundtrack characterizes that journey as one back towards some of the pleasures they had initially fled. Perhaps what one notices the most when tracing the path taken from the 1970s texts *(Thriller, Jeanne Dielman,* and *Film about a Woman Who ...)* via the 1980s *(The Tango Lesson, Nuit et jour,* and *Privilege)* is a more liberated attitude towards conventional visual pleasure. This is not to say that these three filmmakers revert to objectification or even voyeurism: their cameras still refuse to assume these attitudes. Instead, there is an overt sense of "knowingness" (one could almost say "wisdom") that replaces the tight-lipped denial of the 1970s.

Privilege provides our critical frame here, as the aging process, change, and history form the core of Rainer's film. Ostensibly about menopause, *Privilege* retains the multiple layers of discourse found in *The Man Who Envied Women*[17] as well as the disruptive and anti-seductive strategies of *Film about a Woman Who* .... The difference between *Privilege, Film about a Woman Who* ..., and *The Man Who Envied Women* can be explained by a key moment from the film itself. The main character, Jenny (played by Alice Spivak), is expressing her distress at discovering that, when she entered middle age, men stopped looking at her. The scene is interrupted by an inter-title that reads, "having passed the frontier of attractiveness to men, she is now on the 'other side' of privilege." Having for years attempted to *avoid*, to disrupt, or to appropriate the dominant male gaze, what *Privilege* seems to suggest is that, in fact, that gaze is lifted simply through the aging process, with the depressing realization that, as Jenny later says, "men's desire for me was the lynch-pin of my identity."

To return our discussion to our three filmmakers, I wish to substitute for privilege "visual pleasure," which situates Jenny in the classic position of the woman in dominant cinema, defined only by what she represents for men. With such a substitution in place, *Thriller, Jeanne Dielman*, and *Film about a Woman Who* ... become visual pleasure films – films that engage directly with Mulvey's article and all that moment represents in feminist film history. However, *Privilege, Nuit et jour*, and *The Tango Lesson* operate on "the other side" of visual pleasure. If we explore this comparison between the postmenopausal and the postvisual further, within the text of *Privilege* it is suggested that menopause destroys not only female desire but also women's desirability; in filmic terms an undesirable woman would produce the epitome of the uncinematic – a woman who is no longer circumscribed by the male gaze or defined by male desire and who, therefore, refuses to signify "woman." It is precisely this "uncinematic" woman that Potter, Akerman, and Rainer cast in their postvisual pleasure films – *The Tango Lesson, Nuit et jour*, and *Privilege*. Thus, the more relaxed attitude to conventional visual pleasure noted earlier is possible because of the different signification of the female body for these filmmakers. This change manifests itself in different ways in each film, as I will now briefly discuss.

As they move towards the 1990s, all three filmmakers seem to have more control over their work. Taking Potter first, this shift is directly figured in her films as she graduates from *Thriller*, which takes a pre-existing narrative and questions how it is put together around the woman, to *The Tango Lesson*, in which she is fully in control of the narrative and plays a filmmaker writing a script for a film. This control is visually underlined by an emphasis on Potter's gaze. As she moves through Paris, supposedly planning the visuals for the film script she is writing, we see *with* her both literally (as we follow her gaze along a stone wall with her hands marking out footsteps) and figuratively (as the scene she has imagined, in which her main actor's feet replace her hands, is shown to us in sumptuous colour).

While the command the woman has over the narrative and imaging process has changed here, the way of seeing has not, and it is evident that the tactile evocation of space that opens *Gold Diggers* is amplified in *The Tango Lesson* through creative use of sound and image. *The Tango Lesson* features an emphasis on a sensual gaze alert to light, movement, and shades in black and white or colour and that therefore creates highly tangible spaces that charge the bodies moving through them with energy. It is perhaps in this overemphasis of the materiality of the framed that Potter retains her commitment to non-illusionism: there is still a diegetic space and characters who belong to that fictional world, but we are *also* drawn to other things in the frame.

The "pleasurable open-ended contemplation" that Annette Kuhn suggested *Thriller* offered is fulfilled in *The Tango Lesson* by the use of mise-en-scène; however, to this Potter adds another dimension created by a more thematic use of the female gaze. Having trouble writing her script, Sally goes to Paris where she wastes time taking tango lessons from a dancer, Pablo. The power struggle that develops between Pablo and Sally is not figured through who looks but, rather, through who is looked at. Thus, in their main argument, Sally demands that Pablo look at her, accusing him: "You don't know how to use your eyes. You only want to be looked at, not to look. That's why you don't see, that's why you know nothing about cinema." On the one hand one might suggest that little has changed from Mimi in *Thriller* – the almost invisible and certainly overlooked victim – to Sally in *The Tango Lesson,* still demanding to be seen. In fact, everything has changed once we realize that Sally is able to take control of her own image and demand an acknowledgment of her "to-be-looked-at-ness" because such a position is no longer threatening.

Rainer also makes an appearance in both her films, yet in *Privilege* she seems more assured, playing herself and then an alias, Yvonne Washington, who is leading the questioning of the main subject, Jenny. As noted previously, of the three filmmakers Rainer compromises her style the least over her twenty-year career; however, even she tackles issues her earlier films avoided. In *Film about a Woman Who …* Rainer investigates autobiography and relationships between the sexes while formally disrupting the viewers' visual pleasure. The women in her dramas are rarely filmed to seduce; instead the viewer is made to feel discomfort. One scene in particular can be singled out as an example of Rainer's anti-seductive practice; a close-up shot frames Rainer from knees to chest and a man and woman by her side slowly pull down her skirt to reveal her underwear. We could think of this scene as a "strategy of demystification" (Mary Ann Doane)[18] of the female body. In *Privilege* this demystifying practice finds less place, though we might suggest that visual pleasure is denied through the mixing of media, when the film begins with a film image then cuts to an unflattering grainy video footage. The effect on Jenny is that she suddenly seems to age before our eyes.

Akerman also allows something that she had formerly denied: the nude female body. Her development is from the repressed Jeanne Dielman, whose whole existence depends upon a strict regimen that values rituals and repetition over any kind of pleasure, and who is filmed in an extremely anti-seductive manner, to the character of "Julie" in *Nuit et jour* who exudes sexuality. Over the course of the film Julie flits between two lovers, wandering around Paris with a vacant smile on her face and being frequently filmed in the nude. It is here that *Nuit et jour* takes up the representation of the female body that was a central part of *Jeanne Dielman* and Akerman's first film, *Je tu il elle* (1974), and connects it forcefully with the notion of what Sandy Flitterman-Lewis terms "la jouissance du voir" or "an erotics of vision unhampered by the strictures of voyeuristic definition."[19] Over the course of her career Akerman's gaze has always favoured this erotics of vision; however, it is only in her postvisual pleasure phase that she has been able to turn it onto the female body.

I have hoped to show through these brief examples the continuity of ideas in the films of Potter, Akerman, and Rainer, as each works from a postvisual pleasure position. What is important here is the fact that this postvisual pleasure position could only have been achieved by going through and past the visual pleasure period, for it demanded the sense of continuity and change that comes from twenty-five years of developing work. Finally, in reply to the plea by Potter's heroine in *Gold Diggers*, Potter, Akerman, and Rainer did indeed give her back her pleasure; however, this was never going to be the visual pleasure described by Mulvey. Instead, as I have discussed here, it is a carefully developed and negotiated pleasure that shows clear traces of its history of evolution and now needs to be reconnected to the feminist film theory that was once its interpreter.

Notes

1 Sue Thornham, *Passionate Detachment: An Introduction to Feminist Film Theory* (Oxford: Oxford University Press, 1997).
2 Maggie Humm, *Feminism and Film* (Edinburgh/Bloomington and Indianapolis: Edinburgh University Press/Indiana University Press, 1997).
3 Patricia Mellencamp, *A Fine Romance: Five Ages of Film Feminism* (Philadelphia: Temple University Press, 1995).
4 B. Ruby Rich, *Chick Flicks: Theories and Memories of the Feminist Film Movement* (Durham and London: Duke University Press, 1998).
5 Humm, *Feminism and Film*, 36.
6 Ibid., viii.
7 This is not to suggest that these three are the only examples that could be used here. Others include Helma Sanders Brahms, Helke Sander, or Lizzie Borden; that is, filmmakers who began their careers in the 1970s and have continued to make feature-length films through the 1980s and 1990s.

8 Molly Haskell, *From Reverence to Rape: The Treatment of Women in the Movies*, 2nd ed. (Chicago: University of Chicago Press, 1987).

9 Marjorie Rosen, *Popcorn Venus: Women, Movies and the American Dream* (New York: Coward, McCann and Geohagen, 1973).

10 Laura Mulvey, "Visual Pleasure and Narrative Cinema," *Screen* 16, 3 (Autumn 1975): 6-18.

11 Rich, *Chick Flicks*, 105.

12 "Interview with Yvonne Rainer," Mitchell Rosenbaum in Yvonne Rainer, *The Films of Yvonne Rainer* (Bloomington and Indianapolis: Indiana University Press, 1989), 41.

13 B. Ruby Rich, "In the Name of Feminist Film Criticism," in *Jump Cut: Hollywood, Politics and Counter-Cinema*, ed. Peter Steven (Toronto: Between the Lines, 1985), 208-30.

14 Annette Kuhn, *Women's Pictures: Feminism and Cinema*, 2nd ed. (London: Verso, 1994), 163.

15 Judith Mayne, *The Woman at the Keyhole: Feminism and Women's Cinema* (Bloomington and Indianapolis: Indiana University Press, 1990), 55. Mayne also mentions Ursula Reuter Christiansen's *The Executioner* (Denmark, 1972) and Valie Export's *Invisible Adversaries* (West Germany, 1976).

16 Kuhn, *Women's Pictures*, 165.

17 This film makes some reference to this subject. At one point Yvonne Rainer enters the field, bends her head sideways in front of the camera, takes off her glasses, and says: "Will all menstruating women please leave the theatre?" and leaves. This is then shortly followed by Trisha's remarks that men, with their castration complex, are both fascinated and repelled by women's periods and that, in our culture, this causes postmenopausal women to be denied sexual powers.

18 Mary Ann Doane, *The Desire to Desire: The Woman's Film of the 1940s* (London: Macmillan, 1987), 36.

19 Sandy Flitterman-Lewis, *To Desire Differently: Feminism and the French Cinema* (Urbana: University of Illinois Press, 1990), 21.

Part 2

Close-up on the Life and Works
of Auteures from Europe

This part focuses on several individual women filmmakers whose body of work is very strongly marked by their life and personality as well as by their particular style of directing. Their careers span several decades, and their work shows elements of both continuity and change, reflecting developments in their own lives, the political context, and the movie industry.

Steven Taubeneck begins by providing an introduction to the films of German director Helma Sanders Brahms, who was present at the first weekend of the "Women Filmmakers: Refocusing" events in Vancouver. Sanders Brahms's films, especially the classic *Germany, Pale Mother,* have enjoyed extraordinary success beyond Germany, not only in terms of recognition for their aesthetic qualities, but for their contribution to reflection on the situation of postwar and post-Wall Germany. Yet these films are extremely hard to obtain, which means that few people are able to view them. In an interview with Judith Plessis and Taubeneck, Sanders Brahms shares some of her experiences, including those pertaining to the obstacles she currently encounters as a woman of her generation, in trying to make new films. Some of the more practical points she makes are developed further in a panel discussion in which she participated and that is included in Part 4, as is Ute Lischke's discussion of the context of her films in relation to other German filmmakers.

Her triumphs and difficulties are echoed by another famous German director of the same generation, Margarethe von Trotta, in an interview held at the University of Victoria (British Columbia). While most of her films are more accessible on video (and with subtitles in English), von Trotta is equally controversial in her choice of themes. Her film *The Promise,* which deals with the fall of the Berlin Wall, provides an interesting point of comparison with Sanders Brahms's *The Apple Trees,* which presents a different focus on issues related to that event. Another of her best known films, *The Second Awakening of Christa Klages,* is analyzed in detail by Siew Jin Ooi, who illustrates how feminism and other aspects of radical politics are linked in von Trotta's work.

The last chapters in this section deal with two other major European directors, Agnieszka Holland and Sally Potter. B. Amarillis Lugo de Fabritz concentrates on two of Holland's films: *Provincial Actors*, which was filmed in Poland, and *Europa, Europa*, which was filmed in exile. This chapter complements Janina Falkowska's discussion of the effects of political change on the careers of women filmmakers from Poland (see Chapter 15). The analysis by Corinn Columpar of Potter's *The Tango Lesson* can be read as a sequel to Catherine Fowler's discussion of cinefeminism's "middle age" (Chapter 4).

5 Helma Sanders Brahms: An Introduction
Steven Taubeneck

Helma Sanders Brahms was born in 1940, in the northwestern German town of Emden. The light in many of her films is a northern light, grey and darkly bright under low-hanging clouds, and may resemble the light she saw in the skies of her childhood. She described her childhood in a recent interview: "The first time I saw a film I knew it was my thing. I had a lonely childhood. When I was ten years old, my parents sent me on Sunday mornings to matinees. There were often fairy-tale films showing. There was one that I especially liked, and afterwards I went to the cashier and said: 'I want my money back for the other films since they were so bad.' I thought: 'I don't want such bad films to be made.' The one film I liked was *La Belle et la Bête* (*Beauty and the Beast*), by Cocteau. From that time on, I was convinced that I would make films." Her story reveals her strong commitment to: (1) make better films, (2) rely on fantasy and imagination, and (3) resist the conventions of the culture industry. It also reveals one source of her insights into the loneliness of childhood.

It may be difficult today to imagine what the situation was like in Germany during the 1950s. Germany had just fought two world wars in a period of thirty-one years, from 1914 to 1945. This was undoubtedly the "age of catastrophe," as the historian Eric Hobsbawm has called it, not only for Germany but for the entire world. Violence and destruction had shaken humanity on a scale never known before, leaving over 50 million dead or wounded. Millions of refugees had fled into postwar Germany, while the country itself had been split under the superpowers in the Cold War. Some people like to describe the 1950s as a kind of "golden age," but it is more likely that, in the case of Germany at least, it was a time of shock, of paralysis, in which people tried to survive as best they could by forgetting or repressing what had just happened, what they had just done. Helma Sanders Brahms's film, *Germany, Pale Mother* (1979), graphically depicts the shock that many felt in the aftermath of the war. In this film, she tells the story of her mother and the inner war she entered after the outer war had ended. Many of Sanders Brahms's films spring from this time, from her confrontation with the Second World War and her experiences during the immediate postwar period. Another example is the more recent film *Mein Herz – niemandem!*, or *My Heart Is Mine Alone* (1997), which tells the amazing story of Else Lasker-Scholer and Gottfried Benn. Both films offer a sustained reflection on the tragedies and ironies of the mid-twentieth century.

The film industry in West Germany during the 1950s and 1960s was dominated by two major tendencies arising from the end of the war. First, since

the cinemas and distribution of films were in the hands of the allied powers, the films shown in West Germany were largely American. Second, when
German producers appealed to the government for funds, the government
would, in order to get around American censorship, encourage only the
most politically innocuous and cheaply made films. What came to be known
as a "Bavarian cottage industry" arose in both TV and the film industry,
which produced many kitschy "Heimatfilme," or films about happy domes-
ticity. Above all, these films tend to show women as housewives, loving
mothers, and supporters of their husbands. It is probably these films, among
others, that so disturbed Helma Sanders Brahms as a child that she asked for
her money back from the theatre.

During those years, the West German government's position towards filmmakers was ambiguous and frustrating. The film industry was losing customers, cinemas were closing, and most people were staying at home to
watch television. In order to improve the situation, the government awarded
tax breaks, organized a film subsidies bill, and gave state film prizes. Yet
these apparent blessings proved to be curses, for they brought a kind of
bureaucratic control that was hostile to experimental and socially critical
artists. In response, twenty-six artists gathered in 1962 to protest the situation with a manifesto. The Oberhausen Manifesto, as the document is now
called, signalled the first appearance of the New German Cinema.

At that time Helma Sanders Brahms was studying drama, German, and
English in Hanover and Cologne. In 1965 she completed her exams to be a
schoolteacher. Her knowledge of literature from her studies and personal
interest is clearly shown in her films, for example in her use of Bertolt Brecht's
poem "Deutschland" ("Germany") in her film *Germany, Pale Mother*. Brecht
begins his poem: "May others speak of their disgrace, / I speak of mine. / O
Germany, pale mother! / How you sit, defiled, / among nations. / From among
the corrupted ones, you stand out." Sanders Brahms's narrator recites the
poem in the film to set the sufferings of her family within the broader context of Germany's general desecration. Film and literature are interwoven
to add a lyrical, but also critical, effect to the presentation. Brecht's poem
critically comments on the story shown in the film. Further, the fairy tale
from the Grimm brothers, called *The Robber Bride*, offers a critical counterpoint to the rape of the mother in the film. Sanders Brahms has often mixed
literature into her films, either by using literary texts as part of the script or
by drawing on the lives of actual writers (e.g., the poet Heinrich von Kleist
in the 1977 film *Heinrich*). The tension between literature and visual imagery
creates a critical, reflective interaction in her films. Perhaps Sanders Brahms
can best be seen as a modern-day Scheherazade, someone who, through her
stories, attempts to have a deep, improving effect on her audience.

After she had completed her teacher's exam, Sanders Brahms worked as a
television announcer and began filming TV documentaries. While filming

a documentary in Italy in 1967, she met the directors Corbucci and Pasolini and became an assistant director on Pasolini's *Medea* in 1969. She set up her own production company in 1970 and made her directorial debut with the documentary *Angelika Urban, Salesgirl Engaged to Be Married*. Since her first films, Sanders Brahms has used a mixture of documentary-like realism with personal experience, fantasy, literature, and political commentary. The result is a distinctive kind of fantastic realism that combines Brecht and Pasolini with a more feminist and personal, highly cultured yet critical, aesthetic. Not only her choice of themes, but also the ways she presents her material, add a personal and feminist edge to the critical perspectives inherited from the older male filmmakers.

For many in the New German Cinema, the 1970s was a time in which they continued their love/hate relationship with the American film industry. West German government money began going to so-called "good" films, which, at that time, were crowd-pleasing films, and this was clearly a standard of filmmaking that young German directors were unwilling to recognize. Separated by considerable distance between themselves and the sympathies of their audiences, the young German producer-directors were in the awkward position of trying to teach their German audiences a language they neither knew nor enjoyed. In short, they were attempting to build a German industry to which most Germans couldn't relate. People came to the cinema to be entertained and to forget about, or repress, the past, but the films of the New German Cinema were not primarily entertaining and did seek to address the past critically.

Eventually, to be sure, many directors chose the simpler route of standard Hollywood-style commercial cinema. But, true to her commitment to improve the industry, Helma Sanders Brahms consistently made films that graphically explored the real, existing problems in everyday West German life by resisting more common types of plots and themes. These include the film *Violence* (1971), an "anti-road movie," which alternates static road maps with a tale of how two assembly-line workers kill an immigrant. She built on her experience as a documentary filmmaker and, by developing a plot aimed against the conventional road movie style, created a moving critique of workers' and immigrants' relations in West Germany. In another film about workers, called *The Employee* (1972), she traces a computer programmer's descent into madness, while her *Last Days of Gomorrah* (1974) shows a future society in which television gratifies all desires. The more commercially successful New German films adapted political commentary to the conventions of mainstream cinema. But Sanders Brahms, in her 1970s "workers' films," resisted the temptation to succumb to mainstream expectations. She consistently made films that confronted her audiences with uncomfortable social commentary. Perhaps not surprisingly, her German audience was uncomfortable with her films.

Nevertheless, though West Germany's production subsidy system tended to restrict the number and kinds of films to be made, it also enabled women directors to work in numbers unparalleled in other nations. Women directors created a virtual wing of the New German Cinema, due at least in part to the ambitious funding programs launched by television and government agencies. Helma Sanders Brahms was one of the most visible representatives of a boom in films that used art-cinema strategies to investigate women's issues. Margaretha von Trotta was another important member of this group. Consider, for example, *The Lost Honour of Katharina Blum,* a film she made with Volker Schlöndorff in 1975. The film shows a woman accused of aiding a terrorist being hounded by the police and the scandal-mongering press. Another important member of this group was Helke Sander, who had been a student activist in 1968 and a co-founder of the German women's liberation movement. After several short films linked to the women's movement, including one on the side effects of contraception, in 1978 Sander made *The All-Around Reduced Personality: Redupers,* the story of a photographer who shows unofficial images of West Berlin and encounters opposition to publishing them. One of the most powerful women's films from the late 1970s was Jutta Brückner's *Hungerjahre (Years of Hunger,* 1979). In a voice-over from the late 1970s, the lead character Ursula recalls growing up in the politically and sexually repressive 1950s. Cold War ideology and a strict family life confused Ursula as she grew into sexual maturity. Brückner employs unexpected voice-overs and an uncertain ending (in which Ursula may or may not have committed suicide) in order to create painful ambiguities of plot and meaning that highlight her lead character's sufferings. The film uses a psychological narrative style of realism, in which scenes combine uncoordinated juxtapositions to exemplify the movements of memory. From their choice of themes to their techniques, women directors in the New German Cinema were creating a politically effective alternative to mainstream, Hollywood-style forms.

Yet perhaps no one has so divided opinion among critics and audiences as Helma Sanders Brahms. Throughout her films, she has dealt with the many traumas of German social history: the Second World War, the Holocaust, the inequalities of the postwar period, and the tensions of the recent unification between East and West. For her courage, she has been honoured in Sweden, Africa, France, and, especially, Japan. In 1997, she received an honour for her life's work at the Tokyo Film Festival. But in Germany, perhaps because of her tendency to dig into the hornets' nest of German history, she has been relentlessly criticized. Like a few of her colleagues from the New German Cinema, Sanders Brahms has remained at odds with conventional viewers.

Undoubtedly her film *Germany, Pale Mother* represents a high point in her production, and it is around this film that the controversy has swirled. Kevin

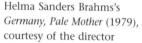
Helma Sanders Brahms's
Germany, Pale Mother (1979),
courtesy of the director

Thomas, a film critic from Los Angeles, wanted to nominate the film for an Oscar. Next to films by Fellini, Godard, Kurosawa, Truffaut, and Visconti, *Germany, Pale Mother* is often included among the top international films of the last fifty years. In this film Sanders Brahms mixes poetry, fairy tales, documentary footage, and personal experience to create an important statement on the effects of the Second World War on postwar Germany. The external war of the 1940s becomes the internal war of the 1950s as the film confronts the viewer with a graphic and disturbing, yet sympathetic, picture of a family and a nation in turmoil. In Germany the film has not received the general recognition it has outside the country, remaining relatively unknown.

The film begins with a reading of Bertolt Brecht's poem entitled "Deutschland." The poem is shown as a text, as words on the screen. The next scene depicts two men rowing, watching a woman on the shore being hounded by a Nazi with a large dog. The tension between the text, on the one hand, and the visual scene, on the other, establishes a narrative and a metanarrative simultaneously. From the outset, we are evidently confronted with a story and a critical commentary on it. As a "pale mother," Germany is a ghostly figure, a woman who gives birth to sickness, infection, and, in this case, oppression and violence. The notion of a "pale motherhood" captures the process of haunting that occurs in the film, from the language and the nation to the mother and her daughter.

The film tells a story that it is important to tell but that rarely gets told in history books: the story of a family as it falls apart under the stress of war and its aftermath. It is not only the mother and daughter who suffer; by the end of the film the husband/father becomes suicidal. Indeed, the father is shown relatively sympathetically in the film as an unwitting oppressor, an unknowing vehicle for the oppressions of war. The ambiguity of the film's ending raises several questions that remain unanswered: How could the Germans have embarked on the war in the first place? Was it perhaps true that civilians suffered more than soldiers during the war? How could people have tolerated the enormous sexism, racism, and violence of those years? How could they overlook the transference of stress from wartime to the postwar situation?

Above all, by raising questions about that time, Sanders Brahms reminds us of the issues that remain unsolved in our own time. She has shown that we may not be as enlightened or as progressive as we might like to think. A tragic and tumultuous period of Germany's history may not in fact have ended with the fall of the Berlin Wall; it may just be entering a different phase, whose consequences we can only barely glimpse. By focusing clear, unsentimental attention on the often forgotten stories of the past, Helma Sanders Brahms shows us how to view the past so that we can be better prepared for what may be coming in the future. Though we might not have changed as much as we think, by pointing out where we have failed to change, she suggests ways of making change possible.

Filmography: Helma Sanders Brahms (Director)

1970	*Angelika Urban, Verkäuferin, verlobt*
1971	*Gewalt* (TV)
1971	*Die Industrielle Reservearmee* (TV)
1972	*Der Angestellte* (TV)
1973	*Die Maschine*
1974	*Die Letzten Tage von Gomorrha* (TV)
1975	*Shirins Hochzeit* (TV)
1975	*Unter dem Pflaster ist der Strand*
1975	*Erdbeben in Chili* (TV)
1977	*Heinrich*
1979	*Deutschland, bleiche Mutter (Germany, Pale Mother)*
1981	*Die Berührte (No Mercy No Future)*
1982	*Filles héréditaires (The Heiress)*
1985	*Alte Liebe* (TV)
1985	*Flügel und Fesseln (The Future of Emily)*
1986	*Laputa*
1987	*Felix*

1988   *Manöver*
1992   *Apfelbäume (Apple Trees)*
1995   *Jetzt leben – Juden in Berlin*
1995   *Lumière et Compagnie*
1997   *Mein Herz – niemandem! (My Heart Is Mine Alone)*
2002   *Clara* (in progress)

---

6   Interview and Excerpts from a Master Class with Helma Sanders Brahms

Conducted by Judith Plessis, Steven Taubeneck, and Penelope Buitenhuis

---

Steven Taubeneck: I've seen *Germany, Pale Mother* several times already and I've used it in classes, and I'm always impressed at the wonderful mixture of intimacy and breadth that the film has. By telling a family story the film gets very close to the most intimate relationships. That's even a part of the camera work, the close-ups of the characters and so on. But through that intimacy and the enormous range of characters there emerges a real documentary sense of the period, of the history. It seems to me that both the intimacy and the breadth are figured in the idea of the mother's language, German, the "Muttersprache" that the daughter learns from the mother, and the idea of learning the language from the mother is accompanied by learning about the nation from the father. I want to ask you first about your relation to the language, to German and this notion of a "Muttersprache," because the "mother language" seems such an important part of this film and of all your films.

Helma Sanders Brahms: Yes, it is very important, since [here] we are mainly among women, to think that the greatest cultural deed in mankind – for the very survival of mankind from day to day, year to year, century to century and millennium to millennium – is that women teach their children to speak. They teach the children to walk erect, and they teach the children to speak, and if they did not teach the children to speak or to walk, you can see that it would be very difficult for human beings to become human. As most of you are women, I think that is the thing you should remember, it is the most important cultural thing, even more than museums, theatres, and films. It's a fact that women teach language. The ability to speak and the ability to walk erect, this knowledge is passed from generation to generation by women. One of my favourite books is *The*

Arabian Nights, because for me the true heroine in the history of mankind is Scheherazade, the woman who teaches a man culture. I don't know whether you know the story, it is the story of a man who has been deeply disappointed by his wife and because of that he cuts off the heads of all the women that he has slept with, the morning after. He is a big sultan, a big Raja, so he can do that. One day he meets this woman who has studied all the sciences of the time and knows the history of mankind. She decides to marry this man because she thinks she can put an end to his barbarism. So she starts to teach him what mankind is. She tells him stories, storytelling is the means to teach this man human language, that means not killing. Understanding is another theme of their dialogue. It's about speaking, teaching how to speak, not to kill but to speak. I found out about Scheherazade when I was seven years old, when my parents gave me a book inherited from my grandfather, the complete edition of *The Thousand and One Nights.* My parents thought it was just a collection of fairy tales but it was the unabridged collection. I was just seven years old, and I read all about men making love with men and men making love with their horses, women enchanting men into storms so that they could beat them, and all kinds of sexual obsessions. When I started to meet my first lovers at the age of fifteen, you know, with pimples, I expected from them something that would come up to my standards. And that was impossible, just impossible. So, when I was nineteen I went to Paris, and I bought a ticket to the Folies Bergères because I thought at last I would see something that would come up to this standard. But again I was disappointed because it was just naked women, and I felt: "My God, humanity has lost a lot of knowledge of these things." But this is another story.

Judith Plessis: Well, those are wonderful stories. My question is also about storytelling: *Germany, Pale Mother* is an extremely powerful film on the personal and political levels. How much of the film is autobiographical?

HSB: It's difficult to give a percentage; I could say all of it or I could say none of it. When you see the film, you can see that when I tell the story of my mother to my daughter, I am telling the story of generations, I am trying to give another interpretation of what generations are. It is a very feminist interpretation. But when I was a child I saw men who were disabled, totally mentally and physically destroyed. They had tried to win a victory in a war that was not theirs, it was the war of Hitler and his people but they had made it their war and now they had come back. Even today, when I went down Water Street here, I saw a man with a T-shirt that reminded me of that time. It said something like "We will fight to the end." When I see things like that, they remind me of what Hitler said. And I guess I was brought up with a deep disbelief in all such phrases,

Director Helma Sanders
Brahms in Vancouver
(1999), courtesy of Judith
Plessis

anything that speaks about fighting until the end, or fighting until there is a final victory. If you ever see a human being dying, you will understand that there is no victory for human beings, the victory is always in the hands of death. That is what you know when you are a woman and you see your own parents dying and you try to help them die. Dying is a very difficult thing, I can tell you. When you hear this talk of a final victory, you understand how silly all these ideas are.

Question from the floor: What about the opening sequence, the scene with the girl and the mother, is that fiction or autobiography?

HSB: Both.

JP: She is a storyteller.

HSB: Yes, I'm a storyteller, I could not make the film with my mother though I must tell you that my mother was more beautiful than the actress I had, but by the time I made the film my mother was an old woman. I could not bring her back to her own youth, even if I had wanted to, so I chose an actress and it was a fiction. There is no possibility to be entirely true to something. You just have to invent, even to be true. That means that choosing an actress is already a fictitious act, you say: "This is my mother," but there is an actress who will replace her. In this case at first I had an actress who wouldn't really cooperate, although she was much more like my mother than the actress I finally found [laughter from the audience]. Yes, I mean she looked liked my mother, but she was not like my mother in other ways. And then I was on the plane between Berlin and Munich with my little daughter, she was one-and-a-half years old and sitting on my lap, and she just left me, because she had seen a person that she liked as much as me and wanted to hug her, and she did, and I turned around and I saw it was Eva Mattes. Eva was at that time full of pimples and rather fat and she had just starred in one of her other films, but somehow there was something in her eyes that made me think, that's her, my daughter has selected her. So when we left the aircraft, I asked: "Do you want to play the role of your life?" And she said, "Yes, why not?" "But you have to lose at least ten kilos of weight," I said, "You have to get very thin, very beautiful." She said, "Yes, in two months I'll be like you want me to be," and she was. So this fabulous creature reinvented herself, she didn't eat any more, and after two months she was slim and had no more pimples. She was beautiful and looked like my mother. That was fiction in a way, too. You understand what I mean?

ST: Part of the intimacy of film is in its beauty; it is certainly very graphic and very disturbing, but also very beautiful. Part of the beauty is in the music, on the one hand, and the house, on the other. The house somehow captures the sadness and the attractiveness of the family. I wonder if you could describe how you came to the music and how you came to the house.

HSB: I had to shoot this film in one house: the scenes in the house in Berlin and the scenes in the house where I was born, all the houses you see in the film, all the rooms, are in the same house. It is one big house in a very beautiful spot in Berlin near a lake, and we simply did small things: added a piece of furniture, or a lamp or something, and it worked. It was because I was with my daughter and I had to find a way to shoot a film and live with my daughter at the same time. She wanted to be with me and it was very difficult because actors are like little children. They want to be hugged, they want to be loved, so they were very jealous of my child. And I had brought with me from Munich the woman who had been helping me all the time, cleaning, cooking, and taking care of my child. I brought her because I loved her very much. But she was a Bavarian, and when she stated her demands she meant them. When she got to Berlin she took her bag and caught the next train home. She didn't want to stay so there I was, I had the child and I had this film to make and I had no help. When my actors arrived I even had to cook myself, and we had decided that the actors were living with us in this house and were not going to a hotel. So everyone slept in this house, which made it like a very special family. I cooked myself for these forty people, with my child on my back, while making the film. I don't understand how I did it. But it was a time when people came and helped me, and things were somehow manageable, but it was very, very difficult.

JP: Helma, as you know, the title of this conference is "Women Filmmakers: Refocusing." It has been twenty years since you filmed *Germany, Pale Mother;* how do you feel about this film today?

HSB: I can't watch it anymore. I have seen my parents die, I helped them die, and I can't see the film, it is too close to me. I am happy that you still love it because somehow my parents survive in this film and that's good. I think that my daughter, too, is proud of the film, she has presented it for me several times in different countries. I'm very happy that I have made something that my daughter is proud of. That's what I wanted and I hope the film will survive even longer; it's good to have done something that is living. I must tell you that when I made the film it was entered in the Berlin festival and it was a huge success with the audience; they stood for four minutes applauding. But the German press destroyed it completely, in a way that prevented cinemas from showing the film. Then I had to go to Paris, to the women's film festival. It was one of the first meetings of this festival, and the film was shown there. I went there and I said to myself: "My God, what will come out of this? I'm here and the film will be shown and I have to face the audience. What will happen after the massacre by the German press?" I went into this huge cinema with more than a thousand seats and it was packed – people were sitting on all the stairs and everywhere. Then the lights were coming up and I stood there and there was complete silence, nobody lifted their hands to applaud, and I said to myself: "My God. What did I do?" All of a sudden I said: "I'm sorry, but I made this film. Maybe you don't like it, but I can only say it's my film." Then all these people, more than a thousand, stood up and came towards me. They didn't applaud, but they wanted to take me in their arms, I think that was one of the greatest moments of my life. When something like that happens it's worth living, you know.

Question from the floor: Was there a technical problem when the rape scene occurred? At that point the sound was cut out. Was that supposed to happen then? Was it meant to be silent?

HSB: You are right, any sound was too banal for the moment. I think sound is much less powerful than what people imagine. Our imagination goes much further, and sometimes you just have to trust in the imaginations of your audience. You will get stronger effects this way than if you prepare everything for everybody. Cinema works a lot with the subconscious and you have to be aware of that. The main thing is that when you make a film you have to think on different levels, from the intellectual to the sensual to the subconscious. The use of fairy tales, for example, is very much linked to the subconscious. Fairy tales and myths are always working with the subconscious, and when people are open to them they work wonderfully well. I have shown my films in many, many countries with entirely different cultures, in India and Japan and Africa. Somehow, it works. I don't know why exactly, but they understand it immediately. Maybe there is a subconscious flow in mankind that makes these things work especially well.

Sanders Brahms comments on the film *Apple Trees* (1992): Excerpts from a master class facilitated by Penelope Buitenhuis

Penelope Buitenhuis: I'm really pleased to present Helma Sanders Brahms from Berlin. Some of you saw her films that were shown this week at the Cinémathèque. She has made twenty-three films since 1970 and won many awards.

HSB: We'll be talking about my work, which is mostly about trying to write German history from my point of view because Germany is the country I know best. What is rewriting history from a female point of view? A female point of view in my case does not always have a woman as protagonist of the film. I have also made films about men, such as one about a man who committed suicide. Writing history from a woman's point of view means to write history from the point of view of the victim rather than the point of view of those who are victorious. In Germany, as you know, there was this long period where the country was cut up into two sides, like a schizophrenic person. One side was behind the so-called Iron Curtain and the other side was part of the West. Yet on both sides it was Germany. I would like to show you another example of a film, *Apple Trees* (*Apfelbäume*) that I did on the German situation. It's about the time of the Reunification, but it starts in the East. It tells the story of how there is a quarrel involving this young man who really believes in socialism (that's why he resents the people who are in power), and it gets very violent. They are watching on a television screen the things that are happening in Berlin ... and they are very happy that they can get out. That's the moment when the woman goes to West Berlin, in 1992.

PB: Did you shoot this film like a documentary?

HSB: Yes, this is almost documentary filming. In the scenes with the actors, I had to be very fast because when they were pulling these trees out of the ground, I went to the place, and I didn't have the money yet to make the film. I went there with the actors and I did these scenes over the fields and in the trees that were still there. I mean, the big trees were pulled out and you can see afterwards that she is walking around the stumps that are lying there. I made this footage first. My cameraman did it for nothing and afterwards we got the money to make the film. That's the way the film started. The people all came from the East and their story is something I had to understand. When I went there, I saw all these trees lying there and I started to think about the film. I went to people and asked them how they had lived and I tried to show that in the film. In that film I tried to have an epic style, not always as slow as it is in these scenes, but mostly it has a quiet flow because of the trees. In fact, the trees are the main characters, they are the protagonists of the film. I made the film in such a way that you see the apple trees in all seasons and you see the apples fall to the ground. They are picked and collected in an industrial way, and the modern methods of treating the apples are shown.

PB: I'm curious about whether the apple trees are a metaphor for something else.

HSB: Of course they are a metaphor! They are a metaphor for many things. You remember, at the beginning, the grandmother and the child are talking about paradise. It's the socialist paradise that's shown in this film, which doesn't work at all, of course. In a way it's a sort of paradise, until the apple trees are destroyed. In France, the film was shown under the title *The Fruit of Paradise*. This pulling up of the trees shows the degradation of the GDR [German Democratic Republic].

PB: I'm still confused about the political context of the apple trees and why they are being destroyed. Why *are* they being destroyed?

HSB: This is the founding of Berlin, as it will be in the future, one of the metropolises of Europe. Everyone expects it to grow as fast as Paris and London have grown. And these areas will be full of all the buildings and activities where they have industry and have to load and unload the trucks. All the stuff that is around a big city. Right now, it's not there yet. These fields where the trees were are still like a desert. There is a German law that says if there are trees on the land, then they have to pay more taxes than if there are no trees. So people who own that land are waiting for the price to go up, and they pulled out the apple trees so that they do not have to pay so much tax.

PB: How was the film received outside of Germany?

HSB: It did quite well in France, and it went to Japan where it was really successful. It was the topic of many articles, from an artistic and also a political point of view. Much more than in Germany, where people feel wounded by my films.

PB: Are your films available here in Canada?

HSB: One of them is available now through Multimedia in Chicago, through their catalogue. But the other films, not yet, unfortunately.

This interview is drawn from discussions with Margarethe von Trotta that took place at a March 1998 conference at the University of Victoria, organized by Dr. Peter Golz (Germanic Studies), the Women's Scholar's Series, the Film Studies Program of the University of Victoria, and the Goethe Institute of Vancouver. Von Trotta's comments come from a public question-and-answer period called "Never Stop Being Curious" and a discussion forum following the screening of her 1995 film, *The Promise*. Von Trotta answers questions about many aspects of her earlier films and discusses the recurring political and personal themes that she brings to her work as an author and director.

When the Goethe Institute presented a successful festival of von Trotta's films in Vancouver in 1996, it described her as the most important female German film director: "Her films give a clear emphasis to feminine aspects: the fates of women form the clear focus of her pictures – albeit the fates of women who intervene very deliberately in political activity. She is an unambiguous part of the tradition of the political film, which takes a topical or historical event as its 'fuse,' so to speak, to give a personal judgment of the state of society."[1]

In this interview, von Trotta sheds new light on important motifs in her work, such as the Doppelgänger, the effects of prison on her characters, and her representations of women's friendships. In the second part of the discussion, von Trotta talks about the mixed reactions to *The Promise*, the first major film to deal with the psychological traumas of reunification after the dismantling of the Berlin Wall.

Q: You are considered one of the great European filmmakers. What other filmmakers have influenced your work?

MvT: Alfred Hitchcock and Ingmar Bergman were masters for me in the beginning. It was the time of the "nouvelle vague" in France; my area during my university studies in Paris was cinema in general. The first time I saw Bergman's films it was a cultural shock for me. In Germany I was used to light comedies, or nostalgia films – films that did not deal with reality or real issues. It was just an escape. Then, all of sudden, in Paris I was confronted with the work of Ingmar Bergman. I thought it would be wonderful to make films as he did. But I knew it was not possible for a woman, so I went on being an actress. The New German Cinema began in 1965. I met and worked with Volker Schlöndorff before becoming

Director Margarethe von Trotta, courtesy of
the director

his assistant and then screenwriter for his films. In *The Lost Honour of
Katharina Blum* we wrote the script and directed the film together.

Q: Is the duality that you represent in your films a result of the way you saw
the division between East and West Germany?

MvT: First and foremost, I see duality within my characters. For example,
the double self – the other side of yourself – is always very important. I
use this Doppelgänger motif extensively. Each chooses what the other
chooses not to be. Two people within one person. If you look at my films
you will always find this duality. It comes from my personal experience
because I need two people to describe my contradictions. In duality, there
are always mirror images; therefore you often find mirrors in my films.
This theme of duality is common in Romanticism, and German culture is
very linked to Romanticism. In *Rosa Luxemburg,* there are two people: the
strong, political woman on one side, and on the other side, an emotional
woman who loves animals and birds, and feels comfortable in her solitude. I like contradictions.

Q: Are there other major themes that emerge in your films?

MvT: A second theme is the prison. After *Rosa Luxemburg,* a critic wrote that
all my films are prison films. Prison is not only a prison with walls and

confinement; one can also be in prison in one's own country or in a love affair. The idea of being a prisoner is one of the main themes in my films. There are so many ways of feeling like a prisoner.

Q: What does making films represent to you?

MvT: As an author and director, I feel cinema allows for cultural expression as well as self-expression. You can express your cultural background and portray your own experiences at the same time. It is also a sort of therapy. It is many things at once. You become like a medium of your experiences. Do you want me to say that I make films to change the world? You can never ask an artist why he does what he does. He has to do it. I don't attempt to know it all. I like to joke around with what is in a film. My motivation has never been to stand up in front of the world or to be famous but, rather, to liberate myself from a burden. One would have more influence to change the world as a politician or priest.

Q: How do you represent women's friendships?

MvT: I don't idealize women's friendships. I show the difficulties, but, most importantly, I prove that women's relationships with other women is an important theme to explore in films.

Q: Do you think the period of high glory is over for German cinema?

MvT: The New German Cinema slowed down in the 1980s, and it is true that the films today are not as strong as those from the beginning of the '70s. But the new films are much more multicultural. People are making films now without knowing why they are making them.

Q: How do you see a film? How do you translate the writing into an image of the film? Are you driven by images?

MvT: When I work from a text such as an authentic letter, I want to portray the emotional side, but that comes to me naturally. I go mainly with emotions, not with documentary facts. I try to recreate the emotion I feel. My individual process is as follows: I write the script first. I have some of the images in mind but not all. Of course, any filmmaker is dependent on places and actors. Then I choose my director of photography. We talk about the general atmosphere, and then we base it on a specific painter and the mood that his art would create. Then we go and find locations. Finally, we make a real storyboard.

Q: How did the film *The Promise* come to be?

MvT: Perhaps I should first tell you a bit about how it came to be a film titled *The Promise*. At the beginning, the original title was "The Wall Years," but the distributor feared that with the word "Wall" nobody would come. Enough about the wall, the title was somewhat depressing and so we had to change it. In the end, we chose *The Promise*, which is much more American in its positive thinking.

To date, it is the only feature film about the Wall years. The initial idea came from an Italian producer who went to Berlin on New Year's Eve '89 and saw all the enthusiasm about the new situation. He came back to where I was living in Italy at the time and said I had to make a film about this, about the Wall years. In the beginning, I hesitated; it was all so new and we didn't know how it would turn out or whether the interest would last or not. But he insisted (in Italy *Die bleierne Zeit* had been a big success), and he felt that, as a German, I had a responsibility to my country and my culture, and to other countries, to speak about this situation in Germany. I didn't live in Berlin at the time so I didn't dare to write it myself. I asked Peter Schneider, who is a well known author in Germany, to help me. He lived in Berlin from '61 (the year the Wall was built) on. He had previously written essays about the situation. He had many friends in Berlin and was one of the leaders of the '68 student movement. He was one of the first leftists who had been very critical of the East, so during the Wall years he did a lot of research about the situation. I asked him if he was available to write a script with me, and although he hesitated in the beginning he finally accepted. In '92, we started doing new research and interviewing people. That was the first moment the East Germans were able to really tell their stories. We started to write in '90, the film was done in '93, and it came out only in '94 for the Berlin Film Festival. As five years had already passed, and the situation was totally different from when we had started to write, we thought we might be only one of many films on this topic. But in fact nobody else in Germany had made a fiction film about this period. When we realized we were the only ones, we felt we had to respond to every demand, to every situation, to everything. When we started to write, we asked ourselves how we could tell all the stories of this time. We couldn't do it in one film, and so we chose only certain moments in the life of this imaginary couple: they are either together or hoping to come together. When their relationship is interrupted, the film is interrupted, too, and then it jumps to the next chapter where they can meet again and so on. At the beginning of each chapter, we showed the image of the Wall, and scenes from the West, how it was at this time. And, each time, the Wall was different because there were four generations of walls. At the beginning, it was very primitive, with stones and barbed wire, and then it became more and more solid and higher and higher. The absurdity of it is that from the third generation on, it was built by West German companies because they had better materials. During our research we even found a document showing that they planned to make a fifth generation of the Wall: one in the East, the death strip, one at the West side, a little strip in between, and another wall. Absurd. Completely obsessed by walls.

Q: When you were making *The Promise*, did you meet many people who had had relationships and love stories like those in the movie?

MvT: In all the details, the film is authentic. We really did a lot of research, but we invented the story of the couple. Peter Schneider wanted to make

Gone with the Wind or something! He had the idea; it was all new for me because I had done so many films about sisters and women's friendships and never a love story. To us, it seemed like the right story to tell. The amusing thing is that after the film came out in Germany, we got letters from women who said that was exactly their story. One even wrote me to tell me that, after the Wall came down, although the couple had had other partners in-between, they had found each other again and finally married. So, some happy endings do exist in the world.

Q: The impact of the situation on family and extended families in Berlin must have affected millions of people.

MvT: Yes, absolutely. Millions. It was the capital; it was a big city.

Q: Did you intend the film to be a personal story or the story of a whole people?

MvT: You saw the documents at the beginning. I tried to show that it was not only a personal story that happened in Berlin, but an international situation. That's why I started with the international scene, showing Kruschev and Kennedy. Then I moved to Germany and to Berlin. Then to people, groups of people, and the individuals. It became more and more personal. Then the individual stories began and that was my way of leading people to one of the stories, one of the possible stories. It's not the story of the whole nation.

Q: Why do you think that there had been no other such films made about the coming down of the Wall at the time your film came out?

MvT: I don't know. I think because I didn't live there – I lived in Italy and had for three years at the time – and perhaps my distance from Germany gave me the courage, or the ignorance, or the innocence. It allowed me to believe that I could do it. The Germans themselves were too paralyzed and are still more paralyzed now.

Q: I often wonder what happened to all the German dissidents, all the people who were instrumental in the Wall coming down. What has happened to them?

MvT: Yes, these East Germans have been lost in a way ...

Q: Will you tell us a little bit about the projects that you have on the go or are considering doing next?

MvT: So many people say that I have to make a sequel to this movie. Peter and I have already started to think about it, but we think we have to wait some time yet. If we make another movie, it would not be with the same people, it would just be the story of how things went for Germany after the last film.

Q: Was there a difference in the way the film was received in East Germany compared to West Germany? How was it received in general?

MvT: There was a lot of discussion in Berlin. There were also many people who didn't like it at all because every Berliner has his own story and it was difficult to satisfy them all. I'll tell you how things developed in the period from '89 to '95. The actor who plays the older woman in the film is from East Berlin. When I gave her the script in '91, she was enthusiastic about it, and she said it was such a good story, it was all true, and I was not denouncing anybody. She told me details from her own life. But when the film came out (and the film was exactly the same as the script), she was completely against it. She suddenly said East Germany had not been like that and that they had not suffered as much. That was very interesting for me, and I couldn't blame her. They began to see their own past with softer eyes than in the beginning. I have a friend who did a book with East Germans, and when the book came out all the people denied having said what they did, even though she had the tapes. But they didn't deny it on purpose; they really had had another opinion before. I believe that the gap between the two sides is growing greater and greater. Every time I go to Berlin, people seem to hate one another more. They're travelling less often from one side to the other. They are less and less curious, and once again in prison. Now the wall is in their heads.

Q: Do you consider yourself a historian?

MvT: No, not really. I'm interested in history. I'm interested and I live in a country where there's a very important and very cruel history to tell. I began with *Rosa Luxemburg* at the beginning of the century and with *Bleierne Zeit* after the war, the fifties to the eighties. But I need historians to help me when I'm doing a film. And I have a son who is a historian, so that helps.

Q: When you first showed the film, how was the response in Germany? Was the general response positive?

MvT: In Berlin, it was rather aggressive. But in Berlin, German films are always received with aggression. I don't know why. There were a lot of discussions in both the East and the West, just as we are discussing now, and the responses were more or less the same: very positive.

Q: What was the response to your film at the Berlin Film Festival in comparison with that of other films?

MvT: There were no other German films at this festival because German filmmakers already know that this festival is very dangerous for them, and therefore they prefer not to go. I had had the same experience myself already with another film, and I knew it was a bit like that. We managed, but we had to be brave. People asked us why we wanted to go there and subject ourselves to the criticism. I could have gone to Venice with the film, but then I would have felt like a coward. With a film like this, I had to go to Berlin.

Q: Do you think that the reception of your films is more negative because you are a woman?

MvT: I think it is always a little bit difficult when you are a woman making a film. You are criticized more perhaps than your male colleagues are. I don't know about this film per se, but in general I would say a woman filmmaker has more difficulties.

Note

1   "A tribute to Margarethe von Trotta," Goethe-Institut Vancouver, Fall 1996.

8   Changing Identity: Margarethe von Trotta's *The Second Awakening of Christa Klages*
Siew Jin Ooi

"I wanted to make films from the beginning," Margarethe von Trotta is recorded as saying in an interview with Renate Fischetti.[1] In the 1960s in Germany, however, few opportunities presented themselves for doing so: "I wanted to direct – and then again not. I didn't have a role model. Back then, at the beginning of the 1960s, there still weren't any female directors in the Federal Republic. So I became an actress first."[2] After a brief spell in theatre, von Trotta acted in numerous films by various directors, including such luminaries of the New German Cinema as Rainer Werner Fassbinder, Herbert Achternbusch, and Volker Schlöndorff.[3] Although she was widely recognized as an actor – even playing herself, "the famous film star Margarethe von Trotta,"[4] in Achternbusch's *Das Andeschser Gefühl* (*The Andechs Feeling,* 1974)[5] – von Trotta also worked with Schlöndorff behind the camera, collaborating with him on scripts for such films as *Der plötzliche Reichtum der armen Leute von Kombach* (*The Sudden Wealth of the Poor People of Kombach,* 1971), and serving as an assistant director on *Die Moral der Ruth Halbfass* (*The Morals of Ruth Halbfass,* 1970), and as co-director for their highly successful adaptation of Heinrich Böll's *Die verlorene Ehre der Katharina Blum* (*The Lost Honour of Katharina Blum,* 1975). It was not until 1977 that von Trotta finally made her debut as a director in her own right with the feature film *Das zweite Erwachen der Christa Klages* (*The Second Awakening of Christa Klages),* which premiered to much acclaim at the 1978 Berlin Film Festival and proved a success with both the public and the critics upon its release in Germany.

The film was inspired by the real-life experience of a young woman, Margit Czenki, who robbed a bank in order to prevent a daycare centre from being closed, and this is the model for the film's main character, Christa Klages. It is important to realize that the political climate in which von Trotta made her film was one of profound conservatism. Student protests on West German

Margarethe von Trotta's *The Second Awakening of Christa Klages* (1977), courtesy of Bioskop Films

university campuses against conservative university structures and inadequate conditions in the late 1950s soon developed into protests against the capitalist values of West German society and government, the rearmament of their country, the Vietnam War, and dictatorial regimes. While a political organization – the German Socialist Students Union (SDS) – emerged from this, political extremists ventured into terrorist activity, founding the Red Army Faction (RAF). Terrorism increased its presence throughout the 1960s and 1970s, culminating in October 1977 with the assassination of the president of the Employers' Association, Hans Martin Schleyer; the hijack of a Lufthansa aircraft to Mogadishu; and the apparent suicides of three key members of the Baader-Meinhof group – as the RAF came to be known during that period – in Stammhein prison while under maximum security.[6] The federal government moved to counter the rise of terrorist activity with the introduction of the *Berufsverbot* in 1971, a decree aimed at preventing radicals from assuming positions within the civil service.[7] Nor was the film industry exempt from censorship: virtually dependent on the federal government for financial support, the German film industry was governed by a law that forbade offending against the Constitution (amongst other things). Unless they were privately funded, films that dealt overtly with politically and socially sensitive issues simply could not be produced.[8] *Christa Klages*, however, is not aimed at providing a titillating account of urban terrorism. The film does not end with the robbery as dénouement; rather, it uses it as the event that sets off everything else. Yet, it cannot be denied that *Christa Klages* presents, if only obliquely, a critique of the political situation of the day.

Combined with this thread of terrorism is a concern for feminist issues that permeates the whole film, as evidenced by the motivations for the robbery as well as by von Trotta's treatment of the individual development of three women. The student protests, with their stand against oppression and authoritarianism, provided a space within which the new women's movement could emerge in Germany during the 1960s. The director Helke Sander is generally credited with bringing the women's movement into the media, and hence, to public attention, at an SDS conference in 1968 when she spoke up against the lack of representation of women's issues within the student movement itself. With regard to film, Sander also co-organized, with Claudia von Alemann, the inaugural International Women's Film Seminar in West Berlin in 1973, the first of its kind in the Federal Republic.[9] In 1974, Sander also founded the journal *Frauen und Film,* which is today "the oldest feminist journal on film anywhere."[10] Although avenues for the discussion of film within a feminist context were emerging, the practice of feminist filmmaking encountered many barriers in the early years of the 1970s: it was commonly assumed that women who could be called feminists simply could not be objective about matters related to the women's movement. If women filmmakers addressed issues raised by the women's movement, then they were likely to be labelled feminists regardless of whether or not they had any association with the movement. Women filmmakers who were involved or even thought to be associated with the women's movement were prevented from making films on the basis of their allegiances, whether real or assumed.[11] It was not until the second half of the 1970s that women filmmakers would be permitted to focus their cameras on issues related to the women's movement. Despite the gains that had been achieved by the movement,[12] it was still a time when "the majority of the public, who at any rate felt no special sympathies for the new women's movement, was under the impression that feminism was necessarily proclamatory, rigorous and, for that matter, not especially entertaining."[13] It was within this context that von Trotta's film was screened.

Although reviewers were divided as to the feminist nature of the film when it was released in Germany,[14] the majority, in praising *Christa Klages,* latched on to the very lack of "ideological heavy-handedness" that was perceived to typify contemporary feminist cinema and would "use quite a bit of space in their articles to embrace the feminist content on the one hand, and to distance themselves and the film from the women's movement on the other."[15] Although a participant in the women's movement, von Trotta herself – aiming, perhaps, as Ward suggests, for a mainstream audience – was loath to see *Christa Klages* labelled as a "woman's [sic] film," and she is on record as describing the women's cinema of the day as a "thought ghetto."[16] While this might have been due, as Ward observes, to a lack of "vocal solidarity" that would lead to the "ambivalence" with which von Trotta's later films would be received by feminist critics,[17] the feminist slant of *Christa Klages* is undeniable. While the relationships that develop between the women and the film's male characters are important to the plot, the relationships that form between these women cannot be dismissed; namely, Christa, who had set up an alternative daycare centre three years prior to the film's opening; Ingrid, a friend to whom Christa turns for help after the holdup; and Lena, Christa's hostage during the robbery, who comes to conduct her own search for her captor. These relationships are the film's driving force and, given the way they challenge the established institutions of mainstream society, arguably its most subversive aspect. In order to understand how the bonds that develop between the women can assume such significance, it is necessary to investigate the question of identity, of who these women are and how they have constructed their lives.

The importance of the theme of identity is apparent from the opening sequences: the camera tracks down a long corridor before cutting to a woman who sits alone in an empty room; the camera closes in on her face and a voice intones: "I had to create my own prison before I could realize what had happened with me."[18] It is important to note that the German reads: "Ich mußte mir erst mein eigenes Gefängnis schaffen, um zu begreifen, was mit mir geschehen war." The German uses not "was mir geschehen war" – which would translate as "what had happened to me" – but "was *mit* mir geschehen war" (my emphasis) – "what had happened *with* me." Whereas the former construction suggests the effect of external forces, the latter suggests the play of internal, psychological processes.[19] The focus on identity is thus visually and linguistically communicated. Even during the holdup, instead of highlighting the action or the danger inherent in such a situation, the two shots that dominate this scene focus on Christa with Lena in her grip. The first, in medium close-up, draws attention to the pair by filling the screen with their image as well as by the amount of time that the camera spends on them. And, although Christa points a gun at Lena's head, the second shot presents a close-up that focuses not on the gun and the danger to Lena but, rather, on Lena's face – a face that, remarkably, shows more curiosity than fear. Attention is also drawn to this by the music, which changes from that in the previous scene to four chords that descend to approximately a four-second silence in the middle of this shot and are repeated before the scene changes again. There is nothing to distract from Lena's face and those eyes searching Christa's impassive visage.

Lena

The experience is one that has a profound impact on Lena's life. Until then her life is one that has been conducted wholly within the bounds of regulation and convention. She is the perfect employee, with an impeccable record for punctuality and generally toeing the line. As she lives alone, without a partner and with no evidence of extracurricular activities, it can be seen that her daily orbit is influenced only by the pull of work and home. The traditional slant of Lena's dreams and aspirations, and the narrow scope of her life, may be observed in those scenes that show her in her apartment, in her personal world. The first scene in Lena's apartment depicts her jotting down Lotto numbers from an oversized television set. The one-room apartment and these cramped quarters heighten the hugeness of the screen. All of this suggests that this television is a channel for Lena's dreaming, a means of escaping temporarily from the everyday; but it is also a medium through which she may hope for a more permanent escape. The size of the television simultaneously reflects the breadth of her dreams and the lack of opportunities available to her for realizing such an escape. A desire to escape from the life she currently leads may also be seen in the cylindrical lamp with a picture of Niagara Falls; the positioning of the lamp next to her bed reinforces the idea that it is an outlet for her dreams. The lamp is again lit up in the second scene set in Lena's apartment, accompanied by the strains of "Un bel dì" from Puccini's *Madama Butterfly,* Cio-Cio-San's aria, as she literally and figuratively waits for her ship to come in, bearing with it her husband, Pinkerton. That this scene immediately follows Lena's visit to the daycare centre suggests that Lena, too, dreams of marriage and children.

Lena's initial curiosity develops into a full-blown search on her part for the physical person that is Christa Klages as well as for the person behind the mask. Lena's fascination with Christa can be understood as a part of her desire to escape the life she knows. This can be seen in her action of comparing her own photograph with Christa's by the light of her lamp as she lies in bed. The music that plays during this shot is also significant: these are the same chords that play over the close-up of Lena's face during the hostage sequence. The music further suggests the idea of curiosity on Lena's part; that the music reoccurs in a sequence pertaining to Lena's dreams brings to the sequence in which it first occurs the idea that Lena's curiosity while a hostage is related to her desire for a world beyond that which she already knows. She sees in Christa a woman who has experienced far more than she herself has ever experienced or even imagined. Christa provides Lena with the impetus to look beyond her own life, to entertain notions that do not exist in the bourgeois world. Lena's visits to the alternative daycare centre[20] bring her face to face with a world that does not feel any compulsion to conform. Christa's actions also expose Lena to one of the chief motivators of the world in which she moves: money. This is first seen when her manager instructs her to calculate the bank's foreign currency losses using the exchange rate from a date prior to the robbery's execution. Money as motivator rears its ugly head again when the landlord finally evicts the daycare centre from its premises because of its inability to keep up with the rent. That the centre is to be replaced by a sex shop further indicates the primacy of the role played by money in the bourgeois world, overriding all questions of honour and morality.[21]

In trying to find Christa, Lena learns about a world beyond her own. In the process she learns more about the world in which she moves, about the values upon which it is built. Lena's refusal to identify Christa as her captor demonstrates the extent to which she has been changed by Christa's actions. In asking Christa to remove her stocking and sunglasses, Lena demonstrates her ability to look beyond the mask, beyond the shadow of terrorism, to see the person that is Christa. Furthermore, the change of tense between the question, "Was that the woman?" and her answer, "No, it's definitely not her," seems to suggest an understanding that the person standing before her is no longer the same person who pinioned her from behind so long ago.[22]

Ingrid

While Lena carries out her search for Christa, Christa and Werner search for a haven and somebody who will transport the money from the holdup to the daycare centre. They find both in Ingrid, a friend from Christa's schooldays. Ingrid has already achieved Lena's dream of marriage and seems contentedly ensconced in a comfortable middle-class existence, her husband Heinz's lifetime position with the army ensuring that they will have few material concerns. She is an acquiescent, and at times, fear-ridden woman whose sphere of activity, like Lena's, does not extend beyond home and work – only, in this case, work takes place at home, where Ingrid receives customers as a beautician.[23] This emphasis on appearance in her work is paralleled in her personal life, which, beyond the surface, is far from rosy.

Ingrid's unhappiness within her marriage can be understood to be the result of the nature of the relationship between her and her husband. Given that he comes home only on weekends and that this is his time for indulging his passion for bat hunting, Ingrid seems to function more as a trophy to him, a part of the middle-class existence he has bought for himself. Ingrid's desires are no concern of his, and this is made painfully clear with the topic of children. Although she may laugh as she exhibits to Christa her birthday present to Heinz, a marble egg inscribed with the words "Please fertilize," this sequence grotesquely illustrates the depth of Ingrid's desire for children and her inability to give full voice to this desire. Narrow though this dream may be in scope, it would at least provide Ingrid with an escape from her present life of almost complete isolation. That she is incapable of achieving even this much is reflective not only of the opportunities available to her for realizing any other dreams she may have, but also of the true nature of her marriage. It is a relationship in which her desires and the voice with which she would give those desires expression are, and always have been, subjugated to the will of her husband. Heinz's unwelcoming, even hostile attitude towards the presence of Christa and Werner suggests that he will brook no interlopers. It is a state of absolute domination, as is vividly illustrated by the bats mounted around the apartment (even in the toilet). Their eerie presence serves as a constant reminder of Heinz's authority and, in denying her even the freedom to decorate the traditionally female space of the home, further conveys his supremacy in this relationship.

That Ingrid's initial appearance of contentment hides a darker core can be seen to be foreshadowed in the way the shot of Lena listening to *Madama Butterfly* cuts abruptly to the scene of Ingrid screaming. While Cio-Cio-San sings of hope and optimism, the reality is that Pinkerton has already taken a "proper" wife at home in the United States. Just as Cio-Cio-San's dream of marriage proves to be an empty one, so, too, Ingrid's experience demonstrates that Lena's ideal may, in fact, be not a dream at all but a nightmare. Ingrid's screaming does not end until she is in Portugal, away from Heinz. That the camera tilts up from Christa's sleeping form to the bats on the wall even before Christa sits up further suggests, even at this stage, that Heinz is responsible for Ingrid's fear.

The reappearance of Christa in Ingrid's life is an event that throws Ingrid's discontent with her own life into high relief. Christa not only brings with her a sense of true community, in her sharing of ideas and experiences that Ingrid had left behind with her schooldays, but she also reawakens Ingrid's old envy of Christa's autonomy. Ingrid's receptiveness to Werner's advances reflects the depth of her dissatisfaction with her life, as does the fact that she is able to argue with Heinz in the face of his displeasure after only a few days of renewed contact with Christa. Christa's presence makes Ingrid realize the emptiness of her marriage and enables her to overcome her fears of possible consequences in order to do as she wishes. Thus Ingrid assists Christa, although Werner's death makes the danger of involvement clear.

Ingrid transgresses the limits of her life as Heinz's wife and its concomitant world of conformity. Testimony to this change occurs when Ingrid, who must first lie to Heinz and customs officials to reach her destination, joins Christa in Portugal, where it may be inferred that a lesbian relationship develops between the two women. As well, instead of returning "home to mother" after being thrown out by Heinz, Ingrid joins the daycare community, more at home with its ideology than in the world of convention. Ingrid's ability to overcome her fear allows her to escape the isolation of her marriage and to live in a world where her desires need not be subjugated to anybody else's.

Christa

Christa's actions change not only the lives of Lena and Ingrid, but also her own. Christa is a woman who has already gone through the ritual of getting married and exchanging recipes with other housewives before realizing that was not really her style; she now has Werner as her occasional partner-in-bed, her partner-in-crime. Her marriage did, however, leave her at least one positive thing – her daughter, Mischa, for whose sake, it would seem, Christa established the daycare centre. Christa is unrestrained by convention and tradition, and unimpressed by authority. She is what is known as a "free-thinker," except that she's not a thinker. She is not given to contemplation, and this becomes ever clearer as the film progresses.

It is apparent from the start that the robbery was not fully thought out. Wolfgang, Christa's second accomplice, has no alternative escape plan; Christa and Werner have no concrete plans for getting the money to the daycare centre, relying on the goodwill of others. The sheer disbelief with which Christa greets Ingrid's news that her colleagues would not take the money because the means did not justify the ends makes it clear that the robbery was not an issue that Christa had discussed with them; it had never crossed her mind that it would be rejected. The sheer panic that Werner's death induces in Christa makes it plain that the possible consequences of her actions had not been fully thought out. There is greater value to Christa in taking action than in having a discussion.

Personal independence and action are important to her, and her stay in the cooperative in Portugal allows her both. While Christa may come to understand that there is importance in talking – in discussion and communication – and while she may be happy living in the cooperative, it must be noted that she is still moving in isolation, still operating alone. This is made clear when Christa returns to Germany, a period characterized by two concepts that are alien to her: waiting and contemplation. Still unwilling to risk arrest by facing the past and revealing herself, Christa maintains her distance from her friends, and it becomes evident during this time of solitude[24] that she is still unable to understand that she needs others. The motif of the leaky faucet in the apartment she rents can be seen to reflect this. Although the landlady offers to have the faucet fixed, Christa states that she will repair it herself. Despite Christa's claim to self-sufficiency, it is not until some unspecified period later, when the landlady brings a plumber in, that the faucet is repaired. This incident not only suggests that help is available even when least expected, but also that Christa is still unable to relinquish her belief in her ability to single-handedly change the world around her. This interpretation is further heightened by the positioning, between these two scenes, of an episode in which Christa again rejects an offer of help after an unexpected encounter with a friend.

While she may already have been free of the restraints laid down by mainstream society, Christa's preference for action over thought has isolated her from others who might be sympathetic to her beliefs and has deprived her of the mutual support that can be derived from the sharing of ideas. This is a lesson that Christa learns only at the film's end. When she does rejoin her daughter and friends, it appears to be as a result of realizing that her self-imposed exile was a prison in itself. It is only when Lena, understanding the reason behind Christa's actions, refuses to identify Christa as her captor that Christa comes to her "second awakening," finally understanding that help can come from the most unlikely sources, that she cannot always act in isolation from others, and that there is strength in working in conjunction with them.

As the three women change in their outlook, they move from isolated, solitary lives to a world of solidarity and co-existence, united by their common beliefs. This movement away from isolation to a sense of community is a theme common to many of von Trotta's works,[25] but it is the concept of unity that provides this film's subversive edge. Lena's act of solidarity is an act of overt subversiveness in its direct refusal to uphold and affirm established mainstream values that overlook human needs. More than that, Lena's position illustrates the power that an individual can wield over others, whether another individual or a public institution, and that it is up to the individual to make an informed decision rather than blindly follow the usual procedures laid out by the powers that be. Ingrid's decision to follow her own desires, which lead her first to join the farming cooperative and then the daycare community, is also an act of subversiveness. It might be less overt than Lena's, in that she does not oppose a public institution, but in demonstrating the power of an individual over her own happiness, her choice questions the private institution of marriage as a source of fulfilment and suggests that happiness can be found in activities and areas beyond the mainstream. In contrast to that of Lena and Ingrid, Christa's awakening is not to the power of the individual but, rather, to the power of solidarity and to the recognition that much can be achieved through working with others. Furthermore, the change in Christa not only leaves its mark within the film's story, but, even more, on the film's audience, especially since this is Christa's narration. The events related in the film are already over by the time the film begins, and Christa's stunned gaze is an image that remains with the viewer long after the screen is blank. It seems clear that von Trotta wishes her audience to experience, as her characters have, an awakening, or second awakening.

In an interview with Willi Bär about *Christa Klages*, von Trotta and her co-scriptwriter, Luisa Francia, observe:

> The path ... that these three women take could be the path of a single woman ... It begins with Lena, the conventional employee, with her traditional, interchangeable wishes for marriage and a small household ... Ingrid, the second woman, already possesses everything that Lena still dreams of: her

own apartment, furniture à la "Home Beautiful," and a husband with a lifetime position ... Now Christa Klages has already left these phases behind her. She has left marriage and small household, and has sought a new path for herself and her child, but also for others.[26]

It can be seen that this is the path that von Trotta herself had taken. Having worked as a secretary before serving in Paris as an *au pair*, von Trotta briefly interrupted her subsequent theatrical acting career by her marriage and consequent child. Although she returned to her profession during that period, she divorced her husband after only a few years, around which time her progression through the ranks of filmmaking began. It is interesting to note that, in the film, the money from the robbery finally finds its way to Christa's childcare group through anonymous donations that are clearly from Hans, the pastor whom Christa had befriended after the robbery and who assisted her in evading the authorities. Von Trotta, too, was assisted by a man in bringing her own project to fruition: in trying to fund *Christa Klages,* she encountered much resistance to her attempt to change her identity from scriptwriter and leading actress for Schlöndorff to director in her own right. It was only when Schlöndorff, her husband at the time, guaranteed the funders the intervention of his proven directorial ability in the event that von Trotta should be incapable of completing the film that she received any money at all.[27] While von Trotta may, in this regard, have been more privileged than most other female filmmakers of the day – especially since Schlöndorff was also a part owner of Bioskop Films, which co-produced *Christa Klages* with WDR television – it may be seen that this was not a position that she abused. *Christa Klages* was awarded a Federal Film Prize, the Filmband in Silver, and, with it, 300,000 DM, which would later be used to partially fund von Trotta's third and most widely acclaimed film to date, *Marianne and Juliane.*[28] As one of the first female directors of the New German Cinema to attain national and international prominence, von Trotta has served not only as a role model, but also as a collaborator and mentor for subsequent generations of German female filmmakers. Dagmar Hirtz, who worked as a film editor before directing her first feature film, *Unerreichbare Nähe* (*Final Call,* 1984), observes: "For me, meeting women like Margarethe von Trotta (who co-wrote the screenplay) – who preceded me along this path, who had the confidence, who fought for and successfully realized their own films – has been crucial."[29] Margit Czenki, the erstwhile bank robber whose story forms the basis of *Christa Klages,* acted in the film and worked as a scriptwriter for von Trotta in later productions. She also collaborated with other directors before going on to direct her own feature film, *Komplizinnen* (*Accomplices,* 1988). Von Trotta herself is unequivocal about her position: "I would support every woman who has the desire to make films ... I would, however, support a man equally, only men normally have it easier."[30] It is worth noting, too, that von Trotta's working style has been described as being "very partnerlike."[31] Hanna Schygulla, contrasting von Trotta's style with that of male directors who are usually "like a father or a lover," observes that she "likes to be a sister."[32] Furthermore, von Trotta's concern for her actors' "well-being"[33] and comfort is well documented.[34] In working with her crew members and using their strengths to contribute to her vision, it seems clear that von Trotta has herself undergone the "second awakening" she would invoke in others, and the fruits of this are clear from the success not only of *Christa Klages,* but also of her subsequent films.

Notes

1 Interview in Renate Fischetti, "Ich wollte von Anfang an Filme machen," in Renate Fischetti, *Das neue Kino – Acht Porträts von deutschen Regisseurinnen* (Frankfurt am Main: tende, 1992), 161. All translations are my own unless otherwise stated.
2 In Ingeborg Weber, "Bei Dreharbeiten mit Margarethe von Trotta," in *Margarethe von Trotta, Die bleierne Zeit,* ed. Hans Jürgen Weber (Frankfurt am Main: Fischer, 1981), 86.
3 It is not uncommon for female directors to have originally begun in acting, whether studying it or working in the industry; other examples from the New German Cinema include Doris Dörrie, Helke Sander, Helma Sanders Brahms, and May Spils.
4 Thomas Elsaesser, "Mother Courage and Divided Daughter," *Monthly Film Bulletin* 50, 594 (1983): 176.
5 Original film titles are provided with the titles under which they were released in North America; any reference to the film thereafter will use the North American release title (which may or may not be a literal translation of the German).
6 Von Trotta would later use the imprisonment and subsequent deaths of the Baader-Meinhof members as the basis for her third film, *Die bleierne Zeit (Marianne and Juliane).*
7 This included a variety of professions, ranging from teachers and judges to dustmen and gravediggers, comprising some 16 percent of the labour force. See Julia Knight, *Women and the New German Cinema* (London: Verso, 1992), 39. Those who "overtly – in demonstrations, writings or speeches – expressed sympathy or agreement with 'terrorists' or 'extremists'" could also be branded as *Sympathisanten,* sympathisers (see Thomas Elsaesser, *New German Cinema: A History* [London: Macmillan, 1989], 237) and could be subjected to media and police harassment. Most famous, perhaps, are Heinrich Böll's experiences after the publication of an article he wrote requesting pardon for Ulrike Meinhof. This article was used as the basis for his novel, *Die verlorene Ehre der Katharina Blum (The Lost Honour of Katharina Blum)* and was subsequently adapted into the film by Schlöndorff and von Trotta.
8 Neither the collective effort, *Deutschland im Herbst (Germany in Autumn),* nor Fassbinder's *Die dritte Generation (The Third Generation)* received funding from either television or the state. See Jan Dawson's "The Sacred Terror: Shadows of Terrorism in the New German Cinema," *Sight and Sound* 48, 4 (Autumn 1979): 242-5, for a discussion of the restrictions facing filmmakers during that period and the depictions that were achieved. See also Dawson's "A Labyrinth of Subsidies: The Origins of the New German Cinema," *Sight and Sound* 50, 1 (Winter 1980/1): 14-20, for a discussion of the policies regarding film subsidies.
9 For the ways in which it differed from women's film festivals in other countries, see Knight, *Women and the New German Cinema,* 102 ff.
10 Sandra Frieden, Richard W. McCormick, Vibeke R. Petersen, and Laurie Melissa Vogelsang, eds. "Introduction," in *Gender and German Cinema: Feminist Interventions.* Vol. 1: *Gender and Representation in New German Cinema* (Providence, RI: Berg, 1993), 2.
11 See discussion in Knight, *Women and the New German Cinema,* 94 ff.
12 Edith Hoshino Altbach observes: "In the 1970s, a young feminist from the United States could go to any major West German city and find much to remind her of home." Cited in

"The New German Women's Movement," in *German Feminism: Readings in Politics and Literature*, ed. Edith Hoshino Altbach, Jeanette Clausen, Dagmar Schultz, Naomi Stephan (New York: State University of New York, 1984), 7.

13 Renate Möhrmann, "The Second Awakening of Christa Klages," *Gender and German Cinema* 1: 77.

14 Möhrmann, "The Second Awakening of Christa Klages," 76.

15 Jenifer K. Ward, "Enacting the Different Voice: Christa Klages and Feminist History," *Women in German Yearbook* 11 (1995): 53.

16 Quoted in Ward, "Enacting the Different Voice," 54.

17 Ibid., 53-4.

18 Margarethe von Trotta and Luisa Francia, *Das zweite Erwachen der Christa Klages* (Frankfurt am Main: Fischer, 1980), 13. The subtitles provided in the Water Bearer video of the film read: "I had to create my own jail before I realised what had happened to me," which misses the subtlety of von Trotta's and Francia's phrasing.

19 This interpretation of the German can also be seen in Ward, "Enacting the Different Voice," 61-2.

20 Instead of *Kindergarten*, the script uses *Kinderladen*, which is described as a "(left-wing) play-group" in the *Collins German-English, English-German Dictionary* (London: Collins, 1980), 389. This anti-authoritarian childcare initiative was organized before the new German women's movement but was quickly taken up by the movement. See Knight, *Women and the New German Cinema*, 75.

21 See Ward, "Enacting the Different Voice," esp. 55-61, for a discussion of the film's moral code.

22 Martin Donougho makes note, too, of the change of tense, but he remarks only that it is "ambiguous." See "Margarethe von Trotta: Gynemagoguery and the Dilemmas of a Film-maker," in *Literature/Film Quarterly* 16, 1 (1988): 153. Also, the subtitles provided for Lena's response in the Water Bearer video of the film read: "No, I'm positive it wasn't," which conveys nothing of the change of tense that occurs in the German.

23 At least two customers are served in the course of the film: one, Frau Wurm, is named in the film but unseen by the audience; the other, Frau Kuchenbrod, is visible to the audience but named only in the script. Both names seem suggestive of the type of life that is led by Ingrid. "Kuchenbrod" is formed from *Kuchen* (cake) and "Brod," which has the same pronunciation as *Brot* (bread); both are products of the kitchen, the area to which women are traditionally relegated. *Wurm* (worm) calls up images of the dark, dank earth that the creatures inhabit, suggesting not only the restrictions on Ingrid's movements, but also a downtrodden, doormat life.

24 The script is divided into five sections, each of which corresponds to Christa's experiences during the course of the film: (1) Approach, (2) Friendship, (3) Community, (4) Solitude, and (5) The Second Awakening.

25 Such as *Marianne and Juliane, Heller Wahn (Sheer Madness)*, and even *Schwestern, oder die Balance des Glücks (Sisters, or The Balance of Happiness)*.

26 In Willi Bär, "'Den Mut zum Ausbruch nicht verlieren': Gespräch mit Margarethe von Trotta und Luisa Francia," in von Trotta and Francia, *Das zweite Erwachen der Christa Klages*, 94-5.

27 In an interview with Fischetti. See Fishcetti, "Ich wollte von Anfang an Filme machen," 163-4.

28 A breakdown of the sources of funding for the film is provided in von Trotta, *Die bleierne Zeit*, 112. For a list of prizes that were awarded to the film, see Renate Fischetti, "Preise und Auszeichnungen," in Fischetti, *Das neue Kino*, 325-6.

29 Quoted in Knight, *Women and the New German Cinema*, 171.

30 Fischetti, "Ich wollte von Anfang an Filme machen," 166.

31 Quoted in H.-B. Moeller, "Women's Cinema: The Case of Margarethe von Trotta," in *Film Criticism* 9 (1984): 114.

32 Quoted in Knight, *Women and the New German Cinema*, 93.

33 Margarethe von Trotta, "*Schwestern, oder die Balance des Glücks* – Tagebuch," in Margarethe von Trotta, *Schwestern, oder die Balance des Glücks*, ed. Willi Bär and Hans Jürgen Weber (Frankfurt am Main: Fischer, 1979), 143.

34   See, for example, Margarethe von Trotta, *"Schwestern, oder die Balance des Glücks* – Tagebuch,"
     95, 116, 123, 125, 143-7; See also, "Interview mit Konstantin Wecker," in von Trotta,
     Schwestern, oder die Balance des Glücks, 165-6; "Interview mit Kameramann Franz Rath," in
     von Trotta, *Die bleierne Zeit,* 97-102.

Filmography: Margarethe von Trotta (Director)

1975	*Die verlorene Ehre der Katharina Blum* oder: *Wie Gewalt entstehen und wohin sie führen kann* (The Lost Honour of Katharina Blum)
1978	*Das zweite Erwachen der Christa Klages* (The Second Awakening of Christa Klages)
1979	*Schwestern, oder die Balance des Glücks* (Sisters, or The Balance of Happiness)
1981	*Die bleierne Zeit* (Marianne and Juliane)
1983	*Heller Wahn*
1986	*Rosa Luxemburg*
1988	*Felix*
1988	*Paura e amore* (Three Sisters) (Love and Fear)
1990	*L'Africaine* (The African Woman),
1993	*Il lungo silenzio* (The Long Silence)
1995	*Das Versprechen* (The Promise)
1997	*Winterkind* (TV)
1999	*Dunkle Tage* (TV)
1999	*Mit fünfzig küssen Männer anders* (TV)
2000	*Jahrestage* (mini TV Series)
2001	*Rosenstraße*

9   Agnieszka Holland:
Continuity, the Self, and Artistic Vision

B. Amarillis Lugo de Fabritz

As we watched freedom come to each country in turn, the question for
me was what would now happen to these directors [Holland, Mészáros,
and Chytilova]? Having perfected the art of speaking indirectly, would
they have to create a whole new cinema now that they could tell the
truth straight on? How would the Velvet Revolution affect the idiosyncratic, forceful people these women had to be to have major film careers
in that early time?

— Barbara Quart[1]

One of the techniques Agnieszka Holland perfected to enable her to "speak
indirectly" in the films she made in Poland involved positing her political
discourse in the form of character-based narratives. These personal narratives focus simultaneously on the way individuals construct their identities, their selves, and the extent to which these identities constitute a cultural

Agnieszka Holland's *Europa, Europa* (1990), courtesy of the Film
Reference Library, Toronto

construct. The tension that arises between individuals' efforts to construct
their desired identities and the way culture frustrates them becomes the
storehouse for Holland's indirect political discourse. The competition between these agendas serves as an allegory for the state of Polish society as
well as for the role of the Polish state during the late Soviet period. Holland
did not abandon the use of the personal narrative as a political device following her exile to the West in 1981; instead, she adapted the layering of
political symbolism to the exploration of the nature of fascism in the supposedly civilized cultures of Europe during the Second World War.

Here I analyze Holland's use of the politically inscribed personal narrative in two films – one, *Provincial Actors* (1978), representing her Polish period, and the other, *Europa, Europa* (1990), representing her exile. Technically,
these films fall under two distinct ideologically prescribed forms of cinematic storytelling: socialist realism and the Western European Holocaust
narrative. In the case of *Provincial Actors,* the personal narrative worked within
a well established system of interpretation. The reader of socialist realist
literature and/or viewer of socialist realist art took for granted the need to
read at the level of allegory in order to fully understand what the artist
wanted to communicate. Any plot deviation from the legislatively decreed
rules of socialist realism was easily discernible, and such deviations became
a clearly marked initial "road map" to guide initiated readers through the

viewing and interpreting of the film. In the case of *Europa, Europa,* which was made outside the realm of socialist realist aesthetics, Holland chose to depict the Holocaust in terms of a picaresque personal narrative. This allows the film to abandon another typical, though unwritten, convention – that of representing the Holocaust as the collective experience of a passive community. Instead, *Europa, Europa* offers an exploration of the appeal and interaction of the different ideologies that vied for control of Eastern Europe during the Second World War.

Poland

In Poland, Agnieszka Holland belonged to the group of filmmakers that defined what constitutes "classic" communist-era Polish film, Andrzej Wajda's Unit X. Unit X produced Wajda's war trilogy and his *Man of Marble* and *Man of Iron* series, but it also provided the training ground for other outstanding non-classic Polish directors, such as Polanski and Kieslowski. *Man of Marble* and *Man of Iron* in particular helped define late Soviet period Polish filmmaking, which is summarized as follows by David Paul: "In Communist countries it is taken as a given that the arts, including cinema, have political significance."[2]

In Soviet period Poland, socialist realism was a legislatively ordained set of criteria that filmmakers were required to meet. As described by Michalek and Turaj, it dictated that art must portray a positive hero in the leading role, a person who struggles for socialist ideals. The work of art must focus on class struggle between the new socialist order and the old capitalist order (or its remnants), and the socialist order must prove victorious. Further, the work of art must glorify the leading role of the Communist party. There must be a correct examination of the character and behaviour of social types, a description of a type that enhances the schematic message.[3] As such, socialist realism constituted part of the Soviet influenced Polish regime's attempt to use cultural institutions, in this case the arts, to promote the Marxist-Leninist ideological principles (in their totalitarian form) within traditionally Roman Catholic Polish society.

Unlike Wajda, whose style leaned towards historical epics and who was engaged in a direct discourse with the conventions of socialist realism, Holland favoured a personal style of narrative that was not easily classified under these conventions. She capitalized on the unwritten interpretive contract that existed between artists and audience during the late Soviet period. By the late 1970s, the centrally planned Soviet system had established a set of living conditions that provided, as it were, a centrally planned cultural experience, with a centrally shared political, social, and material existence. The centralized and standardized nature of the Soviet totalitarian experience meant that everyone shared similar educational and career paths. Uniform standards for social and economic advancement produced shared social processes across the Soviet bloc. Thus, simply knowing what city a person came from enabled one to know their social status, education, and occupation. These conditions produced a curiously homogenous artistic discourse.

A shared symbolic system led to a shared set of expectations on the part of the artists, particularly when it came to the design of their work. This amounted to a "reading contract" that envisioned an implied reader who would carry out an intensive decoding of the interpretive elements of artistic works. Readers, in turn, envisioned an ideal work of extreme narrative economy.[4]

Provincial Actors, at first glance, is the story of a provincial theatre filled with frustrated actors. The main character of the film, Chris, finally gets the lead in Stanislaw Wyspianski's *Liberation*, an ambitious and mysterious play. He hopes this role will prove to be his big break, since a director from the Lodz acting school is coming to see the play. However, due to the constant cuts and compromises made by the production's director, the production ends up being mediocre.

Behind this surface plot, Holland develops an allegory of the state of Polish society through her depiction of the way the different characters' identities are constructed and deconstructed by the communist system. Chris is married to Anna, a puppet operator in the provincial puppet theatre. She is treated as an inferior by her husband's colleagues and is constantly put down by her husband for being merely a puppet artist. Her appearance is plain. Her haircut is a blunt bob, and at night she wears a frumpy cotton nightgown. She speaks with little or no emotion during her first few scenes in the film.

Signs of greater tension, however, are built into her simple, quiet appearance. She takes pills, presumably tranquilizers, on a consistent basis; frequently breaks into tears of frustration; and she makes some fairly insightful comments to her husband regarding the politics of theatre censorship – comments that point to hidden knowledge. When her husband comes home after the director makes the first serious set of cuts from the play, she asks him why he gets so involved in the play, since there's no truth in it. She accuses him of getting exalted to hide the fact that he is a cold egoist.

Slowly, the film builds a picture of Anna's past identity. She runs into an old schoolmate when she goes to do a performance with the puppet theatre in Warsaw. Her friend comments that Anna always had confidence as a young woman. The viewer discovers that Anna used to be smart and energetic. She used to be good at physics and seemed to be a promising ice skater. Her friend admired her for her confidence. This encounter, of course, serves not only to contrast Anna's provincial existence with the "elite" existence of Warsaw, but also to add to the mystery of what turned Anna into the depressed woman she is now.

Cinematically, the scene where Anna first runs into this friend proves particularly interesting. Holland skilfully integrates the angles of her medium shots of her characters with the symbolic load of the geographical site to highlight Anna's dislocation in greater Polish society. Anna first runs into her friend accidentally after a rehearsal, outside the Palace of Culture in Warsaw. This alone loads the scene with great irony, since it is Anna, the "non-serious" artist in the family, who gets to perform in Warsaw, instead of her husband, the "serious" artist. If anything, the totalitarian social structure exacerbated the split between "big town" and "country" existence. Only the elite lived in the capital city. Performing in the capital city reflected a level of recognition of excellence – at least theoretically. The fact that what has been recognized is the puppet theatre points to an uncomfortable relationship in the capital's perception of the province.

When Anna speaks with her friend outside the Palace of Culture, she looks visibly ill at ease. Her unstylish dress contrasts with her friend's brightly coloured blazer, a sign of her status as a fully empowered working member of the capital's society. Anna's body language grows increasingly distorted as she tries to position herself to block her friend's view of the large poster that announces her puppet theatre. In a way, she tries to pass for someone that she is not, as she uses her body to avoid the topic of her membership in the puppet theatre.

The tension between Anna's body and the body of Warsaw further increases when Anna goes to visit her friend's apartment for dinner. Her body seems lost in the vast space of the chair she occupies. She clutches her purse like a shield against the openness of the living room. The living room alone seems twice as large as her apartment back in the provinces. She runs into the bathroom to consume more tranquilizers. Anna does everything except express vocally her discomfort and displacement within this element of society. All this works to visually discredit the friend's comments on Anna as a confident, intelligent, athletic young woman.

The rest of Anna's story is revealed as her husband has drinks with an old schoolmate who has become an actor in Lodz. The schoolmate reveals that Anna had managed to enter acting school in Lodz, the centre for film production in Poland. (The reputation of the Lodz school is analogous to the reputation of Julliard and Yale in the United States: high-quality and elite.) She, however, had been kicked out of the program because she had "no natural aptitude for acting." After a pause, Chris elaborates: "Wrong mental attitude." These descriptions are all buzzwords to say that Anna had real talent and that she approached acting as art "with a capital A." The directors in Lodz need such good actors, but, as stated by the director who comes to see Chris act during the first dress rehearsal of his play, "I need useful all-around guys more." Individuality has become a detrimental quality; conformity to institutional ideological attitudes is what the system values. The artist as creator has been replaced by the artist-as-cookie-cutter – producer of hundreds of performances of Maiakovsky's plays.

Thus, Anna's identity as a mere puppet performer and wife of a ne'er-do-well provincial artist is the result of the box the Communist regime has put her in because she does not conform to the rules it has set out for its artists. What she really was – a vibrant, athletic young woman with potentially great artistic talent – has been sacrificed for the sake of producing an individual capable of functioning within the constraints of totalitarian society.

Anna also plays at her role of Chris's wife. As the movie progresses, the viewer sees how Anna and Chris's relationship has deteriorated to the point where it has become dysfunctional. He treats her in a cold and distant manner. As noted earlier, Chris tends to treat Anna as an artistic and personal inferior. He repeatedly puts down her job and orders her to complete tasks that reinforce a traditional male-female patriarchal marital order. This is illustrated in a scene where Chris and his father and another male actor from the theatre sit watching a televised performance in Chris and Anna's apartment. Anna tries to inquire about the progress of the play. Chris's response is to order Anna to make sandwiches. Anna, in turn, expresses her increasing frustration by pumping herself full of pills and having ever more frequent temper tantrums.

Anna and Chris's relationship has also deteriorated at a sexual level. Particularly telling is the scene when Anna tries on a new, sexy negligee. This piece of distinctly feminine clothing is quite a luxury, especially if one is familiar with the low quality of clothing produced under the Communist regime. Her behaviour towards it shows how much she appreciates its novelty, carefully stroking it and fluffing out its long skirt in strikingly romantic gestures. Chris's response is to say, "It is nice," then to go straight to sleep. The next morning, the negligee appears in the trash can, which is exactly where their sexual relationship seems to be.

These private scenes contradict Chris and Anna's public behaviour. Outside their cramped apartment, they affect the pose of a united couple. Together, they attend the requisite March 8 theatre party, and Anna attends the play's premiere as the dutiful wife. When Anna visits her friend in Warsaw, she tells her that she has already been married ten years and that she still loves Chris. Chris, for his part, simply waves his wedding ring at his friend Michael when Michael asks him whether he's married or not. Both Anna and Chris have become so used to playing their roles of husband and wife that they can't get away from them, even after Anna moves out of the apartment. After Anna moves out, Chris gets horribly drunk, breaks the theatre marquee case, and proceeds to stumble into Anna's puppet theatre performance. Anna runs to Chris's side and, instead of kicking him out, cradles him in her arms like a baby. As she rocks him, she tells him that they'll move to another town – Warsaw or Lodz – in spite of the fact that she had just moved out of their apartment.

The point of this scene is to complete the depiction of "true believers" as those whose dreams are crushed by the system. The system assigns them other identities so that they will better fit into the totalitarian social structure. Anna loses her dream of acting, becoming a mere puppet performer. Chris loses his opportunity to act in Lodz because they need "useful all-around guys" more than good actors. The film's main plot line depicts Chris's losing battle with the director from Warsaw. This director carries out a series of extensive cuts to the play's original text because "Adam couldn't stand on stage for four hours," presumably the length of the unabridged play. The cuts, however, are an act of censorship, removing the play's elements of poetic nationalism and muting its desired aesthetic effect. *Liberation* becomes the ironic reference to Chris and Anna's aborted artistic aspirations.

What Agnieszka Holland has achieved is a dual narrative. A superficial narrative exists at the level of what normally would be considered as "plot." Chris's attempts to impress the important director from the big city dominate this level of narrative. The secondary narrative unfolds within the context of the main character's body. The true effect of the totalitarian regime at the cultural level manifests itself in the body of Anna, a body increasingly impaired by the "dumbing down" of its senses, reflected through Anna's growing drug addiction. The potential fullness and beauty of society, reflected in Anna's attempt at a manifestation of sexual desire, ends up, just like Anna's beautiful nightgown, in the refuse heap.

Exile

Agnieszka Holland continued making films following her exile by the Jaruzelski regime. In 1990, she finished the film *Europa, Europa,* her fifth film since *Provincial Actors.* Here, her focus turns from Soviet Communist totalitarian society to fascist totalitarian society. Once again, she proceeds to create a film that theoretically belongs to a specific genre, the Holocaust film, but one that refuses to be easily qualified by the conventions of the traditional Holocaust film narrative. The Holocaust film has evolved a set of conventions represented by films such as *Shoah* and *Schindler's List:* dark and humourless, they most often emphasize the role of Jews not only as victims, but also as one collective victim. Typically, in these films the human individual takes second place to the weight of historical events on the collectivity. *Schindler's List* serves as a particularly good example of the genre. The emphasis of the film falls on Schindler's legacy, the number of Jews that survived, rather than on Schindler's many personal weaknesses. And even though the film would generally be considered a "fictional" narrative, its attention to detail and to the historical representation of its characters blurs the line between the veracity attributed to documentary and the artistic "vision" of fiction.

In *Europa, Europa*, Holland turns to a personal narrative, in this case the story of Solomon Perel and his adventures during the Second World War, in order to construct an alternative vision of the Holocaust narrative. The emphasis on the individual experience achieves various effects within the film. Most notably, by moving the film's discourse away from the traditional depiction of the Holocaust as a communal event, it allows it to become an experience to be interpreted by the main character and, through his eyes, by the viewers. The Holocaust becomes something more than an episode with a single, hermetically sealed interpretation. Suddenly, the treatment of the Holocaust expands from the depiction of an impersonal massacre to an analysis of the psychology that could allow such a massacre to occur.

The film presents a picaresque character as hero. The plot depicts Solly jumping from master to master in order to improve his social status in a highly hierarchical order. The mobility provided by the framework of the picaresque narrative structure allows the film to present a full range of ideologically defined characters in situations that help to explicate their ideological motivations. Holland chooses to present Solly's mentor figures as appealing characters so that the viewer can see the mosaic of ideology that made up Eastern Europe during the Second World War.

The depiction of Solly's interaction with each of these characters also allows the viewer to start to perceive the appeal of the different ideologies represented by the characters as well as the power that mastery of their ideological discourse would represent. In the course of the film, Solly finds a mentor figure for each of the major ideological groups he encounters: his father for Judaism, Inna for Communism, and the German general who wants to adopt him for Nazism. All of these mentor figures initiate Solly into their respective community of believers. Inna serves as Solly's guide in the Komsomol; the general arranges for Solly to gain entrance into the Hitler Youth academy; and the film's first two scenes depict Solly as he undergoes the two defining Jewish initiation rituals: the bris and the bar mitzvah.

In the meantime, Solly's ability to internalize each system's discourse is converted into power within each of these ideological systems. His ability to master Russian and Marxist rhetoric in Russian gains him entrance into the Komsomol and proves useful in his future dealings with Soviet troops. His mastery of educated German becomes a discursive sign that marks him as Volksdeutsch, pure German. His ability to interpret both languages literally saves his life when German troops capture him as he tries to escape with the other members of the Soviet orphanage. His control of German allows him to gain credibility in the eyes of his German captors against Zenek's attempt to point out to the German soldiers that he is a Jew.

Solly's ability to change identity, chameleon-like, according to the discursive code he is utilizing, serves to highlight how identity is a manufactured cultural construct. Solly's imposture is played out in dramas of recognition and misrecognition. Identities supposedly based on biological criteria become secondary to the person's ability to master the discourse of that society.[5] Solly's mastery of German disguises his circumcised penis. In one of the film's many coincidental meetings, Solly befriends Robert, a poetry-quoting homosexual German soldier. Robert's military behaviour helps cover his sexual orientation, which would have sent him to the concentration camp as quickly as Solly would have been had the other Germans found out. In turn, it allows Robert to interact with Solly at the externally dictated military level as well as at the internally dictated aesthetic level, as both wistfully exchange verses from Goethe over the campfire. In a similar way, Solly's ability to master Marxist discourse gains him the acceptance of the class-discriminating Russians, despite his bourgeois background.

The story's structure as a picaresque narrative also allows Holland to comment on the implications of geography for the war experience. As Susan Linville notes: "For Solly Perel, the political flux of this Eastern setting means he can be embraced or rejected in dizzying succession on the basis of his (presumed) race, class, or nationality. Indeed, the East creates a 'perfect' environment for a Zelig-like personality."[6] By focusing on Solly's migration, the story highlights the international dimension of the Second World War. The diversity of ideologies and cultures he interacts with generalizes the narrative for the viewer and expands the frame of its reference beyond the individual experience of persecuted Jews, or Poles, or European homosexuals.

By way of the picaresque personal narrative, Holland transcends the convention that dictates that the Holocaust is to be depicted within the framework of victimizer and victimized, and posits the European war experience in terms of a dialogic ideological process. Holland tries to convey this aspect of the war experience through her continual merging of visual elements of the Nazi and Soviet systems in Solly's dreams. As Solly penetrates deeper and deeper into the Nazi structure, and as he finds himself forced to suppress his experiences as a Jew from his conscious existence, he finds his subconscious trying to make sense of his greater world through his dreams. One dream in particular is significant: he finds himself back in his old Soviet orphanage, re-viewing the dropping of candies during a Komsomol lecture on the importance of atheism. Suddenly, Hitler and Stalin come together in a waltz and, later, in the form of a statue. Their waltzing makes oblique reference to the equally well choreographed foreign policy conducted by the Stalinist regime in Eastern Europe, as Stalin appeased Hitler by ceding Poland to Germany in the Molotov-Ribbentrop Pact.

The waltzing scene has a further level of symbolism for the viewer who is familiar with the Soviet period's interpretive contract. Connecting the

German and Soviet totalitarian leaders in a dance can only remind this type of viewer of the many times Poland found itself partitioned as a result of German and Russian politics throughout the nineteenth and twentieth centuries, including the failed attempt by Stalin to lead the newly formed Soviet army in the occupation of the Ukraine and Poland at the end of the First World War. Solly's interpretation of Hitler's and Stalin's politics as a choreographed dance points to the Polish view that Russia (here the Soviet Union) and Germany have long manipulated politics in Eastern Europe, particularly in Poland.

The dream scene further points to another stylistic innovation that separates *Europa, Europa* from other Holocaust narratives, whether Western, such as *Schindler's List,* or East European, such as *Dita Saxova* and *The Shop on Main Street:* the insanity of the Holocaust can be presented in terms of a Bakhtinian carnivalesque model.[7] It may be no coincidence that a form borrowed from a medieval literary text transferred qualities of the medieval carnival feast into the cinematic form. The movie abounds with humorous scenes that serve to point to the nature of the power structure during the war as well as to the inversion of that power structure (represented by Solly's presence). Solly becomes the main agent for the presentation of the carnivalesque since, according to the ideological constructs of both systems in which he seeks refuge, he has no claim to the privileged positions he achieves.

According to Communist ideology, Solly's background as the son of a bourgeois Jewish shopkeeper should make him ineligible for membership in the party. He finally gains membership in the elite Komsomol by presenting a compelling class on atheism. (The presentation is interrupted by a Polish Roman Catholic, who denounces the principle of Communist atheism.) Solly, as well as the Communists in the orphanage, gains the upper hand in the eyes of the small children through a carefully staged candy rainfall. Each child's individual standing as a powerless orphan becomes temporarily suspended in the collective ritual of joining the Communist ranks, represented by their chaotic and gleeful acceptance of the candy.

Solly's rise through the ranks of the Nazi youth is also marked by a series of carefully staged rituals that consistently reiterate the collective mentality of the Nazi movement while simultaneously pointing to Solly as an inversion of the social order advocated by Nazism. Two scenes in particular stand out as illustrative of the carnivalesque element of the movie. The first takes place in the train carrying Solly to the Nazi school. Solly's shared birthday with Hitler, as well as his dark hair, lead to his deflowering by his Nazi escort. His sexual initiation while being ceremonially escorted by a representative of the power that desires to kill him for his biological background is, in one of the most humorous moments in the film, canivalesquely capped by his howls out the train window following his experience. Indeed, his rise through the social ranks is marked by his increased desirability as a sexual object.

The second scene takes place when Solly, now called Jupp, enters the Nazi Youth school. The scene is striking in its staging. The sea of Hitler Youth uniforms illuminated by lighted torches creates a festive flavour. The enthusiasm seen in the boys' faces as they pledge allegiance to Hitler is intoxicating. This ceremony of form as presented in these details, however, contains one visually minor but symbolically critical subversion: Jupp does not pledge allegiance to a live being but, rather, to the inanimate bust of Hitler in the courtyard. A binary dynamic emerges: the children, the least powerful members of the Nazi order, temporarily gain dominance within the context of the ceremony in which they pledge loyalty to the Nazi order. However, they pledge loyalty not to a living order, but to an artificial, plastic one.

Once again, Holland has managed to put together a dual narrative. The ostensibly main narrative deals with nothing more than the Holocaust itself, and the way the Jews found themselves betrayed by both the Soviets and the Germans. The progress of the war becomes the major driving force in this plot, as characters move along with the war front. The real narrative, however, revolves around Solly's struggle to stay alive and the way his body disassociates him from the people around him. Most of Solly's adventure reflects his efforts to conceal his circumcision. Particularly during his membership with the Hitler Youth, he finds himself forced to continually conceal his member. The only person in the German army who finds out his secret, ironically, has a secret of his own: homosexuality.

Solly's adventures raise the question of how an ideological system and its manifestation as a cultural and/or political system comes to define masculinity, and they address the contradictions that can exist between simultaneously active ideological constructs. Within Jewish culture, circumcision introduced the male child into the Jewish male collective. However, within Nazi culture, a Jewish male body, no matter how fertile, bears marks that define it as unacceptable and, thus, subject to being destroyed by the new Nazi order. Paternity in Nazi Germany became displaced as young boys were taken away to Hitler Youth boarding schools. Young girls (such as Solly's romantic interest at the Hitler Youth school, Leni, a viciously anti-Semitic blonde) desire to get pregnant not to start families with the boys from the school but, rather, to have "Hitler babies" and to hand them over to Nazi institutions to be raised. Adults could only stare in amazement as their children became the physical manifestations of the new ideological system.

The element of multilingualism, Solly's ability to survive due to his ability to mimic the linguistic code surrounding him, defines the second, picaresque, narrative of the body. In contrast to *Provincial Actors'* Anna, whose body existed in a constant state of tension in Polish society, Solly, as picaresque male hero, points to the body's (and thus the individual's) ability to camouflage itself to obtain social acceptance. Solly's state of adolescence adds symbolic weight to the notion of adaptive mutation. His adolescent age means that he is undergoing society's "masculinity rituals." Mastering the social skills required to assume his position as an adult man in society provides a level of freedom for the flow of the narrative. His ability to shift from one system to another, from one master to another, as he searches for a place to finally ascend to the state of adulthood, facilitates his role as narrator of the differences and similarities between the Soviet and Nazi systems.

In *Europa, Europa* Holland improves on *Provincial Actors* by intensifying the moments of intimacy in which the main character displays his disjunction from the society to which he belongs. In a poignantly comic moment, Solly, alone in the shower, tries to "sew" a new hood for his penis, with negative results. However, probably the most lyrical moment of the film occurs when Solly stares out his dormitory window, fogs the windowpane, and draws a star of David. That moment evokes many different images. It reminds the viewer of the ever-present social mark used against the Jews, and it recalls, at a very distant level, Kristallnacht, when, in 1938, the windows of Jewish homes were shattered by German crowds, initiating the intensive stage of Hitler's assault on Jews.[8] Most important, it lets the viewer know that no matter how well Solly hides from the Jewish ghettos, he is aware of the Judaism he carries inside, which is as integral to his being as is the air he breathes on the windowpane.

These two films demonstrate how Agnieszka Holland puts the lessons she learned about "speaking indirectly" (during her Unit X days) to good use. Having developed the personal narrative as an effective means to symbolically portray inscribed political discourse, as seen in *Provincial Actors*, in *Europa, Europa* she proceeds to explore how a different narrative framework can accommodate the construction of her semiotic system. In both, she explores the limits of such generic classifications as "socialist realism" and the "holocaust film."

Holland continued to develop her inscribed political discourse in her later films. Wrapped around the body of Mary Lennox, the girl from *The Secret Garden* (1993), is a secondary narrative of the meaning and legacy of colonialism. *Washington Square* (1997) wraps a discourse on the nature of beauty (and who determines what constitutes it) around the body of its heroine, Catherine Sloper. Most interesting in this continuum, however, is Holland's 1999 film *The Third Miracle*, in which the discourse rests in a "non-body," the body of a dead woman, Helen O'Regan, who is being studied for beatification and eventual canonization by the Roman Catholic Church. There, the not so hidden secondary narrative deals with the nature of purity and how the body engenders it.

All of these films challenge our position as viewers, moving us from passive witnesses to active readers of the film text. Holland's films push one to see how the ideological pronouncements of various cultural and political systems manifest themselves on the body. This, perhaps, is the greatest legacy this East European filmmaker has made to our conscience as Western consumers of cinematic art.

Notes

1 Barbara Quart, "Three Central European Women Directors Revisited," *Cineaste* 19, 4: 58.
2 David Paul, "The Esthetics of Courage: The Political Climate for the Cinema in Poland and Hungary," *Cineaste* 14, 4: 16.
3 Boleslaw Michalek and Frank Turaj, *The Modern Cinema of Poland* (Bloomington: Indiana University Press, 1988), 9-10.
4 This presentation of a reading contract relies on some of the theoretical constructs found in Seymour Chatman's *Story and Discourse: Narrative Structure in Fiction and Film* (Ithaca/London: Cornell University Press, 1978).
5 Susan E. Linville. "*Europa, Europa*: A Test Case for German National Cinema," *Wide Angle* 16, 3: 40-3.
6 Linville, "*Europa, Europa*," 48.
7 Bakhtin developed this concept in *Voprosy literatury i estetiki*, translated as *The Dialogic Imagination: Four Essays by M.M. Bakhtin* (Austin: University of Texas Press, 1981), 165.
8 In November 1938, with Kristallnacht (the "Night of Broken Glass"), what had previously been an economic attack against German and Austrian Jews transformed into a physical attack. Synagogues and Jewish-owned stores and homes were destroyed, Jewish men arrested, and individuals murdered.

10   The Dancing Body: Sally Potter as a Feminist Auteure

Corinn Columpar

The year is 1997. A filmmaker writes, directs, and stars in a movie that treads the line between reality and fiction, explores the personal and professional stakes of the creative process with acute self-reflexivity, and pairs its protagonist with a younger lover. How does this highly personal project fare under public scrutiny? If the filmmaker in question is Woody Allen, it fares quite well. Reviews of his film *Deconstructing Harry* lauded Allen for his "brazenly autobiographical" writing and his "unapologetic exploration of the artist as asshole" while deeming the film "complex," "terrifically liberating," "honest," "multi-layered," and "scathingly good."[1] Even his reduction of women to fodder for his sexual appetite and his relegation of non-White actors to the role of prostitute were written off as personal quirks or "meta-jokes."[2] If the filmmaker in question is Sally Potter, however, the public is not so generous. Critics took Potter to task for her film *The Tango Lesson*, designating the work as "an act of wild hubris" employing a "self-admiring gaze" and featuring "a woman smothering herself with her own affection."[3] Given their resistance to the film, some reviewers even had difficulty conceding the indisputable: that Potter is an accomplished dancer worthy of the camera's scrutiny.

In a review that is fairly anomalous within critical circles, insofar as it acknowledges the effect of Potter's gender on her film's reception, Roger Ebert of the *Chicago Sun Times,* in order to reveal one aspect of the gendered double standard fuelling criticisms of *The Tango Lesson,* reminds readers of the regularity with which films romantically pair men with women half their age.[4] Yet Potter's transgression is not limited to her decision to play the film director, Sally, who becomes romantically involved with Pablo Veron, a professional tango dancer several years her junior; rather, it is in making herself the subject of her art that she commits her most egregious assault on gender norms. While Allen's self-indulgence is greeted with a chorus of kudos and the occasional bemused "tsk, tsk," Potter's is considered unfeminine and, thus, gravely inappropriate and egotistical. In short, if Harry were to meet Sally it would be on a textual terrain reserved for male subjectivity.

The reviews of *The Tango Lesson* are noteworthy not only for their tendency to conflate female autonomy and authorship with narcissism, but also for their failure to engage with the film on its own terms. *The Tango Lesson* is assailed repeatedly for that which it is not, yet the extent to which various reviews contradict one another in the process of deploying this common critique suggests confusion over what it, in fact, is. While some critics bemoan the film's lack of passion, others call for a more ironic tone, and still others demand a greater degree of intellectual rigour. Read within the context of Potter's other work, however, *The Tango Lesson* emerges as something quite other than the cinematic paradigms against which it is being measured, for it is not a pure musical, a pure melodrama, or a pure intellectual exercise; rather, in exploring female subjectivity and corporeality while disrupting the conventions of an illusionistic cinema, it is a work that returns to those thematic and formal preoccupations that define Potter's oeuvre. Furthermore, while investigating how the female body is implicated in narrative and form, emotion and theory, experience and representation, *The Tango Lesson* also makes explicit the extent to which dance has influenced Potter by infusing her method as filmmaker and shaping her understanding of sexual politics.

Potter has a long history of involvement with dance, extending from her years as a professional dancer in London to her most recent, self-proclaimed obsession with tango and the dance culture of Buenos Aires. In some ways her career as a dancer has been quite distinct from her career as a filmmaker. Aside from one film that was made for integration into a live dance

Film poster for Sally Potter's *The Tango Lesson* (1997)

performance, Potter ceased her experimentation with film during the years she "trod the boards"[5] with Richard Alston's company Strider and her own Limited Dance Company, formed in association with Jack Landsley in 1974. In 1979 she returned to her first love, cinema, and made *Thriller*, which incorporated her experience with performance, yet marked her movement away from it. After *Thriller* found an enthusiastic audience in festival patrons and feminist academics alike, Potter dedicated herself entirely to filmmaking, and in the last two decades she has put out six films, including four narrative features: *The Gold Diggers* (1983), *Orlando* (1993), *The Tango Lesson* (1997), and *The Man Who Cried* (2000). The separation, however, between Potter's work with dance, on the one hand, and film, on the other, is not as definitive as this resumé might suggest. For example, when describing her approach to filmmaking Potter cites her experience in the dance studio as instrumental in her training for a role behind the camera, where discipline, the ability to collaborate, and an understanding of choreography are imperative. Furthermore, dance is central to many of the texts themselves. For example, the dancing body is featured in *Thriller*, which deconstructs Puccini's opera La Bohème; in *The Gold Diggers*, which incorporates avant-garde musical numbers; and in *The Tango Lesson*, which chronicles Sally's immersion into a world of new rhythms and steps. Yet, it is in her heightened awareness of what Norman Bryson calls "social kinetics,"[6] or the choreographic nature of daily life, that Potter's experience with dance most subtly, yet most profoundly, informs her work. Thus, even though *Orlando* is a film in which dance per se has no bearing upon the narrative, it is marked by its maker in that it foregrounds the issue of how socially structured movement serves to gender bodies.

This pervasive influence of dance imbues Potter's work with a unique aesthetic and subversive potential. In the introduction to her anthology *Meaning in Motion: New Cultural Studies of Dance,* Jane Desmond suggests the theoretical possibilities of dance when she asks, "since dance takes the body as its primary medium, can it provide a potential utopian site for imagining what a feminist politics of the body might look like?"[7] As an activity and an art form, dance allows for a conception of the female body as both lived and gazed upon, suffused with subjectivity and available for specularization. By extension, dance on film has the power to complicate any simple theoretical reduction of woman to fetishistic object for a male spectator and to facilitate a feminine and/or feminist re-visioning of the female body. Yet the extent to which a particular film is able to realize such a re-visioning and create a set of imagery resistant to cooptation depends on how it contextualizes its dancing bodies narratively and formally. Thus, *The Tango Lesson* (as both an individual text and one component of a larger auteurist project) can serve to initiate a discussion of whether Potter, with her cinema of the body in motion, could be the author of the political vision suggested by Desmond's query.

The Tango Lesson takes as its subject a filmmaker named Sally who, at the film's outset, is in the process of developing ideas for a new project entitled *Rage,* which features a publicity-starved fashion designer who murders the models in his employ. While staying in Paris and labouring over the screenplay for *Rage,* Sally happens upon a theatrical performance of the tango starring the legendary Pablo Veron, becomes mesmerized by the dance, and arranges after the show for private instruction. The story that ensues is broken up into a series of "lessons," some having to do with dance and others related to the romantic relationship that blossoms between teacher and student. Sally eventually abandons her current project and decides to make a film about tango starring Pablo and other dancers whom she meets during her visit to Buenos Aires. Given this plot, with its self-reflexive structure and focus on artistic agency, the relationship at the film's centre is one of considerable complexity in that power and the question of who is leading whom are continually under negotiation. Potter foregrounds both the corporeal and the specular so that the politics of the gaze, around which the field of feminist film theory has emerged, becomes profoundly implicated in a politics of the body, concerned with how gender is made to matter.

While most of the critics who berate Potter for taking viewers with her on an extended ego trip cite her decision to star in *The Tango Lesson* as her biggest mistake, it is almost certainly her presence behind rather than in front of the camera that proves so threatening. The division of labour that Laura Mulvey identified as structuring classical Hollywood cinema – "In a world ordered by sexual imbalance, pleasure has been split between active/male and passive/female"[8] – is subverted in this film, which is explicitly constructed as the vision of both Potter (the director) and Sally (the character). Not only does the film's self-reflexivity make it impossible to forget Potter's role as author, but the viewer also repeatedly gains access to Sally's ideas for *Rage* when the black-and-white footage capturing Sally and Pablo's mutual engagement is interrupted by fleeting images drenched in vibrant colour. Despite her status as one of relatively few women working in a male-dominated industry, Sally/Potter does not construct her vision as a privilege that she has usurped so much as a desire that she has indulged and a skill that she has honed. And, significantly, Pablo does not have access to this desire or skill. During a climactic fight she tells him why he cannot recognize what she does for a living: "You don't know how to use your eyes. You only want to be looked at, not to look. That's why you don't see, that's why you know nothing about cinema!"

That Pablo functions as the primary object of Sally's gaze (not to mention the gaze of a host of diegetic spectators as well as viewers taking in Potter's film) is indeed important in that it allows for a neat reversal of conventional looking relations. Yet Potter is not simply interested in re-gendering the gaze so as to turn the male gaze on its head while maintaining a scopic economy that disempowers through objectification; rather, what makes *The Tango Lesson* so politically productive is the manner in which it constructs Pablo as spectacle. It is important to acknowledge that Pablo's specularization is not unprecedented since, as both Steve Neale and Steven Cohan contend in their contributions to the anthology *Screening the Male: Exploring Masculinities in Hollywood Cinema*, the one type of male body that is routinely put on display is that of the dancer or musical performer.[9] Yet those performers (and their directors) have gone to great lengths, through a variety of means, to diffuse the threat of feminization associated with such displays. Cohan argues that, in the case of Fred Astaire, for example, narrative-stopping dance numbers function as highly theatricalized performances of masculinity insofar as Astaire's star persona overshadows the diegetic and narrative context of his movement. Certainly a similar argument could be made with regard to Pablo, since the extent to which his character is a fiction or a fact is intentionally made ambiguous. More important, however, Pablo is not mere spectacle; he transcends the iconic status of the fetishized female star theorized by Mulvey in that his specularization is thoroughly implicated in his embodiment and, thus, his subjectivity. While

Sally's labour is wedded to her artistic vision, Pablo identifies himself first and foremost as a dancer whose understanding of himself is derived largely, if not entirely, from the experience of his own corporeality in conjunction with the attention of an admiring audience.

Potter constructs Pablo as a thoroughly embodied performer and a continually performing body by erasing the distinction between spectacle and narrative that is inherent in the structure of the typical musical. When Pablo asks Sally, towards the end of the film, how many numbers he will have in the movie that she is setting out to make, the question emerges as strikingly inadequate given all that has preceded it. For, in *The Tango Lesson*, not only do midnight strolls slip seamlessly into tango combinations and mundane chores into occasions for syncopated solos (both of which are things one might see in a Gene Kelly musical, for example), but even an act as simple as lighting a cigarette has a distinctly performative flair when undertaken by Pablo. This heightened sense of performance that imbues Pablo's every move inevitably incites awareness of how all bodies both make and bear meaning continually throughout the film – how a hand gesture can communicate the word croissant, how a turning of the head can betray jealousy, or how a missed dance step can signal discord between dancers/lovers.

As suggested by the fact that Pablo and Sally move continually between English, Spanish, and French when conversing, one of the primary issues to be worked through in *The Tango Lesson* is that of (mis)communication. Sally is fluent in the language of images and practised in the art of looking, while Pablo is fluent in the language of movement and practised in the art of performance; for them to understand one another, a common ground must be forged. The challenges that Sally faces when she starts taking lessons from Pablo are those of recognizing "how intricate [tango is] from the inside"[10] and, thus, of understanding how to fully inhabit or fully embody the movement. This is an endeavour that entails, in Pablo's words, throwing everything from the past away and relearning how to do something as basic as walking. Sally throws her heart and soul into this "lesson," seeking to meet Pablo on a utopian terrain of perfectly harmonized movement and connectedness. In the process, she necessarily seeks out a site removed from looking relations that position her as bearer of the gaze and Pablo as its recipient. In return she asks of Pablo that he similarly divest himself of this scopic economy, becoming frustrated when she senses that her partner is giving more of himself to their audience than to her.

This attention to corporeality offers as a horizon of possibility the articulation of a female subjectivity grounded in embodiment. As mentioned before, Potter has consistently explored the role of the female body in both art and culture at large, and in some ways *The Tango Lesson* marks the culmination of this personal and professional project. Potter presents a version of herself struggling to construct an understanding of self and of the other that takes place outside of the scopic economy that, on the one hand, has routinely reduced woman to image throughout film history, and, on the other, inspires Potter to create. In doing so, she draws in important ways on earlier projects. In *Thriller*, Potter places Puccini's working-class heroine Mimi at the centre of an investigation into her own death. As she looks for clues, deconstructing and reconstructing the opera from the perspective of its silenced victim, she asks why it is her life that is sacrificed in the name of tragedy rather than, for example, the life of Rodolfo, her starving artist lover. One issue raised repeatedly in the process of this questioning is the extent to which her death is aestheticized. Remembering how she was taken from Rodolfo's room after passing away, she says, "Oh Mimi, you were carried from the room. Lifted up and taken out of there. Carried away from the attic. Yes. In arabesque, in arabesque. Yes, I was. That's important. I was in arabesque. Frozen in arabesque." This pose of beautified suffering haunts the text as it is assumed repeatedly by Mimi's on-screen double in a type of visual refrain. Furthermore, the extent to which it is a specifically feminized pose – one reserved for the female body as textual martyr – is made evident when roles are reversed (a man poses in arabesque while a woman supports him) with absurd results. While Potter demystifies dramatic conventions in *Thriller*, it is more general social conventions that are the object of her scrutiny in *Orlando*. In this cinematic adaptation of Virginia Woolf's novel, Potter once again deploys from a site of alterity a critique of, among other things, the manner in which gender is embodied. Yet in this case that alterity is one associated not with a tragic heroine but, rather, with a uniquely triumphant character who lives for 400 years, changing sex midway through his/her lifespan. In many ways, *Orlando* works as a comedy of manners in which markers of gender (and particularly markers of femininity, since Orlando starts his trajectory as a man and then must adapt to womanhood) are profoundly defamiliarized. Through the choreography of Orlando's movements, as she struggles, for example, to navigate narrow walkways or sit comfortably in the cumbersome dresses that become her uniform in the wake of the "transformation," Potter manages to foreground the performative nature of gender in certain scenes without recourse to a single line of dialogue.

With its aesthetics of performance, *The Tango Lesson* synthesizes the elements of *Thriller* and *Orlando* discussed above. While *Thriller* attends to the issue of how the female body functions narratively and is figured visually within the arts, and while *Orlando* is concerned with the social construction of gender in British daily life, *The Tango Lesson* renders moot the distinction between art and life. As a result, the issue of who should lead whom has implications that are both professional and romantic, political and personal. Furthermore, *Rage*, the film that Sally is conjuring up when she first encounters Pablo, invokes both *Thriller* and *Orlando* in a more specific manner, adding another layer of self-reflexivity to the text. The production values and visual texture of *Rage* are identical to those of *Orlando*, while Sally's description of it as a meditation on the glamourization of death marks a return to the subject matter of *Thriller*. By incorporating, at some level, her prior films into the very fabric of *The Tango Lesson*, Potter acknowledges the shift that her work has taken with this production. The difference between the film that the semi-fictional Sally sets out to make, on the one hand, and ends up making, on the other, mirrors the difference between Potter's earlier works and *The Tango Lesson*. In both cases she ultimately creates a movie that is grounded in experience and that, consequently, is more personal and more pragmatic than anything she had done before. As a result, she constructs a movie that demands not only a critique of existing gender norms, but also an attempt to negotiate and/or transcend them and to conceptualize the female body and female subjectivity anew.

In the end, however, the practised embodiment that emerges, in part or fully, in the process of dancing is not intended to replace Sally's vision, for she remains an artist working in a visual medium; rather, it is a means of exploring ways to construct the female body as empowered, fully present, and subjectified when in front of as well as behind the camera. Some of the most satisfying moments of the film, in fact, are those in which Sally and Pablo seem to transcend their linguistic differences (so to speak) and the lived body and the imaged body merge. While the film's ending, with its graceful dance steps and climactic kiss, suggests such a reconciliation, the most striking image is that which graces the film's promotional poster, taken from a scene of literal reconciliation in which Sally and Pablo make up after a big fight. At the top of the image is a life-sized religious painting of Jacob wrestling with an angel, and, while the narrative context of the painting bespeaks an antagonism, their bodies are positioned in a manner suggestive of the tango. Beneath the painting Sally and Pablo assume the same position, thus simultaneously reproducing and resignifying the iconography and, consequently, raising the spectre of both the experiential and the pictorial. Quite deliberately, Potter has frozen this fleeting filmic moment into an enduring still image, for it captures the complexity of her project. What she sees and feels, what we see and know, is that at that moment no one is leading, no one is following, and a feminist re-visioning of the body is indeed under way.

Notes

1 In an article entitled *"Deconstructing Harry:* Dark Laughter When Life Is All Halloween," Janet Maslin uses the phrases "terrifically liberating," "brazenly autobiographical," and "brazenly good." (*The New York Times on the Web,* 12 December 1997, <http://www.nytimes.com/library/film/121297harry-film-review.html>). The remaining quotations are from Holly Hertzel's review of the film on her Web page (*Movie Review Ring,* accessed 15 March 1999, <http://www.geocities.com/Hollywood/Lot/3000/harry.html>).

2 Andrea Chase, "Movie Review of *Deconstructing Harry,*" *Movie Magazine International,* 24 December 1997, <http://www.shoestring.org/mmi_revs/deconstructing-harry.html>.

3 While the first quoted phrase is from Janet Maslin's article "*The Tango Lesson:* Filmmaker Falls for the Tango in Paris" (*New York Times* on the Web, 14 November 1997, <http://www.nytimes.com/library/film/111497tango-film-review.html>), the remaining two are from Jack Matthews's review entitled "*Tango Lesson* Struggles to Get the Steps Right" (*Los Angeles Times* online reviews, 24 December 1997, <http://accessatlanta.hollywood.com/videoguide/movies/tango/review>).

4 Roger Ebert, "Review of *The Tango Lesson,*" *Chicago Sun Times* online reviews, accessed 10 March 1999, <http://www.suntimes.com/ebert/ebert_reviews/1997/12/121903.html>.

5 Scott MacDonald, "Interview with Sally Potter," *Camera Obscura* 35, 197.

6 Norman Bryson, "Cultural Studies and Dance History," Jane Desmond, ed., *Meaning in Motion: New Cultural Studies of Dance* (Durham, NC: Duke University Press, 1997), 75.

7 Jane Desmond, "Introduction," in Desmond, *Meaning in Motion,* 2.

8 Laura Mulvey, "Visual Pleasure and Narrative Cinema," in *Issues in Feminist Film Criticism,* ed. Patricia Erens (Bloomington: Indiana University Press, 1990), 33.

9 Steven Cohan, "'Feminizing' the Song-and-Dance Man: Fred Astaire and the Spectacle of Masculinity in the Hollywood Musical," in Steven Cohan and Ina Rae Hark, eds., *Screening the Male: Exploring Masculinities in Hollywood Cinema* (New York: Routledge, 1993), 46-69; and Steve Neale, "Masculinity as Spectacle: Reflections on Men and Mainstream Cinema," in ibid., 9-22.

10 Henri Béhar, "Sally Potter on *The Tango Lesson,*" *Film Scouts LLC,* 4 November 1997, <http://filmscouts.com/scripts/interview.cfm?File=sal-pot>.

Filmography: Sally Potter (Director)

1979   *The London Story*
1979   *Thriller*
1983   *The Gold Diggers* (also writer and editor)
1986   *Tears Laughter Fear and Rage* (TV)
1988   *Women Filmmakers in Russia* (a.k.a. *I Am an Ox, I Am a Horse, I Am a Man, I Am a Woman*) (documentary)
1993   *Orlando* (also writer and composer)
1997   *The Tango Lesson* (also writer, composer, and actor)
2000   *The Man Who Cried* (also writer and story idea)

Women in the Mainstream:
Using Popular Genres in Europe

Part 3 is devoted to a discussion of films by women directors in Europe, beginning with German filmmaker Doris Dörrie's *Nobody Loves Me* (1995). Kathryn Barnwell and Marni Stanley, who both teach Women's Studies at Malaspina College on Vancouver Island, look at this film's treatment of issues of gender, race, class, and sexual orientation. Does the use of comedy make a political message more effective, more palatable? Or does it trivialize the tragic experiences of racial and sexual minorities? Intertextual allusions to *Black Orpheus* and the carnivalesque blur the boundaries of realism and fantasy, and the director's claim to be promulgating multiculturalism is shown to be problematic.

Brigitte Rollet and Caroline Eades both survey a substantial number of recent films directed by French women – films that exploit mainstream genres, including comedy, in various ways. Rollet relates the history of women's filmmaking in France to political events such as May 1968, and to changes in the industry following the formation of the European Union. She discusses French attitudes towards feminism, which are very different from those in England or North America. Contemporary women directors in France mostly reject being labelled by their gender, and many aim for mainstream success. Yet their use of masculine genres, such as the road movie or thriller, may be transgressive in relation to the male models, and they challenge masculine hegemony in the film industry by achieving box-office success – particularly Coline Serreau (with comedy) and Josiane Balasko (with comedy and crime). Rollet's filmography provides the background to Eades's discussion of three successful recent films (by Veysset, Merlet, and Roüan, respectively) as illustrations of the ideological and aesthetic preoccupations of contemporary women directors. These directors feature strong but ambiguous central female characters – characters who reflect some of their own experiences. In a panel discussion in Part 4, Eades contributes further to an understanding of the present position of women feature filmmakers in France.

In a chapter originally written and presented in French (as were those by Eades, Mounsef, and Rollet), Josette Déléas turns to the work of prominent Italian director Lina Wertmüller. In *Seven Beauties* Wertmüller, like Dörrie, exploits the carnivalesque, exposing social mechanisms through parodic use of the grotesque. Like Dörrie and some contemporary French directors, she provokes a debate over what is laughable and what is not, as well as over the specificity (or lack of it) of women's perceptions and representations as illustrated by their use of male-dominated film genres.

11 The Vanishing Healer in Doris Dörrie's *Nobody Loves Me*

Kathryn Barnwell and Marni Stanley

Doris Dörrie was born in Hanover (then in East Germany) in 1955. She studied drama in the US and continued her training at the Academy of Television and Film in Munich, where she now lives and works. Her output includes a number of documentaries and ten feature films, among them the internationally successful *Men* (1986), as well as seven volumes of short stories, a novel, a play, and three children's books. In 2001 she stage-directed Mozart's *Cosi fan tutte* at the state opera house in Berlin. Her work often addresses male-female relationships, as is the case in her popular comedy *Keiner liebt mich* (*Nobody Loves Me*, 1995), where issues of race and sexual orientation are also central.[1]

Synopsis Part 1: The Central Female Character in Search of a (Straight, White) Man

An attractive, intelligent woman who is about to turn thirty, Fanny Fink lives alone in a graffiti-covered housing project, and has a job frisking female passengers at the Cologne airport. She has been single for the past four years and her isolation has made her cynical about love and relationships with men. A friend tells her that a woman over thirty has a better chance of being hit by an atomic bomb than getting married, and her mother asks her if her biological clock is digital (since she can't seem to hear it ticking). Fanny still hopes to find the right man, and makes a video for a dating service. In it, however, she offers this off-putting advice to any potential date: "If I were you, I wouldn't love me." Nevertheless, she is trying to improve her self-image by listening to esteem-building tapes at night: "I am strong. I am smart. I love and am loved." She also attends a night course on "conscious dying," in which participants are encouraged to make friends with death by sleeping in their own coffins, planning their own suicides, and writing their own epitaphs. Her clothes, apartment, car, and jewellery are all decorated with skeletons. She seems, in short, to be obsessed with death, and pessimistic in spite of her attempts to find New Age solutions to her problems.

Synopsis Part 2: The Men in Fanny's Life – Black and White

Fanny meets a Black tenant in her apartment building, Orfeo de Altamar, who turns out to be a gay palm-reader and psychic. He tells her that the man of her dreams is blond, handsome, and associated with the number

Doris Dörrie's *Keiner liebt mich/Nobody Loves Me* (1995), courtesy of the Film Reference Library, Toronto

twenty-three. Consequently, when Lothar, the new building manager, appears and is tall, blond, and has the licence-plate number 2323, Fanny sets out to seduce him. Orfeo gives her lessons in femininity, lending her his drag outfits. Although Lothar appears initially to be friendly and helpful, his hidden agenda is to clear the building of its eccentric tenants, beginning with Orfeo, to make way for a more lucrative project. Fanny aggressively pursues Lothar, meeting him by deliberately bumping into his expensive car, which she does not yet realize is the place he calls home. While not exactly the man she sought in her advertisement ("not a smoker or a drinker, with good health insurance and an apartment of his own"), Lothar at first looks like quite a good catch. However, he soon reveals himself to be self-centred, greedy, unfaithful (he sleeps with other women including her best friend) and, like Fanny, obsessed with death.

Her friendship with Orfeo develops, when she asks him to move in with her after his eviction from his apartment down the hall. He is seen in various scenes that emphasize his blackness and his gayness: "worshipping" a fetish, painting his body with tribal African flare, lip-synching Billie Holiday's "Lover Man" at a gay bar. He seems, in contrast to Fanny, to be full of life, although he is actually dying of a mysterious disease (identified only as not being AIDS). As Orfeo becomes physically weaker, he assures Fanny that he will be transported back to where he came from: not Africa, but a distant star. His death is transformed into a triumphal departure, and his body disappears. Fanny drops her now useless coffin off the balcony onto Lothar's car and invites her neighbours in to celebrate. Among the disparate collection of eccentrics is a young White man who had previously made several overtures to Fanny. He removes his jacket to reveal the number twenty-three on his jersey.

One review of the film calls it "charming, emotionally perceptive," "uplifting," and claims that through her friendship with Orfeo, Fanny "learns a lesson about what real love is." Dörrie is quoted as saying that it reflects "the prevalent aspects of the modern German character: isolation and an almost obsessive tendency to wonder about death." There is, however, more to the film than that.[2]

Dörrie's Purpose: Sexual and Racial Politics

In an interview about her film, Dörrie says:

> I wanted to tell the story of a young, self-centred woman who lives alone and is unhappy even though she has all she needs. This, to me, is the situation many young people find themselves in today and, furthermore, I saw it as a synonym for Germany's current position in the world. I am preoccupied with the fact that Germans seem unable to be happy with what they have and, as a result, isolate their country from the rest of Europe. I believe that multiculturalism is the only way forward in Germany. This alone can teach compassion, and I wanted to explore this in *Nobody Loves Me*.[3]

This view ignores the particular implications of the fact that Orfeo is Black, in the German context. Racism in Germany in this century has an almost unspeakable history. It is clear that this character would not have survived the Nazi years, because of either his race or his sexual orientation. His presence even now is an anomaly, since postwar legislation in Germany has made it impossible for *Gastarbeiter* (foreign workers, most of whom are Turkish) to become citizens, even into the second or third generation of residence in Germany. In *Nobody Loves Me*, Dörrie deals with gender and class concerns with a deft wit, but she ultimately fails to address the issues raised by the transformation of Germany into a multiracial community. Race receives only token treatment, since although Orfeo is more able to help Fanny than the White Germans around her, death/disappearance seems to be the only solution to his own situation. Having fulfilled his healing role, he conveniently vanishes.

Lothar is also central to Dörrie's handling of both gender and class politics. On one hand, he is Fanny's initial object of desire. He has perfected a "sensitive new age male" façade, complete with a ponytail (which Fanny later steals, along with his Armani suit, in a symbolic vengeful castration). Yet behind it hides a deceitful libertine, who sleeps with one woman after another because he is unsure of his own sexual potency. His dealings with the tenants demonstrate a ruthless hypocrisy. While appearing to be sorry for the inconvenience renovations are causing them, in reality he is aiming to rid the building of its eccentric collection of inhabitants. When the water supply is cut off, he has it reinstated for ten minutes so that Fanny can make him a cup of coffee, and he evicts Orfeo even after he has finally managed to pay his rent. The class politics in the film centre on Lothar, as the representative of the exploitative "owners." But this is a comedy, and the class conflict is handled with a light touch. We see the tenants surviving their siege and creating community through shared difficulties. We cheer when Fanny, in the closing shot, conveys her choice of life over death by destroying Lothar's beloved and expensive car with her coffin. However, the fact that he has no building/home other than the car complicates his role as representative of capitalist exploiters.

Like Orfeo's, Lothar's role is ambivalent. The comedic elements in the film camouflage the incongruities, which are acceptable as part of a carnivalesque depiction of the trials of modern loneliness and homelessness, as well as of race relations.

The Carnivalesque

Dörrie ensures that Orfeo's first appearance is ironic, as it inverts the stereotype of a lone Black male as threatening to White womanhood. He and Fanny first meet in the elevator. Orfeo is in full "tribal" makeup (which portrays a mix of black and white: shaved head with alternating white spots and stripes, hands and arms painted in a skeleton design) and belligerently blows smoke in Fanny's face. She panics when the elevator stops, the lights go out, and pushing the buttons has no effect. Orfeo performs a wild dance and chant, which apparently restarts the elevator, and presents his business card with a flourish. His professional activities (as psychic, palm-reader, and performer) are unable to support him financially, but he has another kind of power.

The story takes place during the time of the annual Cologne Carnival (in late February-early March), which justifies the eruptions of carnival revellers that occur throughout. These are the only scenes in which non-White faces (other than Orfeo's) are depicted: some are Whites in blackface, some are Blacks in elaborately designed "tribal" costumes and makeup. Difference, or otherness, is accepted in the Carnival as a colourful and entertaining performance. However, in reality, no matter how many disguises Orfeo tries, he cannot find a performance of Blackness that will provide economic viability in Dörrie's Cologne.

From his multiple marginalized positions, Orfeo attempts to find an acceptable masquerade. He is poor, lonely, unwelcome in Germany, and sick. His vulnerability is underlined by the physical representation of his abject body postures: crouching in the elevator or outside Fanny's door, lying unconscious in the hallway of the building, weeping in Fanny's arms as he becomes sicker and weaker. He has tried a variety of strategies to succeed economically, but no attempt on his part to play roles more acceptable to the White majority (whether defying or catering to their prejudices) can change how he is viewed and how he is treated. For his day work as a psychic he dresses in imitation of a tribal African man whose photo he keeps in his apartment. At night, he works as a drag performer in a gay bar, but he has been rejected by his well-to-do lover who works in television. While Orfeo transforms himself in a variety of ways in his continual struggle to fit in, his lover, who is a newsreader and whom we see at the bar and on screen, is successful in the public sphere with virtually unaltered appearance. In one scene Orfeo sits in a public market, advertizing that he will read palms; when he gets no response, he flips over his sign to the other side, which appeals for donations to send him "back" to Africa (although he was born in Germany). This latter appeal elicits an immediate donation. The implication is that many Germans want people like him simply to disappear.

Saving Eurydice

The film makes obvious use of the Orpheus/Eurydice myth, via echoes of *Black Orpheus*. Both films are set in carnival; both re-enact the mythic descent into hell and the attempt to save Eurydice. In spite of the motif of masquerade introduced by carnival, and underscored by duplicitous characters such as Lothar, the connection between Fanny and Orfeo is shown to be genuine. The film establishes a psychic as well as physical connection between the two, initially based on their shared experience of rejection and betrayal in love. At one point, Orfeo, recently betrayed by his lover, is up on the roof in tears, looking at the carnival lights below and clearly contemplating suicide. The film cuts to Fanny, who suddenly jolts awake calling his name. After Orfeo's eviction, when he moves in with Fanny, we learn that his mysterious disease may be related to the scar below his left breast and, therefore, to his heart. As Orfeo becomes weaker, Fanny becomes stronger: she nurses him, feeds him his favourite elixir (Veuve Clicquot champagne), washes his body, and sleeps in the same bed. Other than sex, there is no intimacy that they do not share. Each says to the other: "I love you," the first time for both that love has been reciprocal.

In spite of this closeness, however, it is clear that Orfeo's life and death serve to relieve Fanny of the responsibility of acknowledging the role that racism and homophobia have played in his suffering. In his role as guide, Orfeo offers her a series of "tutorials" on life. "Is the glass half empty or half full?" sums up the choice before Fanny, though not before Orfeo. He points out to her that she is, in fact, quite lucky compared to him: she has a job, a family, a place to live, and "the right skin colour." For his part, he tells Fanny of his "true" origins: he is an extraterrestrial alien who will be taken home. On the night of his death, Fanny paints his head with the African "tribal" motif he has worn earlier, dresses him in Lothar's now fetishized

Armani suit, and carries him to her coffin, placing in it the gold bar that she has purchased for him with her savings. She lights candles and plays the tape of aircraft taking off that she has made at his request. Out in the hall the tenants have gathered in a panic at the magnitude of the sound (now well beyond what her tape deck could produce). Cut to the roof, where a landing strip of lights has been laid out and Orfeo's large fetish figure now stands. Cut to hallway and a bright light under Fanny's door. When she re-enters her apartment, Orfeo's body has vanished.

Realism, Fantasy, and Comedy

Nobody Loves Me reverses the original myth, as Orfeo saves Fanny but is unable to save himself. The primary difference between this version of the myth and others is that Orpheus and Eurydice are not of the same race. Because Dörrie's Orfeo is helpmate and guide, not partner, to his Eurydice (Fanny), his separation from her is what saves her. Up until the disappearance of his body, it is possible to see in Orfeo's sense of himself as an extraterrestrial alien an attempt on his part to explain the degree of his suffering as a marginalized other. By making what at first appears to be a fantasy finally appear to be true, Dörrie takes the edge off the racial politics of the film; she invites us to read Orfeo's marginalization and ultimate exclusion as science fiction rather than as present and historical reality. Orfeo's apotheosis renders him more mythic than material, suggesting that his death has served to save Fanny – a sacrifice that enables her to set aside her fear of death and, in so doing, embrace life. This narrative twist leaves her both physically and politically unencumbered.

Orfeo's mythic status is reinforced by several associations evoked throughout the film, besides *Black Orpheus*. He is linked with the Tarot card of the Hanged Man, and his masquerade as Death is in keeping with a common carnival motif. On Fanny's dreaded thirtieth birthday, he welcomes her home painted in elaborately detailed skeletal body paint, embraces her recalling the German folkloric motif of "Death and the Maiden," and dances with her to Edith Piaf's "Non, je ne regrette rien," which becomes the film's theme song.

Orfeo is part of an established tradition in Western cinema: the person of colour who acts as a guide or impetus for a transformation of the White protagonist. This character is removed by death or left behind after the protagonist has found whatever was absent from his or her life (passion, life force, joy, creativity, or enhanced understanding). Examples are Chingachgook in *The Last of the Mohicans*, Old Lodge Skins in *Little Big Man*, Wind in his Hair in *Dances with Wolves*, the eponymous general in *The Bitter Tea of General Yen*, or Susie Wong in *The World of Susie Wong*, who all serve to reawaken the life force in the White protagonist or teach an important lesson. They then either die or are shown receding into the distance as the protagonist returns to real life. Orfeo's death is tidier than most, since his alien accomplices remove his body, leaving Fanny nothing more to contend with than a silver ring (with a black triangle) and a new joy in life. This futuristic turn of events reminds us that the film follows a conventional comedic trajectory: the central character begins with her life in a mess – depressed and death-obsessed – and ends with love and a life wish. This is also guilt-free comedy because, while Orfeo may be sacrificed, his vanishing is represented not as death but as transcendence.

What Is the Message?

Looking beyond the Fanny plot to the larger class plot, we see that Orfeo's disappearance seemingly mocks the seriousnesss of Dörrie's attack on post-war German materialism, since he takes Lothar's Armani suit and Fanny's savings (in the form of the gold bar) with him when he disappears. But this serves to reiterate Dörrie's point that Fanny, like many Germans of her generation, is unhappy in spite of having everything. At the film's end, Fanny has not only lost her savings, but she is also still living a much reduced and inconvenienced life without running water and other amenities. Yet her zest for life has been restored, partly through her acceptance of these material losses. She is pictured dancing in the midst of chaos, not meditating on her own death as she was in an early scene.

Since Dörrie sees "multiculturalism" to be the main concern of *Nobody Loves Me,* it is surprising that it is represented by only one character of colour (played by one of the few Black professional actors in Germany) and by fleeting shots of carnival revellers in the streets. In theory, carnival is idealized as an expression of the triumph of anarchy over rules and prohibitions, emotion over intellect, participation over spectatorship, community over hierarchy, as is the case in *Nobody Loves Me.* Politically, on the other hand, carnival, and the comedic/fantastic genre it represents, can too readily serve simply as an outlet for otherwise repressed feelings and modes of social interaction. It merely gives the illusion of an inclusive society that is not, in fact, politically or socially possible. In *Nobody Loves Me* the sole, token Black figure (who seemingly must represent all Blacks and queers and "aliens" in Germany) reminds us that the film has no truly multiracial vision. Dörrie offers her predominantly White audience this lesson: multiculturalism only *looks* scary (as Orfeo does at first), but there are substantial benefits to the White majority in embracing it. They can be absolved of guilt for past systemic racism and homophobia. Their moribund culture (represented by Fanny's dissatisfaction with all that she has) can be revitalized by experts in love and life (the heretofore marginalized Others); and these experts/ Others will (and this may be the unconscious desire expressed in the film) then disappear without a trace.

In the penultimate scene, Fanny and her fellow tenants gather in her apartment to celebrate their survival. Here her new love interest (Anton) is revealed and shown to be the man Orfeo had predicted would appear. What is disturbing about the scene, given all that Fanny has learned from Orfeo and the transformations he has wrought in her life, is that we are again given an all-White world. As the tenants start to dance, the camera pulls back and we see that the occupants of the room (and, it is implied, of the whole apartment building) are White. Fanny has laid claim to Orfeo's knowledge and powers, demonstrated by her ability to restart the faulty elevator herself. So, what further need is there for multiculturalism now?

Notes

1   Information and parts of synopsis from various Web sites, including <http://www.eonline.com/Facts/Movies> and <www.hollywood.com/celebs>. 104 min. Direction and screenplay: Doris Dörrie. Actors: Fanny Fink – Maria Schrader; Orfeo de Altamar – Pierre Sanoussi-Bliss; Lothar Sticker – Michael von Au. From a story by the director.

2   Review by James Berardinelli (1996), available at <http://movie-reviews.colossus.net/movies/n/nobody_loves.html>. See also Bruce Kirkland in the *Toronto Sun* (2 December 1995).

3   Doris Dörrie, Interview, January 1998, <http://www.libertynet.org/ritzfilm>.

Filmography: Doris Dörrie (Director)

1976   *Ob's stürmt oder schneit*
1977   *Ene, mene, mink*
1977   *The First Waltz (Der erste Waltz)*
1978   *Hättest was Gescheites gelernt* (TV)
1978   *Alt werden in der Fremde*
1979   *Paula aus Portugal*
1980   *Vom Romantik keine Spur* (TV)
1981   *Dazwischen* (TV)
1983   *Straight through the Heart (Mitten ins Herz)* (TV)
1985   *In the Belly of the Whale (Im Innern des Wals)*
1986   *Men (Männer)*
1986   *Paradise (Paradies)*
1987   *Me and Him (Er und Ich)*
1989   *Love in Germany*
1989   *Money (Geld)*
1992   *Happy Birthday, Türke*
1993   *Was darf's denn sein?* (TV)
1995   *Nobody Loves Me (Keiner liebt mich)*
1998   *Am I Beautiful (Bin ich schön?)*
2001   *Enlightenment Guaranteed (Erleuchtigung Garantiert)*
2002   *Naked (Nackt)*

12 Women Directors and Genre Films in France
Brigitte Rollet

This chapter aims to address the evolution of women's recent contributions to the making of popular genres of film in contemporary French cinema in order to assess not only the way they reappropriate genres that, until recently, were male preserves, but also the potential (or real) level of transgressiveness of their films. Concentrating on France's most popular genres, such as comedy and crime films, or male-dominated genres like the road movie, this analysis questions women's input into, and impact upon, these genres from a feminist perspective. A brief historical overview of the history of women and film in France is needed in order to make these changes visible and to contextualize the films in question. I then consider whether these films do or could achieve the aims of 1970s feminist films and feminist film theory, and offer an analysis of some genre films made by French women directors in the 1990s.

During the first fifty years of French cinema, women filmmakers were interested in what later came to be known as genre films.[1] However, just prior to May 1968 and in its aftermath, they followed very different paths. The 1970s represent a key moment in the history of women in France in general and within French cinema in particular.[2] The creation of various women's groups and movements contributed to major changes regarding women's lives in France, especially in the field of sexuality and contraception. However, despite the influence of these groups on the development of feminist thought and theories, it is important to note the paradoxical situation within the French film industry, as highlighted by Ginette Vincendeau.[3] While Anglo-Saxon feminist film theory(ies) was (were) strongly influenced by various French schools of thought (from which they often originated), they were not known in France itself. This major lack of theoretical and analytical support does not mean that female directors in France were not making "feminist" films, although the word probably had (and still has) a different meaning in France than it does in Great Britain or the United States. When considering films made by women in France, it is essential to keep in mind the strong and persistent misogyny of French society and culture, which heavily influences the creation, production, distribution, and reception of this work. Another key aspect of France is its specific and asexual conception of citizenship. The French republican "universalism" inherited from the 1789 revolution claims the equality of French citizens whatever their sex, class, or ethnic background, therefore denying any "specific" treatment for one group or the other and rejecting the idea of *communautarisme*.[4] Although this does not entirely justify the lack of commitment of some female directors, it is worth considering when analyzing their films, as it affects the way most women see themselves as directors; they recurrently reject the label *film de femme* and often deny the importance of their gender in their filmmaking practices.

The 1970s was a decade when more women than ever started making films in France.[5] While some female directors opted for documentaries as a powerful weapon and means of making women visible, others chose fiction, portraying, in *drames psychologiques* (psychological dramas), female characters whose lives were sometimes inspired by their own experience.[6] Often autobiographical, these films also gave visibility to women confronting dilemmas that were at the top of the agenda of the women's movement and women filmmakers in the 1970s, such as women's alienation (Chantal Akerman's *Jeanne Dielman*, 1975), female sexuality (films by Nelly Kaplan, Catherine Breillat, and Christine Pascal), the heterosexual couple (Yannick Bellon's *La Femme de Jean*, 1973, and Nadine Trintignant's films), rape (Bellon's *L'Amour violé*, 1976), and so on. This tendency of women's filmmaking in the 1970s is in line with what was advocated by Anglo-Saxon feminist writers and film critics at the time. However, by expressing and emphasizing the subjectivity of their authors, and by offering various "testimonies" of the lives of contemporary female characters, these films were generally more concerned with content than with filmic form. With the exception of Marguerite Duras and Agnès Varda, few female directors renewed cinematographic language in the way advocated by the recently developed feminist film theory:[7] most of them felt a more urgent need to offer positive and varied images of women – images that were as far as possible from those of the stereotypical women traditionally found in male-authored films. Most women filmmakers, however, at last gave their female characters a voice and an eye, creating new perspectives and points of view and reversing the traditionally male gaze. They also indirectly or directly addressed a French female audience, usually neglected in French cinema (another consequence of universalism).

It should not be surprising, in this context, to notice the lack of interest female directors had in popular genres. "Popular" is to be understood here not only as a genre favoured by the majority, but also as a genre belonging to so-called "low-brow" culture. The New Wave and *politique des auteurs* in France emphasized an elitist conception of culture and placed high art in opposition to mass entertainment. By denying the impact of the social, political, and cultural context that affects cultural productions, and by posing the director as the sole author of his/her text,[8] New Wave directors reinforced the dichotomy (still in place in France today) between popular (i.e., commercial) and *auteur* cinema. The latter is best defined, on the one hand, by its emphasis on and concern with the expression of subjectivity via specific filmic forms and styles, and, on the other, by its indifference to narrative content. By contrast, popular genres, such as comedy and crime films, follow and rely upon accepted patterns, formats, and styles that have little to do with the auteur's "high" conception of cinema. Interestingly, the dichotomy of high culture/popular culture has never benefited women; on the contrary, it has indirectly reinforced male predominance over culture. Women were not only long denied "auteur" status (and cinema is not the only cultural field in which women were long excluded from the canon), but they were also not seen as "able" to make genre films.

One may wonder whether women directors in France in the 1970s wanted to make genre film at all, considering the characteristics of such films. Genre criticism has emphasized the importance of the economic element, a key aspect in the development of such films, as "generic production grew out of the attempt to repeat and build on initial successes."[9] Although the French film industry could not be compared with the Hollywood studio's system of filmmaking, it is nonetheless clear that the development of popular genres such as comedy and crime film in the history of French cinema could be seen as following similar economic imperatives. Another major aspect of genre films is the importance of conventional modes of representation, since the genres in question "provide a framework of structuring rules, in the shape of patterns (forms, styles, structures) which act as a form of 'supervision' over the production work of filmmakers and the audience's reading."[10] In other words, genre films could be seen as the least likely to provide women filmmakers with the opportunity to challenge a patriarchal film industry by creating effective alternatives to the dominant forms of representation. However, Jean-Louis Bourget's comment about Hollywood genres, that "whenever an art form is highly conventional, the opportunity for subtle irony or distanciation presents itself all the more readily,"[11] suggests the possibility of transgression – something Jacqueline Audry did try in the French cinema after the Second World War.

Beyond the economic and narrative conditions that could justify women's possible reluctance and inability to make genre films, the implicit or explicit content of such films is surely the major explanation. Comedy, crime films, and road movies have always been, in one way or another, male genres, both in the crew and the gender of the protagonists as well as with regard to the targeted audiences. Each genre expresses its "maleness" in different ways. Road movies and crime films usually allow traditional, and therefore reassuring, representations of masculinity and "male" heroism. Usually set in a non-domestic environment (the road and the public sphere), they epitomize a social world and order from which women are either excluded or marginalized. Male bonding in road movies echoes the classic masculine duet of detectives/cops or the almost male-only space of the crime film. As for comedies, although women are present, they have long been the target of jokes and the butt of male comics. From a narrative

Josiane Balasko's *Gazon maudit/French Twist* (1995), courtesy of the
Film Reference Library, Toronto

perspective, most comedies and crime films made by male directors in France
offer(ed) a closing epilogue as a way of bringing back order. An initial disorder, based on various sorts of reversals that were at the core of a large
majority of French comedies until the 1970s (reversal of situations, of identities, etc.), is eventually resolved at the end of the films and order "apparently" prevails. Similarly, crime films generally create an expectation (which
is eventually fulfilled) regarding the outcome of the story, with an emphasis
on the "why," "how," or "who." Road movies are different, and their ending is often problematic. Since the journey (physical and symbolic) is the
major aspect of such films, the epilogue (i.e., the end of the journey) can
take various forms. However, the link made between the road and criminality
often leads to the death of the protagonists, and it is rare to find a "happier"
alternative to such a doomed epilogue.

It seems, therefore, that women's making/rewriting of popular genres in
French cinema is based on multiple forms of transgression, if only due to
patriarchal assumptions that women are unfunny as well as non-violent,
domesticated, and outside history. The same ideological system perpetuates
another belief, whereby female directors cannot be successful, and therefore, their films cannot attract the large audiences of their male counterparts. As I show below, women's interests in such genres are varied, and
their films, be they labelled "comedy," "road movie," or "thriller," often
have little in common with those of their male equivalents.

Comedy and thrillers, the two most popular genres in 1970s France (in
terms of box office success) allowed for interesting changes. The *comique au
féminin* emerged in France in the aftermath of May '68 via the *café-théâtres*
that flourished at the time and that allowed women to create their own

Coline Serreau's *Trois hommes et un couffin/Three Men and a Cradle* (1985), courtesy of the Film Reference Library, Toronto

"one woman shows."[12] The success of women on stage, and their reappropriation of laughter as a weapon, was highly significant in a country like France (and probably many others), where misogyny was/is a trademark of comedy. As shown by Kathleen Rowe,[13] women's appropriation of laughter was an interesting and important development in women's emancipation, and it allowed them to express anger, a feeling they could rarely articulate. Luce Irigaray's rhetorical question (quoted by Rowe) "Isn't laughter the first form of liberation from a secular oppression?" is echoed by Ruby Rich's comment about what she calls the "Medusan film," which has "revolutionary potential as a deflator of the patriarchal order."[14] Far from providing the sort of escapism traditionally found in male comedies, laughter could become a powerful tool for women directors.

When considering the recent comedies made by women in France (see filmography below), there is a clear sense that, since the mid-1980s, not only are more female directors than ever making comedies, but some of them have also succeeded in "reordering the signs within the convention, giving us unfamiliar images of women," as Ann Kaplan wrote more than twenty years ago.[15] This tendency should not be optimistically exaggerated, since many comedies made by women in France are not transgressive as such and do not challenge the conventional modes of representation (although they often give the main role to a female character).

Among those who successfully rewrite the genre, the names of Coline Serreau and Josiane Balasko stand out. Both have achieved box office successes: Coline Serreau is the only woman in the top twenty most successful directors since the beginning of the Fifth Republic (1958), thanks to the unexpected success of *Trois hommes et un couffin* (1985).[16] The second woman is Balasko, with *Gazon maudit* ten years later (1995).[17] Although the commercial success of a film is not in itself proof of its quality, both films have had a major impact (1) on the history of the genre and (2) on the history of women directors. Proving that a woman could make comedies was one thing, attaining success was another. Not only did Serreau open the way to other female directors (if only by "reassuring" producers!), she also showed how the genre could be used as a powerful and efficient vehicle for the expression of women's concerns. Despite the negative reception of the film by feminists in the United States, *Trois hommes et un couffin* (which Serreau herself considers her most feminist film to date) was a way for the director not only to challenge traditional representations of masculinity, but also to question motherhood and fatherhood in a country long known for the importance of its centuries-old family policies.[18] Similarly, ten years later Balasko shook conventional representations of family life and couples by offering the first French lesbian comedy. She rewrote and subverted both the French comedy and vaudeville. Beyond the obvious "excesses" of the *café-théâtre* tradition, *Gazon maudit* offers a positive portrayal of a lesbian character (played by Balasko herself), while allowing the audience to laugh with (and not at) the heroine.[19] Other directors offering transgressive characters and situations include Catherine Corsini and Valérie Lemercier.

The situation is rather different with thrillers. The 1970s were not that different (in terms of audience) from the previous decades, when the French *polar* (crime film) attracted millions of French (mainly male) spectators. Like the American *film noir,* which greatly influenced the *polar* in the 1950s and 1960s, French crime films created what was almost a male-only world, where women's roles were limited to those of victims or witnesses.[20] In the 1970s, one could wonder whether the large number of *polars* made by male directors at the time did not serve to reinforce and consolidate a more traditional representation of masculinity and of male heroism at a time when feminism and the women's movements were shaking (to say the least) what had, until then, been seen as a solid construction.[21]

Within this context, women directors' general lack of interest in the genre is not surprising. Most of those who made crime stories from the 1980s onwards neither confronted the overt misogyny of the genre nor questioned women's roles within it. A large majority of the films (see filmography below) reproduce the traditional patterns of their male counterparts, either by casting their female characters as victims or witnesses, or by excluding them. The issue of women's violence and women's response to male violence is rarely addressed. The few films in which women are portrayed as killers do not link murder and gender. Ginette Vincendeau states that "the French *policier* [made by male directors] never showed much interest in the social origins of crime."[22] A similar comment could be made about the lack of "sexualization" of crime. A handful of films, however, subvert the rules, if only in the way they constantly borrow narrative devices belonging to other genres. Thus, the only two crime films representing women on the "side of the law" could also be described as comedies. Indeed, both *Les Keufs*, directed by Josiane Balasko (who also plays the main female role) in 1987 and *Pas très catholique* by Tonie Marshall in 1994 (with *café-théâtre* actress Anémone in the leading part), exploit the format of crime stories while creating laughter. The two films offer comic parodies: in the case of Balasko, it is of the cop film; in the case of Marshall, it is of the detective film à la Bogart.

More important, in my view, is the way they both portray unconventional female characters who transgress the boundaries of socially and sexually acceptable behaviour. The two female characters directly or indirectly mock the rules of femininity, either by "masquerading as a woman" or by rejecting the role(s) that other characters expect them to play. Both are in control of their lives and their bodies, in tune with their desires, and in constant rebellion against hierarchy, hypocrisy, and injustice. Unlike the majority of crime films directed by male directors, solving a crime is not the raison d'être of these films; far from being their prime concern, the crime they are dealing with soon becomes a secondary narrative, allowing the main story to concentrate on specific and intimate moments in the lives of the characters. More than Balasko's film, Marshall's film could fulfil the expectations of a contemporary feminist audience not only in the way it questions accepted beliefs about women and motherhood, or women and sexuality, but also in that it offers a highly enjoyable portrait of a woman who is not punished by (or for) her lifestyle (be it her bisexuality or her earlier abandonment of her child and husband).

Similarly, one of the road movies listed in the filmography below, *Personne ne m'aime* directed by Marion Vernoux (in the same year as Marshall's film), offers something rare in French (and women's) cinema. It is true that, in the history of French cinema, the road movie is minor. There are, indeed, only a handful of male-authored French films that could be described as such.[23] This, in my view, makes women's contributions to the genre even more interesting. Originating from the United States, the road movie was a buddy movie, long characterized by the White, heterosexual-male status of its protagonists (although there were occurrences of couples on the road and on the run). The potential dangers inherent in travel made women's presence problematic in such films, as was obvious in Ridley Scott's *Thelma and Louise* (1991).[24] Rebellion is often the common point among those taking to the road, and this rebellion has a different meaning when women are on the road. Not all the road movies made by women are of interest from a feminist perspective.

After Agnès Varda's acclaimed *Sans toit ni loi* (*Vagabond*, 1985), a couple of road movies made by women opted for a single female traveller, including Laetitia Masson's controversial *A vendre* (1997).[25] Vernoux's *Personne ne m'aime*, like most interesting genre films made by women, combines various narrative traditions, including comedy. Starring well known celebrities from the New Wave (Bulle Ogier, Bernadette Laffont, and Jean-Pierre Léaud),[26] the film follows four women who end up travelling together in a minibus. The intertextual reference to the New Wave, created by the presence of such actresses but also by specific cinematographic practices, is then denied, first by the director herself but even, more clearly, by the content of the film. Unlike the New Wave tendency to make what Geneviève Sellier calls "un cinéma à la première personne du masculin singulier,"[27] the film multiplies women's voices, creating "un cinéma à la troisième personne du féminin pluriel." Although the journey is the main narrative element of the film, several flashbacks offer a secondary narrative dealing mainly with the difficulty of a mother-daughter relationship. The film also allows the development of female bonding in the camper, all the women sharing (often in a comic fashion) parts of their experiences as lovers, wives, and/or mothers. The fragmented narration and choice of sixteen-millimetre film (then converted into thirty-five) and low-key lighting not only express the director's rejection of the gloss and perfection of contemporary filmic images (like the so-called *"cinéma du look,"* for example), but also refuses the artificial construction of feminine beauty inherent in most films starring women. Without falling into voyeurism by emphasizing the aging process of the New Wave "muses," the film nonetheless creates a "realist" atmosphere reinforced by the use of a lightweight camera. This realism is then contradicted by the recurrence of characters directly addressing the camera and the audience.

In conclusion, it appears that the genre films highlighted above give women directors the possibility of creating female characters who escape the sexual stereotypes upon which these genres are often based. Because the temporary or permanent lack (or absence) of order and/or norms is a common ingredient in comedies, as well as in road movies and crime films, these films can transgress the social and sexual norms that prevail in other, more realist, films. Far from offering the final return to order typical of conservative popular genres, the directors often subvert the conventions of the genre by suggesting another conception of order as well as a nontraditional ending. Similarly, issues that are often at the core of contemporary female-authored films (such as parenthood, sexuality, making and breaking of relationships, etc.) are raised, albeit in a very different form, in most recent genre films made by women.

These directors address women's issues and rewrite popular genres, often succeeding in creating hybrid genres. This "hybridity" could be seen as another form of transgression, since it suggests the breaking of boundaries between different sorts of narratives: many films mix popular genres and issues traditionally associated with melodrama and "women's films." The recurrent choice of open endings in these films also expresses a refusal to be constrained within the reductive framework of such genres, signalling a clear departure from their traditional and conservative structures. These films could be labelled auteur genre cinema, as they seem to follow the view according to which "there can be a coincidence between genre and author, which enables the director to use its conventions as a kind of shorthand, enabling him or her to go straight to the heart of his/her concerns and to express them at a formal level through the interplay of genre convention and motif."[28] Although they are, unfortunately, a minority, some genre films allow women directors, among other things, to make strong statements about gender identity and gender roles, while subverting conventional narrative frameworks.

Notes

1 See the early comedies made by the pioneer of women's filmmaking, Alice Guy-Blaché, at the end of the nineteenth century, the costume dramas of Jacqueline Audry, and the comedies of Andrée Feix after the Second World War.
2 See Brigitte Rollet, "Femmes cinéastes en France: après Mai 68," *Clio: Femmes, Histoire et Société* 10 (2000): 233-48.
3 Ginette Vincendeau, "Women's Cinema, Film Theory and Feminism in France," *Screen* 28, 4 (1987): 4-18.
4 The recent debates and reactions around *parité* (equal political representation between the sexes) and the *Pacs* (*Pacte Civil de Solidarité*), a domestic bill that was seen by its opponents as specifically benefiting gay and lesbian couples, have highlighted the fierce opposition to the recognition of groups based on their sex or sexual orientation (or, in other cases, their ethnic background).
5 See Annick Blondel, "Cinéma des femmes, cinéma féministe ou cinéma féminin?" (PhD diss., EHESS, 1981).
6 See Monique Martineau, "Le Cinéma au féminisme," *CinéAction* 9 (1979).
7 See Claire Johnston, "Women's Cinema as Counter Cinema," in *Movies and Methods: An Anthology*, ed. Bill Nichols (Berkeley: University of California Press, 1976), 208-17.
8 Although the word *auteur* is considered "gender neutral," therefore complying with the French tradition of universalism, it is very much male-dominated. See G. Sellier, "Images de femmes dans les films de la Nouvelle Vague," *Clio: Femmes, Histoire et Société* 10 (2000): 216-32.
9 Pam Cook, *The Cinema Book* (London: London Film Institute, 1990), 62.
10 Ibid., 58.
11 Jean-Louis Bourget, "Social Implications in Hollywood Genres," in *Film Genre: Theory and Criticism*, ed. B.K. Grant (Metuchen: Scarecrow Press, 1977), 62-72.
12 Or more than one, if one thinks of the trio *Les Trois Jeanne*, who became famous in the mid-1970s.

13 *The Unruly Woman: Gender and the Genres of Laughter* (Austin: Texas University Press, 1995).
14 B. Ruby Rich, "In the Name of Feminist Film Criticism," in *Jump Cut: Hollywood, Politics and Counter-Cinema*, ed. Peter Steven (Toronto: Between the Lines, 1985), 208-30.
15 E. Ann Kaplan, "Aspects of British Feminist Film Theory," *Jump Cut* 12/13 (December 1976): 52.
16 The film, seen by more than ten million spectators in France, was at the top of box office ratings for 1985 (ahead of *Rambo*) and was remade as *Three Men and a Baby*.
17 The film was second at the 1995 box office, with around five million spectators.
18 See Brigitte Rollet, *Coline Serreau* (Manchester: Manchester University Press, 1998).
19 See Brigitte Rollet, "Transgressive masquerades at the *fin de siècle* ? *Gazon maudit* and *Pédale douce*," in *Perspectives on the Fin de siècle in Nineteenth and Twentieth Century France*, ed. T. Unwin and K. Chadwick (Lampeter: Edward Mellen, 2000), 139-53.
20 It is worth noting here that the key ingredient of the American *film noir* – namely, the *femme fatale* – is extremely rare in French detective stories. Isabelle Huppert's character in C. Pascal's *La Garce* is the only one reminiscent of this tradition.
21 See Martin O'Shaughnessy, "'Bebel,' un héros dans un monde en crise," *Un Siècle d'anti-féminisme*, ed C. Bard (Paris: Fayard, 1999), 367-77.
22 *The Companion to French Cinema* (London: Cassel and British Film Institute, 1996), 118.
23 Georges-Henry Clouzot's *Le Salaire de la peur* (1953), Jean-Luc Godard's *Pierrot le fou* (1965) and *Week-end* (1967), Bertrand Blier's *Les Valseuses* (1974), Claude Miller's *Mortelle randonnée* (1985), and Manuel Poirier's *Western* (1997). Miller's film is the only one starring a female protagonist (who is also a murderer).
24 See the December 1991 issue of *Cineaste* for a discussion about the film and its link with feminism.
25 There are interesting similarities between the films of Varda and Masson, which I have analyzed elsewhere.
26 They all star in other recent films made by women.
27 "La Nouvelle Vague: un cinéma à la première personne du masculin singulier," *Iris* 24 (Fall 1997): 77-89.
28 Cook, *The Cinema Book*, 63.

Filmography

Comedy
1946 *Il suffit d'une fois*. Direction: Andrée Feix
1947 *Capitaine Blomet*. Direction: Andrée Feix
1969 *La Fiancée du pirate*. Direction: Nelly Kaplan
1971 *Papa les petits bateaux*. Direction: Nelly Kaplan
1973 *Colinot trousse-chemise*. Direction: Nina Companeez
1975 *Le Futur aux trousses*. Direction: Dolores Grassian
1976 *Comme sur des roulettes*. Direction: Nina Companeez
1976 *Néa*. Direction: Nelly Kaplan
1977 *Pourquoi pas!* Direction: Coline Serreau
1977 *Le Dernier Baiser*. Direction: Dolores Grassian
1978 *Vas-y maman*. Direction: Nicole de Buron
1979 *Charles et Lucie*. Direction: Nelly Kaplan
1982 *Qu'est-ce qu'on attend pour être heureux!* Direction: Coline Serreau
1984 *Les Nanas*. Direction: Annick Lanoé
1985 *Trois hommes et un couffin*. Direction: Coline Serreau
1985 *Sac de noeuds*. Direction: Josiane Balasko
1986 *Pékin Central*. Direction: Camille de Casabianca
1987 *Les Keufs*. Direction: Josiane Balasko
1988 *Les Surprises de l'amour*. Direction: Caroline Chomienne
1989 *Pentimento*. Direction: Tonie Marshall
1989 *Romuald et Juliette*. Direction: Coline Serreau

1990   *Le Jour des rois.* Direction: Marie-Claude Treilhou
1991   *Plaisir d'amour.* Direction: Nelly Kaplan
1991   *Ma vie est un enfer.* Direction: Josiane Balasko
1992   *Les Mamies.* Direction: Annick Lanoé
1992   *La Crise.* Direction: Coline Serreau
1993   *Toxic Affair.* Direction: Philomène Esposito
1993   *Pas d'amour sans amour.* Direction: Evelyne Dress
1993   *Elles ne pensent qu'à ça.* Direction: Charlotte Dubreuil
1993   *Les gens normaux n'ont rien d'exceptionnel.* Direction: Laurence Ferreira Barbosa
1994   *Pas très catholique.* Direction: Tonie Marshall
1994   *Personne ne m'aime.* Direction: Marion Vernoux
1995   *Augustin.* Direction: Agnès Fontaine
1995   *Gazon maudit.* Direction: Josiane Balasko
1995   *Le Fabuleux destin de Madame Petlet.* Direction: Camille de Casabianca
1995   *Dieu, l'amant de ma mère et le fils du charcutier.* Direction: Aline Isserman.
1996   *La Belle Verte.* Direction: Coline Serreau
1996   *Romaine.* Direction: Agnès Obadia
1997   *Quadrille.* Direction: Valérie Lemercier
1997   *J'ai horreur de l'amour.* Direction: Laurence Ferreira Barbosa
1998   *Un cri d'amour.* Direction: Josiane Balasko
1999   *La Nouvelle Eve.* Direction: Catherine Corsini
1999   *Mon père, ma mère, mes frères et mes soeurs.* Direction: Charlotte de Turkheim
1999   *Augustin, roi du Kung fu.* Direction: Agnès Fontaine
1999   *Le Derrière.* Direction: Valérie Lemercier
1999   *La Bûche.* Direction: Danielle Thompson
2000   *Aïe.* Direction: Sophie Fillières
2000   *Ça ira mieux demain.* Direction: Jeanne Labrune
2000   *Du poil sous les roses.* Direction: Agnès Obadia
2000   *Epouse-moi.* Direction: Harriet Martin
2000   *Le Goût des autres.* Direction: Agnès Jaoui

Polars

1981   *Neige.* Direction: Juliet Berto
1982-3   *Cap Canaille.* Direction: Juliet Berto
1984   *La Triche.* Direction: Yannick Bellon
1984   *La Garce.* Direction: Christine Pascal
1984   *L'Intrus.* Direction: Irène Jouannet
1986   *Signé Charlotte.* Direction: Caroline Huppert
1987   *Les Keufs.* Direction: Josiane Balasko
1988   *Fréquence Meurtre.* Direction: Elisabeth Rappeneau
1989   *Peaux de vaches.* Direction: Patricia Mazuy
1990   *Plein fer.* Direction: Josée Dayan
1991   *Border Line.* Direction: Danielle Dubroux
1991   *Sale comme un ange.* Direction: Catherine Breillat
1992   *Max et Jérémie.* Direction: Claire Devers
1994   *J'ai pas sommeil.* Direction: Claire Denis
1994   *Pas très catholique.* Direction: Tonie Marshall
1996   *Un Samedi sur la terre.* Direction: Diane Bertrand
1996   *Le Journal du séducteur.* Direction: Danielle Dubroux
1996   *Parfait amour!* Direction: Catherine Breillat
1997   *Nettoyage à sec.* Direction: Anne Fontaine
1998   *L'Examen de minuit.* Direction: Danielle Dubroux
1998   *L'Inconnu de Strasbourg.* Direction: Valérie Sarmiento
1998   *Place Vendôme.* Direction: Nicole Garcia
1999   *Toni.* Direction: Philomène Esposito

Road Movies
1962   *Les Petits matins.* Direction: Jacqueline Audry
1977   *Le Camion.* Direction: Marguerite Duras
1979   *Premier voyage.* Direction: Nadine Trintignant
1980   *Cocktail molotov.* Direction: Diane Kurys
1985   *Sans toit ni loi.* Direction: Agnès Varda
1986   *Signé Charlotte.* Direction: Caroline Huppert
1987   *L'Accroche-coeur.* Direction: Chantal Picault
1990   *Un weekend sur deux.* Direction: Nicole Garcia
1992   *Le Petit Prince a dit.* Direction: Christine Pascal
1994   *Personne ne m'aime.* Direction: Marion Vernoux
1994   *La Piste du télégraphe.* Direction: Liliane de Kermadec
1995   *Pullman paradis.* Direction: Michèle Rosier
1995   *Les Fugueuses.* Direction: Nadine Trintignant
1997   *No Sex Last Night.* Direction: Sophie Calle, Greg Shepard
1997   *A vendre.* Direction: Laetitia Masson
2000   *Princesses.* Direction: Sylvie Verheyde
2000   *Baise-moi.* Direction: Virgine Despentes

13   Mainstreaming the Margins in France: Three Films *au Féminin*
Caroline Eades

In France, films directed by women are rarely designated by film distributors, critics, and television programmers as belonging to a specific category such as "women's cinema," which would set them apart from films directed by men.[1] One reason for this could be the socio-political environment and the history of feminism in France: for the past twenty years, the status of women and their overall situation have slightly improved, more as a consequence of the actions of individuals, trade unions, and national representatives than, for instance, as a consequence of the activity of French feminist organizations in support of women artists. Another reason might be the particularities of French state funding and the television quota system, which largely contributed to the steady development of French film production (the largest in Europe, with over 150 films per year). This system is also designed to give first-time directors access to commercial production and distribution;[2] the number of women directors has progressively increased due to the incremental effect of this system as well as to the growing participation of women in all fields of activity (rather than due to specific regulation).

Moreover, in France women have always been involved in the film profession outside the coveted field of directing (mise-en-scène), even though their participation is minimal and not often publicized. Alice Guy Blaché (who started out as Léon Gaumont's secretary), Christine Gouze-Rênal, Monique Annaud, and Albina du Boisrouvray have been as successful as have their male counterparts in mainstream film production. In a recent television interview, Catherine Deneuve acknowledged that, as an actor, she enjoyed seeing more and more women technicians on film sets. A career in film production or acting can also lead women (as well as men) to filmmaking, as was the case for former editors Jackie Raynal, Marie-Geneviève Ripeau, and Nadine Trintignant, as well as for actresses such as Musidora, Christine Pascal, Juliet Berto, and Virginie Thévenet, to name only a few.[3] Last, the growing participation of women in screenwriting[4] contributed to the development of stories featuring original and realistic female characters and provided challenging roles to well known actresses – for instance Nicole Garcia in Brigitte Roüan's *Outremer* (1990) and Nathalie Baye in Tonie Marshall's *Vénus Beauté Institut* (1998). They also provided such roles to new talent like Valérie Mairesse and Sandrine Bonnaire (in Agnès Varda's *L'Une chante l'autre pas* [1976] and *Sans toit ni loi* [1985], respectively), or more recently, Karin Viard (in Catherine Corsini's *La Nouvelle Eve* [1999]) and Caroline Ducey (in Catherine Breillat's *Romance X* [1999]).

To summarize, a small group of professional women have had access to film production throughout the years, just as they have broken into other artistic or economic sectors in France, thanks mostly to personal connections and opportunities rather than to an organized and deliberate policy. Therefore, it seems difficult to find common characteristics in the variety of films that have resulted from women's collaboration at different levels of responsibility, for diverse motives, and with various financial resources. However, if we restrict the target of our investigation to three films directed by contemporary French women – Sandrine Veysset's *Y aura-t-il de la neige à Noël?* (1996), Agnès Merlet's *Artemisia* (1997), and Brigitte Roüan's *Post coitum animal triste* (1998) – then we can observe the presence of recurrent thematic or stylistic elements that might constitute a common response to the ideological and aesthetic demands made specifically on women.

Most of these films focus on the accurate description of a social group and a working community (the rural world in *Y aura-t-il de la neige à Noël?*, the book publishing world in *Post coitum animal triste*, Italian artists in the Baroque era in *Artemisia*). In order to achieve a realistic effect, the geographical location of these stories is precisely defined (the Southeast of France, Paris, Tuscany) and the rituals of daily life, such as eating and drinking, are emphasized by the narration, as in the recurrent breakfast scene in *Post coitum animal triste*. The action involves the use of common objects and props (a heater in *Y aura-t-il de la neige à Noël?* and a meat-fork in *Post coitum animal triste*), which assume a specific narrative role as death instruments. These films have a linear narrative structure: even if *Post coitum animal triste* begins with a puzzling montage of Mme Lepluche's crime and Diane's love affair with Emilio, both stories end up merging, from a narrative stand-point, when Diane's husband becomes Mme Lepluche's attorney and, from a symbolic standpoint, when marital infidelity stands out as the main theme of the film. Last, camera position, movement, and framing concur to create in these films an unobtrusive approach to the characters and a close follow-ing of the action, which seems to conform to a rather conventional film style and to achieve transparency, realism, and identification.

The realistic dimension of these films is also developed through the spe-cific dynamics of the narrative, which could be described as centripetal. This inward motion is, for instance, implemented by a progressive shrink-ing of the characters' environment throughout the films. They become re-luctant to leave their homes: Diane comes back from the ski resort earlier than expected, the mother in *Y aura-t-il de la neige à Noël?* refuses to go to the school Christmas raffle, Artemisia hesitates to go outside to paint natu-ral landscapes. In the end, it seems that they all prefer to stay confined to their bedrooms.

One could relate these representations of women to the conventional social and symbolic opposition between women's confinement and men's mobility. But in these films it is the male character who finds himself im-prisoned – by his legitimate family in *Y aura-t-il de la neige à Noël?* by justice in *Artemisia,* and by his professional commitment in *Post coitum animal triste* – whereas the female character easily moves about in her rural or urban environment. In this open space, she has the opportunity to meet second-ary male figures who, far from constituting a threat, provide her better ac-cess to the outside world. What is at stake in these films is precisely the process that will make her forsake this opportunity in favour of her domes-tic quarters and her inside world.

The dynamic pattern of the narrative is thus perceptible at a more per-sonal and physical level: instead of exploring her surroundings, the female character sets about discovering her own body, either through her reflec-tion in a mirror or through sexual experiences that help her raise her con-sciousness (not so much of the other as of herself). This concern for the inner body could explain why feeling is more important than looking: what matters is not so much what someone else is seeing but, rather, whether one is comfortable, warm, and contented. These films avoid the traditional opposition between nature and culture for the benefit of an intimate and sensorial experience: the body is perceived from the inside and not from the other's point of view.

Agnès Merlet's *Artemisia* (1997)

Comfort, for instance, is at the centre of the main character's preoccupations in *Y aura-t-il de la neige à Noël?:* she struggles to provide her children with food, light, and heat, whereas their father offers to buy them a television. Physical comfort is also present in *Post coitum animal triste* through allusions to food consumption: Diane is shown several times making nocturnal visits to the refrigerator, her family has a particular breakfast ritual, Mme Lepluche kills her husband during lunch. In *Artemisia*, details related to the care of the body are even given a substantial part in the development of the plot: Artemisia's father starts suspecting his daughter's involvement with her painting-instructor Tassi when he notices that she is not as suntanned as her servant and understands that she does not spend her days flying a kite on the beach.[5] The body is mostly shown in trivial activities and usually deprived of its dramatic or erotic aspect, which is to say its narrative use is as a metonymical instrument for suffering or seduction. The mise-en-scène of sex in these films even tends to emphasize its playful or even ridiculous characteristics and to undermine its manipulative dimension.

The fact that the main character of these films is a woman implies that male characters are generally treated as secondary by the narrative discourse or the mise-en-scène. Although an essential figure in *Y aura-t-il de la neige à Noël?* the father is often shown with his face half-lit or obscured by elements of the set (a window frame or the truck windshield). In *Post coitum animal triste* long shots are used to present Diane's lover as a silhouette: his face is revealed to the spectators only in the second half of the film through Diane's vision (after he has left her and his body is out of her reach). In *Artemisia* the male body is reduced to a painter's model (i.e., a complex form), a combination of muscles and flesh, an aesthetic object. Setting the male figure at the fringe of the image could be interpreted as the effect of the inward and introspective perspective chosen by these women filmmakers. Moreover, in *Y aura-t-il de la neige à Noël?* and *Post coitum animal triste*, the age and the gender of the main character, the intimate nature of the story, and a series of hints (e.g., the character's first name, Blandine, sounds much like the director's first name, Sandrine; Brigitte Roüan plays the part of the main character of her film) suggest that the author is recalling memories rather than inventing a pure fiction: the narrative dynamics appear to contribute to the implementation of an autobiographical project.

From an ideological standpoint, it seems that this pattern also constitutes a key to the interpretation of the individual's relationship to the institution. These films do not offer an explicit representation of women's fight for their right not to be oppressed. On the contrary, the female characters' social environment seems somehow rather tolerant: Artemisia's dream of becoming a painter is fulfilled, bigamy seems to be accepted in *Y aura-t-il de la neige à Noël?* and adultery is not punished in *Post coitum animal triste*. Obstacles to the female character's sexual behaviour come mostly from members of her family (Artemisia's father, Diane's husband, the children in *Y aura-t-il de la neige à Noël?*), especially when an awkward situation cannot be solved by a social institution (i.e., marriage).

If there is no happy ending, it is not because the representative of the Law prevails over the female character's point of view or decision: on the contrary, the judges in *Artemisia*, the husband/lawyer in *Post coitum animal triste*, and the schoolmaster in *Y aura-t-il de la neige à Noël?* turn out to be inefficient supporters rather than declared opponents. The father's role is rather ambiguous: in *Artemisia*, the father is both a negative and a positive figure, an adversary and a model, sometimes supporting her career as a painter, sometimes depriving her of her work and her lover. The father figure is often duplicated by other male characters who share the same ambivalence: the schoolmaster in *Y aura-t-il de la neige à Noël?* lends the mother a heater before a cold Christmas night without foreseeing that she will use it to asphyxiate her children during their sleep; the judge in *Artemisia* agrees to expose her to torture in order to find the truth that could save her.

Secondary female characters are treated somewhat differently. The heroine's mother is always mentioned in these films:[6] she even stands as an explicit referential figure when the story verges on autobiography. However, the narrative defines her as an outsider: she belongs to another time, a time when a woman's destiny was a story of submission, oppression, and eventually rebellion. These stories are told from the daughter's perspective: anchored in the present, retrospection does not lead so much to a nostalgic evocation as to an objective account of the past, which is then considered as a necessary but transitory step. Symbolically, the main character in

Y aura-t-il de la neige à Noël? lost her mother when she was very young, as did Artemisia and Diane.

As for other secondary female characters, far from embodying an overly optimistic conception of women's solidarity, they are depicted as much more negative than their male counterparts, especially towards other women: Tassi's sister, the nuns, and the stepmother in Agnès Merlet's film all contribute to Artemisia's misfortune. Sandrine Veysset's main character unsuccessfully vies with other female farm workers and the legitimate family of her children's father for care and attention. The fact that these films seem to present a rather conventional definition of relations between women (i.e., as tainted by individualism and rivalry) could be considered, however, as a narrative device: the interaction between the heroine and secondary characters becomes part of the process that leads the main character towards isolation and introspection.

Indeed, it seems that social exclusion is finally internalized by the main character through personal doubt, self-questioning, and denial of the outside world. And here resides the real motive of the female characters' failure. In these films, the major handicap to equality between women and men in the professional world, whether artistic or agricultural, is certainly not competence or dedication, but it also cannot be reduced to immediate social factors. The fact that female characters lack any entrepreneurial spirit, are unwilling to take any risks, and refuse to comply with the system plays a large part in their misfortune. This is shown by Artemisia's refusal to yield to the compromises of commissioned art, Diane's reluctance to dissociate her professional life from her private life, and the mother's ambiguous choice in *Y aura-t-il de la neige à Noël?* (she does not want to take her children to the confined environment of social housing but ends up exposing them to the brutality of their father, the hardship of agricultural work, and extreme lack of comfort on a miserable farm). In these films, the main characters are progressively led towards victimization by the dynamics of the narrative, until they end up behaving as their own enemies: in *Y aura-t-il de la neige à Noël?* the mother smashes her children's playground to prevent the father from doing it himself; in *Post coitum animal triste,* Diane nurtures her own depression. Male characters may be responsible for the female characters' situation and subsequent actions; however, after an initial rebellious phase, women end up assuming the blame and hurting themselves.

Although the main characters are endowed with remarkable qualities such as courage, dignity, a sense of humour, and the ability to love, it seems that in these films, under the cover of autobiography and realism, the unfolding of the plot, the characterization of the heroines, the structure of the narrative, and the process of identification[7] concur to justify and reinforce the image of women as systematic victims of others and of themselves. Nonetheless, although the main characters stand out as responsible for their own fates – however influenced by circumstances, men, and other women they may be – one should not overlook the obvious fact that the authors of these films chose to maintain a clear distance between themselves and their characters through the use of special effects, an aesthetic concern for the image, and a personal reflection on art and representation.

In the early period of cinema, pioneers such as Méliès or the Lumière brothers used to insert special effects (*trucages*) into their films, even in documentary series, in order to familiarize the viewers with the incredible technical potentialities of their new art.[8] Since then, what has become a rhetorical or stylistic figure has served various purposes according to the genre of the film: to enhance action, to build a science-fiction environment, to introduce a dream or fantasy sequence. In films that seem to claim a realistic perspective, the presence of patently "artificial" images represents a significant break in the overall narrative and aesthetic composition.

These images can be divided into two categories: some of them form the prologue or the beginning of the film and, as such, create a temporary unsettling effect on the viewers rather than providing them with immediate and easy access to the fictional world; others occur unexpectedly here and there throughout the film and reflect the main character's distorted point of view on her environment (in my examples, the blurred courtroom in *Artemisia*, Mme Lepluche's elongated cell in *Post coitum animal triste*, the fade to black on desolate farmland in *Y aura-t-il de la neige à Noël?*).[9]

When set in prologues, special effects seem to contribute to the filmmaker's appropriation of the image: she presents herself within the film as the author by emphasizing the constructed dimension of the cinematic image over its realistic quality.[10] Such an introduction to the film narrative could be considered as an equivalent to what, in literature, is termed the "autobiographical pact" (a term coined by Philippe Lejeune[11]) – the initial contract set by the author with the reader, establishing the status of the narrative either as a fictitious story or as a "real" account.

In these films, artificial images simultaneously underline and undermine the autobiographical dimension of the plots.[12] On the one hand, they point to the author as the narrator of a story that could be her own, as we mentioned earlier. On the other hand, they create an immediate distancing effect by revealing the process of storytelling and filmmaking and putting the emphasis on how and why the story is told: autobiography is thus set within the context of history, possibly, in *Y aura-t-il de la neige à Noël?*, the history of ordinary women's oppression. In *Artemisia*, the opening special effects subdue the obvious biographical and historical dimension of the film in order to immediately draw the viewer's attention to the aesthetic issues that will be developed by the narrative discourse.

Therefore the director not only presents herself as a referential model for the main character, but also claims her status as narrator and author of a film. The opening scene in *Y aura-t-il de la neige à Noël?* is characterized by a fast and hectic pace that differs from the slow and controlled rhythm of the rest of the film. Sandrine Veysset resorts at first to a filmic style that recalls home movies and amateur recordings, then promptly dismisses it, thereby underlining the qualities of her film as a fiction, an aesthetic composition, a work of art. The beginning of Brigitte Roüan's film allows for a similar interpretation. It could be considered a sensational opening, with the film-maker proving her ability to seduce her audience through her mastery of the potential offered by film as an art; that is, the ability not only to tell a story, but also to film it.[13] The first images in Agnès Merlet's film progressively reveal a voyeuristic eye: the extreme close-ups, the low lighting, and the fragmented editing in these shots contrast with the clarity and the neutrality of the verbal commentary. At one and the same time, the reflexive dimension of the prologue seems to address the spectator's expectations and the filmmaker's objective (i.e., the transformation of words into images, the movement from ear to eye). This opening is, therefore, poetic in both senses of the term: it provides a lyrical beginning to the narrative and it refers to the creative work of the author, which develops from screenwriting to filming, from the pen to the camera.

Moreover, the final scenes in *Y aura-t-il de la neige à Noël?* and *Artemisia* function as an echo of the prologues. Although they feature conventional stylistic figures (frame-in-the-frame, or direct address to the viewer) instead of special effects, they achieve the same result as the opening shots; that is, they pull the viewer away from the fictional world and the process of identification. The film narrative, however realistic it may appear, is therefore embedded in the presentation of the story as a narration and as a cinematic construction.

The self-referential introduction of the author at the beginning of her film replaces a more traditional access to the fictional world and could be interpreted as the filmmaker's denial of all ambiguity concerning the relation of the narrator to the story. It also establishes her right and ability to master a language, more precisely, the cinematographic language that stands out as different from verbal language. In this regard it is significant that female characters are often shown in situations where they are denied, or diverted from, the use of verbal language. Artemisia's father speaks for her when dealing with customers; in *Post coitum animal triste* Diane's job consists of helping other people express themselves through writing; and Mme Lepluche remains silent while her lawyer prepares for her defence.[14] The author of the film, therefore, differentiates herself clearly from her character, not only because she has access to verbal language through dialogue, but also because she found in the filmic image an alternative to any potential or actual obstacle to her right to express herself.

Finally, the use of artificial images could also be a way for the filmmaker to situate her work within an aesthetic tradition. Special effects abound in the works of the formalist avant-garde of the 1920s, from Germaine Dulac to the surrealists, and can be found in the first features of Jean Renoir and Marcel Carné at the onset of "poetic realism" (as well as, more recently, in the films of Agnès Varda, Marguerite Duras, and the Left Bank cineasts who set themselves apart from New Wave aesthetics). As a matter of fact, one could consider Roüan's visual transposition of verbal puns[15] in *Post coitum animal triste* to be reminiscent of Buñuel and Dali's famous shots of the sliced moon/eye or the hand full of ants in *Un chien andalou*. Special effects are used to convey the same message as words, only they do so through the photographic image, thus pointing to their ability to represent real, symbolic, and imaginary objects.

During her lover's trial, Artemisia's vision is presented through distorted images that reflect her distress; this is the same way that special effects were used in *réalisme poétique* to represent a projection of the character's subjectivity on his or her surroundings.[16] However, in Agnès Merlet's film, such an alteration of the forms and shapes of the world as we know it could also be considered to be an allusion to the very subject of the film (i.e., artistic representation as imitation and deformation of reality). This could explain why Merlet found it necessary to add special effects to her character's dialogue and performance in order to express Artemisia's state of mind. This choice implies that, in these films, the treatment of ideological issues, historical references, and personal experiences cannot be separated from aesthetic concerns, which, therefore, become part of the narrative and, beyond the difference of subject, set Agnès Merlet's work apart from contemporary social dramas directed by Robert Guédiguian, Bertrand Tavernier, Mathieu Kassovitz, and the group of young filmmakers somewhat hastily labelled *la Nouvelle Vague* (Arnaud Dépleschin, Olivier Assayas, Bruno Podalydès, Cédric Klapisch).

If special effects function as an indicator of the author's claimed relationship to the image, they also contribute to the narrative per se as a reflection of a similar characteristic to be found in female characters. The imaginary is present in many of these films through allusions to mythical figures, but it should be noted that Medea in Veysset's film, Judith in Merlet's, and Sappho in Roüan's, are mentioned not so much in regard to their literary sources as to their pictorial representations, paintings, or photographs. Moreover, these figures are inserted into the film as cameos that serve to establish a visual connection between the mythical and the contemporary characters: this provides not only a possible coincidence between them, but also an argument in favour of women's vocation for visual representation (i.e., their ability to represent the world through images and to assert themselves both as objects and subjects of these images). In these films, women's destiny seems linked to the question of the imaginary. In other words, the issue of representation is essential to understanding the way the female characters run their lives. Veysset's and Merlet's heroines have a premonitory dream of their future as a mother or as a painter. Diane describes the writing of a book not so much as an intellectual and verbal task, but as a work of the senses and the imagination: *Post coitum animal triste* ends with a shot that represents Lesbos's rocky seaside as Diane's idyllic setting for a new start in life, as well as the cover picture of the book she strove to edit throughout the film.

The representation of fantasy is important because this type of image concerns both myth and experience, the collective as well as the individual, the spectator as much as the author.[17] In these films, special effects are subjected to an inverted treatment: instead of projecting the subject into the realm of fantasy and giving the appearance of real life to the figments of the characters' imagination, artificial images are used to obliterate any claim that fantasies might have to realism. This is in order to emphasize their spectacular dimension and to turn them into an object of mockery. The young couple making love on the beach (or Tassi's orgy) becomes for Artemisia a voyeuristic entertainment, an amusing peep-show, not far from the burlesque beginnings of cinema; the child's routine behind her parents' bedroom door in *Y aura-t-il de la neige à Noël?* resembles a vaudeville scene; Diane's revenge verges on slapstick when she butts her former lover or relieves herself on his doormat. We are not far, here, from Mary Ann Doane's definition of "masquerade" in cinema,[18] combining the Bakhtinian acceptance of the term with the issue of the female gaze: fantasy is presented in its carnivalesque aspect, which implies both inversion and derision in the evocation of "low material." By contrast, the reality of love appears harsh, brutal, and cruel, and, as such, cannot be represented through images. The father's attempt at seducing his daughter in *Y aura-t-il de la neige à Noël?* or Diane's lover's departure in *Post coitum animal triste* are not visually represented; they are conveyed to the viewers by a verbal narration. As Edgar Morin observes, "what prevents the objective truth of the film from being integrated into the practical as serious is the self-consciousness of the aesthetic."[19] Special effects can be considered, then, as direct and obvious preliminaries or reminders of the aesthetic argument of these films: the image is artificial by nature.

Eluding or distorting reality does not, however, totally preclude mimesis, and it should be understood as part of a specific project that consists of freeing the cinematographic art and the filmic narrative from audio-visual domination, from the traditional combination of the verbal with the visual, from the heritage of both the literary and the pictorial arts. The aim of these films is to achieve another kind of connection, which recalls once more the avant-garde of the 1920s:[20] cinema refers to reality as the synthesis of all sensorial experiences, including touch and smell (and, in *Petits arrangements avec les morts,* even a sixth sense).

By disengaging the filmic experience from its usual expectations, the artificial images single out the eye in its organic dimension, beyond, or rather "before," its function: both the act of looking and the object of the gaze lose their priority. In order to escape from the dictatorship of the look, and maybe to take an ironic distance from psychoanalysis, these films play on the notion of seeing and not seeing through basic perception: the father switches the lights off to save on electricity in *Y aura-t-il de la neige à Noël?*, Diane hides in dark staircases and bedrooms in *Post coitum animal triste*, Artemisia shuts her eyes in front of the chapel paintings. These recurrent scenes focus on the function/dysfunction of the eye – the characters' as well as the spectators' – at its most elementary level. This could serve to emphasize, from an intradiegetic or an extradiegetic perspective, either the possibility of resorting to other senses besides vision and audition (dialogue is not used to compensate for the eye's inadequacy in these examples) or the physical nature of experience, in contact with the real world or with representation.

The organic aspect of the visual experience, therefore, often points to the limits of representation, for instance through the conventional theme of the mirror, which is associated in *Artemisia* with the secret drawings of a young novice and in *Post coitum animal triste* with the breakdown of a middle-aged woman abandoned by her young lover. These films also denounce the traps of representation through the use of distorted images as metaphors for mental or ideological manipulation. As a matter of fact, the idea that the outside world could be organized and structured like a painting or a theatrical play in order to influence and to control people is far from being a novelty in the artistic field, including cinema.[21] But if, in these films, the illusory nature of representation refers to psychological and social manoeuvring, it remains embedded in a general reflection on art. Artemisia's access to womanhood is depicted as a consequence of her education and her experience as a painter.[22] *Post coitum animal triste* emphasizes the material aspect of art, the concrete dimension of creativity, the daily task of the artist through Diane's constant support of a young novelist: their common accomplishment is shown at the end of the film when he is presented in the printer's shop with the very first copy of his book. The insertion of artificial images at the beginning or throughout the film is, therefore, consistent with the overall project of these directors, which aims not only to provide a realistic description of people and their milieux, but also to define art as a personal and physical struggle with this reality.

The story of *Artemisia* makes this film more explicit than the others in this regard.[23] The eponymous character is reluctant to follow Tassi's advice when he teaches her to use a grid to fragment reality (i.e., the landscape stretching under their eyes) in order to understand its underlying cohesion, to reconstruct its coherence, and to represent its totality. What Artemisia is supposed to learn from a master in the art of painting in seventeenth-century Italy could be related to the conception of realism in cinema, which Eisenstein and the Russian formalists developed in the twenties with dialectical montage, also called "montage of attractions." But her first artistic experiments are shown as the result of her personal experience of the outside world as fragmented, irrational, inconsistent, whether it is the reflection of a body in a small mirror, the partial view of a fresco, or the discovery of the realities of adult life. Totality and coherence can be reached only through art, which is an objective in itself and not an exercise in reconstruction. In order to represent reality, she has then to undertake a personal quest that requires a sensorial awareness of the outside world as well as an intimate self-oriented meditation, as Tarkovski depicted in his film on Andrei Roublev's metaphysical and artistic itinerary in fifteenth-century Russia.

French contemporary women filmmakers Veysset, Merlet, and Roüan present an alternative to "women's cinema" and to French independent cinema. Their films feature strong and engaging female characters, but they remain ambiguous, or at least open to interpretation with regard to the motives of their misfortune and their attitude towards adversity – from total submission to senseless provocation to self-destruction. The fact that the narrative is organized around such characters draws these films away from topics that are much favoured by French independent filmmakers and disparaged by the critics – the *ménage à trois* and the endless squabbling of unhappy couples.[24]

One could safely suggest that the choice of characters and the dynamics of the narrative that appear to be common to these three filmmakers have been influenced by the referential world and their own social and personal experience as women. But it seems that aesthetic concern prevails in the sense that the sufferings of Veysset's "mother," Diane, Artemisia, Zaza, France, Nénette, and many others are, first and foremost, objects of fiction; that is the expressive products of artists who use the narrative structure and the mise-en-scène of their films to establish themselves as authors, to inscribe themselves in the history of cinema, and to assert a common standpoint on their artistic practice that cannot be separated from their own stories as individuals and as women.

Notes

1 On the Franco-German cultural channel Arte or the state television station France 3, weekly film series (*Thema, Cinéma de minuit*) usually feature national cinemas, famous directors, or various themes (e.g., "A Car Named Desire," "No Sex Please, I'm the President"). The presentation of women's cinema as such remains an exception: pay television station Canal Plus scheduled a special program entitled *Cinéma au féminin* on 16 September 1999 for the opening of a new festival on women directors in Arcachon. Canal Plus's subscribers magazine advertised this program with the headline "When Women Filmmakers Talk about Sex."

2 Funding for first-time directors is mainly provided by the Ministry of Culture (through an advance on box-office income) and by French television stations which are required by law to program recent French films.

3 For further references on French women filmmakers, see Paule Lejeune, *Le Cinéma des femmes* (Paris: Atlas Herminier, 1987).

4 Brigitte Roüan and Josiane Balasko, for instance, wrote scenarios for their own films (*Outremer, Sac de noeuds*) as well as for other directors (Philippe Le Guay's *L'Année Juliette,* Jean-Marie Poiré's *Les Hommes préfèrent les grosses*).

5 In contrast, in Pascale Ferran's *Petits arrangements avec les morts* (1993), Zaza is often shown sunbathing on the beach when she tries to find a reprieve from her past and present troublesome life.

6 Mothers are also essential characters in Brigitte Roüan's *Outremer* (1990), Antonia Bird's *Face* (1997), and Marleen Gorris's *Antonia's Line* (1995).

7 In this regard, Sandrine Veysset's mise-en-scène puts particular emphasis on the newborn child, Rémi. She forces the spectator to share the mother's constant awareness of her baby's whereabouts, whether it is present in the frame or not, in its mother's care or in other people's, including the viewer's (who sometimes is the only one looking at/after the child).

8 For details on the aesthetics of early cinema, see, for instance, Noël Burch, *Life to Those Shadows* (London: British Film Institute, 1990).

9 Special effects are also used to depict the characters' troubled vision of the outside world in Pascale Ferran's *Petits arrangements avec les morts* (with Zaza's glowing tree) and in Claire Denis's *Nénette et Boni* (1996) (with an extreme close-up of the baker's pastries).

10 Chantal Akerman, in *Jeanne Dielman, 23 quai du commerce, 1080 Bruxelles* (1975), gave a striking example of how women filmmakers and spectators could be led by the mise-en-scène to assume their point of view as subjects. By contrast, the filmic image was then given an "objective," over-realistic, almost documentary quality that is now discarded because of the need to enhance the creative contribution of the author as a visual artist.

11 Philippe Lejeune, *Le Pacte autobiographique* (Paris: Seuil, 1975).

12 In this regard, artificial images constitute the "poetic signified" with "its ambivalent status: it is both (i.e. at the same time and not successively) concrete and general and, as such, dismisses individualization: it is a non-individual concrete that reaches the general," Julia Kristeva, *Sèméiotikè, Recherches pour une sémanalyse* (Paris: Seuil, 1969), 191.

13 So did Laetitia Masson who, at the beginning of her film *A vendre* (1997), presents a parodic medley of various genres with video-clip images of love-making, a documentary-like interview of the main character's parents, and the voice-over of a "film noir" private investigator.

14 In Laurence Ferreira Barbosa's *Les gens normaux n'ont rien d'exceptionnel* (1993), Martine, the main character, suffers from amnesia; so does Zaza in Pascale Ferran's *Petits arrangements avec les morts,* when her parents are unable or unwilling to talk to her or to their other children after her sister's death.

15 For instance, the image of Diane gliding in the streets on top of a cloud after a night with her lover is to be understood as the illustration of the French phrase *être sur un nuage* (to be on a cloud, i.e., to be happy).

16 In *l'Atalante* (1934), Jean Vigo uses double exposure to render the depressive bargeman's vision of his absent wife floating under the water in her wedding gown.

17 See Judith Mayne, *Cinema and Spectatorship* (London and New York: Routledge, 1993), 88: "the value of fantasy for psychoanalytic readings of the cinema needs to be seen less in

terms of a 'better' analogy than dreams, the mirror stage, or the imaginary, and more in terms of the series of questions it can engender."

18 Mary Ann Doane, "Masquerade Reconsidered: Further Thoughts on the Female Spectator," *Discourse* 11 (Fall/Winter 1988-9): 42-54.

19 Edgar Morin, *Le Cinéma ou l'homme imaginaire* (Paris: Minuit, 1956), 161 (my translation).

20 French filmmakers Jean Epstein, Abel Gance, René Clair, and Marcel l'Herbier intended to achieve through cinema the synthesis of all other arts, as claimed by *Il Manifesto della Cinematografia Futurista* in 1916. At that time, French writers and critics interested in cinema marvelled at its ability to create a unique fusion of the perceptive and the emotional (see Jeanne-Marie Clerc, *Littérature et cinéma* [Paris: Nathan, 1993], 18-9).

21 See, for instance, Peter Greenaway's films *The Draughtsman's Contract* (1982), *Drowning by Numbers* (1988), and *The Baby of Macon* (1993).

22 Even Laetitia Masson's *A vendre*, which seems at first to focus on France Robert's emotional and sexual itinerary, takes a reflexive turn at the end when the heroine meets a woman painter and, as an echo to the portraits ostentatiously hung in some of her lovers' apartments, raises the issue of responsibility in art.

23 The aesthetic dimension of *Artemisia* sets it apart from other films directed by women – such as Patricia Mazuy's *Saint-Cyr* (2000), Suzanne Schiffman's *Le Moine et la sorcière* (1986), Véra Belmont's *Marquise* (1997), and Nina Companeez's *L'Allée du roi* (1996) – that also intend to rehabilitate women as important political figures ignored by centuries of patriarchal history.

24 These subjects are far from being typical of films directed by men, as is demonstrated by Catherine Corsini's *La Nouvelle Eve* (1999) and Jeanne Labrune's *Si je t'aime ... prends garde à toi* (1998).

14   Lina Wertmüller: The Grotesque in *Seven Beauties*

Josette Déléas

While it might be said that Lina Wertmüller's films have left the critics somewhat indifferent over the last fifteen years, this was not the case during the 1970s, when any new release by the Italian director was sure to provoke passionate debates ranging from dithyrambic praise to virulent anathema. It was in 1976, after the American première of her film *Pasqualino Settebellezze (Seven Beauties)*, that the director would ignite a major controversy. For some she became the equal of the greatest film directors overnight, the one whom, from then on, a mocking Roman journalist called: "Santa Lina di New York."[1] For others, she was nothing but a reactionary misogynist whose aesthetics were rather conventional.[2] Such extreme reactions are in perfect accord with the carnivalesque logic of a filmic world in which the filmmaker is all too eager to debase the sacred and the religious while elevating the lower and the vulgar through the use of comedy.

By creating an audacious parallel between the misadventures of her Sicilian macho, the buffoon Pasqualino Settebellezze, and the horror of the concentration camps, Wertmüller was being true to the Italian tradition of folk comedy. As Jurij Lotman (1976, 22) notes, in puppet theatre and la commedia dell'arte, "death can be a comic episode, murder – a buffonade, suffering – a parody." He adds:

> The unpitying nature of Italian (and not only Italian) folk theatre is organically connected with its conventionality. The audience remembers that these are puppets or maskers on the stage and perceives their death or suffering, beatings or misfortunes, not as death or suffering of real people, but in a spirit of carnival or ritual.[3]

The grotesque stylization found in the carnivalesque world provided Wertmüller with the various elements that she would use in her most successful works (like *Seven Beauties*) to expose the social mechanisms that shape and control the individual through concepts like masculinity or institutions like the family. These elements have been clearly identified by William and Joan Magretta in "Lina Wertmüller and the Tradition of Italian Carnivalesque Comedy: Caricatural Characters, Parodic Situations, the Absence of Mimesis, and the Use of *Lazzi*."[4] *Lazzi* are scenic means found in the commedia dell'arte; they are used to express emotions or simply as buffoonish episodes destined to entertain the public. Finally, the filmmaker gives her dialogues the earthiness and vitality of carnivalesque language.

The first shot of *Seven Beauties* seems far removed from a festive carnival evocation. It is a freeze frame of Mussolini and Hitler, in a medium shot, talking with one another while shaking hands. Il Duce is on the left and Hitler is on the right, occupying the onscreen position where a character normally acquires the greatest importance. Almost immediately, thanks to an optical effect, the title *Seven Beauties* surges from the background to stop in between the two men and unites them by forming a horizontal line that extends from Mussolini's right shoulder to Hitler's left shoulder. To establish the significance of this shot in the film narrative, the director makes it stand apart in its stillness and deadly silence before reanimating it as the first moving image of a contrasting montage sequence punctuated by a very eloquent and loud soundtrack. It took just one titled shot for Wertmüller to introduce her filmic discourse and challenge the viewer.

How can we connect two historical figures known for their monstrous megalomania with a title evocative of fairy tales and perfection? The director may have chosen the number seven because of its ambivalence and its association with the devil. As Catherine Pont-Humbert explains in her *Dictionnaire des symboles, des rites et des croyances,* this number is linked to "Satan who tries to imitate God."[5] But the word "beauties" remains puzzling.

Lina Wertmüller's *Pasqualino Settebellezze/Seven Beauties* (1976), courtesy of the Film Reference Library, Toronto

In fact, what this first titled image clearly signals is the filmmaker's use of the grotesque, which, according to Friedrich Schlegel, is composed of the "clashing contrast between form and content, the unstable mixture of heterogeneous elements, the explosive force of the paradoxical," and which he finds both "ridiculous and terrifying."[6] This will be confirmed when cabaret music, as unexpected as the title, brings the two fanatical conquerors back to life and changes them into laughable and laughing buffoons. Their metamorphosis will be evoked in a later sequence, when Pasqualino's older sister is being booed on the cheap burlesque theatre stage. As she is trying to perform, she exhibits her big thigh decorated with a black garter and a patriotic cockade and shakes her generous body, draped in a tri-coloured fabric emblazoned with the colours of the Italian flag. We find these same colours both on a huge paper cockade that weighs heavily on her left ear and on the ample scarf that wraps the other two hefty dancers who accompany her. The satirical metonymy becomes quite audacious and irreverent when Concettina turns her back to the male viewers, who insult her, and shakes her tri-coloured behind topped with an oversized bow.

Clearly, Lina Wertmüller wishes to ridicule fascist nationalism, whose destructive nature she denounces in the first sequence, where shots of war are intercut with shots of Mussolini and Hitler, while a mocking voice off-screen recites a litany punctuated by a refrain sometimes pronounced in a tone of disbelief, but more often in one of banter: "Oh! Yeah!" While bombs explode, houses collapse, planes burn, and corpses pile up, the extradiegetic narrator apostrophizes those who no longer know how to laugh: the machos, the credulous Christians, men from the right, fatalists, capitalists, the oblivious, the apolitical, the aware, the obedient, the victims, the believers, the naive, and so on. It is somewhat difficult to grasp all the references in this verbal flood, but when the omniscient voice concludes "those who now say let's play ... Oh! Yeah, oh! Yeah, oh! Yeah," while bombs are heard, what is being denounced by the soundtrack at the very instant when Pasqualino is thrown to the ground (wrapped in bandages from which he tries to free himself) is the murderous irresponsibility of those who play at war. After being shown several times since the middle of the opening sequence in very short and dark shots, intercut with fragments from archival footage, he is finally introduced into the story. Since he is still an unknown figure, he symbolizes the individual drama clearly inscribed in the collective tragedy of a world in which the need to dominate, to appropriate, and to reproduce leads straight to the Apocalypse. What Pasqualino's misadventures will confirm, and what constitutes a recurring theme in Wertmüller's major works, is the "powerlessness of individuals who have been manipulated and controlled through patriarchy and its institutions; and they are about being resistant, either intentionally or unintentionally, to alternative ideologies."[7]

Pasqualino is among the individuals who resist because they have only one goal: to survive at any cost. At the beginning of the film, in the company of Francesco, a deserter like himself, he witnesses the execution of Jews from his hiding place but fails to understand his companion's reaction. After they flee, Francesco talks about his feeling of shame and insists on the necessity of saying "no" to fascism, to war. But for Pasqualino, the equation is simple: to intervene, in this case, would have resulted in a meaningless suicide. In fact, all his actions are those of a coward whose machismo the director mocks. During the first flashback, when he enters the cabaret where his sister is making a spectacle of herself, he is portrayed as a caricature. Only the lower part of his legs appears onscreen as he descends the stairs, feet spread apart, shoes shining brightly. The legs stop, the trousers are pulled up aggressively: the camera, while working its way up his body, confirms that a man has just asserted himself with his crotch. In this shot verticality is clearly linked to masculinity, as it is throughout the film settings, such as the phallic forest where Pasqualino and Francesco meet, and through the camera movements when the director chooses a pan or a tracking shot. The pan up Pasqualino's body ends on a close-up of his face shrouded in darkness. He wears the same hat as do film noir heroes, smokes with a passion similar to Humphrey Bogart's, and sets his felt hat straight like the main character in *The Maltese Falcon;* but the position of his hat, his cigarette-holder (which cuts across the frame), and the excessive smoke that he fiercely exhales change him into a buffoon.[8] Here Wertmüller is interested in play-ing with the detective genre, as she does later with the western, when Pasqualino, reassured by the revolver hanging from his belt, provokes Totonno, Concettina's pimp. This latter scene comprises shots that alter-nate between close-ups of the two enemies and long shots where both are located in opposite corners of the frame. The actors' positions and their movements, punctuated by the passionate accents of a Spanish musical score, transform this scene into a pure parody of western films.

However, since parody in Wertmüller's world is always linked to the gro-tesque, her caricatures contain an unexpected blend of heterogeneous and incompatible elements. This confusion amounts to a tension, which, as Philip Thomson explains in his study of the grotesque, is not part of caricature. To return to Pasqualino's entrance into the burlesque cabaret, as he descends the stairs his steps follow exactly the tempo of the music that accompanies his sister's grotesque movements. For this reason, he is also the target of obscenities and insulting mockeries from the crowd of male spectators. The filmmaker reinforces this deliberate analogy by cutting to a close-up of a laughing old man, whose toothless mouth is a yawning chasm where the macho's pretentiousness is swallowed up. He is now reduced to a mere pup-pet, like the character whose performance in the next shot evokes that of a wooden marionette. This Chaplinesque figure will remain quite visible in the next scene. He is reflected in the mirror of Concettina's dressing room, located on the right of the frame in the background, at the same time as Pasqualino, on the left, insults his sister while brandishing his male "val-ues." He orders her to marry Totonno to save the family honour. Pasqualino then descends the dressing room stairs, as he had descended the cabaret ones upon his arrival, but he now occupies the right of the frame, while on the left the mime keeps on performing. The parallel between the two now indistinguishable characters is firmly established.

Thus Pasqualino is a puppet, but a dangerous one. When the filmmaker chooses to insert the close-up of the old man's gaping mouth and the shot of the mime before Pasqualino enters his sister's dressing room, she intro-duces a serious note into her filmic discourse. Bakhtin explains that, in grotesque realism, the gaping mouth plays a major role: "This is, of course, related to the lower stratum; it is *the open gate leading downward into the bodily underworld*. The gaping mouth is related to the image of *swallowing*, this most ancient symbol of *death and destruction*."[9] This last comment takes us back to the first image of the film, which we can finally understand. But in order to do so, we need to review the scene near the end of the film, when Pasqualino explains the origin of his nickname: Seven Beauties. It was given to him in his native village to acknowledge his success with women in spite of his lack of charm. The irony of the title-shot of the film is now specified, while simultaneously the director identifies the origin of the will to conquer. It is anchored in the supreme machismo that led to fascist madness and perpetuates itself in destructive power games between men and women. To mock it, Wertmüller echoes Rabelaisian mirth by directing the viewers' captive attention to the old man's face, as he bursts out laughing in a room filled with obscene men. As Bakhtin points out,

> the people's festive laughter … is also directed at those who laugh … This is one of the essential differences of the people's festive laughter from the pure satire of modern times. The satirist whose laughter is negative places himself above the object of his mockery, he is opposed to it. The wholeness of the world's comic aspect is destroyed, and that which appears comic becomes a private reaction. The people's ambivalent laughter, on the other hand, expresses the point of view of the whole world; he who is laughing also belongs to it.[10]

If we put aside the filmic discourse momentarily, in order to restrict attention to the film's diegesis, it becomes obvious that the male spectators of the burlesque theatre are laughing at Concettina. Like her six sisters, she is ugly and fat, hence the contemptuous irony that seems to permeate the film's title – a title that the director will deliberately explain only later. In fact, by playing up the physical ugliness, the generous bodies of the seven sisters, the filmmaker emphasizes the artistic logic of the grotesque body, the body that, in its protuberances, "ignores the closed, smooth, and impenetrable surface of the body and retains only its excrescences (sprouts, buds) and orifices, only that which leads beyond the body's limited space or into the body's depths. Mountains and abysses, such is the relief of the grotesque body; or speaking in architectural terms, towers and subterranean passages."[11]

Bakhtin's definition helps us to understand Wertmüller's aesthetic choices in representing her female characters, particularly with regard to her introduction of Concettina. When the filmmaker cuts from the close-up of the woman's thigh adorned with the tri-coloured cockade to a low angle close-up of her face exhibiting a huge protruding wart, she elevates the character's gaping mouth and underscores both the higher and the lower stratum, the salient and the hollow. Concettina's physical appearance is a reminder that the grotesque body is a body that exists outside of social norms. As Foucault demonstrated, norms act as one of the main instruments of power of the modern era,[12] and Wertmüller, an anarchist from a tender age, revels in opposing them. By choosing fleshy women for her mise-en-scène, she calls to mind the grotesque tradition of Western culture, in which the presence of the fat woman in the carnival, like that of her sisters – the bearded woman, the dwarf, and the giant – is a call for social change.

What the director subverts here, as in all her most significant films, is the bourgeois world order. In this she differs from Rabelais, who, according to some theorists, made the "material bodily principle [... play] a predominant role," exalting it and thus making his works "a typical manifestation of the Renaissance bourgeois character, that is, of its material interest in 'economic man.'"[13] Wertmüller, who grew up during the Second World War and knew about Hiroshima, does not have the optimism of the Renaissance man, whose hypertrophic images precipitate the individual towards the lower stratum for rejuvenation: "To degrade an object does not imply merely hurling it into the void of nonexistence, into absolute destruction, but to hurl it down to the reproductive lower stratum, the zone in which conception and a new birth take place."[14] In Rabelais's world, Gargantua's grotesque devouring body acts as a metaphor for the "social, utopian, and historic theme, and above all [for] the theme of the change of epochs and the renewal of culture."[15] In Wertmüller's world the fat women's bodies are intended to jostle the conscience of a capitalist society guided by a single goal: profit. As Jean Beaudrillard explains, "just as during the Middle Ages, society found its balance between God and the Devil, so ours finds its balance between consumption and its denunciation."[16] In fact, according to Maud Ellmann, "fat ... has come to represent the very hallmark of modernity."[17] She comments further:

> The fat woman, particularly if she is nonwhite and working-class, has come to embody everything the prosperous must disavow: imperialism, exploitation, surplus value, maternity, morality, abjection and unloveliness. Heavier with projections than with flesh, she siphons off this guilt, desire and denial, leaving her idealized counterpart behind: the kind of woman one sees on billboards, sleek and streamlined like the cars that she is often used to advertise, bathed in the radiance of the commodity.[18]

It is with the image of woman as merchandise that *Seven Beauties* ends. All the women surrounding Pasqualino – his sisters, his mother, and even his young fiancée – have become prostitutes while he was in a concentration camp. That their johns are the American soldiers who came to free Italy amounts to the ultimate irony. As the editing and the shot composition of their bedrooms indicate, they are now similar to the dolls that, among small American flags, decorate their dresser. The director's point is clear. In a world that has as its only goal to produce and to reproduce, there is no room left for innocence. Everything is for sale. Everything can be bought. Pasqualino accepts the idea that his pretty fiancée is no longer a virgin because she has made a lot of money and because his only desire is to have "twenty-five, thirty children." He remembers Pedro's message but gives it his own misinterpretation. The Spanish anarchist who chose to die in the concentration camp is the filmmaker's spokesman, and even today Wertmüller shares his belief. Before committing suicide, Pedro dreams of a world where human beings would curb procreation in order to restore harmony within nature and find inner peace. Pasqualino, in his blind stupidity, sees only one way to resist the dangers of overpopulation: to contribute to it! To Carolina, his fiancée, he declares: "In a few years we'll start killing each other for a glass of water ... for a chunk of bread ... That's why there have to be a lot of us, in order to defend ourselves." For Wertmüller, this choice is a fatal one. So, in the last shot, when Pasqualino repeats after his mother, "Yeah ... I am alive," the director drowns half of his face in darkness to contradict him, closing her circular tragi-comedy on a sombre note recalling the opening freeze-frame, which, in its silent fixity, acts as a sinister prophet of the Apocalypse. According to Jean Beaudrillard, "every form of power, every situation speaks of itself by denial, in order to attempt to escape, by simulation of death, its real agony. Power can stage its own murder in order to rediscover a glimmer of existence and legitimacy."[19]

Concettina tries to undermine this semblance of existence and legitimacy. A grotesque figure because of both her physical appearance and her behaviour, she is in fact the unruly woman who attempts to oppose the male order. She makes a spectacle of herself in a world where women have no right to do so, a world where women become spectacles only inadvertently, through an accidental breakdown of the limits imposed on them by a society that does not allow their bodies to exist outside of the norm.[20] Concettina reclaims this right by exhibiting and defending her ugliness. She replies to the raucous male audience's obscene noises, shouts, and jeers with insults and rude gestures duplicating those of the males. But by acting out the machismo she intends to confront, although she intends to dismantle it, she ends up reinforcing the renewal of the existing social structure. In this, she is the direct descendant of the unruly carnivalesque woman of the Middle Ages. Natalie Davis helps us understand the role played by the uncontrolled woman in our society in her study on women and carnival: "Play with an unruly woman is partly a chance for a temporary release from the traditional and stable hierarchy; but it is also part of the conflict which arises from efforts to change the basic distribution of power within society."[21]

This basic distribution is well established in *Seven Beauties* thanks to the complicity of the women surrounding Pasqualino. The women who make mattresses with his sisters laugh when he pinches their behinds. Concettina, whom he abuses physically and verbally, prostitutes herself to pay for his lawyer's fees when he goes to prison after accidentally "murdering" Totonno. After he rapes the hysterical woman in the psychiatric hospital, he must endure a freezing shower and electric shock treatment, but the motherly older female doctor removes his straightjacket and discharges him. As for his mother, she keeps him in a childish state and nurtures his machismo. He will remember her comments about women, as he thinks of how he discovered them as sexual objects in his early childhood, and finally recalls his first intercourse in order to find the strength to penetrate the "sadistic pile of frozen Teutonic dough"[22] that is Hilde's body. In this scene, where the monstrously animalistic commandant of the camp trades Pasqualino's life for his erection, Wertmüller stretches the unthinkable to the limit. In a work largely devoted to a study of Rabelais's works, Schneegans explains: "Through the medium of the exaggeration of the abnormal a moral and social blow is dealt to the aberration."[23] What confirms the key significance of this sequence is that it foreshadows the scene where Pasqualino's vitality proves hideously destructive, when he has to kill his friend Francesco following Hilde's brutal orders. At this moment, the director leaves behind the comedic tradition by underscoring the fact that there is no distinction between the world of comedy, where characters escape from the consequences of their acts, and the moral universe where they carry the responsibility of *our* beliefs and *our* actions. As Annie Leclerc, the French feminist philosopher, reminds women: "As long as we are accomplices to man's oppressions, as long as we repeat them upon our children, fabricating at will vigorous oppressors or docile victims of oppression, never, never shall we be free."[24]

The message is serious, but to deliver it Wertmüller wants to provoke our laughter – not an escapist kind of laughter, of course, but one that springs from awareness.[25] To succeed, in the true spirit of Italian comedy, she erases from her narrative all traces of Aristotelian mimesis. As Allardyce Nicoll explains, evoking the imaginary world of the *commedia:* "What might have been thoroughly distasteful with a comedy naturalistically presented can here be accepted within the framework of the palpably fictitious."[26] In *Seven Beauties* the fictitious becomes palpable thanks to a remarkably orchestrated mise-en-scène, to which the editing and music add a comedic element. For instance, in the scene where Pasqualino arrives at an isolated chalet in the forest, he is attracted by a woman's voice. Soon he discovers a voluptuous pianist, scantily clad, who is singing Wagner's *Traüme (Dreams)*. As Joan and William Magretta point out, "the comic effect arises particularly out of the ludicrous incongruity of Pasqualino's very real predicament as a man in imminent danger and the quasi-fantastic scene of this sensual woman singing almost orgiastically in the middle of nowhere."[27] Soon after, Pasqualino will be arrested, and it is *The Ride of the Valkyries* that "welcomes" him to the concentration camp, shrouded in the same artificial blue shades that bathed the forest. In the camp he meets Hilde. The critics call her "more stupendous than any stereotype of a Wagnerian soprano" and note "the additional comic contrast of this hideous 'Angel of Death' with the Valkyries who chose the heroes to be slain in battle and then conducted them to Valhalla."[28]

To add a light touch to her sombre scenes the director finds inspiration in the *lazzi* from the commedia dell'arte, pantomimes destined to illustrate certain situations, to depict a character. When Pasqualino gathers all his courage to seduce Hilde while she is inspecting the prisoners, he tries, like a pitiful Don Juan,

> to hum seductively at her, but the high-pitched sound which emerges is feeble and tremulous. Some time later, after the prisoners have been ordered back to their quarters, Pasqualino remains in the prison courtyard. In a brilliant pantomime, Pasqualino licks his fingers and then wets his face with his spittle in order to put some life into his pallid complexion. He readjusts his prisoner's cap, placing it at a ludicrously rakish angle, and then tries to whistle at the Commandant as she walks by him. Here the grotesqueness of the comedy is based on two ludicrous incongruities: first, there is the disparity between Pasqualino's conventional gestures of courtship and the monstrosity he woos; second, his behavior is suited to the everyday world but fantastically inappropriate in a death camp, a fact underlined by Pasqualino's pathetic attempt to transform his prisoner's outfit into a rake's costume.[29]

While an excessive stylization and the presence of incongruous elements characterize the mise-en-scène of *Seven Beauties* and its cinematography, absolute realism colours the language of its characters. They express themselves the way people from the lower stratum of society express themselves. As Bakhtin explains, when people who are familiar with one another laugh and insult each other, their speech is filled with grotesque images of the body: "The body copulates, defecates, overeats, and men's speech is flooded with genitals, bellies, defecations, urine, diseases, the nose, the mouth, the cut-up corpse."[30] For instance, when Concettina first appears in the burlesque theatre she is singing a song about the Fascists "rationing everything." The lyrics end on the following note: "One thing I ask you, please don't ration my lover's tool, or all hell will break loose!"[31] Or, in a preceding scene, Francesco talks about the inhumanity of war and says to Pasqualino: "You can't obey people who send you out to fight with poor clothing in a climate where when you blow your nose the snot is crystallized! When you take a crap, you shit icicles!"[32] In addition, it is interesting to note that, in the original version of the film, the Sicilian characters speak the local dialect of Naples. According to Dietrich (in Pulcinella): "The peculiar and extremely free humorous language of Sicily and southern Italy, the similar media of the Attelanae and later of Pulcinella's own linguistic clownery were born on the confines of languages and cultures, which not only were in direct contact but were in a certain way interwoven."[33] As Bakhtin points out, "In the system of one language, closed to all others, the image is too strictly imprisoned to allow that 'truly divine boldness and shamelessness,' which Dietrich finds in the farce of southern Italy, in the Attelanae (as far as we can judge them), and in Pulcinella's folk humour."[34] Without any doubt the Sicilian viewers must have enjoyed this untranslatable impudence, which is an essential part of the joyous licence of the grotesque.

While most viewers, on the other hand, are less able, and often unable, to grasp some of the film's linguistic nuances, they can all rediscover the earthiness of popular language, "the cheerful vulgarity [which] is the wit of the poor, their last and extreme defence."[35] Wertmüller uses this vulgarity first to ensure that her political message is well understood by the lower classes to whom her films are primarily directed, and, second, to disturb the conscience of a bourgeoisie whose hypocritical "sensitivity" is offended by a vulgarity that they once invented. In her world, as in Rabelais's world "the freedom of laughter, consecrated by the tradition of popular-festive forms, [is] raised to a higher level of ideological consciousness, thanks to the victory over linguistic dogmatism."[36] It is in the same subversive spirit that she plays with the macabre and the grotesque, not so much to undermine these as to expose the hidden nature of the patriarchal system that traps individuals within destructive norms. The grotesque aesthetics that can also be defined as the "ambivalent abnormal"[37] allows her to create a filmic world where hyperbolic images, incongruous situations, a shock montage, and a sarcastic soundtrack generate laughter. Delighted to be able to use a crude image, Wertmüller declared in an interview that laughter is "the Vaseline that makes the ideas penetrate better not in the ass, but in the brain. In the heart."[38] She is, therefore, completely aware of the power of the grotesque to trigger emotional as well as reasoned reactions, and she sees "comedy as the enemy of myth." She explains further:

> It frightens me when the face of power is presented with seriousness. As for the leftists, it is very important that people preserve the ability to laugh at themselves. We must laugh about ourselves, and other people too, all the time, knowing that other people are also ourselves. It is a sign of great civilisation, because it is a sign of self-criticism, from discussion, from polemic, from the vitality that these bring to our search for a new society.[39]

By maintaining tension between what is laughable and what is not, and by preserving "the unresolved clash of incompatibles in work and response,"[40] Lina Wertmüller sends a message that resists attempts at theoretical reduction but provokes a debate, triggering the controversy without which there is no freedom.

Notes

1 Comment cited in Lucy Quacinella, "How Left Is Lina?" *Cineaste 7* (Fall 1976), 15.

2 See, among other comments, Pauline Kael in her article, "Seven Fatties," *New Yorker*, 16 February 1976, 109.

3 Jurij Lotman, *Semiotics of Cinema*, trans. Mark E Suino (Ann Arbor, MI: Department of Slavic Languages and Literature, University of Michigan, 1976), 22.

4 William R. Magretta and Joan Magretta, "Lina Wertmüller and the Tradition of Italian Carnivalesque Comedy: Caricatural Characters, Parodic Situations, the Absence of Mimesis, and the Use of *Lazzi*," *Genre* 11 (Spring 1979): 25-43.

5 "The number seven symbolises a completed, closed cycle, perfection. By associating the four, which is the symbol of the earth, with its four cardinal points, and the three, symbol of the sky, it represents a universal whole. But seven is also the number of the devil, of Satan, who tries to imitate God. The infernal beast of the Apocalypse, the great red dragon, has seven heads, each covered with a diadem. All the Apocalypse is built around the number seven: seven churches from Asia, seven stars, seven gold chandeliers, the book sealed with seven seals, seven angels and their seven trumpets, etc." See Catherine Pont-Humbert, *Dictionnaire des symboles, des rites et des croyances* (Paris: Editions Jean-Claude Lattès, 1995), 376 (my translation).

6 This is how Wolfgang Kayser, referring to fragments 75, 305, and 389 in the first volume of Schlegel's *Athenäum*, summarizes Schlegel's definition of grotesqueness. See Wolfgang Kayser, *The Grotesque in Art and Literature*, trans. Ulrich Weisstein (New York: Routledge, 1994), 53. Cited in Philip Thomson, *The Grotesque* (London: Methuen, 1972), 16.

7 Grace Russo Bellaro. "Gender, Role and Sexual Identity in the Works of D.H. Lawrence, Lina Wertmüller, and Jean Genet" (PhD diss., State University of New York, 1993), 198.

8 This is how Wertmüller describes her character in her script: "Flared nostrils, half-open, heavy-lidded eyes: his mouth is twisted in a mean grimace and smoke curls out of the side of it. His hands are pushed deep into his jacket pockets. Pasqualino stands still, smoke pouring out of his mouth and nose." "*Seven Beauties*," *The Screenplays of Lina Wertmüller*, trans. Steven Wagner (New York: Quadrangle/The New York Times Book Co., 1977), scene 7, 275.

9 Mikhail Bakhtin, *Rabelais and His World* (Cambridge: MIT Press, 1968), 325.

10 Ibid., 12.

11 Ibid., 317-8.

12 Mary Russo quotes Foucault in her *The Female Grotesque, Risk, Excess and Modernity* (New York/London: Routledge, 1994), 10. "In a sense," Foucault writes, "the power of normalization imposes homogeneity, but it individualizes by making it possible to measure gaps, to determine levels, to fix specialities and to render the differences useful by fitting them into one another." See Michel Foucault, *Discipline and Punish: The Birth of the Prison*, trans. Alan Sheridan (New York: Vintage Books, 1979), 184.

13 Bakhtin, *Rabelais*, 18.

14 Ibid., 21.

15 Ibid., 325.

16 "Comme la société du Moyen Age s'équilibrait sur Dieu ET sur le Diable, ainsi la nôtre s'équilibre sur la consommation ET sur sa dénonciation." Jean Beaudrillard, *La Société de Consommation* (Paris: Editions Denoël, Collection Folio, 1970), 316.

17 Cited in Mary Russo, *The Female Grotesque*, 23.

18 Ibid., 24.

19 Cited in Russo, *The Female Grotesque*, 124.

20 Ibid., 53.

21 Ibid.

22 Jack Kroll, "Wertmüller's Inferno," *Newsweek* 86, 4 (26 January 1976): 79.

23 Heinrich Schneegans, *Geschichte der grotesken Satire* (Strassburg: K.J. Trubner, 1894). Bakhtin says of Schneegans: "He is the most consistent interpreter of the purely satirical grotesque. In his mind the latter is always negative, it is the exaggeration of the abnormal, an exaggeration that is incredible and therefore becomes fantastic. Through the medium of the

exaggeration of the abnormal a moral and social blow is dealt to the aberration. Such is the gist of Scheegans's analysis" (Bakhtin, *Rabelais*, 45).

24 "Tant que nous serons complices quelque part des oppressions de l'homme, tant que nous les répéterons sur nos enfants, fabriquant en veux-tu en voilà de vigoureux oppresseurs ou de dociles opprimés, jamais, jamais nous ne serons libres." See Annie Leclerc, *Parole de femme* (Paris: Editions Grasset et Fasquelle, Collection Livre de poche, 1974), 87.

25 Lina Wertmüller has repeatedly insisted on the importance of a liberating laughter. See Beatrice Stiglitz's article "Images of Extremity," *Holding the Vision: Essays on Film,* ed. Douglas Radcliff-Umstead (Kent State University: International Film Society, 1983), 32-6, where she quotes Paul Zimerman, who, in "The Passionate Assassin" (*Newsweek,* 29 April 1974), 98, 99-103, discusses the importance of laughter in Wertmüller's world.

26 Allardyce Nicoll, *The World of Harlequin: A Critical Study of the Commedia dell'Arte* (Cambridge: Cambridge University Press, 1963), 149. See also Magretta and Magretta, "Lina Wertmüller," 35.

27 Magretta and Magretta, "Lina Wertmüller," 38.

28 Ibid.

29 Ibid., 40.

30 Bakhtin, *Rabelais*, 319.

31 Wertmüller, *The Screenplays*, 274.

32 Ibid., 271.

33 Summarized by Bakhtin in *Rabelais*, 472.

34 Bakhtin, *Rabelais*, 472.

35 Wertmüller's comment quoted in Peter Biskind, "Lina Wertmüller: The Politics of Private Life," *Film Quarterly* 28, 2 (Winter 1974-5): 11.

36 Bakhtin, *Rabelais*, 473.

37 Thomson, *The Grotesque*, 27.

38 Comment during an interview with Peter Biskind in "Interview with Lina Wertmüller," quoted in Karyn Kay and Gerald Peary, ed., *Women and the Cinema* (New York: Dutton, 1976), 332.

39 Ibid., 330.

40 Thomson, *The Grotesque*, 27.

Part 4

Focus on Conditions of Production: Training, Funding, Distribution

In Part 4, three chapters provide an overview of the situation of women filmmakers in specific geographical and political contexts. The first, by Janina Falkowska, talks about a generation of Polish women filmmakers, including Agnieszka Holland, who experienced dramatic political changes in their country, causing some of them, like Holland, to leave and continue their careers elsewhere. This decision affected their access to resources as well as the type of films they make and the language in which they are made. In Poland under Communism, in spite of a strong cinematographic culture, opportunities for women directors were limited. Most were restricted to making films for children and adolescents. Feminist content was not welcome, as gender issues were considered irrelevant and a purely Western preoccupation. Holland and Sass, like others who managed to make original and successful films, frequently depict women in distress – alone, impoverished, and alienated. Falkowska demonstrates that the meagre output of women directors became even worse in the post-Communism free market economy. Ute Lischke echoes some of these comments in her discussion of women filmmakers in East Germany. Changes since reunification have had significant effects on the careers of several other German filmmakers featured elsewhere in this book (Sanders Brahms, von Trotta, Dörrie). Economic and political transformations, through censorship and market forces, have affected both the conditions of film production and the content of their films. Lischke's example filmmaker, Helke Misselwitz, is one of the few East German filmmakers able to weather the changes brought by reunification.

Suzanne Buchan provides an introduction to the very different filmmaking scene in Switzerland, a small multilingual country with significant minorities. Government subsidies enable filmmakers there to survive the competition from surrounding countries (with larger populations) and the domination of American films. Women filmmakers tend to know and support each other, and to rely on training opportunities and partnerships abroad. Her observations are confirmed in an interview conducted with

Swiss filmmaker Patricia Plattner, whose film *Made in India* is discussed in Chapter 18.

Two panels follow, each with several filmmakers who were present at the "Women Filmmakers: Refocusing" events. Their personal experiences provide further first-hand evidence of the obstacles women filmmakers face and the resourcefulness they show in overcoming them. The first, on feature making, brings together Patricia Plattner and two women with vast experience, Helma Sanders Brahms and Anne Wheeler, a prominent Canadian feature film director, and the French critic, Caroline Eades. The second panel, with several Canadian documentary makers, covers issues of collective identities (Loretta Todd is a First Nations filmmaker, Nicole Giguère is from Quebec) and government funding and institutions (Brenda Longfellow and Aerlyn Weissman), as well as problems raised when dealing with controversial subjects. All address television as almost the only outlet for documentaries today and how that affects aesthetic choices. This subject comes up again in Part 8 in relation to other aspects of the Canadian context. We find out from all these directors what it takes to make a film in terms of training, equipment, skills, collaboration, and money.

15 Agnieszka Holland, Barbara Sass, and Dorota Kędzierzawska in the World of Male Polish Filmmaking
Janina Falkowska

In the preponderantly male world of Polish cinema, those few female film-makers who achieve prominence are an exception to the rule. Eclipsed by the likes of Krzysztof Zanussi, Andrzej Wajda, or the late Krzysztof Kieślowski, women who have dared enter the male world of film production have found themselves expending a significant amount of energy in overcoming deeply entrenched gender barriers. Agnieszka Holland, Barbara Sass, and Dorota Kędzierzawska each persevered to produce remarkable films dealing with political, social, and cultural issues centring on the lives of women, children, and families. Agnieszka Holland (before her Hollywood career) and both Dorota Kędzierzawska and Barbara Sass (throughout their careers) all deal with the problems of the underprivileged, the socially deprived, the poor, and the abandoned. Holland's early films, *A Woman Alone* (1981) and *Angry Harvest* (1985), present women in claustrophobic situations: the former, as prisoners of the political system; the latter, as prisoners of war. Barbara Sass creates excruciating portraits of female alcoholics or ambitious, independent women who end up bitter and alone. Finally, Dorota Kędzierzawska depicts the world of the utterly disenfranchised – abandoned children, impoverished women, and Gypsies, all of whom are generally alienated (politically and culturally) within Polish society.

In her essay, "A Wormwood Wreath: Polish Women's Cinema,"[1] Grażyna Stachówna presents statistical information and many historical details relating to the position of women filmmakers in Poland. She notes that women filmmakers were few and far between. For instance, of the 369 films made in Poland between the years 1902 and 1939, only five women – Nina Niovilla, Marta Flanz, Zofia Dromlewiczowa, Wanda Jakubowska, and Franciszka Themerson – managed to make a few films. After 1945, women's position in the Polish film industry remained practically unchanged. For thirty years, only five women directors of feature films found a place among the veritable army of male directors: Wanda Jakubowska, Ewa Petelska, Maria Kaniewska, Halina Bielińska, and Anna Sokołowska. Further, the latter three produced films only within the genres "traditionally 'recommended' to women directors, that is, films for children and adolescents, melodramas and, sometimes, historical romances."[2]

In the 1970s many women pursued careers as film directors, but only a few have achieved any real success. With determination and talent, five of

Barbara Sass's *Pakuszenie/The Temptation* (1995), courtesy of Agencja Produkcji Filmowej

these artists, Agnieszka Holland, Barbara Sass, Magdalena Łazarkiewicz, Maria Zmarz-Koczanowicz, and Dorota Kędzierzawska, courageously created their films. Even during the extraordinary period between 1980 and 1985 in Poland, the time of Solidarity with its liberated thinking and robust cultural creativity (partly curtailed by the introduction of Martial Law in 1981), few films were made by women. At that time, as Stachówna notes,

> there were 198 new feature films shown, among which only seven were made by women: Barbara Sass (three films), Agnieszka Holland, Ewa Kruk, Anna Sokołowska and Hanka Włodarczyk (one film each). Women's voices were also audible in three films co-directed by Ewa Petelska (together with her husband) and one film made by the Hungarian Márta Mészáros (a Polish and Hungarian production). After the political change in 1989 (this year marks the official abolition of the Socialist system in all the countries of Eastern and Central Europe), there were 38 premieres: only one of those new films was directed by a woman. In 1990 the proportion of women to men was 1:21, in 1991 0:20, in 1992 1.5:15.5 (the Łazarkiewiczs made one film together, *Odjazd/Departure*), in 1993 3:26, in 1994 1:15, in 1995 1:14 and in 1996 2:20.[3]

Women are treated less seriously than male directors, are given no leeway, and, as a result, are forced to prove that they are at least as tough and resourceful as their male counterparts. One source of this mode of thinking lies in the political developments that occurred after 1945, whereby women were granted the constitutional guarantee of equal rights. One might argue, in fact, that women's emancipation was enforced by the communist regime only as it suited the government's agenda. Badly needed for the reconstruction of Poland after the Second World War, women were directed to work in construction sites and factory lots. With their children taken care of by extended families or community daycare centres, they worked physically as hard and as long as did the men.

Although the rights equality postulate was seen as a positive phenomenon by the society at large, the toll on families and on women's physical health was huge. Further, women's labour was not rewarded with the same pay accorded men, nor were women given managerial positions – a problem that persists in Poland today. And that lack of understanding and respect for women's specific situation, paired with a traditionalist, patriarchal approach to women, has translated into a general misconception of their situation as artists.[4]

The difficulty of the female filmmakers' situation in Poland is corroborated by the fact that their films are rarely discussed by critics as "women-made films," despite the terrible demands placed on women filmmakers by the industry. As well, critics rarely describe films produced by women as being "from a woman's perspective." Similarly, journalists in Poland rarely ask women directors questions concerning gender or feminist perspective, typically avoiding the subject, as though it were too intimate or shameful.[5] As Stachówna notes, "Avoiding raising the question of the director's sex results from the critic's fear of being accused of 'sexism' or 'feminism.' Both notions are suspect in Poland where they are still regarded as 'foreign' – i.e. non-authentic, ridiculous and compromising."[6]

Reluctance to recognise gender as an issue results from the very traditional nature of Polish culture. Opinions as to "appropriate behaviours" for men and women have evolved extremely slowly; religious convictions, which preserve an extraordinarily conservative distribution of roles and duties in family and society, maintain a strong influence. In the rare case when a female filmmaker is asked whether she can or should separate her gender from her work, her answer is similar to that given by Dorota Kędzierzawska: "While I work on a film I never think about the fact that I am a woman. All I know is that I want to make a film that I will be able to acknowledge as my own ... There is in fact only one specific thing in the work of a woman director: *she cannot show her physical weakness* [emphasis added]. Nobody should ever notice that after 14 hours of work I nearly collapse ... I am a film director, the rest is irrelevant."[7] This situation is a sad comment not only on the ignorance of Polish critics regarding major social movements, such as feminism, but also on their lack of understanding of the gender restrictions that negatively affect the process of film production.

One of the outcomes of such a situation is that Polish film criticism fails to offer a gender perspective. There are few studies concerning the image of

Polish women in the films of various historic periods,[8] no feminist interpretations of Polish films (to date),[9] and, finally, although there are articles written on particular women filmmakers in Polish weeklies and monthlies, there is not a single article analyzing the collective creativity of Polish women directors. This latter fact is particularly surprising when one considers the wealth of gender analysis elsewhere, especially in articles and books written by American feminists. Sadly, this lack of attention to female artists and practitioners is conspicuous throughout Eastern Europe (a fact generally acknowledged at annual conferences organized by the International Society for the Study of European Ideas in Europe).[10]

As if responding to this lack of interest, Polish women directors do not manifest their female identity in interviews or official speeches; instead, they describe themselves as representatives of their artistic generation. For example, Agnieszka Holland identifies herself first and foremost as a member of the 1968 generation and the group of filmmakers belonging to the "Cinema of Moral Concern"[11] rather than as a woman filmmaker. Forced to emigrate for political reasons, in one interview she describes her moral dilemma upon leaving Poland at the commencement of Martial Law: "Before the 13th of December [1981, when Martial Law was established in Poland], I went to Sweden for two weeks ... If I had come back to Poland, I would have had trouble."[12] Magda Łazarkiewicz, as well, defines herself simply as a member of the so-called Martial Law Generation.[13]

Poland's three most prominent women filmmakers – Agnieszka Holland, Barbara Sass, and Dorota Kędzierzawska – all completed a formal film education. Agnieszka Holland studied at FAMU (the Prague Film School), Barbara Sass at the Łódź Film School, and Dorota Kędzierzawska at WGIK (Moscow Film School) and the Łódź Film School. All three worked under the guidance of the great Polish and Soviet male filmmakers: Holland under Andrzej Wajda, Sass under Wajda and Wojciech Has, and Kędzierzawska under Soviet filmmakers. The three women deal with a diversity of issues, not all of which are labelled "women's problems." Holland moved from endemic sociological and cultural issues to more global political themes and, later, in her Hollywood career, to the themes of alienation and otherness. Barbara Sass and Dorota Kędzierzawska are more consistent in their choice of themes. While Sass concentrates on the depiction of strong female characters, Kędzierzawska's films deal with children and the underprivileged. All three filmmakers, however, insightfully depict women, both older and younger, within a specifically Polish context. Although many other themes related to the political and social specificity of Poland are present in all their films, I will concentrate here on their depictions of women and children.

In several of Agnieszka Holland's films, *Aktorzy prowincjonalni* (*Provincial Actors*, 1978) *Gorączka* (*Fever,*1980), *Kobieta samotna* (*A Woman Alone*, 1981), *Bittere Ernte* (*Angry Harvest*, 1985), and *Washington Square* (1997), the main characters are women – young or old, small or large, naive or experienced. Inevitably, they have to deal with some difficulty in their private or professional lives. Frustrated and unhappy, they are exhausted by their duties, their unrequited loves, and their unrealized dreams. Holland's most touching depiction of a woman occurs in *Kobieta samotna* (*A Woman Alone*, 1981), which deals with issues of loneliness and helplessness within a distinctly Polish socio-political context.

The main character in the film, Irena Misiak (Maria Chwalibóg), belongs to the lowest economic sector of Polish society. Living in squalor (in an appalling one-bedroom apartment), she leads the sad life of a single parent with a young son and earns very little as a postal worker. She has been abandoned by her husband and rejected by her family, and feels isolated in a society that cares for neither her social nor emotional needs. Irena meets Jacek, a young disabled man who feels as lonely and as helpless as she does. Their friendship gives Irena some consolation but not enough courage to persevere in such adverse conditions. Pushed to extremes by poverty and her son Boguś's problems at school, Irena steals money from her workplace, leaves her son in an orphanage, and flees to Jacek's apartment. Together, they decide to escape from Poland, planning to use the US embassy in Warsaw as an escape route. However, when they stop at the motel on their way to Warsaw, Irena, riddled by guilt, reveals the theft to Jacek. Driven by a bizarre feeling of compassion, Jacek suffocates Irena with a pillow and approaches the embassy in Warsaw alone, wired with a bomb. Once in the embassy, he is approached by the security men and led away. This shocking ending provides a pessimistic but appropriate conclusion to two lives dictated by misery and hopelessness. As Grażyna Stachówna comments, "Holland builds with paralysing determination this sombre and cruel vision of a reality in which morality is not respected; there are no lasting values nor any hope for a better future. She destroys any illusion as to so-called moral justice, family loyalty, or maternal love. Such a frustrating reality dehumanises people and condemns them to follow purely biological instincts; only the fittest and the most hardened have a chance of survival."[14]

A Woman Alone departs from clichéd images of that stereotypical, subtle female sensitivity and imagination endorsed in those Polish films produced by more conventional male and female filmmakers.[15] Holland does not shy away from brutality, ugliness, and cruelty in her presentation of the shocking aspects of the human soul (whether male or female). She seems curiously reluctant to impart sentimentalism and an easy sympathy with suffering. Her emotionally withdrawn style in this and other films, referred to as "masculine" by some critics, contradicts many spectators' expectations regarding the work of a female director, particularly in dealing with such intensely brutal social circumstances. This reversal of expectations constitutes one of the remarkable strengths of Agnieszka Holland's films.

A Woman Alone is a dark, emotional description of the state of the lower classes in a Poland overcome by despair and a sense of helplessness. The choice of colour scheme, aggressive framing, and intense close-ups and music all contribute to what is an almost neorealist creation. There is a passionate twist to this pseudo-documentary, a kind of cruel excess in its presentation of those who are most oppressed by the system, a depiction very similar to that which occurs in *Angry Harvest*. Like *Angry Harvest*, which is devoted to the events of the Second World War, *A Woman Alone* presents the entanglements of history from the highly personalized perspective of Irena, a woman unable to overcome adversity.

In *Angry Harvest*, Holland depicts a woman who is a victim of both history and the particular conditions that history has created. The film tells the story of Róża, a Jewish woman saved from incarceration by "a good German," Leon, who hides her in the basement of his house, feeds her, and tends to her needs. What begins as an act of good will turns into a horrific story of sadism and cruelty when Leon realizes that he is physically attracted to Róża. The woman's fortuitous escape from Wiedeń by cargo train, then by foot through the woods to Leon's house, is thus transformed into an ominous journey into death, realized when Róża finally commits suicide. As in *A Woman Alone*, the narrative offers no escape for the woman, who is circumscribed not only by oppressive historical circumstances, but also by her no less burdensome female sexuality.

In both films, Holland paints a grim, though excruciatingly honest, portrait of women. She presents them as historical subjects, in unusual and life-threatening situations, but permits them to remain honest to themselves despite their desperate circumstances. These women are simple people who believe in a moral order that values pride and trust in others. Yet the world that surrounds such people condemns them to death. As moral innocents, they accept the surrounding world, becoming its victims in the process. From her early television films, depicting the problems of adoption (*Niedzielne dzieci* [*Sunday Children*, 1976]) and the dilemmas of married couples (*Coś za coś* [*Something for Something*, 1977]), to her fiction films (*Aktorzy prowincjonalni* [*Provincial Actors*, 1978]) and onwards, Holland's protagonists – female and male – are painted with bold, severe strokes, without any sentimentality or exaggeration, and with an open and honest exposition of their motivations. It is in this sense that critics have admired her films, saying that they are made "as if by a man."

In *Zabić księdza* (*To Kill a Priest*, 1987) and *Europa, Europa* (1990), both later films made abroad, Holland addresses twentieth-century terrorism in

Central Europe and the historical complexities of the Second World War. In both films, women play marginal roles; the psychological dilemmas and ethical problems are solved by male protagonists. Yet, as in her films portraying women, the honesty of the characters and the situations in which they find themselves point to Holland's understanding of the individual as a subject of history. In *Olivier, Olivier* (1991), *The Secret Garden* (1993), *Total Eclipse* (1995), and *Washington Square* (1997), Holland deals with issues of independence and loneliness. General themes of duality of vision and ambiguity in the experiencing of fate are presented with respect for human choices, whether made by men or women.

Agnieszka Holland is a filmmaker who defies categorization: she refuses to be grouped with women directors who portray only women. She calls herself a professional filmmaker who happens to be a woman. All of her films' renderings of women seem to confirm this ideological position. Similarly, she is distinguished from other famous representatives of "the Cinema of Moral Concern," such as Andrzej Wajda and Krzysztof Zanussi. She is distinct in her style and less emotional than other Polish film artists in her presentation of political and social realities, yet her depiction of them is astute. Mariola Jankun-Dopartowa describes Agnieszka Holland's individuality as a positive factor: "she belongs to those masters of cinema, for whom distance is a condition of life and creativity, as indispensable as light or breathing."[16]

∾

Barbara Sass, on the other hand, makes women the singular subject of her films. She portrays them with brutal honesty, without any idealization of either their strengths or their weaknesses. In her first film, *Bez miłości* (*Without Love*, 1980), Sass introduces a new kind of a Polish woman into the cultural discourse. Strong, independent, and exceptionally courageous, her heroines are often played by the director's favourite actress and close personal friend, Dorota Stalińska (she appears in, for example, *Debiutantka* [*Debutante*, 1981] and *Krzyk* [*The Shout*, 1982]). Joanna Korska writes that

> the "liberated woman" in Barbara Sass's films wears trousers, jumps over waste containers, and practices judo. She does not eat but drinks coffee or alcohol and takes drugs instead of having a good night's rest. She is extremely dynamic, rarely reflects, acts too much. She is able to write, talk and make phone calls at the same time. She is despotic, her language is strong and she does anything not to show her weaknesses, even to herself. This liberated woman has no husband, only lovers and no children ... because they are an obstacle to her professional career.[17]

Without Love (1980) tells the story of Ewa Bracka, a young journalist whose life centres on her career to such an extent that she allows her daughter to be brought up by someone else. Ewa is not happy, however; although she works hard at her profession, she is not particularly successful. Constantly seeking new lovers, she has a predilection for weak and unreliable men. Driven to succeed at all costs, Ewa wrongly uses the photo of a drunken young girl to illustrate an article for a writing competition. As a result the girl attempts to commit suicide, and Ewa is reprimanded by her superiors for her unethical behaviour. With her strong woman's mask fallen low, Ewa reveals her true face: that of a weak, terrified, and helpless creature. Still, after this distressing experience, she is nevertheless able to drag herself back to life.

With the exception of *Pajęczarki* (*Spider Women*, 1993), a comedy about the adventures of two sisters who climb high-rises to rob affluent business-men, all of Sass's films are gloomy portraits of women in distress (see Sass's filmography at the end of the chapter). For example, in *Debutante* (1981), another Ewa, this one a young architect, opposes her male colleague and superior at work, taking sides with his wife and his female assistant. And in *The Shout* (1982), another young woman, Marianna, unsuccessfully tries to rebuild her life against all odds.

A strong but fractured woman is also present in the figure of Katarzyna (Anna Dymna) in *Tylko strach* (*Only Fear*, 1993). An alcoholic, Katarzyna leads a double life. During the day, she is a successful television journalist but at night she drinks heavily to alleviate the stress related to both her professional life and her unstable private relations with men. At an Alcoholics Anonymous meeting, Katarzyna is asked to take care of Bożena (Magda Segda), a newcomer, who drinks because she is tired of her family "duties" and of the lack of any professional perspective. Thanks to their friendship both women become stronger and more capable of battling their alcoholism.

Sass depicts relationships between women in a unique way within Polish cinema: female friendship is a means of saving the sanity, and even the lives, of her distressed heroines. In interviews, however, Sass, like Agnieszka Holland, refuses any connection with "feminism." Yet she admits that she wants her films to be acknowledged as "presented by a woman, manifesting a female sensibility and system of values ... so that one can easily see they are made by a woman."[18] Sass's films are highly personal: they are based on her own experience (she often wrote her own screenplays), and feature strong heroines who struggle against alcoholism, delinquency, bad living conditions, and restrictive working environments in order to attain self-sufficiency. In the process, they often adopt the ruthless methods and cyni-cism of their opponents, thus losing their inner calm and their sensitivity to human suffering.

∾

After Poland's transition to capitalism in 1989, the nation's film industry flourished. Women, however, produced fewer films than ever before. The majority of films produced after 1989 were centred on discernibly "male" things (i.e., the mafia, politics), which paid little heed to female sensibilities. Some women filmmakers, such as Dorota Kędzierzawska, persisted in their desire to produce films portraying the world of emotions, insecurities, and despair, especially as these phenomena are experienced by women and children. In the 1990s, which were dominated by aggressively market-driven film productions,[19] Kędzierzawska's delicately poetic films *Diabły, diabły* (*Devils, Devils*, 1991) and *Wrony* (*Crows*, 1994) depict the inner world of the most disconsolate members of Polish society – neglected children – and are thus strikingly at odds with the predominantly entertaining films of that period.

In *Crows*, Wrona, a ten-year-old girl, is the only child of a hard-working and depressed mother. Left on her own, Wrona spends much of her time wandering the streets of a seaside town. She desperately needs her mother's love, but, unable to get it, she instead kidnaps a charming four-year-old girl, Maleństwo ("The Little One"), from her loving parents' house. Both girls spend the day on the beach: in a series of touching scenes, Wrona takes care of the child as well as she is able. She soon realizes, however, in

Dorota Kędzierzawska's *Wrony/Crows* (1994), courtesy of Studio Filmowe "Oko"

alternating moments of love and anger, that she is unable to adequately care for the child and returns Maleństwo to her parents. Delicate, yet without idealizing childhood, the film haunts spectators with its portrayal of loneliness and hunger for basic human emotions and feelings.

Although marketed as a film about children, *Crows,* with its presentation of human helplessness in the face of indifference to emotional needs, nevertheless appeals to a larger public. This film deservedly received the prestigious Coup de Coeur Award at the 1994 Cannes Festival – an award that is usually given for the best film about children. In *Devils, Devils,* a thirteen-year-old girl, Mała ("Little"), joins a group of Gypsies who have arrived in her small town. Mystified by their exotic culture, Mała spends hours dancing and singing with them. They thus generously fulfill her need for tender familial relations, so lacking in her own family, and offer her freedom and spontaneity. When they fold their tents to leave, Mała begs them to take her.

In both *Crows* and *Devils, Devils,* young girls, and their desire to be loved and respected, are portrayed with affection and understanding. But these protagonists also fulfill another role: they are subtle *porte paroles* used to show the truth about the lonely, the unloved, and the rootless generally.[20] In this sense, these films reflect the frustrations and unhappiness of the Poles experiencing hardship and poverty in the new, capitalist Poland. Like the girls in Kędzierzawska's films, Poland's poor long for acceptance and respect. Like them, they remain unloved and abandoned by a ruthless political system that pays more attention to the success of its own international economy than to the needs of its citizens.

In 1998, Dorota Kędzierzawska produced the film *Nic* (*Nothing*). It is the shocking story of a young, underprivileged woman with two children who decides to kill her newly born child because her socio-economic position makes it impossible for her to raise it properly. Referring to a disastrous Polish Seym ruling on abortion in Poland,[21] in this devastating film Kędzierzawska comments on the inaccessibility of abortion to poor women. Shot with orange, yellow, and brown filters, the film oscillates between themes of compassion and tenderness (e.g., when the mother is portrayed with her two older children) and despair and loneliness (e.g., when her husband leaves her alone in the sparse apartment). These colours turn to dark tones in the sequence portraying the gloomy dark night of the last child's murder. The film's female protagonist says little throughout the film; she does not even try to defend herself at the trial. She does not understand the social circumstances of her miserable life: devastated by her act and misunderstood by the judges, she resignedly accepts the condemnation of the penal system and goes to jail.

Nothing openly addresses the issue of abortion or presents the woman as a victim of the social order. Unlike the heroines of Barbara Sass's films, the protagonists in Kędzierzawska's films are powerless victims who are unable to express their anger. Their literal and symbolic silence bespeaks the helplessness of Polish citizens during the contemporary period. In recognition of her sensitivity in presenting the social realities of Poland, in 1998 Dorota Kędzierzawska received a prestigious prize from *Polityka*, a weekly journal devoted to the discussion of political topics in Poland. She was praised for her depiction of abandoned children, impoverished women, and Gypsies, and for her revealing treatment of the lonely and the alienated – issues rarely portrayed in the Polish cinema of the 1990s.

Films made by Polish women directors over the last two decades communicate a pessimistic message of frustration, suffering, and death – a message that is the result of the economic, cultural, social, and ideological conditions of life in Poland. Agnieszka Holland, Barbara Sass, and Dorota Kędzierzawska have resorted to quasi-documentary techniques in their portrayal of women: their characters are realistically depicted, without embellishment, and with all their mundane problems. In Holland's films, the heroines are not stereotypically attractive – they have torn underwear and adopt unappealing poses – because their body images are not as important as their social problems and dilemmas. Barbara Sass's alcoholic women are as disturbing and as revolting as are their male counterparts. And Kędzierzawska's underprivileged provide a sad testimony to socialism's neglect of the weakest members of society. In all of their respective films, the disempowered are representative of real people who are subjects of history and victims of social oppression.

Filmographies

Agnieszka Holland
1975   *Wieczór u Abdona (An Evening with Abdon).* Production: Wilhelm Hollender, Zespół Filmowy X, WFF Łódź.
1976   *Niedzielne dzieci (Sunday Children).* Production: TVP.
1976   *Zdjęcia próbne (First takes).* Production: Zbigniew Wołłoczko, Zespół Filmowy X, WFF Wrocław.
1977   *Coś za coś (Something for Something).* Production: TVP.
1978   *Aktorzy prowincjonalni (Provincial Actors).* Production: Michał Szczerbic, Zespół Filmowy X, WFF Łódź.
1980   *Gorączka (Fever).* Production: Michał Szczerbic, Zespół Filmowy X, WFF Łódź.
1981   *Kobieta samotna (A Woman Alone).* Production: Zespół Filmowy X.
1985   *Bittere Ernte (Angry Harvest).* Production: CCC Filmkunst, Admiral Film and Zweites Deutsches Fernsehen, Germany.
1987   *Zabić księdza (To Kill a Priest).* Production: Columbia Pictures Corporation, J.P. Productions Sofima.
1990   *Europa, Europa.* Production: Les Films du Losange, JP Productions Sofima, Filmkunst Berlin.
1991   *Olivier, Olivier.* Production: Oliane Productions.
1993   *Tajemniczy ogród (The Secret Garden).* Production: Warner Bros, Francis Ford Coppola (An American Zoetrope Production).

1995   *Całkowite zaćmienie (Total Eclipse)*. Production: Capitol, New Line, Jean Pierre Ramsay.
1997   *Washington Square*. Production: Solopan and Hollywood Pictures.
1999   *Trzeci cud (The Third Miracle)*. Production: Fred Fuchs and Steven Haft.

Barbara Sass
1980   *Bez miłości (Without Love)*. Production: Zespół Iluzjon.
1981   *Debiutantka (Debutante)*. Production: Ryszard Straszewski, Zespół Kadr, WFD Warszawa.
1982   *Krzyk (The Shout)*. Production: Ryszard Straszewski, Zespół Kadr, WFD Warszawa.
1985   *Dziewczęta z Nowolipek (The Girls from Nowolipki)*. Production: Ryszard Straszewski, Arkadiusz Piechal, Zespół Kadr, WFD Warszawa.
1985   *Rajska jabłoń (Paradise Appletree)*. Production: Ryszard Straszewski, Arkadiusz Piechal, Zespół Kadr, WFD Warszawa.
1987   *W klatce (In a Cage)*. Production: Ryszard Straszewski, Zespół Kadr, WFD Warszawa.
1990   *Historia niemoralna (An Immoral Story)*. Production: Tadeusz Lampka, Zespół Kadr, WFD Warszawa.
1993   *Tylko strach (Only Fear)*. Production: Telewizja Polska S.A.
1993   *Pajęczarki (SpiderWomen)*. Production: Tomasz Orlikowski, WFDiF Warszawa.
1995   *Pokuszenie (The Temptation)*. Production: Paweł Bareński, Prostar Holding.
1999   *Jak narkotyk (Like a Drug)*. Production: Akson Studio.

Dorota Kędzierzawska
1991   *Diabły, diabły (Devils, Devils)*. Production: Zespół Indeks TVP.
1994   *Wrony (Crows)*. Production: Zespół "Oko," Telewizja Polska S.A.
1998   *Nic (Nothing)*. Production: TVP, KID FILM, APF, Łódzkie Centrum Filmowe.

Notes

1   Grażyna Stachówna, "A Wormwood Wreath: Polish Women's Cinema," in *The New Polish Cinema: Industry, Genres, Auteurs*, ed. Janina Falkowska and Marek Haltof (Trowbridge, Wiltshire: Flicks Books, forthcoming). (The paper's original title is "Wianek z piołunu. Polskie kino kobiece" and it has been translated by Marta Guzy. This version of the translation is cited in this chapter.) On 19 June 2000, I received official permission from the author of this unpublished paper to cite some statistical material on pages 2-10.
2   Ibid., 5.
3   Ibid., 10.
4   For a discussion of these issues, see Janina Falkowska, "A Case of Mixed Identities: The Representation of Women in Post-Socialist Polish Films," in *Women in Central and Eastern Europe* (Special Issue), *Canadian Woman Studies* 16, 1 (1996), 35-7.
5   See Stachówna, "Wormwood Wreath," 8-9, for similar suggestions.
6   Ibid., 7.
7   Translated from Polish: "Pracując nad filmem nigdy nie myślę o tym, że jestem kobietą. Wiem tylko, że chcę zrobić taki film, który będę mogła uznać za własny ... Właściwie tylko jedno w sytuacji kobiety reżysera jest specyficzne: nie może on okazać swojej fizycznej słabości. Nikt nie powinien dostrzec, że po czternastu godzinach zajęć jestem ledwie żywa ... Jestem reżyserem, reszta nie ma nic do rzeczy." Bożena Janicka, "Sama nie wiem dlaczego" ("I Don't Know Why") *Kino* 2 (February 1995): 21.
8   An article by Joanna Pyszny about the Polish School of filmmaking, "Kobieta w filmach Szkoły Polskiej" ("A Woman in the Films of the Polish School of Cinema"), in *Polska Szkoła Filmowa. Poetyka i tradycja (The Polish School of Cinema. Poetics and Tradition)*, ed. Jan Trzynadlowski (Wrocław: Ossolineum, 1976) is an exception here. See also Grażyna Stachówna's work about Polish and international female filmmakers, *Kobieta z kamerą (A Woman with a Camera)* (Kraków: Wydawnictwo Uniwersytetu Jagiellońskiego, 1998).
9   Only recently did women dare to protest against the extremely misogynist films produced in Poland in the 1990s. See, for example, Bożena Umińska, "Kwiat, zero, ścierka" ("A Flower, a Zero and a Rug"), *Kino* 4 (April 1992): 8-11; and Bożena Janicka, "Tato, córeczka i inne kobiety" ("A Father, a Daughter and Other Women"), *Kino* 1 (January 1996): 11.

10 For instance, during the International Society for the Study of European Ideas meeting, which took place at the University for Humanist Studies in Utrecht, The Netherlands, August 19-24 1996, several panels dealt with the lack of gender perspective in research and writings on women from the Eastern European countries.

11 Tadeusz Sobolewski, "Wyzwoliłam się – mówi Agnieszka Holland" ("I Liberated Myself – Says Agnieszka Holland"), *Kino* 12 (December 1992): 7-8.

12 Translated from Polish: "Przed 13 grudnia wyjechałam na dwa tygodnie do Szwecji ... gdybym wówczas wróciła, miałabym nieprzyjemności." Zbigniew Benedyktowicz, "Nowa gra–mówi Agnieszka Holland," ("A New Game – Says Agnieszka Holland"), *Kino* 2 (February 1992): 12-16.

13 Piotr Wasilewski, *Świadectwa metryk. Polskie kino młodych w latach osiemdziesiątych* (*Birth Certificates: The New Polish Cinema of the Eighties*) (Kraków: Oficyna Obecnych, 1990), 91-5.

14 Stachówna, "Wormwood Wreath," 13.

15 With the exception of these three women filmmakers, all Polish film directors present women as "beautiful objects of desire, constantly pursued by men but usually rendered powerless by a patriarchal system. These women cannot choose another path of development and growth. As Krystyna Janda has stated in a *Cineaste* interview, women were usually 'flowers to look at and admire which just floated across the screen and really didn't hold power' (Szporer 13). In all these films, the undercurrent of misogyny is present albeit carefully concealed by the veil of Polish romanticism and a Slavic form of gallantry which originated in seventeenth century France" (Falkowska, "A Case of Mixed Identities," 37). Examples of both men and women filmmakers succumbing to such depictions of women in their films include the following: Ewa and Czesław Petelscy, Jan Rybkowski, Maria Kaniewska, and Stanisław Bareja.

16 Mariola Jankun-Dopartowa, "Reżyserka samotna" ("The Lonely Filmmaker"), *Kino* 12 (December 1997): 29. Translated from Polish: "Osobność Holland nie jest przejawem alienacji – reżyserka należy do tych twórców, dla których dystans jest warunkiem życia i tworzenia, niezbędnym niczym światło i oddech."

17 Translated from Polish: "'Kobieta wyzwolona' z filmów Barbara Sass biega w spodniach, przeskakuje kosze na śmieci, trenuje judo. Pali zamiast jeść, pije kawę, alkohol lub zażywa środki pobudzające zamiast się dobrze wyspać. Jest niezwykle dynamiczna, rzadko się zastanawia, za dużo działa. Potrafi równocześnie pisać, rozmawiać, telefonować. Jest apodyktyczna, używa dosadnego języka i stara się nie okazywać słabości nawet przed sobą samą. Kobieta wyzwolona nie ma męża tylko kochanków i nie ma dziecka ... ponieważ dzieci przeszkadzają w karierze zawodowej." Joanna Korska, "Barbara Sass: Kobieta pod presją w Polsce lat osiemdziesiątych" ("The Woman under Pressure in the Eighties"), in *Kobieta z kamerą,* ed. Grażyna Stachówna (Kraków: Wydawnictwo Uniwersytetu Jagiellońskiego, 1998), 82-3.

18 Translated from Polish: "który opowiada kobieta, reprezentuje kobiecy typ wrażliwości i system ocen ... by było widać, że zrobiła go kobieta." Korska, "Barbara Sass," 71.

19 See Marek Haltof, "Polish Films with an American Accent: New Action Cinema in Poland" in *The New Polish Cinema: Industry, Genres, Auteurs,* ed. Janina Falkowska and Marek Haltof (Trowbridge, Wiltshire: Flicks Books, forthcoming).

20 Bożena Janicka, "Elf i ptaki," ("The Elf and the Birds"), *Kino* 12 (December 1994): 8.

21 The Polish Seym ruling on abortion, "The Ruling on Protection of Life and the Human Fetus," no. 162 (285) II *Cadence*, 2 April 1997.

The Films of Helke Misselwitz: Reconstructing
Gender and Identity in the Former GDR
Ute Lischke

During a period when there was a distinct absence of women directors making films at the DEFA,[1] Helke Misselwitz was one of the few women to make
an impact. She achieved an international breakthrough with her black-and-
white documentary *Winter Adé* (*Winter Farewell*, 1988), which received the
Silver Dove at the Leipzig Documentary Film Festival. This was followed by
her first feature film, *Herzsprung* (*Heart Leap*, 1992), which appeared after
the reunification of Germany in 1989 and was made in co-production with
a revamped DEFA and the German television channel ZDF. Her perseverance in studying film (she had failed the entrance exam the first time because, in the political discussion portion of the test, she had said nothing)
reveals her tenacity. She resisted and took on the task of criticizing the regime and the social conditions that made life especially difficult for women
in the former GDR.

Misselwitz's work has much in common with her West German female
counterparts. As Julia Knight has pointed out,[2] the work of women filmmakers in Germany has always been marginalized. This evaluation of wom-
en's filmmaking role in West Germany is surprising since, during the 1980s,
the peak period of New German Cinema, the number of women filmmakers, in comparison with the number of male filmmakers, was proportion-
ally higher than it was in any other film-producing country.[3] Although
women making films in Germany had come from "extremely restrictive
social, economic and institutional conditions that had denied most women
access to the means of feature film production throughout the history of
German cinema,"[4] by the 1980s new government subsidy programs enabled
women to make a breakthrough into feature film production. This is at-
tested to by a diversity of work by such filmmakers as Helma Sanders Brahms,
Margarethe von Trotta, Helke Sander, Ulrike Ottinger, and Doris Dörrie,
whose films focus on the presentation of alternative images and feminist
representations. Yet, despite the apparent success of these filmmakers, their
works continue to be marginalized.

The situation for women filmmakers in the former GDR was equally difficult but for different reasons. Women were hindered by restrictions on their
work. As directors, they were usually relegated to documentary filmmaking,
television studios, or youth films. Within the DEFA, women worked as
scriptwriters, editors, and cutters, rarely as directors of feature films. Notable exceptions are Evelyn Schmidt and Iris Gusner. After reunification, both

Photo from the shoot of Helke Misselwitz's *Winter Adé* (1988), courtesy of the director. Misselwitz is second from the left.

men and women faced serious difficulties in adapting to the capitalist mode of filmmaking when they went from full employment in the DEFA to a competitive marketing and funding system that was completely alien to them. It is a tribute to Helke Misselwitz that she is one of the few German filmmakers from the former GDR who has continued to make films after reunification.

Misselwitz trained, apprenticed, and worked as a carpenter and physiotherapist before finally attending film school in Babelsberg. For her, becoming a filmmaker was the fulfilment of a dream. No other medium allowed her to express herself in this way. Like those of her West German counterparts, her films are an expression and exploration of the female body and identity. They give meaning to the lives of individuals who otherwise lacked a sense of self within a collective, and by then thoroughly bankrupt, society. Through her female protagonists, Misselwitz makes some important observations about German society, both East and West. The difficult issues of gender relations are a mirror through which Misselwitz hopes that German society can envision a better future. This chapter is an exploration of Misselwitz's attempt to construct a distinct German female identity in her films made both before and after German unification as well as of her attempt to establish her own identity and place within a unified Germany.

Autobiography and History

In the last thirty years, the relationship of autobiography to women's writing, women's film, and German history has been a crucial one. In the 1980s a number of critical studies appeared in Germany that dealt with female autobiographical writings. Diaries, journals, letters, and notebooks were reclaimed and re-examined – as were films by such filmmakers as Margarethe von Trotta, Jutta Brückner, Helma Sanders Brahms, Helke Sander, Ula Stöckl, and Helke Misselwitz – to reveal women's interaction in the private and the public spheres. Often, these women were found to have been denied access to what Foucault calls "technologies of the self,"[5] various techniques through which human beings come to know who they are. Women's private and public spaces remained circumscribed. Both Susanne Zantop[6] and Barbara Kosta[7] highlight the fact that, even when women wrote or made films, they worked at the margins of literary and film movements defined by men and their works. For this reason women had to learn to establish their own spaces, their own genres, and their own readership. Women writers cultivated the same genres for centuries, constantly expanding, adapting, and refining them, whereas male *authors* created seemingly new, original ways of expression. Women's forms did not change substantially until the late twentieth century, when the medium of film gave an added visual dimension to their writings.

In Germany, women's representation not only contends with gender issues, but also with the task of confronting Germany's twentieth-century fascist past. Filmic texts have explored experiences that often do not accord with official history, and they include experiences particular to women. Autobiography has explored divergent selves as textual surfaces upon which the socio-historical context has left its traces. During a period of historical and personal transition in Germany in the 1970s, writers and filmmakers began to re-examine their own positions within a discourse that shaped personal and national identity.[8] Following the period of the German student movement of the late 1960s – a period of rebellion and upheaval against self-serving institutions, including universities – many women took up the pen. While they attempted to come to terms with personal and public conflicts, they also had to deal with the issue of *Vergangenheitsbewältigung* – mourning their past. One reason for participating in the process of *Vergangenheitsbewältigung* stems from the loss of the female voice and place in German history. Paradoxically, the 1970s became, for German women, both a time for mourning and a reawakening of self. During this period, new forms of autobiographical expression emerged, supplying the text with new roles and characters, and uncovering repressed knowledge hitherto excluded from cultural consciousness. The dramatis personae are the women themselves as they see and assign meaning to their lives, and as they define their relationships to the subject position and to authority.

During the 1970s writers such as Christa Wolf, Ruth Rehmann, Jutta Heinrich, Elfriede Jelinek, and Helga Schubert, and filmmakers/writers such as Helma Sanders Brahms, Jutta Brückner, Margarethe von Trotta, and Helke Sander, are representative of German women who pursued autobiographical explorations in new forms and spaces in an attempt to explore and uncover repressed truths about the "self." In the former GDR, women writers such as Christa Wolf had already become successful at breaking through the traditional borders in their writings. And, by the time the wall dividing East and West Germany had crumbled, these writers and filmmakers were using their work as a means of rebelling against an increasingly technocratic and hostile German society.

Some women, among them Jutta Brückner, found themselves silenced, unable to write. Brückner wrote about her futile attempt to write and the discovery that she could communicate much better by making a film. Her film *Hungerjahre* (*Years of Hunger*, 1980) and Helma Sanders Brahms's *Deutschland, bleiche Mutter* (*Germany, Pale Mother*, 1979-80) are known as *Frauenfilme*, or women's films, made by women during a time marked by postwar repression of memory and personal reflection. The sheer abundance of these texts, the number of works authored by women, and what seems to be the paradoxical appearance of these autobiographical explorations at a time when philosophers and critics alike were challenging the concepts of the self, self-representation, and notions of authorship, all call for a reconceptualization of autobiographical expression.

Jutta Brückner came to film precisely because she found this medium created a more viable public space for women's experience than did writing and offered her an opportunity to seek expression of her ideas that literature had denied her. For her, film visualized, rather than simply imagined, women's physical presence, permitting an intensity of identification that literature could not achieve. In all her film work she has tried to find new forms with which to narrate women's experiences and to allow women to recognize their own space. Much like Brückner, Misselwitz has established herself as a feminist autobiographical filmmaker. She, too, is able to forge new connections to history and to our understandings of historical practice. With reunification we are entering a new phase of development, and women's active participation in shaping the developments of the era is especially important. Female identity is different from male identity and much more dramatically bound to the body and to one's role in society. Autobiographical writing, as construction of the body's identity in an image, is an attempt at self-creation grounded in the logic of Western individualism. No woman today escapes this self-creation, even though it assumes different forms from those handed down to them by the traditional culture for men.

In a personal interview I had with Helke Misselwitz, she emphasized that her autobiographical scripts deliver an "alternative" film to which the moviegoer relates on a personal level. The film world is one that requires the viewer to think and experience on an emotional as well as on an intellectual level. Misselwitz's films reflect on her personal history and exhibit self-effacement, submissiveness, and self-objectification. Like many other female autobiographers, she takes a close look at how she is shaped as a historical subject, as a woman in her specificity, and how that specificity is anchored in and directed by socio-historical formations.[9] Experience is a complex combination of meaning effects, habits, dispositions, associations, and perceptions, all of which result from the semiotic interaction of self and outer world. Autobiographical filmmaking functions therapeutically by providing the potential to identify oneself as subject. In addition, the various renditions of women's own lives allow other notions of self to emerge.

Misselwitz acknowledged that she always identified her own space with that of the kitchen. She reflected: "I wanted the kitchen to become the dominant room, also for communication. I always saw that the women were busy and that in the kitchen they were not cut off from life, but the children and the men came there" (author interview with Helke Misselwitz, 23 February 1997). She also acknowledged that even though the state purported to support women's equality, in reality women carried the double and difficult burden of balancing work and family life. Indeed, Misselwitz's own career was often hampered, as she says, by a demanding husband who stole her "body" from her "mind" and her professional work. Furthermore, she was relegated first to television and then to the documentary division of the DEFA. The regular working hours there accommodated home life as opposed to the more hectic schedule and longer hours involved in a career making feature films. Misselwitz confessed that it was difficult for women to make films at the DEFA:

> It was generally difficult for people who had a different view of the world, or an urge to show different people. For them it was always difficult at the DEFA, but it was especially difficult for women. There were only two or three women directors who were allowed to make feature films and they only made very few films. (Author interview with Helke Misselwitz, 23 February 1997)

Researchers have argued that the criticism that led to the dismantling of the regime in the former GDR in November 1989 first surfaced in the visual media in documentary films. Misselwitz's *Winter Adé* (1988) is one such documentary, and it focuses on East German women. Travelling through the GDR, the filmmaker interviews women factory workers, single mothers, and teenagers about their everyday existence. They all represent the point of view of women talking from inside their double burden of domestic and work spaces and relate the dissatisfaction of women's lives within a system that cultivated pessimism. *Winter Adé* is an exceedingly honest portrayal of the social, political, and economic landscape of the pre-*Wende* (reunification) GDR, a snapshot of the period of transition immediately preceding the fall of the Berlin Wall. Drawing large audiences in public cinemas, the film became exceptionally popular and was a cult hit in the United States. It is apparent that German reunification has clear implications for German film production. Dissatisfaction with and criticism of a bankrupt socialist regime, provided through alternative images of women's lives, was finally able to reach a wider audience. A re-examination of women's lives within that context became the focus of an open discussion in Germany, Europe, and North America.

Partisan and Critic

Throughout her filmmaking career, Misselwitz fought censorship. Before 1989, she was critical of the GDR; after 1989, she recognized that unification was not without its problems. The films she made during this period reveal her unhappiness with the imperialistic attitude of the West (West Germany, the United States). It is clear that her allegiance remains with the East (East Germany, Poland), as she reveals in her relationship with the Polish man in her film *Engelchen* (*Little Angel*, 1996): the East is gentler, kinder, and more understanding than the West. The East is the female side, or the bride forced into a shotgun wedding with the West.[10] This leaves unresolved not only the issues regarding cultural production between East and West, but also the nature of identity itself within a unified Germany.

In her next film, the documentary *Sperrmüll* (*Trash*, 1989-90), Misselwitz monitors the fall of the Berlin Wall. Her film must be understood within the context of the dissolution of the East German state. The intention of this project was to demonstrate the conflicts that arise when families split up as a result of reunification. Whereas the mother follows her desire to live in the West, her son stays behind and witnesses unification without great enthusiasm. He visits his mother in West Berlin but decides to remain in the GDR because he is convinced that the East is the better place to live. Monitored in long interviews, conflicts arise. Political and socio-economic complications in the divided countries are played out on a personal level within the private sphere. They also affect the self-perception of the protagonists.

Much like other *Wende* films made around this period, such as Helma Sanders Brahms's *Apfelbäume* (*Apple Trees,* 1992), Ula Stöckl's *Das alte Lied* (*Pits,* 1991), and Margarethe von Trotta's *Das Versprechen* (*The Promise,* 1994), Misselwitz, too, presents a critical review of the socio-political changes that occurred within a condensed period of rapid transitions. The drama and tragedy of a divided Berlin is reflected in this contemporary tale of family separation, generational conflict, and shifting ideological convictions. The filmmaker explores the changing living conditions of the West. But instead of addressing East-West polarization only in an abstract way, Misselwitz concentrates on the visual representation of space from a subjective, partial point of view – a powerful narrative strategy that gives value to a woman's testimony. In this counter-representation, the recollections of a female protagonist set the parameters within which to describe the complex phenomenon of unification, represented in the private sphere. Significantly, Misselwitz deconstructs the myth that life in the West is better than life in the East, and she addresses the problems that result from unification. She allows women to recount their experiences, tell stories of repression, and voice their frustration with their limited choices; however, the lifestyle of the West is not presented as a positive alternative.

Herzsprung (1992) was Misselwitz's first feature film. Unlike her black-and-white documentaries, it is slick and glitzy in its production. Yet the heroine, Johanna, reminiscent of Brecht's *Die heilige Johanna der Schlachthöfe* (*St. Joan of the Stockyards*), becomes a victim of reunification. Here the director takes a critical look at women's lives after unification. Reunification has become a dialectic of violence personified by Johanna, who is a victim of both the economy and male violence, a personification of the fate of the GDR, which is also vulnerable to aggression and violence, the "Ossie" dominated by the "Wessie."[11]

In *Engelchen* (*Little Angel*, 1996), Misselwitz's second feature film, she again looks at the effects of the darker side of life on a woman's thoughts, actions, and experiences. The protagonist, Ramona Schneider, is the "little angel," the innocent female partner of the shotgun wedding, who is unable to survive the effects of unification. A sensitive young woman, she leads a lonely and bleak existence – one that is equivalent to that of women in the former GDR. She lives in an uncaring world near the Ostkreuz train station in East Berlin. One day, she meets a handsome Polish man selling cigarettes on the black market. He has connections to Berlin's underground and is involved in shady dealings. The two fall in love, but happiness is short-lived. In our interview, Misselwitz acknowledged that this film came out of a personal experience with a Polish man. The film reveals that, even though she is critical of the system in the former GDR, her sympathies lie more with the caring males of the Eastern bloc countries than with the brash West.

Through autobiography, or narrative of self-discovery, Misselwitz makes herself, her body, the subject of her own work. She becomes her own textual production. Life is processed, remembered, restaged, and interpreted, and a second reading of experience is filtered through present needs and desires. The past is a series of stories narrated in order to invest it with a specific meaning and coherence. Key experiences are assembled to reveal events central to the formation of an identity of the self. Misselwitz, in her autobiographical films, has revealed that the identity of the German female who grew up in the East is distinctly different from that of her sister who grew up in the West. She has also shown that her allegiance is more to the East than to the West, while making it clear that the female voice has been and continues to be repressed and devalued in the East as well as in the West. Through her confrontation with Germany's past and the process of historical and personal transition, she helps to shape both her personal and national identity. The identity of the German female self is in the *doing* of things distinctively female within her body; it is not a recreation of male-centred identity, much less of the male expectations of what the female should be doing. Instead of the German female self constructed by West German males as *good* girls *(Little Angel)* of the *Kinder, Kirche, Küche* (children, church, kitchen) variety, we have, through the message of Misselwitz's films, *bad* girls who go everywhere. In focusing on the female body and the female self, Misselwitz has helped to reshape and refocus German (and European) cinema in the 1990s.

At this particular juncture, when European cinema is facing a number of challenges, ranging from almost insurmountable competition from Hollywood, financial and funding difficulties, audience lethargy, issues of national identity and co-production, and the complex mechanism of promotion and marketing of European films, filmmakers are attempting to face the challenge of continuing to produce national and European cinema. Given recent discussions around the rebirth of national cinemas in Europe, the growing number of networks of movie houses to draw in even larger audiences, and the enormous potential for development in the Eastern bloc, Misselwitz appears to be in the vanguard of this transformation.

Acknowledgment

I would like to thank the SSHRC for providing me with a research grant which has enabled me to carry out research on women and DEFA films.

Notes

1   The DEFA or *Deutsche Film-AG* (German Film Company) was founded on 17 May 1946 by the Soviet military and became the official film company that served the former German Democratic Republic as a state company with a monopoly of film production. The DEFA studio for feature films used, since 1947, the premises of the former UFA (Universum-Film Aktiengesellschaft founded in 1917) film studio space in Neu Babelsberg. Until 1991, the DEFA produced about eight hundred feature films, as well as television, documentary, and animation films. After reunification, the DEFA came into the hands of Treuhand, the official German holding company, and was sold in August 1992 to a French consortium, the Compagnie Générale des Eaux, of which Volker Schlöndorff is a member.
2   Julia Knight, *Women and the New German Cinema* (London: Verso, 1992).
3   Ibid., 2.
4   Ibid., 16-7.
5   Michel Foucault, *The Archaeology of Knowledge,* trans. A.M.S. Smith (London: Harper Colophon, 1972).
6   Susanne Zantop, *Trivial Pursuits? An Introduction to German Women's Writing from the Middle Ages to 1830: An Anthology* (Lincoln: University of Nebraska Press, 1990).
7   Barbara Kosta, *Recasting Autobiography: Women's Counterfictions in Contemporary German Literature and Film* (Ithaca: Cornell University Press, 1994).

8   Kosta, *Recasting Autobiography*, 35-6.
9   Teresa de Lauretis, *Technologies of Gender: Essays on Theory, Film, and Fiction* (Bloomington: Indiana University Press, 1987), 18.
10 Alison Lewis, "Unity Begins Together: Analyzing the Trauma of German Unification," *New German Critique* 64 (Winter 1995): 135.
11 See Lewis, "Unity Begins Together."

17   "Cinéma des Copines" and an Interview with Patricia Plattner
Suzanne Buchan

From a political standpoint, the inclusion of Switzerland in a conference on European women filmmakers may seem questionable, since Switzerland, at least up to now, has not been a member of the new European constellation. In 1992, a public referendum rejected Switzerland's entry into the European Economic Community. In the past, its political neutrality was a distinguishing feature; on current maps, it lies in isolation, surrounded by the new European Union. This changed status of Switzerland in Europe is the choice of its inhabitants, and it carries serious social, political, and economic consequences. Its national film production, often a reflection and barometer of internal issues, has also been affected by this decision. This chapter investigates pertinent socio-political and cultural aspects of the status and development of women's filmmaking in Switzerland.

There were nonetheless some convincing reasons for including a discussion on Swiss filmmakers in the Vancouver "Refocusing" conference. There are a number of interesting parallels between independent filmmaking in Switzerland and in Canada. Both countries have multilingual regions. Indeed, Canada's bilingualism and its established immigrant populations may be seen as an early stage of Switzerland's situation with four official languages. As far as film production is concerned, this results in tendencies and differences that are not only linguistic and demographic, but also geographical. There is a cultural distinction in Canada between the east and the west, with Quebec occupying a unique geographical, linguistic, and cultural position; in Switzerland, one metaphorically speaks of the "fried potato trench," the Röstigraben, which invisibly but markedly separates the German- and French-speaking mentalities. And the Francophone Suisse Romande, like Quebec, pursues a stimulating cultural exchange with France.

In both countries, interest in other cultures is a predominant theme in particular areas of film production. This asserts itself in different ways: in

Canada, the themes of immigration and identity are often bound up with the personal history of the filmmaker or reflect Canada's population as a country of immigrants; in Switzerland, a country where foreigners account for 20 percent of the total population, the interest in other cultures, either abroad or in relation to their impact on Swiss society, is predominantly addressed by Swiss nationals, often in the form of documentary or narrative films. Another shared feature between the two countries is that both have a federal film funding program; Switzerland has the Swiss Federal Film Commission (a public institution with the mandate to promote and finance Swiss film productions), and Canada has Telefilm Canada.

In order to establish the context and conditions for women working within the cinematic medium, I briefly review the development of film culture in Switzerland and then move on to discuss certain thematic and aesthetic features that identify Swiss women's filmmaking, their representations of women in film, and their ongoing contribution to feminist politics in Switzerland and in its film branch.

Swiss Film Politics

Switzerland's complex historical, political, and cultural development can provide some insights into its film production system and trends. There are a number of factors that have had a direct effect on film politics and have produced a complex and difficult situation for filmmakers.

Until 1963, film in Switzerland was a mirror for the changes the country experienced after the Second World War. According to film historian Martin Schaub, the previous "discursive conflict culture" gave way to a period of consumerism, conservatism, and political disengagement. In film culture, this was reflected by an "Americanization" of the cinema. In 1960, Switzerland imported 459 films (thirty-five-millimetre features), which accounted for 98.7 percent of total film offerings in the country.[1] The Swiss identity was in a state of dissolution, the result of a cultural colonization that had begun after the war. Young filmmakers responded to this with a decision to make films *about* Switzerland *in* Switzerland, thus defining New Swiss Film as a conscious attempt to correct Americanization and to reorient towards national culture. Unfortunately, despite a number of box office successes in the 1980s and early 1990s, American dominance continues to prevail, with Swiss films representing a meagre 2 percent of cinema screenings in 1998.

Although a federal film law was introduced in 1963 with the mandate to support Swiss film, this radical new beginning was, to a great extent, financed by the filmmakers themselves, by foundations, and by financial awards. This persistent labyrinth of applications, interviews, submissions, and statistics remains the dominant mode of financing for filmmakers in Switzerland, and, as a rule, the more often a filmmaker has struggled through it, the greater her/his chances of future funding. Filmmaking is often referred to (in political publications and statistics) as involving "father-and-son" cooperation, with little mention of women. Young filmmakers of the New Swiss Film of the late 1980s opposed the dominance of established filmmakers in the funding system but had to resort to self-financing. Together with the absence of major studios and the newly imposed limitations on international co-productions, this system, as we will see, has proven to be a particular obstacle for women filmmakers.

Women Filmmakers in Switzerland

Filmmaking in Switzerland remains a male-dominated domain, and this appears to be self-evident, although a number of Swiss women have achieved critical acclaim for their work in documentary, narrative, and experimental film. The majority of women's films continue the traditional focus on ethnographic, cultural, or social themes; the intrinsic difference between films made by women and those made by men is the subject matter. Women filmmakers reveal the historical status of women within Switzerland's social and economic fabric, celebrate unrecognized achievements of women in other countries, and/or concentrate on the search for identity. Some of their films are purely documentary in nature; others locate similar themes within a fictional narrative.

If one considers the different language regions of Switzerland, the dominant areas of production remain the German- and the French-speaking areas. The Italian part of Switzerland is referred to as a "deserto cinematografico."[2] A number of collectives and independent film production companies (or participation in such ventures) started in the German-speaking part of Switzerland, although in recent years these have waned. In an interview Gertrud Pinkus, director of *Il Valore Della Donna è il Suo Silenzio* (1980) and *Anna Göldin – letzte Hexe* (1991), points out that most of the films made by socially engaged women filmmakers are circulated by the sixteen-millimetre distribution centres of religious institutions, whose main function is to deliver films for schools and private screenings. Although the films are rented on a regular basis, these viewers are not included in official cinema statistics and, as a result, the films are not considered box office successes.[3] This can be fatal for filmmakers applying for funding for new projects, since box office success is often a prerequisite for new grants.

Partnerships

Women have often made their films in conjunction with male collaborators, frequently husbands or partners. This form of organization and production made the first women's film work in Swiss cinema possible.[4] The cooperation between Urs and Marlies Graf, Walter Marti and Reni Mertens,

Hans Stürm and Beatrice Leuthold, and June Kovach and Alexander J. Seiler contributed to a number of successful film projects. It was not until the mid-1970s that women began to work independently and, in close contact with the feminist movement, to organize themselves, concentrating on films focused on the various and changing roles of women in society. Until the establishment of the Women's Liberation Movement in 1969, only two women were independent directors,[5] Isa Hesse and Jacqueline Veuve.

Cinéma des Copines

In the 1960s and 1970s, professional training for women was mainly autodidactic; they gained experience on the job as apprentices, and the number of films they made remained minimal. Before the founding of Swiss film schools in the late 1980s, the only option for women was to attend film schools abroad. As well, many women filmmakers were (and still are) not able to undertake their own projects and worked as editors or in other capacities for their male colleagues.

A solution to this exclusion of women was the formation of various collectives to collaborate with other women filmmakers. Known as *cinéma des copines,* this form of working together over a long period of time with a number of other women filmmakers and without financial support, was often the only way for Swiss women filmmakers to finish a film and make their mark in the cinema landscape. A number of them, such as Pippilotti Rist, Anka Schmid, and Tania Stöcklin, have done this. A benefit of this form of mostly unpaid cooperation was the network of personal contacts that grew with each film.

Engagement in film politics in order to promote women filmmakers remains an issue for many. The 1992 vote not to join the European Union had negative consequences for filmmakers who had hoped to have access to additional funding outside of Switzerland. The pending decision to now join the European Union, with the consequence that Switzerland will no longer occupy its unique position of isolation and exclusion, should bring new opportunities for co-productions.

Representation of Women

The female protagonists represented by male filmmakers are generally informed by the latter's particular ideologies or their personal experiences of women, as well as by a patriarchal view of Swiss structures and traditions. Few women are the subjects of documentaries by men. This changed in the 1970s and was, in part, the result of feminist politics. A new sensitivity emerged, for instance, in films by Claude Goretta and Alain Tanner – films that can even be described as having a feminist standpoint. Women characters convey the more humanist and "better" message of the authors, but they remain idealizations. In contrast to the works of their male colleagues, a number of women's fiction films reveal an intensely personal style that may well reflect the filmmakers' professional marginalization within a male-dominated branch of film. Women made films about recognizably real women, identity, and sexuality, and they made visible the processes involved in coming to terms with an often conflicting sense of identity within the strictures of Swiss society.

It would be a questionable undertaking to propose a set of themes that is unique to, and identifies the work of, women filmmakers in Switzerland (or in any other nation). But there are some general themes that take on a certain slant when seen through Swiss society and culture. As was the case in many other countries, the cinematic feminist perspective grew out of the feminist movement, which eventually led to the search for a discourse on female identity.[6] These issues included 1970s social criticism based on the resumption of socio-political discussions, which had stopped during the booming Swiss economic period. A new focus to the feminist perspective came with the revival of the culture of democratic conflict, and representations of women's status and roles became an important contribution to a critique of the conservative and patriarchal suppression of women in Swiss society. In-depth and very intimate portraits of individual members of minorities and disadvantaged groups also began to appear.

The majority of films made by women after the 1975 founding of the Women Filmmakers of Switzerland Association (*Frauen-filmschaffende Schweiz* FFS)[7] were of a taboo-breaking and informative nature, a feature shared with many films made by women in the 1970s throughout the Western world. In this respect Swiss filmmakers did not differ from their foreign colleagues. Yet women in Switzerland did not experience the favourable results of feminism, in terms of social status, enjoyed by their North American counterparts. And even today Switzerland remains dominated by a patriarchal system within which women have little power, in spite of the ongoing discourses around equity in politics and the economy.

Documentary was and is a favoured form of film, and it can involve ethnography, participant observation, montage, cinematic intervention, and/or mixed fictional/non-fictional forms. Narrative films have investigated the personal experiences and daily lives of women, at the same time reflecting upon issues unique to Swiss identity and the cultural diversity of the Swiss immigrant population (which is not an integrated part of a cultural mosaic but, rather, remains suppressed and ignored by the majority of Swiss nationals).

The Ongoing Struggle of Feminist Discourse

In a critical review of Swiss film from 1896 to 1987 published by the Swiss Film Centre, a chapter entitled "Männersache" (men's affairs) begins with the following statement: "Filmemachen ist in der Regel noch Männersache, nicht nur in der Schweiz, aber in der Schweiz besonders"[8] (Filmmaking remains a man's affair, not only in Switzerland, but especially in Switzerland). This tongue-in-cheek comment from one of the best known Swiss film historians and journalists demonstrates the dominant critical and journalistic attitude towards filmmaking by women. Instead of pursuing the reasons for this, the author chooses to investigate the image of women in films made by men, completely bypassing an issue that continues to be a problem – the fact that women working in Swiss cinema are not given the critical attention their work needs, which, in turn, cuts them off from limited funding sources.

The Facts Revealed: *CUT*

A small number of publications have focused on the situation of women working in the Swiss film industry, most notably *CUT: Women Film and Video Makers in Switzerland from the Beginnings to 1994: The Current State of Affairs*, edited and with contributions by Brigitte Blöchlinger, Alexandra Schneider, Cecilia Hausheer, and Connie Betz. It is currently available only in German. This book remains the most comprehensive publication on women's filmmaking in Switzerland. The fact that all but one of the authors studied (or were research assistants) at the Seminar for Cinema Studies at the University of Zürich is an indication of the contribution film studies has made to researching and making available important information on the status, aesthetics, and development of Swiss women filmmakers. Without doubt, the 1989 appointment of experimental filmmaker and film theorist Professor Christine Noll Brinckmann as head of this newly established program contributed to the realization of the project. Until the book was published, most of the accumulated information was scattered in private archives or studios and was difficult to find.

Besides the direct reference to the fact that many women work as film cutters, the book's title also acknowledges the importance of video as a means of expression. Video has enabled many to undertake projects that, had they been shot on sixteen- or thirty-five-millimetre film, might never have been completed. Switzerland has an impressive number of video artists who have embraced new technology and the freedom it provides, and recent innovations in digital imagery have made equipment even more accessible. *CUT* also includes comprehensive filmographies and biographies of women film- and videomakers.

The Future

A study of federal film support, the most important source of film funding in Switzerland, revealed that, between 1981 and 1992, a total of 437 grants were given out – 82.8 percent for productions submitted by men, 12.8

percent for those submitted by women, and 4.8 percent for mixed projects.[9] The study further showed that women with university degrees have a better chance of receiving a grant than do those without them. During the period studied, the majority of films documented were made without federal support, through unpaid work, private financing, unpaid salaries, and so on. Unfortunately, *cinéma des copines* is still a dominant form of film production, which may be one reason why the majority of films made by women are short. The analysts come to the conclusion that the aforementioned federal support statistics are related to the general social asymmetry regarding gender.

Despite the recent establishment of film schools that provide much needed employment, many Swiss women filmmakers must still look for work abroad – as film editors, directors' assistants, or production assistants. Yet there are some positive developments on the horizon that should enable a growing number of film school graduates and others to realize their projects. Support for first films is now more possible through increasing television and federal financing; established filmmakers can gain access to funding for Swiss productions that are co-produced with other countries; and, as has already been mentioned, Switzerland's potential entry into the European Union should bring further opportunities. Film schools are an additional networking source, and their collaboration with Swiss television has resulted in broader audience awareness.

Gertrud Pinkus offers some words of advice based on experience to women filmmakers:

> Be capable of many things. Be diverse. Master technical aspects. Do as much as possible by yourself in order to remain independent. Do not rely on people who always know everything better and are more clever ... You have to be able to take the camera out of the cameraman's hand. In certain situations you have to be able to say: I'll do that myself. You have to be able to fire your woman editor. Because a film is not social work. It is subject to very tough pressures of business and competition – as is artistic expression.[10]

An Exemplary Filmmaker: Patricia Plattner

A filmmaker who exemplifies the diverse qualifications and talents of many Swiss filmmakers is Patricia Plattner, who participated in the "Refocusing" conference. After a fine arts education, she spent many years abroad gathering the experiences and impressions that identify her work. Graphic artist, author, producer, ethnographer, documentary filmmaker, director, artistic director, and screenplay writer, Plattner is gifted with the diverse abilities which have enabled her to carry out numerous commissions and to complete films

Il faut savoir perdre pour mieux gagner !

From Patricia Plattner's *Piano Panier ou La Recherche de l'équateur* (1989), courtesy of the director

that reflect a unique personal style. Plattner's *Piano Panier* (1989), for example, is an introspective film that reveals the dynamics of a long-time friendship between two women. We see their arguments and laughter; but the film also takes time to show the development of conflict over petty differences and the deeper meaning of superficially banal routines. *Made in India* (1998), her documentary on the complex process involved in the astonishingly successful union organizing activities of low caste Indian women, is not simply a socio-political document. At the visual level the film oscillates between anthropological sensitivity and the sheer joy of presentation.

Plattner is considered to be a prominent member of the new generation of women filmmakers in Switzerland; other names include Véronique Göel, and Anka Schmid and Tania Stöcklin (who have collaborated on a number of productions, continuing the idea of *cinéma des copines*). Like many of her female colleagues, Plattner has an impressive and diverse curriculum vitae and is consistently active in political and cultural issues. She works for a number of European and Swiss television producers, and has her own production company. Her development and success as a filmmaker are due, in part, to her ability to collaborate outside of Switzerland and to find markets for her work beyond her own small country.

∾

The following is excerpted from a public interview that took place during the "Women Filmmakers: Refocusing" conference prior to the screening of an excerpt from *Piano Panier* viewed in its thirty-five-millimetre version.

(The film was shot on sixteen-millimetre film but transferred to thirty-five-millimetre film for wider distribution.)

Suzanne Buchan: Patricia Plattner is a well known filmmaker in Switzerland, but how many people here had ever seen a Swiss film before this week? Only two of you, and I'm not surprised! It's a pity because there are a number of very good and diverse filmmakers in Switzerland, and Patricia is a good example of their talents and originality. Like many others, she began as something else. Before making films she graduated in 1975 from the Higher School of Visual Arts in Geneva, in painting and photography. Between 1976 and 1983 she was active in various fields, including performance, and received a number of grants from the Swiss federal government for work in the fine arts. She won several prizes, including one for an architectural design for a kindergarten. Some of the money she received allowed her to embark on a long career as a traveller. Her films speak from her experiences in many places. The first big journey she undertook was around the world. She went from Japan to California, where people suggested she should visit Vancouver. Here she dropped in at the Western Front for two weeks, and made her first video, an experimental film.

Patricia returned to Switzerland, and with friends and colleagues founded a graphics studio called Les Studios Lolos. She still works there as a graphic designer and continues painting and photography. Between 1982 and 1984 she did what most would-be filmmakers at that time had to do, since there were no training schools: in order to obtain the necessary experience she apprenticed herself to an established filmmaker. In 1985 she founded her own production company, Light Night, and made a number of films for the francophone Swiss television company TSR. In 1986 her first short film, *La Dame de Pique* (*The Queen of Spades*), won the first of many film prizes that she has received from the Swiss federal government. There is one particular committee that recognizes aesthetic quality rather than box-office success, and Patricia has received a number of its awards. In 1989 she won several prizes for her first full-length feature film, *Piano Panier,* which we will see today. She went on to produce or co-produce a number of films in the early nineties and to write several scripts. The path from being an assistant to becoming a director and producer is a familiar one. Her work has been mostly with francophone filmmakers, but she also co-produced a film with Manoel de Oliveira in 1993. Patricia has made several documentary films, worked for television, and is a consultant for various film organizations in Switzerland. Her latest film (1998) is a documentary, *Made in India,* about lower caste women organizing in India. She is well qualified to give us a sense of what it is like at present to be a woman filmmaker in Switzerland.

Patricia Plattner: First, you have to be very determined, you have to fight, and it's better not to start as late as I did. I was over thirty when I made my first film. Because there was no film school I could attend, working in cinema for me was a distant dream. It was only little by little that I was introduced into this profession. Once I saw that maybe it was possible for me to do something in film, I tried to be as versatile as possible, becoming a producer and also knowledgeable about cultural policy in the country, and proficient at making funding applications. I met with some success; otherwise I would have been discouraged by the difficulty of going on. Maybe I am a bit too pessimistic, and talk too much about financing, but I think you all know how important it is. As you know, Switzerland is a very small country and distribution of all films, not just those by women, is difficult. It's depressing, so I'll try not to focus only on this side of filmmaking!

SB: Maybe you could tell us something about how *Piano Panier* developed? Where did the idea for that film come from, and how was it funded?

PP: Well, I had been reading a novel by a Swiss author that I really liked and wanted to base my script on that book, but it was a very difficult project. The story was situated in Sri Lanka on an archaeological site. Production costs would be high, and there was a war going on in Sri Lanka, so people were afraid. I tried to raise money for it, but with no success. Then I met a Portuguese producer, Pavlo Branco, who also works in France and is a well known producer in Europe. He has helped a lot of young (and not so young) filmmakers. He advised me to drop that idea ("If you still like it in three years' time, do it") and to write a very simple script for a story set in Portugal, where he has a team of technicians who work twelve months a year for him. He also told me to use young, unknown actors, who wouldn't cost too much. So I thought, "Here's a challenge!" and went to stay in a little house in Portugal for a month (the one that appears near the beginning of *Piano Panier*). The house was empty, and I was there just with my computer. I had an idea for the story of two young women friends who live in Geneva, one Swiss and one Portuguese. We have a lot of Portuguese workers in the French part of Switzerland; in the German part there are more from Turkey. I was interested in exploring their friendship, coming from different backgrounds, and thought the Swiss girl could visit her friend's family in Portugal. By making the two main characters in their early twenties, I could use young actors. For the Swiss woman I used a stage actress; it was her first film but she won a prize in Germany for this role and has gone on to act in other films. The Portuguese actress had already made a few films in Portugal, and the actor who plays her fiancé is now well known there. I also thought of using the empty house where I was staying (there was just a mattress!). And I spoke to the lady who ran the restaurant where I went to have coffee, who said I could shoot there. So I wrote the script in four weeks and managed to obtain funding very quickly. The whole thing only cost just over $400,000 Canadian, which is a very low budget. Three months later I was shooting in Portugal. I had a Swiss cameraman, who since has worked on other films with me, and the rest of the crew was Portuguese. Fortunately Portuguese is not that different from French, and most of them could speak French! So that is how my first feature film was made. People liked it, and it gave me the opportunity to do other films afterwards. Eight years later I can see a lot of mistakes in it, but it still has a certain freshness and shows me I've made some progress since then, too!

SB: In the film, Marie, the Swiss girl, plays a piano piece called "Piano Panier," which explains the film's title. At the beginning she decides to leave her lover, a married man with children. Her friend, Filipa, tries to console her by suggesting that she go to Portugal with her. They have known each other since childhood but have been out of touch. Marie does not expect that Filipa will get married while she is in Portugal. She has difficulty adjusting to Portuguese family life, especially the religious context. Although she believes herself to be culturally sensitive and aware (she practises Tai Chi and is learning Thai), she is really in search of her own identity rather than interested in learning about theirs. The two friends spend some time together in the isolated house by the sea (where Patricia stayed), and the film depicts the conflicts and ambivalences as well as the closeness of their friendship. They separate after an argument, but their friendship finally overcomes their differences, and Marie attends Filipa's wedding in Lisbon after all. The film is a reflection on the nature of women's relationships with other women, and how their relationships with men affect them, as well as on cultural difference and divergent expectations.

Questions after the screening focused upon intercultural communication, including differences in the significance of physical contact between people of the same sex. Asked whether this aspect of the film was meant to raise questions about the characters' sexual orientation, Patricia Plattner said that this was not conscious on her part.

For a discussion with Patricia Plattner on the making of her documentary *Made in India*, see Chapter 29.

Notes

1 Martin Schaub, "Die eigene Angelegenheiten," in *Vergangenheit und Gegenwart des Schweizer Films (1896-1987): Eine kritische Wertung*, ed. Martin und Martin Schaube Schlappner (Basel: Stroemfeld/Roter Stern, 1987), 74.
2 Connie Betz and Alexandra Schneider, "Wege zum Film: Ausbildung, Arbeitsweise, Subventionspraxis," in *CUT: Film- und Videomacherinnen Schweiz, von den Anfängen bis 1994: Eine Bestandsaufnahme*, ed. Brigitte Blöchlinger (Basel: Stroemfeld, 1995), 23.

3 Ursula Ganz-Blättler, "Erfolg hat viele Gesichte: Léa Pool, Gertrud Pinkus, Greti Kläy im Gespräch, in Blöchlinger," *CUT*, 39.
4 Betz and Schneider, "Wege zum Film," 23.
5 Cecilia Hausheer, "Frauen, Bilder, Politik: Aufbruch in den siebziger Jahren," in Blöchlinger, *CUT*, 43.
6 Ibid., 45.
7 All translations by the author.
8 Schaub, "Die eigene Angelegenheiten," 139.
9 Betz und Schneider, "Wege zum Film," 29-30.
10 Hausheer, "Frauen, Bilder, Politik," 42.

For **Patricia Plattner**'s filmography, see Chapter 18.

18   Making Feature Films: Panel Discussion with Helma Sanders Brahms (Germany), Caroline Eades (France), Patricia Plattner (Switzerland), and Anne Wheeler (Canada)
Moderated by Jacqueline Levitin

Jacqueline Levitin: Anne Wheeler is a Canadian filmmaker whose history in filmmaking is almost as long as Helma's. What we have here are women from different countries who can perhaps compare the situation of women in the practical realm of filmmaking. The first question I'd like to start with is: looking at the last ten years, what are the projects that you wanted to push through but weren't able to? And what are the projects that you ended up with and for what reason? Who would like to start? Anne?

Anne Wheeler: That could be a very long answer. I guess the Canadian film industry has gone through ebbs and tides. About ten years ago it was quite rich and people were making fairly large films, and I could almost get anything made within reason. Because of our distribution problems in this country and, with only thirty million people, there seems to be more of an emphasis on television. So, a lot of my projects became television rather than feature, though I felt some of them should have been feature, and that put me into a mould that I didn't really want to get put into, and it's been very hard to break out of the television mould and get back into features. But obviously the higher budget for features, being this close to the States, not going with an American lead: those are all problems that we face here. Being so close to America, it's very hard to make the films you want without them becoming somebody else's films. I certainly have projects right now that I would like to make but they are higher budget, with higher production value. It's much easier to get the two- or three-million-dollar small feature films done.

JL: Could you just quickly elaborate on how the situation has changed in Canada? Why has it changed?

AW: Well, I think a lot of the government agencies were very enthusiastic in the 1980s, and there have been a lot of cutbacks since then. We don't have a Channel Four; in England you have the television and the feature film distributors cooperating but you don't have that here. So you have to do one or the other. There has actually been a lot more opportunity to reach a greater audience and to do things with more creative independence on television than there has been in feature. Because if you go into feature you end up having to go into American distribution, American stars: all of that is a great push. So you almost have more creative freedom in the television realm.

Helma Sanders Brahms: When you look back, ten years ago it was the fall of the Wall, and the fall of the Wall in Germany changed almost everything. I was able to make one film that deals with the fall of the Wall called *Apple Trees*. It spoke about a situation that, in 1990, was happening all around Berlin in what before had been the GDR [the German Democratic Republic], socialist Germany. Around Berlin there had been enormous plantations of apple trees because the GDR didn't have access to the markets for fruits – for oranges, for bananas, and all that. So they tried to have as many apple trees as possible so that all the citizens could at least have apples. In the mid-1970s they had a lot of apple trees planted, and in 1990 these apple trees were all torn out of the ground, which meant that ten million apple trees were all lying in the fields. Imagine ten million apple trees with their roots up to the sky. This was an image that was so impressive that I made a film about it, telling the story of these apple trees through the story of a young couple that, in the beginning, was quite enthusiastic about socialism. I was able to make it rather quickly after the fall of the Wall.

I had another project then – the story of a Jewish woman who had fallen in love with a young German man who turned out to be a very great poet of the twentieth century, one of the greatest in the German language. She also was one of the greatest poets in the German language. But she was Jewish and he became a Nazi. This is the conflict of the story. And I thought this was a great story because it revealed so much about the relationships between Germans and Jews, their approach to culture and to what was their common language. I tried to get this film financed, but it took me five years and finally I could only make a small film – a mixture of documentary and fiction. It was only possible that way, and it made me so sad that I could not really make the film I wanted and I got

Photo of Anne Wheeler,
courtesy of the director

very ill because of it. I got cancer, and I went through a very serious operation, and I became what I have always been – an Amazon, but this time really, physically. [Sanders Brahms opens her jacket abruptly and reveals that she has undergone a mastectomy.]

I have another project that seems to have the same destiny but I think maybe this time it will be different. It's a film about a great woman, one of the greatest in Germany: the very independent, very loving, very wonderful Clara Schumann. Clara Schumann was the wife of Robert Schumann, and she was the greatest pianist of her time. She was really a star of the nineteenth century, a star like today we have stars on the music scene. She had a very, very tough life. I have Isabelle Huppert to play the woman, which I think is wonderful because she is just the right person. I have the Berlin Philharmonic Orchestra to play the music, which is I think the greatest orchestra in the world. But I don't have the money yet. I have a Hungarian co-production to help me, I have a French co-production: they have been true to me for four years now. Everyone has stuck by me, but still I can't finance the film. There is a lot of money in Germany for films but – I don't know – it's become very, very difficult for me. It's almost impossible right now to make films, even though I have had five films in Cannes and I have almost all the international awards you can have in the cinema industry. One of my films is said to be one of the classics of film – *Germany, Pale Mother*. In spite of that I can't get the money. That is my situation.

Patricia Plattner: In Switzerland, where I come from and where I live, the situation is not very good. I don't know if you have seen a Swiss film in the last month but I would be surprised if you have. We have quite a lot of difficulties because there is no local film industry in our country, unlike France or Germany. The country is very small. We have three different languages: French, German, and Italian. So, as a French speaker (I live in the French-speaking part), I can say that I don't have a market for my films in Switzerland: it's impossible because there are only two and a half million people in the French-speaking part. That is why for the two features I made, I co-produced with France. They were distributed in France and the first one was very low budget. But for the second one, I tried to do something a little more ambitious and so I needed a third country. I found a third country in Europe, but then Switzerland refused to be part of the common market. So for us it's more and more difficult to get money from other European countries because we are "out of Europe."

We have a tradition in Switzerland that documentary film is very important. One of the reasons is probably economic because it's true that we can shoot a nice documentary film with money that we can find in Switzerland. I'm sure Swiss filmmakers would make more feature films if it was easier for them to find the financing. Also, in Switzerland we don't have a long tradition in filmmaking; we had no school, no university. I think the first film school was in the eighties or end of the seventies. Now we have a little school in Geneva, a little one in Zurich, a little one in Lausanne, but maybe only eighteen students can go to film school in Switzerland. So we don't have the film school tradition like you have in Poland, for instance.

JL: What about you, what would you like to do?

PP: Well, I would really like to make another feature film. But I did two feature films, each five years apart, which I think is not good timing. I would like to do more. The second feature I did, *The Crystal Book,* I really wanted to do and I spent about six years trying to find the funding. But I got it. As we have all these financial problems, in order to make a feature that you would like to see on the screen, you have to wait a long time. I've been out there doing very low-, low-, low-budget films. After that, it's very difficult to see them because there is no money for the distribution. Most of us also shoot documentaries.

JL: Did you get involved in producing?

PP: Yes, that's important. Most of us in Switzerland are producers as well as directors. Most have their own production company. I also co-produce French films. We cooperate because we need to.

Caroline Eades: I guess I'm the happy one because I'm not a filmmaker. I think that the situation is slightly different in France. It's slightly different because, in 1993, it was the beginning of the war between American film producers and French film producers, and also between distributors. I'm referring to the GATT [General Agreement on Tariffs and Trade] agreement of course, and the reaction that it raised in France. There has been a real effort to try to defend French film, to compensate for the importation of American productions. The government started to support more new directors whether they were male or female. I would bluntly compare the situation to wars in general in that it can be good to women in some regards, as when men had to go to the front and women had to go to work in the factories. It's more or less the same in the movie industry: when we need women then we can go and get them.

The other important factor is the change in the television landscape in France. The development of Canal Plus certainly contributed to bringing financial support that was needed for new projects. And because France is one of the major players in the European development, French directors can also look to European funding more easily than directors from other countries. So, I would say that for some women filmmakers, especially young ones, there was certainly a sort of conjunction of different changes, different improvements, that could explain why some of them had their films produced.

The problem usually comes with the second or third film. They don't expect you to really succeed with the first film. However, if you do succeed then the pressure is immense, it is really intense. In France, failure is not allowed. Failure is a very bad thing, perhaps even more so in the arts, and in something as fickle as the movie business. We have a lot of film directors – and I wouldn't make too much difference between men and women here – who really can't make more than three or four films.

The situation has been improving since 1993, but I would say, unfortunately, there are some black clouds on the horizon. First, the Ministry of Culture is not as well funded as it used to be. The other problem is the television system, since Canal Plus is coming under fire because the advantages that this particular channel got are not legally accepted anymore. Also, last year was a very bad year as far as French film distribution is concerned. Which is to say the audience is not responding well. They are going to see American films. We produced 180 films last year but distributors are not so interested in producing something out of the mainstream, something that does not attract the audience as well as American films. Maybe in one way we are losing the war and everybody is a victim in that situation.

JL: Caroline raised the question of both gender and generations in her comments and I'd like to explore it a bit further. In your experience, is there respect for the "elder stateswomen" of filmmaking? Are women who are experienced filmmakers treated differently from males who are experienced filmmakers? Do you also find that there is economic investment in the newer filmmakers, but only for a short time?

AW: I think that for all filmmakers it's almost easier in this country to get your first film made because there's a lot of programs for emerging filmmakers. The second film is usually more difficult. A lot of people fall down and fail because, with the first film, everybody was very generous and gave them gifts in terms of their time and energy. But for the second film it's, "Okay, you've made one, let's see how you do on your own now," and people withdraw their support to a degree. I think it's particularly hard for somebody who has been around a long time to be seen as having something new to say and as a viable commodity in the market here. For those who don't know, Canadian filmmakers only hold 2 percent of our theatrical audience right now. It's very, very low, and that 2 percent includes mainly the larger male-driven films – mostly from central Canada, of course. We have more problems being out in the west because it's such a huge country.

I think older women filmmakers are seen to be nurturing. I do a lot of mentoring. We are considered to be teachers, to take on a lot of responsibility in bringing new people into the industry. I suppose because of our feminine qualities we are seen to not be as aggressive, as competitive, to sort of "give over" to the newer generation and to be very generous on that level. Which is a wonderful thing, and I do a lot of that and I get a lot from it. But I think that probably men in my position do not get nearly as many people coming for help as I do. I probably have six to ten requests a week from people coming into my office with problems or scripts, and asking "Can I mentor them?" or "Could I do this or that?" And some of them are very talented, and I am usually involved with four to six filmmakers at a time, trying to get their first or second films made. I don't think that it's the same situation with men. I think that men are considered to be going on their own quest and their own career, and people wouldn't think of bothering them with that amount of energy, that's for sure.

In terms of subject matter, if you make one film about sisters, you've made *all* films about sisters. It seems if you come to a second film about sisterhood, or motherhood, or anything about the relationships that women have with other people, be they men or women, if you've made one film like that, it's considered already done. Whereas you can have many thousands of male buddy movies. But two in a row of friendships between women of whatever ages and orientation, it's called duplication. So I guess there is more pressure on women to come up with something that's completely unique, that hasn't been done before.

PP: I would say that when I started about fifteen years ago, being a woman was not a disadvantage. I had the feeling that there was an expectation and maybe that we even got help before the film was done because people were expecting something. But then I have the feeling that the response from the critics was much harder for the women filmmakers than it was for men filmmakers. We were supported on one hand, and on the other the critics were more difficult for us.

HSB: There are a lot of things that are going through my head while I listen to these very moving statements. It seems we all have the same experiences in some way or another. We all have so much difficulty getting our films made and then, when they are made, we all have these terrible problems with the critics. In film we speak of "shooting," and there is something fatal in it.

The idea that cinema might be different from what Hollywood movies were, that was something that moved young people in the early seventies very much. I remind you that in 1968 [Jean-Luc] Godard took a knife and sliced the screen in Cannes to say, "This cinema is over. We need a new cinema, a fresh cinema." Because we were overfed on these films of the fifties and sixties. And if you look at them today you see how most of them – not all of them, certainly not Kazan and other great directors – most of them are really boring and sad. Myself, I felt like I was touched with this knife that said, "Look! Cinema can be different, cinema must be different!"

Inventing a new film is in a way inventing the world again. It means you get into a dark room, the light is going down, you are in a belly, you know you are born into a new world that is coming up. And the wonderful thing that moved us so very much in the early seventies was the fact that, in a way, we were allowed to recreate the world.

I admire this generation of the French, this nation, because it was really generous to me. The French are the ones who normally gave me money for films. The French love to have something to fight for. But now we have come back to the cinema like it was before. You must see that 1989, in a way, was a decisive moment that marked the end of European cinema. The fall of the Wall meant that America gained at that very same moment 600 million spectators. The first films that went over the torn-down Iron Curtain were free copies sent by the American film industry. They were shown all over, and they destroyed the film industries of Poland and the Soviet Union, of Hungary, of Czechoslovakia. And Germany cooperated in this.

CE: The question of generation and gender is certainly interesting because, in our country, youth is such an important thing in culture and advertisement and so forth. First, I notice that most of my students and most young people in France, who are the audience of cinema, don't know the works of the former generation of women filmmakers – Chantal Akerman, Agnès Varda – because they can't see them. Chris Marker's film *La Jetée* [1963] has been extremely popular for the past three years because it was the inspiration for the American film by British director Terry Gilliam, *The Twelve Monkeys*, and suddenly all my students wanted to see Chris

Marker's film. So it was quite interesting to see how we have to use commercial mainstream movies to get them interested in what is part of our patrimony, or matrimony. The second thing is, young women directors are very interesting for the media. Promotion is, of course, very important, and they would rather invite a beautiful young face, a woman's face, than a man's face on one of the radio or television shows promoting films. It's very interesting to see how the interest in women filmmakers can be perverted by the media system. So, a young woman filmmaker might have a better chance than an older one. It doesn't mean that the older women are not still doing films, but it's true that they have another barrier to face, not only while making their films but also in promoting them. On the other hand, you have to use the system, and this may be what some of the young women filmmakers are doing in this regard.

Question from the floor: Do you ever feel discouraged, as a woman filmmaker, to the point of giving up?

AW: In a way I did give up after I did four features in five years and couldn't get distribution for them. And I guess in a way I slid into television because I found it a lot more supportive of subjects that were of interest to me, and the producers were very supportive of letting me do creatively what I wanted to do. But of course I had the yen to get back to the big screen. I feel like I am not giving up at all. In fact, I have become a bit more aggressive and the film that we've just put out, *Better than Chocolate,* which just came back from Berlin, is very different from anything I've ever done before. It's sort of an attempt to grab a younger audience: it's a lesbian love story between two young women. It's very funny. It's full of music. Perhaps I'm bending my style to grab an audience, but I feel like it's what we have to do. And we did it for very, very little money. We structured it altogether differently. The main players of the film own the film, so we did it for less than what an episode of *X-Files* would cost. So, it was – "Okay, I'll try and make a film that makes money. Okay, so I'll have a lot of music, a fair amount of sex, beautiful young women. Let's go for it." And the film is very funny. I mean people do find it tremendously entertaining, and it's selling extremely well. It's sort of an attempt to make an entertaining kind of film, but it's also an attempt to get into the arena of money-making films.

What is happening is very depressing and we can get really, really down by it. But I guess I always get a glimmer of hope that the American market keeps aiming for the lowest common denominator, and there is a huge number of people out there that want something more intelligent, that want to be challenged a bit more by what they are watching. And I know my films are probably more accessible in the States than something that was put out in German or French as a first language. I'm continually getting letters and feedback from people who want to buy my films. I think there is a growing public out there that is becoming more aware, more cognizant of what it's missed out on and that is very tired of the formulas, the formula films that continually get played over and over again. So, I guess it's a matter of trying to identify that audience, helping them find something that's more interesting. Because there is a huge audience out there that's really tired of the American film.

HSB: As for me, I can say that I don't give up at all. Not giving up – I mean it's just trying to go as far you can go with what you want to do. And how you have to change yourself in order to go with what is possible. Just recently I went through a workshop on script writing – after having done so many films. It was given by a guy from Hollywood, and I just wanted to see what I could learn from him. Maybe he could have learned a lot from me, but I mean, why should I try and teach him? I wanted to learn how I could change my script according to the possibilities. And what I learned was that if you want to talk to a huge audience you have to talk in a simple way so that a huge audience can understand you. It's just wanting to reach as many people as possible and that's good, I think. We have grown up with a certain arrogance; the generation of the seventies was used to a certain audience, a highly cultured audience in Europe. But this audience is not there anymore. We have to find out how we can combine the knowledge of Hollywood – how to approach a big audience – with our cultural background.

PP: To give up – I don't think so. Because you love what you do so much that you don't want to stop. You still hope that you will be able to do what you would like. And myself, because I studied fine arts and have done quite a lot of painting and graphic design, when I feel frustrated waiting for finances, I go back to drawing some posters. I like writing a new script. And I'm now also producing a first feature for people younger than I. So, I'm still working more or less in cinema but sometimes doing something a little bit on the side. Last year, for instance, I was the artistic director for a big show in the Geneva museum about the education of young girls in Geneva during the last two centuries. So I had to find photographic and video documentation and such. I would prefer to shoot one feature film a year; that would be my dream. But if I have to wait a little bit more, I think I have many other things around that I can do that will nourish my work.

Filmographies

Patricia Plattner

1986   *La Dame de Pique.* Director, writer, producer (fiction, 22 min., 16 mm)
1989   *Piano Panier ou La recherche de l'équateur.* Director, writer, producer (fiction, 95 min., 35 mm blow up)
1990   *Des Tableaux qui bougent, portrait de G. Schwizqebel.* Director, writer

1991	*Le Sismographe, la lune et le léopard.* Director, writer, producer (documentary, S-Beta, 50 min.)
1993	*Le Hibou et la Baleine – Nicolas Bouvier.* Director, writer, producer (57 min., 16 mm, with Swiss TV)
1994	*Le Livre de Cristal.* Director, co-writer, producer (fiction, 110 min., 35 mm)
1996	*Hotel Abyssinie.* Director, co-writer (documentary, 61 min., 35 mm blow up)
1997	*Une Histoire qui enjambe les Alpes.* Director, writer (documentary, 38 min., video for Swiss TV)
1998	*Made in India.* Director, writer, producer (documentary, 91 min., 35 mm blow up)
1999	*Maéstro, Maéstro! Herbert Von Karajan.* Director, writer (documentary, 85 min., Beta D)
2002	*Les Petites Couleurs.* Director, producer (feature, 94 min., 35 mm)
2002	*Couleurs à vendre.* Director, writer, co-producer (documentary, 52 min., video)

Anne Wheeler (Films for Television and Theatrical Release)

1985-6	*Loyalties.* Director, co-producer (theatrical)
1987-8	*Cowboys Don't Cry.* Director, writer, associate producer (theatrical)
1988-9	*Bye Bye Blues.* Director, writer, producer (theatrical)
1989-90	*Angel Square.* Director, co-writer (theatrical)
1991-2	*The Diviners.* Director (feature-length TV)
1994	*Other Women's Children.* Director (feature-length TV)
1995	*The War Between Us.* Director, script editor (feature-length TV)
1996	*Mother Trucker: The Diana Kilmury Story.* Writer, producer (TV)
1997	*The Sleep Room.* Director, (miniseries for CBC TV)
1998	*Better than Chocolate.* Director (theatrical)
1999-2000	*Marine Life.* Director (theatrical)
2000-1	*Suddenly Naked.* Director, executive producer (theatrical)
2001	*Edge of Madness.* Director, writer (theatrical)
2001-2	*The Investigation.* Director (CTV Canada)

For **Helma Sanders Brahms**'s filmography, see Chapter 5.
For **Margarethe von Trotta**'s filmography, see Chapter 7.

19   Making Documentary Films: Panel Discussion with Nicole Giguère, Brenda Longfellow, Loretta Todd, and Aerlyn Weissman

Conducted by Michelle Bjornson

Michelle Bjornson, the facilitator of the following panel on documentary filmmaking with Canadian filmmakers, is herself a filmmaker. Her film on feminist educator Dr. E. Margaret Fulton, *A Round Peg*, won a Silver Apple Award in 1998 from the National Educational Media Network.

Nicole Giguère is a Quebec writer, producer, and filmmaker who has been involved in film and television for twenty-five years. Her many films range from documentaries on Quebec history, to women's humour, rock music, aging, and, most recently, the Barbie doll. (See Chapter 34, where she talks more about filmmaking in Quebec.)

Brenda Longfellow is a director, producer, and professor of film at York University, Ontario. Her documentary on poet Gwendolyn MacEwen won the 1999 Genie Award for Best Short Documentary. She has written extensively on feminist and Canadian cinema and is the co-editor of an anthology on Canadian women's cinema, *Gendering the Nation.*

Loretta Todd is a Vancouver-based First Nations filmmaker. Her films include *Forgotten Warriors* (nominated for Best Short Documentary at the Genie Awards in 1997), *Hands of History* (1994), and *The Learning Path* (1991). (See also Chapter 36.)

Aerlyn Weissman was co-director of the National Film Board's award-winning documentary *Forbidden Love: The Unashamed Stories of Lesbian Lives*

Panel at "Women Filmmakers: Refocusing" conference in Vancouver (1999), courtesy of Jacqueline Levitin. *Clockwise, from top left:* Nicole Giguère, Loretta Todd, Aerlyn Weissman, and Brenda Longfellow.

(1992) and has worked on film projects from Hollywood to the Himalayas. She has received two Gemini Awards for recording excellence. Currently, she mentors at the Gulf Islands Film and Television School on Galiano Island, British Columbia.

Michelle Bjornson: I am going to be asking some questions that I ask myself when I start films, coming from a filmmaker's point of view as opposed to an academic point of view. One of them is: How do you position yourself between the need to fill purely aesthetic or artistic concerns, and the ethics or the responsibility of portraying and documenting the subject or theme that you are dealing with?

Aerlyn Weissman: I mostly feel as though those two things are not separate. For me, the central ideas and metaphors of the piece that I am working on dictate the aesthetics. I try to start from putting my heart at the centre. That's a survival choice, because if your work takes two or four years to actually come to fruition, you had better love what you're doing. Once I am working from that place, the aesthetic choices – expressing those ideas, those situations, those stories – really come from there. They are not arbitrary. You are given the story, and you are chosen to tell the story as much as you choose to tell it, so you must listen to the demands of your material and often – always in fact – it tells you, even in some detail, how it wants to be told.

Loretta Todd: Trinh Minh-ha said something in *Woman, Native, Other* about existing "before the word" or existing "with the word." She was talking about writing, and I thought, well, that applies to making film, too. Do you exist before the making of the film or do you exist with the making of the film? So, in a sense, I would agree that the aesthetic definitely comes out of the experience of being in the story. However, as much as I'm trying to find a place to represent the story (the theme and the people who are a part of that story), I'm at the same time very conscious of commenting on what that story and their aesthetic mean to me. So I would have to say that I try to find a place for my voice. That might make my documentary style not different from anybody else's but definitely distinctly my own.

Nicole Giguère: I want to add that, for me, the content is very important because often, especially when you work for television, yours will be the only film for two or five years to be made on that subject. If you've got the money to do something on that subject, nobody else will be able to get it. So I have in mind that I should say all that is possible on the subject, but I have to say it my way, too. I've been making documentaries for twenty-five years now. With every film I try something new. There is always something to discover, or to learn, or to try. I find something every time. That is why I'm still making documentaries.

Brenda Longfellow: I think no one on this panel is an industrial kind of filmmaker, so that issue of form is something that is present in all of the work represented here, which is very unique in the field of documentary filmmaking. I am very interested in a kind of practice that thinks about its own form and the ways and the modes by which we tell histories. We are now at a time in women's film history when, unlike twenty years ago, the issue isn't so much "let us in, let us in." The issue is fighting for unique voices within the field of documentary filmmaking. Twenty years ago you could make a film on a Canada Council Grant with a little bit of money from the National Film Board. Now, almost exclusively, the only way to make documentaries is for television. We have to fight hard and long for aesthetic and artistic documentaries because the tendency in television is for very formulaic, very conventional, voice-of-god style narration, without any aesthetic vision at all.

MB: That leads into my next question: If you were asked to name a bias from which you make your films, what would that be?

AW: I'm a party girl [laughter]. I like to have fun with my work. I find it very difficult to do a piece about a person or a group of people that I really don't like and I really do not want to spend time with. I've liked the people in my work. I like their histories. I like their stories. I don't do confrontational or investigative type of work; it doesn't suit my interests or my temperament. I am sure I have other biases but that is a very important one and it's rarely discussed.

LT: I have been told, in a memo from a project that I worked on for the History Channel recently, that I am "too Native" and "too arty." I do not even know what being "too Native" means. I suspect other people would say that I am not Native enough. My bias is a thing about affection – allowing a personal relationship to develop within the making of the story, which tends to be contrary to what a documentary is supposed to be. A documentary is supposed to be about maintaining an objective distance from the story. Beyond that, my biases are aesthetic. I like a lot of movement, I like a lot of lighting – which means you can't just get things on the fly. You have to set up shots. You have to spend time ensuring you have the budget to arrange that kind of filmmaking. Often, the way things are going now, the money to do that isn't there. You then have to decide what you can achieve aesthetically with the budget that you have. I love the idea of the camera caressing the subject or the actor, whoever it happens to be. I like to spend time to create that kind of emotional landscape between the viewer and the subject.

NG: Filmmaking is a wonderful way to meet people and to discover things. When you arrive to prepare a film, or with a microphone or a camera, you ask questions of people you don't know. You can ask very intimate questions and go rapidly to a very strong relationship with people who otherwise you wouldn't meet in your daily life. I like to meet different people and to keep a relationship with those people. Aesthetically, I love music. I have written a lot of original songs in my work, so this would be my bias.

BL: I mainly work in biography, and all the biographies I have done have been about women, so I guess that is my bias. I am especially interested in historic subjects and using a biography as a way to think through as deeply as possible the contradictions that women live with. I've often chosen subjects where there has been dissonance between the public image of the woman and her private experience. Like *Shadow Maker,* my film about Gwendolyn MacEwen: she was a famous poet when she was nineteen years old and was considered to be very elegant, brilliant, much more of a public figure than Margaret Atwood at that point. But in her private life a lot of other things were going on. I am interested in thinking about how lives intersect with history, that field of feminist investigation where the private and the public intersect. I like to investigate the image while I am telling the story and to make people conscious of how images are found and retrieved and which images are missing. With biography, too, I am trying to preserve a sense of the mystery of the subject. That relates back to television, where so much is about information and making people believe that they have heard everything, and a closure is imposed on the subject. I like films that are more open-ended and leave questions with viewers.

MB: Do you make films differently from the hierarchical film model? What experience have you had with collaboration and its pitfalls and benefits?

AW: First, I'd have to say that men collaborate on their films but they don't call their collaborators co-directors. They call them researchers or associate producers. There is a certain level of fraud that goes on in that way. The so-called "solo artists" mostly aren't. In any case, we all know this process is actually collaborative. I think if you're working with someone that you have an ongoing communication with, it can't help but benefit your project. You have more eyes, more ears, and more sensibility. Now, having said that – maybe I'm just getting old and bossy or something – for the things I do now, I don't choose to collaborate. I was very happy with the collaborations that I did and it may happen again in the future, but I turn into a little Napoleon when I get on the set now.

MB: You've talked about the limitations of television. Can you comment on what you feel are the limitations right now that you face, either in your own personal development or the greater outside world that we are making films in?

AW: I think that the institutions that produce and fund our work have been cut back or have disappeared entirely. I'm thinking of Studio D at the National Film Board,[1] of those who now believe "PC" stands for "politically correct" rather than "politically conscious." Everything is for broadcast, and the implications of that, I think, are first of all a general dumbing down. Only a very narrow, moral universe is allowed to be presented on television, and there is an emphasis – it isn't new, but continues – on confrontation and sensationalism. Just try saying the words "portrait of a community" to a broadcaster and watch them glaze over like a doughnut. Communities, very specific communities, are briefly raided for their interesting stories for a presumed mainstream, White, middle-class, heterosexual audience. When you go back two years later to make another piece, you are told, "we've done a show on ____" (fill in the blank – any marginalized community). After Lynne Fernie and I did *Fiction and Other Truths: A Film About Jane Rule,* for the next two years Rudy Buttignol at TV Ontario told everybody who came to him with a portrait of a woman writer, "We've done that." He only stopped because Lynne cornered him at a party and, I think, threatened his life if he didn't stop [laughter]. You're told, after a few films have been made from your community, "Well, the playing field is all even now, and now you can go line up with all the American episodic stuff to get your little piece of the action," which all seems to feature aliens. Aliens never go out of style. So you think, maybe I should develop a script on gay and lesbian aliens. Which brings me back to dumbing down. I am being a bit facetious, but there is some truth in how all of that works in television.

LT: There was a golden era in Vancouver at the CBC in the documentary department that I came across when I was doing research for my biography of Chief Dan George. If you go to the archives and look at the films there – they were made primarily by White, middle-class men, with one woman, I think, working as an editor – they made some really remarkable films and experimental television. They were left alone by the bureaucracy in Toronto and most of their stuff never got national exposure. When I saw the dismantling of what's called the "golden era of television," it was not necessarily sad for me because I thought that perhaps we can rebuild something that reflects the kind of complexity that really exists in this country. But what is being rebuilt in the Canadian context of documentary and television is essentially very market-driven, and it definitely assumes a very limited scope and openness to different points of view in terms of the audience. There is no appreciation of the craft of filmmaking and experience. But if you say that in Canada, then "you are whining" – "you had your chance and now you should be giving other people this opportunity." I've stood many times behind many people and given them the opportunity to tell their own stories; I feel I've paid my dues that way. But this trend now of "Here's the money, go make a film" is a way of atrophying the real talent and the real experience that have been built up. Somebody comes along, and if they are prepared to do it cheaply, quickly, and without any depth, they get the money. I've definitely had some good experiences and some bad experiences in television. With the Chief Dan George biography, although it falls within a basic biography format, CBC gave me freedom to explore it in all kinds of different ways. On the other hand, I did a biography recently for the History Channel where that was not allowed at all. There was an expectation in terms of what the formula was and how that formula would be followed. People in the funding agencies now are not fighting for the same freedom that they enjoyed when they were making films.

NG: I am working with the Directors Association in Quebec and we are fighting with broadcasters. We are fighting with producers, too. Directors are the only ones on the crew without a union contract or the protection of basic conditions. But this must be very depressing for young people or students to hear. They always hear the same thing from us: "Oh, it's very hard to find money, it's getting harder and harder." Trying to say something positive, I could say we are getting to see more and more documentaries. Even if it's not the kind of documentaries that we like to make, there is an opening right now because of the new channels on TV that focus on documentaries. Wherever we look internationally, in France or in Europe, there's more recognition of documentaries. That is the good news.

BL: Fifteen or twenty years ago there was a non-theatrical circuit. There were rep houses and theatres that would show documentaries in 16 millimetre. I teach at a university. We show nothing in 16 millimetre anymore; everything is video. What that means is that, where feminist documentary filmmaking was about building communities, especially in the first stages, like other kinds of political filmmaking, now with television it is also about commodification. CTV [a private network] did a series a couple of years ago called *Women: A True Story*. Huge amounts of money were spent on it. It was billed as their radical, feminist entry into private broadcasting prime time, and it was a disaster. Many of the directors left, some were fired, it was a tremendous problem. What has to be negotiated is that fine line between getting attention and commodifying women as a kind of specular interest. A number of documentaries have been produced over the last little while about women in washrooms or the silly things that women do – that's commodification. It's moving outside of the feminist movement. It addresses an interest in women's lives but in a totally commodifying, exhibitionist way. European channels are better. Channel Four in the UK, for example, has a stream called *Out on Tuesday* of gay and lesbian work. They commission a lot of really interesting films. There's no reason why that can't be done in Canada. That's what has to be pushed. But it's a very difficult and sometimes dangerous struggle.

AW: It's good to think about some of those larger contexts. I do some teaching and mentoring at GIFTS, the Gulf Islands Film and Television School. Something like 300 kids a year come through a program where, in small teams, they make a five-minute video – think of the idea, write it, storyboard it, shoot it, cut it, and then show it – in a week. And the quality of the work is stunning. The kids are an inspiration to work with. Multiply that by the number of ads you see every week for film schools and various media programs. The second most popular course of study in the United States today (the first one is business) is television and media. Enormous numbers of young people are becoming involved with this field, with the art and the way that we communicate today. This is possible in part because of the changes in technology. Digital video has revolutionized filmmaking. I've heard people say, "What am I going to tell all these kids? There are only sixteen story editor jobs in this country." Well, I can say they are not after your story editor job. They are going to create their own realities and their own worlds of media communication. At GIFTS, these videos go directly to broadcast on the Internet. That, to me, is the hope of the future – to hear the voices that we have not been able to hear because of issues around access. But on the other end of all this – if you look at the business pages – BC Tel is now BC Telus, AT&T is now part of something else, and America Online is now alive in Netscape. At the same time we're seeing an enormous concentration of corporate ownership of the outlets for our work. There is a fragmentation and, at the same time, increasing control, and it's a bottom-line economic agenda. It is not a people-community-growing-awareness-learning agenda. Quite the contrary. It's not in their interest for anyone to get too enlightened about anything. We are caught in the middle now, and it's going to be very interesting to see how things shake out.

LT: I guess I am sort of a classicist within my cultural context, within the cultural community of Aboriginal expression, where song and dance and story and creating were available to everybody to do, and there was no distinction between creating and everyday life. Still, there were certain people who were valued for their ability to have visions and to interpret dreams, who functioned as visionaries. Those people served a very central purpose within the community as being part of the continuum, being able to express certain principles by which we lived our life, such as our covenant with the Creator, like our relationship to other beings within the universe.[2] I think what makes filmmakers great is the willingness to embrace that role of visionary and dreamer and to be able to interpret something back to the people. When I spoke to the students studying film, I said the thing about Canada is that you're always told that you are not great. You are not allowed to embrace your greatness. So how can you find it within yourself to be able to serve the people? As a classicist – that is, coming from a tradition in which my skill as a storyteller is really based on how good I was at learning the skills of the storytellers who came before me – when students aren't interested, for example, in the work of editors in the past, I think it's a real shame. An Aboriginal channel has been recently announced, and it will be interesting to see whether it's able to do that – if it's able to create the sort of transformative mechanism within Canada that people talked about when radio and broadcasting first came into being. Not just for Aboriginal people but for the whole concept of broadcasting in and of itself.

Notes

1   See Diane Burgess's chapter on Studio D, Chapter 38, this volume.
2   For more on this subject, see Chapter 37, this volume.

Filmographies

Michelle Bjornson (Director)

1986   *Cheek to Cheek* (experimental drama, 6 min., 16 mm)
1987   *End of the Game* (drama, 17 min., 16 mm)
1990   *The Mailboat Doesn't Stop Here Any More* (docu-drama, 30 min., 16 mm)
1993   *It Will Not Last the Night* (documentary, 60 min., 16 mm)
1997   *A Round Peg* (documentary, 60 min., Beta SP)

Brenda Longfellow

1987   *Our Marilyn*. Writer, director, optical printer (27 min., 16 mm)
1992   *Gerda*. Writer, director (feature, 88 min., 16 mm)
1996   *A Balkan Journey: Fragments from the Other Side War*. Writer, director, co-producer (52 min., 16 mm)
1998   *Shadow Maker/Gwendolyn MacEwen, Poet*. Writer, director (56 min., 16 mm)
2002   *Tina in Mexico*. Writer, director, editor (83 min., 16 mm)

Loretta Todd

1991   *The Learning Path*. Writer, director (53 min., 16 mm)
1994   *Hands of History*. Writer, director (52 min., 16 mm)
1997   *Forgotten Warriors*. Writer, director (51 min., 16 mm)
1998   *Today Is a Good Day – Remembering Chief Dan George*. Writer, director, producer (45 min., Beta SP)

Aerlyn Weissman

1987   *A Winter Tan*. Co-director, sound (drama, 91 min.)
1992   *Forbidden Love: The Unashamed Stories of Lesbian Lives*. Co-director (84 min.)
1995   *Fiction and Other Truths: A Film About Jane Rule*. Co-director (57 min.)
2002   *Little Sister's vs. Big Brothers*. Director (documentary)

Nicole Giguère – see Chapter 34

Part 5

Women's Films through a Postcolonial Lens

While Parts 1 through 4 dealt with film history, theory, and filmmakers mainly from Europe or North America, the second half of this book looks at film cultures within other contexts, including Asian, African, and Latin American countries, as well as at films by members of minority communities in Canada and elsewhere. These chapters bear out Ann Kaplan's claim in Chapter 1 that, currently, the creative energy of these new filmmakers is transforming the world of cinema and providing a counter-trend to mainstream Hollywood movies.

African cinema is represented by two Kenyan filmmakers who are discussed by Beatrice Wanjiku Mukora. One, Wanjiru Kinyanjui, was trained in Europe and received foreign funding to make *Battle of the Sacred Tree*, whereas the other, Anne Mungai, studied filmmaking in Kenya, and her film *Saikati* was made with fewer resources. Both represent African women caught between "traditional" customs and Western influences. But Mukora uses African feminist theory to demonstrate that these dichotomies are not fixed and simply gender-based. According to non-Western models, we can understand the heroines of these women filmmakers as living multiple and complex identities.

In Malaysia, where a film industry has existed since the 1930s, it is only recently that film has been seen as a means to represent and construct a national identity. Gaik Cheng Khoo discusses the work of Malay filmmaker Shuhaimi Baba and other members of the Malaysian "New Wave." The cultural results of economic and political developments are as striking here as they are in Eastern Europe, and they are taking place in a multiracial context where the government subsidizes Malay productions to compete with "Bollywood" as well as Hollywood. Baba's films incorporate Malay custom, including notions of sexuality, in order to reinforce a Malay cultural identity resistant to revivalist Islam as well as to Western homogenization. Her female characters remain Malay while embracing modernity, in a balancing act reiterated in all three of her films, including one that features a young filmmaker taking up the mantle of an illustrious female veteran of cinema.

A team of four specialists in Hispanic studies, led by Rita de Grandis of the University of British Columbia, presents the films of Argentinian director María Luisa Bemberg, which are often set in the historical past. Three are discussed: *Miss Mary; I, the Worst of All;* and *I Don't Want to Talk about It*. All three provide insights into the intersections of gender, power, and knowledge in various situations. Her representations of women range from members of a traditional patriarchal household, to an exceptional nun, to the relationship between a powerful small-town storekeeper and her "abnormal" daughter. The scene in Argentina is very different from that in Cuba. Susan Lord provides an overview of the documentaries made by Afro-Cuban Sara Gómez (best known for her feature film *De cierta manera/One Way or Another*). Lord demonstrates how Gómez raised gender and ethnic issues in a changing revolutionary context.

The final chapter in Part 5 consists of a presentation/interview by Agnes Huang and Larissa Lai with Chinese filmmaker Yue-Qing Yang, who now lives in Vancouver. Yang's *Nu Shu: A Hidden Language of Women in China* was well received at the "Women Filmmakers: Refocusing" conference, where she also talked about her attempts to make a film on footbinding. In this case, film serves literally to document the recent history of a generation of women before it disappears. As a transnational filmmaker, Yue-Qing connects Part 5 to Part 6, which deals with crossing cultural boundaries.

20 Beyond Tradition and Modernity: Representations of Identity in Two Kenyan Films

Beatrice Wanjiku Mukora

> Africa is in search of an identity. We are divided in ourselves between the past African tradition and the more recent, but widely approved, Western ones. In all walks of life, we are split.
>
> — Wanjiru Kinyanjui, Kenyan filmmaker

Although Kenya has one of the oldest film industries in Africa, it continues to occupy a narrow space in film scholarship. In fact, the Anglo-African film scene in general, with the exception of Ghana and Nigeria, remains one of the most under-theorized areas in African cinema. The film industry in Kenya has its roots in the British colonial administration where it was introduced to produce educational tools. Today, it is an active industry producing local films that deal with the turmoil of post-independence. These films, like most African films, reflect the cultural way of life of Kenyans who continue to deal with the tension between tradition and modernity.

As human beings, we are involved in a constant process of redefining ourselves according to our experiences, background, gender, kinship, and even geography. Why do we need an identity? The process of redefinition is a means of keeping us balanced and addressing the different experiences that we encounter. As redefinition draws in historical and present experiences, it allows us to shape the future. As many scholars interested in studies of identity formation agree, presuming the precarious nature of identity is key to comprehending that we are constantly between worlds or phases. Stuart Hall points out that "identities are never unified, [but rather] increasingly fragmented and fractured; never singular but multiply constructed across different, often intersecting and antagonistic discourses, practices and positions. They are subject to a radical historicization, and are constantly in the process of change and transformation."[1] For once-colonized people, identity is linked to phenomena that are embedded in historical colonial practices and the aftermath of postcolonialism.

The presence of colonial structures engendered tensions between tradition and modernity. For example, urbanization as a product of colonialism is a great force, and it continues to incite these tensions. Still today, Africans straddle the two "models" of tradition and modernity. The tension generated by these opposing models is basic to cultural production as it is represented in literary work, film, and theatre in almost all colonized African nations. The process of rediscovering identity by positioning oneself between oppositions has been symbolic and thematic in Kenyan cinema and literature.

Ngugi wa Thiong'o, a Kenyan scholar and writer, has touched on this issue through the representation of his characters. Muthoni, in his novel, *The River Between,* is presented as a woman located between two ideological positions: Christianity and "traditional" (pre-colonial) Kikuyu religion. Although her father is a steadfast Christian, she continues to embrace traditional Kikuyu values and practices because they accord her an identity within a larger cultural and ethnic society. Two films, Wanjiru Kinyanjui's *Battle of the Sacred Tree* (1994) and Anne Mungai's *Saikati* (1992) similarly revolve around women who, like Muthoni, find solace in traditional values while engaging in so-called "modern" practices. The tension between the opposing models and the features they contain is both expression and symptom of the postcolonial state. A comparison of the two filmmakers' backgrounds in film training offers an interesting case that helps to elucidate these so-called oppositions.

Wanjiru Kinyanjui received her film training in Europe. Her film, largely financially supported, produced, and distributed by two European film companies – Birne Film (Germany) and Flamingo Films (France) – is of higher quality and has a more focused plot than does Anne Mungai's *Saikati.* Anne Mungai was trained in film at the Kenya Institute of Mass Communication. With poor financial support and distribution (both coming primarily from the Kenya Institute), and with equipment from the Fredrick Engel Foundation, *Saikati* suffers from a digressive plot and substandard levels of production. Nonetheless, one could discern that, with modern filming equipment, *Saikati* would have been as good a film as *Battle.* I must, therefore (as advised by a colleague), "cut Mungai some slack" ideologically and focus on the film's content.

According to Mbye Cham, "in *Saikati,* its numerous technical and artistic shortcomings notwithstanding, Anne Mungai attempts a balanced look at female sexuality in urban Kenya and at both the 'push' and the 'pull' factors that account for the rural urban drift."[2] Both films serve as a rich resource for understanding the complexities of the postcolonial situation, the multiple locations of postcolonial subjects. Their narratives focus on the prime symptom of the postcolonial state – the breakdown of nationalism – in order to raise questions of identity through an investigation of class, ethnicity, gender, age group, and sexuality.

Like postindependence African novels, postindependence films struggle to represent indigenous experiences. They illustrate the contested aspects of contemporary, partially urbanized Kenyan society, and attempt to centre peripheral subjects. Both *Saikati* and *Battle* work against depictions of

African women as ineffectual figures occupying the margins of human activity. However, to avoid generalization and slippage, it is important to emphasize that the representations of gender and sexuality vary in the two films according to the different agendas and goals of the respective filmmakers.

In this chapter I wish to examine two major phenomena. The first involves how both films inscribe women within the clashes of tradition and modernity, within the complexities of these spaces and their inherent contradictions. I contend that binarisms such as urban/rural, modern/traditional, and so on are artificially created and furthered by the Western value system – a system that continues to prevail in postcolonial Africa and that is reflected in African films. The second, and related, phenomenon involves looking at how African feminist thought is engaged with the cultural conditions that predominate in Kenyan cinema and, in so doing, reveals binary oppositions as spurious constructs. In women's pursuit of self-definition and self-determination, it is imperative that they move beyond set dichotomies by making use of their multiple identities and influences, all of which are located on a continuum between tradition (at one end) and modernity (at the other).

Manthia Diawara makes a valid point when he posits that African films belong to a social realist narrative tradition that tends to "thematise current socio-cultural issues,"[3] thereby joining in the contestation of, and struggle for identity within, the postcolonial site. According to Diawara, "social realist films" are a reflection of these forms of tension. Situating and elaborating these tensions is central to this chapter, which hopes to understand the ongoing conflicts faced by postcolonial subjects like Muthoni.

African feminism, according to Obioma Nnaemeka, "establishes its identity through resistance – it *is* because it *resists.*"[4] Her concern is that Western versions of feminism may have proven ineffectual within the African context because African women have a different set of priorities. She points to the "most recurrent and contentious areas of disagreement and resistance – radical feminism, motherhood, language, sexuality, priorities, (gender) separatism, and *universalism.*"[5] Although Nnaemeka agrees that "feminist scholarship remains one of the most powerful critical and analytical tools with immense possibilities for fostering intellectual maturity and social change,"[6] the frequent inappropriateness of its aims has allowed African women theorists to create a new structure of analysis – one that omits the questionable and presumptuous conceptual frameworks that external feminist theories have imposed upon African women's experience.

The intervention of African feminist theory has challenged dominant discourses grounded in Western thought, while making a concerted effort to reclaim both the individuality and heterogeneity of African subjects. According to Sheila Petty, who believes that this movement is just beginning to gain momentum, the heated debates indicate that the African feminist framework is applicable to African cinema, especially since African film-makers, like African writers, commonly use devices such as decentred narra-tive structures (drawn from oral tradition) to tell their stories (personal communication, 14 December 1998). African feminist theorists have inter-vened powerfully in order to elaborate the significance of complexities, para-doxes, and possibilities of difference.

Nnaemeka suggests that the binary divisions that are set out in literature by feminist authors should not be interpreted as oppositional but, rather, as complementary because "they give life, vibrancy and meaning."[7] The inter-stitial space, often seen as ambiguous and grey, is where meaning represents the complexities and multiplicity of postcolonial subjects. The dotted boundaries of this space allow the conflation of features that are seemingly positioned as polar opposites. The women in these films can be viewed as accommodating their individual experiences to changing socio-cultural cir-cumstances rather than as being in conflict with them.

I maintain that conceptual frameworks must be contained within an Af-rican context. It is only logical that feminist theories emerging from Afri-can discourses and experiences should be inherently African. I have chosen to call upon African feminist theories because, first, they provide a theoreti-cal base from which the "gaze" is African rather than African-filtered-through-Western-eyes, and, second, because they break African dependency upon Western theory (Sheila Petty, personal communication, 14 December 1998). African feminist approaches to theory examine the themes and topics that engage women writers and filmmakers, their language and characteriza-tion, the forms they use, and their images.

Saikati

Saikati is primarily a story about a Maasai girl (named Saikati) who is being forced to marry the chief's son. The marriage would entail an end to the possibility of her gaining an education. Her cousin Monica, who is from Nairobi (the capital of Kenya), comes to the Mara (the rural area where Saikati and her family live) for a visit and discovers Saikati's predicament. Monica offers Saikati a solution: return with her to Nairobi, find employ-ment there, and assist her family financially. With Saikati's mother's con-sent, after hefty persuasion, they set out for Nairobi early next morning.

Saikati soon discovers that her cousin is a prostitute and that, together with her lover, Hamish, she has covertly planned a similar job for her. Scared and alienated, she decides to return to the Mara and the comfort of her family. Alex, a British tourist whom Monica had arranged to initiate Saikati into the world of prostitution, feels badly about how events have turned out and offers her a ride back to her village. The journey from Nairobi to the Mara is met with obstacles, some posed solely by Monica's stubbornness.

Finally, Saikati returns to the Mara, where her family receives her with joy. We lose sight of Monica and the British tourists and assume that she continues to be "trapped" in the urban life and the profession of prostitution. The film leaves the viewer content that Saikati appears to have finally found her identity and sense of self through the unprecedented journey to Nairobi and back, which she has come to view as an "ill-conceived attempt to run away from forced marriage."[8]

Saikati is replete with binary oppositions. The opening of the film forecasts the dilemmas to be represented throughout. We see Saikati in her school uniform, which symbolizes the so-called modern institution of learning. She then changes into Maasai dress upon returning to the *manyatta,* the Maasai traditional dwelling place. This is resonant of Ngugi wa Thiong'o's description of the schizophrenic colonial child who is taught English at school but who switches to the language and cultural practices of the family when he/she returns to his/her compound.[9]

As Sheila Petty points out, "*Saikati* evolved out of Mungai's own personal experiences within the dichotomies of tradition and modernity in Kenyan society."[10] For Mungai, women's issues reflect the struggle between the traditional and the modern. In an interview with Mbye Cham at the Second Annual Festival of African Cinema in Milan, Mungai describes the trap within which rural women find themselves: "Most women marry early and sometimes not out of their own consent. Because they marry early and then start having children early, and these children in turn, marry early, the trend of women getting no education just goes on and on. Okay, traditionally, the culture is one where every woman is born looking forward to getting married, but you can still get educated and get a husband."[11]

The questionable generalization of the last statement notwithstanding, Mungai rightly describes women in rural areas as receiving little or no education. The urban lifestyle, with its rewards of money and pleasure, is what lures rural girls like Monica to the city. In the same interview, Mungai agreed that there are other reasons why girls like Monica abandon rural life for the city (e.g., lack of money for tuition, early pregnancy). She maintains, however, that "Saikati could have chosen to follow the *good* city life, but she chose to go back home because she had *a goal* to achieve."[12]

The condemnation of city life brings one back to Diawara's argument that social realist films present the issues of difference from a traditional position. Mungai represents the disadvantages of the rural life as she is well aware that girls in rural areas have no opportunities for education or for ultimately bettering the lives of their families and relatives. At the same time, at the film's end/turning point, Monica, the disenchanted urbanite who confuses liberation (i.e., from the stranglehold of forced marriage) with prostitution, recedes into the background with the British tourists. Saikati

Wanjiru Kinyanjui's *Battle of the Sacred Tree* (1995)

begins to negotiate her identity within the urban setting and to recognize that the *good* life of the bright-lit city is an illusion. It is here that her process of self-determination begins: although she rejects tradition, she cannot physically situate herself within the ultra-modern site of Nairobi. Saikati effectively goes beyond the oppositions of tradition and modernity by not being imprisoned within either; that is, in going to the city she gives up tradition, but only in order to continue her education (embracing modernity). I contend that *Saikati*'s point is that binarisms should be avoided. Saikati ultimately comes to believe that she must return to the village (i.e., embrace tradition) and find a solution to her desire for education (i.e., retain modernity) without losing her indigenous identity. In a sense, Mungai does not so much create a binary opposition as challenge its existence.

Battle of the Sacred Tree

Battle of the Sacred Tree reflects the clashes between Christianity and Kikuyu religious practices. The main character, Mumbi, leaves Nairobi for Githunguri, a rural area outside the city, in order to escape her husband's physical (and mental) abuse. Early one morning, together with her daughter, she returns to her father's house. Chagrined by her decision to leave her affluent husband, her father questions her about it. Mumbi explains that she could no longer withstand her husband's drunken behaviour and that she needed to be independent. Her father, failing to grasp her logic, dismisses her, proclaiming, "To be independent is to be proud."

In her efforts to be productive in her new home, Mumbi opts to join the Christian's women union, which engages in income-generating projects. While the Christian women deliberate over Mumbi's induction into their committee, they are not able to forget that she dishonoured the Christian institution of marriage: "a woman who cannot keep a husband is definitely a prostitute." As a result of this debate, an old acquaintance offers Mumbi employment at the local bar. Reacting to her unrighteous decision to take this job, the committee rejects Mumbi's application, equating her new-found job with promiscuity. A dispute then occurs between the Christian women and Mumbi concerning the *Mugumo* tree, which the women believe is representative of backward and primitive ways of worshipping. As one of the committee women declares, "the tree reminds us of the days of darkness." Mumbi and her father (who practises traditional medicine) find themselves aligned as both are against the cutting down of the tree, which symbolizes a facet of Kikuyu history. Mumbi's faction wins the battle and the tree remains standing in Githunguri.

Mumbi, like Saikati, is caught between lifestyles located at opposite ends of a binary axis – a polarization that serves to blur the complex relationship between them. She makes use of an array of identities and a multiplicity of positions in order to challenge both modern and traditional concepts, both of which serve to conceal the history of women and the Kikuyu people. For example, she challenges the subordinate position of the lowly abused wife, a position that her father seems to feel is traditional. Resisting this type of objectification, she points to a goat and asks her father, *"Agorire ta bori erea?"* ("Did he buy me like that goat?").

African feminist theory maintains that the most important challenge to the African woman remains "her own self-perceptions since it is she who has to define her own freedom" and take responsibility for her own self-determination. Thus, postcolonial women need to challenge both the gender hierarchies and the dominant power structures within their communities.[13]

In order to cultivate and negotiate an identity, Mumbi confronts hermetically closed structures (not necessarily patriarchal or Western) that go beyond notions of binaries. Nnaemeka points out that the "African woman is a creation of historical and current forces that are simultaneously internally generated and externally induced."[14] Mumbi's choice to work at the bar, and her determination not to have the tree cut down, are influenced by external and internal factors that, if placed as either traditional or modern, would be rendered reductionist.

An African Feminist Framework

An African feminist framework serves to develop an African female aesthetic because it simultaneously demands a new examination of the principles of composition and expression.[15] It takes into account the fact that certain inequities and limitations existed/exist within traditional societies and that, while colonialism reinforced them, it also introduced others.[16] Furthermore, an African feminist framework recognizes a common struggle with African men to remove the yoke of foreign domination and European/

American exploitation.[17] *Battle* offers a clear example of this when the men and women work together to reject the women's Christian union's demands that the *Mugumo* tree be cut down. Mumbi and Wanjiku (an employee of one of the Christian women) work together with her father, the chief of the town, the headmaster of a local school, and the men who frequent the bar in order to undermine the Christian women's campaign.

Priorities that other models of feminism decry as forms of oppression or victimization – such as motherhood, the resilience of men and women to colonial oppression, woman-to-woman violence, and female power hierarchies – are central in African feminism. Nnaemeka advocates replacing the male/female dichotomy with a "matrix of domination" because this "focuses on the nexus of interlocking systems of oppression where oppressor/ oppressed positions shift."[18] This approach is useful because it transcends gender, providing a flexible way of looking at hierarchies within either gender. Furthermore, in *Battle,* to speak of the Christian women and Mumbi as equals because they both belong to the rural sphere would be useless because difference in religious orientation is more critical than are identities of gender and/or location.

African feminism attacks the static binary divisions that prevailed during colonialism and neocolonialism because they conceal complexities and the various differences between women. The intervals and interstices in between the dichotomies are key in illustrating that the binarisms in both films are by no means neatly separated dichotomies. Multiple identities co-exist, with a plurality of affiliations in between them. Saikati is at once rural and urban, and Mumbi displays characteristics traditionally attributed to men.

African feminism's adherence to the traditional is grounded in the desire to choose and to control one's life without having to give up what is African in one's identity. Women like Saikati, Mumbi, and Muthoni are concerned with equity rather than repudiation or adherence to the traditional. Perhaps both filmmakers, in their effort to rehumanize their characters, are asking whether their cultures should not evolve so as to contain all that any African woman can be. The difficulties inherent within postcolonial definitions, therefore, can be rescued by employing African feminist thought as presented by such people as Nnaemeka, Davies, or Nfah-Abbenyi, all of whom agree that it is misleading to argue about women in postcolonial terms.

Petty warns that "ideally an African feminist film should strive not simply to synthesize feminist and pan-African ideas but to balance concerns so that binary oppositions are not created wherein one term takes precedence over another" (personal communication, 19 February 1999). The foregrounding of ambivalence does not necessarily negate any particular lifestyle but, instead, points to the individualization of the subject. In an interview at the Biannual FESPACO in Ouagadougou, Petty asked Anne Mungai whether she considered herself a feminist and whether *Saikati* was a feminist film. Mungai responded as follows:

> That is very difficult to say because in my country, when you say you're feminist you are saying that you want to be like a man. In those terms, I do not agree. I do not believe I'm like a man. What I believe in I do not exactly call it feminism, and this is what comes out in my film. I don't know if you'd call it feminism, but what I believe and what I wanted to show in my film is that although men, according to culture are in charge, women have to have a say. When you're not allowed to express your feelings, it is a kind of oppression. I just believe that it is a human right for women to talk, to be allowed to have a voice. That is what I am advocating in my film and that is what I believe in. Women must be given a voice. (Interview with Sheila Petty, 27 February 1993, Ouagadougou)

African feminist approaches continue to challenge dominant discourses grounded in Western thought, while making a concerted effort to reclaim the individuality and heterogeneity of subjects. To construe that Kenyans are a monolithic group, both fixed and static, is to deny the difference and diversity that exist in the local milieu. Additionally, to construe that African female subjects adhere to either construct (tradition or modernity) is to simplify the paradoxes and dilemmas that beset women in the multiplicity of positions.

This chapter began by positing that the effects of colonialism are articulated through film and literary work because both are interested in rewriting Kenyan history while simultaneously celebrating and critiquing precolonial traditions. Indigenous filmmaking in Kenya began as a counter-colonial discourse similar to that found in the work of such novelists as Meja Mwangi, Grace Ogot, and Ngugi wa Thiong'o. Working against the grain of colonial discourse is a preoccupation of African feminist theorists, as is the deconstruction of the lingering binarisms that limit our ability to understand the vagaries and frustrations of postcolonial women.

Notes
1 Stuart Hall, "Who Needs 'Identity'?" In *Questions of Cultural Identity*, ed. Stuart Hall and Paul du Gay (London: Sage, 1996), 4.
2 Mbye Cham, "African Women and Cinema: A Conversation with Anne Mungai," *Research in African Literature* 25 (Fall 1994): 93-104.
3 Manthia Diawara, *African Cinema: Politics and Culture* (Bloomington and Indianapolis: Indiana University Press, 1992), 141.
4 Obioma Nnaemeka, "Sisterhood, Feminisms, and Power: From Africa to the Diaspora," in *Sisterhood, Feminisms, and Power: From Africa to the Diaspora*, ed. O. Nnaemeka (Trenton: Africa World Press, 1997), 6 (emphasis in original).

5 Ibid. (emphasis mine).
6 Obioma Nnaemeka, "Feminism, Rebellious Women and Cultural Boundaries: Rereading Flora Nwapa and her Compatriots." *Research in African Literature* 26, 2 (Summer 1995): 81.
7 Nnaemeka, "Sisterhood, Feminisms, and Power," 3.
8 Sheila Petty, "How an African Woman Can Be: African Women Filmmakers Construct Women," *Discourse* 18, 3 (Spring 1996): 85.
9 Ngugi wa Thiong'o, *Decolonising the Mind: The Politics of Language in African Literature* (London: James Currey, 1986).
10 Petty, "How an African Woman Can Be," 83.
11 Cham, "African Women and Cinema," 99.
12 Ibid., 100 (emphasis mine).
13 Juliana Makuchi Nfah-Abbenyi, *Gender in African Women's Writing: Identity, Sexuality, and Difference* (Bloomington: Indiana University Press, 1997), 31.
14 Nnaemeka, "Sisterhood, Feminisms, and Power," 14.
15 Carole Boyce Davies, "Introduction: Feminist Consciousness and African Literary Criticism," in *Ngambika: Studies of Women in African Literature,* ed. Carole Boyce Davies and Anne Adams Graves (Trenton, NJ: African World Press, 1986), 15.
16 Ibid., 9.
17 Ibid., 8.
18 Nnaemeka, "Sisterhood, Feminisms, and Power," 20.

Filmographies

Wanjiru Kinyanjui
1987   *... When Joined by a Stranger* (documentary, video)
1988   *A Lover and Killer of Colour* (short fiction)
1988   *The Reunion* (video)
1990   *The Bird with the Broken Wing* (video)
1991   *African Time* (documentary)
1992   *Black in the Western World* (documentary)
1992   *Clara Has Two Countries* (video)
1993   *Vitico – a Living Legend* (documentary)
1995   *Battle of the Sacred Tree* (feature)
1996-7 *Shot in Nairobi* (TV)
        Daudi's Dream (feature, video)
        Kenyan Teenage Girls (documentary)

Anne Mungai
1980   *Nkomani Clinic* (short)
1980   *The Beggar's Husband* (short)
1981   *The Tomorrow's Adult Citizens* (short)
1982   *Together We Build* (short feature)
1986   *Wekesa at Crossroads* (short feature)
1990   *Productive Farmlands* (short)
1991   *Faith* (short)
1991   *Root 1* (52 min.)
1993   *Saikati* (feature)
1993   *Pongezi* (short)
1994   *Usilie Mtoto wa Africa/Don't Cry Child of Afrika* (43 min.)
1998   *Tough Choices* (52 min.)
1998   *Saikati The Enkabaani* (feature)

21 Shuhaimi Baba and the Malaysian New Wave: Negotiating the Recuperation of Malay Custom (Adat)

Gaik Cheng Khoo

Malaysia has had a minor film industry since the 1930s. Traditionally considered as commercial entertainment, it is only in the last twenty years that the medium of film has been explored by filmmakers and cultural and film critics as a discursive form representing national identity. More important, the work of ethnic Malay filmmakers of the Malaysian New Wave in the 1990s demonstrates both a conscious and unconscious desire to recover the indigenous roots of Malay culture. This recuperation takes a different form for female filmmakers than it does for male filmmakers. I will explore this difference by examining the films of New Wave female filmmaker Shuhaimi Baba. However, to better understand the motivations behind the New Wave filmmakers' cultural work, I will first provide some general information on Malaysia and its film industry.

Background on Malaysia

The need to archive and recuperate the past stems from the effects of a state-led modernization project that rapidly thrust Malaysia from developing nation status (during the 1970s) to its current status as an emerging tiger economy (beginning in the early to mid-1990s). Among many things, modernity meant urbanization and mass migration from rural areas to cities as people sought work in the manufacturing sector as opposed to the agricultural sector. The present effects of modernity must be attributed to the success (or partial success) of the National Economic Policy (NEP), which was instituted in 1971 after the race riots between the Chinese and the Malay populations on 13 May 1969. The ethnic social make-up of Malaysia today consists roughly of 60 percent indigenous Muslim Malays, 30 percent Chinese, 9 percent Indians, and 1 percent "others" (Eurasians, foreigners, etc.). Based on the theory that economic disparity between the Chinese and Malays was largely responsible for the race riots, the NEP was an affirmative action plan whose purpose was to redistribute wealth, then largely accumulated in the pockets of foreigners and Chinese, to the indigenous Malays.[1] The NEP's success is reflected in the birth of a broad, wealthy, predominantly urban Malay middle class that has access to higher education in local and foreign universities. This modernity, which is akin to Westernization, has also implied a focus on the individual subject, thus raising awareness of issues concerning individual freedoms and women's rights, and leading to the Domestic Violence Act, 1994. It is also a period that has seen an increase in divorce cases and, as AIDS emerges within public forums, an awareness of sexuality.

Malaysian Cinema

As noted earlier, filmmaking in Malaysia dates back to the 1930s. In a way, the ethnic division of labour within the early Malay studio system (1930-70) reflected the division of ethnic social spheres in colonial Malaya. Chinese entrepreneurs – the Shaw Brothers, Ho Ah Loke, and Loke Wan Tho of Cathay Keris – owned the two major studios during the 1950s. Behind the all-Malay cast were hired directors from India and film crews from Hong Kong, both national groups having had a much longer film tradition and more experience with cinema production than had Malayans. While, by the 1960s, more Malays gradually moved "backstage" into the arena of directing films, few non-Malays worked as actors, as the dialogue then and now is conducted in Malay so as to cater to a Malay majority audience. When the studio era ended in the late 1960s, Malay cinema entered a decade-long slump. During the "Independent Era," from 1976 to 1986, the NEP sense of national pride motivated individual Malay actors, with the help of Malay politicians, to turn their hand to the economic venture of film production and filmmaking.[2] Malays began to dominate the industry at all levels not just as performers, but also as producers, directors, and screenwriters. At the same time, government support for the local film industry was slow to take off. Nevertheless, by 1992 there were signs of a revival in the sagging Malay film industry, with the advent of young Malay filmmaker Aziz M. Osman's controversial film *Fantasia*.[3] Malaysian critics have hailed the 1990s group of filmmakers "The Malaysian New Wave." In step with contemporary globalizing influences, Hollywood dominates local cinemas and video stores. Malaysian filmmakers who were sent overseas under the NEP to study returned to make films influenced by Western classical cinema. Generally, Malaysian film and television productions over the last two decades have been very commercial, using urban settings that are similar to the hegemonic urban society that most Malaysians have come to inhabit. While, in the past, "the film contents and styles were Indian and the dialects were a mixture of bazaar Malay, Indonesian and Chinese,"[4] today, the language used is official Bahasa Malaysia (Malay), with some English words thrown in for a modern effect.

Despite the influences from Hollywood and "Bollywood" (Bombay cinema, specifically, Hindi musicals), some filmmakers, such as U-Wei Hj. Shaari, Adman Salleh, Shuhaimi Baba, and Mahadi J. Murat, strive to give Malaysian cinema a more unique artistic and commercial identity – an identity that would reflect Malaysia's place within global modernity. By "global modernity," I refer not only to the Hollywood style of filmmaking or storytelling

serum hidup mereka

dibelai harapan dan

kasih halus

menyelubungi pengorbanan

dan perjuangan

menentang kebencian

dan pengkhianatan

se/ubung

SHUHAIMI BABA

Advertisement for Shuhaimi Baba's *Selubung* (1995)

(e.g., Aziz M. Osman's *Back to the Future* imitation, *XX Ray*), which spells a certain cultural homogenization and the eventual doom of alterity, but also to cultural flows from the Middle East, such as a globalizing Islam that, since the late 1970s, has had a substantial impact on Malay society. During this period, Malay students sent to universities abroad under the NEP came into contact with Middle Eastern students (who were resisting American imperialism in their home countries) and their ideas of a revivalist Islam. Indeed, Shuhaimi Baba's first film, *Selubung* (1992), exemplifies this situation by centring on a group of Malaysian students at the University of Perth who get involved with a Muslim fundamentalist movement on campus. Malay students exposed to *dakwah* (proselytizing) abroad spread the word/movement throughout Malaysian university campuses and colleges when they return. Today, one of the most visible legacies of the *dakwah* movement is the wearing of the *tudung* (head covering) by many Malay women. Interestingly, however, Malay films seldom show women wearing the *tudung*. The reason for this could have to do with the desire to attract a larger audience, since Malay cinema's roots are in commercial entertainment rather than artistic expression.

Advertisement from Shuhaimi Baba's *Ringgit Kasorrga* (1994)

Nevertheless, revivalist Islam, responding to Westernization, cultural im-perialism, and an overall sense of rapid modernization in Malaysia itself, has exerted considerable pressures on local gender relations and discourses on sexuality. Many progressive Malays view the impact of Islamic revival-ism as repressive of Malay sexuality. For Malays, religious orientation and ethnic identity have been intertwined with the early beginnings of Malay civilization in the 1400s (i.e., if you are Malay, you are born Muslim). Crit-ics of revivalist Islam, such as Malaysian anthropologist Wazir Jahan Karim, view resurgent Islam more as an Arabicization that threatens to transform their culture and purge their *adat* (Malay custom). Some staunch Muslims, on the other hand, regard some forms of *adat* as heathen superstition that adulterate Islamic practice and undermine Islamic beliefs. This is because *adat* contains Hindu and animistic elements derived from the area's pre-Islamic era. Hence, as a response to Islamic repression, filmmakers like Ad-man Salleh, Mahadi J. Murat, Shuhaimi Baba, and U-Wei incorporate the uniqueness of *adat* into their films. However, Shuhaimi Baba's form and method of recuperating *adat* differs from that of her male peers above. Her particular filmmaker's vision constructs a specific Malay identity, embed-ded in *adat,* but which does not eschew modernity for its female characters. She is one of two Malay female filmmakers currently in control of writing, directing, and producing her own films (the other is Erma Fatima).[5]

Adat and the New Wave Filmmakers

Some of the ways *adat* is represented by the Malaysian New Wave involve the use of black magic (in *Amok*); traditional forms of healing such as *susuk* and massage; local practices like *nasi kangkang* and *puja pantai*;[6] traditional performative arts like the beating of the large drum, *rebana* (in *Selubung*); and the Malay martial arts, *silat* (in *Amok*). Joel Kahn puts forth a theory of "the representation of a Malay imaginary constructed in recent years by members of the Malaysian intelligentsia," a portrayal of the subalternization of the Malay as poor villagers. In the case of Malay writer Shahnon Ahmad's novels, Kahn shows this construction and positive evaluation of the subaltern Malay to be "intimately bound up in the processes of identity construction and reconstruction that have emerged in the context of 'modernization' of Malaysian society instigated by the so-called 'NEP.'"[7] Kahn believes that the tourist industry, the domestic leisure and entertainment industries, as well as architecture and urban planning all serve to reconnect the urban Malay middle classes to "the essence of Malayness."[8] This includes, for example, adherence to Islam, a portrayal of Malay life as largely rural-based, an emphasis on a Malay sense of community (as opposed to individualism), and the importance of spiritual values in the lives of traditional Malay villagers. The construction of Malay myth and tradition occurs in Baba's films, too. In a personal interview, she explained that the idea of the lucky flying moths in *Selubung* was not derived from any specific local belief. It was only after she had written the scenes that she discovered that there was an existing superstition that moths were lucky. Hence, in the process of recuperating tradition or custom, new myths will be reconstructed or created.

The focus of such a reconstruction is interesting in that certain images, representations, or issues are selected and celebrated over others. For example, male filmmakers are preoccupied with focusing on the question of uncontrollable female libidinal desires. In such representations, modernity (female emancipation, female sexual power, and self-autonomy) is partly if not fully responsible for the sexual licence of the female character. (See, for example, the representation of Natalie, Wan's American girlfriend in Adman Salleh's 1994 film, *Amok*).

I would argue that male fears of the emancipated modern woman, one who is beyond the control of male desires, underlie the representations of the sexualized woman in films such as *Amok* and *Perempuan, Isteri Dan ... ?* (U-Wei).[9] What makes this representation of the sexualized woman unique is that her sexuality is symbolized by her wearing only a *sarung* tied around her midriff (the act of *berkemban*). This image evokes an earthiness and raw sensuality that is rooted in the imagery of the *kampung* (village), suggesting a kind of Malay essentialist femininity before the advent of urban modernity, before the period of *dakwah* activism. This representation of native, female sexuality results from recuperating an essential Malayness, or an essentialized ethnicity, that is cathected onto the body of the gendered Other. Thus, in the process of reclaiming ethnic roots while resisting a homogeneous global modernity and fundamentalist Islam, an elision of another kind occurs, for privileging ethnicity in this case means sacrificing gender politics. That, to me, problematizes the focus of contemporary male Malay filmmakers on recuperating *adat* through the image of "the woman in a *sarung."*

For women filmmakers like Shuhaimi Baba and Erma Fatima, the focus on the representation of modern female characters does not revolve around female sexual emancipation. Nor does modernity signify sexual licence for their female characters. Instead, their female characters embrace modernity and are comfortable with it without going overboard. They not only dress in Western-style clothing, but they are also progressive, independent, strong-minded, and articulate, speaking a mixture of Malay and English. This is hardly surprising as Baba, a progressive Malay/Muslim in her late forties, studied English literature at the University of Malaya before obtaining a film diploma from the Beaconsfield Studio (in the United Kingdom) in 1980. Shuhaimi Baba and Erma Fatima's films imply that it is not necessary for their male counterparts to remind the Malay woman about her own "essential" pre-*dakwah* sexuality or to free her from her own Islamicized sexual inhibitions and repressions; rather, their female characters' desires revolve around other crucial issues: career choices; emotional relationships with friends, family, and the potential romantic partner; and, last, how to lead a productive, satisfactory life as a decent human being in a rapidly industrializing society. In all of Baba's three films, *Selubung* (1992), *Ringgit Kasorrga* (1994), and *Layar Lara* (1997), there is evidence of the dynamic between rural and urban spaces: the juxtaposition of *kampungs* and urban skylines, people inhabiting the older, slower, and more traditional pace of life, and those who work and play in the big bad city. Finding a balance between the two is a key theme.

The attempt to find a balanced representation of, and a positive role for, the Malay woman in modern times is tricky. It involves balancing her ethnic identity so as to resist homogeneous globalizing cultures while, at the same time, liberating her from any kind of patriarchal constrictions: it is to present her, paradoxically, as an individual living as part of a community. The heroines in Baba's first two films clearly reflect this cultural balance as they both grow up in the *kampung* but now work in the city. Moreover, this balance is visually encoded when, in the city, they dress in urban Western work clothes but at home in the *kampung* they wear batik.

Next, by analyzing her film *Layar Lara*,[10] I would like to illustrate how Baba recuperates *adat*.

Layar Lara

In this film, the female protaganist, Ena, has lost her cultural equilibrium and must regain it in order to be successfully inculcated into an idealized modern Malaysian community. By "an idealized modern Malaysian community," I am referring to the relocation of traditional ideas of community from the *kampung* to the city. Ena has to learn to adapt to the community around her, whether it is a village or urban community, by shedding her egocentric behaviour and cavalier attitude towards acting (the film is about a film crew), and by being more considerate of other people. In the end, Ena becomes a member of the film crew/family when she recedes into the background and acknowledges that she is merely one cog in the machinery of filmmaking.

In the end, she learns (the hard way) how to get her priorities straight, choosing a serious career over her sexist rocker boyfriend, and becoming just another film crew member as opposed to a prima donna. This position, between individual and community, resembles the gender bilaterality that is found in *adat*, which acknowledges gender hierarchies "but attempts to reduce their importance through reinforcing values of generosity, generalized reciprocity, co-operation and sharing."[11] This view of *adat* is very evident in *Layar Lara:* Ena gets a humiliating scolding from her superior, Malik, who almost hits her on the head because he is so frustrated with her. As the director, Malik controls the film production and also takes on the role of the disciplining father for the seemingly fatherless Ena. Yet, he is also portrayed as vulnerable and as reliant upon his efficient female assistant, Zizie, as well as upon the cooperation of the rest of the crew. Ultimately, it is the generosity of the film crew, to whom Malik also defers, that allows Ena back into the production. In the closing scene, when they meet at a coffee stall and he shows his frustration by breaking a plastic chair, Ena is no longer frightened by his violence, as she had been in a similar scene at the beginning of the film. In the earlier scene she left hurriedly with her boyfriend to escape Malik's anger; in the later scene, Malik puts his arm around her shoulder and she leaves with him and the others.

In *Layar Lara,* the greedy urban developers and real estate agent, who is played by Ena in the film-within-a-film, illustrate the degree to which urban Malay values in the post-NEP period are divorced from their *kampung* roots and traditions. The 1990s urban Malay value system, as *Layar Lara* suggests, is cut off from its past by its attempt to be modern and to catch up with the developed West. To its detriment, it has abandoned its own indigenous and localized history, a history that has yet to be told in full. Yet, a consistent theme throughout the postmodernity[12] of *Layar Lara* seems to involve continuity between the old and new. Thus, although we see a clip of Ena in a rock video that is influenced by MTV, we also see her watching a television re-run of *Asmara Juita*, starring Auntie Zai, Ena's favourite local actress. While watching the black-and-white film with rapt attention, Ena mouths Auntie Zai's lines and gestures, clearly learned by heart. These two generations of actors, signifying the disparity between old and new Malays, are later brought together in a scene where they re-enact parts from Auntie Zai's past performances, a *purba*, or historical/period film, and then, later, go on to improvise a modern scene where they prepare to ascend a Kuala Lumpur skyscraper together. It has long been Auntie Zai's desire to view the city from the top of the skyscraper. She has written letters to the building owner asking for permission but, to her disappointment, has never received a reply. Ena realizes the extent of the disparity between Auntie Zai's generation and hers when she sees that the letters are written in Jawi (Arabic). She then suggests that there is no need to seek permission and that they should just go in a chauffeur-driven car. The two women play-act the scene, using gestures and body movements accompanied by some playful dialogue to suggest that they are dressing in diamonds and engaging in upper-class snobbery. Auntie Zai's desire to ascend the skyscraper is a modernist ambition, signifying the woman's ready acceptance of modernity; it is only Auntie Zai's traditional baggage (i.e., the Arabic writing few people can understand these days and her observation of formal processes) that prevents her from achieving her heart's desire. Yet, with the guidance of Ena – the younger, modern Malay woman – she learns to overcome these hierarchical barriers through a shared imaginative space. It is in the space of impromptu dialogue and creative performance that the two women form a bond across their generational and temporal differences.

Finally, *Layar Lara* recuperates a different kind of *adat:* instead of focusing on the *wayang kulit* (shadow puppetry) and on black magic, the film pays tribute to the actors of another kind of *wayang*, the *wayang gambar* (movies/cinema), and the magic here is that evoked by the silver screen. According to Baba, it is a magic that is irresistible, attracting actors to participate more fully in the art of visual storytelling by turning their hand to directing and producing.[13] Unlike Mahadi J. Murat's nationalist *Sayang Salmah* (1994) and Erma Fatima's *Jimi Asmara* (1994), which feature 1990s actors playing characters set in the past (Malaya during the 1950s and 1960s) and which are shot in a beautiful golden hue, Baba brings real Malay veteran actors into her film, suturing a kind of bond between the past and present of Malay cinema. Nowhere is this suturing clearer than in the scene where Ena role plays with Auntie Zai, the two women coordinating their dance movements in an improvisatory choreography, reflecting a creative and imaginative space where the old and the younger generation of female Malay actors can meet and bond.

Ostensibly, the film seems apolitical – revolving around the antics of Ena, a spoiled, young female actor, and a group of old film veterans, led by Auntie Zai, who would like a part in the film her nephew is working on. However, as *Layar Lara* approaches its conclusion, the parallels between the lives of the actors and their roles in the film-within-a-film reinforce each other as fact and fiction coalesce. *Layar Lara* saves the best for last: while the film-within-a-film has so far featured Ena and Malik as the main characters, the most important role in it is given to Auntie Zai. We see her throughout most of *Layar Lara* as an aging, slightly senile former actress whose dying wish is to appear on the big screen one last time, even if only as an extra. In this last role, where she plays an old village woman, she stands as a symbol of the displaced Old Malay, or *Melayu Lama*, whose identity is being rudely severed from that of the land by the crass materialism and corporate greed of the new generation, the *Melayu Baru*: "Hey, kid," she says, "come here. You think it's easy to get land these days? You! You take this land. Take it! Take it, but don't pull the wool over our eyes! We've all lived here for generations. This land is our flesh. You think money can buy heritage? There is no price in exchange for our roots and heritage" (my translation). Because she dies before the scene is shown, her bit part poignantly crystallizes her moment in cinematic history – a moment that she had waited so long to recapture. This poignancy is further enhanced by inserting this climactic scene from the film-within-a-film between scenes of Seniwati (the title for a female thespian) Zai's funeral, and using both slow motion and the haunting sound of the *seruling* (a Malay wooden flute).

Layar Lara succeeds in recuperating Malay cinematic history by reviving interest in Seniwati Zai as a famous and talented film veteran from the studio days. In the closing scene, Malik expresses a wish to hold a benefit in honour of Seniwati Zai and to make a film about her life. Moreover, as the scene closes and before the credits appear, there is a dedication in English to the real-life film veterans of Cathay Keris Studio. Simultaneously, the film projects a sense of disbelief in, or cynicism towards, the whole symbolic network that is contemporary Malaysian politics.[14] I do not read such disbelief, as expressed by Auntie Zai's impassioned cry, "This land is our flesh," as a critique of, or as outright resistance to, modernity. After all, one of Auntie Zai's other long-time wishes is to ascend a skyscraper, a symbol of modernity, to view the city from its roof. It seems to me that this disbelief reflects a resistance towards capitalism and its values rather than towards modernity per se. More than that, the metaphor reminds the viewers that the identity of the (old) Malays is autochthonous (in light of the modern political and nationalist construction of Malay ethnic identity),[15] and the struggle between the developers and the villagers for land raises the question of the existence and effectiveness of the Malay Land Reservation Act, which was introduced precisely to protect this aspect of Malay identity.[16] *Layar Lara* shows the difference between the *Melayu Baru*, as portrayed both by Ena's spoiled, fake, sexually manipulative behaviour and by her role as the real estate agent who has sex with a married male villager in order to obtain the land grant, and the *Melayu Lama*, as embodied by the film veterans and Auntie Zai's role as a vocal villager. It does this in order to critique the former for their neglect of their past, their roots, *adat,* and their lack of respect for the experience of their elders.

I would like to conclude with a quote from Shuhaimi Baba that captures the idea of women embracing modernity. Speaking about *Layar Lara,* she says, "We have to let the past go. Pay tribute to them [the stars of yester-year] and then bid them goodbye graciously." She says her film is about a young actor taking over the role of her predecessor: "The aging actor dies and Ena becomes more realistic. [She] takes over" (personal interview, Petaling Jaya, Malaysia, July 1998). Baba's reference to an older woman passing the torch to her younger successor evokes a sense of continuity that is reminiscent of the relationship between Mastura, the heroine of *Selubung,* and Dr. Sardar, her female mentor. Both the female successors are young, independent-minded women who are savvy, dynamic, and more than able to stand up to any modern challenges that the future might pose. As much as *Layar Lara* is about recuperating *adat,* Baba's statement displays an un-shakeable and optimistic sense of trust in the members of the younger generation of Malaysians as they fearlessly look ahead to modernity.

Notes

1 The term "Malay" denotes both the indigenous ethnic group living in Malaysia and their language. "Malayans" denotes the inhabitants of Malaya, including all ethnicities, prior to 1963. In 1963, Malaya was renamed Malaysia to include not only Peninsular Malaya but also Singapore as well as Sabah and Sarawak on the island of Borneo.

2 Azad Khan Hatta, *The Malay Cinema* (Bangi, Selangor, Malaysia: UKMP, 1997), 119.

3 *Fantasia* got into trouble with the censorship board for being anti-Islamic. Throughout the 1980s and 1990s, as fundamentalist Islamic ideas permeated the secular government there was a systematic effort to purify ethnic Malay Muslim culture and purge it of its underlying animist and Hindu elements.

4 Hatta, *Malay Cinema,* 90.

5 Baba explains that she writes her own screenplays because there are few good scriptwriters in Malaysia, and the current system does not encourage quality scripts because it pays so little.

6 *Susuk* is the custom of inserting golden needles under one's skin in order to preserve one's youth and beauty, as featured in *Selubung.* Literally, *nasi kangkang* means "squatted rice," and it refers to the menstruating woman's act of squatting over and peeing into her husband's rice in order to assert control over him. The female protagonist gains the upper hand over her husband in *Perempuan, Isteri Dan ... ?* after he has unknowingly eaten the rice, or *nasi kangkang,* she serves him. *Puja pantai* refers to greeting and appeasing sea spirits through the use of chants and prayers (also shown in *Selubung*).

7 Joel S. Kahn, "Subalternity and the Construction of Malay Identity," in *Modernity and Identity: Asian Illustrations,* ed. Alberto Gomes (Bundoora, Australia: La Trobe University Press, 1994), 26.

8 Ibid., 36.

9 For a detailed analysis of the recuperation of *adat* through the representation of native female sexuality in *Perempuan, Isteri Dan ... ?* see my "What Is It to Be a Man? Hyper-masculinity in Contemporary Malaysian Cinema," *West Coast Line* 34, 2 (Fall 2000): 43-60.

10 *Layar Lara* garnered Baba the best director award at the Brussels Independent International Film Festival in 1997 as well as the jury award at the Pyongyang Film Festival the following year.

11 Jahan Karim Wazir, *Women between Adat and Islam* (Boulder, CO: Westview Press, 1992), 5.

12 Postmodern because the film employs a pastiche of film styles: from a pop music video to a black-and-white Malay melodrama from the 1950s, which typically featured a mother-in-law and her daughter-in-law competing for the son's attention. In the case of *Asmara Juita*, it is the daughter-in-law who is wicked.

13 Personal interview, Petaling Jaya, Malaysia, July 1998. I was asking her about who the other Malay female filmmakers were and about the reasons for actresses becoming directors.

14 "Disbelief" and "cynicism" derive from the Lacanian psychoanalytical vocabulary of Slavoj Zizek and Renata Salecl. See Renata Salecl, "Do We Still Believe in Authorities?" transcript of speech given at "The Role of the University," conference held at the University of British Columbia, 26 October 1998. See also Slavoj Zizek, "How Did Marx Invent the Symptom?" in *Mapping Ideology,* ed. Slavoj Zizek (New York: Verso, 1994), 311-4.

15 See Adrian Vickers, "'Malay Identity': Modernity, Invented Tradition, and Forms of Knowledge," *RIMA* 31, 1 (1997): 173-211.

16 The Malay Land Act was part of British colonial policy, the strategy of which was to divide and conquer the various races. It was meant to keep land in the hands of the Malays. What *Layar Lara* suggests is that, under the present government, which inherited and kept the act, it is Malay capitalists rather than other racial groups who are oppressing (*menganiayai*) fellow Malays by trying to buy off their heritage and uprooting them. The word *akar umbi,* which roughly translates as "roots," is used in the dialogue.

Filmography

1992 *Selubung.* Direction: Shuhaimi Baba, with Deanna Yusoff, M. Nasir, and Ida Nerina; production: Identity Entertainers.

1992 *XX Ray.* Direction: Aziz M. Osman, with Aziz M. Osman, Vi Anastasia, and Faizal Hussein; production: Nizarman.

1994 *Amok.* Direction: Adman Salleh, with Nasir Bilal Khan, Ramona Rahman, and Hans Isaac; production: Nizarman.

1994 *Jimi Asmara.* Direction: Erma Fatima, with Hani Mohsen, Rosyam Noor, and Maizurah Hamzah; production: BNE Studio.

1994 *Perempuan, Isteri Dan ... ?* Direction: U-Wei Haji Shaari, with Sofia Jane Hisham and Nasir Bilal Khan; production: Berjaya Fp.

1994 *Ringgit Kasorrga.* Direction: Shuhaimi Baba, with Deanna Yusoff, Tiara Jacquelina, Hans Isaac, and Zaidi Omar; production: Persona Pictures.

1994 *Sayang Salmah.* Direction: Mahadi J. Murat, with Azhar Sulaiman, Sidi Oraza, Fauziah Nawawi, Norish arman, and Sofia Jane; production: Grand Brilliance and Perkasa Filem.

1997 *Layar Lara.* Direction: Shuhaimi Baba, with Man Bai, Ida Nerina, and Azean Irdawaty; production: Persona Pictures.

22 Representation of Women in the Films of María Luisa Bemberg

Maria de los Angeles Carbonetti, Rita de Grandis, Mónica Escudero, and Omar Rodríguez

The cinematic work of Argentine filmmaker María Luisa Bemberg (1922-95) constitutes a well defined corpus. In it, the intersections of gender, class, and power are systematically examined to account for the limited options available to women in a society marked by a strong patriarchal gender hierarchy. Alberto Ciria has said that, in her movies, issues of gender are subordinated to those of class and power.[1] We, however, believe that, although his statement is accurate, when dealing with gender one is inevitably confronted with issues of power. We can therefore pose the following questions: How does Bemberg treat gender and power? What kinds of institutions does she blame for the subordination of women? And what alternatives, if any, does she propose?

In order to reflect upon these issues, Bemberg usually sets her films in the historical past and within the confines of the privileged classes: her female characters – Sor Juana, Miss Mary, and Leonor – either belong to the upper and upper-middle classes or move within those circles. This is significant because, as educated and privileged women, they can afford to look inside themselves, reflect upon their inner conflicts, and, in so doing, gain awareness. Within their historical and social setting, these female characters develop a consciousness that enables them to become fully aware of the societal conditioning imposed upon their personal and social behaviour. In their quest for self-definition their consciousness allows them to challenge, and at times to transgress, the traditional boundaries within which they are confined.

We will show how this transgression and its consequences take place in three films: *Miss Mary* (1986), *Yo, la peor de todas* (I, the Worst of All, 1990), and *De eso no se habla* (I Don't Want to Talk about It, 1993). The order of presentation is according to year of production, and it is possible to observe the progress from a very simple articulation of form and content (as in *Miss Mary*) to a complex development of plot and characters (as in *I Don't Want to Talk about It*).

Miss Mary: A Feminine Gaze Filtered through the English Language

In *Miss Mary* (1986) the variables of class, gender, and power appear mediated by a cultural appropriation of the symbolic capital attributed to English culture, the culture of prestige that assigns power to a certain class – the Argentinean aristocracy. Here, culture and class are articulated through the interaction between an English governess and an aristocratic Argentine family at the beginning of the twentieth century, reflecting a period of strong English influence in the economic development of modern Argentina during the 1880s. Within this context, the feminine gaze of Miss Mary Mulligan is that of an outsider, as she is marginalized both as a woman and as a foreign employee. Her job as a governess assigns her an intermediary role, halfway between the servants (who have access to the private rooms only for domestic tasks) and the masters (those who, like friends and family, share the dining table and the living room).

María Luisa Bemberg's *Miss Mary* (1986), courtesy of the Film Reference Library, Toronto

As an Englishwoman, Miss Mary shares with the ruling class a culture of prestige that other European cultures, such as the Italian or Spanish, did not have at that time in Argentina. She embodies a set of manners with which the upper-class family identifies and that they expect their children to acquire through her services as a governess. This cultural background creates a further ambiguity in that it blurs the boundaries between the Argentines (the natives) and the foreigners. Within this dynamic the land-owning family buys an elite European language and culture – French or English, the two languages of prestige – absorbing its traditions and customs to form an "Argentine" upper-class culture. This aspect of the film evokes autobiographical data since, in several interviews, María Luisa Bemberg recalls that she never attended regular schools as she was educated at home by English and French governesses. Her father believed that a woman did not need to be either intelligent or cultivated; it was enough for a girl to be pretty and virtuous, and to have appropriate social skills.[2] According to her own statements, she and her two sisters could not even go out on their own, let alone receive institutional education. While her brothers attended school and graduated from Harvard University (one has a PhD, the other is an economist), the three girls stayed at home and learned the manners and subjects a woman of the time should know ("from twenty-two substitute mothers").[3] Governesses were responsible for transposing the "authentic" culture of Europe to the would-be aristocratic agro-cultural oligarchy of Buenos Aires. For Miss Mary it is not clear who comprises the ruling class.

This becomes evident when she wonders what would have happened to her had she been sent to India instead of Argentina. In India it was very clear that the English were the dominant group, whereas in Argentina, although the dominant culture was English, the dominant class was not.

What emerges clearly in the film is Miss Mary's self-awareness of being a woman and a subordinated employee. The interview with Señor Alfredo foregrounds the social space allotted to her and also the construction of gender, according to which the girls' educational expectations are established. In the dialogue between employer and employee sexual control is never explicitly expressed, but it is hinted at. Alfredo says, "My girls must never to be out of sight," and Miss Mary answers, "Girls under my supervision have always achieved matrimony in the proper manner." Her role is to protect their virginity.

Señor Alfredo warns Mary about the inherent consequences of her own femininity, the risks of her own youth, beauty, and sexuality. This warning reflects a Victorian morality that Mary Mullighan knows very well. For Señor Alfredo, religion is also a central aspect of the children's education. In answer to a question about her religious background ("Are you a Catholic?"), Mary replies laconically: "It is in the contract." Her Irish name and religion add irony to her situation as "English." Other areas of knowledge, such as history and geography, will occupy a secondary place. Religion is fundamental to sexual control of the girls and, at the same time, to Miss Mary's own sexual control.

The interview foreshadows the conflict that will evolve when Miss Mary becomes amorously involved with the family's elder son. Her transgression (both "moral" and in relation to her employment contract) relates directly to her own sexuality. In a parallel plot, Terry, one of the daughters, is penalized for a similar "sin" as she is obliged to marry because she has had sex with a friend. The family re-establish order. Since obedience to the authoritarian family institution is unavoidable, we can ask what the differences are between Miss Mary and the other women in the family, all of whom are neurotic and sick. At this level, there is no longer a distinction between a foreigner and a native, a subordinated employer and a subordinated daughter or wife. They all share a common destiny as women and are punished if they rebel. The only difference lies in Miss Mary's self-awareness and knowledge of her subordinated position as the family's employee and as a woman, along with her perception of the other women's subordinate role within the family structure.

I, the Worst of All: Feminine Knowledge as Bait

In his study of Argentine cinema, Alberto Ciria devotes a chapter to the work of María Luisa Bemberg and concludes that, even though her main characters are consistently women, feminist perspectives are not the director's fundamental concern. Ciria believes "that it is in her analysis of power that Bemberg's films become more relevant and dynamic in regard to contemporary issues."[4] Surprisingly, he seems to ignore power as one of the most fertile terrains upon which to engage a gender-related discussion.

The conflict that *I, the Worst of All* explores in depth is based upon the relations among Sor (Sister) Juana, the Church, and the Crown, and it focuses almost exclusively on institutional power structures. The gender dynamic is thoroughly subordinated to the Church and the Crown. This dynamic, which recurs in Bemberg's other films, illustrates the inevitable exertion of institutional power over individuals, particularly women. Sor Juana is depicted, on one hand, as a member of the convent community at the mercy of the ecclesiastical hierarchy and, on the other hand, as dependent upon the protection of the Crown. Consequently, she lacks any means of effectively challenging the status quo, unless they are bestowed upon her by a powerful third party. Systematically, Bemberg removes Sor Juana from a position of active resistance to one of passive acceptance. She lacks the knowledge necessary to transgress the all-powerful social institutions, despite her assertion that, as a poet-nun, she has a certain kind of knowledge and that "knowledge is a transgression, and especially for a woman." A close analysis of the aesthetics as well as of the contents of the film shows that the role assigned to the poet-nun and her knowledge is never an active one but, rather, is tantamount to the passive role of bait – always acted upon but never acting.

There are two crucial scenes in which this passivity is clear. The first involves the climax of the subplot between the viceroy's wife, María Luisa Paredes, and the poet. The most intimate moment of their relationship is completely dominated by the marquise, countess de Paredes. The scene is set in the darkness of Sor Juana's chamber, where a black background isolates the characters from the room, stressing the actual encounter. The mise-en-scène favours the predominance of María Luisa as she is on the left side of the frame (the first place where one's eyes go, at least if one's eyes are Western), looking at Sor Juana, who remains on the right side. The countess de Paredes is the only active element of the scene. Even the camera is inert; an immobile lens takes in the action. As for Sor Juana, she simply follows the orders of the Crown as spoken by María Luisa: "Take off the veil. It is an order. All of it ... This Juana is mine, only mine." Sor Juana stays quiet, despite all her love poems dedicated to the marquise, despite all the lust of her gaze. In the most erotic moment of the film, she is portrayed as passive.

The second scene shows Sor Juana finally taking part in the politics of the Church as she writes the controversial *Athenagoric Letter*, the document that eventually leads to her ruin. In planning a conspiracy to harass the fanatical archbishop of Mexico, Monsignor Francisco de Aguiar y Seijas, both the bishop of Puebla (Manuel Fernández de Santa Cruz) and the new viceroy of

New Spain (the marquis de la Laguna) make use of Sor Juana's skills. As in the scene with the countess, Sor Juana is again appointed by others to perform. The conversation between monsignor and Sor Juana is, through the use of alternate shots, treated as a conventional dialogue; however, while close-ups are used for Bishop Fernández de Santa Cruz, shots from head to waist are used for Sor Juana, thus establishing the ascendancy of the former over the latter. Her words *"you have given me* the chance to respond to the archbishop" and "I only wrote it because *you ordered me to"* (our emphasis) summarize her role as receiver. In short, in two of the film's key scenes Bemberg does not hesitate to depict Sor Juana and her knowledge as completely subordinate to institutional power.

I Don't Want to Talk about It: The Unrealized Subject

I Don't Want to Talk about It is set in the past, as are *Miss Mary* and *I, the Worst of All*, and more precisely in the 1940s in a small rural town where both protagonists – Charlotte, who is a dwarf, and her mother, Leonor – are able to enjoy privileged status thanks to Leonor's economic power. She runs what appears to be the only store in town, which not only provides her with the means to live well, educate her daughter with the best teachers, and be the centre of the town's cultural life, but also gives her power over people's lives and institutions. Since she is the sole supplier of the essentials of life, she holds the key to the inhabitants' survival and can succeed in making the population of the town accomplices in her denial of her daughter's condition. However, this is not, in our opinion, the main point of the film. We believe that the main point of the film lies in Leonor's experience of having a handicapped child – an experience that awakens in her a different sense of the meaning of humanity. The whole film can be seen as her struggle against society's definition (which she shares) of what is normal and what is not. In other words, the tension in the film lies in Leonor's inner conflict: on the one hand, her love for her daughter allows her to reject societal constructs of the ideal woman; on the other hand, the patriarchal system encourages her to see her daughter as deviant.

This tension is particularly explicit in three scenes. In the first, Charlotte is dancing to Bizet's *Carmen* in front of the mirror, and we see the desperation and anguish provoked by Leonor's awareness of her daughter's sexual awakening. She realizes that, despite her efforts to raise her as "normal," Charlotte's chances of developing her sexuality are quite limited in a society that determines women's sexual roles largely according to their looks. In the second scene, at the piano recital, Leonor asks Charlotte not to take a bow so that people will not see her shortness. She is the one who has pushed for her daughter to perform, yet she is terrified of what others may think of her daughter's appearance. The third scene occurs at her daughter's

María Luisa Bemberg's *De eso no se habla/I Don't Want to Talk about It* (1993), courtesy of the Film Reference Library, Toronto

wedding. Leonor insists on Charlotte being given away by the major, not because of his position but, rather, because he is in a wheelchair and this would create the visual illusion of a "normal" looking couple. This strategy of normalization is subverted, however, by her hysterical laughter when Charlotte walks away on the arm of her new husband, who happens to be the most sought-after bachelor in town. Even though Leonor challenges society by developing her daughter's musical potential, she is caught in the web of traditional conventions steeped in patriarchy. She finally loses her battle when she sees Charlotte, who has found her own "normal" habitat, going away with the circus. In the end, Leonor locks herself up for life, an obvious allusion to the cage within which we all live, alienated from one another by a system that commodifies humanity. Little Charlotte is to be consumed by spectators who will pay to see her perform.

Leonor's actions are consistent throughout the film, whereas Charlotte's are not. Charlotte appears to be a self-assured young woman who knows who she is and, in fact, seems to understand better than her mother that it is one's humanity, not appearance, that defines a person. In the first of the three scenes mentioned above, she is aware and seemingly comfortable with her incipient sexuality; in the second, she is able to confront her mother at the concert by standing up to take a bow, asserting herself and her short-ness. Similarly, with regard to her marriage, she never questions Ludovico d'Andrea's motives in marrying her, nor does she think it odd (as does the rest of the town), and she accepts his offer only after careful consideration. At this point, she is unknowingly transgressing the boundaries of social acceptability, but her level of consciousness is not equal to her actions. This is why, later, she is so easily lured away by the circus life. Her mother, by "not talking about it," has prevented Charlotte from really grasping the meaning of both their choices. Charlotte never understands that, with her mother's support and Ludovico's love, she could have defied society; instead, she allows herself to be taken over by conformity, thus destroying her subversive potential. In joining the circus, she unwittingly conforms to a pre-assigned role for dwarves rather than challenging society's expectations.

Both Leonor and Charlotte (to different degrees) are caught up in the contradiction inherent within the social definition of difference. Don Ludovico d'Andrea, however, is able to bridge that gap and can see in Charlotte the woman she really is. In the scene that takes place in the stable, we are witness to the transcending power of love, as Ludovico discovers Charlotte's womanhood. As she gallops on her horse, a symbol of sexuality, passion, and desire, she appears to become one with the beast, sharing its symbolism. It is at this moment that Ludovico appreciates Charlotte's inner self and is, therefore, capable of appreciating her humanness. On the horse, her height is irrelevant, and he feels her female power and her inner beauty. This discovery clearly confounds him and he unsuccessfully tries to deny it, but his love eventually leads him to marry her. With this act he is transgressing society's rules and, as is the case for any Bemberg character who dares do so, he is defeated. When he loses Charlotte to the circus, his life loses meaning and he disappears, probably drowning himself.

We can conclude, then, that there are several different levels of transgression in the film, all of which lead to failure. Defying society, Leonor builds a protective wall around her daughter only to find, at the end, that it has become a cage; Charlotte's attempt at "normality" fails because of her inability to see herself as Ludovico sees her; and, finally, Ludovico, probably the most tragic of the three characters, loses his life. His fate is only fitting, as he is the biggest transgressor in the story. He had all the attributes deemed desirable in a patriarchal society: he was good-looking, well off, and educated; he could have "had" all the women he wanted, as long as they were normal. Yet he chose Charlotte, thus violating the proper code of behaviour. And, to ensure the restoration of order, he had to be punished.

The three examples briefly examined here illustrate the strong relationship between power and gender in Bemberg's films. Power is a central concern and manifests itself in a variety of ways in relation to gender as a socio-historical construct. On the one hand, power is fundamentally, visibly, and identifiably embodied in institutions that deal with prohibition, boundaries, and the regulation of social behaviour: the Church (represented by the archbishop of Mexico in *I, the Worst of All*), social class (represented by the father in *Miss Mary*), and money (represented by Leonor, the financially independent mother in *I Don't Want to Talk about It*).

On the other hand, power also manifests itself intersubjectively as a constitutive element of identity formation. From a psychoanalytic perspective (a perspective with which María Luisa Bemberg was very well acquainted), the power dynamics that results from intersubjective relations are complex, for the subject may be both powerless and powerful. Bemberg develops her female characters within this dialectical opposition, focusing on the ambivalent role of gender and sexuality. Her treatment of subjectivity is linked to the notion of desire. In *I, the Worst of All* Sor Juana is the object of desire for the viceroy's wife and the Church authorities. From this perspective, power results from the self investing power in the other. For example, the Marquise de Paredes and the bishop of Puebla both, for different reasons, invest Sor Juana with power. They want something that they do not have (knowledge, wisdom), and they project their desire onto Sor Juana. Here, power manifests itself as a relationship between subjectivity and desire. The powerful subject desires the other, because the latter possesses something that the former does not. The marquise de Paredes and the bishop of Puebla desire Sor Juana because both recognize her intelligence. The first object of desire for the marquise (a woman aware of her subordinate position in relation to her husband and the Crown) is to be noticed by Sor Juana. Both the marquise and Sor Juana share being marginalized as women, but the latter embodies a knowledge and freedom of self-expression to which the former lacks access. From this point of view, Sor Juana is both powerless and powerful. She transgresses the limits of the allowed knowledge available to women, but she does not reclaim any form of power other than the desire to know, the freedom to continue her quest for knowledge. This is transgressive insofar as it implies a form of knowledge that reveals its gendered nature and could be used to overthrow male authority. Her knowledge has a seductive force because of its ability to reveal society's limiting mechanisms.

This form of intersubjective power also appears in *I Don't Want to Talk about It*, but in a different way. Here we have a mother-daughter pair, with Leonor embodying the symbolic order and creating, physically as well as figuratively, the existential prison that Charlotte inhabits. Paradoxically, Leonor constrains Charlotte because she wants society to change its perception of people who are small. She desires to alter the social order, to make her daughter "normal" in a revised symbolic order. In fact, her socioeconomic position within her community allows her to prevent the whole town from enforcing the social norm that confines dwarves to certain roles. On the other hand, the daughter does not know, does not even have access to, the symbolic order of which her mother is so aware; the mother's imposed order is the only one Charlotte experiences. Suddenly, when the circus comes to town, Charlotte sees herself reflected in the other dwarves that are passing through, immediately identifies with them, and liberates herself by running away from home and joining them. Paradoxically, her liberating act involves conforming to the symbolic order her mother worked so hard to prevent her from knowing. Bemberg's portrayal of the relationship between mother and daughter shows the inevitable contradiction within which they are both caught. The mother's efforts to separate her daughter from social prescriptions and perceptions return Charlotte to the symbolic order, an order from which she was removed and which she envisions as liberating. The inescapability of these unconscious societal parameters – parameters that repress and prohibit – has achieved its full dimension. Charlotte returns to being what society always supposed her to be (a circus freak), as does Sor Juana, who finishes her days as a nun, in the only place allowed for nuns.

María Luisa Bemberg's characters, particularly her women characters (but also Ludovico d'Andrea in *I Don't Want to Talk about It*) are caught in the contradiction that opposes their inner desire and outside order. Bemberg is acutely aware of the repressive symbolic order that limits the actions of her female characters. She represents women as engaged in a process of self-reflection that leads them to attempt to resist the system, although they are not able to overcome it. Miss Mary is punished, Sor Juana is silenced, and Charlotte is self-banished. In the final scenes of these films we see the institutions finishing their macabre job, ensuring that, paradoxically, these women know "how things are." In spite and because of their efforts to transform their situations, they end up being trapped within mechanisms of exclusion.

María Luisa Bemberg develops her female characters within the tension that surrounds power, gender, and identity. Power is conveyed as both a social construct that totally determines behaviour and as a psychological trait of identity. The subject is constituted by, and develops around, a desire to resist and challenge the symbolic order. This subject attempts, by searching for a potentially transgressive form of knowledge, to break away from the "feminine" mould of passivity. Finally, all Bemberg's female characters fail to achieve the desired freedom and agency because the law of social prohibition exerts its ultimate power to re-establish the symbolic order of discourse.

Notes

1   Alberto Ciria, *Más allá de la pantalla: Cine argentino, historia y política* (Buenos Aires: Ediciones de la Flor, 1995).
2   Luis Trelles Plazaloa, *Cine y Mujer en América Latina* (Puerto Rico: Editorial de la Universidad de Puerto Rico, 1991), 110.
3   Leila Guerreiro, "María Luisa Bemberg," in *Mujeres argentinas*, ed. María Ester de Miguel (Buenos Aires: Alfaguara, 1998), 160.
4   Ciria, *Más allá de la pantalla*, 176.

Filmography: María Luisa Bemberg

1970   *Crónica de una señora.* Direction: Raúl de la Torre; screenplay: María Luisa Bemberg.

1972   *El mundo de la mujer* (short film) (direction, production, and screenplay)

1974   *Triángulo de cuatro.* Direction: Fernando Ayala; screenplay: María Luisa Bemberg.

1978   *Juguetes* (short film) (direction, production, and screenplay)

1980   *Momentos.* Direction: María Luisa Bemberg; production: GEA Cinematográfica; screenplay: María Luisa Bemberg and Marcelo Pichón Riviere.

1982   *Señora de nadie.* Direction: María Luisa Bemberg; production: Lita Stantic, GEA Cinematográfica; screenplay: María Luisa Bemberg.

1984   *Camila.* Direction: María Luisa Bemberg; production: Lita Stantic, GEA Cinematográfica (Buenos Aires) and Impala (Madrid).

1986   *Miss Mary.* Direction: María Luisa Bemberg; production: Lita Stantic, GEA Cinematográfica.

1990   *Yo, la peor de todas.* Direction: María Luisa Bemberg; production: Lita Stantic, GEA Cinematográfica.

1992   *De eso no se habla.* Direction: María Luisa Bemberg; production: Oscar Kramer; production: María Luisa Bemberg and Aura Films (Italy); screenplay: María Luisa Bemberg and Jorge Goldenberg.

23   Temporality and Identity in Sara Gómez's Documentaries[1]

Susan Lord

The central purpose of this chapter is to refocus on Sara Gómez's filmmaking by way of her documentaries. In doing so, I also introduce some theoretical and methodological problems raised by the cross-cultural encounter particular to undertaking an analysis of Gomez's documentaries.[2] I develop the claim that the politics of time induces one of several disjunctions that must be recognized in the act of analysis and that, without recognizing these, the writer would not only lose the opportunity for critical self-reflection and decolonization, but also reproduce the imperial imaginary by effectively transposing a chronotope of Western and postrevolutionary culture.[3]

The documentaries made by Gómez in the first decade of the Cuban Revolution[4] insist on the reality, immediacy, and contemporaneity of the social subjects on screen. Thirty-some years later, in another country, that present-tense is at once palpable and remote, making it, according to some, all the more "real." And to write about the double-time of these representations and referents is to participate in the production of certain narratives of revolution, nation, colonialism, and so on and, thus, to participate (at least implicitly) in the erasure of others. In the early stages of a research project, such as this, the tendency is to identify with the images through structures

Sara Gómez (1943-74)

of fiction and fantasy, nostalgia and rescue, and so on, as opposed to through those structures of judgement that are afforded to the historian or anthropologist. (Clearly, neither "side" goes uninformed by the other at any stage of research.) Here and now, in the era of George W. Bush and global corporate capital, where socialism has become homeless, as I watch the films I think about revolutionary Cuba's formative years from a position between activist and scholar, friend and stranger, participant and observer; that is, as one whose identification is phenomenological and psychological, ethical and political.

The phrase "the politics of time" refers to the analytical lens through which I view these films and navigate the viewing positions afforded by them: to highlight not just the different cultures of time and the forms of labour presented as content in the films, but also their value as representations. In the socio-cultural history of modernity that forms the context of emergence for those representations, the measure of value is performed according to where one is in the evolutionary stream of time. Johannes Fabian's *Time and the Other* offers a critique of the moral, ethical, and epistemological consequences of anthropology's deployment of the tool of evolutionary time – the sequentialization/spatialization of time – as key to the advancement of colonialism.[5] He argues that the history of the discipline of anthropology reveals that the use of naturalized-spatialized time is almost invariably for the purpose of distancing those who are observed from the time of the observer. Yet, a critical praxis can be built through, first of all, a recognition of coeval temporality: the contemporaneity and simultaneity/ synchrony of observer/observed. By introducing this concept here, I hope to resist the lure of the anthropological gaze.

The late Afro-Cuban filmmaker Sara Gómez is recognized by scholars, filmmakers, and cineastes as having made profound and lasting contributions to Cuban cinema, women's cinema, and postcolonial cinema: she remains the only woman to have made a feature film in Cuba; she is one of a very few Afro-Cubans to have made films in the Instituto Cubano del Arte e Industria Cinematográphicas (ICAIC); and her work has inspired a new generation of Cuban media artists. As is well known, Gómez died of asthma in 1974 before she could complete the editing of *De cierta manera* (*One Way or Another*), the only feature-length film she made after ten prolific years as a director of short documentaries. The feature was completed by Gómez's colleagues at the ICAIC in 1977 and went on to receive tremendous critical and scholarly attention. It continues to focus attention and debate about Cuban culture and society.[6] This film presented North American and British feminist film critics and theorists with one of the first "non-Western" films by a woman, thus marking the canon's shift away from complete Eurocentrism. It is remarkable for its portrayal of complex social, racial, and sexual relationships, and for its inventive strategies for giving such relationships a mode of representation adequate to their complexities. The film has, in fact, become foundational to new Cuban cinema and to feminist film culture.

All of this well deserved attention given to her one feature film has, strangely, done nothing to encourage distribution and analysis of her earlier short films, inside or outside of Cuba: thirteen documentaries of between eight and forty minutes in length, addressing a range of themes from Afro-Cuban musical traditions to autobiography. The exception to the dearth of distribution in Canada was the festival of new Cuban Film and Video curated by David McIntosh and Ricardo Acosta for the Euclid Theatre in Toronto in 1994. The program presented a number of Gómez's films as precursors to the work by the young contemporary media artists who deal with issues of identity and difference. The only English-language account of Gómez's documentaries is Michael Chanan's descriptive analysis of half the films in his seminal 1985 book *The Cuban Image: Cinema and Cultural Politics in Cuba* – as yet the only book in English on Cuban film. Some analysis and description of approximately half of the documentaries appear in the 1989 special issue on Gómez of the journal *Cine Cubano*; yet, ten years later, in the special issue celebrating the fortieth anniversary of the ICAIC, neither Gómez's name nor her image, nor stills from her films, are given a place in those pages. The tangle of speculations about what has inspired such an uneven memory for her and her work in the various branches of film studies deserves a future analysis. I raise the matter here mainly to underscore the fact that, as with any auteur, Gómez and her films are variously claimed and, apparently, dis-claimed.

The documentaries were made in the period when the "double vocation" of artistic and political experimentation was the norm[7] and before what is referred to as "the grey years" (the Sovietization of culture).[8] Chronologically, the titles are: *Iré a Santiago* (1964), *Excursion a Vuelta Abajo* (*Trip to Vuelta*

Abajo, 1965), and *Crónica de mi familia (Chronicle of My Family*, 1966). There follows a trio of films on the Isle of Pines (1967-9): *En la otra isla (On the Other Island), Una isla para Miguel (An Island for Miguel)*, and *Isla de Tesoro (Treasure Island)*. Then there are *Y ... tenemos sabor (And We've Got Taste*, 1968); *Poder local, poder popular (Local Power, Popular Power*, 1970); *Un documental a proposito del transito (A Documentary about Traffic*, 1971); and *Mi aporte (My Contribution*, 1970). Finally, we have a pair of films about pre-natal and first-year child care: *Atención pre-natal* (1972) and *Año uno: Sobre horas extras y trabajo voluntario (On Extra Hours and Volunteer Labour*, 1973). Each of these short films is strikingly different in style and each stretches the limits of documentary conventions. I believe that this experimentation participates in the New Cuban Cinema's creative revolution by signifying a response to those elements of history, memory, and everyday life that are frozen out of the frame of dominant narratives of nation and subjectivity. Whether the subject matter concerns local cultural and political critiques of national work programs *(Año uno)* and election processes *(Poder local, poder popular)* or the maternal lines and race politics within a family *(Crónica de mi familia)*, the films consistently bring to the frame marginal identities. Central to both the modes of representation and the subject matter is the issue of time itself. Along with strategies that reflect on the temporality of film processes (shot duration, montage rhythm, and narrative), the cultures of time represented in the films include the subjective worlds of memory and everyday life *(Crónica de mi familia)*, the uneven development of social chronotopes (the Isle of Pines trilogy), and the different or contesting temporalities formed by cultural memory and practices *(Y ... tenemos sabor, Crónica)* as well as by gender difference *(Mi aporte)*.

One set of questions I attempt to work through came about as a result of the difficulty I had "knowing" the work at this particular stage of my research. The partial and contingent truths that form the always receding goal of documentary[9] are temporalized at two sites for any investigation of documentary meaning: the writer (her subjectivity limited by forgetting and ever-partial knowledge) and the film (disjunctions that form the work's present-tense viewing context as well as the ever-accruing mediations that adhere, so to speak, to the signifying system and the sign's receding referent). With this condition in mind, my positioning of the work, together with the work's positioning of me, constitutes one of many potential lines of inquiry about the work and the cultural memory that the work labours to produce. Feminist theory and epistemology have long argued the contingency of the subject; and critical ethnographic theory has brought the critique of the imperial imaginary to bear upon the knowledge claims of anthropological and ethnographic records. In what follows, I utilize some of those insights to sketch these lines of inquiry for analyzing documentary from a cross-cultural, feminist perspective. The first is from the point of view of feminist documentary theory; the second develops from the typologies and history of Latin American documentary theory; the third issues from the contestation over "popular" culture and the meaning of transculturation; and the fourth emerges from a postcolonial reflection on the encounter between critic and text.

First, however, some observations about the works of Gómez. Gómez's films are consistently about marginalization "today" – a condition that is a result of long and deep cultural histories that inform each other across the colonial divide. Particularly attentive to the status of women and the value of machismo, as well as Afro-Cuban culture and enduring racism, the films also address how that marginalization is a cultural problem for the revolution's political aim to unify a people, a popular culture, and a nation. Thus, rather than performing the discourse of margin versus centre, the films adjust the frame so as to take up the radical claims for a new society based upon cultural difference and expressed through popular democracy. Most of these documentaries present a view of participation practised fundamentally as critical engagement. *Mi aporte* is one of the best examples of the extent to which Gómez's filmmaking and the social subjects of those films together embody radical, participatory democracy (thus participating in the larger project within modernity of the democratization of culture).

Collaboratively made in 1970 by six people at the ICAIC, with Gómez as the premiere director, *Mi aporte* begins as an ostensible report card on women in the new society. Addressed to Camilo Cienfuegos (a revolutionary hero who died in 1960), the film begins with the announcement that it will show women's contribution to the sugar harvest and, thus, to the revolution. The first of its three parts opens with an interviewer introducing women (young and old, White, Mulatto, and Black) who work at the sugar plant and asking them what they do in a style typical of *cine reportaje* (reportage). The responses to questions about their work lead to a discussion on issues of childcare and the difficulties of combining work, childrearing, and homemaking. These testimonies are intercut – in such a way as to suggest an interruption of the women's stories – with a male worker's analysis of his female comrades' ineffective labour due to their physical weakness, pregnancy, and/or absenteeism due to childcare exigencies. Included in this first part is also a short section where a paternalistic-sounding voice-over describes the progress of women's integration into the labour force, while the image track shows women peering out of their windows and doors. This image track is eventually synchronized with those women's voices – many of them single mothers – as they tell how they are unable to go to work because there is no one to look after the children and not enough daycare in the area. An intertitle in a bold, black font on white background appears on the screen: "The woman who lives in this house cannot work because her husband doesn't want her to." It appears that the specific woman referred to is the one we have just seen knitting and heard talking about the choice between marriage or work. However, the "response" provided is footage of a daycare, with children singing, eating healthy lunches, playing, and so on. This first section ends with the following intertitle: "Have we created the condition for the formation of the new woman?"

As with the film's overall structure, this trio of title-sequence-title articulates the issue dialectically, with the synthesis offering not a resolution to the thesis/antithesis but another question. (The example also illustrates the use of different "languages" – linguistic and filmic – which I will only note here.) Section 2 takes up this question by way of a discussion between four women (all of them students and professionals), Gómez among them, filmed in a *cinéma vérité* style, with synched-sound and little editing. The content of the discussion is most clearly summarized in the following remark: "To have a job is fundamental for me … [it is the way to be] part of the building of society … But the practical reality is very different: it is hard to have a home, a baby, and try to be active at work." Halfway through this section, the discussion is played over an image-track composed of footage seen in Section 1. This discussion ends with "FIN," but then a third section begins, turning the film into a process documentary: a group of women from a tobacco factory, having now watched the film, are themselves filmed having a discussion about the issues raised by the film and its subjects. Their critique echoes the one heard in the previous section: the report card is not so much reporting on women's contributions as on the failure of the revolution to deal with cultural issues specific to gender and machismo. The women articulate how this, too, is their work, their contribution. The film ends with the words: "End of Report [*reportaje*]."

Feminist Documentary

If we read *Mi aporte* through documentary typologies developed in the North, such as those formulated by Bill Nichols and Julia Lesage, we are given a set of meanings and values associated with consciousness-raising, interactive and reflective structures, and feminist dialogics. This lens gives us a feminist documentary in the mode defined by Lesage as follows:

> Cinéma vérité documentary filmmaking had features that made it an attractive and useful mode of artistic and political expression for women learning filmmaking in the late 1960s. It not only demanded less mastery of the medium than Hollywood or experimental film, but also the very documentary recording of women's real environments and their stories immediately established and valorized a new order of cinematic iconography,

connotation, and range of subject matter in the portrayal of women's lives. ... The feminist documentarist uses the film medium to convey a new and heightened sense of women's identity, expressed both through the subject's story and through the tangible details of the subject's milieu ... The realist feminist documentaries represent a use of, yet a shift in, the aesthetics of cinéma vérité, due to the feminist filmmakers' close identification with their subjects, participation in the women's movement, and sense of the film's intended effect. The structure of the consciousness-raising group becomes the deep structure repeated over and over in these films.[10]

This typology yields one set of truths applicable to *Mi aporte:* feminist collectivities develop a critical consciousness among participants; the shift in iconography based on this critical consciousness is capable of contributing to social change; direct speech and storytelling are transmissible through the film's structure, which itself reflects a "decolonized" reflexive structure of feminist consciousness; and, of course, the focus is on gender roles as the deep structure in the determination of cultural and social value. What this perspective cannot "see" is the critical engagement with the deep, formal structures of Latin American documentary and the dialectic between gender and colonialism as well as between gender and class.

Latin American Documentary

In documentary literature, it is now commonplace for writers to turn to Bill Nichols's 1991 delineation of the main documentary "modes": expository, observational, interactive, and reflexive.[11] However, this is but one version of a set of articulations he and Julianne Burton developed over the course of a decade. Burton's "Democratizing Documentary: Modes of Address in the Latin American Cinema, 1958-72," first published in 1984, and Michael Chanan's "Rediscovering Documentary: Cultural Context and Intentionality" present a history of the modes employed by Gómez as well as analyses of how these modes function within a Latin American perspective; they perform the analysis for a "northern" viewer.[12] Burton's introduction states:

From the inception of the social documentary movement in the mid-to-late fifties, Latin American filmmakers began experimenting with a broad range of strategies designed to eliminate, supplant, or subvert the standard documentary mode of address: the anonymous, omniscient, ahistorical "voice of God." ... Long before the technological innovations in sound recording associated with "direct cinema" and "cinéma vérité" were widely available in the region, Latin American filmmakers explored indirect and observational modes in an attempt to pluralize and democratize modes of documentary address ... In their drive to subvert or eliminate the authoritarian narrator, some filmmakers substituted intertitles ... [and ceded the voice-of-God to] on-camera and/or on-microphone presence of the filmmakers or their surrogates, and the self-presentation of social actors.[13]

The issue of voice-over and its function as a trace of the presence of the disembodied patriarchal authority has long been the subject of feminist and feminist-postcolonial critique. Clearly, feminist and decolonizing cinemas overlap in their subversion of that type of authority. And this is certainly true for *Mi aporte*: the direct critique of machismo and the formal choice to have women speak directly and in voice-over, as well as the decision to have the director, her microphone, and the social actors all registered as collaborators in the construction of this representation, all participate equally in feminist and decolonizing principles. However, in the case of Latin America in general and Cuba in particular, the voice-of-God was never only, or even initially, a patriarchal figure: it was the master, the colonizer, the imperialist. Gómez's contribution to an already highly politicized, specifically decolonizing, formal strategy was to reveal gender as another culture of authority that oppresses women by marginalizing their participation and devaluing their time (the latter point is especially clear in *Año uno*). These two critiques – the decolonizing and the feminist – do not collapse into one another when viewed through the lens of Latin American documentary tradition; nor is the gendered analysis a mere supplement. By critically engaging in this decolonizing project, Gómez declares herself a full participant as critic and comrade. For example, her use of intertitles, in this and other films, declares her solidarity with the experimental documentary project developed by her ICAIC colleague, Santiago Alvarez, whose film *NOW!* (1965) is perhaps best known. As Burton has pointed out, the genealogy of experimentalism that Alvarez embodies extends from Vertov and is translated through the particular aesthetics and politics of Latin America. Understanding and taking a place in this project underscores the experimental process of popular democracy and authorizes an Afro-Cuban woman to explicitly and critically engage with the deeply problematic issue of women's autonomy.

Turning now to Chanan's typology of Cuban documentary, we will see how fully Gómez participates and experiments with tradition. Chanan takes the ICAIC's content-driven typology of Cuban documentary and reformulates it through the lens of intentionality, thus providing a means through which to see the politics of form. These categories are derived from the most frequently used terms in Latin American documentary theory and criticism: *cine didáctico, cine testimonia, cine denuncia, cine encuesta, cine rescate, cine celebrativo, cine ensayo, cine reportaje, cine de combate*. As Chanan explains:

The distinctive feature of all the terms listed is precisely their intentional character. They indicate a variety of purposes: to teach, to offer testimony, to denounce, to investigate, to bring history alive, to celebrate revolutionary achievement, to provide space for reflection, to report, to express solidarity, to militate for a cause. These are all needs of revolutionary struggle, both before and after the conquest of power, when they become part of the process of consolidating, deepening, and extending the revolution.[14]

Gómez's *Mi aporte* clearly presents itself as an instance of *cine reportaje;* however, the report card on women's progress is formally provided by employing some of the other "traditions." For instance, it investigates and protests the unequal development of women and men; it rescues women's voices from silence, and, by offering the women a role not only in the representation itself, but also in the interpretation of the images produced, it extends the *cine didáctico* intention ("to impart the means for the acquisition of more and better knowledge upon which action may be premised") into the heart of the lifeworld – the home and childrearing. Again, the dialectical structure of the film is especially noteworthy because it presents a means by which to think critically rather than just a content that requires consideration. One signature of Gómez's authorship in this collaborative film is the retelling and recontextualization of images seen earlier. Clearly, this is not unique to her, but it does disclose her abiding commitment to provide the means for the interrogation of representations, even her own. Repetition recontextualizes the Vertovian "fragments of actuality," it realizes a politics of time through form, and it constitutes an important part of the dialectical structure of both *Mi aporte* and her later feature film *De cierta manera.* Given that the latter was edited by her colleagues after her death and that footage was lost due to damage, *Mi aporte* provides an important clue to the postproduction presence of the director.[15]

Transculturation and Popular Culture

Issues related to the interconnection between popular culture, race, and cultural difference are less central to *Mi aporte* than they are to some of Gómez's other documentaries, particularly *Iré a Santiago, Crónica de mi familia,* the trio of films on the Isle of Pines, *Y ... tenemos sabor,* and *Poder local, poder popular.* Nonetheless, cultural traditions and gender-power issues occupy an important place in the image repertoire and the politics of representation of *Mi aporte.* Afro-Cuban women were the most marginalized Cubans before the revolution. *Mi aporte's* "report" remembers this reality by ensuring that their voices and images contribute to the ongoing work of the popular struggle for equality. Significantly, as with gender issues, Gómez does not collapse cultural difference into a singular narrative of nation and revolution. The critical consciousness embodied in the films and their social subjects presents a version of Cuban culture and society as the double-time of nationalism and cultural difference, first articulated as "transculturation" by Fernando Ortiz in his 1940 ethnographic study *Contrapunteo Cubano del Tabaco y el Azúcar* (*Cuban Counterpoint: Tobacco and Sugar*): "I am of the opinion that the word *transculturation* better expresses the different phases of the process of transition from one culture to another because this does not consist merely in acquiring another culture, which is what the English word *acculturation* really implies, but the process also necessarily involves the loss or uprooting of a previous culture, which could be defined as a deculturation."[16] That the women of *Mi aporte* are seen working in the sugar warehouse and the tobacco factory, that they are White, Mulatto, and Black side by side, and that they all experience the as yet unrealized promise of gender equality but articulate that expectation differently according to their cultural contexts – all this together signifies an attempt on the part of Gómez to present the culture of gender as a transcultural phenomenon.

William Rowe and Vivian Schelling have argued that mixed-race, or *mestizaje,* identity can function for the state as a sign of racial harmony, thus obscuring the power held by a particular group.[17] However, from the freeze-frame at the beginning of Alea's *Memories of Underdevelopment* to Giral's *Maria Antonia,* to any of Gómez's films, the Mulatto/Afro-Cuban identity functions as an especially powerful sign of the violence of the history of the encounter of cultural difference – an image not necessarily subsumable within the narratives of Cuban national or revolutionary identity. But the deployment of such images is consonant with the decolonizing aims of Cuban revolutionary and experimental culture. Zuzana Pick argues that the ideology of *mestizaje* is a site of cultural difference as opposed to diversity;[18] Franco writes that it is *mestizaje* that separates Latin America from all other colonial ventures and that its cultural manifestation is not simply hybridity but a radical fragmentation that defies categorization.[19]

Rowe and Schelling make a case for understanding popular culture in Latin America: "When popular culture is defined not as an object, a meaning or a social group, but as a site – or, more accurately, a series of dispersed sites – then it generates a principle of opposition to the idea ... of the national body as a single body."[20] What is "popular" and what is "folklore" in Cuba after the revolution presents an interesting problem for Afro-Cuban identity. The early work of the revolution saw marginalized popular traditions gain centrality and authority in the project of building a new national culture. The New Theatre movement performed plays aimed at both political and aesthetic education through the use of themes pertinent to the audience/community's concerns, and the use of music, masks, and so on reflected local cultural traditions. These dispersed sites of cultural practice, rooted in tradition but transformed by revolutionary purpose, did permit previously marginalized cultures to participate in the project. However, after the Bay of Pigs in 1961,[21] when Castro declared "within the revolution everything, outside the revolution, nothing" – and we must see "revolution" and "Cuba" to be interchangeable now – local cultural traditions with religious connotations and ritual value were remarginalized as "folklore" and then housed in national institutions such as the Folklore Group. According to Rowe and Schelling, Cuban socialism thus repeats the enlightenment-modernity trajectory of educating "the people" as a unified body away from superstition and irrationalisms.

Gómez's work marks this shift as a double danger. First, when museofied as "folklore" – as a "distanced past" and a sign of underdevelopment – the problematic ritualized orders of a patriarchal governance (such as Abakua[22]) are reproduced or repeated within social relations. Not subject to historical transformations – to coeval temporal creation and communications with other institutions – the religious practitioners are thus not subjects of history. The second danger is that, given that these folkloric practices are AFRO-Cuban, this marginalization reassigns a racial difference to an already historically repressed group. Hence, Gómez's films seek to reframe these cultural practices as popular subjects of and in history. History, however, is not accorded a single formation of monumental or revolutionary time; for Gómez, the specificity of cultural memory requires that the revolutionary narrative be dispersed and popular.

Postcolonial Encounters

The distance and difference of time and space presented by the documentaries demand of the non-Cuban viewer a type of self-reflection qualitatively different from the engagement proffered by *De cierta manera* and other narrative films of the period. Surprisingly little has been written about the issues of viewing and analyzing documentary films across cultural difference. Further work, beyond what I introduce here, can be effectively undertaken by juxtaposing Vivian Sobchack's phenomenology of nonfiction film viewing with the concept of the "contact zone," developed by Mary Louise Pratt.[23] Extrapolating from the work of Jean-Pierre Meunier, Sobchack theorizes the documentary viewing experience as one that is primarily about comprehension rather than evocation. (The reverse is true for the home movie or *film-souvenir*.)

> Identification in the documentary experience involves a *process of learning* that occurs *contemporaneously* with viewing the film. Nonetheless, given the cultural knowledge we have of our life-world, which includes the

already posited existence of people and events we know (if only through mediation of some type), we still take up the objective specificity of a particular documentary image as a *general* form.[24]

One could thus say that the chronotope of documentary spectatorship is the experience of being between the nostalgia (what Meunier calls "empty sympathy") of the home movie and the intensified "present-tense" of consciousness of the fiction film. As Sobchack writes: "Each documentary image, then, possesses a general existential reality presented across multiple specific views. The specific information in each image is retained and integrated with subsequent images to form our cumulative knowledge of that general reality we know exists or has existed 'elsewhere' in our life-world. Thus documentary consciousness is structured as a particular temporal relation between the past and the present."[25] This condition of viewing in double-time is intensified when the historical reality of the document is of a culture not one's own, thus suspending or at least complicating the references to "elsewhere" in *our* lifeworld.

The contact zone designates "the social spaces where disparate cultures meet, clash, and grapple with each other, often in highly asymmetrical relations of domination and subordination – like colonialism, slavery, or their aftermaths as they are lived out across the globe today."[26] I suggest that the scene of engagement with the films of Gómez – or the scene of any cross-cultural film viewership and analysis – is a contact zone: "the spatial and temporal co-presence of subjects previously separated by geographic and historical disjunctures, and whose trajectories now intersect ... A 'contact' perspective emphasizes how subjects are constituted in and by their relations to each other ... copresence, interaction, interlocking understandings and practices, often within radically asymmetrical relations of power."[27] Clearly, the encounter with images cannot be equated with an encounter with the social subjects of those images. However, the cross-cultural encounter with documentary images can be a cognitive and emotional, ethical and political experience that engenders a different analytic language, a "contact language" that itself requires a relinquishing of tools that work perfectly well elsewhere. By employing Pratt's concept of the contact zone together with Ortiz's concept of "transculturation" to analyze the films and the forms of knowledge produced by such analysis, one may be to able to give historical and political bases to Sobchack's phenomenological approach to viewing nonfiction film.

Sara Gómez's documentaries are original and committed works that offer contemporary viewers, scholars, and filmmakers insight into the possibilities for autobiographical and auto-ethnographic film, framing the dialectic of race, gender, and revolution in a form appropriate to the content, and opening future paths for decolonizing cinemas. Not suited to the discourses of "hybrid cinema," which describe the film production of a postcolonial consciousness, Gómez's work stages and reveals the encounters between different structures of power, between marginality and authority, and between contesting ideologies of gender and race. The politics of form is consistent with a cultural politics of *mestizaje*. The particularity of ethnicity and gender identity is, however, inconsistent with the synthesizing and equalizing task of the revolution. Gómez's work consistently refocuses the *unfinished* work of the popular struggle for social change. In doing so, however, she also represents Afro-Cuban traditions as parts of a historical and material culture that is embodied in everyday life. Cultural memory is thus represented in the present tense, subject to social, political, and subjective revisions. The reframing of women's and Afro-Cuban culture does not function within the tradition of salvage ethnography; rather, they are presented as problematic but rich and complex living cultures, long subject to historical time, and brought into dialogue with revolutionary aims.

Acknowledgments

This chapter is made possible thanks to the generous support of SSHRC and the dedicated research assistance given me by Marlena Little. Thanks to David McIntosh for introducing me to Gómez's documentaries.

Notes

1 The following pages represent the initial stage of a larger research project in which I will analyze Gómez's work in terms of the social and cultural construction of temporality and its vital role in transculturation as well as in relation to similar thematic and formal strategies in work by women in postcolonial and decolonizing contexts. Her work can be seen as initiating reflection on the transcultural conditions that represent the power and authority of tradition and the self-certainty and promises of modernity in tension and in doubt. This encounter renders an especially complicated yet productive space for the appearance of women as agents of social change and cultural expression. For, as culturally specific gender roles and temporal realities are threatened by the standard time of modernization and commodification, a view of the gains and losses brought by the encounter becomes tangible and available to critique and reflection. The appearance of this "new woman" as an agent rather than symbol depends upon collectivities and new formations of social relations. This describes precisely the project expressed by Gómez.
    As yet, only Gómez's feature, *De cierta manera*, is available in distribution.

2 The literature on ethnography and ethnographic film has grown considerably in the last decade; the same is true for feminist documentary. However, what is lacking is a meta-theory or methodology for undertaking critical analyses of documentaries from another culture and time. Hence, the work I undertake here is largely extrapolated from methods meant for other forms of writing and research: anthropology, ethnographic filmmaking and research, fiction film theory, and so on.

3 "Chronotope" is used in cultural theory and film theory to refer to fundamental forms of self-understanding held by identities and cultures. This term originates in M.M. Bakhtin's "Forms of Time and of the Chronotope in the Novel," in *The Dialogic Imagination: Four Essays* (Austin: University of Texas Press, 1981). He writes: "We will name *chronotope* (literally 'time space') the intrinsic contectedness of temporal and spatial relationships that are artistically expressed in literature ... In the literary artistic chronotope, spatial and temporal indicators are fused into one carefully thought-out, concrete whole. Time, as it were, thickens, takes on flesh, becomes artistically visible; likewise, space becomes charged and

responsive to the movements of time, plot and history. This intersection of axes and fusion of indicators characterized the artistic chronotope" (84).

4   1 January 1959 marks the fall of the government of Fulgencio Batista and the beginning of Fidel Castro's revolutionary government. (Editor's note.)

5   Johannes Fabian, *Time and the Other: How Anthropology Makes Its Other* (New York: Columbia University Press, 1983), writes: "[evolutionary time] promoted a scheme in terms of which not only past cultures, but all living societies were irrevocably placed on a temporal slope, a stream of Time – some upstream, others downstream. Civilization, evolution, development, acculturation, modernization (and their cousins, industrialization, urbanization) are all terms whose conceptual content derives, in ways that can be specified, from evolutionary Time." Written in 1983, this critique of Eurocentric modern anthropology is now familiar, and specific variants have been taken up in ethnography and documentary film studies to discuss the content of the ethnographic document and the relationship between the filmmaker and the social actors. It has not been employed in a meta-critical manner to discuss the scene of viewing ethnographic (etc.) documentary. This is one arena I hope to develop in the larger project.

6   For a recent exchange about identity, revolutionary cinema, and critique that finds *De cierta manera* a focal point, see the series of essays and replies in *Screen*: Catherine Davies, "Reply to John Hess," *Screen* 40, 2 (Summer 1999): 208-11; Davies, "Modernity, Masculinity and Imperfect Cinema in Cuba," *Screen* 38: 4 (Winter 1997): 245-59; John Hess, "No mas Habermas, or ... Rethinking Cuban Cinema in the 1990s," *Screen* 40: 2 (Summer 1999): 203-7; Oscar Quiros, "Critical Mass of Cuban Cinema: Art as the Vanguard of Society," *Screen* 37, 3 (1996): 279-93.

7   Ana López, "Revolution and Dreams: The Cuban Documentary Today," *Studies in Latin American Popular Culture* 11 (1992): 46-7.

8   For more on the history of Cuban documentary see López, "Revolution and Dreams, 45-57; Michael Chanan, *The Cuban Image: Cinema and Cultural Politics in Cuba* (London/Indiana: British Film Institute/Indiana University Press, 1985); Michael Chanan, "Rediscovering Documentary: Cultural Context and Intentionality," in *The Social Documentary in Latin America*, ed. J. Burton (Pittsburgh: University of Pittsburgh Press, 1990); and Julianne Burton "Democratizing Documentary: Modes of Address in the Latin American Cinema," in *The Social Documentary in Latin America*, ed. J. Burton (Pittsburgh: University of Pittsburgh Press, 1990).

9   See Linda Williams, "Mirrors Without Memories," in *Documenting the Documentary: Close Readings of Documentary Film and Video*, ed. B. Grant and J. Sloniowski (Detroit: Wayne State University Press, 1998), 386-7.

10   Julia Lesage, "Feminist Documentary: Aesthetics and Politics," in *Show Us Life: Toward the History and Aesthetics of the Committed Documentary*, ed. Thomas Waugh (Metuchen, NJ: Scarecrow Press, 1984), 231, 246.

11   Bill Nichols, *Representing Reality: Issues and Concepts in Documentary* (Bloomington and Indianapolis: Indiana University Press, 1991). See esp. the chapter titled "Documentary Modes of Representation."

12   Burton, "Democratizing Documentary"; Chanan, "Rediscovering Documentary."

13   Burton, "Democratizing Documentary," 49.

14   Chanan, *The Cuban Image*, 37.

15   "The editing, at the moment of her death, was well advanced. Most sequences were already cut, and the commentary had beeen planned, though not all of it written" (Chanan, *The Cuban Image*, 282).

16   Fernando Ortiz, *Cuban Counterpoint: Tobacco and Sugar*, trans. Harriet de Onís (New York: A.A. Knopf, 1947), 102. The following assemblage of quotations provides a summary of the concept of "transculturation": "Among all peoples historical evolution has always meant a vital change from one culture to another at tempos varying from gradual to sudden. But in Cuba the cultures that have influenced the formation of its folk have been so many and so diverse in their spatial position and their structural composition that this vast blend of races and cultures overshadows in importance every other historical phenomenon. Even

economic phenomena, the most basic factors of social existence, in Cuba are almost always conditioned by the different cultures. ... The whole gamut of culture run by Europe in a span of more than four millenniums took place in Cuba in less than four centuries ... The Negroes brought with their bodies their souls but not their institutions nor their implements. They were of different regions, races, languages, cultures, classes, ages, sexes, thrown promiscuously into the slave ships, and socially equalized by the same system of slavery. They arrived deracinated, wounded, shattered, like the cane of the fields, and like it they were ground and crushed to extract the juice of their labor. No other human element has had to suffer such a profound and repeated change of surrounding, cultures, class, and conscience ... To a greater or lesser degree, whites and Negroes were in the same state of dissociation in Cuba. All those above and below, living together in the same atmosphere of terror and oppression, the oppressed in terror of punishment, the oppressor in terror of reprisals, all beside justice, beside adjustment, beside themselves" (98-102).

17 William Rowe and Vivian Schelling, *Memory and Modernity: Popular Culture in Latin America* (London: Verso, 1991).

18 Zuzana Pick, *The New Latin American Cinema: A Continental Project* (Austin: University of Texas Press, 1993).

19 The importance of the mestizo/a identity and its problem for claiming "the popular" cannot be overestimated. As Jean Franco, *Critical Passions: Selected Essays*, ed. Mary Louise Pratt and Kathleen Newman (Durham and London: Duke University Press, 1999), writes, "the cultural manifestation [of mestizaje] is not simply hybridity but its multifaceted and evanescent surface can be read as so many personal and fragmented histories that it defies categorization" (211). The discourses of abjection, margin, and periphery continue to pervade Latin American cultural theory, clearly serving as a corrective to anyone trying to analyze those cultural representations through Northern frameworks of power plays and dispersals. As Franco has written across a number of articles, the language of "periphery" adequately describes the distinctions between metropolitan and rural cultures and social formations. The meaning produced by the centre loses its substance and sense in the marginal cultural reality. The periphery describes those moments when enlightenment narrative fails to offer universal explanatory power: the project of the centre is misrecognized at the periphery.

20 Rowe and Schelling, *Memory and Modernity*, 2.

21 The Bay of Pigs invasion took place on a south shore of Cuba on 17 April 1961, a mere two years after the victory of the Revolution. Through the CIA training of Cuban émigrés, and with the help of dictatorships in Nicaragua and Guatemala, the United States, under Kennedy, invaded the island. Within seventy-two hours, the counter-revolutionaries surrendered. Eventually 1,197 of them were returned to the US in exchange for 53 million dollars worth of medicine and food.

22 Abakua is a social formation scrutinized by Gómez in *De cierta manera*. It is a male secret society founded in Havana in the nineteenth century by the Africans of Calabar. It is known also as *ñañiguismo*. See Pedro Perez Sarduy and Jean Stubbs, eds., *AfroCuba: An Anthology of Cuban Writing on Race, Politics, and Culture* (New York: Ocean Press, 1993).

23 See Mary Louise Pratt, *Imperial Eyes: Travel Writing and Transculturation* (London: Routledge, 1992).

24 Ibid., 249.

25 Vivian Sobchack, "Nonfictional Film Experience," in *Collecting Visible Evidence*, ed. Jane Gaines and Michael Renov (Minneapolis and London: Minnesota University Press, 1999), 250.

26 Pratt, *Imperial Eyes*, 7.

27 Ibid., 9.

Sprung from Sisterhood: Interview
with Yue-Qing Yang on Making *Nu Shu:*
A Hidden Language of Women in China
Conducted by Larissa Lai and Agnes Huang

> East of the Guilin hills of China, there is a secret hidden in the
> mountain villages ... No man could read it. Not even the emperor
> knew about it, for it was forbidden. The secret is Nu Shu, meaning
> women's writing.

These are the words that lead into the opening credits of Yue-Qing Yang's
film, *Nu Shu: A Hidden Language of Women in China*. Completed as an independent production, the film celebrates the unique language system created and used exclusively by Chinese women in Hunan province. For several
centuries, and perhaps even a millennium, these women in southern China
communicated with each other in a script that only they could understand.
This "secret" script was called Nu Shu. "Nu" means "women," and "shu"
means "writing" – thus "women's writing." Nu Shu was revolutionary on a
number of levels. As a language, Nu Shu represented a completely new system: it was syllabic, whereas Chinese (Nan Shu, or men's writing) was
pictographic. Nu Shu also signified the revolution of women against male
dominance, and of the Southern Yao people against the Northern Confucian Han Chinese culture.[1]

As a language created by and for women, it is not surprising that Nu Shu
sprang out of the sisterhood of women. Many of the Nu Shu women in a
particular village were sworn sisters, bonded for life. Nu Shu was embedded
in the everyday practices of these women (such as weaving), and it was
written on the everyday things they used (such as fans, handkerchiefs, and
clothing items). As it was sung and often written in seven-character phrases,
Nu Shu was also very poetic.

Until recently, Nu Shu remained "secret" – unacknowledged outside the
region. It wasn't until the 1980s that Nu Shu was "recognized" by academics and authorities as a language system. There is now a Nu Shu dictionary,
and many of the songs have been translated into Chinese. Sadly, though,
Nu Shu was devastated during the revolutions that purported to liberate
women. After the Communist liberation of 1949, Nu Shu customs (along
with many customs in local regions) were indiscriminately abolished. By
the 1960s, and particularly during the Cultural Revolution, Nu Shu was

Yue-Qing Yang's *Nu Shu*:
*A Hidden Language of Women
in China* (1999), courtesy of
the director

virtually extinguished. Today, there are just a few Yao women who can read and write Nu Shu.

There are several different stories as to the origins of Nu Shu. Although it is not certain who started Nu Shu, all the legends agree on one point: it was a most gifted young woman, and she created this language by transforming the Chinese she knew through embroidery and weaving patterns. One scholar noted that, in Han Chinese areas, the oppression of women was greater than it was in the Yao regions; yet that was not where Nu Shu was invented. Yue-Qing Yang concludes that "perhaps it wasn't oppression that initiated Nu Shu's invention, though this undoubtedly explains its secret use. Its creation may be better explained by the relative freedom and equality of Yao culture, which allowed women's natural creativity to flourish."

Yang was born and raised in Shandong province in eastern China. Although she was trained as a biologist in both China and Canada, *Nu Shu* is not her first foray into the filmmaking world. In 1989, Yang made her first documentary, *The Chinese Forest Frog*, which won the Shennong Honour Award.

As a feminist, Yang says she is "dedicated to uncovering and telling the stories of Chinese women." Her next project is to expand her ten-minute demo film, *Footbinding: The Three Inch Golden Lotus*, into an hour-long documentary. Just before *Nu Shu*'s premiere in Vancouver in June 1999, Larissa Lai and Agnes Huang had the opportunity to interview Yue-Qing Yang.

Larissa Lai: How did you first hear of Nu Shu?

Yue-Qing Yang: I first heard about Nu Shu from a friend. In the 1980s, when Nu Shu was first recognized as a written language, China's Central Television Station made a national news broadcast about it. The news broadcast was shown in Canada, which is how some people here heard about it. Then, at the fourth United Nations World Conference on Women in Beijing, where I was presenting my video on footbinding, I met a woman from the Taiwan Women's Bookstore. We talked about Nu Shu. And later I found a researcher at a local university in Beijing who also knew about it.

LL: I like the self-reflexivity in your film: you place yourself as a narrator from the very beginning. You start by talking about searching out Nu Shu in Hunan province. Later on, there's a segment about a woman you interviewed named Wu. You explain how your crew forgot to give her a red money packet, which was given to all the other women, so she was beaten by her husband and forbidden to come back the next day. Could you talk about why you decided to include yourself in the body of the film instead of making the film as a conventional, distanced documentary?

YQY: It was easier for me to tell a story, and it was clearer why I was telling this story when I linked it with my own process of finding out what Nu Shu is all about. Nu Shu says a lot about the past and present status of women. Not many people know about Nu Shu, even in China. Sadly, we don't know how popular Nu Shu was before it was destroyed because there is no record of its herstory.

LL: What kinds of things did women write about in Nu Shu?

YQY: Women wrote Nu Shu most before they got married and after their husbands died. Before their marriages, they mainly wrote about sisterhood, and after their husbands died, they mainly wrote about widowhood. Most of the writings during widowhood were autobiographic. The tradition has carried on even today. A few women still go to Huan-Yi, the only woman of her generation still living who can read and write Nu Shu, and ask her to write about their lives.

LL: So Nu Shu as a language is still alive then?

YQY: I wouldn't say that. Nu Shu is not naturally alive; it is interfered with. There was a break in the use of Nu Shu during the Cultural Revolution (1966-76). There are two reasons some women have come back to Nu Shu. One is that elder women only know Nu Shu; they don't know Nan Shu. The other is the attention Nu Shu women have received from researchers interested in the subject.

LL: Is there any interest among young Hunanese women in learning Nu Shu, or is it purely an academic pursuit?

YQY: It's mostly academic. Young women nowadays don't learn anything about Nu Shu when they're in school. It would be a totally new thing for them to learn. Before the 1930s, when young women weren't allowed to get a formal education, they learned Nu Shu from other women. When they were allowed to attend school to learn Nan Shu, they still went to other women to learn Nu Shu, so they received a double education. During the Cultural Revolution, a number of women were publicly prosecuted for using Nu Shu. This was a strong message from the authorities telling women to shut up. In fact, when the Communists took over in 1949, they abolished many of the local customs: everything old, which was considered backward, was abolished. In the early stages, what many women wanted to abandon and what the Communists wanted to abandon was the same: the "backward" traditions.

I was very influenced by Communism's strong stance on the equality of women. The Communists improved women's status; in order to get women's support, the Communists had to give women freedom. Women supported the Communist revolution because from the revolution women stood to gain the most. And with women's support, the men supporting the revolution gained the most.

It's interesting that the Communist feminist movement didn't make a link with Nu Shu, which sends me a message that the feminist movement in China was and is very male-oriented!

Agnes Huang: Why wouldn't the feminist movement consider Nu Shu "feminist"?

YQY: Even today, prominent feminists in China don't think Nu Shu is feminist because it's not about "political" rights. Yet when I got to Hunan, I felt so empowered by these women. These women are the strongest source of the feminist movement in China. Our mothers and grandmothers – who had bound feet and who looked very "backward" – survived; they brought up families, they were abused, they suffered, but they survived. Our feminist source is not the middle-class, British, go-to-the-streets-and-ask-for-our-rights style. That is not our way. Look what Nu Shu says about marriage: "Zhi yuan huang di zhi cuo li" (This damn emperor made the wrong custom / why should I have to be married away). This statement to me is so enlightening. Confucians for thousands of years have been saying, "Jia tien xia" (Family under heaven). So if these women are saying Confucian marriage is wrong, then they're also saying the whole patriarchal system is wrong.

LL: It's interesting that the bulk of Nu Shu writing takes place before marriage and after widowhood. These are the moments when women are the most independent, the moments that seem to be the most ideal states.

YQY: What the women wrote and received in Nu Shu, they never let their husbands see. Most of their stories were about their husbands. In that case, it was inconvenient to be married because there were men in the house. When their husbands died, there were no limits.

AH: It isn't clear to me from your film whether all women and girls learned Nu Shu or if only specific women and girls learned Nu Shu and became sworn sisters.

YQY: Nu Shu was available to all the women. However, not every woman knew how to write. In each village, there were a few women who were good at Nu Shu and they acted as scribes for other women.

LL: Could you talk about the sworn sisterhoods? How were they organized, how did they come to be, what were their roots, and did they constitute some sort of feminist practice?

YQY: Sworn sisterhoods have a long tradition in China. It's parallel to brotherhoods. A man's friends were other men, never women. Men respected their mother because she brought them up, not because she was a person. In order to respect their father and the emperor, men had to respect their mother. Within marriage, men and women didn't have any intimacy at all. The family was totally functional – to bring up children, to let the husband's blood-line continue. Confucius said, "Brother is like my hand / wife is like my clothes." Clothes can be taken off and thrown away and you can get another set, but you cannot chop off your hand and get another one. Under these beliefs, a lot of sworn brotherhoods formed. Women's sisterhood has never been recognized. The difference in these areas of Hunan province is that the women there have similar ceremonies [to those of] men when they form their sworn sisterhoods. This kind of practice is allowed, while in the North, any kind of sisterhood remains hidden.

LL: Why do you think that is?

YQY: The Yao culture is more equal in nature. When Confucius was alive, no one accepted his ideas. When he went to the South to publicize his thinking, he was laughed at for his patriarchal ideas. After Confucius died, his ideas were adopted by the emperor because he found it was the best way to support his power. Today in China, I think we've abandoned our cultural identity – in the way we dress and the way we manage our country. Before, Mainland China put forth a strong identity, saying we're Communists, we're Chinese. But since the open door policy in the late 1980s, which opened China to foreign investment, people in China have been unquestioningly adopting things from the West, particularly America. When I see the young people playing rock-n-roll – lousy rock-n-roll – I think, "Wow, Chinese people have abandoned their identity and their souls too."

I think the Yao system is more democratic than today's Western democracy. Women in Canada still get married and change their last names to their husband's – marrying into *his* family. So even in this society where many women see themselves as feminist, I haven't seen any system better than the Yaos', where men marry into women's families as well as the other way around. That was another discovery I found very empowering. We have lots of resources in China. In the past, we overlooked the Yao people because we thought they were barbarians. In the present, we overlook them because they're not modern enough. We should learn to pay more attention to their ideas of equality and not just who's in power.

AH: Did the Yao people have their own written language?

YQY: Historically, they may have had some symbols they carved in stone or embroidered into patterns. Over the years though, that was probably lost. Later on, the emperor forbade anyone to make their own script, so the Yao people don't have their own written language now.

AH: Do you know if Nu Shu came out of the Yao language?

YQY: There's no evidence of that. The evidence is that Nu Shu describes words and concepts in the Chinese language itself. It's kind of a local dialect.

LL: I found the idea that Nu Shu may have come out of embroidery very interesting. In one of the Nu Shu songs, the women sing, "Women embroider / Men study books." There seems to be a sense of equality, a balance between these two practices.

YQY: Men have Nan Shu; women have Nu Shu. Men have their male brothers; women have their female sisters. So yes, they had a strong sense of equality.

LL: There's very much a sense of empowerment – empowerment embedded in women's practices.

AH: Nu Shu script was often written on fans and handkerchiefs and embroidered into quilts and clothing. Was this done on purpose so nobody knew the women were passing letters to each other?

YQY: First of all, the summers in Hunan are very hot and long. Fans are popular as a gift. There's a poem called "Chu shan" – a fan is a pleasant gift because it can bring comfort to you. A handkerchief is also very common and handy. Even the third daybook, which was written in Nu Shu and explained the ceremony Yao women held on the third day after marriage, was used to hold embroidery patterns. Nu Shu wasn't secret in the village itself.

LL: I'm amazed at how the practice of Nu Shu is embedded in everyday life.

YQY: It's very organic. Nu Shu is more alive as a language because it uses things the women use in their day-to-day lives.

LL: It would be really interesting to go to Guangzhou and hook up with the descendants of these Nu Shu women, to see how they live their lives.

YQY: The Nu Shu customs died and young Yao women mostly learn Chinese Nan Shu and adopt "modern" lives. Some young women know Nu Shu, but it's like, "When the earth is gone, how long can a flower stay?" Nu Shu is like a flower that grows in the air.

Acknowledgment
Originally published in *Kinesis,* June 1999.

Note
1 Located in South China, the Yao people are an ethnic group, of which there are many in China in addition to the dominant Han people (92 percent of the population). The Yao people are in the majority in Jian-yong county of Hunan, where Yue-Qing Yang did her research on Nu Shu.

Part 6

National and Cultural Montages: Crossing Boundaries

One remarkable aspect of the "Women Filmmakers: Refocusing" conference was the strong presence of filmmakers with connections to India. Although several had the experience of filming in India but living elsewhere, they were otherwise very different. This section begins with a chapter by Jacqueline Levitin, which introduces the works of Deepa Mehta, a well known Canadian director of Indian origin whose feature films (especially *Fire* and the currently suspended *Water*) have been highly controversial in India. Excerpts from an interview and a master class conducted at the conference convey the wealth of experience that Mehta was willing to share. Her stories of confrontation and collaboration, as well as the technical information she provided, were eye-opening in terms of enabling people to recognize the risks and challenges faced by a filmmaker who bridges two cultures.

Similar issues emerged in very different ways from the interview and master class with British documentary maker Pratibha Parmar, whose films are introduced by Tracy Prince. They have also provoked debate, especially in feminist circles, since Parmar is not afraid to tackle such sensitive topics as female excision in Africa, sex and people with disabilities, South Asian gays and lesbians, racism in Britain, and women stars of the popular music scene. In spite of her success with documentaries, Parmar also dreams of finding the funding to produce a full-length feature film. Like several other participants, she acknowledges the contribution of British television's Channel Four in making it possible for large audiences to see films that expose the lives and preoccupations of people of colour and lesbians and gays in Britain.

The experience of Raman Mann, a prize-winning Indian documentary maker who lives and works in India is very different from the experiences of Mehta and Parmar, who have both filmed in India and in the West (Canada, the US, and the UK). Many of Mann's films in Hindi are primarily aimed at educating rural women about health and environmental issues, while those in English are made for a specific purpose (e.g., *Barred from Life* helped to free some women who were serving life sentences). An interview with Patricia

Plattner (who, in Chapter 17, talks about her experiences as a Swiss film-maker) addresses her experience of filming *Made in India*. This visually stunning feature-length documentary on rural women's organizing is aimed primarily at a Western audience, the hope being that it will focus attention on the success of these women's model and that it might be imitated in other parts of the world.

These filmmakers have very different experiences accessing funding and other resources, including equipment and the latest technology, as well as in their contacts with local people involving language and other types of cultural communication. Their films are made with different intentions, in very different styles. While Bollywood is not represented here, the work of these extremely determined, creative, and successful women illustrates the range of films being made in India.

25 An Introduction to Deepa Mehta: Making Films in Canada and India

With extracts from an interview conducted by Kass Banning[1]

Jacqueline Levitin

Kass Banning: East and West. Your work of course is a hybrid of these influences. Could you address how you perhaps come to blur the boundaries – what is authentic Indian, what is authentic Canadian cinema, etc.?

Deepa Mehta: You know, I really don't give a damn anymore ... It's so irrelevant! The point is, can I – do I – have the ability to do a film that I really believe in? And that's what it's about. Because if I start thinking about "Am I too Western, am I too Eastern?" I'd never be able to do anything.

Draping a bright orange shawl over her black *salwar kameez*, Deepa Mehta seems both distantly self-confident and tentatively ready for communication as she addresses the Vancouver audience of her master class. After four feature films, she is Canada's most internationally renowned woman filmmaker. A description of Mehta that includes a national designation such as this, however, is awkward given Mehta's pronounced dislike for labels and her frequent ambivalence, even annoyance, in response to queries about what "being Canadian" means to her. At the time of her appearance at the "Women Filmmakers: Refocusing" conference she had lived an equal measure of her life in India, her country of origin, and in Canada, where she immigrated in 1973. However, more recently this balance is tipping towards India. Frustrated with restrictions on her filmmaking career in Canada, Mehta has been returning to India for at least a good portion of each year. She explains that, at this point, she wants only to produce stories that impassion her and that these stories are Indian stories. Telling these stories in India, however, has added "controversial" to the "renowned woman filmmaker" label. Mehta wants her films to stir audiences to thought rather than simply to entertain. And, recognizing her challenge to the patriarchal family, militant Hindu fundamentalists reacted strongly to *Fire* (1996), the first film she produced in India. But Mehta also pays a great deal of attention to the aesthetics and narratives of her films, and, while audiences in Canada or India may be enticed to the theatre by her films' notoriety, they most often find themselves moved and entertained. The ability to manipulate content, aesthetics, and perhaps, controversy defines Mehta's special talent as an independent filmmaker competing in the global market. A more precise description of Mehta, then, might be as a transnational filmmaker attuned to the cinematic traditions of two very dissimilar societies,[2] a feminist with a distaste for rigid nationalisms and oppressive power relations, and an independent filmmaker with an early-honed instinct for the art of film exhibition. Each of these terms deserves to be investigated in more detail.

"Born to the Cinema"

Growing up in India in a comfortably well off family, Mehta recalls wanting to be a doctor in order to save those less fortunate than herself.[3] Instead, philosophy became her field of study at the University of New Delhi. Mehta was born in 1950 in Amritsar, a city on India's border with Pakistan and home to many Hindus and Sikhs who fled the newly created Pakistan at the time of Partition in 1947. It is as Partition, and not as independence from Britain, that most Indians recall 1947 and the events precipitated by Britain's seemingly off-handed division of colonial Indian territory according to the proportion of Hindu and Muslim populations. Mehta grew up hearing stories of the rapes and massacres that occurred as millions relocated to their religious community's side of the border, and Partition is the story of her second film made in India, *Earth* (1998). Originally from Lahore, her father's family was among those forced to flee. In Amritsar, he became a film distributor, owning a few movie theatres where he showed mostly Hindi popular cinema. Mehta recalls watching these films from an early age, mesmerized by the extravagant intrigues, passion, songs, and dance. Years later, while debating whether to continue on to a PhD, she was invited to work for a production company making documentaries for the Indian government. Intrigued by the filmmaking process and by the world of ideas that documentary cinema offered, Mehta agreed to work as the company assistant and typist, fully knowing she had no typing skills. Although her shortcomings as a typist were soon discovered, Mehta was allowed to stay on. In the company, she learned editing, sound, camera work, and how to put a story together; and she directed her first documentary, a film about a child bride. It was while making another documentary that she met her Canadian husband-to-be, Paul Saltzman. ("We were both trying to interview the same woman.") In 1973, she followed Saltzman to Canada where they formed a film production company, Sunrise Films.

At Sunrise, Mehta edited, produced, and directed for television, including for the series *Danger Bay*. In 1985, she directed a more personal television special, *Travelling Light: the Photojournalism of Dilip Mehta*, on the well known photojournalist who is also her brother and business partner.[4] The film received three Gemini (Canada's television awards) nominations, and her first international acclaim when it was judged a finalist at the 1987 New York International Film and Television Festival. This was followed by *Martha, Ruth & Edie* (1987), a television feature produced and co-directed by Mehta, which screened at the Cannes International Film Festival in 1988 and later won the Best Feature Film Award at the 11th International Women's Film Festival in Florence, Italy. Her 1988 television drama, *Inside Stories,* received a Gemini nomination for Best Performance by a Lead Actress. Already an award-winning and seasoned director, Deepa Mehta experienced her real break with the success of her feature film debut, *Sam & Me,* in 1991.

Sam & Me tells the story of Nik, a young Indian who arrives in Canada with an immigrant's hopes and expectations, only to be pushed into taking a job as the caretaker of the elderly, though feisty, father of his obsequious uncle's employer. In Canada, Mehta had also experienced the "immigrant's story." Despite her many career successes, life in Canada shocked Mehta. Growing up in privilege had not prepared her to be treated as a member of a "visible minority." *Sam & Me* was written in collaboration with Ranjit Chowdhry, who plays Nik and who was, himself, a recent arrival to Canada. ("I wrote the story for *Sam & Me* and Ranjit wrote the screenplay ... He's an extremely funny and a bright and an irreverent kind of person. I love him dearly. And he's a fine actor as well. We worked very closely on the script. And I've tried to use him as much as I can in my films.")[5] The dialogue of *Sam & Me* recalls the immigrant experience with a knowing but ironic humour: "Have you seen Gandhi picture?" Nik's Indian cab driver friend recites, imitating his Caucasian fares for Nik, "Indian food very spicy. Indian saris very pretty," but his demonstration client fails to perform on cue. In an interview not long after the film's release,[6] Mehta recalls her own experiences with a similar humour, but also with still stinging bruises (she remembers strangers calling her "Paki bitch" on the street) and a contempt for her new countrymen's paternalism and ignorance. In early years, she told the interviewer, people at parties would ask, "Does she speak English?" – not addressing themselves to her but to her husband. Personal and professional problems plagued Mehta as she made *Sam & Me.* The breakup of her marriage occurred during the film's production, and Telefilm Canada, the federal film and television financing agency, did not agree to Sunrise Films' requests for funding. Sunrise was forced to look to Britain's groundbreaking Channel Four for the missing financing.

Transnational Filmmaker

Although Mehta recalls that she "would have died" if she had been unable to make the deeply personal *Sam & Me,*[7] the changed direction that she took following the success of that film led to a temporary dead end. *Sam & Me* earned Mehta an honourable mention in the Camera d'or (first feature category) at the Cannes Film Festival in 1991 and a startling offer to direct

Deepa Mehta's *Fire* (1996), courtesy of the Film Reference Library, Toronto

first one, then another, episode of George Lucas's television series, *The Young Indiana Jones Chronicles* (*Benares*, 1992) and *Travels with Father* (a movie of the week, 1994). Although these were not personal projects like *Sam & Me*, Mehta felt honoured to be chosen for the director role, and the experience was a pleasant one. Lucas, she says, treated her with respect and support.[8] However, between the two *Young Indiana Jones* episodes came an offer to direct a big budget feature, *Camilla* (1994), a Canadian/UK co-production with stars Jessica Tandy, Bridget Fonda, and Tandy's husband, Hume Cronyn.[9] Mehta liked the script. A road movie, *Camilla*, like *Sam & Me*, told of a friendship across generations – here between an elderly woman escaping a well intentioned but insensitive son, and a young woman whose personal confidence blooms under the old woman's tutelage. Shooting went so well that Mehta did not foresee what was to come: "I was naive," she later explained. "I had assumed I'd get to see the final cut." By the time the studio had finished test marketing the film and "soliciting 'everyone's opinion,'" *Camilla* was "unrecognizable to her." "I learned the hard way, but it was a good lesson."[10]

Blamed for the film's lack of success, Mehta found herself unable to get work. It was then that she decided to make only those films that impassioned her[11] and never again to lose artistic control. However, her next project, *Fire*, about the pressures of tradition within an extended Indian family (a story that impassioned her), did not fit easily into the Canadian scene. Mehta, who this time wrote the script herself, could not imagine her story taking place in Canada, although shooting in India would disqualify her for Canadian government-supported financing; technically, it would no longer be considered a "Canadian" film. Unwilling to compromise, she

Deepa Mehta's *Camilla* (1993), courtesy of the Film Reference
Library, Toronto

Deepa Mehta's *Sam & Me* (1990), courtesy of the Film Reference
Library, Toronto

went to India anyway. "I'm talking about my work here," she clarified for
an audience member who asked her to elaborate on her sense of nationality. "I'm not talking about myself as a person in that sense. I find that I
don't know what defines Canadian film anymore. Because I think that the
definition is difficult as far as a person like me is concerned, a hybrid person
who can move from continent to continent. And at this point in my life,
I'm looking at things that interest me and they all happen to be in India. I
make those films – whether it's *Fire, Earth,* or *Water,* and they are not considered Canadian films. So what am I? I feel like I've been really rejected

and marginalized by Canada because I don't fit into any of the categories that are laid out by the government that defines what a Canadian film is."[12]

Fire was executive-produced by Mehta's companion, David Hamilton, thereby keeping financial and aesthetic control "in the family." Like *Sam & Me*, *Fire* had personal resonance for the filmmaker. Radha, the self-sacrificing wife in *Fire* (played by the highly respected Shabana Azmi), is seduced by her younger and equally unhappy sister-in-law, and agonizes over leaving her husband. Mehta explains that, despite being a supporter of feminist independence, she too had to struggle against ingrained cultural tradition in order to end her marriage.[13] *Fire*, Mehta says, is a film about choices and not simply a narrative about sisters-in-law who develop a lesbian relationship. It is the sisters-in-laws' rebellion against the role women are traditionally expected to accept, she insists, not their lesbianism, that made *Fire* so controversial in India and that explains its universal appeal:

> Mr. Bal Thackeray [local leader of Shiv Sena, a militant Hindu nationalist party] said, "There is no way that *Fire* can ever be screened there – not only in Bombay but in the whole province." And the next day the same thing happened in Delhi, and it was closed down there, with the result that *Fire* became an issue. I mean it wasn't really about *Fire* then. It was about freedom of expression for the people who are for it. It was a very good vehicle for lesbians because Mr. Thackeray was saying that lesbians don't exist in India. And suddenly there were protests and there were marches, and women carrying banners saying, "We are lesbian and we are Indian." And that was a bit of a shock to a lot of people. But more than that, for me, what was fascinating was women who were middle-class housewives who came out in support of *Fire* – who weren't the so-called academics or intellectuals or lesbians, who didn't have labels, who just felt that *Fire* spoke to them. Which is what I see when I think of *Fire* and somebody asks me, "What is *Fire*?" And they say, "Isn't it a lesbian film?" And I say, "No it isn't." Because it's a film about choices. And within that, a certain, very important aspect of it is about a choice that they make, which is a lesbian choice. The film is about choices. So when I saw that people actually had gotten that – the housewives really had put down their vegetables and their cooking and everything aside and were saying, "How dare somebody tell us that this film is not meant for us. We've seen it and if we haven't, we want to have the choice to decide what's good for us and what's not. And who cares about Indian culture anyway?" – that was amazing and I think that that's what really escalated the whole *Fire* controversy. Mr. Thackeray had thought that he could do this because he had been doing it in the past and there would be no backlash. And he was counting on support especially from women who would say, "Yes, you're right; this film is not for our eyes. It doesn't reflect our problems, or it doesn't talk about us in any context." And the

opposite happened. So when they stood up and the protest marches started and the all-night vigils, it wasn't about *Fire*. It was about where India is and where Indian women are at this point in history. And that for me is an incredible bonus as a filmmaker. I didn't expect it; I wasn't looking for it. I was really surprised and very heartened because ... you do a film and then you hope people will go and see it. But you don't expect that it might, at least have the potential perhaps, to bring about a change, which they feel is needed in this society. And that's what happened with *Fire*.[14]

It has been argued that Mehta's comments (she is not a lesbian herself) minimize the particularity of her characters' choice to enter a lesbian relationship and thus also the support she received early on from the lesbian community in India, who defended the film against Hindu fundamentalists.[15] However, her comments here and elsewhere indicate that she wanted to deal not with the particularity of a choice but, rather, with choice as a human right that women have been denied. A similar tendency to abandon partisanship for a broader, ethical position already marked *Sam & Me*, a film that denounces racism, but not only racism against South Asians. The film is an assault on narrow-mindedness generally, and none of its characters is blameless.[16]

Straddling Aesthetic Traditions

In contrast to her earlier work, Mehta's Partition story, *Earth* (1998), begins to resemble a "mainstream Indian film." Unlike *Fire*, which was shot in English and only later translated into Hindi, *Earth*, from the beginning, spoke the languages of India.[17] And surprisingly, although the Partition story is already well known in South Asia but not abroad, the film seems to be primarily directed to an Indian audience because of its choice of well known actors and a popular composer and lyricist as well as its use of unexplained visual clues – clues that are beyond the comprehension of most non-South Asians. The screenplay, as written by Mehta, moves beyond the narrow perspective of Lenny, the child witness to Partition, which is emphasized by Pakistani Parsi writer Bapsi Sidhwa in *Cracking India*, the novel upon which the film was based.[18] This perspective is enlarged to encompass and to accent a cross-ethnic love triangle: Shanta, the *ayah* (Lenny's nanny, sensually played by Nandita Das, the younger sister-in-law of *Fire*), is a Hindu and is loved by two men – Masseur, whom she eventually chooses, and his rival, Ice Candy Man, both Muslims. Partition becomes both backdrop to and catalyst for the love triangle's tragic outcome, an emotional narrative that, in contrast to Sidhwa's understated novel, is reminiscent of popular Hindi cinema's sensationalism.

Following *Earth*, Mehta initiated production on *Water*, the third in her trilogy of films that began with *Fire*. "I think that what really links them all [the trilogy] for me is an exploration of passion and different aspects of it. So it's passion that unites them."[19] Hindu fundamentalist opposition, however, has managed to thwart the production of *Water*. In February 2000, Shiv Sena, whose women's wing, Mahila Agadhi, had earlier led the protest against theatres showing *Fire,* and the Rastriya Swayangsevak Sangh (RSS) organized demonstrations that destroyed the set of *Water* only a few days after shooting began.[20] They spread rumours about the film's lurid and anti-Hindu content. *Water*'s story of widows taking shelter in a house in the holy city of Benares in the 1930s – one widow is driven to prostitution – was said to tarnish the image of widowhood, while the romantic involvement of another widow, a Brahman (the highest Hindu caste), was variously reputed to be with a man from the lowest caste or even a Brahman priest, shocking defenders of the officially condemned, but still practised, caste system.[21] Responding to calls to reveal her film script, the producers invited respected Hindu leaders to study the screenplay. Approval and an apology from one of the holiest and most respected of these leaders did not dissuade Mehta's adversaries. Death threats were issued and Mehta's effigy was burned in protest.

Although the producers had obtained all necessary clearances from both federal and state authorities to begin shooting,[22] and despite a public outcry from those who rallied to Mehta's defence, neither government took responsibility to protect the production against the demonstrators. (The Bharatiya Janatha Party [BJP], the governing party in India, is politically linked to some of the militant groups allegedly involved in the disturbances.)[23] Not only were the perpetrators of the violence not arrested, but officials also accused Mehta's crew of inciting violence merely by being in the city. They were forced to flee. Still later, Mehta's opponents accused her of plagiarism to further discredit her and the film,[24] and rumours circulated that the film was anti-Gandhi, possibly to cool support from those Congress Party-run states that offered the production a new location. As Bapsi Sidhwa reasoned in a letter to the major daily newspaper, the *Hindustan Times,* arguing against the claim of plagiarism, "should not those who have so relentlessly attacked Deepa for making a film about Hindu widows be sitting at Gangopadhyay's doorstep protesting his book, if they consider him the source of her inspiration? The most unfortunate part of all this is that it has managed to deflect attention from the real issue, which is the demise of a film before the first shot has even taken place."[25]

While this is not the first attack of its kind in India, it is likely that *Fire*'s reputation for challenging religious tradition made Mehta the particular object of fundamentalist ire, from Muslims as well as Hindus, and a pawn in the long-standing civil war between the left and the right, the secular and the theocratic.[26] As a response to yet another story of female rebellion (the scenario of *Water* questions customs that require widows to renounce life but say nothing about widowers), the uncensored violence of those who feel attacked by Mehta's liberal message have this time made it impossible for Mehta to turn controversy to her advantage.

The role of a transnational independent filmmaker is difficult. A seemingly tough and fiery character, Mehta has been able to assume this role better than most. While in film circles the rule is that all publicity, good or bad, increases box office, this is not the case if such publicity results in the film not being made. Mehta's strength to fight the shameless means of her detractors comes, in part, from the support given to her by her associates. A caring director, she has won the respect and friendship of both her actors and crew, and they have remained strongly loyal throughout her troubles. (Director of photography Giles Nuttgens, line producer/producer Anne Masson, production designer Aradhana Seth, and editor Barry Farrell have worked with Mehta for several films.) The professional alienation she describes feeling in Canada is, for the moment at least, matched by rejection in India, where troubled memories of colonization and suspicions about the influences of globalization can be stirred up against any and all foreigners. To those now calling the tune, Mehta's class and British education as well as her Canadian citizenship mark her as an outsider in a country where she had expected to feel at home. This blow is a hard one for a filmmaker who has continually fought for tolerance for all differences. The significant lesson Mehta calls upon from her years of filmmaking is, simply, to persevere.

Postscript

Following unsuccessful efforts to keep the production of *Water* going, Mehta returned to Canada. She has put off further production on the film "until the political climate in India changes." In 2002, her company completed a comedy entitled *Bollywood Hollywood* (Bollywood is named after Bombay, India's film capital), this time with Telefilm Canada's cooperation and financial support. She is scheduled to begin another production, this one for Columbia-Tri-Star, an adaptation of Alice Walker's *By the Light of My Father's Smile*.[27]

Notes

1 I am indebted to Kass Banning of York University in Toronto, who conducted a public interview with Deepa Mehta for the "Women Filmmakers: Refocusing" conference held in Vancouver on 27 March 1999.

2 I further develop the notion of Deepa Mehta as a transnational filmmaker in "Deepa Mehta As Transitional Filmmaker, or 'You Can't Go Home Again,'" in the anthology, *North of Everything: English Canadian Cinema since 1980,* ed. William Beard and Jerry White (Edmonton: University of Alberta Press, 2002).

3 "I wanted to be a doctor. I wanted to save lives. All these people that I saw wounded and living miserable lives in India. I wanted to do something to help." Janis Cole and Holly Dale in *Calling the Shots: Profiles of Women Filmmakers* (Kingston: Quarry Press, 1993), 136.

4 Dilip Mehta was co-founder of Sunrise Films, along with Mehta and Saltzman. Cole and Dale, *Calling the Shots*, 135.

5 He also plays the pivotal role of family servant in *Fire.* "I really wanted him to be in *Earth* but his Hindi is not very good and *Earth* is in Hindi. So that was that." Public interview with Kass Banning at "Women Filmmakers: Refocusing" conference (hereafter referred to as public interview with Kass Banning).

6   "Mehtamorphosis," *Chatelaine* 66, 11 (November 1993): 58-61.

7   Public interview with Kass Banning.

8   Ibid.

9   At $11 million, *Camilla* was "reportedly the largest budget in Canadian film history to be handed to a woman director." Cole and Dale, *Calling the Shots*, 135.

10 Kathleen Wilkinson, "Filmmaker Deepa Mehta Is on Fire," *Lesbian News* 23, 2 (September 1997): 38.

11 Ibid.

12 Similarly, Mehta relates that she had not received money from the Canadian government for *Sam & Me* because it "wasn't considered a Canadian film" (public interview with Kass Banning, 1999). Mehta's frequent mention of her dealings with Canadian and Ontario film funders gives the impression that she was personally attacked by these agencies. While the calculation of Canadianness according to the nationality or immigration status of a film's key personnel is meant to protect the Canadian film industry from American domination, and the "point system" is intended to be employed indiscriminately, it could be argued that restrictions on the location of production and on the citizenship of actors disproportionately impinge upon immigrant filmmakers such as Mehta. Mehta was more forthcoming (and perhaps less angry) in 1993, when she told Janis Cole and Holly Dale that Ranjit Chowdhry had simply arrived in Canada too recently to be considered Canadian and for their film to have access to pre-production funding. Other actors in the film were also not Canadian. See Cole and Dale, *Calling the Shots*, 137. Mehta's assertion that, in Canada, a visible-minority filmmaker is channelled into making only "immigrant" stories rings true for many filmmakers, as does her argument that making films to fit financing agency categories stifles a film's "passion": "Americans come here. They hire Canadian actors to play two-bit roles and things that are so American, and *they* get the money. And these co-production treaties – if you have a treaty with one country, you can have 10 percent of this and 5 percent of that – I don't know how it helps our industry. You're getting crew members and you're getting a story that's set in Regina, but does the film have any passion? Does it have any belief? Is it something that moves you? That doesn't seem to matter, because it fills that form." Public interview with Kass Banning.

13 Wilkinson, "Filmmaker Deepa Mehta Is on Fire," 38.

14 Public interview with Kass Banning.

15 See Rima Banerji, "Still on Fire," *Manushi* 113 (July 1999): 18-21. "Mehta's refusal to take a public stand supportive of lesbians is insulting and demeaning when originally so much of the hype mentioned the same-sex relationship as the film's core. After all, there is a difference between saying *Fire* is not a lesbian film (as Mehta has done) versus suggesting it is not only a lesbian film, and has multiple possibilities embedded in it. By making the former statement, Mehta has alienated precisely that segment of viewers which has been at the forefront of defending the substance of *Fire* on her behalf, and protecting it from attack by fundamentalists" (20). In contrast to Banerji, other writers have recognized the more radical aspect of the film in that its lesbian narrative takes place within the context of the traditional family and not in an "elsewhere." See Geeta Patel, "Trial by Fire: A Local/Global View – Talking with Geeta Patel," *Gay Community News* 24, 2 (Fall 1998): 10-7. Patel also offers an excellent discussion of the local and global meanings of *Fire*. See also Ratna Kapur's "Too Hot to Handle: The Cultural Politics of *Fire*," *Feminist Review* 64 (Spring 2000): 53-64, for a lucid discussion of the struggle over the meaning of tradition in India as exemplified by reactions to *Fire*.

16 See Kass Banning's discussion of *Sam & Me* in "Playing in the Light: Canadianizing Race and Nation," in *Gendering the Nation: Canadian Women's Cinema*, ed. Kay Armatage, Kass Banning, Brenda Longfellow, and Janine Marchessault (Toronto: University of Toronto Press, 1999), 291-310. I also further develop the notion of Mehta's attack on intolerance in "Deepa Mehta As Transitional Filmmaker."

17 The film is in Urdu, Punjabi, and Gujarati as well as English, representative of languages spoken in India's northwest.

18 The book was originally published as *Ice Candy Man*. Parsis were considered neutral in the Partition conflict.

19 Public interview with Kass Banning.
20 Shiv Sena (warriors of the god Shiva) are militantly Hindu nationalist and anti-Muslim. At the time, with the Hindu nationalist Bharagiya Janata party (BJP), they were the governing party of the western state of Maharashtra, whose capital is Mumbai. The RSS is the principal Hindu organization in India.
21 According to Hindu traditional practices, widows were considered to be bad luck, were often blamed for their husbands' deaths, and were prohibited from remarrying. (Laws since 1947 have tried to reverse this practice.) A woman ceased to be part of her own family when she married and, as a widow, had nowhere to go. According to Sutapa Mukerjee, Varanasi (Benares), a Hindu holy city, is currently home to some 2,000 abandoned widows. (See Sutapa Mukerjee, "Widows Defend Film-maker's Vision of Their Lives," *Vancouver Sun*, 12 February 2000, E21.) Amitabh Bhattacharya, a Sanskrit scholar and a Brahman, is quoted in a discussion concerning opposition to the film: "In the early part of the century, about half the widows here [Benares] ended up as prostitutes, about a quarter were concubines for wealthy Brahmans, and a quarter remained pure for God." See Robert Marquand, "Film Stirs Hindu Radical Rage," *Christian Science Monitor*, 14 February 2000, 1.
22 Only foreign-funded films must seek approval from the federal government's Ministry of Information and Broadcasting. The government instituted this procedure in the early 1970s following the release of French director Louis Malle's documentary series on India, which was criticized for showing the country in a bad light.
23 The Bharatiya Janatha Party heads a federal coalition of Hindu fundamentalist parties.
24 Marquand, "Film Stirs Hindu Radical Rage," gives an excellent summary of events, although his coverage does not include the later accusations of plagiarism.
25 Republished on the World Socialist Web Site, <http://www.wsws.org/articles/2000/may2000/dm2-m19_prn.shtml>
26 Although Shiv Sena is anti-Muslim, some fundamentalist Muslim groups joined their attack on the film by proclaiming a *fatwah* against actor Shabana Azmi for performing Hindu rituals while acting. No other Muslim actors have similarly been singled out, nor have there been protests against the many popular Hindi films shot in Benares that feature sex and violence. For more information on the events, and reactions from both sides, see the on-line Indian journal *Rediff* at <http://www.rediff.com>.
27 I interviewed Deepa Mehta by telephone on 17 August 2001.

Filmography: Deepa Mehta

1974	*At 99: A Portrait of Louise Tandy Murch* (documentary short)
1985	*K.Y.T.E.S.: How We Dream Ourselves* (documentary)
1985	*Travelling Light: The Photojournalism of Dilip Mehta* (CBC TV special)
1987	*Martha, Ruth & Edie* (co-director) (TV feature)
1988	*Inside Stories* (TV drama)
1990	*Sam & Me* (feature)
1992	*Benares* (episode of *The Young Indiana Jones Chronicles*, ABC TV)
1993	*Camilla* (feature, Miramax Release)
1994	*Travels with Father* (movie of the week and final episode of *The Young Indiana Jones Chronicles*, ABC TV)
1996	*Fire* (feature)
1998	*Earth* (feature)
	Water (production temporarily halted) (feature)
2002	*Bollywood Hollywood* (feature)
(in progress)	*By the Light of My Father's Smile* (feature, Columbia-Tri-Star)

26 Excerpts from a Master Class with Deepa Mehta
Moderated by Sharon McGowan

Sharon McGowan: Are there any directors whose fiction work you admire and whose work influenced the way you approached your first picture?

Deepa Mehta: Satyajit Ray. He's the greatest humanist filmmaker that I've ever known. His work is simple, very complex yet uncomplicated. That is the beauty of it. I do not wish to emulate it, but I wish at some point I could reach his vision on some level.

SM: Was there any film in particular that moved you?

DM: *Pather Panchali*, his first film in the Apu trilogy. To this day it moves me tremendously. And the other one that I really love is *Ganashatra*. It's a pretty amazing film that talks about women with such empathy. He's a really sensitive filmmaker.

SM: You didn't write the script for *Sam & Me*. You wrote the original story and then you collaborated with a screenwriter, but you are writing all your scripts now. How did you feel about writing when you first started moving into fiction?

DM: The first script that I wrote was *Fire*. I wrote it in about three days. Then I started looking for a writer to see if I could translate my story into a screenplay. I found out that I couldn't find anybody who actually got into the story entirely and wrote what I wanted to say. Maybe that was a blessing, as it really meant that I was left with my story and myself. So I did it, and I wrote the script the way I would film it. That's the wonderful thing about writing the script yourself. There is a feeling of total integration. I wrote *Earth* and I'm writing *Water* right now.

SM: I've noticed in your movies that your casts are always really large. You seem to work with stories that feature a number of characters bouncing off of each other. Your first film, *Sam & Me*, was already like that.

DM: Well, you always worry that the story is going to run out. It's not that I'm against doing something with just two protagonists, it's just that I find that life is larger, and it's very interesting getting different viewpoints, seeing how people react to the same situation in different ways. I find it fascinating because it enlarges the world I'm trying to explore. It's not that I can't do it with two people, it's just that I seem to gravitate to stories that bounce off many people because I like different perspectives.

SM: What do you do in an audition session?

DM: I never do screen tests because I find that it makes the actors self-conscious. I don't sit behind a desk and talk to them and ask them to

Deepa Mehta, courtesy of the director

read. I don't ask them to do any readings, ever. If I find that somebody's interesting, I usually spend one half day with them, just talking to them about anything. I will go out for a meal, sitting down and asking them things. When I cast for *Fire*, I did not have any idea what Nandita Das would look like on screen as she had never worked in feature film before, but I knew she was right the minute I saw her, from her theatre experience, the fact that she was a social activist and a very caring person, and very alive. I just knew it. Then I spent time with her. Line readings a director can change. That's the easy part. If you give me a line reading and I don't like it, it's very easy for me to ask you to say it differently, but that's no gauge of what I feel. I know instinctively whether you are right for the part or not. Auditions are very humiliating for actors. I hate the thought of somebody coming there, standing outside and being nervous and learning their lines and coming in, while I'm just going to sit there to make a judgment. If I say "no" you're going to be devastated for the next ten days! It's really sad, the whole thing. I think to be an actor takes such courage because you put yourself out there. If as a director I can't respect that, I don't think I should be called a director. I never put any actors through that process. That's what works for me. I'm not saying that it should work for you, but that's the way I do it.

SM: So how would you work with a group of actors? You said at the screening that you like to rehearse for two and a half weeks. Can you explain what that process involves?

DM: I work with one actor on the character for a couple days and focus on the usual stuff: what the background story is, and where he is going, where he is at this point in the script, why they are doing what they do. I ask the actors if they are confused about anything in the script, so they are entirely comfortable with where they are. If they have any questions, that's the time to ask me. I do that with every actor. I try to spend time with each of them individually. Then what I do is pair them off according to the screen time that they are going to be spending with one another. They go through line readings, and spend time together and talk over their scene together. They can rehearse their lines together – I never rehearse lines with the actors because I like that spontaneity to come when I'm shooting. I want them to think of every scene that they do in the context of the whole film. We are not filming in sequence because that's not the way it's done; we are filming by location. They should have the whole picture in mind, not just the scene they are doing that day. So when they do the scene and say their lines there's a freshness to it. If that doesn't work, you change it on the spot.

SM: Have you ever been in the rehearsal process and run into the problem of an actor not understanding a character the way you saw it? How would you deal with that?

DM: I think it happens a lot. It's not that they don't understand it as much as not being comfortable with the line as it's written because they feel that the character would not say it this way. When that happens, I always ask how they think the character would say it, and then they say it and if it works for me without changing the script, that's fine.

SM: So you've never run into a serious problem with that?

DM: No. One very interesting time was in a scene in *Fire* towards the end of the film, where Radha is telling Sita what brought her to the place she is at. She is talking about the fact that she can't have kids and the whole process of her husband lying next to her abstaining from sex to test his own strength and perseverance. The scene was [originally] written as a flashback between Radha and her husband, Ashok. You see Ashok coming to Radha and asking her, "Will you lie next to me?" We had been shooting for about eighteen days and had really gotten into it when I felt that the flashback was pathetic, disgusting. Fine, I'm the director and the writer, and I sleep with the producer (he's my husband), so that's fine, too! [laughter] So I vetoed the whole scene. The whole scene had to be rewritten and I was quite pleased with it and showed it to Shabana [Azmi, who plays Radha] and Shabana was upset because she loved the flashback and had grown attached to it. Before we knew it, it was the day of the shooting and Shabana was feeling very uncomfortable. The lights were on, the camera department was waiting. I tried to talk to her, to flatter her ego. I said this was an opportunity – two whole pages of dialogue. But she is very intelligent. If an actor is intelligent that is such a bonus! I realized she had agreed to do it – she is very professional – but her heart was not in it. So I decided to shoot the flashback *and* the new scene and then make the decision. I think that was a very good thing to do. It cost us a bit more and it was a hard day of shooting, but she felt comfortable and secure because her passion for the part had not been disregarded. It was not a case of "I am the director, you are the actor." It was about accommodating an actor who really felt, passionately, that that was the way it should be done. Now she just loves the new scene. She said, "I'm so glad you threw away the other one."

[A scene from *Fire* is shown to the audience.]

Q: What I loved about the film was that you've got visual metaphors and language metaphors. Everything in the film is a metaphor. How do you do that?

DM: I have no clue. I've always been a sucker for metaphors, so ... It just seemed India and life as I know it was so complex and everything reflects on everything else. Something is being said, but it really means something else. It is an exploration of all that.

Q: A lot of the language, although important to the story, was also poetic. Does writing dialogue come easily for you?

DM: Very easily. I really enjoy it. It's not that it's always perfect – I often change a couple of words – but I love writing dialogue. What takes time is for the story to culminate in my head. I can't just write an outline. I have a very difficult time doing that. Because I write the way I would like to direct something, it means it is far more detail-oriented. For *Fire*, I wrote the outline after I wrote the third draft, when all the details were there – the colours, the wardrobe, even the camera moves.

Q: That's what I was wondering, if you saw the composition as you were writing? Your films are beautifully composed.

DM: Yes, I did. Of course it has to be changed because the location is never the same as you imagine. Although after working with [cinematographer] Giles Nuttgens for three films, we both understand that the movement of the actors dictates the camera moves and not the other way. We can accommodate changes easily. When I discuss what the colours are going to be, or what the look of the film is, we usually talk about the emotional centre of the scene in terms of what is important and how it should be revealed. Then we get a small camera on set before we shoot, in case there are changes.

Q: One of the things I found interesting in the film was the mother-child question. At first, I was a little shocked, and then it became deep and complex. Was it intentional or did it just happen?

DM: It is a basic part of our culture in India. They say that a woman is a mother first, then a wife, a sister, a daughter, and then a woman herself. Women are defined by their relationships. It was there for a reason.

Q: There's this beautiful story between the two women, but all around it you bring in the politics of what's going on in the country with the fundamentalists. Would you comment on your intention in the writing or the response to *Fire* in India?

DM: The political response was very different from the average cinemagoer's response. There were people who loved it, and I think some in India were appalled. Nobody was indifferent to it, and that is what's fascinating. The reaction of the fundamentalists to the film could happen to anything that challenges the patriarchal society, and that was the problem with *Fire*. The lesbian relationship was the most obvious thing for them to hang on to. I found out in talking on panels to people from Shiv Sena [which violently opposed the screening of the film] that what really offended people was that the women have a choice: "How dare you portray women who choose to go against the traditional ways?" The fundamentalists wanted to uphold tradition and the other people were saying, "We make up our own minds." Surely the point about traditional values is that they have to be questioned all the time. Otherwise, we'll be stuck; there'll never be any change. We would just accept things the way they are.

Q: Something that struck me when I saw the film is the different focus points that you have. There isn't just one character's story, there's something going on in the lives of every one of these characters. It's a different kind of writing from the Hollywood model. Could you tell us about the process of writing a script, maybe taking us through *Fire*.

DM: I hadn't ever read a book about how to write a screenplay, which is just as well. I had a story in my head about Radha and Sita. The focus was on them, their lives in a contemporary Indian middle-class household. I expanded from that. Radha looks after her mother-in-law who has had a stroke and can't talk, but who really represents tradition.

Q: Were you thinking about people in your own life?

DM: Not really. But certainly there is a short story that I've read that deeply influenced me, called "Lihaaf," written in the 1940s in Urdu by a woman writer called Ismat Chughtai. It's a very beautiful short story. That certainly had some influence. But it was more, "How can something capture the atmosphere in which one loves, or can love?" So it's ideas and not just "this is my aunt and this is my mother." Yes, it has a lot to do with life in a joint family and that does come from experience. I was brought up in a joint family in India. In some ways, it connects to something tangible which is mine, but not all of it.

Q: The atmosphere that you built on the set is partly due to so many warm colours. How do you work with your creative team, with the lighting, to build up that atmosphere?

DM: Going back to the script, every script, whether it's something that I've written or even something that I've been asked to direct which is not my own, it evokes colours in me. I remember finishing *Fire* and thinking that this film must be white, orange, and green. I didn't even intellectually think why it evoked those colours. Obviously, orange, the colour of fire; green, paternity; white, purity: you can go into that. I take my daughter's colouring pencils and I actually do a colour palette for the film. And this is before I talk to anybody, before I've seen any sets. That's my first reaction when I read a script – to do a colour palette for it. Then I sit with my production designer and talk about what the film is about and why certain colours are important and why the elimination of certain colours is also extremely important. So, there's no blue in *Fire* at all. The colour blue does not exist; it's a coldness that I wanted to keep away from the women's story. Once I've talked to my production designer and I've seen the tapestry or the upholstery that's going to be on the chair, or the carpet, then I bring in the costume designer to discuss what the characters will wear and against what background. I take a deep interest in all that, and in fact, it's usually written in my scripts, down to the detail "the women are drying their orange-coloured sari on the roof." Once I've got that done, I sit with my cinematographer and discuss lighting. What is going to work with the colours I've chosen? But everything is from the script. We all get together and I work very closely with my production team. I trust Giles [Nuttgens] implicitly, but we discuss the warmth of the lighting, the highlights, the fact that I hate moonlight-blue nights: they're so absurd. Just that kind of thing.

Q: Was it in the back of your mind that those colours are in the flag of India as well?

DM: That's right. I thought about that later.

Q: You mentioned that you sent your first draft to your cinematographer and your editor and production designer. Do you storyboard?

DM: No. I never storyboard. I can't draw. My greatest concern is telling somebody what I want to see. I discuss it with Giles on set. When something's there in writing, people tend to refer to it, and if you change it, people think you're doing somebody a disservice. Who needs it?

Q: One scene in *Fire* really struck me in terms of the cinematography. People are dancing and they come in and out of focus, but it's very quick. You get a sense of a documentary background because it's so realist: you would never see somebody really in focus if you were that close to them. I was wondering whether you choreographed that section or whether that was the cinematographer.

DM: It was him. He used a hand-held camera, took about eight takes, and we edited the ones that were in focus or close to focus. That's where the editor comes in. That's what happens when you work with a cinematographer, editor, and production designer. They get what the film is about and they respect that.

Q: I was wondering about space in *Fire,* and the fact that there is this space, which men have absolutely no power over because it's so interior.

DM: Yes, you're absolutely right. We talked about it a lot. To explore that interior space, I really needed them to be upstairs. The upstairs space, I decided, actually had no boundaries, so the internal had a chance to breathe.

Q: In the clip from *Sam & Me,* when the character comes out and dances, the music is from a live recording shot in front of a huge audience. It seemed to me that, by implication, you were talking about all those men in the audience.

DM: Yes, the song is from a popular film. The audience is largely male at that moment because they are watching a film in which there's a woman dancing, watched by men. So yes, they are watching this man who is imitating this woman being watched by those men. I have fun doing things like that.

Q: Was there any reason for a man to perform this woman character?

DM: No, it was theatre – street theatre, particularly. This happens in all countries in the world, especially in India, China, Southeast Asia. So there is no sociological reason. It's reality.

Q: I was wondering what the budget for *Fire* was.

DM: The budget for *Fire* was $1.6 million and the budget for *Earth* was $3.2 [million].

SM: This is a broader question. What are your central premises about the responsibilities of a filmmaker and producer?

DM: I don't think I have any, because if I did, I would not do what I want to do, which might be considered politically incorrect. I'm not naive: I know that films are very powerful. But I certainly don't say, "I'm going to make a film that has a social message," or "Because I'm coloured or I'm a woman it has to be this way, otherwise it might be misinterpreted." I want to be free to explore everything, even something that doesn't make me look too good. If I want to explore it, it has to come from a place of honesty and not what is expected of me because I happen to be non-White or a woman.

Q: As a director-writer, you have a lot of control. I was wondering what kind of hints you would give writers (and directors) to ensure that the symbols and metaphors in the writing are transmitted when two people are involved.

DM: I don't think that's my type of work. If I get scripts from somebody else in such a detailed state I always send them back and say, "You have to direct it yourself." Really. My scripts work for me because I know I'm going to direct them. When I get a script, I read it from the outside. I look for a story that moves me, that is passionate, that is funny. What I don't want is somebody telling me to use a particular lens now, or pan from here to here, or have the camera zoom in.

Q: Do you find there is a difference between Canadian crews and the crews you work with in India?

DM: No, my crew is very eclectic. My cameraman is British, his first assistant is French, and his third assistant is Italian. The make-up person I use is Canadian, the hairdresser is Canadian, the script supervisor is Canadian, the dolly grip is British, the sound guy is from LA.

SM: How about advice for the future?

DM: Don't give up. What happens in Canada is that you give up because it's so difficult to get the money. Don't let that get you down. There are other avenues. There is a whole other world that exists outside Canada. Don't be limited to what is expected of you. Don't write for film financiers like Telefilm. Don't write for the Canada Council crowd. Write because you want to. I've been in that space where I've said "I'll make a compromise," and, luckily, I didn't. I don't regret it. It makes it tougher, but don't make that compromise to get the money to do the film that you really want to do. That's saying goodbye to it.

27 The Post of Colonial in the Works of Pratibha Parmar: *Kiss My Chuddies*
Tracy Prince

I had a different title planned for this chapter (it was "Between Visibility and Invisibility"), but after talking to Pratibha Parmar at the "Women Filmmakers: Refocusing" conference, I *had* to change it to *Kiss My Chuddies*.

Pratibha Parmar's *Warrior Marks* (1993), courtesy of Women Make Movies, NY

Pratibha knows that my research focuses on issues of race *and* national identity, so she was telling me about a great new wildly popular Asian comedy on British TV called *Goodness Gracious Me.* What is interesting is how the Asian comics take on current issues in Britain and have White audiences rolling with laughter when confronted with their own racism. On the show, the comics often say "kiss my chuddies," a Punjabi word for knickers, for undies, and now all across Britain people have picked up the saying. What does this have to do with Pratibha Parmar's work, you might ask? Well, in the same way that Indian food has become typical British fare and "kiss my chuddies" has entered the lingo as a commonplace exclamation, Pratibha's films and criticism have worked to make commonplace an altered view of gender and of British national identity.

Born in Kenya and living in England since the mid-1960s, Parmar is no stranger to the alienation strategies inherent within institutionalized efforts to solidify ethnically derived versions of national identity. As a founding member of Black Women Talk (the first Black British women's publishing house), and in her commissioned works for BBC's Channel Four, with a

Pratibha Parmar's
Wavelengths (1997), courtesy
of Women Make Movies, NY

segment devoted to gay and lesbian issues entitled "Out on Tuesday," Parmar
has worked to combat racist, sexist, and homophobic ideas that are so deeply
culturally embedded that they are thought of as constituting "common
sense." As she and the other authors of *The Empire Strikes Back* discuss,[1] it
was taken over as a "common sense" logic, that immigrants and British-
born people of colour have marred the vision that defines Britain. She explains in *Queer Looks,* "There is a particular history that informs the thematic
concerns of my work as much as my aesthetic sensibilities. That history is
about a forced migration to an England that is intensely xenophobic and
insular, an England that is so infused with outdated notions of itself as the
Mother Country for its ex-colonial subjects that it refuses to look at the ashes
of its own images as a decaying nation, let alone a long-dead empire."[2]

Parmar has been ahead of her time on many issues. She and Val Amos led
an early charge with their critique of Eurocentric versions of feminism in
the *Feminist Review* in 1984, well before this became a more mainstream
argument. As she writes, "little attention has been given to the lives of black
women."[3] In her critique of the White women's liberation movement she

shows that "the specificity of black women's experiences of racism, which have been structured by racially constructed gender roles" has been by-passed.[4] Also among those leading the charge critiquing race relations in Britain, she accomplished this in her criticism and activism and in such films as *The Colour of Britain* and the more recent *Brimful of Asia*, the two films upon which I will focus here. In 1982, she was writing about race issues in Britain in a book entitled *The Empire Strikes Back: Race and Racism in 70s Britain*. It preceded the much read *The Empire Writes Back* by seven years and was written when the words "postcolonial" and "neoimperial" weren't the academic buzzwords they are today.

What Parmar shows us in her films and criticism is an early and astute analysis of the real life application of what, in postcolonial theory, often remains fairly abstract. This is my favourite part of Pratibha's work. Rather than abstracted jargon, Parmar's films use popular culture, art, dance, personal reflections, and, yes, a few high-flying intellectuals to speak to such issues as Paki-bashing (the subject of *Sari Red*), what it means to be British (*The Colour of Britain* and *Brimful of Asia*), and the image of Black and Asian sexuality that is often presented as exoticized, "full of Eastern promise," permissive, and so on (*Memory Pictures, Flesh and Paper, Khush,* and *Wavelengths*). More specifically, Parmar's work could be said to add a caveat to Paul Gilroy's *There Ain't No Black in the Union Jack*: there ain't no Black women and no one seems to have thought about lesbians at all. Parmar's career has often revolved around exposing and analyzing what Gwendolyn Foster has described as "the racist colonization of Black female subjectivity and Black women's images, stories, identities, and spectatorship."[5] Her work is pivotal because it deals explicitly with what White feminists have often left out. Again according to Foster, "if, as bell hooks states, some feminist theorists have been guilty of erasing black women as spectators, they have been equally guilty of ignoring black and Asian women as cultural artists."[6] Parmar's work pushes the words "Black" and "Asian," along with revised notions of gender and sexuality, into current definitions of Britishness and Englishness.

Parmar's work is unique in that it is obviously grounded in postcolonial theory and an activist's sense of the political realities of these theories: Parmar has a long history of activism and academic criticism associated with issues surrounding race and nation. The result is that, in her films, there is ample evidence of theory in practice. In *The Colour of Britain*, for example, we get lots of satisfaction from seeing the application of postcolonial theory. If you'd like to begin to understand the arguments of postcolonial critics about the "location of culture," "essentialism," or "imagined communities," then watch this film. Parmar shows artists, choreographers, directors, dancers, and actors actively imagining a different national identity as they engage in their daily efforts to change the old common-sense logic regarding the colour of Britain. When it comes to essentialism, artist Anish Kapoor argues that he doesn't want to be expected to stand in for the quintessential Asian whose work "represents" an ethnic minority in Britain. He would rather his work represent the current art scene in Britain. A choreographer whose work is highlighted puts it best when she says that the situation will be more equitable one day, when her dance troupe is sent by the British Council to India to showcase "British" culture. These examples provide us with information about widely varying locations of culture.

The idea of a "threatening" Black presence in Britain has been pervasive since the increased immigration following the Second World War. And the fear of the loss of all that is "English" and "wholesome" has been systematically and overtly tied to the increased postwar immigration rates of people of colour. The efforts to define what it means to be British and what it means to be English have often been thinly disguised efforts to retain a White image of nationality. As is discussed in *The Empire Strikes Back*, it is crucial to be aware of the logic within which "a reworking of the concepts of 'nation' and 'citizen' has taken place [– a reworking that] aims to deny even the possibility that black people can share the native population's attachment to the national culture – God, Queen and country."[7] The authors quote a *Daily Telegraph* article from 1979, which states that "the United Kingdom is the national homeland of the English, Scots, Welsh, Ulster-men ... They wish to survive as an identifiable national entity ... they have been willing to work, suffer and die for it. By contrast, for the jet-age migrants, Britain is simply a haven of convenience where they acquire rights without national obligation."[8] The *Empire Strikes Back*'s argument revolves around how ideas such as these "accord with a mythology which has very deep roots in English popular culture ... [which depends on] the kind of historical forgetfulness which reworks the whole meaning of 'Britishness' in powerful images of the purity of nation, family and way of life, now jeopardized by the alien, external wedge."[9]

Brimful of Asia shows the current situation in British race relations by looking at the members of a younger generation who are now defining "Britishness." Parmar celebrates the cultural explosion in Britain that is being called "New Asian Cool." By offering the views of the fashion and music industry, a close-up of a trendy night club, and an interview with the editor of *2nd Generation* magazine, the film charts the emergence of a lively, pop-culture take on the colour of Britain. The view is that of people of colour who were born in Britain and who, with a new common-sense logic, take for granted their "Britishness." *Brimful of Asia* shows the *changed* colour of Britain, with the cultural producers whose works are highlighted showing that they routinely draw upon their various cultural locations. As the press release for the film explains, for the second generation, the new attitude is no longer an "uneasy juggling act between two value-systems" but, rather, a "totally new and amorphous amalgamation of global influences."[10] The artists and writers featured show that they are drawing upon a wide-ranging base of cultural knowledges in order to create a new Britain.

Like some of the people featured in both films, Parmar refuses to be defined as an artist doing work "from the margin"; rather, she says that her work comes from a "resistance to that marginalization."[11] In an interview with Trinh Minh-ha, Parmar asked: "Are we victims of fragmentation or, precisely because of our cultural hybridity and post-colonial experiences of displacement and marginality, are we a synthesis placed very much in the center?"[12] As Parmar explains, her work reflects upon "the process through which I constantly negotiate the borderlines between shifting territories ... between the margin and the center ... between inclusion and exclusion ... between visibility and invisibility."[13] These two films focus on such shifting territories, and the historical and current efforts at exclusion are undermined by a resituated centre. The young generation in *Brimful of Asia* and the artists in *The Colour of Britain* are shifting the centre, refusing to work out of the margins, and negotiating the borderlines of identity construction. They are moving towards a post in (post)colonial and are making White Brits understand what "kiss my chuddies" means.

Notes

1 Pratibha Parmar, "Gender, Race and Class: Asian Women in Resistance," in *The Empire Strikes Back: Race and Racism in 70s Britain,* Centre for Contemporary Cultural Studies, University of Birmingham (London: Hutchinson, 1982). I am purposefully vague throughout the chapter when referring to the authors of this book. It was a collaboratively authored and edited book put out by the University of Birmingham's Centre for Contemporary Cultural Studies. Thus, specific editors are not listed.

2 Pratibha Parmar, Martha Gever, and John Greyson, *Queer Looks: Perspectives on Lesbian and Gay Film and Video* (Toronto: Between the Lines, 1993), 5.

3 Ibid., 236.

4 Ibid., 237.

5 Gwendolyn Audrey Foster, *Women Filmmakers of the African and Asian Diaspora: Decolonizing the Gaze, Locating Subjectivity* (Carbondale, IL: Southern Illinois University Press, 1997), 2.

6 Ibid., 3.

7 Introduction to *The Empire Strikes Back*, 29.

8 *The Empire Strikes Back*, 30.

9 Ibid.

10 Promotional material for *Brimful of Asia*.

11 Parmar, Gever, and Greyson, *Queer Looks*, 5.

12 Trinh Minh-ha, *Framer Framed* (New York: Routledge, 1992), 156.

13 Parmar, Gever, and Greyson, *Queer Looks*, 5.

Filmography: Pratibha Parmar (Director)
Some descriptions have been excerpted from Parmar's Web site, <http://www.tibha.demon.co.uk/index.html>.

Bhangra Jig (1990): A vibrant short video about how young Asian people in Scotland celebrate desire and self-pride through dance and music.

Brimful of Asia (1998): Parmar explores the explosion of second-generation Asian talent in mainstream British culture. Features musicians Talvin Singh, Asian Dub Foundation, and Cornershop, as well as fashion designers and writers.

The Colour of Britain (1994): A look at the work of artists who have been at the forefront of redefining British culture and the image of the nation itself. Different ideas of what and who is British are offered up by the work of artists such as Anish Kapoor, Jatinder Verma of Tara Arts Theatre Company, and dancer-choreographer Shobana Jeyasingh.

Double the Trouble, Twice the Fun (1992): "We're crippled and queer, we've always been here," sing the a cappella group, The Tokens, with saucy signing, taking queer reclamation into yet another dimension.

Flesh and Paper (1990): A short video weaving a sensual tapestry of the life and writing of Indian lesbian poet and writer, Suniti Namjoshi.

Jodie: An Icon (1996): The phenomenon that has made Hollywood actress Jodie Foster an icon for lesbians who identify with her, and who adore and celebrate the screen personas of her remarkable career.

Khush (1991): "Khush" means ecstatic pleasure in Urdu. For South Asian lesbians and gay men in Britain, North America, and India, the term captures the blissful intricacies of being queer and of colour.

Memsahib Rita (1994): A twenty-minute drama produced for the series *Siren Spirits* weaving four tales of magic and mystery.

A Place of Rage (1991): Within the context of the civil rights, Black power, and feminist movements, this exuberant celebration of African American women and their achievements features interviews with Angela Davis, June Jordan, and Alice Walker.

The Righteous Babes (1998): A fast-paced rock-video-styled documentary, this film explores the role of feminism in popular music and the influence this has on modern women.

Sita Gita (2000): A half-hour dramatic monologue in which Nina Wadia explores the dualities of a young Asian woman's life. Sita is a hard-working student studying law and taking care of her father and brothers while Gita is a lap dancer in a club, earning money to buy her independence. How does she reconcile these two aspects of herself?

Warrior Marks (1993): Alice Walker and Pratibha Parmar present an hour-long documentary on female genital mutilation in Africa.

Wavelengths (1997): A short dramatic film about the time-honoured quest for love and human intimacy. This stylish, witty, and warm movie set in gay bars, in dreams, in advertisements, and cyberspace delights in the gloss of the world it depicts as it explores one woman's foray into cybersex looking for emotionally safer sex.

28 Interview and Excerpts from a Master Class with Pratibha Parmar
Conducted by E. Ann Kaplan

The discussion that follows took place on 26 March 1999 at the University of British Columbia, following a screening of *The Righteous Babes* and *Brimful of Asia*.[1]

Ann Kaplan: Can you tell us about how you began making films – some of the broader interests and projects and training you had before that?

Pratibha Parmar, courtesy of
Jacqueline Levitin

Pratibha Parmar: I started making videos and films in 1986. Prior to this I
had been doing a number of things, including a PhD at Birmingham University in the Department of Cultural and Contemporary Studies. I was
part of a group of postgraduate students of Asian and Afro-Caribbean
descent, Black-British as we defined ourselves at that time. We were all
working on issues of race in Britain and we co-edited a book called *The
Empire Strikes Back: Race and Racism in 70s Britain,* published in 1982. The
thesis I was working on for my PhD was on issues around South Asian
women workers and the relationship between race, gender, and class, as
played out in these women's lives. I was motivated to do this work primarily because my own mother was a home machinist. We had come to
England as immigrants, when I was eleven, from Kenya. I had vivid memories of growing up with my mother working at home for very little money,
sewing pillowcases and dresses. I was the first person in my family to
actually go on to higher education at a university. So I was very interested
in looking at my own personal history and experience and the general
experience of Asian women. In the sixties there had been a real movement of Asian women's resistance in the workplace, fighting for union
recognition, and equal pay ... all those things fed into my theoretical
academic interests.

AK: Why film, though? Did you continue writing?

PP: Well, one of the other things I'd got involved in was working with
young South Asian women. I started to use video and photography with
these young women, as a way of articulating their own experiences emotionally – their experiences in the family and in the wider culture where

they experienced themselves as part of a minority. One of the ideas we came up with was a series of three posters with a group of young Asian women, called "In Our Own Image." One of them depicted a young South Asian woman doing self-defence, with a quote at the bottom from a ten- or twelve-year-old who said, "If anyone calls me a 'Paki' I'll go kick their head in." We called the poster "Self-Defence is No Offence." The poster was displayed in lots of schools and colleges by teachers doing anti-racist work. In some schools the poster was actually torn down by the head teacher on the basis that it was inciting violence. This controversy made it into the ten o'clock news on television and there was a debate. What had started for me as a really small thing, about defining yourself against certain kinds of racist stereotypes, had completely challenged people's conceptions and they'd found it very threatening. It was then that I realized the power of creating representations from your own subjective position rather than from how other people define you. I think that is what made me decide that I wanted to work in the television industry in Britain. At that time there were very few Black or Asian people working in this area, and I wanted to begin to create films and programs that have images and stories from those communities.

AK: Looking back over the films you have been making for more than ten years now, I find a range of different kinds of projects. Could you tell us how you see your ideas changing, as you confront different political and social realities?

PP: I suppose one of the important things is that I never went to film school, so filmmaking comes out of my activist background in many ways. The kinds of films I've made have very much related to the political and social movements that I have been a part of at different times. I was an activist in the anti-racist movement in the seventies, when the National Front and the British National Party [two right-wing organizations] were very active. I was part of a group of people who organized pickets or demonstrations and rallies, and spoke on the radio, trying to ban these people from talking. What motivated me to make films and programs was partly, obviously, dictated by the historical-political moment. *Sari Red,* one of my first videos, is about a young South Asian woman who was killed by three White men on the streets of London just because she defended herself against their racist abuse. When I heard about this I thought, "that could have so easily been me" – you know, if I was walking down the street and somebody threw racist invective at me, I would shout back, too. And this woman did that and she was killed. These guys were in a van and they went onto the pavement where she was and crushed her against the wall. When I found out about that I was furious, I was very upset, and I felt she was only one of many victims of racism, and it still goes on. The many racist murders taking place were reduced to statistics, and I wanted to do something that actually rendered this woman's life in a very personal way, that didn't just reduce it to another statistic. So I met with the campaign that was trying to obtain justice, to bring her killers into court. Then I wrote a poem. Actually, I don't know if it's a poem, I don't know what a poem is, I just wrote something emotional and very personal about her death and made the video *Sari Red.*

I made *Khush* at another moment in time, about another issue. When I first came out as a lesbian, I didn't know any other South Asian people who were gay or lesbian, and for many years I felt I was the only one. As time went on, and I was travelling around, I began to meet South Asian lesbians and gay men in Canada and in the US, and I knew about a movement coming up in India. To me it was very exciting because I'd felt like I was the only one, and I was suddenly coming across all these other South Asian lesbian and gay people. I wanted to make a film that would reflect the dialogues and conversations that many of us as South Asian gay people were having across the continents. I decided to make a film that was not in any way about explaining who we are but actually celebrating who we were and affirming ourselves to ourselves.

AK: You're known as a documentary filmmaker, but this isn't really quite accurate, is it? It seems to me a problematic label because many of your films combine non-fictional sections with dramatized episodes very effectively. Perhaps the most dramatic example of that is *Double the Trouble, Twice the Fun.* Other films, like *Khush,* also combine them. Could you talk about how and why you evolved this interesting sort of in-between cinematic technique? Were there any theoretical concerns, such as problematizing fictionalization, or implying that documentary filmmaking is as fictional as dramatized episodes are? What were you hoping to achieve with this very interesting in-between strategy?

PP: I think it is partly because I didn't have any kind of formal training, I learned just by making my films and my videos. I taught myself and I asked people around me. Since I didn't know what the rules were, I didn't have anything to follow. I began to create my own style. It comes from my experience, so it's not just about being influenced by cinema, but also by literature. I want to incorporate performance, art, dance, memory fragments, notions of exile, location, identity – all those things from different modes of storytelling. In the UK in the seventies and the eighties there was a very vibrant literary culture coming out of the Black and Asian communities, particularly poetry. I wanted to use poetry in my films. There was also an explosion of dance performances, and I am fascinated by dance, I love the ways dance can begin to tell you stories in a way interviews might not. So I wanted to explore all those things. Another thing was that television seemed to me so bland most of the time (and still does). Since I was working in television, I wanted to challenge the traditional documentary mode – that is, the voice of God telling you what you are watching and how to understand it. So there are a number of different things that influenced and determined my style, which came out of my personal and political experiences.

AK: Watching and thinking about your films over the years, I've noticed that you make very few films about the family. There's one haunting short film, *Memsahib Rita,* one of my favourites, in which you do deal with a family situation. It's about a teenager who is living with her aunt and her father because her Caucasian mother is dead. There are a lot of flash-backs. Of course, the context is still racist Britain. That film was so inter-esting, and I felt you must have a lot to say about family and race. Are you deliberately avoiding the Freudian family romance, or do you want to get away from feminist preoccupations with issues related to melodrama and soap operas? Or do you just want to represent women moving in differ-ent spheres, aside from the family?

PP: I don't know, it hasn't been a deliberate choice; I don't think I've said that I don't want to go anywhere near the family. Part of it is obviously to do with the fact that I began at a time when there were very few of us from the Asian and the Black communities in Britain making films and videos. So we were almost obliged to depict these communities, with our own sense of responsibility, and we had to begin by filling in the ab-sences, challenging the stereotypes, dealing with the external representa-tions of us. That was the first step in a way. That's obviously changed, and thank goodness there's no longer that kind of burden of responsibility, of representation, that many of us were thrust into. I've had to think about my own relationship to my family, in the last year or so, because my mother had a very serious stroke. That made me really question my own role within the family. For many years I was living this sort of double life because I wasn't really out to my family but I was very much out else-where. Yet I was very close to them and afraid of losing them if I did confront them with my sexuality. It took a long time to bridge that gap, perhaps because I didn't want to rock the boat. I know that sometime I will do a feature narrative that will be quite personal, when I [am] emo-tionally ready to do something on my personal life.

AK: Your 1993 film *Warrior Marks* has been much talked about and debated and there have been many, many reactions. I wonder if you could say something about the kind of impact that film has had?

PP: Well, yes, that film has had a huge impact everywhere and a very interesting one too. I made the film in collaboration with Alice Walker, and with an African women's organization called FORWARD Interna-tional, based in London, in 1994. *Warrior Marks* came out of a particular movement against female genital mutilation [FGM]. FORWARD International was working closely with Alice Walker on its campaigns on FGM. She had just published a novel called *Possessing the Secret of Joy,* which explored that subject. When Alice finished writing the novel, she sent me the manuscript and asked if I would be interested in working with her on making a documentary about this subject. I read the novel and was completely blown away by it. I had known about FGM but not in any real depth. I talked to Alice and we decided to work on it with FORWARD. After we finished the film we wrote a book about the making of the film, so that the process and collaboration have been well documented. But since the film has been out in the world, I have been pleasantly surprised by the kind of impact it's had in terms of actually instigating change. A year after we'd completed the film we were invited to Ghana for the first ever Africa-wide Amnesty International conference to show the film and talk about it. This conference was lead by African activists working with Amnesty International, which was beginning to mount an Africa-wide campaign on female genital mutilation. They were interested in the film and it has been used by these groups locally to talk about the issue. We've had lots of screenings everywhere and it was shown on television in a couple of countries, but for me its concrete use was the most important consequence. I believe that the film has helped to raise consciousness about FGM and also broken the international as well as the cultural taboo that has stopped action being taken. It is no longer acceptable for worldwide welfare agencies to say, "We can't interfere with this since it's a cultural issue." I also believe that the fact that someone of Alice Walker's reputation has spoken out against this has made it possible for many more thousands of women to speak out against it. The fact that this is a human rights issue and not a cultural issue is now much more widely accepted, and this, in turn, helps the grassroots organizations to be funded and supported in their work against FGM. Soon after the film came out, Amnesty International in the UK accepted FGM as a human rights issue. Many other things influenced that decision, but for sure the film helped.

Another area in which the film generated debate was amongst academic feminists. Now I could take them on, and their criticisms, and I will one day when I don't have other priorities.

AK: As a film critic, I'm always trying to figure out what spectator position a filmmaker is trying to construct for me. One of the things I value about your work – and that facilitates working with you – is that you are a writer as well as a filmmaker, and you have a theoretical background that permits fruitful dialogue. Sometimes it's very difficult for critics and filmmakers to find a common language. My question is, how much do you, as the filmmaker, actually think about the spectators? Do you aim a film at a specific audience? Obviously there are specific causes that you want to address, but how far do you imagine spectator response? You said you were surprised by some responses to *Warrior Marks*. Did you mean that it was hard to figure out how an audience might react to that film?

PP: When I'm making a film it's very intuitive a lot of the time. I never consciously think: "I'm making this film and I want it to be seen by this group of people, and this is how these different groups are going to respond to it." If I did that I couldn't allow my own creativity to emerge in any way, I'd be making something very prescriptive. One of the first times I was forced to think about who I was making my work for was when I was invited to show my first two videos, *Sari Red* and *Emergence*, to the Robert Flaherty seminar [in the US] in 1989. It was the first time that seminar had focused on work by what they called Black and Third World video filmmakers. Those seminars are interesting events, intense in all kinds of ways, but this one was very interesting to me because *Sari Red* was shown alongside a film by a Black British director based in London, John Akomfrah. In these seminars you don't know when they're going to show your film, but when they do you're questioned, so you have to go to every event of the week in case it's your turn. Every time you're thinking, "Oh my God, is this going to be my film?" and you get really tense about it. Eventually they showed *Sari Red* and then they showed John's film, I think it was *Testament,* and we had to go up and be questioned [the Flaherty seminars are known for their very intense, heavy, questioning]. I was just starting out, I didn't even feel I had the right to call myself a filmmaker, I'd only made two little videos and they'd been self-funded, so I was amazed that I was even there. A discussion came up and a professor from some university in LA said, "Well, I found both *Sari Red* and *Testament* difficult to decipher and to understand, because they are speaking with cultural symbols and codes that are internal to those communities, they were not in any way universal." So I said, "Well, by universal you mean a White, male, heterosexual perspective? You know, I've always had to decipher those codes and educate myself to understand what that culture is, so I think you probably need to go and educate yourself." I didn't know who he was, to me he was just a man in the audience. I didn't realize what impact my remarks would have. There was an uproar. There were some people who reacted quite badly, I think. They were thinking, "How dare this little brown girl, from wherever she is from, question this well known man in this way and tell him to go and educate himself?" That incident was written up in the *Village Voice*, and what a fuss about nothing! It made me realize how different the whole question of race was in the US then it was in Britain because in Britain it would have caused a little stir, maybe, but it wouldn't have been so unusual. It seemed that in the US context it was really rare for someone like me to be questioning the authority of this man. So it made me think about different spectator positions. When I'm making films from my particular subjective position, of course, I use the kind of cultural, political, and social background and symbols and signs that are very natural to me. Certain audiences might not plug into that, but I don't think, "Well then, I'm going to have to try and explain it to them."

AK: Your films clearly are about topics that you think are important and you are generous in discussing them. Maybe we could talk a little about *The Colour of Britain*. It illuminated beautifully the split between (1) recognition of the greatness of art produced by people of colour in Britain and (2) Britain not wanting to be represented by minority artists internationally. With that film I thought you were trying to expose a real schism in the British national identity. Could you talk about your interest (in *Brimful of Asia* as well) in giving space for artists of colour who may not get as much attention as they deserve in the country where they live? Channel Four in England shows these films, and getting attention for them seems like an act of generosity on your part. I was also impressed with how you got the artists to cooperate so wonderfully with you.

PP: For *The Colour of Britain* it was actually quite difficult to get the artists to cooperate. It's about British-Asian artists who have made it into the mainstream. All three artists, in theatre, dance, and sculpture, had been the cultural ambassadors for Britain at international artistic events. One had been at the Venice Biennale representing Britain. Another was trained in Indian classical dance and has been creating incredible choreographical pieces using classical Indian dance steps with avant-garde Western music, creating a synthesis that's absolutely wonderful. In this film I wanted to show that in spite of all the discussions of hybridity and diasporic aesthetics, these artists who were being celebrated in the mainstream would be just as likely as anyone else to be victims of racist abuse when walking down the main street at home. The schism, as you call it, was that: What does this say about Britain? What does this say about our position as South Asian people within Britain? These questions are what I wanted to explore in that film, to show how this is not about marginality but about the core of what British culture is. In a sense *Brimful of Asia* is a continuation of the same thing, but with a very different generation and in popular culture rather than the so-called higher arts.

AK: We have just seen *Righteous Babes,* where a number of prominent female vocal artists express their views. Do you have a position, in terms of what they're doing? You present the artists, critics, and fans very appreciatively, but might one question some of their comments? [Laughter]

PP: What are you trying to get at, Ann? Are you being Canadian here? Just be direct! [Laughter]

AK: Well, I'll try to be direct. I'm fascinated with *Righteous Babes*. I was struck when some of these women said, "I just want it all." I kept thinking, that's fine, to want it all, but what about all the other people, what about welfare women, women who can't get it all, people who are out of work, and so on? I was hoping for some sort of social consciousness, which many of these women seemed oblivious to. They want to be represented as powerful, and obviously my work on Madonna totally validated that view. I agree that this is extremely important as a step, in terms of real empowerment. But I wondered why you didn't push the envelope. I understand that the style of both films was to let the artists and critics have their say. But what do you think about some of the positions articulated by your subjects?

PP: I'm still in some respects an old-fashioned socialist feminist myself, in that I believe that equality has not been achieved as yet. In fact, the gaps between different groups of women are getting larger internationally, and the reality of the majority of women's lives is that a lot of them live in poverty, or in low paid employment, and a lot of women are single mothers without any support. I don't deny all those social realities. *Righteous Babes* had quite a specific focus and is deliberately limited to looking at popular culture and feminism, at where the young women today are getting their so-called feminist role models. And they certainly aren't getting them from the likes of us. They're not getting them from books, either. That was the way that I learned about feminist writings and about the politics of feminism, through reading and writing and going to women's consciousness-raising groups. Women's consciousness-raising groups don't exist anymore as we have known them. I was really interested and intrigued to find out where these young women are finding their role models. I think that popular culture is a very important area of intervention for us as feminists. I wanted to make an intervention in mainstream television, so that a film like that could be watched by a million people who would begin to associate feminism with music and begin to make connections between feminist ideals and their manifestation in popular culture. It was important to me to use the word "feminist" in a mainstream medium like television, to make an argument for feminism by saying that feminism is very much alive, and [to] do it in an accessible way without "dumbing" down.

AK: Actually, the critique that Ani Difranco makes about the Spice Girls is what I was hoping for more of! I still have two more questions. One is about the soundtracks to your films: *Warrior Marks*, for instance, has a very complicated soundtrack, and *Double the Trouble, Twice the Fun,* and

Khush do too. All of them have a very interesting mix of different kinds of music. For example, the Gregorian chant that comes suddenly into *Warrior Marks* conveys a sense of the horror of the infibulation. How do you work up these tracks? And what's your input?

PP: I'm very much there with the sound, right from the beginning. For me sound has always been a priority: and it's one of the key layers in my films. It's not there as wallpaper or something that bridges the gaps between interviews. The soundtrack has its own kind of storytelling that works in its own way, in the way that dance does in my films. So I work with a composer very closely and we listen to a lot of different music, particularly for the three films you mentioned, but he's done others as well, like *Sari Red* and *Memory Pictures*. It's the same composer; we've built up a very good relationship over the years. We've just created these soundscapes that speak in another way of what we're trying to say.

AK: The last question is inevitable, talking to an independent filmmaker in this era: it's about the funding situation. How much is it your choice, for instance, to do documentary, or is it largely because that's what you could get funding for, and does Channel Four accommodate documentary films? When we talked in 1994 you told me about wanting to do a drama feature. I wonder what happened to that, and how much the kinds of funding available has determined what you are able to do. Do you see a way out of that, and is a feature film still a project?

PP: Well, funding is not one of my favourite topics, as you know. I really hate raising funding for my films. I've made quite a few now, but every time I finish a film I feel as if I'm back to square one, having to prove myself all over again. People say, well you've got a portfolio of films now, you should have doors just being opened to you, but in fact I think the doors are closing more and more for independent filmmakers in the UK. Channel Four was set up with a remit to make programs for minority groups, by minority program makers; and minority, for them, meant women, people of colour, lesbians and gays, disabled people. Never mind that women are 50 percent of the population, we're still like a minority. Since Channel Four was specifically set up to cater for these groups it did provide openings for many of us in the early years. We could go in there and say, "OK, these are the things we want to do." But in the last three years, their commitment to their original remit has changed drastically, and, in fact, documentary programs are decreasing rapidly, especially those that are in any way seen to be political. Reality TV has taken over and ratings are what it's all about.

AK: Why is that?

PP: There's talk about Channel Four being privatized. The concern now is for ratings and drawing in the advertisers, and advertisers are going to go for chat shows, and *Oprah* or American re-runs, *Friends*, and *Ally McBeal* and all that kind of thing, which is what Channel Four is now saturated with. I think that funding is actually getting harder, rather than easier, for many of us, particularly for me. As you know, my body of work is not exactly commercial or marketable: it's about so-called minorities or about subjects that are not often tackled on television. I suppose the reason why I've made mostly documentaries is that I work in the television industry. I've made a deliberate choice to make interventions within British culture through my films. It's not for want of trying to make feature films that I haven't made one yet. I've been attempting to make feature dramas for a few years now, but you know the kind I want to make are not necessarily seen to be very profitable commercial properties.

I am currently working on a few feature dramas; they are all at the early stage of development and one of them is an adaptation of Alice Walker's novel, *Possessing the Secret of Joy*.

AK: And you don't want to compromise, I assume.

PP: I don't know if it is even a question of compromise; for me, it's about what other stories I want to tell. Making films is so damn difficult and takes so much energy and so much time. You get exhausted and you don't have a life when you are involved in a production. When I make a film, I give everything to it. I don't take on something 50 percent or 60 percent; I give my heart and soul to it, and do it with passion and zeal. If I'm going to make narrative features, which are even more time-consuming, then I want to make stories that I feel completely passionate about. There aren't that many stories out there that I feel that way about. Scripts have come my way, and producers have said, "You're hot at the moment, look at this script and let's do this together," and I've read them. I was actually offered a script by the BBC, and it was half a million pounds, which is more than a million Canadian dollars. But the story was about a young Asian woman being beaten up by her father and running away from home, just the sort of stereotyped story of young Asian women which I have been working against, to show that this is not the only thing in our lives. When I was offered this script, I thought, "God, it's my first big drama break, a million-dollar budget, prime-time TV, a feature film that will be released theatrically!" I spent two weeks in angst about it, getting really ill, and in the end I just had to say I couldn't do it.

AK: There's no way of taking a project like that and transforming it?

PP: Believe me, I did try! [Laughter]

Pratibha Parmar: Excerpts from a Master Class, Facilitated by Peggy Thompson

Peggy Thompson: Today we are going to focus on the nuts and bolts of filmmaking, on the process, beginning with some scenes from *Double the Trouble, Twice the Fun*.

Prathiba Parmar: In this session one of the things I'd like to discuss is directing sensitive scenes, particularly sex scenes or lovemaking scenes. In my first documentary, *Khush*, I started exploring that area. There is a sensual interplay between two women throughout the film, and they kiss at the end. Some of the techniques I used in that film to disrupt traditional documentary narrative form were drama and dance, and archival film footage from Bollywood. *Double the Trouble, Twice the Fun* is one of the first films I made that isn't based on an idea of my own. I was approached by an Indian writer who was disabled and gay and had just moved to England – Firdaus Kanga. His whole journey was about looking for other people like himself, and he wanted to make a film about disabled gay and lesbian people, allowing them to talk about their experiences. I enjoyed meeting him and we began work on it for BBC Channel Four. At that time [1992-3] they were doing a series every week for six weeks called "Out," which actually gave some lesbians and gays a chance to do some work for a large audience. We went to meet people in various communities, political activists as well as those who weren't particularly involved, and he wrote a moving drama piece about making love with another man for the first time. He wanted to include that, and I thought, "How am I going to do this? Where will I find gay, disabled actors?" But we did find one, and another who is not gay but who agreed to play the part. Actually shooting that scene was, at that point in my career, one of the hardest things I'd had to do. I realized that being a director isn't just about technical know-how, where the cameras are, and what kind of lighting I wanted, but about being a friend, an observer, someone the actors could feel relaxed with. We talked it through, and the scene was tender and intimate. My camerawoman was saying, "How are you going to do this? How many shots? How many sequences?" I felt we just had to go with what happened. We didn't know how many takes it would need. In the end we just rehearsed it once, with a closed set and a minimal crew, shot it as one scene. We did the whole scene on a track to avoid different set-ups and changing the camera position. That allowed us to move with the actors; they did what felt natural to them and we followed. We only had to do two takes in the end because it took a lot of emotional courage for the actors to do it, and I didn't want to get into voyeurism. It's a fine line.

Question: Can you talk about the inclusion of signing for the deaf in that film using overlay?

PP: I wanted to foreground the signer rather than the speaker. That was an ideological and political decision, to challenge people by reminding them of the deaf community. I hadn't seen that done anywhere, so I had to think about how to do it aesthetically, and I had to do research because it was shot on video. I talked to editors about how to do it. Video technology was less sophisticated then than it is now. Layering these different images was incredibly expensive and time-consuming.

Q: Did your budget support that?

PP: I told them at Channel Four that we really needed it, and that it had emerged during the process of making the film, and they came up with the money. Those were the good old days of Channel Four!

Q: When you include interviews in your films do you pre-plan them?

PP: One of my first jobs was not as a director or producer but as a researcher for a series of historical documentaries on Black people in the UK, and I was trained to do "pre-interviews" for possible interviewees. I transcribed the tapes and the director went through them and picked the bits he wanted. He thought the people would say the same things with a camera there, but that wasn't what happened: some refused. It seemed like a too pre-scripted way of making a documentary, though a lot of TV is done that way. I talk to the possible people on the phone first, then I meet them, then I come back with my camera crew. They aren't just providing sound-bites, they're people with their particular experiences, and I want them as relaxed as possible.

Q: You have made several documentaries about artists. That type of film is almost impossible now in Canada because topics have to be "broadcastable." How do you do it?

PP: Now it would be more difficult to get the funding. There's been a dumbing down of television. For *The Colour of Britain* we got some funding from the arts council. That film provided a different kind of technical challenge because of the dance. I grew up in a culture where we were exposed to dance through live performances and through watching Bollywood movies. Dance evokes emotion in visceral ways, and it can tell you so much: facial expressions, gestures with the hands ... I really wanted to incorporate it into my work.

Q: What about the film you made for Channel Four about Jodie Foster? How did you manage to do it without her permission and without interviewing her?

PP: It's a film about an icon for a series called "Icons," without the icon! It was done respectfully. I was interested in deconstructing the whole process of how an icon is created and why and how Jodie Foster became one for so many women. We needed to show clips from films like *The Silence of the Lambs,* and the lawyers told us we could use clips from movies if it was for educational purposes, without permission or paying for it. Legally this is called "fair usage" and it exists in Canada too. It's very useful. You just have to make sure the clips are relevant to the discussion. When the film was finished it was shown in LA at the film festival. I sent Jodie a fax reminding her that I had let her know about the film and that now it was complete. It got good reviews and her PR company asked for a copy of it.

I sent it and never heard anything back. I can't imagine she wouldn't have liked it. It is, as someone said, a video Valentine from her fans.

Q: Do you have an open structure when filming a documentary? Can the unexpected happen?

PP: Sometimes it does, for example in the Jodie Foster film a woman appeared with a dog when we were shooting. She said she was interested because she was always being mistaken for Jodie. So we included a scene with her being asked if she was Jodie; it was improvised and turned out great. You have to have certain themes but also be flexible on the day.

Q: What differences have you found when you have made drama films?

PP: I've actually done two short dramas. One was for a BBC series of four twenty-minute films by Black and Asian women writers and directors. I chose a script set in London, where I grew up, about a young South Asian woman coming to terms with having a White mother, and her father's preoccupation with a romanticized image of his dead White wife. A lot of it takes place in the woman's imagination, and it was tough doing it. I never went to film school, so I did what I did when I began making documentaries: I asked people, read books, harassed technicians ... If people share their process with you, it gets demystified. That's why I always talk about my process, to encourage people and say, "Well, you know, anyone can do it if they really want to: I did!" You don't have to have special skills, they can be learned. For that film I did a lot of unpaid work. I made a shot list with something like forty shots, when there was only time for five or six! It got me to think, to learn the language of drama. When it was done I saw that I still needed to practise certain specific skills.

Q: How did you find working with the actors?

PP: I knew I would want to make more drama films, so I went and did a three-month acting course with other actors to learn their language and see what it involves. I actually enjoyed it and learned to communicate with them much better. Partly because I was never going to be an actor myself, I was relaxed. It was a real compliment when an actor later told me, "You really are an actor's director."

Q: How do you maintain your sense of self while working as part of a creative team?

PP: I think film is a totally collaborative process. It's not just about one actor or just the producer. I try to treat everyone as equals, it's not just about my vision as director. For example, in *Double the Trouble, Twice the Fun*, I worked closely with the set designer, who had strong ideas about what she wanted to do. We discussed some of the effects I was trying to achieve with colour. For some of the interviews I had a back projector behind the person, projecting vibrant images of flowers, textures ... It was an idea that came from a woman I interviewed who was blind but could follow textures and feel shapes. It created different visual layers in the film. We also needed a certain kind of light projection for the signing, to create the mood.

Q: Is it important for you to work with female cinematographers?

PP: I worked a lot with one in particular, but I lost her when she moved away from the UK. We were shooting a documentary about the Civil Rights Movement in the US, in San Francisco, and she ended up doing an exchange with someone from there. And now she's teaching cinema studies in Texas. I was very sad to lose her.

Q: What about the script? What sort of editorial control do you have outside the production?

PP: That's changed. At the time when I made *Double the Trouble* the commissioning editor would just come in at the rough-cut stage and again for the fine-cutting. Now it's more hands-on. For *Righteous Babes* I had umpteen visits and I constantly had to fax drafts of the commentary for their approval.

Q: How do you reconcile your planning of the set design and visuals with the effect of spontaneity that you want to create? There's such a beautiful sense of effervescence and spontaneity in your work.

PP: Thank you very much, that's a lovely thing to hear! I plan, but I also only do things that I feel really passionate about. The only time I did something just for the money, I wasn't happy with the result. After that I said no to things that I can't put my signature to. I went into filmmaking quite late (I was thirty-one) because I wanted to say something through this medium. Even during the worst times of frustration I feel blessed that I've found something that I feel good about and that I've been able to do.

Note

1 This interview is complementary to another one conducted by E. Ann Kaplan, "An Interview with Pratibha Parmar," *Quarterly Review of Film and Video* 17, 2 (2000): 85–105.

---

29 Documentaries Made in India: Raman Mann and Patricia Plattner
Collated by Valerie Raoul

Deepa Mehta's experience of resistance to her feature films and Pratibha Parmar's comments on her experimental short films on Indian lesbians and artists provide examples of controversial topics addressed by filmmakers of Indian background who live in Western countries. They illustrate the range of treatments possible, from full-length feature films with potential for large-scale commercial success to low-budget experimental shorts. At the "Women Filmmakers: Refocusing" events we also had the opportunity to see and to discuss some more traditional documentary films about India that had been made there by three other women. Award-winning Indian director Raman Mann was in Vancouver as a Shastri scholar at Simon Fraser University; Swiss filmmaker Patricia Plattner was present both weekends for screenings of her feature-length documentary *Made in India;* and Evelyn Nodwell of Vancouver spoke about her video based on interviews with women involved in the environmental movement in India.[1] This section brings together some of the material from Raman Mann's paper and extracts from interviews with Patricia Plattner in order to take a closer look at the implications involved if the filmmaker is from India or from the West. The most obvious disparities may be in access to resources, but the filmmaker's degree of connection to the West also affects the choice of topic, the final product, the language used, and where and how the film is shown. Both Mann and Plattner have made films to raise awareness about women's efforts in India to improve their living conditions, but the kind of production team they work with is very different, as are their sources of funding, their communication with the women being filmed, the importance of aesthetic effect in the film, and the audience the film seeks to address. The East-West connection goes both ways, as this comparison shows: Plattner took her experience of filming in Europe to India, while Mann brought her familiarity with Indian prisons to her subsequent project on women in jail in Canada.

Raman Mann: Making Educational Films about Women in India

Raman Mann is an independent Indian documentary video-filmmaker based in New Delhi. Her original training was in foods and nutrition, and home economics. As a filmmaker she is self-taught, although she completed a film appreciation certificate through the Indian National Film Archives in New Delhi. For her projects, someone else (usually from India) wields the camera, but she is the one who decides what is filmed and how, and she works with an editor on the final product. Mann has produced more than thirty videos and films, twenty to thirty minutes long, many of which have an educational function. The topics are wide-ranging (see appended filmography). A number focus on health issues, including twenty-three training modules on diarrhoea management and others on vaccination techniques, family planning, and community-based rehabilitation for people with disabilities. Several deal with human rights and crime, such as an advocacy film on prisoners' rights aimed at prison staff and police, and an exposure of the smuggling of antiques out of India. Two were made as TV specials: the story of a four-year-old girl prodigy for Indian TV, and, for Britain's Channel Four, an account of a twelve-year-old boy raised in England who returns to the land of his birth for the first time. Funding to make these films has come from many sources, including various levels of government in India as well as business, international non-governmental organizations and development funding agencies, UNICEF, and the Indian Human Rights Commission. Several of Mann's films in Hindi are about women, from *Alka Sharma* (*No Dowry*) (1993) to *New Horizons* (1993), on rural women's agricultural cooperatives, and *Compassion* (1993), on sensitization to violence against women. Since 1993 Mann has also made films in English, two of which have attracted a good deal of attention. The first was *Call of the Forest* (1993, 25 minutes), which documented the collective action taken by Gond tribal women in Central India to save their trees. This film received the UK International Award for best video related to women and development in 1994 from the British Council and One World Broadcasting Trust. It has been screened worldwide at festivals and used by many environmental agencies and groups. In 1996 *Barred from Life* (27 minutes), a film on women prisoners serving life sentences in India, achieved a comparable success and was selected for the Créteil International Festival of Women's Films (Paris 1996). While in Canada, Raman Mann was working on a documentary on women in prison here. Recalling her experience of filming in Indian prisons, she shared her reactions with us.

Raman Mann: For me, as a middle-class Indian woman living in India in comfortable surroundings, the experience of working with women in poverty in rural villages and urban slums has been an eye-opener. It has been a learning experience, meeting women who know the true meaning of survival and the struggles that go with it. The experience has also been full of spontaneous friendship with other women, establishing bonds. I have seen indigenous women in Bastar [central India] in the forefront of the fight to save the forests, women in Gujarat taking over failed milk cooperatives and bio-gas plants from the men and turning them into a success, women in the sex trade in Bengal organizing sericulture cooperatives, and women in Murshidabar starting village schools. With the help of government-sponsored programs and volunteer agencies, these women are determined to save their children from sinking into the surrounding social morass. Their ethos is one of self-empowerment, and they are breaking time-worn stereotypes and demolishing some pervasive myths about poor women in India. My films can make their efforts known to others in India and elsewhere.

My first documentary on women in prisons started with an article in an Indian magazine called *Frontline* on women serving life sentences in the state of Uttar Pradesh in North India. I read it by chance, on a flight to London, when I was going to receive my first international award for *Call of the Forest*, on International Women's Day, 1994. The article brought out the various and arbitrary ways in which the criminal justice system interprets the meaning of a "life term." The women's stories exposed the contradictory and stereotypical ways in which different agencies within the system regard the cases of women prisoners. I determined then that I wanted to make a film to draw attention to their plight, that might even contribute to gaining the release of some women.

The excruciating job of obtaining funding to produce the film took over nine months. Then one day the British Council and the Foreign and Commonwealth Office in New Delhi called to tell me that they had approved the proposal I had made through UNIFEM. They would provide funds to make this documentary on women serving life sentences in India for the United Nations Conference in Beijing in 1995. My friends and I had a celebration! *Barred from Life* became possible.

Prisons in India are a legacy of British colonial rule. The same buildings are still functioning, and the Indian Penal Code in operation today is based to a great extent on the colonial penal code established in 1860, three years after the tumult of 1857, which Indians call their First War of Independence and the British the Indian Mutiny. The prison manual of 1894 was still in use until 1998, and when I went in 1995 to film in the women's prison in Lucknow, in North India, it was the only one available. Even in 1998, when I filmed a second documentary on prisons, a photocopy of the new one had only just been received.

I concentrated on Lucknow Women's Prison, where I was able to meet thirty-three women who had been imprisoned for periods ranging from fourteen to twenty-seven years. I discovered that almost all these prisoners came from poor, rural families. Typically, they were illiterate and unaware of their legal rights, hence completely powerless. Comparing the officials' accounts of why the women were in jail with the women's own stories of their experiences revealed a sharp contrast. The manner in which they were convicted in the first instance was often strange. Indifferent government lawyers, self-serving prison officials, and even a few "social workers" all seemed to have played a part in denying these women their legal and human rights. The film shows how the prison staff hid from some of the women the fact that they were entitled by law to be released because it was in their own interests to keep them in jail. Custodial staff did not want to lose their jobs or access to supplies because of a reduction in the number of prisoners. The women prisoners in question, as well as an ex-prisoner, Phoolan Devi [India's well known "Bandit Queen," of the film of the same name], talked about their experiences in prison, providing telling examples of the harsh realities of prison life and of the official apathy and insensitivity towards women prisoners in general.

The film shows how the prison doctor and a lawyer (who provided his services free of charge) worked relentlessly, motivated by their own personal commitment to this cause, to obtain the women's release. Finally they succeeded. The observations of the State High Court judge who announced that they were to be freed contradicted official claims that the justice system normally protects the legal rights of prisoners. Clearly, the women were released only through the efforts of clear-sighted, empathetic, and outspoken individuals, such as the male doctor, lawyer, and judge.

In India, prisons for women are an extension of everyday patriarchal structures and cultural boundaries. Normally controlled by their fathers, brothers, husbands, and sometimes sons, women become twice-controlled in jail. Having grown up in a social prison, as it were, women in prison (especially those – the majority – from the poor classes) learn to accept the paternalistic control of the prison staff. All their lives women try to live up to the roles expected of them, as obedient, dutiful daughters, wives, and mothers. The penal system assumes that women who end up in prison need an even greater degree of control, management, or treatment. Male officials nearly always step forward as spokespersons for them, assuming that they have greater knowledge and authority than the women themselves, even to tell their story.

The crimes of women in almost 95 percent of the cases in India are petty thefts or offences attributable to poverty. Most women, as elsewhere in the world, are found guilty only of non-violent crimes. Some of the women I worked with for the film had killed as a last resort, in sheer despair and desperate self-defence. Similar cases are reported by battered and abused women the world over, regardless of culture. We were happy that the women were released, but the stigma of having been in prison is even greater for women than for men. In India women who return from prison are rarely accepted back into their villages or even into their families. Ostracism is a serious stumbling block in helping in their rehabilitation and reintegration into society. Life outside prison is also difficult for them as they have become institutionalized. As one woman poignantly said: "You can never leave prison, because prison never leaves you."

I would like to share the anguish expressed by some women I have met in prisons. In Lucknow I was asked, "Why are you making this film? Are you going to help us? Do you think you can help us in this living hell?" In Punjab I was told, "Every night I despair. I lie awake thinking of my children. Where are they now? My husband's family threw me out on the road. They took away my children. I had so many dreams for them." In British Columbia, Canada, I heard, "I was no-one's child. My mother gave me up ... I've been pushed through forty foster homes, abused, beaten, and now I'm in prison. They keep sending me back." In Saskatchewan, an Aboriginal woman explained, "My father beat up my mother when he was drunk. I wandered out of the house ... A big man came driving by in a car. He said he'd help me. He drove me to the forest and raped me. I was only three years old." The women I met challenged me: "Where were all the social workers when we needed help? Where was all your research? Why does the media show us as monsters in prison? No one deserves this!"

Interestingly, the perceptions of women prisoners, and the realities of their life in jail, are quite similar in England, Canada, and India. The differences are as much a matter of the degree of hardship and access to resources as of culture. The women's stories are disturbingly alike. I was silent because I had no answers to give them. Most of us have been spared the hell these women have lived through. Documentary films can at least make some of their stories known and sometimes even contribute to change.

Patricia Plattner: Looking at Women Working Together in India

Extracts from an interview with Patricia Plattner

Patricia Plattner's stunningly beautiful ninety-minute documentary *Made in India* (1998) focuses on the Self-Employed Women's Association (SEWA) movement in Gujarat. It received its North American premiere in Vancouver at the first weekend of the "Women Filmmakers: Refocusing" conference

Patricia Plattner's *Made in India* (1998)

and was shown again to an enthusiastic audience the following week. Plattner shared some of her experiences working on this film in India after the screenings.

Question: How did you come to make *Made in India*?

Patricia Plattner: I've been to India (Gujarat) many times over the last twenty years, before shooting *Made in India*. At first I was thinking of making a film about the architecture, but when I met the women I changed my mind. The first time I went alone and stayed five weeks, it was then that I met people involved in SEWA, the movement that has enabled about 250,000 poor lower caste women to organize themselves into a union. I was not sure I would go back to make a film. I was just so surprised to see what was happening there. I wanted to make a film about these women, so I began interviewing them and writing about them. When I came back to Switzerland with this idea it was not difficult, for once, to obtain funding. It was not an expensive film. We have a government cultural office that provides funding for films, and they offered me funding very quickly. Since I didn't ask for much money, the television company was also willing to support the film.

So I went back again for another five weeks, and with SEWA's help I chose the six women who would participate. I told them I wanted three from the city and three from the countryside, of different ages and religious backgrounds, because there are Hindus, Muslims, and Christians. I met twenty-four women, and spent one day following them, then I selected six. For the crew, I thought it would be good to go in with an all-female team. No men are allowed to be members of SEWA, and I also noticed that it was very important to be all women in order to get into the houses and to make sure that the men left us alone. In fact, whenever the husbands were there (and I thought it would be good to interview the husbands as well), the women would only say "yes" or "no," whereas when there were no men around they really opened up. It took a few more months before we could start shooting. In India the paperwork, customs, and things like that are very difficult, and it was complicated to get permission. So it was some time before we could go back for another five weeks to shoot the film.

Q: Have the women in the film seen it, and, if so, what do they think of it?

PP: No, they haven't seen it yet on a large screen. I did send the tape, and they have seen that and are very happy with it. But they don't understand the parts in English because they don't speak English, only "hello," "thank you," "good-bye" ... But I'm looking forward to watching it with them. I want them to see how beautiful they look on the big screen! Actually, the film has only been screened once so far (March 1999), in Geneva on International Women's Day. It will be screened at festivals and I hope it will be shown in commercial theatres, in Switzerland at least. Documentaries do get shown in cinemas in Switzerland. I'm also doing a shorter fifty-minute version for television (this one is ninety minutes). I really want as many people as possible to see the film because of its political message. I want women in Africa and South America to see it because SEWA is really a good model of organization. But I may have to cut out some of the women, so it won't be the same film, it will be less complete. I'll probably have to use more commentary too rather than letting the women speak for themselves with sub-titles.

Q: Are there other films about the SEWA movement? Are there films made by Indian women?

PP: Yes, there are short informational videos, maybe a bit too explanatory and didactic for a Western audience. They are used to train women, and the people who make them welcome feedback. Unfortunately they don't have very good quality equipment, and most of their films are not subtitled in English. Some are translated with an English voice-over, which tends to be annoying and sound didactic.

Q: Did you use any digital equipment?

PP: Yes. For some other scenes it was easier to have the smaller camera and not to need so many lights. Two of the women we filmed live in the desert, where there is no electricity, so it would have been difficult to shoot in thirty-five millimetre; video was much easier. We had to recharge the batteries overnight. Video is also cheaper, but the big camera is still expensive to rent (and heavy), and the transfer to thirty-five millimetre is expensive. Shooting with a digital camera can end up costing almost the same price as shooting in film. I expect it will become cheaper very soon.

Q: Did you already know about SEWA before you decided to make the film?

PP: No, I met with the SEWA people after I had decided to make a film in India. But I was encouraged to make it about SEWA because their general secretary and other officials spoke good English, and were very helpful when I met them, and introduced me to the right people. I was very impressed, and they were happy when I decided to make the film about them. Of course, they are already quite well known in North America, and maybe in Great Britain a little, but not in the rest of Europe, especially French-speaking countries. You know, India, for French people, it's not on their map! They have an interest in African films because of their former colonies there. SEWA people do come to international events in Geneva, and it's good for them if they can be better known here. The more Western help they can get, the better, so that they can grow, and extra money would enable them to get better video equipment, for example. The SEWA people were enthusiastic, but they didn't tell me what to do or say. I really wrote the script; I just told them I wanted to be with some women, and they provided contacts for me. We did pay them something for helping us to organize the shooting, finding a car and a driver, things like that. I always needed to have someone there to translate. Fortunately I can communicate in English, as it would not have been possible in French!

Q: Did you have any difficulty finding an all-female crew?

PP: No, not really. I just needed someone for camera, someone for sound, and a general assistant; and I used people I had already worked with in Europe. And it was good to be all women, especially when we were sleeping in the villages. I was most surprised by the camerawoman. She had been an assistant to my other cameraman for two of my other films, so I knew her quite well. It was the first time she was really responsible, and she was so happy. I had more trouble finding a soundwoman. I don't know if you have many here in Canada. I would have thought there would be plenty of them, but there were only two or three available. The only problem was that we had to carry about 200 kilos every day because we couldn't leave anything in the car, and we were in a place where you couldn't bring the car close to where we wanted to film. There was just a little path. And it was very hot, forty-two degrees during the day and thirty-nine at night. So we four girls loaded up every day, and when we came back we were tired! I did notice that when you have men they can carry quite a lot more. Fortunately, Séverine, the camerawoman, is a very good technician, because we had some technical problems with the machinery in remote places, and she knew how to handle everything. People think women are not such good technicians, but some are very good!

Filmography: Raman Mann

1993   *Call of the Forest* (English, 25 min.), Norwegian Agency for Development Cooperation. Winner, International Award for Women in Development Video, UK, 1994, best of 78 films from 23 countries.

1993   *Solidarity* (Hindi, 25 min.), Ministry of Human Resource Development, India (rural women's cooperatives)

1993   *Compassion* (Hindi, 20 min.), Ministry of Human Resource Development, India (violence against women)

1993   *New Horizons* (Hindi, 28 min.), NORAD and Ministry of Human Resource, India Development (rural women's cooperatives)

1993   *Payal Ladha. A Face in the Crowd* (English, 12 min.), Doordarshan (Indian TV, about a child prodigy)

1993   Several training films on health issues, immunization, vaccination, etc.

1993   Twenty-three training modules on diarrhoea management, UNICEF, South Asia Regional Office.

1993   *Alka Sharma/No Dowry* (Hindi, 23 min.), Doordarshan (Indian TV)

1995   *Citizen 2000: To the Golden Temple* (English, 30 min.), Channel 4 TV, UK (Critics' Choice of the Week)

1995   *Saath Saath/Together We Progress* (Hindi, 25 min.), Ministry of Rural Areas and Employment, India (development/tribal people)

1995   *My Safety, Your Safety* (English, 25 min.), Airports Authority of India

1996   *Under the Hammer* (English, 50 min.), Channel 4 TV, UK (on international smuggling of antiques and art treasures).

1996   *Seeing Green, Seeing Clean* (English, 25 min.), Norwegian Agency for Development Co-operation

1996   *Barred from Life* (English, 27 min.), British Council/British Overseas Development Administration, New Delhi. Selected for Créteil International Women's Film Festival, France, 1996.

1996   *Global Efforts in Community-Based Rehabilitation for People with Disabilities* (English, 45 min.) Rehabilitation International, USA

1999   *In the Best Interest of the Child* (English, 25 min.), UNICEF, India Country Office (documentary on child rights)

1999   *Media against Trafficking* (English, 25 min.), Canadian International Development Agency and the Commonwealth Human Rights Initiative (sensitizing the media on producing communications on the issue of trafficking in women and children in the South Asian region)

2000   *Our Lives in our Hands* (English, 25 min.), NORAD and Youth for Action in India (rural women's self-managed watershed management projects and micro-credit societies)

2001   *Waiting For Justice* (English, 39 min.), Amnesty International, Netherlands Chapter (torture as an instrument of interrogation and punishment)

For **Patricia Plattner**'s filmography, see Chapter 18.

Note

1 Evelyn Nodwell is an anthropologist attached to the Centre for India and South Asia Research (Institute of Asian Research, University of British Columbia) who also teaches at Simon Fraser University. Her video, *Grassroots Development,* was based on an exchange project between India and Canada, and it looked at how rural people deal with environmental crises. Her focus was on village women's experiences in Jhabua, a remote tribal area of India. She has since produced a second video about the project, in cooperation with the Knowledge Network (BC Educational TV), entitled *From the Ground Up.* It discusses the exchange of Canadian and Indian researchers and how distant communities can learn from each other.

Part 7

Representations of and by Minority Women

The original division of the "Women Filmmakers: Refocusing" events into two separate weekends, one focused on Europe and the other on "post-colonial contexts," obscured a fact that soon became apparent: European countries, the former colonizers, are as "postcolonial" as are their former colonies. The connections between them also remain, especially in the form of minority communities constituted by first- and second-generation Europeans whose cultural background is marked by the experience of having been colonized. The Indian community in Britain represented by Parmar is one obvious example (see Chapters 27 and 28). Carrie Tarr, in her discussion of the representation in recent French films of French women of Maghrebi (North African) heritage, provides a complement to Chapters 12 and 13 on French cinema, by Rollet and Eades, respectively. Plattner's comments on the community of Portuguese workers in Geneva (represented in her film *Piano Panier*, which is discussed in an interview in Chapter 17) provide yet another angle on minority experiences in Europe.

Europe is, however, not the only part of the world where diversity is the rule rather than the exception. Khoo's comments on Malaysian cinema (in Chapter 21) remind us of that multiracial society in Asia. Communities are not homogeneous in Africa either, and Lesley Marx introduces us to the work of a successful White South African woman filmmaker, Katinka Heyns, whom she interviewed. Heyns has made three feature films that both celebrate and question her Afrikaner heritage. Inverting stereotyped images of figures in an African landscape, her depiction of Africa provides an unusual point of comparison with the films made by Black women in Kenya described by Mukora (see Chapter 20).

Both North and South America also have their share of minorities, as does Central America (see Chapter 23, on Sara Gómez of Cuba). This is illustrated here by filmmaker Guita Schyfter (born in Costa Rica and now residing in Mexico), who was interviewed in Vancouver on making her film *Like a Bride*. Based on a novel about two Jewish girls – one from a traditional

Sephardic family, the other from a "progressive" family of European origin – the film deals sensitively with intergenerational conflict as well as issues of cultural identity, assimilation, and loyalty. This interview can be read in conjunction with Chapter 22, which deals with Argentinian filmmaker María Luisa Bemberg. Elena Feder goes on to distinguish Latino/Latina film in Canada from its counterpart in the US. She focuses in particular on two Chilean-born immigrants to Canada, Marilú Mallet (see also Chapter 34 on Quebec filmmakers) and Claudia Morgado, who makes experimental films using forms and themes (including lesbian subject matter) that unassumingly cross several boundaries.

Mainstream French cinema has, until recently, tended to ignore, marginalize, or stereotype representations of its ethnic minority "Others," working to maintain the hegemony of a White, patriarchal, Eurocentric understanding of Frenchness.[1] However, "Beur cinema"[2] of the mid-1980s (films by and/or about the problematic identity of "second-generation" postwar immigrants from France's former empire in the Maghreb) and *banlieue* cinema of the mid-1990s (films set in the multi-ethnic working-class housing estates on the periphery of France's major cities) have turned French cinema into a site of struggle for alternative constructions of French national identity.

Male-authored Beur and *banlieue* films have privileged the experiences of young men of Maghrebi origin, occasionally in relation to the older generation, represented through stereotypical, traditional mothers and impotent fathers, but rarely in relation to young women. Indeed, apart from Rachid Bouchareb's *Cheb* (1991) and Malik Chibane's first two films, *Hexagone* (1994) and *Douce France* (1995), few films take seriously the issues of integration and identity facing young second-generation women. Young women of Maghrebi origin have been equally marginalized in women's films addressing questions of ethnicity and identity (filmmakers such as Claire Denis, Claire Devers, and Laetitia Masson, for example, have chosen to focus predominantly on male characters of African or French Caribbean origin). To date only two White women's films foreground the presence of women of Maghrebi origin in France, *Les Histoires d'amour finissent mal en général* (*Love Stories Usually End in Tears*) by Anne Fontaine (1993) and *Clubbed to Death* by Yolande Zauberman (1997). However, since 1996 there have been two first features by young French women of Algerian origin: *Souviens-toi de moi* (*Remember Me*) by Zaïda Ghorab-Volta (1996) and *Sous les pieds des femmes* (*Where Women Tread*) by Rachida Krim (1997).[3]

This chapter looks at how *Souviens-toi de moi* and *Sous les pieds des femmes* represent both first- and second-generation women immigrants of Maghrebi origin in comparison with *Les Histoires d'amour finissent mal en général* and *Clubbed to Death*. It aims to assess the extent to which the divided Beur subject of the 1980s has been replaced in the 1990s by a more confident, hybrid, and, in this instance, female subject – a subject able to negotiate positively between different cultures and to challenge the assumption of French Republican discourses that women's path to liberation from the Islamic sex/gender system lies in assimilation into Western culture.[4] It should be noted that French film culture has not been permeated by the debates about ethnicity, identity, and representation that underpin much independent Black filmmaking in Britain and North America (and elsewhere) and that the subject matter and style of the films discussed here can be attributed in large measure to their need to address a majority audience.

French Women's Films

In *Les Histoires d'amour finissent mal en général,* her first feature film, Fontaine takes a (relatively) light-hearted look at the problems faced by Zina (Nora), a young *beurette* from the *banlieue* who is also a streetwise Parisienne. Zina (whose mother has returned to Algeria) embodies the divided postcolonial subject, torn, somewhat schematically, between Slim, her Beur fiancé (whose stereotypically oppressive mother embodies traditional Algerian family values) and Frédéric, her White French actor lover (whose elegant mother appears to be a racist). Unable to commit herself to either man – Slim being too dull, Frédéric being too unreliable – Zina ends up on her wedding day losing them both. But the film avoids dealing seriously with the issues of identity and belonging it raises, getting rid of the woebegone Zina by having her hitch a ride from a stranger and head off for Marseilles. Zina may be a survivor, but her denial of her origins does not lead to her acceptance within French society, and she remains a divided subject rather than one who can celebrate her bicultural identity.[5]

Clubbed to Death clearly aims to celebrate a multi-ethnic, multicultural France. Zauberman's track record includes the much lauded documentaries, *Classified People* (1987), which denounces apartheid, and *Caste criminelle* (1989), which denounces the caste system in India, as well as a stylish black-and-white first feature, *Ivan et Abraham* (1992), which exposes anti-Semitism in 1930s Poland. *Clubbed to Death* foregrounds the interracial love affair between Lola (Elodie Bouchez), a young, promiscuous (White) French girl, and Emir (Roschdy Zem), a handsome but impotent man of unspecified ethnic origin, who meet by chance at a "rave" in the exoticized "Third World" space of a Parisian *banlieue*. Their encounter allows Emir to save himself from entrapment in a culture of drugs and violence, but only by rejecting his relationship with Saïda, a woman of Maghrebi origin, hauntingly played by Béatrice Dalle. In this film, Saïda, an exotic dancer and drug addict who is alienated from her roots, is set up as the object of a voyeuristic gaze and is denied the subjectivity and narrative agency accorded to her White rival.

It is notable that both *Les Histoires d'amour finissent mal en général* and *Clubbed to Death* construct young women of Maghrebi origin who are dislocated from a family context but unable to successfully cross cultures. Even more disturbing is the absence of women of Maghrebi origin in *L'Autre côté de la mer* (*The Other Shore*) (1997), a first feature by documentary filmmaker

Dominique Cabrera, herself a *pied noir* (the name given to French colonialists in Algeria). This film is organized around the encounter between Georges, a *pied noir* (Claude Brasseur) back in France for an eye operation, and Tarek, an assimilated Beur eye surgeon (Roschdy Zem) who has never set foot in Algeria. Tarek's problematic identity is traced back to his suppression of his Algerian roots on the death of his immigrant father and is symbolized by his decision to marry a White Frenchwoman. Women of Maghrebi origin have therefore disappeared from the film, from which position they can function only as the site of a lost authenticity rather than as fluid, post-colonial subjects in their own right.

Maghrebi-French Women's Films

The gaps and inadequacies in films such as these, and the general need to counteract French media stereotyping of Maghrebi women as either victims of the Islamic patriarchal system or exotic, sexualized Others, underline the importance of women of Maghrebi origin taking up questions of representation for themselves. In fact, since the early 1980s, Maghrebi women have been making video documentaries and short fiction films, predating the Beur cinema phenomenon of the mid-1980s. Their particular concern with working out women's problematic identities in relation to the patriarchal values of the Algerian immigrant family is taken up in both *Souviens-toi de moi* and *Sous les pieds des femmes*.

Souviens-toi de moi (**Remember Me**)

Zaïda Ghorab-Volta, who grew up in the Parisian *banlieue* in an immigrant Algerian family, devised the screenplay for *Souviens-toi de moi* in 1987 but was refused the *avance sur recettes* (an advance on box office receipts), and the film was shot on weekends, with a cast of amateurs and on a shoestring budget, over a period of nine years.[6] Ghorab-Volta not only wrote and directed the film (which is dedicated to her female cousins in Algeria), but she also plays the central role of Mimouna, her screen presence giving the film semi-autobiographical authenticity. The film expresses the existential anguish of a young woman of Maghrebi origin whose fractured, nomadic self is manifest in a loosely episodic, discontinuous narrative structure, which cuts between the dark, claustrophobic family space in the *banlieue* and the more open, public spaces of the city. Abrupt transitions in the editing, the poignant strains of the original string-based musical score, the off-centre framing and blocking within the frame, and the naturalistic, semi-improvised acting style all work to reinforce Mimouna's lack of a coherent, centred sense of self.

Outside the home, Mimouna's life is compartmentalized into activities involving White French people, and she is obliged to hide these from her family, particularly her fraught relationship with her unsatisfactory lover, Jacques, and her dead-end job in a school canteen. Inside the home, the film offers harrowing scenes of conflict between the generations as mother and daughters scream at each other (in their different languages) and the father chides his son for not having a job and not keeping a proper eye on his sisters. The lack of intimacy or communication is reflected in the way individuals are separated within the frame, or caught alone, in doorways or at windows. Yet the mise-en-scène invites sympathy for both parents and children, for the parents are visibly suffering from their inability either to live out or let go of their traditional identities. And in each instance Mimouna finds temporary solace in the company of other young women, be it her White girlfriends or her younger sister.

The tensions in and between home and the outside world are temporarily halted by the introduction of a third term in the third part of the film; that is, the family holiday that Mimouna spends in Algeria with her parents. The pace of the editing slows down and the camera pans calmly to and fro over the luminous domestic interiors, where Mimouna wears Algerian dress and laughs and chats with her female cousins (as they criticize arranged marriages and Algerian men). So what does Algeria represent here? Not a historically realistic space but, rather, the Utopian space of the extended Algerian family, where the separation of the sexes allows people to come together and talk as they are unable to do in France, so affirming the value of the parents' cultural background. These scenes allow brief insights into the parents' dilemmas, enabling the spectator (and implicitly Mimouna) to gain more respect for and understanding of their own fractured identities. At the same time, Mimouna is able both to take pleasure in the fact that she comes from a warm, gynocentric Algerian tradition (her cousins tell her they will always be with her) and to recognize her own difference (she does not respond to the call for prayer, and she has to censor what she tells her cousins about her sexual experiences).

The film ends with a subjective tracking shot alongside the Seine in the centre of Paris (a reverse image of the tracking shot into the *banlieue* with which the film opens) and a scene of interracial female friendship as Mimouna and her girlfriends walk by the river discussing their holidays and their relationships and then go off to have a drink. Mimouna is a different person, less aggressive, more at peace with the world, able to laugh at her problems and put her psychologically damaging relationship with Jacques behind her. Though there is no attempt to show any shifts within the immigrant family, the film's fluid ending constructs Mimouna's identity as something changing and in process, suggesting that her renegotiation of her relationship to her Algerian cultural heritage will enable her to be more at ease with her hybrid identity in France.

Sous les pieds des femmes

Rachida Krim, who was born in Alès in 1955, trained as an artist and made a short first film about North African traditions, *El Fatha* (1992), before starting research on *Sous les pieds des femmes*. The film, shot in Cinemascope, commemorates in fiction the memories and experiences of her mother and other Algerian women living in France at the time of the struggle of the Front de la Libération Nationale (FLN) for Algerian independence. It stars Claudia Cardinale as Aya, an Algerian immigrant who has chosen to settle with her family in France but who is forced by an overnight visit from her former lover, Amin (in France for the first time since the war ended some thirty-five years ago), to confront her memories of what took place during the struggle for independence. Krim's position as the daughter who has internalized her mother's history is inscribed within the film through the role of Aya's daughter, Fusilla (Nadia Fares), a young woman married to a White Frenchman with a daughter of her own, who seems completely at ease with her bicultural identity. Despite its (many) faults, particularly its awkward pace and its overly didactic tone, as a woman's film and as a political drama *Sous les pieds des femmes* provides a striking alternative to *Souviens-toi de moi*'s more naturalistic representation of an Algerian immigrant family.

The family in *Sous les pieds des femmes* at first appears to be completely assimilated. However, the eradication of all but the most superficial traces of the family's Algerian heritage (Aya's earrings, the *tajine* dish she serves her French son-in-law) proves, rather, to be a sign of a more pathological attempt to achieve a distance from the past. For Amin's presence draws attention to inner conflicts that Aya has hitherto suppressed but not resolved. In the opening sequence, as Aya pores over her reflection in the bathroom mirror, the split and doubled image of Cardinale's heavily made-up face looks like a mask that the elegant, Westernised woman constantly has to adjust. Repeated shots of her fiddling with her lipstick and eye make-up, or fingering her shoulder-length hair, give way to flashback scenes from 1958 of a completely different Aya, a traditional young Algerian woman with long braids, played by Beur actress, Fejria Deliba. Leaving aside the political correctness or otherwise of casting Cardinale as an Algerian (or the choice of Cardinale as a commercial ploy to bring in audiences), the unavoidable disjunction between Aya's two incarnations produces a problematic Brechtian distanciation effect that may draw attention to the radical (and impossible) change of identity that Aya has undergone but that also, unfortunately, challenges the spectator's ability to sustain identification with the character.

The film demonstrates how Aya's change of identity is related to her participation in the activities of the FLN, which, in turn, was motivated by her transgressive (and reciprocated) desire for Amin, the handsome FLN cell leader who first teaches her to write her name. After witnessing her husband's arrest in a police raid and organizing Amin's escape, Aya is required to abandon her children and to take on the identity of Rose Benoît, a Frenchwoman. Dressed first in a sleeveless blue-spotted summer dress, then, to please Amin, in a more sombre tailored black suit, Aya successfully passes for French, obediently transports arms, and carries out a political assassination. However, when she subsequently changes into a beautiful embroidered Algerian dress (to demonstrate that there are aspects of Algerian culture that French colonial rule has been unable to destroy), Amin is appalled and angry, presumably because Aya's transgressive sexual and political behaviour is not reconcilable with his fixed image of Algerian womanhood. Though Aya attempts to assert her identity, not as Rose Benoît but as "Aya, the daughter of Mohammed and Fatima Bouziane," she is forced to realize that there is an ineradicable distance separating the heroic, liberated woman that she has become from the repressed, Islamic FLN male activist who had earlier authorized the execution of an adulterous couple. The sequence ends with her revolt, a challenge to Amin either to kill her or to accept her as a woman who will never lower her eyes to a man again. But inwardly, as her voice-over reveals, Amin's rejection of her leaves Aya a broken woman.

The film subsequently seeks to retrieve Aya as an empowering model of Algerian womanhood through her renewed confrontation with Amin, in which she works through her bitterness about the past. She tries to make him (and the audience) see that the seeds of the fanaticism to come in postwar contemporary Algeria were already present in the way Amin allowed Islamic law to police their personal relationship. At the same time, she criticizes the Family Code and people's failure to speak out against it, and she chides Amin for allowing his son, an Islamic fundamentalist, to impose the wearing of the veil on his mother. In the end, when she accompanies Amin to the bus stop with her daughter and granddaughter, the setting and musical accompaniment recall the scene of their first embrace when Amin expressed his vision of the future and quoted the Islamic saying, "Where mothers tread lies paradise," to which Aya had replied, "And what about women?" This time it is Aya who comforts Amin and expresses a vision of an Algeria in which men would liberate themselves by liberating women. As the camera pulls away, the image of Amin travelling back towards a troubled Algeria is intercut with images of what he has lost: three generations of women whose place is now in France. At the same time, Amin is at last able to answer Aya's question, his voice-over from the future recognizing that "Where women tread lies truth." Aya's identity as an Algerian woman with a mind of her own has been validated, and the film ends with a close-up of her face, this time looking out on the world rather than within, and, at last, with the hint of a smile on her lips.

Conclusion

These two first features by women of Maghrebi origin are historically significant, whatever their technical shortcomings, and mark an interesting
shift in focus from women of the Beur generation to women of the first
generation.[7] Mimouna, the divided daughter who is initially at odds with
her unassimilated Algerian mother, eventually negotiates a more relational,
syncretic sense of self; Aya, the divided mother whose history provides her
daughter and granddaughter with a more secure sense of their bicultural
identity (Fusilla even wears Aya's blue-spotted Rose Benoît dress at the beginning of the film), eventually works through her troubled identity as a
liberated Algerian woman. Both films affirm the importance of women's
liberation in the face of the more constricting elements of Islamic law. They
do so through portraying characters who may be settled in France but who
do not simply embrace the (relative) freedoms offered by French society;
rather, they recognize the need to negotiate the Algerian dimension of their
identity, particularly in relation to other Algerian women (a dimension that
is absent in the other women's films considered here). Furthermore, by vali-
dating their parents' stories as well as their own, Ghorab-Volta and Krim are
inviting spectators to become more aware of the history of Algerian immigrants in France, and, like Aya's granddaughter within Krim's film, enabling
spectators of Maghrebi origin to renegotiate their relationship with their
Maghrebi heritage and, thereby, cross cultures with pleasure and impunity.[8]

Notes

1 For a general discussion of the representation of France's postcolonial minorities in French
   cinema, see Carrie Tarr, "French Cinema and Post-colonial Minorities," in *Postcolonial
   Cultures in France,* ed. Alec G. Hargreaves and Mark McKinney (London: Routledge, 1997),
   59-83.

2 "Beur" is a term that is derived from French backslang for "Arabe" (Arab) and was first
   coined by the Beurs themselves in the early 1980s. The word draws attention to their
   positioning between two cultures; namely, the Arabo-Berber-Islamic culture of their parents' generation and the secular but often anti-Arab and Islamophobic French culture of
   their schools and peer group. However, the appropriation of the word by the media means
   that it is no longer empowering, and this chapter mostly uses the more neutral but more
   cumbersome (and still problematic) expression "of Maghrebi (or Algerian) origin."

3 Mention should also be made of the TV documentary, *Mémoires d'immigrés,* by Yamina
   Benguigui (1996), which subsequently enjoyed a very successful run in the cinema and
   gave a direct voice to the hitherto unheard stories of first-generation immigrants from the
   Maghreb (Paris: Canal-Editions, 1997).

4 For a discussion of this issue, see Rachel A.D. Boule, "Veiled Objects of (Post)-Colonial
   Desire: Forbidden Women Disrupt the Republican Fraternal Space," *Australian Journal of
   Anthropology,* 5 1 (1994): 113-23.

5 For a more detailed analysis of this film, see Carrie Tarr, "Ethnicity and Identity in Contemporary French Cinema: The Case of the Young Maghrebi-French Woman," *Iris* 24 (1997):
   125-35.

6 She has since co-written the script for Romain Goupil's TV film *Le Voile du silence (The Veil
   of Silence)* (1996), which is about a schoolgirl who chooses to wear the veil, and she has
   made a TV film, *Laisse un peu d'amour (Leave a Bit of Love)* (1998), which is about mother-
   daughter relationships within a White, single-parent, working-class French family.

7 There has been a series of fiction films in the late 1990s showing an interest in retrieving the past of the first generation of immigrants. *Vivre au paradis* by Bourlem Gherdjou (1999), set in the *bidonville* (shanty-town) in Nanterre between the years 1958 and 1962, also includes the figure of a strong female FLN activist.
8 A later version of this article is to be found in Carrie Tarr "Where Women Tread: Daughters and Mothers in *Souviens-toi de moi* and *Sous les pieds des femmes*," in *Women, Immigration and Identities in France*, ed. Jane Freedman and Carrie Tarr (Oxford: Berg, 2000), 153-69.

---

31 Katinka Heyns: Questioning Afrikaans Culture
Lesley Marx

The South African film industry is a very old one, dating back to 1910 and the making of *The Great Kimberley Diamond Robbery*. The subject matter of this film indicates that, right from the start, the interests of those with the money to make films would centre on the White experience of Africa. The great turning point in South African history in the twentieth century was the 1948 election to power of the Afrikaans-dominated Nationalist Party, which duly saw to it that its obsession with White supremacy, Calvinistic morality, and patriarchal control would manifest itself in all forms of cultural expression. One form of this stranglehold on the film industry was the prejudicial subsidy system that ensured the privileging of films made by Whites for Whites (preferably Afrikaans Whites). Distribution and screening venues also heavily favoured the ruling party. There were few Black cinemas, and they were a far cry from the picture palaces that sprang up for White audiences in Johannesburg, Durban, and Cape Town.

Furthermore, films about Afrikaners were encouraged to represent the culture and community in its most idealized form: morally pure women and upright men. The principle of filmmaking centred on entertainment values rather than on provocative experimentation with filmic form and content. Thus, throughout the 1950s and 1960s, large numbers of Afrikaans soap operas and comedies were produced that had nothing to do with the political realities of the day – the increasingly stringent apartheid laws, the sacking of Sophiatown and the birth of Soweto, the pass laws, the banning of protest movements, the slaughter at Sharpeville, and the start of the border wars in Mozambique and Namibia.[1]

There were challenges to this pattern of filmmaking, notably through the efforts of foreign visitors: Donald Swanson and Eric Rutherford produced *Jim Comes to Jo'burg* (aka *African Jim*) in 1949. Playing on the well worn story of the country bumpkin who finds fortune in the city, they exploited a range of stereotypes about Africans and urbanization but, nevertheless, gave Black audiences the pleasure of watching a story with Black actors who went on to become stars and role models. American filmmaker Lionel Rogosin's pioneering *Come Back, Africa* (1959) was much more hard-hitting and looked forward to politically aware films such as *Mapantsula* (1988). A wide range of compelling documentaries and some fine features emerged during the 1980s, and fuller use was made of collaboration with Black writers and actors, even though the directors and producers tended, usually, to be White (and male), replicating international power structures in filmmaking.

With the end of apartheid rule and the success of the African National Congress in the 1994 elections, there were high hopes that the struggles of the South African film industry would be eased through more generous and fully equitable subsidies and through the serious interest of business corporations. At present, these hopes have not been fully realized. Occasionally a new film will appear that is innovative, and there does seem to be some growth in Black filmmaking. The adaptation of Njabulo Ndebele's novella, *Fools* (1998), for example, was written, directed, and produced by Black filmmakers and starred some of South Africa's most notable Black actors. Yet it had almost no publicity and was subject to severely limited screenings, largely in video format on university campuses and in community halls.

Within the context outlined above, Katinka Heyns's career has been privileged: she benefited from being part of the Afrikaans film industry. Indeed, her best opportunities as an actress were given to her by the highly talented Jans Rautenbach, who went on to become her mentor. She learned to make films through working in this environment and was given much support and encouragement. When she launched out independently and set up her own production studios – Sonneblom (Sunflower) – South African Television was ready to give her a great deal of work. She made television dramas and documentaries, and also entered the very lucrative dubbing industry.[2]

Her successful productivity set her apart from other women directors in the country. Not surprisingly, women filmmakers are few and far between in South Africa. While Helena Nogueira and Elaine Proctor immediately come to mind as interesting and risk-taking directors who have tried to challenge the masculine domain of filmmaking, and while there are several excellent documentary filmmakers (such as Lindy Wilson), it is fair to say that only Katinka Heyns has managed to make her mark, with some degree of critical *and* commercial success, in a country that does not treat its own filmmakers with much enthusiasm and that, to an alarming degree, privileges Hollywood over local production.[3]

Notwithstanding the extent to which Heyns was blessed under the old South African system, it must be noted that she came of age amidst a group of Afrikaans artists who were by no means complacent or supportive of the

Katinka Heyns's *Paljas* (1997), courtesy of the director

status quo. Jans Rautenbach was of the same generation as the ground-breaking Afrikaans writers known as Die Sestigers (the Sixties Generation), who contested the dominant system through both formal experimentation and the provocation of their subject matter (André Brink and Breyten Breytenbach are just two of the most well known of these artists). Rautenbach's films explored love across the colour bar (*Katrina*, 1969), the conflict between coloured and White Afrikaans identities (*Die Kandidaat*, 1968), and insanity in a young Afrikaans girl (*Jannie Totsiens*, 1970). These films constantly challenged the Afrikaans community's preferred image of itself as the good, the true, and the beautiful.

On the latter subject, Heyns tells the amusing story of how she, a rather unglamorous woman, was cast in *Katrina*, along with two other not-very-handsome actors, to make up the representative Afrikaans family in the film. Rautenbach was excoriated by Afrikaans critics for casting such "ugly" people as Afrikaners and so giving a "bad impression" of what Afrikaners were like. She herself suffered criticism for casting Aletta Bezuidenhout in her most recent film, *Paljas* (1997). Anant Singh, the producer, thought the film would benefit from being shot in English with Jessica Lange or Meryl Streep in the lead role. Alternatively, he thought, a more conventionally

Katinka Heyns's *Paljas* (1997),
courtesy of the director

Katinka Heyns's *Die Storie van Klara Viljee* (1991), courtesy of the director

beautiful local actress like Sandra Prinsloo might have been better. But Heyns persisted with Bezuidenhout and, more than that, filmed her with almost no make-up (personal interview, January 1999). The result is a very moving portrayal of a disillusioned, hard-working, spiritually drained woman whose strong-boned face takes on a kind of majesty, associated, paradoxically, with the tough sensuality of the landscape that has helped to drain her.

Katinka Heyns is, herself, a tiny woman with white-blonde hair and shocking blue eyes. She introduces her film studio, Sonneblom, with the story of how the buildings were designed to marry the left brain and the right brain and so provide an aesthetically pleasing context for all the hard technology that they house. At their centre is a beautiful, very still, garden, which she describes as the womb out of which have come some of her most creative ideas. From the many blue and terra cotta terraces one looks across the hills of Honeydew in the east Witwatersrand (ridge of white waters), the plateau under which lie all the great coal and gold mines of the province. It is far enough out of Johannesburg and its metropolitan sprawl to still retain some sense of the *veld,* the open country spaces.

The following discussion of Heyns's three feature films focuses on those country spaces and the women who inhabit them. It also suggests some of the ways in which Heyns's films both celebrate and question the Afrikaans culture that is her heritage – the extent to which they are suspended between a challenge to, and a recuperation of, conventions of cultural and female identity.

Heyns's first feature film was made in 1987 and was based on a best-selling novel by feminist writer, Dalene Matthee. Heyns argues that she herself is not a feminist, by which she means a person who believes in gender dichotomies. Yet, she was clearly influenced by Matthee's tendency to dichotomize in her novel. *Fiela se Kind* (Fiela's Child), set in the 1880s, tells the story of a strong coloured woman, Fiela Komotie, who brings up a White castaway child, Benjamin, as her own, until he is twelve. At this point, the census-takers arrive and discover him. They remove him from his home in the Lange Kloof and take him to Knysna, a town on the coast. There they rig an identification ritual by using a poor White Afrikaans woman from the forest whose son had gone missing many years before. She apparently recognizes Benjamin, and he is forced back to the forest under his new name, Lucas van Rooyen.

The first half of the film sets up a rhythm of cross-cutting between the open plains, the mountains, and the wide blue skies of the Lange Kloof on the one hand, and the claustrophobic, dense green undergrowth of the Knysna forests on the other. There are several inversions of stereotyped images of South African figures in a landscape. If the stereotype of the coloured person was that of the idle hedonist, in this film our first image is of a sturdy Fiela yelling at her sons to catch a fine-looking ostrich, a bird that will mark the start of her breed farm.[4] The camera has already revealed, in a slow pan, the vastness of the space she occupies, the comfort of her home, and the assurance with which she sustains this land that was her father's and was left "in her name." She reiterates her name throughout the film, both as self-affirmation and as challenge. Other recurrent motifs are those of all the members of the family working in harmony at their individual tasks, of good meals around the family table, and of the ready supply of clean, strong clothes. It is clear that her foundling child, Benjamin, would be well provided with love and material care in this aspirant middle-class home. Key to the dynamics of the home, though, is the passivity and near-silence of the husband, Selling Komotie, who by the end of the film appears semi-invalided.

By contrast, "Kom-se-Bos," the settlement in the Knysna forest, reveals the derelict despair of a poor White Afrikaans family. The brutality of the father, Elias, takes on Dickensian proportions; the mother, Barta, is cowed into silence for much of the film, and the two younger children, Benjamin (now Lucas) and his supposed sister, Nina, are set to work sawing beams to ensure the subsistence-level lifestyle of the family. Clothed in rags, they either starve or wolf down food brought by sympathetic neighbours. The forest is a space of forced labour or of pursuit: Elias is either in pursuit of the children in order to beat them into submission or in pursuit of elephants to cull. Where Fiela, the coloured woman, cultivates the land and causes the ostriches to go forth and multiply, Elias, the White man, ravages the land and its inhabitants.

Fiela is frequently shot moving powerfully across her farm or with wide skies behind her. Barta van Rooyen, on the other hand, is seldom seen in an open space; she is either huddled in the dark forest or framed by the shadows of her pathetic shack. Her gaunt, tired face is riven with lines; her huge eyes stare with fear and despair. One of the most compelling moments in the film occurs when she tells the truth about her false identification of Benjamin: she moves from the shadow towards an open window and gazes out. Visually, the chiaroscuro suggests both the horror that she has lived through and the tenuousness of the release she has just given herself from the lie that has haunted her. A positive spin on the forest is provided by the dryad-like Nina who collects coloured bottles and plays music on them, who knows the birdsong, and who believes in forest fairies. Her imaginative appropriation of the forest cannot withstand the beatings and bruises inflicted on her by her father, however, and she eventually puts the forest behind her. At the end of the film Barta's monstrous husband lies incapacitated on a bed, having been trampled by one of the elephants he has spent his life trying to trap in order to make a quick buck. It is a fittingly grotesque resolution to this story of the poor White family, presented as a kind of gothic morality tale.

Both narrative lines, that of the coloured family and the poor White family, end with the husband invalided. Where Elias gets his just desserts, one could argue that Fiela's husband seems to have drifted into a stasis that matches his silence. This is used, rather problematically, to affirm Fiela's unassailable strength in the home. We are reminded, though, that this strength is hers only in her home, on her farm. Her courageous trek over the mountains to Knysna to try to claim Benjamin back yields only insult and abuse from the White magistrate.

The film is deeply concerned with an analysis of what it means to be a mother and how the intersection of race, class, and gender affects maternal desire. Both women, coloured and poor White, are portrayed with sympathy but also with an unblinking eye for the ways in which the failures of a social system *and* the failures of personal will may generate tragedy. Barta may have the advantage in terms of race, but she is the helpless victim of patriarchy and is condemned to the breadline by her vicious, lazy husband. Fiela owns land and is inscribed into a better class than Barta. Her dominance in the household, the gentle subservience of her husband, and her feisty dealings with all the men who cross her path, White or coloured, provide a compelling image of female strength. Yet her racial status acts inexorably against her desires until the sentimental ending, when Benjamin is restored to her.

The ideology of the film is deeply vexed at this point, however. It is strongly suggested, through framing and visual emphasis, that Benjamin, her White foundling child, is her favourite. Ultimately, the film is, indeed, about Fiela's child, the boy Benjamin who grows into the man Lucas and rediscovers himself as Benjamin. His burgeoning love for his "sister," Nina, thus becomes safe, and he returns to Fiela to take up the inheritance she bequeaths him. This is a curiously ironic moment in the film: the coloured woman hands over her land to the White man, implicitly endorsing both the preference that she has shown for him and his visual foregrounding at the expense of his coloured siblings. The moment also apparently endorses the sense that he has come into his *rightful* inheritance. Fiela's son, David, has conveniently died, and her other son, Tollie, is an incipient alcoholic (shades of the old stereotypes of idleness and drunkenness that have bedevilled representations of coloured people).

The ending of the film, with its assurance that Benjamin will be a farmer (in fine Afrikaans tradition), is filmed not for irony but, rather, as the resolution to a family romance that effectively reinstates White male ownership of the land and avoids the darker possibilities that the plot had suggested both for miscegenation and for incest. This is not to deny the effectiveness of the film in 1987 South Africa: it gives us images of the pioneer as a coloured woman on the land, and it shows how this woman aspires to a place of economic strength; it also reminds us, shockingly, of the nightmare of White Afrikaans patriarchy.

In 1991, Heyns released *Die Storie van Klara Viljee*. Heyns's husband, the fine Afrikaans novelist Chris Barnard, wrote the screenplay, and she agrees that his influence is to be felt in the full, complex treatment of the male characters. She also speaks of the productive tension between his desire for narrative structure and order and her tendency to let the camera play, to let it go where it wishes and to see what happens. He works with words; she works with images. He plans, she works intuitively (personal interview, January 1999). The fact that the film ends with the dance of male and female suggests her own instinctual attraction to a harmonizing of opposites. One of the ways in which the film avoids simple oppositions is through the depiction of the central characters of Klara and Dawid. Both are victims to patriarchy and prejudice and eventually transcend them.

Die Storie van Klara Viljee is a rich blend of allegory and social realism, as Heyns weaves together vignettes of small-town life and the epic-comic struggle of Klara, first to hide from the demons of her past and then to confront them. The title itself suggests the ways in which the film evokes stories, legends, even myths to suggest the great underlying themes of love, loss, and endurance. The landscape is that of the Arniston dunes and the dramatic south Cape coastline. Arniston means a great deal to Heyns: it is associated with her childhood years, her father, who was a great storyteller, and her early belief in mermaids (personal interview, January 1999). To some extent, *Klara* is a story about a mermaid whose love for the sea is almost destroyed but who recovers her sense of wholeness.

The folktale antecedents of the story are apparent: Klara is the good Afrikaans orphan who falls in love and is betrayed by a ne'er-do-well fisher called Pietman. Klara's counterpart is the tarty and ironically named Engela (Angel), who has produced a child by Pietman but who wrongfully accuses the schoolteacher, Dawid, of being the father. Dawid loses his post but refuses to bow to the prejudices of the town by leaving. He sets up a transport business. Where Engela is left to follow a fairly predictable path into the city and abandons her child to the care of the village, Klara's character takes a different turn.[5] On the supposed death of Pietman, Klara builds herself a cottage behind a sand dune so that she need never see the sea again, and she proceeds to bury herself in solitude against all the pleas of the community. When she discovers that Pietman has fooled both her and the village and is living in Cape Town, she decides to remove the dune, with the help of a shovel and donkey.

Played with impressive toughness and truculence by the beautiful Anna-Mart van der Merwe, Klara emerges as a woman who determines her own destiny in a completely uncompromising fashion. Much of the comedy of the film derives from her successful attempts at fending off interfering men who want to help her shape her destiny. She offers to whip one and shoot another. And Heyns resists the temptation to frame her for her beauty; instead, her large-boned body is emphasized, moving in an ungainly but determined fashion through the village or across the dunes. In terms of the narrative, she is the object of male desire and the masculine gaze, but this conventional, gendered structuring of the male-female dynamic is constantly unsettled by the comic ineptitude of Klara's admirers and by the filmic foregrounding of Klara's relationship with the landscape.

Klara, in the most literal fashion, takes command of the land, reshapes it to reflect her desire, and opens up her view to the sea and the liberation it represents. Of course, this reshaping suggests a kind of wilful imposition that could just as easily be seen as a metaphor for the ruthless colonizing of the land. It is important, then, that Klara's action is preceded by her luxurious swimming in the sea, a baptism and submission to the feminine power of the ocean (very reminiscent of Kate Chopin's heroine in *The Awakening*). The dune is associated with Pietman, the sea with her sensual freedom.

Klara's demolition of the dune serves as a catalyst for the entire village to renew itself: the gardens bloom, the carpenter starts producing beautiful furniture, the mill starts turning, and all the villagers gather to help Klara shovel. The film ends with a Bergmanesque dance on the beach and the promise of a wedding between Klara and the good, kind Dawid. The resonance with Shakespearean comedy is also marked, from the strong attractive heroine to the choric quality of the village idiot and the caricatures of village types.

What is further notable in this film is that the community of women is potent: the land upon which Klara builds her cottage was left her by her mother; Engela's child comes to live with Klara; and Engela's stepmother, the abused second wife of the brutal Doors, escapes to Klara's dune where she helps to plant a garden. Tant Mollie, the telephonist and owner of the local boarding house, and Tant Lissie, the schoolteacher who replaces Dawid, both provide love and support to Klara. The final dance is concerned, though, to reaffirm the harmonious drawing together of men and women in happy couples, in keeping with the folkloric quality of the film.

The importance of music and dancing in *Klara* is even more notable in Heyns's most recent feature film, *Paljas*, released in 1997.[6] The concertina, the piano, the Jew's harp, and the gramophone playing Josef Schmidt and Mario Lanza are deployed at several key moments to counterpoint a narrative about the power of magic to renew a family, a community, and a landscape. The MacDonalds are a working-class family living in the small town of Toorwater, where Hendrik is the stationmaster.

The relationship between Hendrik and his wife, Katrien, is marked by silence and alienation. Her gaunt face is filled with pain and disillusionment, her large capable hands are constantly seen in close-up, working – scrubbing floors, baking bread, chopping pumpkins, feeding the family. These are images traditionally associated with the *boerevrou* ("farm woman"), but this wife is alienated from the land. Hendrik is haunted by nostalgic yearning for the days of their courtship in the wide *veld*, under the full moon, but these romantic images of the landscape have been superseded by the grim realities of domestic drudgery. Katrien's clumsy suitor, Frans, brings more distress than comfort, and her daughter, Emma, has reached the stage of understanding some of the misery in the family. The two women have little connection to the land around them: they are seen largely confined to the domestic space of the kitchen or the dining room. The land does serve as an escape when Hendrik's well meaning but infuriating attempts to *regraas* the world ("shout the world into order") prove too much to bear, and the women rush off to the *veld*. But even here, they invariably encounter men who want to confine them: Frans and Nollie, the awkward but sympathetic suitor to Emma.

Willem, the young son, stopped speaking two years previously. The mystery around the son's muteness is sustained, and it haunts the film and the family. It clearly has something to do with the breakdown of communication between mother and father, which itself is symbolized by the geographical moves the family has made. Katrien speaks the symbolic litany of railway stations across the scrubland of the Karoo, each one poorer and more isolated than the last, marking the downward spiral of Hendrik's career: Touwsrivier ("rope river"), Lydenburg ("town of suffering"), Soekmekaar ("seeking each other"), Twyfelfontein ("fountain of doubt").

But Toorwater means "magic water," and it is here that a circus arrives, leaving behind it the clown, Manuel, who befriends Willem and teaches him magic tricks. The clown is portrayed as a feminine figure, whose make-up becomes a leitmotif throughout the film, echoing Katrien's yearning to wear make-up and earrings, Emma's venturing into womanhood by putting on make-up, Willem's release from his silence through turning into a miniature clown, and his transfer of his clown make-up to his father.

Make-up is partly a metaphor for magical and protean performances of different identities and partly an image of the feminine that enables Hendrik to understand his wife and daughter more fully at the end of the film. The clown with his make-up is also closely tied to lyrical images of the landscape. He first materializes over the horizon of the *veld* leading an elephant and playing his Jew's harp, and he appears to communicate with the moon, an obvious feminine image. Many of the most joyous scenes in the film are of Manuel and Willem, in clown costumes and playing concertinas, dancing across the *veld*.

The transformative powers of the clown and what he represents are eventually felt throughout the town. Toorwater is riddled with Afrikaans Calvinists of an almost caricatured vileness, deeply suspicious of magic, which they read as witchcraft and which must be rooted out. In an especially violent scene, they shoot Manuel as he attempts to escape along the railway track. The far distances of the Karoo, the loneliness of the track with its forlorn promise of travel and adventure, and the prone body of the clown provide moving images of loss and sterility. This turning point in the film leads, however, to the adoption of the clown not only by Willem, but also by his family. By the end of the film, his role as healer affects the entire community. The final scene shows the home of the MacDonalds transformed from a lonely outpost of grief into the centre of the dance, renewed love between Hendrik and Katrien, and burgeoning love between Emma and Nollie, while Willem is seen silhouetted against the sky at the top of a windmill, playing the clown's song on his concertina.

Heyns brings all three of her feature films to a comic resolution that offers the regeneration of family and community. Important to that process is either a strong female character or a magical feminine principle, and their varied engagements with the power of the South African landscape. Fiela, the yeowoman-farmer; Klara, the sculptor of nature; Manuel, the clown who reminds a family of the magic of the *veld:* all these figures in a landscape suggest ways of reconceiving the relationship between the individual and nature by means of an imaginative investment in the reenchanting of the world.

Paljas was entered for a Best Foreign Film Academy Award but never came close to winning. Heyns expresses pleasure that it was considered worth entering and speaks of the mixed reception it has received overseas: very poor responses in Los Angeles, but very good ones in India and Sweden. She suggests that it is difficult to market films abroad that are so closely tied to a sense of place and community (personal interview, January 1999). A recent televised interview with her, shot on the Arniston dunes, reveals her to be full of hopes and dreams and desires for new ventures. Her sense of the magic of place continues strong, as does her commitment to the stories of her people – and her belief in mermaids.

Her films, spanning ten of the most overwhelming years in South African history, certainly offer an intervention and a revisioning in terms of gender politics in Afrikaans society. In terms of the burning issues of race and national identity more broadly, however, Heyns's vision – and this is both a strength and a limitation – remains tied to her own specific cultural loyalties.

Notes

1 For fuller accounts of the history of the South African film industry, see Keyan Tomaselli, *The Cinema of Apartheid: Race and Class in South African Film* (Sandton: Radix, 1989); Peter Davis, *In Darkest Hollywood: Exploring the Jungles of Cinema's South Africa* (Randburg/Athens, OH: Ravan Press/Ohio University Press, 1996); and Rob Nixon, *Homelands, Harlem and Hollywood: South African Culture and the World Beyond* (New York: Routledge, 1994).

2   In the 1990s these opportunites were less and less forthcoming, and the most recent news is that she has decided to close her studios and explore new projects, which may well involve more film work but may take her in new directions altogether.

3   Proctor's very fine film on the traumatizing effects of the border wars, *On the Wire* (1989), and Nogueira's controversial film about lesbian love, *Quest for Love* (1988), were landmarks of the 1980s, but their subsequent work has been intermittent and very badly served by South African distribution. Wilson's *Last Supper at Horstley Street* (1985) is a deeply moving account of the forced removal of a family from District Six, a mixed-race suburb on the slopes of Devil's Peak, which was bulldozed by the authorities in the 1960s.

4   See J.M. Coetzee's exploration of idleness as it was ascribed to both Hottentot and Boer in the early colonial days in *White Writing: On the Culture of Letters in South Africa* (Sandton: Radix, 1988). *Fiela* challenges the attribution of idleness to people of colour and offsets this with the brutal depiction of regressive Boer (Afrikaner) idleness in the form of the stereotype of Elias and the Knysna family, within the melodramatic structure of good versus evil upon which the drama rests. In South Africa, "coloured" refers to people of mixed racial heritage, as opposed to Black South Africans of "pure" African descent.

5   Keyan Tomaselli and Miki van Zyl have offered an exhaustive analysis of the trope of the *boeredogter* ("farm daughter") in the exploration of the rural/urban tension in countless Afrikaans films (see "Themes, Myths and Cultural Indicators: The Structuring of Popular Memories," in *Movies, Moguls, Mavericks: South African Cinema 1979-1991* [Johannesburg: Showdata, 1992]). *Klara Viljee* sustains this narrative as subtext rather than as main plot in the interests of a complex nostalgia for reaffirming the possibilities of the renewal of the village world. It acknowledges the ravages of the urban on the rural but asserts the resilience of the latter.

6   "Paljas" means a magic spell that makes things right again.

Filmography

Primary References

1987   *Fiela se Kind*. Direction: Katinka Heyns; production: Sonneblom Films.
1991   *Die Storie van Klara Viljee*. Direction: Katinka Heyns; production: Sonneblom Films.
1997   *Paljas*. Direction: Katinka Heyns; production: Sonneblom Films.

Secondary References

1949   *Jim Comes to Jo'burg (African Jim)*. Direction: Donald Swanson; production: Warrior Films.
1959   *Come Back, Africa*. Direction: Lionel Rogosin; production: Lionel Rogosin.
1968   *Die Kandidaat*. Direction: Jans Rautenbach; production: Emil Nofal Films.
1969   *Katrina*. Direction: Jans Rautenbach; production: Emil Nofal Films.
1970   *Jannie Totsiens*. Direction: Jans Rautenbach; production: Jans Rautenbach.
1985   *Last Supper at Horstley Street*. Direction: Lindy Wilson; production: Channel Four TV.
1988   *Quest for Love*. Direction: Helena Nogueira; production: Vision International.
1988   *Mapantsula*. Direction: Oliver Schmitz; production: Haverbeam/One Look/Orion Films/Spectrum Films.
1989   *On the Wire*. Direction: Elaine Proctor; production: National Film and TV School, London.
1998   *Fools*. Direction: Ramadan Suleman; production: JBA/Natives at Large/Eban. Multimedia/Framework International/M-Net Africa/The European Union/The SABC.

Conducted by Rita de Grandis and Jan Mennell

Rita de Grandis: Before beginning, I asked Guita how she would introduce herself, and she said, "No superfluous words, let's get straight to the point. You academics are too flamboyant!" So I just want to welcome her and to thank the vice-consul of Mexico here in Vancouver, for without her support, this visit would not have been possible. Even finding out how to get hold of Guita was very difficult, not to mention obtaining the funding that we needed to bring her here. I'll also introduce Jan, from Queen's University in Kingston, Ontario, who will be joining in a three-way conversation with our guest.

Guita Schyfter: I want to thank everyone who made it possible for me to be here. I'll begin with how I got into filmmaking, since everyone asks me that. As this is partly a women's studies audience, you may be interested to know that I began by studying psychology. Around 1970 I had finished my bachelor's degree and then went to New York to visit my sister. I was walking along the street, and there was a big demonstration. I was looking at the people (I'm an expert on demonstrations because I went through 1968 in Mexico) and realized there were only women, and they were holding brassieres and placards saying, "Don't feed a pig tonight." So I arrived at my sister's and asked, "What is this?" and she told me, "That's the Women's Liberation Movement." I asked, "Is the pig a policeman?" and she said, "No, it's the husband." Then she gave me a book by Betty Friedan, and, having read it, I decided to go on to do my Master's in psychology on this women's liberation thing. I wanted to study women's attitudes, how they varied depending on whether they worked outside the home or not. After that I went to a film festival where I saw Agnès Varda's *Happiness,* and I asked, "Can women direct films?" It was a great surprise to me to learn that they could. Ten years later I was in England, working in the field of educational psychology and involved in launching an open university in Mexico. I was attached to a filmmaker over there who made films for TV, and I told her, "I want to do what you do because the truth is I'm not cut out for the academic life!" So I went to the BBC to study television, and when I returned to Mexico I never went back to the university. I started making documentaries instead, and I've been doing that for years now.

RdG: And how did you come to make your first feature film, *Novia que te vea (Like a Bride)?*

GS: I spent some time living in Spain, and while I was there I read a book about writer's block. The author's advice was, "Whenever you want to tell a story, look at your own roots." I thought, if I had to make a documentary about my roots, what would they be? I realized I was Jewish and Costa Rican, but I thought I could never make a documentary about being Jewish. About ten years went by, and when I had the opportunity to make my first feature film in 1992, I remembered that advice. So I decided to talk about what it was like growing up Jewish in a Latin American country.

Jan Mennell [after showing a clip from the very beginning of the film]: There are so many questions raised in this scene. The first is about the Biblical flavour that it has to it. One has the impression of the people arriving in the Promised Land. Was that intentional, especially with the piñata in the scene, in the shape of the six-sided star of David?

GS: No, that's not the point. My immigrant story has to start with their arrival in a different culture. So the whole point is that it is different, and they are dressed differently from the local people. The people at the railway station look at them because they know they are strangers and different from them. Piñatas in Mexico come in all kinds of shapes, but the classical one is this star-shaped one. I put it there to represent a different culture and something that fascinates the young boy.

JM: So the opening scene sets up a major theme throughout the whole movie, which is precisely how it feels to be a Jew in Mexico, and how to relate to the different culture. I know this film is based on a novel of the same title, by Jewish Mexican author Rosa Nissan, published in 1992. I wonder if that scene is taken from it, although the film is substantially different from the novel. In fact you add another character, Rifke, who actually takes over in the film and becomes central. Why did you make that change?

GS: From the beginning, when I decided to make this film, I based the characters on my friends and the people I grew up with or knew or interviewed in Mexico. When I made the film I was not thinking only about the Jews, I was also thinking about all my friends who were not Jews. What I wanted to tell was not just a story about growing up Jewish in a Catholic country, and the decisions you have to make, but also about the differences within the Jewish community. In Mexico and Costa Rica, when people say "Jews" they usually think of a monolithic and secretive group. So I wanted to tell a story about how different we are within the Jewish community. There are all kinds of political and ideological positions, different kinds of food, different mentalities, even different languages. At first I didn't want to talk about the Sephardic Jews, because I didn't know them well. I wanted to talk only about the Ashkenazi Jews of European origin. But then I decided I wanted to show this variety, and when I looked at the book I decided to use the Sephardic family it describes and to add another, an invented Ashkenazi one, more like mine.

JM: So why did you use the book at all?

GS: Because for me it was difficult to make this film; in Latin America, there were no films with Jewish characters that come alive, so I was a little bit afraid. This was my first feature film and I thought everyone would say, "This is probably her life, it's autobiographical." So I wanted to blame someone else, to be able to say, "No, I didn't say that, she did ..." That's why I looked for a book to base the film on. Basically, I wanted to be able to say, "This is not my story, it's her story." Of course the book helped me a lot because it immersed me in a Sephardic culture that I only knew a bit about. It also enriched me because it opened the doors to a lot of Sephardic homes and things like that.

JM: That brings me to another question. As I watched the film I became more and more aware that, in making a difference between the two communities, you were almost establishing a hierarchical relationship between them. The Ashkenazi family is much more flexible, culturally more open, more adaptable. You see it in the scenes with the family: the houses are more open, there's Mexican art in their home, they have integrated more into the Mexican society around them. Whereas in scenes with the Sephardic family, who are from Turkey, they are very closed in, the women especially don't seem to leave the house often. You never see them outside the house, and they never discuss any issues except marriage and food – or their embroidery. So you end up creating, consciously or not, an impression that the Ashkenazi are superior and the Sephardim are backward.

GS: But I didn't say that, Rosa did in her book!

JM: And that is the part of the book you did decide to adapt, right?

GS: That's the way it was in the sixties. At that time the Sephardic community was much more conservative, more traditional, because the Ashkenazi came from a different cultural environment, which was European. So they were more open to art. You know, everybody wanted to get married above all, but among the Ashkenazim it was easier for girls to go to university than among the Sephardim, who were often married when they were fifteen or sixteen years old. Even today the Sephardic women only go out in groups. They were and are just more traditional. That doesn't mean the others are superior. Of course, things have changed because there has been a lot of intermarriage between Sephardic and Ashkenazi Jews, which wasn't allowed at that time. I come from a completely Ashkenazi community in Costa Rica. I never even knew that Sephardic Jews existed until I was about fifteen years old. The film is set in the period when I was that age.

RdG: My next question moves away a bit from the precise historical context of the 1960s to the way you developed your female characters. We know that this is a family history told through an exchange between these two friends and following them through different periods of their lives. In the end they both get married and both have children, fulfilling the traditional maternal role expected of them. Do you believe that maternity is central to women's identity, and was that what you were trying to convey? I get a sense that these two female characters do not really develop a critical distance vis-à-vis the role expected of them, they don't quite accomplish a journey towards autonomy or self-questioning.

GS: [Laughing] I'm sorry, Rita, you didn't pay attention when you watched the movie! Both of them do what, in a sense, they set out to do from the beginning. Oshinica [the Sephardic girl, played by Claudette Maille] has always wanted to be a painter. Her problem is not about wanting to belong, and she has never had any political motivations or interests. Her main motivation is that she wants to be a painter, and in the end she is one. The Ashkenazi girl, Rifke [played by Maya Michalska], has a different problem from the beginning, as she has always wanted to belong in Mexico. She wanted to celebrate Christmas as a child, and she didn't understand why Mexicans knew she was Jewish when she walked down the street. She wants to get lost in the crowd. She's much more politically involved at the university and through the Zionist organization that she joins. All the time she asks herself big questions like, "Should I stay here or go to Israel?" In the end she becomes an anthropologist.

RdG: So the question of their Jewishness is more important than their gendered role within their particular family tradition?

GS: When I was developing the characters, I didn't think about gender roles. What I saw was, "What does this woman want?"

RdG: That reminds me of a remark by María Luisa Bemberg. When she was asked whether the question of maternity was important in defining her female characters, she said, "Not at all." She thought it had been emphasized too much and she preferred to look at other aspects of their development. So in your film, one woman becomes a painter, and the other an academic, but they are finally reconciled with their families, because they both accept marriage, and conflict is ultimately avoided.

GS: They have no other choice, that's just the way it was. For subsequent generations it's different. Now Sephardic girls study at the university too, but for their mothers that would have been impossible. In this film I'm more interested in the question of belonging than in maternity. But I'll tell you that when I finally met Agnès Varda, she said, "You know, I like your film, but that happy ending ... Could Oshinica really paint without her children coming in to bother her?" And I said, "How many issues can you put into one film?" I was more interested in identity and what we can or cannot do, what we want and whether we can get it. Of course, Rifke's mother cries when her daughter goes out with a non-Jewish guy. But they forgive her when she decides that her child will be raised Jewish and have his Bar Mitzvah.

JM: Finally, they do both end up married with children. That role for women is not questioned.

GS: They both do, but others may not have.

JM: At one point in the film, Rifke says she's not going to get married, she wants to study anthropology first.

GS: Yet she's the first to get married, she falls in love, what can I say!

JM [After showing a second clip, where the characters attend a Holy Week play in a neighbouring town]: What does this scene say about the attitudes of Mexicans to Jews?

GS: Well, I think my position is very clear. There is anti-Semitism not only in Mexico but in every Catholic country where they say that the Jews killed their God. This is one of the roots of anti-Semitism.

JM: But another thing comes out through the imagery of the Romans on horseback because the actors in the play are the most indigenous looking people you could find!

GS: They are the real people who put on this play, they are well known for their Easter celebrations. So I asked them to do it, thinking that, when the Spaniards came to America, evangelization was one of their primary goals. And the Indians loved theatre and music, so this is a continuation of their traditions. And all this public theatre about the crucifixion is a way to teach children every year that the Jews killed Jesus. Even if they are dressed as Romans and look Indian, it doesn't matter, that's the message that is conveyed year after year.

RdG: In Mexico there's an ideology about racial harmony that goes back to the idea of unifying the country through a common creed, the idea that a new "fifth race" is being produced, a universal category of human being, depicted in literature and the arts as a symbolic representation of the nation … .

GS: But that's not in this scene; this is just about how for centuries the Catholic Church has told their flock that the Jews killed Jesus and are therefore guilty of a terrible crime. It was even written that Jews should not just be killed, they should be made to suffer because of the death of Jesus. And present-day Jews in Latin America still live with that condemnation, whether they are Sephardic or Ashkenazi. The film's Jewish characters have that experience of anti-Semitism in common – as well as the experience of being expected to get married.

RdG: So the film is about the experience of all immigrant minorities at one level, and how the culture they arrive in affects them, and about different attitudes within the Jewish community, and how they may change, and also about intergenerational conflict, especially for girls ...

GS: That's right.

RdG: Thank you for talking to us. We'll open the discussion to everyone now.

Question from the floor: I noticed the subtitles used expressions like "the melting pot." I was surprised to see that term used. Was the translation a problem?

GS: There were many people involved in the film, from different countries. It was sometimes a linguistic challenge to avoid using terms that some didn't like!

Q: How has your film been received in the rest of Latin America? And by the Jewish community?

GS: People liked it a lot at various festivals. The Jews feel I identify with them. They write me letters saying this is the story of their lives. They had a very positive reaction, they really liked it.

Filmography: Guita Schyfter

1980s Nineteen audio-visual programs for the National Archives of Mexico; also produced three plays by Hugo Hiriart.

1990 *Xochimilco: historia de un paisaje (History of a Landscape)* (documentary, 60 min., 16 mm, 35 mm). ARIEL Award for Best Documentary, Mexican Academy of Cinematographic Arts.

1991 *La Fiesta y la Sombra, retrato de David Silveti (Portrait of David Silveti)* (documentary, 30 min., 35 mm)

1992 *Tamayo* (documentary, 34 min., 35 mm)

1993 *Novia que te vea (Like a Bride)* (feature, 115 min.) Audience Award, Festival of Mexican Cinema, Guadalajara. Heraldo awards for best first feature film, and best screenplay, photography, actress: Mexico, 1994. ARIEL awards for first feature, screenplay, sound, costumes, supporting actress. Opera Prima Award, Rhode Island Film Festival, 1994.

1994 *Sucesos distantes* (feature, 95 min.)

1995 *Diosa de Plata* (photography)

2001 *Las Caras de la luna* (feature, 101 min.)

33 Beyond the Homeland: Latinø-Canadian Film and the Work of Marilú Mallet and Claudia Morgado

Elena Feder

In comparison to parallel areas of scholarly inquiry into marginalized identity formations (such as feminist, queer, Black, and Native American), Latino film studies is a relative newcomer to the North American academic scene. To date practically non-existent in Canada, it began to be constituted as a field of study in the United States as recently as the mid-1980s. The use of the term "Latino," to designate a culturally, economically, ethnically, ra-cially, and nationally diverse set of people according to (loosely) shared linguistic and cultural traditions, dates back approximately to the late 1960s in the US, and is only recently beginning to be used in this sense in this country.[1] As with other subnational-identity markers defined in opposition to any dominant national-identity formation, "Latino" glosses over the widely divergent historical trajectories of the people subsumed under the term. Differences among Latinos are at least as ample as they are among "Anglos" within and between Canada and the United States or, for that matter, in any other ex-colony of Great Britain or the United States where English remains the predominant language.[2]

Gender distinctions complicate the picture further. Both long-term resist-ance and adaptation to colonization, as in the case of Chicanos and Nuyoricans (New Yorkers of Puerto Rican descent) in the United States, and the more short-term experience of exile, dislocation, and integration of Latinos in Canada, are lived and articulated differently by men and women.[3] Their relation to language and translation is also different. Since gender is marked differently in Spanish than in English, I will use the neologism *Latinø* rather than the more cumbersome Latino/a. Imported from yet another alphabet, the letter "ø" stands here as a marker of a politics and a poetics of deconstruction, both always already underpinned by gender and difference. To write about the contribution of women to Latinø-Canadian film or any of the other media arts at this historical juncture is no simple matter. "Latinø-Canadian film" itself cannot become constituted as an object of knowledge in this country until its very existence as a specific practice with a singular history and particular conditions of production is recognized. Since a re-view of its thirty-year history lies beyond the scope of this chapter, I hope that a brief comparative overview of the field on both sides of the US-Canada border will help shed some light on the situation. In the second half, I will discuss in more detail the contribution of two Latinø-Canadian film and video makers, Marilú Mallet and Claudia Morgado Escanilla.

Hispanics, Latinøs, and the W(r)est

In both the United States and Canada, "Hispanic" and "Latino" are terms that are widely used to refer to people of Latin American, Caribbean, and Spanish descent. While the socio-economic history of each of these terms is substantially different on the two sides of the forty-ninth parallel, they share many common traits. In both cases, these terms are used to identify a "mi-nority" group with cultural and racial characteristics that differ from those of the "majority" and that are implicitly associated with inferior social status and limited political power. Both terms tend to erase the historical, political, and socio-economic histories of the groups concerned, while obscuring their different, albeit interrelated, realities. They gather under a common denominator individuals from different (sometimes diametrically opposed) economic classes and socio-political affiliations, generational and educational backgrounds, racial or ethnic characteristics, cultural and religious practices, patterns of migration and assimilation, levels of education and professional training, degrees of linguistic competence and performance, and even experiences of discrimination. The position assumed by Argentinian-born US sociologist, Martha E. Giménez, both exemplifies and sheds more light on this problem:

> Divisions in terms of national origin, social class, ethnicity, race, length of stay in the US, and so forth make it exceedingly problematic to find common cultural denominators in this population beyond the language. And even the language itself divides, for each Latin American country has its own version of Spanish, which is itself divided by region, class, ethnicity, race, etc. Just as heterogeneous are the populations of Mexican, Puerto Rican, and Spanish descent living in this country, in which the younger generations have at best a superficial knowledge of Spanish.[4]

A consensus is slowly building to differentiate "Hispanic" and "Latinø" on the basis of ideological tendencies or social, economic, political, and class histories, even though inclusion in either category will vary according to class and/or political affiliation. Cuban-Americans, for example, are only recently beginning to be included in left-leaning definitions of Latinø. Hispanic, the older of the two terms, largely grew out of the assimilationist and integrationist aspirations of middle-class and professional immigrants to the United States and Canada.[5] In both countries, Hispanic has functioned as an official census category and has surfaced within various institutional settings, often reflecting more than simply a linguistic bias by adding Spain and immigrants of Spanish descent to an already unwieldy mix. The emergence of "Latinø," as a by-product of the radical movement politics of the 1960s, signals a move from middle-class assimilationism towards a more radical assertion of cultural and/or ethnic difference. Avoiding hierarchical inversions of value, most Latinø-US scholars who attempt to define the term today underscore its constructed and contradictory nature, while acknowledging its potential effectiveness as a tool of cultural intervention. Film scholars Chon A. Noriega and Ana M. López, whose introduction to *The Ethnic Eye: Latino Media Arts* remains the most lucid analysis of the subject, suggest that this requires us to look simultaneously to both the future and the past: "to look ahead to a future moment when 'Latino' works might be fully integrated into ... established [narrative, documentary, and experimental] modes and thereby become open to a broader range of inter- and intratextual associations," and also to approach Latinø media arts "through the matrix of [the] differential [yet interrelated] histories" within and between which these texts fluctuate – "the ethnic or subnational (Chicano, Puerto Rican, Cuban American); the interethnic and interminority (relations across communities of gender, race, sexuality and so on); the panethnic or national category for minorities (Latino, Hispanic); the mainstream or national (American [or Canadian]); and the hemispheric or international (Latin American)."[6]

From the Conquest to the struggles of farm workers, students, and civil rights activists in the 1960s, 1970s, and beyond, social, literary, and media historians bracket many constitutive events. These include the 1898 Spanish-American War (when Spain lost the colonies of Cuba and Puerto Rico, the latter annexed by the US); the unremitting violations of citizenship rights inscribed in the 1848 Treaty of Guadalupe Hidalgo (which legally consolidated Mexico's loss of about half of its territory to its northern neighbour); the Vietnam War (when a disproportionate number of Black and Latinø minorities were sent overseas and killed); the Cold War and its attendant Third World anti-colonial and class struggles; the forced immigration of thousands of political refugees as a result of US imperial policies throughout the Americas since the 1930s; and the influx of economic migrants and professionals who have chosen to relocate to the North for a variety of personal reasons.[7] Given that people of Cuban descent constitute the third largest group of Latinøs in the United States, the Cuban Revolution has also come to represent a unique and particularly complex point of historical reference.[8]

The assignation of the term "Latinø" to the otherwise overlooked work by film and video artists of Latin American and Caribbean descent is fraught with the kinds of contradictions that are bound to arise from such a long and complex history. Noriega and López make the ironic observation that, in the United States, the Latinø intelligentsia has sought social and political change through the discursive articulation of an ethnically distinct collective identity, even though Latinø media artists in general (but especially those whose work reflects a concern with post-1960s issues of identity and self-representation) "have rarely ever made 'Latino' works, preferring instead to work at the level of either the subnational or the national itself, speaking either as ethnics or as Americans to both their communities and the nation."[9] This generation of US-Latinø activists, scholars, and media artists came of age during the grassroots and civil rights struggles of the 1960s and 1970s; their aim was to gain access to the mass media, in order to affirm representation and to affect the production of meaning at the national level.

Artistic Output and Panethnic Pigeonholing

The use of biologically determined and subtly racist designations such as Hispanic and Latinø are not simply what Noriega and López define as the "product of a racial politics played out at the national level."[10] Due to the increasing dominance of US mass media worldwide, they have also had a strong impact at the supranational and global levels, often with contradictory effects. Equally ironic is the fact that films like *El Norte, La Bamba, American Me, Stand and Deliver,* and *Mi Familia,* which stand as examples in US film history of the short but significant "Latinø Hollywood" chapter, become "American" films when projected abroad. As a result, they end up bearing all the implications of empire and the forms of desire Hollywood films elicit, including the misconceived notion that success and access to power are equally available to their ego-idealized heroes and heroines, regardless of their darker skin. The marketing of this semblance of homogeneity with the national mean, voided of social and political content and historical referents in the process of both production and consumption, is one of the reasons why not only stereotyped images of Latinøs but the term itself travels with ease across radically different Euro-American contexts. The fact that differences within subnational groups are rarely taken into account has had considerable consequences. More often than not, umbrella terms like Latinø end up disempowering more than enabling the populations they denote. By adding new colours to a multicultural quilt or reifying originary differences while diluting them in an already overheated melting pot, they strengthen racial stereotypes, lead to social strategies and economic policies that exacerbate the ghettoizing of marginalized identity formations, and foster questionable forms of desire and abjection, which end up circulating in both the written and visual vernacular of the day.

One of the more serious dangers of identifying either creative or critical output on the basis of ethnic or panethnic pigeonholing is that it provides a rationale for isolating and shielding artistic output from critical scrutiny and comparative formal or theoretical analyses. Multiculturalist policies notwithstanding, at this historical juncture, Latinø-Canadians of all social, economic, and ideological stripes are left with little choice but to turn into "Native" or "Third World" informants, thereby becoming de facto representatives of the underrepresented.[11] Latin American artists who migrate to the North are surprised to find themselves automatically divested of their national identity, as they become identified with artists in other subnational groups with whom they often have little in common other than language and a vaguely defined sense of a common Latin American heritage. Severed from their interpretive communities and traditional sources of creativity and financial support, they find themselves forced to straddle cultural divides and to diversify their locations of address in order to reflect the fragmentation of their subject positions. This adds a new spin to an established axiom, which wrongly assumes that acknowledgment and recognition are sought solely from the dominant culture, rather than from cultures on both sides of the mirror of identity formation. Although right in other respects, Charles Taylor subscribes implicity to this view in the concluding pages of his *Multiculturalism and the "Politics of Recognition"*:

> The peremptory demand for favorable judgements of worth is paradoxically – perhaps one should say tragically – homogenizing. For it implies that we already have the standards to make such judgements. The standards we have, however, are those of North Atlantic civilization. And so the judgements implicitly and unconsciously will cram the others into our categories ... By implicitly invoking our standards to judge all civilizations and cultures, the politics of difference can end up making everyone the same.[12]

Sensing the need to find alternatives to the imposition of such standards, film and other media artists have availed themselves of a range of established and experimental modes of visual expression, resorting to textual strategies of hybridization (such as mixing genres, styles, cultural and aesthetic codes, and spoken and musical languages) with a view to addressing a non-homogeneous audience – one of diverse, and often conflicting, constituencies and origins. These strategies have allowed them to form alliances with several interpretive communities and, in the best cases, to resist having their work simplified due to a reductive view of ethnicity, gender, and national or subnational identity. For example, Claudia Morgado's experimental short film *Sabor a mí* (*Savour Me,* 1997) has become both a classic Latinø-Canadian film and a cult film in US and Canadian lesbian circles, despite its Spanish title and the use of little known Latinø actors, Latin American music, and pictorial excess. If the growing North American success of Latinø art, music, film, and other media arts is any indication, then speaking from the margins does not need to be an impediment in today's context.[13] Without overestimating the benefits of diasporic or borderline locations, and while acknowledging the limitations of access to representation in terms of bodily identifications, it is important to note that ethnic or panethnic assignations may provide opportunities as well as new challenges, including riding on the funding bandwagon (fellowships, grants, etc.) controlled by academic and institutional sources whose mandates encompass the promotion of cultural diversity.

It is in light of such opportunities and challenges that Noriega and López, who identify themselves as Chicano and Cuban-American, respectively, have chosen to politicize the term Latino "for the benefit of the specific ethnic groups subsumed under that term."[14] At the crossroads of rapidly changing social and cultural movements, their call to practice "a willful ambivalence about critical location, textual classification, and spectatorship/reception –

in short, about the need to name," should be read as an invitation to consider both the dangers and opportunities that such a practice would entail – over and beyond merely US-Latinø interests, and regardless, or perhaps because, of their potential impact worldwide.

From Bananas to Bandanas

The history of both Canadian and US Latino film practice is, in great part, a reflection of progressive integration and resistant adaptation by the conquered and the colonized (and the thousands of economic and ideological migrants, exiles, and refugees from South America, Mexico, and the Caribbean), both to each other and to the nation. In Canada this history can be traced back only to the arrival of the first wave of Chilean political refugees following the overthrow of the Allende government in the early 1970s, whereas US Latinø film history is rooted in a social and cultural formation that spans over 150 years, with Chicano, Puerto Rican, and Cuban filmmakers as the three majoritarian subnational groups. The first generation (late 1960s to early 1980s) of Chicano filmmakers and other cultural workers focused on the exclusion of images of Latinøs from the Hollywood screen. Spearheaded by filmmaker and theorist Jesús Salvador Treviño, the radicalism of this generation was inflected by the films and manifestos of the New Latin American Cinema, including the nearly total absence of women from their scene.[15] In the mid-1980s the focus changed to issues of self-representation and spectatorship, drawing on more than twenty years of work by Black, Chicano, and Puerto Rican cultural workers, on the growing importance of feminist film theory and practice, and on the progressive spread of Third Cinema to include marginal cinemas in the developed world. Since then, not only the Chicano, but also Canadian and US Latinø cinemas have followed a trajectory that continues to bring them into direct negotiation with Hollywood and, to a lesser extent, Mexican and other cinemas in the Spanish-speaking world.[16]

One of the main consequences of this radical shift has been to multiply the coordinates of address and the politics of location for both Latinø media and the critical discourse that takes it as its object of study. Signalling a departure from the movement politics of the 1960s and 1970s, the current generation favours a more personal exploration of the limits and possibilities of specific artistic practices and the immediate and wider contexts within which these are deployed. Noriega and López identify this shift as an undercurrent throughout the essays in their collection, describing it as follows:

> Whereas an intermediate generation of scholars, working under the umbrella of cultural studies, sought to reform Latino cultural nationalism by divesting it of its patriarchal, homophobic privileged agency, the new

generation is more likely to be critical of the underlying nationalist premises themselves – that is, of the discourses of belonging. In many ways, this produces critical work that oscillates between a number of disciplinary locations – body-specific (ethnic, gender, queer), media-specific (film, video, multimedia), and discourse-specific (genre, identity, reception) – without a secure mooring in any one camp.[17]

Judging a Look by Its Cover

These signifying shifts, characteristic of this groundbreaking text, draw attention to the challenges and opportunities involved in representing such an extremely heterogeneous group of artists under as reductive and problematic (albeit strategically useful) a label as Latinø. A closer look at the opening rhetorical strategies of Noriega and López's book, moreover, reveals not only the label's overdetermined history, but also its gender determinants. The silent intertextual exchanges between the cover photo and the book's title signal a break in the traditional mirror of ethnic and gender identification. As with the introduction and essays that follow, the double meanings of the cover photo's caption, *Shoot on Site* (by Harry Gamboa Jr., 1995), are sustained by the ambiguities of the content. Staging the performance of a film shoot, the photograph consists of two women and two men (described as "performers" on the back cover) in the process of filming a scene. Heavily marked as Latinø both by their looks and by their actions, they stand, not coincidentally, on the dividing line of a paved road against the backdrop of a barrio landscape somewhere in East Los Angeles. The reappropriation of space is thus achieved by displacing the everyday violence of "shooting on sight" to the cultural battlefield.

Displacing other preconceptions, yet actually reflecting statistical probability, the filmmaker on this particular site is a woman. We see her squatting to point the heavy camera on her shoulder at the second woman, while the subject of her gaze looks down to address herself directly to the camera. As if commenting tongue-in-cheek on the contradictions inherent in gender, national, and cultural representation, she stands firmly on the pavement, holding a Mexican flag, a bouquet of white lilies (signifier of the Virgin Mary), and an enormous striped- and star-spangled wooden kitchen spoon. Both women have long black hair, wear oversized earrings, and are dressed in black. The filmmaker, whose hair is the more elaborate of the two, wears a black bandana (indicating a difference between gangs), dark glasses, black tights, a T-shirt, spiked heels, and gloves long enough to display an elaborate tattoo on her upper left arm: not exactly a typical look for either kind of shooting. Significantly, the men are mostly in the background, standing expectantly behind and in-between the two women, one ostensibly operating the mike, the other looking intently at the filmed subject while rather superfluously holding a tripod in the air. The set of dialogic exchanges within and between the title, the book, and its cover shows the dominant culture's Latinø Other in the process of *seeing him/herself seeing* as opposed to the self-objectifying seeing him/herself *being seen*. The result is a break in the mirror of identity formation that points to the *provisional* embodiment of a subject that is in the process of refusing to be defined in terms other than its own. It also departs from the self-conscious assumption of a self-defined ethnic eye/I that is at one and the same time an eye/we or communal eye/I – and a critically militant I/we/eye to boot.

The Proof Is in the Salsa

In the production of a shifting subject-effect that is neither singular nor plural, the rhetorical strategy of Noriega and López differs significantly from W.E.B. Dubois and Frantz Fanon's well known articulations of the double consciousness that individual people of colour are forced to internalize.[18] The singularity of a shifting I/we Latinø subject formation, articulated directly and indirectly in *The Ethnic Eye*/I's textual operations, rests as much on a post-1968 understanding of cultural-political militancy as on a Baroque/postmodern Latinø aesthetics, seasoned in the process of transculturation with an excessive, campy performative humour. Framing the struggle for Latinø representation in film and television against the background of the history of Latinø social and political struggle, *The Ethnic Eye* squarely situates the radicalized speaking subject at eye-level with the community that he/she speaks for. Transparency in the articulation of a rhetorical choice sketches the lineaments of a shifting ideological and discursive formation within a culture-specific chronotope, as it did for Fanon. The strategic aim is to embed the lineaments of a shifting discursive formation into a culture-specific chronotope so as to enable the simultaneously singular and plural subject to be seen in the process of breaking away from the imposition of an amnesia-inducing Otherness – be it through the repressive mediation of stereotyping or, even worse, through erasure by censorship.[19]

What emerges from the displacement of this "monøcular" (to coin another neologism) subject of speech by the iconoclastic I/we speaking subject is the discursive gambit of a simultaneously singular and plural "Latinø" *subject of the enunciation* — a subject that is sufficient unto itself yet provisional, firmly grounded in a history of activism and a shifting politics of location that is both playfully serious and perversely aware of the arbitrary and provisional nature of power, including its own.[20] In fact, it is by characterizing their underlying critical strategy as "perverse" that Noriega and López end their introduction, defining it as precisely "the contrariness of refusing fixity, essences, secure locations, singular affiliations"[21] – an unusual, not to mention challenging, place from which to participate in the academic debate on identity politics. This radical departure from the dominant politics of multiculturalism and its homogenizing implications is a crucial de-essentializing move that creates the conditions of visibility for a different social subject: a subject in process, dialogically involved in the (trans)formation of hegemonic thought.

The Other Other Canadians

Whereas Latinøs in the United States trace their history back to the Conquest and are expected to become the largest group of minorities in a few years, Canadians with Latinø ancestry became identifiable as a subnational group only in the early 1970s, and they still represent a negligible fraction of the population. Nevertheless, a large percentage of them, including a substantial number of outstanding women, have been actively involved in practically every aspect of film production since arriving in Canada as political refugees or economic migrants. Working alongside a variety of other media and visual artists, Latinø-Canadian directors, producers, cinematographers, actors, set designers, and so on have produced a substantial body of work. Their contribution to Canadian film history, however, remains to be recognized, let alone critically examined or understood. Although similar concerns and issues of realpolitik have influenced the trajectories of the US and Latinø-Canadian cinemas, until very recently Latinøs in Canada have had little representation at either the national or regional levels. However, taking into account the support offered to Latinø filmmakers by the National Film Board and to Latinø curators by the Canada Council over the last thirty years, it appears that this lack of representation has less to do with institutional resistance than with the fact that Canadian public institutions have little control over the means of distribution of film and other media arts.

This is not to say that Latinøs involved in the film industry have not encountered racism in both its overt and subtle forms. Nor does the acknowledgement of institutional support on the basis of panethnic identities negate the potential for homogenization that lies behind the aim to assimilate newcomers into the Canadian multicultural quilt. In the absence of a long and complex Latinø-Canadian cultural production (which is not to deny the existence of many fine artists),[22] Latinø-Canadian artists remain subject to a double marginalization by the "dominant" national culture – however elusive and conflicted it may be, given Canadian cinema's own self-perception as marginal to Hollywood.[23] Nonetheless, if we look at Latinø-Canadian film from a "perverse" perspective, in the sense outlined above, we can begin identifying conditions and areas of opportunity historically available to Latinøs in this country, and consequently to reappropriate the label in order to further our goals.

In film and video, two main Latinø-Canadian tendencies can be discerned at this time, each broadly equivalent to the two largest waves of immigration of people of Latin American and Caribbean descent to this country. Yet the generational model can be misleading, as there are younger filmmakers whose work resembles tendencies of the first wave and older filmmakers whose work points to directions yet to be explored by the younger generation. As mentioned before, the first wave of Latinø filmmakers is overwhelmingly composed of Chileans who immigrated to Canada in the 1970s and who form part of the larger Chilean exile-cinema movement worldwide.[24] The second wave consists of younger Latinøs who were either born in Canada or immigrated as children or young adults, as well as newcomers from Mexico, the Caribbean, and Central and South America (especially Colombia).[25] Largely oblivious to the homogenizing pitfalls of a politics of recognition, both generations of Latinø-Canadian filmmakers reflect Canada's official multicultural policies, which invite assimilation to a loosely held together *bricolage* model of national identity that encourages the preservation of culture-specific traditions and practices. In addition, both generations of filmmakers address themselves simultaneously to several audiences: their communities of origin; a community of immigrants with shared yet different experiences of exile, assimilation, and discrimination; their host communities of choice; and, in a handful of recent cases, to a wider national audience. While there are several overlapping features in the work produced by the two generations of film and media artists, differences in aesthetic approach and narrative strategy reflect their different degrees of assimilation and levels of investment in local and global cultural capital.

Influenced by two decades of the then vibrant New Latin American Cinema movement, the films of the first generation subscribe to the early avant-garde and Third Cinema axiom of the inseparability of art and politics, as well as to the latter's enticement to experiment with aesthetics, narrative, and performance. Unlike their US counterparts, however, their involvement with the means of distribution and consumption has not taken on the form of a movement politics seeking access to representation beyond the institutional level (e.g., the National Film Board or arts councils). Similarly, although their films have been exhibited in a handful of festivals in Canada and in college and university settings and film festivals abroad, like their US counterparts media artists of this generation rarely identify themselves or their work as Latinø, let alone as Latinø-Canadian.

The films of this generation draw largely on the tragic personal experiences of survivors of the national and international political events of the 1960s, 1970s, and early 1980s. In the case of Latin America, these were defined in terms of the class struggle, with the left being eventually crushed by the most brutal military dictatorships the continent had ever seen. Addressing a common concern with the impact of exile and assimilation on their personal and extended family lives, these filmmakers deal mostly with inherent contradictions in certain situations: left-wing intellectuals being forced to learn manual skills in order to get a job (Jorge Fajardo, *Steel Blues*, a documentary fiction, 1975); the isolation and exploitation of illegal migrant workers (Leutén Rojas's documentary fiction, *Canadian*, 1978, and Luis Oswaldo García and Toni Venturi's documentary, *Under the Table*, 1983); or the frustrations of a relationship lacking a shared language and cultural codes (Leopoldo Gutierrez, *It's Not the Same in English*, 1985).

Not surprisingly, the question of memory emerges as one of the primary concerns of this largely Chilean group of Latinø-Canadian filmmakers. Leutén Rojas's *I Remember Too* (1975), a lyrical investigation of the impact of the 1973 events on the lives of young children of political refugees (rendered through their drawings and off-screen voices), was the earliest treatment of this topic. Looking at Chile from a later perspective, *Récits d'une guerre quotidienne* (*Memoirs of an Everyday War*, 1986), by Gastón Ancelovici and Jaime Barrios, documents the different forms of resistance to the Pinochet government leading up to the referendum that would eventually topple his regime. It remains one of the earliest examples of the returning-exile perspective on Chile.[26]

The Works of Marilú Mallet

A classic of this period, a work on memory, is the trilogy *Il n'y a pas d'oubli* (*There Is No Forgetting*, NFB, 1975), directed by Marilú Mallet (*Lentement*), Jorge Fajardo (*J'explique certaines choses*), and Rodrigo González (*Jours de fer/ Steel Blues*). Each segment of the trilogy deals with different aspects of the contradictions faced by Chilean refugees suddenly thrown into the sociopolitical context of a Quebec still reeling from the FLQ crisis, yet largely impervious to the everyday needs of newcomers whose existence had been reduced to a struggle for economic and emotional survival. Loosely held together by the themes of exile, dislocation, and the sting of memory (lost relatives, friends, dreams, ideals, a place to call home), each of the dramas unfolds along equally steep social and work-related learning curves, albeit in different personal contexts and with different degrees of introspection. The most accomplished of the three is the feature-length segment directed by Mallet, which has since come to be identified with the trilogy itself.

Unlike Fajardo and González, whose directing careers appear to have dwindled after *Il n'y a pas d'oubli* (at least in Canada),[27] Mallet moved on to direct four NFB documentaries over the next eleven years, treating her ongoing exploration of the vicissitudes of the diasporic experience at arm's length in all but one of the four. *Les Borges* (1978) documents the experience of a family who had immigrated to Montreal from Portugal in 1967, while *Child of the Andes* (1988) offers a narrative account of the history and customs of the people of Andahuaylillas, a small town in Peru north of the Chilean border. The story is told through the eyes of ten-year-old Sebastiana against the backdrop of local myths and legends.[28] Shot on location, this fictionalized documentary offers a surprisingly nostalgic "look at a simpler

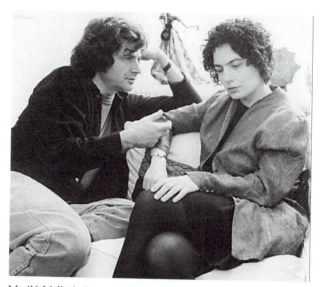

Marilú Mallet's *2, rue de la mémoire* (1996), courtesy of the director

way of life still undisturbed by modern society's technology and materialism."[29] In *Ma chère Amérique* (1989), Mallet returns to her adoptive home to tell the story of two Montreal women: a young Québécoise struggling with the desire for children and aspirations to a musical career, and an older Portuguese immigrant who, as described in the program notes, "sacrificed the love of her children" for work, eventually becoming a millionaire. The exception is her widely distributed *Journal inachevé* (1982; *Unfinished Diary*, 1986), in which Mallet returns to autobiographical concerns and the exploration of the diasporic consciousness that she began to address in her first film.

A strong presence in the festival circuit when it first came out, *Unfinished Diary* has since come to occupy an important place in both Latin American and Latinø film history. This critically acclaimed work, described by a *Globe and Mail* reviewer as "Sad but strong, unsentimental but nostalgic, and thoroughly engrossing,"[30] is a semi-autobiographical docudrama about a Chilean woman film director who, like Mallet herself (once again in the leading role, as in *Lentement*), lives and works in French-speaking Canada. Rhythmically meditative and visually structured to underscore the intense subjectivity of the point of view (voice-over, camera presence, etc.), this often wrenching film takes a hard look at the specific difficulties experienced by women artists in exile, ranging from the misunderstanding and rejection of their work to the power imbalances characteristic of the inter- and intra-ethnocultural relationships with which they have to contend on a daily basis.

Of particular poignancy is the scene where, after a heated discussion with her Australian husband (a filmmaker in his own right) about her work, Mallet's fictional surrogate is driven to near hysteria by the power game governing his passive-aggressive criticism of her purportedly "too subjective" approach to filmmaking. Her candid reaction and the effect of this scene (an uncut static shot from an extremely high angle) is startling. Following this critical moment in the film, and as if to underscore both the solitude of women artists and their need to rely on their immigrant communities, Mallet goes on to interview other exiles (including writer Isabel Allende). This adds a communal dimension to her personal life and relates the experience of her professional and cultural peers to her own artistic vision.

After a thirteen-year hiatus, Mallet returned to filmmaking with *2, rue de la mémoire* (*Suspended Memories*, 1996), a forty-two-minute fiction film that confirmed her as one of the most innovative independent filmmakers in Canada, as well as a beacon of Latinø-Canadian fiction film. An adaptation of one of her own short novellas, shot in Super 16, *Suspended Memories* returns once again to the theme of failed inter-ethnocultural relationships, focusing this time on the unsuccessful struggle to build a relationship between a Chilean émigré and torture survivor and the son of Jewish Holocaust survivors. This film represents a departure from the documentary thrust of Mallet's earlier work. Rather than casting herself in the leading role and once again turning the camera on herself and her family, she uses professional actors and tells a story that is only loosely based on past personal experience. In ways reminiscent of the Magic Realism associated with the literature produced during the Latin American Boom of the 1960s and early 1970s, she freely manipulates sound and image to add an often haunting pictoriality to her signature rhythmic lyricism and meditative, non-linear narration technique. The scene where the ghosts carried by the main character in her memory become "present" around the dinner table is a notable example.

By expressing the relationship between personal histories and a people's history, focusing on the formal interplay of subjective memories and objective times, *Suspended Memories* marks a departure from Mallet's earlier focus on identity and self-representation. In *Double portrait* (2001), however, she comes back to autobiography in order to explore the delicate and conflicted territory of mother/daughter relationships, through her relationship with her own mother. Here she continues to pay close attention to the small details of everyday life, the mainstay of memory, and the splitting that characterizes diasporic identity, yet with a double consciousness of self and/as Other (hence the title) rarely found in the films of her Latinø-Canadian counterparts, both men and women.

The Other Other's Other Within

Some male filmmakers, such as Colombian-born German Gutierrez, have produced documentaries about the life of Latinøs in Montreal (*La Familia Latina,* NFB 1986), or based on return journeys to Latin America (*Vivre en Amazonie* and *Americas 500,* NFB 1993). His treatment of the international drug trade (*Society under the Influence,* 1997) reached a wide audience, showing the links between production in the South and consumption in the North. Others, like Gastón Ancelovici, have gone back to their country of origin (Chile in his case) to make documentary testimonials.[31] Another element just as noteworthy as the recurrent theme of returning South to one's birthplace is the relationship to the "Other within," the Aboriginal populations ("Indians," "Natives," or "First Nations"), in the North and the South.

This theme is important, first because it ties the whole continent together through a shared history of colonization and resistant adaptation spanning over 500 years. It also functions as a thread that links the work of the first generation of Latinø-Canadian filmmakers to the next, and helps to distinguish between them according to subtle yet significant variations. The first generation can be said to displace onto their respective Native "Other within" a personal sense of being othered as a result of becoming a minority in their adopted land. The second generation, however, tends to engage in deeper processes of Other-identification and self-redefinition, departing from the intersections of race, ethnicity, nationality, and gender to arrive at a balkanization of both being and seeing.

Oblivious to discourses of belonging, like the contemporary group of media artists identified by Noriega and López in *The Ethnic Eye,* the artists of this generation resort to strategies of textual and formal hybridization and code-switching. In the process of making their films legible to more than one interpretive community without sacrificing their claim to difference, they offer a palimpsest of accommodation, assimilation, and transnationality, while making ethnic and gender differentiations harder to ascertain. Juan Balmaceda's *Nishin* (1994), for instance, a fast-paced music video co-directed by Native Canadian Keith Herrick, blends together segments of Aboriginal North and South American songs over triumphal images of the people of Chiapas, leading up to the uprising. His eight-minute documentary video *La Shamana* (1997), on the other hand, crosses over the gender divide to tell the story of a young woman's initiation as a spiritual healer and her use of hallucinogens during this process.

In somewhat different fashion, Claudia Medina's *In Between the Middle* (*Entre el medio,* 2001) looks to the history of her own Mexican ancestors for the roots of Native spirituality. Shot in Super 16 on location in Mexico with local actors and mastered on digital beta, this independent twenty-minute short is a rendering of Native spirituality based on stories told by Medina's grandmother, a *curandera,* or healer, who is fictionalized in the film. In this story, a young man and woman, Rafael (José Luis Ordoñez) and Trinidad (Claudia Garcés Rios), inhabit each other's "other side" divided by the invisible and porous wall separating life and death. Trinidad, whose soul abandons her while she dreams, and Rafael, whose spirit cannot find rest since he died far from home, find themselves caught in a nowhere space between life and death until the old *curandera* finally releases them from their respective nightmares. Like Balmaceda, Medina privileges Native American spirituality, underscoring cultural differences in our approaches to death and dying, and blending a coherent narrative with experimental oneiric techniques.

Going a step further in the crossover process, Jorge Manzano's trilingually titled docudrama, *Odenaag Naabndamwin/City of Dreams/Ciudad de Sueños* (1995), imports the testimonial genre, indigenous to Latin American literature, to the Canadian screen.[32] In his next film, *Johnny Greyeyes* (1999), Manzano, who was brought from Chile to Canada as a child, takes the process one step further in telling another bittersweet First Nations story. This time it is about a Native lesbian who finds her way home as a result of falling in love with another inmate after many years in prison. This feature-length film, which received the Freedom Prize at the Vancouver Gay and Lesbian Film Festival and the Bulloch Award for best Canadian film, was billed at the Sundance Festival as a "Native Canadian Drama."

Another successful negotiation of multiple positionalities is illustrated by Colombian-born Jorge Lozano's experimental film *Tampon Thieves* (1995) – a portrayal of the trials and tribulations of a single father faced with raising a teenage daughter on the margins of Torontonian culture, set against the backdrop of gay Latin nightlife. Lozano went on to create, in collaboration with Sinara Rozo, *Living Culture (Cultura Viva),* an interactive multimedia installation exhibited to considerable popular acclaim in Toronto (1997) and Vancouver (1999). In it, digital projection, multiple soundscapes, and artisanal religious artefacts (an altar, votive candles, images and objects related to the modern Venezuelan cult of Maria Leoncia) combine to create a simultaneously sacred and secular space where Aboriginal and Afro-American religious iconography function as a catalyst for popular and elite art forms as well as for national, subnational, and international identity formations.[33]

The Works of Claudia Morgado

Chilean-born Morgado is more typical of the second generation of Latino-Canadian media artists who have received professional training at art schools and institutions throughout the country. In her films an absence of discourses of belonging appears to go hand in hand with a return to classical narrative forms. Issues pertaining to the representation of ethnic, national, or subnational identities are depicted as simply one element among many within the wider cultural field, and experimentation takes other forms. Implicitly uncontested, and therefore exempt from the need for recognition, identity and difference are displaced onto a mise-en-scène where the grain, texture, and flavour of a new Latinø-Canadian identity formation-in-the-making are eloquently yet silently expressed.

A comparison of the representational politics of Claudia Morgado and Javiera Fombona reminds us to be cautious of the broad generalizations that the generational model invites. Venezuelan-born Fombona's experimental video, *The Door* (1997), which takes Canadian society to task for denying equal visibility to lesbians, tends to fall back on a politics of recognition. The underlying strategy of Morgado's films, however, is to take not only homosexuality but also national, ethnic, and linguistic differences for granted, with the result that they come to be perceived as natural or the norm: her aim is to make a financially successful film in a cross-cultural setting where ethnic or linguistic differences and lesbian normalcy are moot.[34]

Like other gay and lesbian Latinø media artists of her generation, Morgado has indirectly benefited from what Negrón-Muntaner describes as "the creation of Latino and independent film/video infrastructures, and ... critical debates around Latino cultural production." These have "laid the groundwork for the production and reception of more recent Latino queer films and videos as media."[35] Born in Chile, Morgado immigrated to Canada in her early twenties and is building her promising career as a *transfrontera* subject with an unabashedly sexually polymorphous Latinø persona. A constant presence in the film festival circuit, her films appeal to many audiences: pan-Latinø and non-Latinø, lesbian and straight, Canadian, Latin American, and international. Situated at the crossroads of multiple social, cultural, formal, and aesthetic divides, her works combine a sleek, focused narrative line with a sophisticated pictorial aestheticism, while incorporating traditional Latin rhythms and a penchant for kitsch. Her use of the *bolero* in the music film *Angustia* (1996) and the experimental short *Sabor a mí* (1997), for example, appeals to and contests the rich tradition of this popular Latin American Romantic musical form; it enables her to displace to a lesbian register forms of masochistic desire that were originally articulated for a heterosexual audience.

In one of her films, the eight-minute *Ode to the Chilotas* (*Oda a las Chilotas*, 1990), Morgado, like Mallet, has chosen to return to the early landscape of her memory. However, she did not engage in an epic quest for national identity, nor did she recreate either the urban setting of her childhood or a rural society with tenuous ties to her personal experience. Rather, she produced an intimate portrait of everyday life in a remote island in Southern Chile where, for centuries, the Chilota have maintained a functional matricentric society. After this visual tribute to a little known slice of women's history, Morgado went on to create the experimental animation short *Spit It Out* (1992). Four years later she made *Angustia*, an innovative and audacious contribution to what Frances Negrón-Muntaner identifies as the "structure of feeling" generated by Latinø gay and lesbian independent film within an "Anglo" context. This "structure of feeling" is constituted by the following six elements:

> formal hybridity (mixing of diverse genres and modes of address), self-reflexivity, the construction of an artist persona often involved in a journey of discovery and confrontation, the representation of geographical dislocation, the [re]contextualization of the subject's drama within the immediate and/or symbolic family, and the self-conscious use of media to construct an alternative reality for the speaking subject/subject of representation.[36]

To a greater or lesser extent, Morgado's films illustrate these characteristics. The affirmation of an immigrant gay/bisexual identity through the use of both Spanish and English is meant, as Negrón-Muntaner points out, to appeal more to gay and lesbian Latinø audiences than to Latin American audiences. However, unlike most US gay and lesbian Latinø films, Morgado's films evince a quest for a language with which to manifest multiple marginalized desires; they could hardly be described as "texts of simultaneous healing and rupture, assimilation ('English') and affirmation of difference (accent), folded maps of journeys of no return that leave the speaking subject always wanting."[37] Both visually and aurally, her films subvert homophobic codes and prevailing racial stereotypes by generating a structure of feeling where excess is privileged over lack, as are diversity and process over singularity and ends. *Angustia*, for instance, simultaneously deconstructs and refigures the naked, blindfolded, and ecstatic woman on whose body the words of the *bolero* are elegantly inscribed. Rather than resorting to the obtuse framing, distorting camera angles or fast-paced montage of her earlier work, Morgado opts for a nimble camera in order to map out the inner and outer surfaces of a static and *ec*static subject. She thereby elicits a re-reading of both words and of the body, that demands sensorial involvement in the spectatorial process.

Further developing her interest in female sexuality and cultural difference, Morgado's next film, the experimental documentary *Unbound* (*Sin ataduras*, 1995) compares individual and cultural differences in women's relationship to their breasts. Released to critical acclaim, this award-winning twenty-minute short is a veritable tour de force that established Morgado as one of the more promising young talents in the Canadian filmmaking scene. She personalizes the political, not least by exposing her own breasts in the opening moments of the film. In the series of vignettes that follow, women from different national, ethnic, and cultural backgrounds candidly describe (often in their own language) their unique (and culturally modulated) relationship to their breasts and its impact on their experience of femininity. With a strong emphasis on the pictoriality that characterizes her work, each vignette is carefully constructed both to mirror each woman's cultural and aesthetic heritage, and to engage in an eclectic dialogue with both the avant-garde and classical pictorial traditions. Allusions range from Botero's signature oversized figures to Caravaggio's lush sensual chiaroscuros, and Morgado's own metaphorical backdrop constructions of culturally specific themes. The result is a dazzling banquet of visual, cultural, and personal constructions of an experience unique to women, celebrating the similarities and differences that both unite and separate them rather than encouraging antagonisms.

Morgado's next film, *Sabor a mí*, represents her first experiment with classical narrative. In this twenty-minute independent film, which is all the more subtly disruptive for its apparent conventionality, Morgado continues to contest dominant modes of representation. Again using *boleros* as the guiding rod of visual and auditory desire, *Sabor a mí* tells a story of seduction between two women who live side by side, one married and straight (played by well known Latinø performer and writer Carmen Aguirre), the other single and a lesbian. Described in festival programs as "a perfectly balanced and cinematically breathtaking ... voyeuristic mecca," this story of lesbian seduction unfolds, with virtually no dialogue, by way of a number of shots and reverse shots that link two neighbouring apartments through an opening in the wall. This brings together two women who watch the most intimate moments of each other's lives only to discover a mutual longing. Encased within an elaborate frame, the wall opening functions here as a visual metaphor that adds a referential and aesthetic dimension to the story.

With *Sabor a mí*, Morgado moves further in the direction of a more explicitly Latinø identity formation, including *boleros*, a Baroque use of colour and space, sparse English dialogue, Latinized objects in the women's living quarters (including a portrait by Argentinean-Canadian painter Nora Patrich), an elaborate hallway altar to the Virgin Mother (under whose gaze the two women "confess" their desire for one another in a silent ceremony that includes communion through blood), and the young daughter's flight through the window on the wings of an angel in the closing shot of the film. This combination authorizes lesbian desire by naturalizing it over and beyond its immediate Latinø context, while also making *Sabor a mí* a Latinø-Canadian film in the most literal sense possible.[38]

This self-referentiality is shared by one other Latinø-Canadian film, the experimental performance piece *Crucero* (*Crossroads*, 1994), the result of a fruitful collaboration between first generation director Ramiro Puerta (a Colombian-Canadian) and writer and actor Guillermo Verdecchia (an

Argentinean-Canadian whose award-winning script and performance the film documents). Framing the conceptual and stylistic concerns of both generations of Latinø-Canadian media artists around questions of social and institutional representation, they explore the in-between space that governs the diasporic experience, offering a humorous, sophisticated, and exacting look at changing notions of a pan-Latinø and, more specifically, Latinø-Canadian identity.[39] By engaging in the postnational reinvention of place from the perspective of hybrid imagined communities, and retracing the fine line that separates the wider contextual whole from the social, historical, and cultural specificities of its constituent parts, Latinø-Canadian filmmakers and media artists are engaged in a diasporic identity formation that is becoming the norm for an ever growing number of people across the globe.

Latinø-Canadian women artists, including filmmakers like Mallet and Morgado, have broached topics of specific interest to them, in new ways that incorporate their own multiple cultural references while appealing to a multiplicity of audiences. Eclectic in their application of form and content, and strategic in their provisional embodiment of subject position and location of address, their works remind us that, while any panethnic integrity is imagined as the integrity of its constituent parts, as a social, political, and critical category, "Latinø" offers an important alternative to a homogenizing politics of recognition defined by the "dominant" culture from "above." One of the most valuable lessons to emerge from this diasporic experience is the confirmation that, eventually, a time comes when, as Ariel Dorfman says, "another language can keep us company as if it were a twin."[40] Perversely or not, given the ongoing budget cuts to education, lacklustre support for the arts, and risks of xenophobia, this knowledge is a gift that will continue to go unrecognized at monøcularism's peril.

Notes

1 Earl Shorris, in *Latinos: A Biography of the People* (New York: Avon Books, 1992), reports that the US Census "was on the verge of" selecting "Latino" as a census category but rejected the idea because of its association with "Ladino," the old Castilian language preserved to this day by descendants of the Jews who left Spain in the fifteenth and sixteenth centuries fleeing the Spanish Inquisition. Shorris dates the idea for his book (published in 1992) as specifically about Latinos back to 1970. The first anthology of Latino literature was Harold Augenbraum and Margarite Fernández Olmos's *The Latino Reader: An American Literary Tradition from 1952 to the Present* (Boston: Houghton Mifflin, 1997).

2 Such is the case in Trinidad, the Philippines, and the Bahamas. I want to thank David Bercovici-Artieda for this observation.

3 I remark on the historicity of such differences not only to complicate the complementary and/or oppositional bonding of both gendered and racialized binary pairs, but also to underscore their provisional and increasingly malleable nature.

4 Martha E. Giménez, "Latinos, Hispanics ... What Next! Some Reflections on the Politics of Identity in the US," *Heresies* 7 (1993): 40.

5 For Shorris and others in the 1990s, the distinction has "less to do with evidence than with politics." See Shorris, *Latinos*, 15.

6 Chon A. Noriega and Ana M. López, *The Ethnic Eye: Latino Media Arts* (Minneapolis: University of Minnesota Press, 1996), xx and xiii.
7 Whereas Augenbraum and Fernández Olmos trace the beginnings of Latinø literary history to the Conquest, Shorris sees the roots of Latinø identity as the amalgamation of three main sources: the already multi-ethnic population of late-Medieval Spain; the remains of the Aztec, Maya, Inca, Toltec, Mexican, and other "Indian" civilizations in the Americas; and the descendants of African, mostly Yoruban, slaves.
8 See Ana M. López, "Greater Cuba," in Noriega and López, *The Ethnic Eye*, 38-58.
9 Noriega and López, *The Ethnic Eye*, xx. Noriega also edited *Chicanos and Film: Representation and Resistance* (Minneapolis: University of Minnesota Press, 1992). Other books on Chicano cinema (by far the most widely studied of the three dominant "Latino" cinemas in the United States), include: Gary D. Keller, ed., *Chicano Cinema: Research, Reviews, and Resources* (Binghamton, NY: Bilingual Review Press, 1985), and his *Hispanics and United States Film: An Overview and Handbook* (Temple, AZ: Bilingual Press, 1994); also Rosa Linda Fregoso, *The Bronze Screen: Chicana and Chicano Film Culture* (Minneapolis: University of Minnesota Press, 1993). In addition to Hadley-Garcia's *Hispanic Hollywood* (New York: Carol Publishing Group, 1993), studies whose aim is to "fuse" or "mediate" the pan-Latino/US-Anglo divide include John King, Ana M. López, Manuel Alvarado, eds., *Mediating Two Worlds: Cinematic Encounters in the Americas* (London: British Film Institute, 1993) and Coco Fusco, *English Is Broken Here: Notes on Cultural Fusion in the Americas* (New York: The New Press, 1995); an early theorization of gender-inflected Latino/Anglo-*mestizo/a* spectatorship is Carmen Huaco-Nuzum's doctoral dissertation, "Mestiza Subjectivity: Representation and Spectatorship in Mexican and Hollywood Films" (University of California, Santa Cruz, 1993). See also the introductory anthology of critical writings by Clara E. Rodríguez, ed., *Latin Looks: Images of Latinas and Latinos in the U.S. Media* (Boulder, CO: Westview Press, 1997), which includes three essays on Puerto Rican cinema. To my knowledge, there are no book-length studies of either Puerto Rican cinema or of what Ana López calls "Greater Cuba" cinema – by which she means both Cuban exile and island cinemas.
10 Noriega and López, *The Ethnic Eye*, xii.
11 Gayatri Spivak, "The Problem of Cultural Self-Representation," in *The Postcolonial Critic: Interviews, Strategies, Dialogues*, ed. Sarah Harasym (New York: Routledge, 1990), 57.
12 Charles Taylor, *Multiculturalism and the "Politics of Recognition"* (New Jersey: Princeton University Press, 1992), 71.
13 Indeed, as Ana López points out, "Exile has become a fashionable position from which to 'speak.' Empowered by modern practices that proclaim the decentredness of contemporary capitalist life and by postcolonial theories of discourse that privilege the hybridity and ambivalence of exile (both inside and outside, belonging yet foreign) as a significant site from which to challenge the oppressive hegemony of the 'center' or the 'national' the exilic experience – along with borders, margins, and peripheries – has become a central metaphor of contemporary multicultural artistic and critical practices." See "Greater Cuba," in Noriega and López, *The Ethnic Eye*, 38.
14 Noriega and López, *The Ethnic Eye*, x.
15 See Noriega's "Imagined Borders: Locating Chicano Cinema in America/América," in *The Ethnic Eye*, 3-21, where he argues that Chicano Cinema "developed not just vis-à-vis Hollywood and the New Latin American Cinema (as well as cinema and television), but through the disavowal of an avant-garde tradition within Chicano cultural production (1965-1975)" (4). See also his above-mentioned *Chicanos and Film*.
16 This point requires more contextualization than can be provided here. To further underscore differences between the US and Canadian contexts in terms of their respective audiences, suffice it to note that by the mid-1980s Televisa, the Mexican film and television conglomerate, had acquired more than a 75 percent interest in the Spanish International Network in the United States. See Gary Keller, *Chicano Cinema*, 20. Keller also reminds us of Carl Mora's observation that "the U.S. market is estimated at 25 million people and represents 40% of Mexico's film export sales. There are about 450 Spanish-language theaters in the U.S. that bring $45 million a year" (20).
17 Noriega and López, *The Ethnic Eye*, ix.

18 W.E.B. Dubois, *The Souls of Black Folk* (New York: Bantam Books, 1989 [1903]), 3. Frantz Fanon, *Peau noire masques blancs* (Paris: Editions du Seuil, 1952), especially the chapter entitled "L'expérience vécue du Noir."

19 As a form of erasure, censorship banishes the repressed, potentially in perpetuity. Not all forms of mediation are the same. For more on the "repression hypothesis," see Michel Foucault, *The History of Sexuality*, vol. 1 (New York: Vintage Books, 1980), 10-13.

20 An interesting debate can arise from comparing comments by Noriega on the subject of activism and the role of "minority" cultural workers within art institutions and the academy (Noriega, "On Curating," *Wide Angle* 17 [1995]: 301-2) and the position adopted by Fatimah Tobing Rony in *The Third Eye: Race, Cinema and Ethnographic Spectacle* (Durham: Duke University Press, 1996).

21 Noriega and López, *The Ethnic Eye*, xx.

22 Among these are writers Carmen Rodríguez (originally from Chile) and Jaime García Arbeláez (from Colombia). Lhasa and other fine songwriters and interpreters have also made a mark in music. In the theatre, writer and performer Carmen Aguirre has been widely recognized for her work with young Latino actors to bring their experiences of exile and dislocation to the stage: *Que pasa con la Raza, eh?* (Vancouver 2000) and *Spics and Spam* (Vancouver 2002). It is impossible, at this point, to determine the number of visual artists working in Canada. In Vancouver alone I would estimate their number at close to thirty.

23 For an excellent analysis of this issue, see Ardele Lister's independent video essay, *Conditional Love – See under Nationalism: Canada* (1997).

24 For more on this movement, see Zuzana Pick, "Chilean Cinema: Ten Years of Exile, 1973-83," *Jump Cut* 32 (April 1986): 66-70.

25 According to a recent estimate, as many as 200,000 to 300,000 Colombians fleeing a fifteen-year-long undeclared civil war have migrated to the United States in the past three years alone. See Michael W. Collier and Eduardo A. Gamarra, "The Colombian Diaspora in South Florida," *LACC*, Working Paper Series no. 1 (May 2001), 1. There are no similar research projects on the Colombian diaspora in Canada.

26 Other notable examples of Chilean exile films of return are: *Miguel Littin clandestino en Chile* (Miguel Littin 1986), also published as a monograph by Gabriel García Márquez; and, more recently, Patricio Guzmán's *La memoria obstinada* (*The Obstinate Memory*)(1997), funded in part by the National Film Board. Guzmán is best known for the New Latin American Cinema classic, *The Battle of Chile* (1975-76). The footage smuggled out of Chile after the 1973 coup was to be edited in Canada before ending up in France.

27 The only other reference I have been able to find to the other two directors is Fajardo's *Le Soulier* (1981), a fifteen-minute short story about a lost shoe, shot in colour in thirty-five millimetre.

28 The child's name may evoke one of the classics of the New Latin American Cinema, Jorge Ruiz's *Vuelve Sebastiana* (Bolivia 1953). Here an Uru child of the same name is also portrayed as the repository of the wisdom of her people, as well as their potential salvation.

29 Quoted from program notes, NFB Web site, <http://www.nfb.ca>.

30 Quoted from ibid.

31 His *Chacabuco, Memories of Silence* (2001) records the memories of survivors of a concentration camp at Chacabuco. Among them are Angel Parra, musician (singer, composer) son of Violeta Parra, who was in Chacabuco from early November 1973 to the end of January 1974 and currently lives in France; the poet Jorge Montealegre, imprisoned in Chacabuco at nineteen years of age; union leader Rafael Salas; architects Andres Crisosto and Adam Policzer; Mariano Requena, MD, who was also Allende's personal physician; and the camp's chaplain and a former commander of the armed forces.

32 Generally exhibiting cross-class and gender alliances, this genre differs from both biography and autobiography in that it allows for the recounting of a personal story by someone other than the subject her/himself without doing away with the subject's first-person narrative voice.

33 Lozano and Cuban-born Ricardo Acosta curated *Crossing Borders*, the first two festivals of Latin American and Latino film and video held in Canada (Toronto 1995 and 1997). My

thanks go to them both for their invaluable help in making possible the 1999 film retrospective, exhibitions, and symposium on *Nations, Pollinations, and Dislocations: Changing Imaginary Borders in the America*, which I curated and organized in Vancouver in 1999.

34 Personal communication, Vancouver, November 1999.

35 Frances Negrón-Muntaner, "Drama Queens: Latino Gay and Lesbian Independent Film/ Video," in Noriega and López, 60.

36 Negrón-Muntaner, 63-4. She takes this concept from Raymond Williams, who defines it as "a social experience which is still in process ... not yet recognized as social but taken to be private, idiosyncratic – and even isolating." Raymond Williams, *Marxism and Literature* (London: Oxford University Press, 1977), 132.

37 Negrón-Muntaner, 64.

38 As Carmen Huaco-Nuzum notes in reference to Frances Salomé España's *Spitfire* (1991), and other films in which the Virgin of Guadalupe and a number of Mesoamerican female deities are used to signal an alternative feminist socio-politics, these elements function as signposts of øther times, desires, and histories through the construction of an alternative Mestiza iconography. See Carmen Huaco-Nuzum, "(Re)constructing Chicana, Mestiza Representation: Frances Salomé España's *Spitfire* (1991)," in Noriega and López, *The Ethnic Eye*, 261-2.

39 Honoured in several festivals, this small jewel of a film received second prize (Coral) for Best Short Film at the Havana International Film Festival, Cuba, 1994; first prize (India Catalina) for Best Short Film at the Cartagena International Film Festival, Colombia, 1995; and Gold Danzante for Best Short Film at the International Short Film Festival, Huesca, Spain, 1995.

40 Ariel Dorfman, *Heading South, Looking North* (New York: Penguin Books, 1998), 6.

Filmographies

Claudia Morgado Escanilla

1988   *Kaos.* Director, writer, producer (16 mm, 6 min.)
1989   *The House of Concord.* Director (promotional documentary, 16 mm, 30 min.)
1989   *Don't Waste Your Time Looking.* Director, writer, producer (16 mm, 5 min.)
1990   *Oda a las Chilotas (Ode to the Chilotas).* Director, writer, producer (16 mm, 8 min.)
1991   *The Pleasure of Silence.* Director, writer, producer (16 mm, 7 min.)
1992   *Spit It Out.* Director, writer, producer (animation, 16 mm, 2 min.)
. 1995   *Unbound (Sin ataduras).* Director, writer, producer (16 mm, 20 min.)
1996   *Angustia (Anguish).* Director, writer (16 mm, 5 min.)
1997   *Sabor a mí (Savour Me).* Director, writer, co-producer (35 mm, 22 min.)
1999   *Succulent, Tasty and Nice.* Director (video, 15 min.)
2000   *Martirio (Sufferance).* Director (16 mm, 16.5 min.)
2002   *Bitten.* Director, co-writer (35 mm, 14 min.)

Marilú Mallet (Director)

1975   *Lentement* (also editor)
1975   *Il n'y a pas d'oubli (There Is No Forgetting)* (99 min.)
1978   *Les Borges* (60 min.)
1982   *Journal inachevé (Unfinished Diary)* (55 min.)
1985   *Mémoires d'un enfant des Andes* (58 min.)
1988   *Child of the Andes* (28 min.)
1989   *Ma chère Amérique* (51 min.)
1996   *2, rue de la mémoire (Suspended Memories)*
2001   *Double portrait* (38 min.)

Part 8

Revisioning Gender and Diversity in Canada

The final part of this book "comes home" to Canada, already represented in earlier sections by Deepa Mehta, Yue-Qing Yang, and Latina immigrant film-makers, as well as on the panels in Chapters 18 and 19. It begins with an overview of the remarkable record of films made by francophone women in Quebec, by Nicole Giguère (also a panel participant) for documentaries, and Jocelyne Denault for feature films. In the following chapter, Carole Ducharme, a Québécoise who now works in British Columbia, discusses the making of *Straight from the Suburbs*. Exploiting comic effect through satirical reversals and caricatural visual techniques, this unique short film provides a direct and highly effective message against homophobia.

The next two chapters focus on another important element in Canadian filmmaking, the work of First Nations women. Unlike immigrant minority communities or even the Québécois, members of First Nations and their ancestors did not come here from somewhere else: on the contrary, their space was invaded by outsiders. In British Columbia, a controversial treaty process has only just begun, and we at the University of British Columbia acknowledge that our campus is built on Musqueam territory. We were fortunate to have a Canadian First Nations filmmaker present, Loretta Todd, who now lives in BC (see Chapter 19). Her work has received considerable acclaim, as is documented in Ken Eisner's interview. He also discusses the work of Arlene Bowman, another filmmaker who has moved to Vancouver. By Todd's estimate, 80 percent of Aboriginal filmmakers in Canada are women, whereas in the United States the reverse is the case. Three other local BC filmmakers are introduced in Eisner's overview: Dana Claxton, Barb Cranmer, and Thirza Cuthand. Their work provides examples for the theoretical discussion by Michelle La Flamme (University of British Columbia), who is herself of mixed ancestry. La Flamme relates the motivation and experimentation of First Nations women filmmakers in British Columbia to postcolonial theory and to the specific political situation and agenda of First Nations in British Columbia – the "final frontier."

The political message of these films is reminiscent of many of those made through Studio D, the women's studio that flourished in Montreal from 1974 until 1996, when the National Film Board closed it down. Diane Burgess traces the legacy of Studio D and raises many questions that connect to issues addressed earlier in this volume. Do women filmmakers (and now minority women) need separate treatment? Does it reinforce stereotypes to expect women's films to espouse causes, especially feminist ones? Her study traces the effects of a separate studio and separate technical training on the output of women's film from both the French and English sides of the NFB, and the relations between government cultural policy and a precarious "national" film industry, to evaluate what exactly is the legacy of the world's first feminist film studio.

These general issues bring us back to those raised at the beginning of this book. The last word is left to camerawoman Zoe Dirse, who recapitulates some of the well known but challenged feminist film theory based on the hegemony of the "male gaze." She uses examples from her own work to reformulate some fundamental questions: What difference does it make when the gaze (and the camera work) belong to a woman? Do women see differently from men? And do women (and men) respond differently when a woman wields the camera? This volume provides not one but many answers to these questions, from various points of view. The debate continues, as does the production of a remarkable range of films by women across the world.

Documentary Filmmaking by Women in Quebec: Nicole Giguère

Vidéo Femmes: A Unique Contribution to Filmmaking in Quebec
Quebec has a strong documentary filmmaking tradition, a historical reality that is internationally recognized. What is known as direct filmmaking, or *cinéma vérité*, grew out of the francophone film-directing program offered by the National Film Board of Canada (NFB) in the 1960s and 1970s. I am not sure if this type of filmmaking has had as much importance in anglophone productions as it has in francophone productions. It was within the context of the NFB's program that we aimed to represent and express aspects of the "real world," which is what I tried to do in my first documentaries, made in 1974-75. At that time we were motivated by an explosion of community and feminist activism. Along with the advent of the handheld camera, this kind of solidarity made production easier and facilitated the broadcasting of audio-visual materials. A handful of colleagues interested in both cinema and social intervention began the group known as Vidéo Femmes. We wanted to produce our own documentaries on subjects of interest to women. We also wanted to ensure the distribution of films and videos created by women from Quebec, both in and beyond Quebec. At the same time other video centres sprang up in Montreal, beginning with Le Vidéographe, which was followed by Coop video and Groupe d'Intervention Vidéo (GIV), both of which also promoted films by women. All these groups still exist and are active in production and private distribution.

Here I will focus upon Vidéo Femmes as I have been personally involved with this organization, which has existed for more than twenty-five years and has enabled many women to become directors. Vidéo Femmes has been consistently recognized and respected in the world of independent films in Quebec, although the group dynamic has changed several times over the years. Recently we have seen a new surge of creativity and a greater diversity of productions, including video art, short films, and experimental films, as well as social documentaries. In terms of distribution, our biggest customer has been the education sector, along with various other groups and associations; recently, however, the cultural sector has begun to be of greater importance. Vidéo Femmes has recently participated in a larger number of festivals, museum exhibits, and international events.

In spite of these activities and a well established reputation, Vidéo Femmes remains (and will remain) a small, independent production house and a non-profit organization that operates on a frugal budget. Our collective subscribes to a form of filmmaking that incorporates an emphasis on artistic expression and social commitment, and this implies a resistance to the norms of larger institutions. Without wishing to underestimate the relative importance of our efforts, it is very difficult for me to assess the contributions made by Vidéo Femmes to the overall development of documentary films by Quebec women. Because we used to favour video, for many years our films were not even considered "cinema." Our early productions were not shown at film festivals and were not listed as part of any film repertoire, which explains why, for a long time, we organized our own festival. These circumstances forced us to develop on the fringe, and even now I have trouble integrating our history into the canon of women's films in cinema.

Certainly the distinctions between using film and using video are much less important in documentary film production today, since sixteen-millimetre film has practically disappeared. Beginners now prefer small digital cameras, and more experienced directors find that this tool affords them a new freedom. Films made by Vidéo Femmes are now often broadcast on television and are admitted to almost all film festivals and independent film events. Today, Vidéo Femmes appears less like a fringe group and more like an independent production house. Through all the changes, it has managed to maintain its own particular objectives and modes of production.

The Role of the National Film Board of Canada (NFB)/ Office Nationale du Film (ONF)

When speaking of a more "institutionalized" documentary form, we must obviously look at the role of the National Film Board of Canada. For productions in English, there was Studio D in Montreal, which was created in 1973 and gave many women directors a chance to gain experience (see Part 8, Chapter 38). It also allowed topics that were considered "women's issues" to be treated on screen and discussed in society at large. This women's studio had a major impact on the direction taken by the NFB across Canada, and it has become an essential point of reference for any discussion of women's film production in this country. Studio D also trained many women to become technicians in the film industry, giving them access to jobs formerly reserved for men.

On the French side, we had a studio called Regards de Femmes. It pursued the same goals as did Studio D, but its existence was much shorter than was that of its English counterpart: it lasted only ten years, from 1986 to 1996. When we examine the productions coming out of these two studios, it seems that films directed by francophones were focused upon personal issues, while films directed by anglophones were focused upon social issues. Today both studios are closed, despite the fact that their films were the most widely sold and watched productions to come out of the NFB. Even though there are still a number of women directors and writers working for the NFB, I personally believe that, with the disappearance of these two studios, both of which had a specific mandate to represent women, there have been fewer films made with women's issues in mind. One thing is certain, the presence of women in technicians' jobs has hardly increased on film sets, and young people can no longer rely on the NFB for training.

Private Production

In Quebec, it is on the private production side that the most change has occurred over the past twenty years. The television networks have turned to the private sector to fill their program schedules, and this has resulted in the growth of companies producing films for television. This new cultural industry affords many opportunities for women to become involved as directors and in various other aspects of television production. With this growth in the private sector, financing for documentary film production has changed a great deal. Before any other financial step is taken, we must first obtain the participation of a network. The result of this is that those who pay the bills have an unavoidable influence on subject matter as well as on the actual production of the documentary. Full-length documentaries have all but disappeared due to lack of financing and broadcasting opportunities. We now live with television's almost complete control of film style, and there are many of us who deplore the fact that a small number of individuals decide the life or death of our projects. I must also mention that, although we have to constantly consider the opinions and demands of television broadcasters, the amount of money they actually invest in our productions is not very high. It is much less than that invested by European broadcasters.

However, through it all, women have remained active and well represented as directors and producers of documentaries, although we often have to conform to the logic of commercial television. We have to contend with an imposed form and style; restrictions on content; and, during production, the physical presence of representatives from many institutions. The multiplication of television networks over the years has permitted a greater production of so-called "documentaries," but we realize that the quality of these works is often poor. This deterioration can be attributed to delays, frequent budget reductions, and the constant need for spectacular, entertaining, and sensationalist productions.

Documentaries often require in-depth research and a long-term commitment. Under the best conditions there is a certain creative liberty in writing and directing documentary film. However, making "real" documentaries, for which one is entirely responsible, is more and more difficult. There are not as many time slots on television for "unique documentaries," thus named in order to distinguish them from the more ubiquitous series and reports. More and more often, the documentary is relegated to special channels, which inevitably means lower viewer ratings and, therefore, lower funding.

The big appetite of specialized channels and their small budgets lead them to prefer quickly produced series, magazine formats, and repeat broadcasting. They also like to acquire shows produced elsewhere rather than at home. The most worrisome thing for women directors is that many of these television shows have the same restricted target audience: men (as demonstrated by their commercials). The result, not surprisingly, is that subjects that openly appeal to women are of much less interest to the networks.

Nevertheless, I find it a positive sign that there is now a greater diversity in television programming and many opportunities for work in directing, which will surely allow more women to enter this field. But I am seriously worried about the commercial objectives of the networks, which are constantly involved in unbridled competition for ratings. This has contributed to a deteriorating work environment for documentary filmmakers in general.

In spite of television's obsession with the "industrial" or mass production of documentaries, some directors, many of whom are women, actually do succeed in making films that stand out. Although many men are involved as documentary directors, I think that this genre of cinema particularly attracts women because it gives them the opportunity to explore different realities and to express their points of view on the world in which they live. Documentary filmmaking probably corresponds to certain preferences that may (justifiably or not) be categorized as "feminine": it requires a lot of commitment, the ability to sustain a relationship with the networks, determination in the face of obstacles, and a good dose of humility. It is definitely not as "glamorous" or as lucrative as is the full-length feature film, where we find mostly male directors.

Some production houses that produce documentaries in which they invest an immense amount of time with no hope of making large sums of money are headed by women (e.g., InformAction [Nathalie Barton], Virage [Monique Simard], and Le Rapide Blanc [Sylvie Van Brabant]). For many years these companies and some others have favoured "author's cinema" and have provided a place for women filmmakers.

Documentary Film Distribution

Some French-language documentary films are translated or subtitled in English; however, in my experience this is not the norm. When a film is shot in English Canada or the United States we may make two versions. English television is sometimes involved in this type of production, which means that an English version is mandatory. The advantage for us is that this facilitates the distribution of the film beyond Quebec. Nevertheless, for reasons that deserve to be studied in greater depth, the distribution of documentary films leaves much to be desired. It is easy to understand why films produced in French are particularly disadvantaged. The francophone market is small, anglophones do not much appreciate subtitled films, and the subjects treated are not necessarily of the same interest to both French and English audiences. In the domain of documentaries, as in many others, Canada is a country of "two solitudes." We often live in different and cloistered universes, never allowing one to penetrate the other.

The Association of Directors of Quebec
(L'Association des Réalisateurs et Réalisatrices du Québec/ARRQ)

The ARRQ represents independent francophone directors in Quebec, and it is the only association recognized by Quebec and Ottawa as doing so. Begun in the 1970s by people involved in film, the ARRQ now includes approximately 250 directors working in the realms of full-length film and television. The association is very active in promoting a variety of causes aimed at improving working conditions for its members. For many years it has tried to obtain a collective agreement between television directors and private producers, and it is also very involved in obtaining copyright protection for directors.

A few years ago an ad hoc documentary committee was formed in order to defend the interests of directors specifically involved in this type of production. A small group of documentary makers is consulted when questions relating to documentaries arise. As for women's participation, we endeavour to make sure women are represented, but there is no committee to deal with our specific needs or interests. This situation leads back to two basic questions: do women filmmakers still need special representation? do they have their own agenda and priorities? In my view, some of us do.

Fiction and Documentary

Some female directors (Mireille Dansereau, Marquise Lepage, and, recently, Catherine Martin) have produced fictional work, but we can still say that this is the exception rather than the rule. At the other end of the spectrum there is Léa Pool, who occasionally produces documentaries but more often directs full-length films. These are two very different worlds, and the passage between them is not easy. There are very few women who can break through into the world of fiction filmmaking, partly because of the enormous budgets involved, the great risks, and the fact that success seems out of reach. Women are often lacking in confidence, and I tend to believe that we have less faith in women than we do in men. Perhaps the subjects that women prefer are less attractive to those (mostly men) who are involved in the decision-making process for big budget movies.

In short, in this area women filmmakers in Quebec face the same obstacles as do women filmmakers in most other places. For us, within the North American context, the barriers are aggravated by the fact that we work in a minority language. Nevertheless, we have achievements of which we can be proud, and some of our work has succeeded in attracting attention in Europe as well as in the anglophone world.

Women Directors Working on French Feature Films in Quebec: Jocelyne Denault

Three Groups of Filmmakers

Women have had a strong presence in Quebec filmmaking from the very beginning,[2] but it was only in the early 1970s that women directors from Quebec began making full-length feature films. As Nicole Giguère mentions, many began by participating in the National Film Board's special programs for women, especially the French language series entitled "En tant que femmes" ("As Women"). In most cases, the films they produced were documentaries or "docu-fictions."[3] A number of male directors had left the NFB to start their own small independent companies, and several women were involved in these, hidden behind a male partner (often their husband or lover) whom they supported, learning on the job. The credits of films from that period often mention the name of a woman who played an ancillary role as "special collaborator" or by assisting with the direction, camera work, or editing. Some of these women, like Aimée Danis and Nicole Lamothe, began to make their own films (mostly shorts). These women are still active, though usually not as directors.

Any description of the situation of women filmmakers in Quebec today must recognize the fact that they include individuals of different ages and that their experience has been very different. They can be roughly divided into three groups. The first group could be called the "pioneers," and it includes those who began in the 1970s, almost all with the NFB series mentioned above (or in its wake). Anne Claire Poirier, Mireille Dansereau, Aimée Danis, Louise Carré, and Hélène Girard are among the best known of these women. Others followed in their footsteps a few years later, but in the private sector. These women included Léa Pool, Micheline Lanctôt, Paule Baillargeon, and Brigitte Sauriol. After them, in the 1980s, came the second group, which was composed of those who are now "seasoned" directors, including Marquise Lepage, Johanne Prégent, Sophie Bissonnette, Marilú Mallet, and Sylvie Groulx. In some cases (e.g., Lepage and Bissonnette), it is their outspoken feminism that distinguishes them from the first category; in others (e.g., Mallet and Prégent) it is the individual (rather than the collective) positions advocated in their films. They are also far more diverse in their training than are members of the first group. Like the first group, most of them learned on the job, but they did so within more varied contexts and continue to be involved in a range of areas such as television series, documentary film, and/or reportage. The third and most recent group is

Julie Hivon's *Crème glacée, chocolat et autres consolations/Ice Cream, Chocolate and Other Consolations* (2001)

composed of emerging "generation X" women, some of whom graduated from film school (e.g., Manon Briand, Catherine Martin, Julie Hivon, and Carole Laganière). Having studied with "the guys," they feel "part of the gang" and are no longer preoccupied with gender struggles either in their lives or in their films. This has led to a shift from the earlier political films to films focused upon a quest for personal happiness. The latter represent a new wave of "films for pleasure." Each of these three groups has its own trademarks, its own major themes, and its own star directors.

The First Women Filmmakers

Since the first women directors in Quebec made their films through the NFB, their work is marked by the realistic documentary genre favoured by that federal agency. Many made their first films in 1975 (International Women's Year), and the results show both the passion of a first venture and that period's sense of commitment to bringing women's issues to the screen. Without being militant radical feminists, several of these women had a message to communicate, and they did so through the medium best suited to that end – the documentary or docu-fiction. The subjects treated reflect women's concerns in the 1970s. These include motherhood (desired or not: *Le Temps de l'avant*), day-care *(A qui appartient ce gage),* marriage and its alternatives *(J'me marie, j'me marie pas),* a historical perspective on women's roles in a patriarchal society *(Les Filles du roy),* or the current situation of women, whether suburban housewives living out the "feminine mystique" denounced by Betty Friedan (*Souris, tu m'inquiètes*) or adolescent girls (*Les Filles, c'est pas pareil*). These are not so much protest films as attempts to allow women's voices to be heard on topics of importance to them. The perspective is constructive rather than fiercely critical. Rather than echoing the more radical feminist demands that were surfacing, they convey a moderate, liberal message aimed at identifying issues and fostering a collaborative solution through working with men.

In the private sector, apart from Mireille Dansereau and Brigitte Sauriol, women were mostly making shorts or using video. In 1972 Dansereau was responsible for the first full-length fiction film made by a woman in Quebec, and it was produced by a private cooperative.[4] *La Vie rêvée* adopts a strong feminist perspective, denouncing the expectations society imposes on women, especially with regard to physical appearance. In a playful manner, the film calls on women to reject the dictates of fashion and to define themselves in ways that differ from that presented by the dominant models. Three years later, Sauriol made *L'Absence*, provoking a debate about the role of the father – a debate that others would extend to the role of the mother.

In attempting to trace the production of feature films by women, one must not ignore this first period, which consisted primarily of non-fiction and which responded to an urgent need to draw attention to many issues. Once this had been accomplished, some directors wanted to move on to more personal questions and to try their hand at full-length fiction films. However, as Nicole Giguère points out, this was not (and still is not) an easy matter.

The 1980s

While still depicting the problems of women in general (which were also their own), women directors of the 1980s had enough confidence to speak out about what they wanted to achieve and how. In the year 1979-80 six full-length films by women made it to the screen. This figure might give the impression that the struggle for equal access to cameras and screens was over; however, in reality, even now the average number of films directed by women each year in Quebec is small. There are usually only two or three, occasionally four, and sometimes none at all.

Among the films of that exceptional year were a romantic comedy by Micheline Lanctôt (*L'Homme à tout faire*), a visual exploration by Léa Pool (*Strass Café*), and an experimental narrative by Paule Baillargeon (*La Cuisine rouge*). These works use non-didactic forms and structures to make their point and to express women's needs and desires. At the same time, other fiction films continued to deal with such serious themes as a woman's relationship to her mother (*L'Arrache-coeur, La Belle Apparence*) or the distress of a sixty-year-old woman who finds herself alone (*Ça peut pas être l'hiver, on a même pas eu d'été*).

During this second period, women's films frequently addressed what might be termed personal problems; however, they were problems with which other women could identify. Apart from *Rien qu'un jeu*, which deals with incest, most of them reflect upon the various stages of life: flashbacks to adolescence (*Sonatine, Marie s'en va-t-en ville*) or to young adulthood (*La Quarantaine, Onzième spéciale*), or reflections upon future plans (*Futur intérieur, Ça peut pas être l'hiver, Salut, Victor*). A recurring secondary theme is the value of solidarity among women during times of stress (*Ça peut pas être l'hiver, Anne Trister, Qui a tiré, Sonatine, Rien qu'un jeu*). Another is the need to redefine love relationships, which are usually depicted as difficult *(Qui a tiré sur nos histoires d'amour? Anne Trister, Blanche est la nuit, A corps perdu)*. Some show an openness to homosexuality that is absent in men's films of the same period (e.g., *Anne Trister*). During the same period Léa Pool, in *La Femme de l'hôtel*, asked an important question about what it means to create a story and whether to do so is not a form of vampirism that draws on other people's lives. It is as though, in retrospect, she is questioning the legitimacy of the documentary fiction of the previous decade.

The 1980s was a period of consolidation for women making feature films, and it confirmed their place in the world of directors; however, their experience (like that of their successors in the 1990s) also illustrates the obstacles they faced. Several of them had to change paths or return to production (Aimée Danis, Louise Carré, Iolande Cadrin-Rossignol) in order to get their films made, and some have subsequently chosen careers in production rather than direction. Others would become (or return to being) editors (Hélène Girard), teachers (Micheline Lanctôt), actors (Micheline Lanctôt, Paule Baillargeon), scriptwriters (Paule Baillargeon), documentary filmmakers (Sophie Bissonnette, Marquise Lepage, Sylvie Groulx), or go back to working for television (Johanne Prégent, Sophie Bissonnette). It is difficult to draw any conclusions about their preferred themes as most of them either make a feature film only every five years or so or have stopped at one. Since the majority of these women filmmakers never went beyond the critical stage of the first or second feature film, it would be dangerous to try to attribute a pattern to their work.

The 1990s and New Arrivals

Quebec's first generation of women filmmakers has been followed by a new generation that shows great promise. The 1990s saw the emergence of young directors who graduated from film programs in Quebec (at the Institut National de l'Image et du Son, Université du Québec à Montréal, Concordia University, and/or Université de Montréal). The young women among them have learned to work with "the guys": they use male crews for their films and expect to be hired on the crews of films directed by men. They believe they "belong" on the inside. Without underestimating the obstacles to making a film, these women do not attribute them to sexism; rather, they see them as common to all filmmakers. They are generally convinced that the barriers faced by their predecessors are no longer there, that the door is wide open to them – until experience dispels this illusion.[5]

Two films illustrate this change of attitude very well. The first appeared in 1991, when six established directors, four men and two women (Denys Arcand, Michel Brault, Atom Egoyan, Jacques Leduc, Léa Pool, and Patricia Rozema), participated in making a film together. The result is a collage of five short films on the same subject, *Montréal vu par ...* Five years later, in 1996, six young filmmakers, three men and three women (Jennifer Alleyn, Manon Briand, Marie-Julie Dallaire, Arto Paramagian, André Turpin, and Denis Villeneuve), also undertook to make a film entitled *Cosmos.* The result is a feature-length film depicting six episodes in the life of a group of characters. The comparison between the two ventures is quite illuminating. In the 1991 film each director worked individually, whereas in the more recent film they all worked together, even going so far as to work on each other's scenes.

The themes chosen by young women filmmakers, and how they treat them, reflect their complicity with their male counterparts; the conflicts represented in their films concern differences of generation rather than gender. In fact, these young women seem impervious to the anxieties and tensions that marked the previous generation. In their films couples are formed and dissolve amicably (as in *Chocolat, crème glacée et autres consolations,* or *Du pic au coeur*), while personal choices seem to be made freely, without opposition *(Deux secondes, Cosmos).* Feminist demands for autonomy and for the right to have a career, so frequent in the films of their elders, are completely absent. These rights are non-negotiable and are taken for granted in the work of Manon Briand, Carole Laganière, Catherine Martin, Julie Hivon, Jennifer Alleyn, Céline Baril, and others who are still at the short film-making stage.

Meanwhile, experienced directors have not given up making films. Whereas during the first period women's films were so few that one could not ignore documentaries, at present fiction films alone are capable of providing a wealth of diversity and information. Over the last ten years, women have concentrated less on men's aggression (as they did in *Rien qu'un jeu* and *Mourir à tue-tête*) than on different types of love, both homosexual *(Lost and Delirious, Emporte-moi, A corps perdu)* and heterosexual *(La Demoiselle sauvage, A corps perdu, Mouvements du désir, Blanche est la nuit, Les Amoureuses, Un léger vertige, Solo, La Position de l'escargot, La Vie d'un héros).* There is still an interest in relationships with the mother *(Les Fantômes des trois Madeleine, L'Ile de sable, Deux actrices)* or father *(La Position de l'escargot, La Fête des rois),* and curiosity about one's origins takes on new significance for some of those directors who are immigrants. Films such as *L'arbre qui dort rêve à ses racines,*

Anne Trister, La Position de l'escargot, and *Journal inachevé* convey the questions raised by the move to Quebec and/or the pain associated with loss.

Films on specific subjects remind us that women can make all kinds of films. Examples such as *La Vie d'un héros* (the Second World War viewed through local events), the thriller *La Fabrication d'un meurtrier,* or the romantic fable *Du pic au coeur* show that women are gaining access to many other forms of cinema besides that embodied by the "cinéma d'auteur" approach to filmmaking. Yet the latter still flourishes, as is indicated by Micheline Lanctôt's *Deux actrices.* It is also necessary to acknowledge the fact that, often, many women abandon the cinema, or at least directing, for reasons that are not unrelated to their sex. Others have found new but relevant paths: Ghyslaine Côté, for example, is the only one to have ventured into children's film (*Pin-Pon: Le film,* 1999, the screen version of a TV show). Another special case is Danièle J. Suissa, who made several feature films between 1975 and 1996, mostly for English language television (*The Morning Man, The Rose Café, The Garnett Princess, No Blame, The Secret of Nandy, Prince Lazure*) as well as two film versions of stage plays (*Evangéline Deusse, Divine Sarah*). Like many others, she has since given up directing films in favour of producing them.

Another unique case involves Denise Filiatrault, who came from the world of live entertainment and television sitcoms. She worked as a scriptwriter and actor as well as in the theatre and is especially known for her work with the *Juste pour rire* (Just for Laughs) festival, for which she was *metteuse en scène.* Comedy is central to her career, and it is not surprising that she brings humour to her direction of films. Her first venture was an adaptation of a play by Michel Tremblay, *C't'à ton tour, Laura Cadieux.* As the author was so well known, directing the film involved little risk. However, she followed up with her own creation, *Laura Cadieux ... la suite,* using the same core characters but inventing funny adventures for them. Among the comical characters she introduces, the women are especially striking: likeable, sensitive, not attractive by Hollywood standards, and touching in their search for love. In a sort of time warp, Filiatrault, Quebec's funniest woman filmmaker, is revealed as an old-fashioned feminist.

Women's Ways of Doing It

Without laying claim to a specifically feminine form of cinematographic writing, it is noticeable that, in Quebec, films made by women use the medium in certain ways. Besides the fact that the camera is generally not intrusive and rarely misleading, its distance from those observed often expresses respect for the characters, avoiding a sense of inquisition or voyeurism. The rhythm of many of these women's films (such as *Les Fantômes des trois Madeleine* or *Futur intérieur*) is meditative rather than brisk or hurried, reflecting a predilection for intimate and personal themes. Relatively speaking, the camera work and rhythm in films by the younger generation are more vibrant, fast-moving, and dynamic (such as *Cosmos* or *Deux secondes*) than are those of the older generation. Some venture into new visual or technical experiments, as in *Du pic au coeur*. The majority of these films by women take place in the present (though they may evoke past events through flashbacks); Micheline Lanctôt's *La Vie d'un héros*, which recounts a childhood memory from the Second World War, is an exception. While the choice of subjects treated by women directors is significant, it is also revealing to note those that they avoid. In Quebec, every male filmmaker worthy of respect has at least one film that is focused upon the political situation. For women directors, politics includes an interest in others and is not restricted to a partisan nationalism.

From one generation to the next, women directors in Quebec have made films that talk about women. If their films have changed, then it is because the situation of women has changed and because they themselves have changed. Filmmakers of the first wave were engaged in collective denunciations, and they were filming "as women" rather than as individuals. They were speaking on behalf of others. Gradually, some began to speak in their own name, while remaining aware that they were expressing what many other women were also experiencing. Now, both established and emerging directors are concentrating on filming itself, on experimenting with the medium and finding new ways to use it for their own ends.

Whether we like it or not, films by women are always situated and assessed in relation to films by men. It is axiomatic that the latter are not compared with the former in the same way. Women filmmakers in Quebec are not furies out to tear men to shreds; they respect them, love them, engage in dialogue with them: but they don't follow male models or heroes. The new generation seems to be telling us that it doesn't need leaders (of either gender) but companions. The members of this generation are happy simply to be able to make movies and, above all, to contribute their own films to Quebec cinema. They have every chance of succeeding.

Notes

1 At the "Women Filmmakers: Refocusing" events in Vancouver, Quebec documentary filmmakers were represented by Nicole Giguère, one of the founders of the Montreal-based collective Vidéo Femmes. Her participation in a panel on the practicalities of making documentary films is recorded in Part 4, Chapter 19. For this section, she agreed to provide more information on this type of filmmaking by women in Quebec. Jocelyne Denault, author of a study of women filmmakers in Quebec that concentrates on the period before 1980, was invited to add a complementary overview showing the relationship in Quebec between documentary and feature filmmakers. Both contributions were translated by Valerie Raoul assisted by Anthea Seles.

2 For more information, see Jocelyne Denault, *Dans l'ombre des projecteurs: Les Québécoises et le cinéma* (Québec: Presses de l'Université du Québec, 1995).

3 This neologism dates from that period and refers to fictions based on intensive research pertaining to the topic treated in the film, either through documentation or interviews with informants.
4 ACPAV, the Association Coopérative de Production Audio-Visuelle.
5 See Marie-Anne Cloutier, "Le joyeux calvaire des cinéastes québécoises," *Châtelaine*, Montreal (September 2001), 46-54.

Films Cited

A corps perdu (1988), Léa Pool (Téléscène Film Group)
A qui appartient ce gage (1973), Susan Gibbard, Clorinda Warny, Francine Saïa, Jeanne Morazain, Marthe Blackburn (NFB)
L'Absence (1975), Brigitte Sauriol (N/A)
Les Amoureuses (1993), Johanne Prégent (NFB)
Anne Trister (1986), Léa Pool (Cinémaginaire)
L'arbre qui dort rêve à ses racines (1992), Michka Saal (NFB)
L'Arrache-coeur (1979), Mireille Dansereau (N/A)
La Belle Apparence (1979), Denyse Benoit (N/A)
Blanche est la nuit (1989), Johanne Prégent (NFB)
Ça peut pas être l'hiver, on a même pas eu d'été (1980), Louise Carré (Maison des Quatre)
Chocolat, crème glacée et autres consolations (2000), Julie Hivon (GPA Films)
Cosmos (1996), Jennifer Alleyn, Manon Briand, Marie-Julie Dallaire, Arto Paramagian, André Turpin, Denis Villeneuve (Malofilm Distr.)
C't'à ton tour, Laura Cadieux (1990), Denise Filiatrault (Cinémaginaire)
La Cuisine rouge (1979), Paule Baillargeon (ACPAV)
La Demoiselle sauvage (1991), Léa Pool (Cinémaginaire)
Deux actrices (1993), Micheline Lanctôt (Stopfilm)
Deux secondes (1998), Manon Briand (France Film)
Divine Sarah (1984), Danièle J. Suissa (N/A)
Du pic au coeur (2000), Céline Baril (N/A)
Emporte-moi (1999), Léa Pool (France Film)
Evangéline Deusse (1984), Danièle J. Suissa (N/A)
La Fabrication d'un meurtrier (1995), Isabelle Poissant (N/A)
Les Fantômes des trois Madeleine (2000), Guylaine Dionne (France Film)
La Femme de l'hôtel (1984), Léa Pool (ACPAV)
La Fête des rois (1994), Marquise Lepage (NFB)
Les Filles, c'est pas pareil (1974), Hélène Girard (NFB)
Les Filles du Roy (1974), Anne Claire Poirier (NFB)
Futur intérieur (1988), Yolaine Rouleau (N/A)
The Garnett Princess (1987), Danièle J. Suissa (N/A)
L'Homme à tout faire (1980), Micheline Lanctôt (Stopfilm)
L'Ile de sable (1999), Johanne Prégent (Film Tonic Inc.)
J'me marie, j'me marie pas (1973), Mireille Dansereau, (NFB)
Journal inachevé (1982), Marilú Mallet (NFB)
Laura Cadieux ... la suite (1999), Denise Filiatrault (Cinémaginaire)
Un léger vertige (1991), Diane Poitras (N/A)
Lost and Delirious (2001), Léa Pool (Cité Amérique)
Marie s'en va-t-en ville (1987), Marquise Lepage (N/A)
Montréal vu par ... (1991), Léa Pool, Patricia Rozema, Denys Arcand, Michel Brault, Atom Egoyan, Jacques Leduc (Cinémaginaire)
The Morning Man (1986), Danièle J. Suissa (N/A)
Mourir à tue-tête (1979), Anne Claire Poirier (NFB)
Mouvements du désir (1994), Léa Pool (Cinémaginaire)
No Blame (1988), Danièle J. Suissa (N/A)
Onzième spéciale (1988), Micheline Lanctôt (NFB)
Pin-Pon: Le film (1999), Ghyslaine Côté (Lions Gate)

La Position de l'escargot (1998), Michka Saal (Remstar Distr.)
Prince Lazure (1992), Danièle J. Suissa (N/A)
La Quarantaine (1982), Anne Claire Poirier (NFB)
Qui a tiré sur nos histoires d'amour? (1986), Louise Carré (Maison des Quatre)
Rien qu'un jeu (1983), Brigitte Sauriol (N/A)
The Rose Café (1987), Danièle J. Suissa (N/A)
Salut, Victor (1988), Anne Claire Poirier (NFB)
The Secret of Nandy (1990), Danièle J. Suissa (N/A)
Solo (1991), Paule Baillargeon (NFB)
Sonatine (1984), Micheline Lanctôt (Stopfilm)
Souris, tu m'inquiètes (1973), Aimée Danis (NFB)
Strass Café (1980), Léa Pool (ACPAV)
Le Temps de l'avant (1975), Anne Claire Poirier (NFB)
La Vie d'un héros (1994), Micheline Lanctôt (Prod. La Fête inc.)
La Vie rêvée (1972), Mireille Dansereau (ACPAV)

---

35 Querying/Queering Stereotypes: Interview with Carole Ducharme on Making *Straight from the Suburbs*
Conducted by Valerie Raoul

At the "Women Filmmakers: Refocusing" conference (March 1999), Canadian filmmaker Carole Ducharme answered questions after a screening of her film *Straight from the Suburbs*. This follow-up interview with Valerie Raoul was conducted after the conference. *Straight from the Suburbs* (1998) is a twenty-four-minute Quebec/British Columbia co-production directed by this filmmaker from Quebec who now lives in Vancouver. It is a comedy in colour, with text in English, and was financed by Société du développement des entreprises culturelles (SODEC, Quebec), Telefilm Canada, and the National Film Board of Canada.

Synopsis (from publicity material)

In a world populated only by Queers, Mary, a troubled teenager, has to tell her two mothers ... she's STRAIGHT! Illustrating what it would be like to be straight in a homosexual society, *Straight from the Suburbs* employs narration straight out of 1950s guidance films, a classic role reversal situation, and a Pop Art sensibility in the set design to create a riotous 24-minute mix of style and substance. In a bucolic world where everyone is happily homosexual, we are introduced to a young girl who lives in a nice house in a nice suburb with her two mothers. Mary has a dilemma: she doesn't know how

Carole Ducharme's *Straight from the Suburbs* (1998),
courtesy of the director

she'll break it to her mothers that she's "different." Although her mothers
are seemingly accepting of Mary's heterosexuality, they do have their concerns. While Betty and Doris ponder the question "What will the neighbors
say?," Mary deals with the difficulties of her blossoming feelings for Brad,
the new straight boy in class.

Director's Notes

In North America in the 1930s to the 1960s, many short "social guidance"
films were made. These "national home movies" were "odes to an idealized
national identity fabricated by the corporations, the institutions and government who made them and whose purpose they served." Those films had
a clear agenda: "to educate, miseducate, convince and condition." Very revealing and hilarious, they "explored the darker side of postwar American
suburbia, a place that shamelessly relegated women to the domestic realm
and checked the behaviour of the unruly teens. Conceived as advertisements for a lifestyle, these wildly entertaining films are a window into our
collective national psyche." *Straight from the Suburbs* is a modern satire of
social guidance films, using genuine phrases taken directly from those films.

Straight from the Suburbs also uses quotations from a *Newsweek* article (17 August 1998) entitled "Gay for Life?" about gays supposedly turning straight. It is fascinating to see that, even today, some people believe that homosexuality is a disorder and that so-called "reparative therapy" can cure lesbians and gays. Even more fascinating is US Senate leader Trent Lott's likening of homosexuality to alcoholism and kleptomania. The 1950s are not over yet!

Valerie Raoul: What led to you to make this film? How does it fit in with what you had done before and the kind of training you had?

Carole Ducharme: In 1996, I had just moved from Montreal to Vancouver and I was working as head of International Co-productions for a film company that thought it would conquer the universe. Meanwhile, I was thinking about all the heterosexual people who have it easy and what it would be like if the world was populated only by lesbians and gays. Then the heterosexuals would understand how it feels to be an outcast and how ridiculous the reasons are behind such discrimination. What better way to try and understand people different from you than to put yourself in their shoes? So I came up with the story of *Straight from the Suburbs*. In 1994, I had written, directed, and produced my first short film, *Love Interruptus*, about the various ways of interrupting love between people. *Straight from the Suburbs* is also about interrupting love between people. I guess I am very interested in this subject.

I obtained a law degree from the University of Montreal in 1987, and worked as an entertainment law lawyer for a couple of years in Montreal before moving to Paris in 1992. There, I worked as a producer and produced a couple of feature films, all international co-productions. I went back to Montreal two years later and stayed there for two years, mainly writing scripts, before moving to Vancouver in 1996. In Vancouver, I worked for an animation production company and produced the animated television series *Cybersix* (a Canada-Japan co-production) broadcast on Teletoon in Canada. So, basically, I had no previous training as a writer-director, and I learned everything while doing my two short films.

VR: What kind of obstacles did you encounter – or encouragement? How did you finance the film, and who else was involved? Would you say it was a team effort?

CD: I received tremendous support from everybody around me when I was writing the script. At that time, I didn't have any financing in place yet and everybody helped me out for free: my story editor, Sylvie Peltier; my production designer, Suzanne Chapman; my co-producer in Montreal, Nathalie Ducharme (who happens to be my younger sister and also plays the teenage girl in the film). We put together a great package, very visual, and we sent it to various funding agencies: Telefilm Canada (Vancouver), the NFB (National Film Board in Vancouver), BC Film (Vancouver), SODEC (Quebec), the Canada Arts Council, BC Arts Council, and the NSI Drama Prize (Alberta). Four weeks later, SODEC agreed to invest $50,000 Canadian in the project. They were extremely supportive. They had previously invested in my first short film to help me finish it. So with that money, we decided to go to Montreal and shoot, even though the other funding agencies hadn't responded yet. We shot for five days in June 1997 and paid everybody on the set. When I came back to Vancouver, I had to keep searching for the necessary funding to pay for the post-production. Since BC Film had not made its decision yet, I sent them the stills from the shoot to reassure them that the film was in the can and that it looked great. But BC Film then refused to finance the project because they didn't like the light in the stills! I explained to them that those were only the stills and that the lights were designed for the sixteen-millimetre camera (Basic Lighting 101). They also said that the script wasn't developed enough. But when a government agency doesn't want to finance your project, they are very good at finding any excuse.

Meanwhile, all the other funding agencies declined to invest in the project. I was stuck with a film in the can and nowhere to go. So I invested my own money to have the sixteen-millimetre film transferred to video and I hired an editor. I got a deal on an editing suite and we did a rough cut. With my rough cut, I reapplied to Telefilm, BC Film, and the NFB. BC Film still declined to invest in the project, so did Telefilm. The NFB told me they didn't have any money left for that fiscal year, but they would have some in the next fiscal year and encouraged me to reapply. So the NFB finally invested $2,500 Canadian, which barely covered the film-to-tape transfer. As for Telefilm, they told me they would not invest unless I had a letter of interest from a broadcaster, a distribution deal, and an official invitation to a recognized film festival. That was their way of saying no. They were very surprised when, a couple of months later, I came back to them with everything they had asked for! They had no choice and reluctantly gave me $15,000 Canadian. And I had one month and a half to finish the film before the Vancouver International Film Festival! The music composer Anne Duranceau had five days to compose five songs. And we recorded the songs in one evening with the fabulous singer Lindsey Davis. It was insane. The copy arrived at the festival the day before the screening in September 1998, a year and three months after the shooting.

Since then, the film has had tremendous success in festivals around the world. Three copies of the film are constantly travelling from one festival to another: France, Germany, UK, Belgium, Portugal, Italy, Australia, Japan, Hawaii, Brazil, USA, Canada, etcetera. Australian television has bought the film. It has won two Nell Shipman Production Excellence Awards –

Best Short Film and Best Musical Score [Seattle, United States, 2000] – and was nominated for two Leo Awards – Best Screenwriting and Best Musical Score [Vancouver, Canada, 1999]. The film was also nominated for Best Short Film at the Jutra Awards [Montreal, Canada, 1999].

You have to be determined, patient, and blindly hopeful to make a film. Here in Canada, where we depend so much on government funding, we develop a love-hate relationship with the government agencies. We love them when they invest in our project and we hate them when they don't. In the meantime, since we never know if a film will be successful, we must enjoy the process all along.

VR: The form you chose is a combination of cartoon, comedy, parody, social satire. Were there models for this? Were the reasons for this style primarily related to the subject matter? Were you thinking of other films about sexual orientation based on role reversals?

CD: The production designer, Suzanne Chapman, suggested that Roy Lichtenstein's pop art painting would suit the world and the theme of the story. And it did. The art director, Roxanne Ducharme (my older sister), used mainly primary colours and dots and lines reminiscent of Roy Lichtenstein's work. For example, the furniture in Mary's room is all painted on the wall. We also used thought bubbles over the heads of the two mothers when they learn that their daughter is a "deviant heterosexual." The mothers appear to be very cool about it, but we can read in the thought bubble what they really think. That is totally Lichtenstein. The costume designer, Linda Brunelle, also followed the same inspiration when choosing the costumes. She focused on dotted patterns and primary colours. The voice-over narrator tells the story, as in those 1950s and 1960s "social guidance" films, as if he was the voice of reason, the voice of God. In those days, a lot of films were made to teach people how to behave properly. In *Straight from the Suburbs,* by reversing the roles and the sexual orientation, we show how ridiculous and funny it is to try and tell people what's right and what's wrong when it comes to sexual orientation. I incorporated into the narration genuine quotes from those social guidance films and also from a *Newsweek* article, where right-wing US politicians condemned homosexuality. The reversal thing is quite exquisite. I didn't have any model and I didn't know any other film about that kind of role reversal.

VR: There are French elements in the film, so it appears to take place in Quebec. Yet the script is in English, and suburbia could be anywhere. Do anglophone and francophone audiences react differently? Do you see the setting as anywhere in North America?

CD: Certain differences in the audience's reaction don't necessarily come from the use of expressions in French but more from the culture of Quebec.

There are a couple of jokes that refer directly to a specific aspect of Quebec culture (for example, when Mary explains to Brad why the French language has disappeared) or of Canadian culture (such as the reference to Canada Customs not having done its job of censuring heterosexual magazines). But those references don't interfere with the overall enjoyment of the film and the understanding of its message. If I look at all the countries where the film has been shown, I think the message is universal: discrimination against lesbians and gays is ridiculous and should be stopped. Although the setting is Quebec (because the narrator says so at the beginning and most of the actors have a French accent), it could well be anywhere in North America.

VR: How have critics reacted to the film? Who is buying or showing it and to what audiences? Have you had some surprises? Were you thinking of the educational uses of this film, in high schools, for example?

CD: The primary market is international film festivals, and it is doing very well. The film has been touring the festival circuit for almost two years now. The next step will be television sales. Australian television has already bought the film. I was surprised to learn that Canada Customs bought a copy of the film for their employees' library! I think that's great. And that is exactly one of the reasons why I made this film, for people to enjoy themselves and laugh but also to make them think about issues like discrimination and homophobia. Other interesting sales of the film include McGill University Hospital in Montreal, and the Gay, Lesbian and Bi-Sexual Community Services Center of Colorado in the US. In Vancouver, Langara College has shown the film in a women's studies class, and UBC has shown it in women's studies and Canadian film classes. When I was writing the script, I was using coarse language sometimes, and my story editor, Sylvie Peltier, kept reminding me about the educational market. So in the end I used only proper and decent language, and I am very happy that I listened to her! A lot of people who see the film tell me I should propose the film to schools, and a number of high school teachers have expressed their interest in showing the film in their classes. I think this is not only a great idea, but also essential. The beauty of *Straight from the Suburbs* is that it is a non-threatening film, full of humour but with a strong message. And that's the best way to make people think without boring them or making them turn the other way and run. So I will explore the educational market with my distributor.

VR: Is this a one-time thing, or do you envisage other films of this type, about homophobia or other issues? What other films do you dream of making?

CD: The issues of discrimination, intolerance, homophobia, injustice, racism, and sexism, are very close to me. Inevitably, those themes will be in my films one way or another. I make films because I want to share some-thing with people; I want them to have a good time watching my movies and I want them to think and reflect on certain issues. There will always be comedy in my films and important issues. I am currently working on a feature film script. It's the story of a little seven-year-old girl growing up in the seventies. On a conceptual level, I dream of making films with positive messages which will help people to find their own truth and to free themselves.

VR: Do you see yourself as part of a community of lesbian filmmakers? Or of women filmmakers making films with a social message? Or of a wider group of filmmakers using humour to get a message across? All or none of the above?

CD: I don't mind labels and I am all of the above. I think I have a moral and social responsibility to make films about women's issues in the broad sense. I think every woman filmmaker should make films with interesting, strong women characters because if we don't do it, nobody will. This doesn't prevent us from making funny, enjoyable films that can be seen by the widest audiences possible. Because it's nice to have a message, to have something to say, but if you have no one to say it to, if nobody is listen-ing or watching, then what's the use?

VR: Do you see attitudes in the film industry and community changing with regard to homophobia? Have depictions of gays and lesbians be-come a marketable commodity? How do you react to a film like *Boys Don't Cry?*

CD: As in every business, you have people who are there to make a differ-ence and people who are there to make a buck. (Personally I would like to do both!) Of course there has been an evolution in the ways lesbians and gays are portrayed in the movies, and I think it's all for the better. We have come out of the era where lesbian and gay films were about the "coming out" theme to an era where lesbians and gays are regular charac-ters (mostly secondary, but it's a start) on prime-time TV series (mostly American). The gays even have their own TV series exclusively dedi-cated to them and their world, the ground-breaking British series *Queer as Folk*. That's great. But that is in TV land. In the real world, there is still a lot of work to do to convert those right-wing homophobes. Film or TV is just one way of contributing to making this world a better place. I really enjoyed *Boys Don't Cry*. I also saw the documentary, *The Brandon Teena Story*. I think *Boys Don't Cry* was very well done and extremely well acted. Those kinds of film are important in trying to raise awareness about some sensitive issues. Those are the films that deserve to exist. They serve a purpose.

VR: What, if anything, did you gain from interacting with other filmmakers and theorists or academics at the "Women Filmmakers: Refocusing" conference?

CD: It is always interesting and refreshing to get out of our own little world and meet other women filmmakers, see their work and hear them talk. We learn all the time. It was a unique opportunity to meet with women filmmakers from around the world. Congratulations on creating this event! I hope there will be another conference soon, although I must admit that, personally, I find the academic conference formula, where one person reads her paper, hard to follow and not as compelling as listening, for example, to a panel or an interview.

VR: What are your current projects?

CD: I have written and directed a half-hour documentary, *The Neighbourhood Kids,* for TFO (The French Television channel in Ontario). It's on the children living in Vancouver's Downtown Eastside, which is known for its drugs, prostitution, and crime. [Since this interview, Carole completed *Man-Made Women,* a one-hour documentary on the Miss Venezuela beauty pageant; she is currently working on a feature film script about a seven-year-old girl who thinks she was born a fish.] I was curious about documentaries and wanted to explore that form, but I must admit I much prefer doing fiction.

VR: Thanks, Carole. Those of us who have seen *Straight from the Suburbs* are certainly looking forward to seeing more films from you. The response at the conference was really positive, and a lot of people want to obtain a copy of the video. *Bonne chance!*

Filmography: Carole Ducharme

1993   *Mon Amie Max* (feature film, drama). Co-producer (France-Canada co-production)

1994   *Love Interruptus* (drama, 16 mm, 8 min., colour). Writer, director, producer, distributor (Montreal: Witness Productions)

1997-8   *Straight from the Suburbs* (comedy, 16 mm, colour). Writer, director, producer (Quebec-BC co-production); produced with Witness Productions (Vancouver) and Big Deal Productions (Montreal)

1999   *Cybersix* (thirteen-part, half-hour animated TV series). Associate producer (Canada-Japan co-production)

1999   *Les Enfants du quartier (The Neighbourhood Kids)* (documentary, 30 min.). Writer, director (Vancouver-Winnipeg)

2000-1   *Man-Made Women* (documentary, 60 min.). Co-writer, co-director, associate producer, sound recordist, co-editor (Vancouver-Montreal-Venezuela)

Shadow and Light:
First Nations Women Filmmakers
Ken Eisner

Loretta Todd

Loretta Todd's Vancouver apartment is filled with radios. Sure, the sun-dappled West End flat – perched on the top floor of a weatherworn four-story building – has other things to offer. There are scads of framed family photos, rows of high-end detective novels, and some black-faced stereo equipment, complete with a satellite hook-up currently tuned to a world-music station. Next to an old easy chair, the current *New Yorker* is folded open to an essay on composer Arnold Schoenberg. But mostly, the visitor is faced by that wall of radios, which range from valuable bakelite numbers from the 1930s to inexpensive reproductions of early transistors. "They all work," says Todd, who grew up in rural Alberta, the middle child of eight siblings who, most of the time, had no TV. "It was a noisy household, and oddly enough, the radio was one way to get some privacy. I remember lying on the bed, a little plastic radio on my chest, and tuning into places around the world. Well, it wasn't really around the world, but they were places I didn't know, where they had wild deejays, and call-in shows, and music I hadn't heard before."

The veteran filmmaker has come some distance from the days when Idaho and Montana seemed like exotic lands, well past the known horizon. Certainly, she couldn't have known she would become a West Coast fixture – a leader, in fact, of a loosely affiliated group of Aboriginal women pointing their cameras confidently into the twenty-first century. Most have had some working connection with Todd, but aside from their determination to depict the lives of people they grew up with, the women who talked to me for the *Georgia Straight*[1] – ranging in age from just over twenty to almost fifty – are about as disparate in style and philosophy as any five artists plucked from the population.

Though not yet forty (or "younger than Madonna," as she prefers to put it), Todd has already raised a daughter – now in her early twenties – worked in the public sector, for government and tribal organizations, and created a steady stream of films, each stylistically stronger than the last. Todd's life trajectory didn't necessarily have "internationally fêted filmmaker" written on it. Her dad was a seasonal bush worker who occasionally roughnecked in the oil industry. With ten people to feed, her mom stayed home a lot. It wasn't all hardscrabble survival, however. "My father used to paint horses," she adds, emphatically. "On paper, or wherever, but often as not, it was on the wall. He would take a pencil and start drawing on the wall, with the

Loretta Todd,
courtesy of Alex
Waterhouse-Hayward

Dana Claxton,
courtesy of the director

Arlene Bowman,
courtesy of Alex
Waterhouse-Hayward

muscle and anatomy there in incredible detail. And my mother was a wonderful singer. So I grew up with this idea of creating for itself, because you have to, with no expectation of applause or anything – but for pleasure."

Both parents have died, but Todd draws comfort from the easy recollection of her parents harmonizing on "My Blue Heaven" – a song also associated with Chief Dan George, the subject of one of her latest films. She recalls a childhood spent visiting relatives in a panoply of urban and reserve situations. "We lived in *all* the worlds: the Indian world, the Métis world, and the White world. That was a facility they gave us, without knowing it – the ability to move between worlds – and that's something you need as a filmmaker, or any kind of artist. Indian people have a much better ability to change and move through time than we are given credit for. You see that in the younger people, who are able to pick up on everything."

As a documentary specialist, Todd cites Americans Errol Morris, Frederick Wiseman, and Barbara Kopple as non-fiction influences – along with the many old National Film Board (NFB) films she got to study at the national archive. What really gets her about the best documentaries isn't the reality, however, but the aesthetics they convey. "I've always loved beauty. I've always loved black-and-white film and a perfectly formed composition. Instinctively, even as a child, I always loved what shadow and light do to an image. Growing up in the Prairies, and watching the light play against birch trees, watching those long, long summer days in northern Alberta, with all the variations that take place over the hours – unlike here, where the long shadows move quickly."

Lately, she's been contemplating the depth of field peculiar to our misty skies and jagged backgrounds. "I hadn't been back to the Prairies in a while, and when I went back there recently, I was struck by how crisp everything was, the way I could see trees way off in the distance: I could see what looked like individual leaves blowing in the wind, and it was such a nostalgic feeling for me, almost like I knew those trees from my childhood." Todd moved here in the early seventies, worked full time for various government bodies, but squeezed in extra hours at film school, studying at Simon Fraser University with camera expert John Houtman. "I went to school in my office clothes; these kids were all dressed in black, smoking cigarettes, and thinking, 'Who's *this* old broad?' But I wasn't actually much older than them, and, intellectually, I was as radical as they came."

In fact, Todd excelled at the kind of analysis prized in academic circles, as her many magazine and catalogue essays attest. But she was never cut out to be a poststructural, Derrida-derived pedant. "In the sixties and seventies, it became all about the surface of things, scratching right on the film and all that, but for me, cinema always had more to do with [Jean] Renoir, and those other great French directors of the thirties and forties – with the beauty of the images themselves." In 1991, after the NFB turned down her original proposal, she landed a privately produced spot addressing the problem of solvent abuse and hasn't stopped in the ensuing years, also turning out short videos and TV segments, and speaking at museums around the world. Now *she's* the one who dresses in black. "I don't think I was ever an earnest social-documentary filmmaker. That wasn't what drove me. I always tried to make my work interpretive. I'm very present in my films. So even if I was making a documentary, I always left a place to express something of myself. In my earliest film, *The Learning Path,* which has a certain naïveté, there are some very haunted images." That film, her first for the initially balking NFB, went inside the minds of former children who grew up at infamous residential schools. "Even in *Hands of History,* which is a pretty straight-forward documentary, I made a point of having no narration, since most films about art have a lot of talking. So every film has had some place for me to develop my artistry." In the case of *Forgotten Warriors,* her study of Aboriginal war veterans, she soon discovered that vital records were often buried or lost. "It was important to me basically to create my own archive, to put us back into the cultural memory."

Todd staged a coup when her next film, *Today Is a Good Day: Remembering Chief Dan George* – partially a product of her own Eagle Eye Films – pre-miered at the 1998 version of the Vancouver International Film Festival: somehow, she managed to fly to LA, shoot a long-awaited interview with Dustin Hoffman (George's co-star in *Little Big Man*), and splice it into her print – all between the first and second screenings of the film. The hour-long documentary, which then got a TV premiere on CBC, went on to the 1999 Sundance Festival, where it was ecstatically received. In fact, that's where the director – who had already taken one of her scripts through a Sundance Institute workshop – hooked up with the executive producer of TV's *Buffy, The Vampire Slayer.* This woman wants to produce Todd's first dramatic feature.

"I don't have any other way to say it," the director admits. "I need the bigger canvas. I also love language, and dramatic film is a way of exploring that." So far, Todd has won awards at the Native American Film Festival, held annually in San Francisco, and at the Talking Pictures Festival in Taos, New Mexico, among others, and she was honoured at Vancouver's first Aboriginal fest, which also took place in '98. "I feel that I can go beyond the experience, into the guts of it, and inhabit it, in a way. Because I don't have any allegiance to any one film style, I can move in all directions at once. I guess I'm at the point now where I want all that. The meat and potatoes I've done; now I want it to be all dessert!"

Arlene Bowman

By Todd's estimate, around 80 percent of Aboriginal filmmakers working in Canada are female; in the United States, the ratio is roughly the opposite. (Ontario's Alanis Obomsawin, maker of *Kanehsatake: 270 Years of Resistance,* is probably the best known on this side of the border.) Arlene Bowman left the States, in fact, for what she found to be a more hospitable climate up North. She has the classic aquiline nose and high cheekbones of an Arizona Navajo – or, more precisely, a member of the Diné nation, albeit a lapsed one.

A small, slim woman, she fled Arizona for Los Angeles to work in the production of films and TV commercials, and to do whatever kind of acting an Indian woman could get in Hollywood. At the same time, she quietly earned a master's degree in film from UCLA, did some programming for California fests, and set out to make movies that are far more instinctively personal than her formal training might lead you to expect. In her signature *Navajo Talking Pictures,* she's seen asking her grandmother for help in making the movie – something the older woman refuses because her granddaughter doesn't know the Diné language – and the film turns out to be about that tussle for recognition. Todd, who greatly admires Bowman's iconoclastic approach, calls this "the end of ethnography" and the start of a more existential trend. "It's for her*self* that Arlene makes films. She's willing to be inexplicable, and I like that – Indian people are always having to explain themselves. Her films are about *her* in this moment, and being able to exist in the moment is the greatest power of the artist."

While shooting *The Song Journey,* an exploration of the female side of the pow-wow highway, Bowman travelled up the Prairies into Canada and ventured out to the Coast. She ended up crashing on Todd's couch for about a month. In 1992, she got a temporary job at Simon Fraser University and has been working on art-project permits ever since.

Subsequently, her work has ranged from the neon-coloured expressionism of *Women and Men Are Good Dancers* to straightforward talking-heads stuff for VTV's magazine-style *First Story* series. Lately, she's been working on experimental video shorts with performance artist Mark McLeod, and now, nearing fifty, she's in the early stages of developing a feature about Aboriginal prostitution. "I'm drawn to what personally affects me," she states. "In October of '98, the cops were cleaning up the women who walk at Main and Broadway, and I got stopped there just because I was on foot. I guess I had the right look. I got mad, but it got me thinking about why this happens in Canada."

Bowman is increasingly drawn to drama, and her work always has a strong musical component. She says Aboriginal visibility in the Vancouver arts scene, and on the street, makes this a fertile place for her to work. "There's just a lot going on, in theatre, visual arts, music – enough to keep me stimulated and open. I always say I'm walking backwards to go forward. I guess I'll keep learning until I'm too old to learn any more."

Dana Claxton

On the polished face of it, Dana Claxton's elegantly assembled work seems to be the product of an haute-bourgeois art-gallery background. Actually, she was into her late twenties before she picked up a Super-8 film camera at Value Village ("for $19.95," she happily recalls) and started shooting everything in sight. "The first film I ever made was called *Grant Her Restitution*, and it was just my sister and myself driving home to Saskatchewan. It was just images, no narration. I was always drawn to media, but it took a while for the elements to come together." She was also galvanized by tours, "as a rather shy observer," of the great museums of Europe and New York.

Claxton, who's just a shade older than Madonna, also worked for a theatre group called Spirit Song and did an occasional fashion column for the *Georgia Straight*. At Vancouver's venerable Video In, she was exposed to twenty years' worth of experimental filmmaking. Today, living in East Vancouver with the influential artist Lawrence Paul, she has already amassed an impressive body of work. Much of it is intended to be seen in galleries rather than theatres. Early last year, she shared a UK show with Black British filmmaker Isaac Julien, and its accompanying essay compared her work to "film noir and the paintings of Caravaggio."

Her self-professed sphere of concern is neocolonialism – an area rich in irony, since it creates so much tension between Aboriginal content and European-based form. "Not that it was ever a strategy, to utilize these Western modes of expression to bring forth an Aboriginal perspective – that does sound straight out of the catalogue, doesn't it? – But those were the tools available to me. I guess I could have painted on robes or teepees, right?" Claxton's earlier shy observations have apparently been replaced by a dryly biting wit. How else can you describe her response to a comment on her fascination with motion? "Oh yeah," she sighs, "the savages are restless over here on East First. Yes, I like moving images, and the juxtaposition with sound. All my short films – since that one with my sister – have these incredible soundscapes, all by Russell Wallace. In my recent installations, I think I've been successful at drawing the viewer into the moment. It's a lot to ask someone to stay in a room for ten or fifteen minutes, so you should give them a nice experience."

While her *Yuxweluptun, Man of Masks,* made for the NFB and currently in wide circulation, is a relatively conventional artist portrait (of Paul, as it happens), she gets to stretch out further in self-produced films like *Buffalo Bone China* and *The Red Paper.* The latter is her most ambitious effort, featuring pseudo-Elizabethan dialogue and black-and-white, sixteen-millimetre photography recalling early Peter Greenaway. "As an artist, other than my critical investigation, I'm not all that calculated. I just *make* it! I can be a flaky artist who just wants to muse on set. 'Oh, let's try *this* now.' Of course, film is such a costly medium, you can't do too much of that."

She also has an hour-long project, called *The People Dance,* which is intended to "incorporate primitivism with postmodernism." It's a step towards feature length, although Claxton says she isn't keen on standard dramatic formats. "I would like to make an experimental feature, but I think I'll always make work of any duration. As they say, it's not about length, it's about content."

Barb Cranmer

Barb Cranmer has no shortage of content to draw upon. Everything about her, from her stocky frame to those piercing dark-ochre eyes, bespeaks solidity. Of the group under discussion, she's the only one actually from this region originally and, in fact, is part of a large, boisterous family that has been central to 'Namgis life and culture for many generations. (Several of her kin were seen displaying their musical knowledge in Annie Frazier Henry's *Singing Our Stories.*) "She's very much talking about the governance of this land, in very specific ways," says Todd, "and she's using film as a vehicle to do that. She serves a very important role, because these things – that often have to do with the actual survival of Aboriginal people – become part of the public record, and part of the generations beyond us. Plus, she has access to this incredible long continuum of people who have pretty much always been here on the Coast."

Cranmer recently moved back to Alert Bay, near the northern tip of Vancouver Island, where she grew up. Until about five years ago, she was doing production work on films by others, such as Todd, doing research and preparation with people being filmed. Recently, she and her Nimkish Wind company partner, Cari Green, returned the favour by producing Todd's *Dan George* film. "I was really lucky," says Cranmer (who's almost Madonna's age), while making a flying visit to a Kitsilano java shop, "getting exposed to the film medium and helping people like Loretta. I found my life's work."

That work started back in 1980, when an educational camera crew came through Alert Bay, offering a quick video course. What resulted was a library of oral histories, taped by elders, many of whom have since died. She stuck with it and moved down to Vancouver to take media courses at Capilano College. Eventually, she made such potent documentaries as *The Washing of Tears* and *Laxwesa Wa: Strength of the River,* both about the reclamation of Aboriginal land and culture.

Since then, she has undertaken three projects – about rendering sacred oil from eulachon, Chilkat blanket weaving, and the rebuilding of a ceremonial bighouse that was torched in a revenge-inspired case of arson. "My style is to find a story, go back into the history, and give it the background you probably don't know about." She's also branching into multimedia, with a CD-ROM series mixing local fishing lore and looming issues (her work life actually started on the boats, with her fisher father), with related Web sites to be built. And she's gathering a small army of younger artists who want to help. "People are very interested in being part of this. All of a sudden, you've got people – young people, especially – who live in remote places but are very technology-literate." In keeping with her own early exposure to filmmaking, she'll be taking four local kids to a media-arts symposium in Penticton.

She's become such a fixture on the filmmaking scene, in fact, that other people are starting to pitch her screenplays. "Two years ago, I would have said, 'No, not at all.' But now I'm starting to feel that that's another learning process I'd like to move into. The documentary process is so serious, it would be kind of nice to do something different. One thing we're looking at is developing a half-hour series, and basing it on our humour. Far too often,

Barb Cranmer, courtesy of Alex Waterhouse-Hayward

Thirza Cuthand, courtesy of Alex Waterhouse-Hayward

our stories are about such serious subjects that I feel it's time to lighten up a bit. We want to go into these communities and find what's funny, because First Nations people really have survived through our humour."

She says the results will be a far cry from TV shows like *The Rez* and *North of 60*. "Those programs had our own people stereotyping our own people. That's *enough* about treatment centres, ya know? Let's look for something new: we're not all recovering alcoholics, so let's see what else we can do!"

Thirza Cuthand

One who has already heard that clarion call is Thirza Cuthand. Presently a student at Emily Carr College, this young filmmaker is dining where ethnic identity is just one of many dishes available on the smorgasbord of self-referencing art. With her razor-cut hair, big shoes, and granny glasses, she fits the riot-grrrl mode. Mostly, though, *she's* the riot. On her super-low-tech videos, she displays the kind of sharp wit and in-your-face energy that Todd sums up as "the courage of the trickster's laugh – coupled with the vulnerability of youth."

Only a little over twenty, the Saskatoon-raised Cuthand comes from a family of artists and filmmakers – her uncle Doug Cuthand is one of the most respected producers in Saskatchewan – but even by their standards, she's out there. Mostly, the shocks come in the form of mordant narration, full of slyly constructed, faux-naive observations about self-discovery ("Every day, when I go to school, I notice that there are a lot less lesbians than I had envisioned the night before"), baby-dyke exploitation ("After that, I avoided her with a ten-foot pole"), and bisexual experimentation ("It felt so sacrilegious, me touching a boy with k.d. lang on the TV").

She may be operating on several margins, but there's also a sense that this woman may be the first person in this crowd to get her own sitcom. The funny-bone attack started when she was sixteen, with cutout figures and hand-painted titles and backgrounds. Over the next few years, she captured everything from small-town isolation to life with her mentally challenged sister to, most recently, a lyrical self-exploration in black-and-white eight millimetre – all under the imprimatur of her own Teensy Nun Productions. "I thought about all these things when I was a kid," she recalls, "and was getting kind of frustrated, wanting to get my voice out there. I just didn't see too many young, biracial dykes on TV." Setting her sights higher than *Jerry Springer*ville, she left what Claxton calls "the land of Cuthands and Cardinals" and moved to Vancouver about three years ago, enrolling at Emily Carr and also hooking up with Video In.

"It's an ever-evolving practice. I started with the voice of this sixteen-year-old girl and now, well, it's not quite *serious*, but there may be an innocence that got lost." To her credit, she does laugh at the absurdity of someone *half* Madonna's age mourning her forfeited youth. Still, Cuthand must be mindful of the challenges of moving from free-for-all camera fun to the controlled artistry people expect of a director wielding expensive equipment under no-nonsense time constraints. "I'm moving into film now, and I have to be conscious of developing my own style. I'd like to add a little bit of experimental stuff in there, without being too esoteric. I like writing, so it will happen."

Her short *Untouchable,* which is about pedophilia among other things, won a best-Canadian-submission at 1998's Out on Screen festival. "But what's interesting is the way my films have been crossing over from the queer festivals to the Native festivals. The response has been surprisingly positive." In one rural setting, she worried how a mixed audience would react to a sequence featuring full genitalia – pierced, no less. "They liked it! It's funny, because I came out here expecting to get involved in the queer community, and I *have,* but I more and more feel part of the Native community. My parents are both biracial, and I'm just now realizing how comfortable I feel making films for Native people. I think it's a community that can contain a lot of different elements."

The new kid on the block is definitely thinking past NFB prototypes. "The documentary approach was pretty restrictive, and I think we're now breaking across boundaries enough to begin to reveal the true extent of our lives. I think that's where we're heading right now. It's hard to talk about serious issues and be funny at the same time. But in my culture, that's the way we approach those issues. Humour is a coping mechanism for people who are oppressed: if you can laugh, you can survive. I'm Cree, and we laugh a *lot.* But basically, I can't help it: I'm always looking for the joke."

Current Focus

So there you have it: a non-movement of loosely aligned, post-something-or-other people, all creating highly intuitive work in which aggressive self-assertion is yielding to subtler, more complicated forms of expression. Of course, given the history that's still hanging ripely in the air, as current as tomorrow's headlines, there'll still be room for undiluted anger. "Oh, I think Indians should yell," Claxton insists. "As long and as *loud* as possible. Most likely, nobody's listening anyway, but at least then you got the pleasure of having yelled."

You can see even in that statement, though, that there's room for real joy in this work. Loretta Todd thinks so. "The fact that people like Dana and Thirza now feel free to pursue interests that are primarily artistic shows you how much things have changed, in just five or so years. I got criticized, back in '91, for being too arty. Now, I have to work not to be seen as too stuffy."

These days, there's more of a risk that Todd will be seen as going Hollywood, but she isn't worried about it. "Given my nomadic childhood, and all that time spent with people from different Native communities, I realize that there are lessons I couldn't possibly have learned any other way," she says, turning down the sounds of far-away Brazil and Senegal so they're left burbling quietly in the background. "People who grow up poor and close to the land tend to love economy of motion and doing things well. I want to tell *our* stories, and there's a certain aesthetic and a kind of intimacy that goes with it. That's something an Aboriginal story tries to create, in the sense that everyone's in this room, together. Often, storytelling is about transformation, and so our stories are about *becoming* – the conflict isn't as evident as it is in European-style stories."

Finally, she figures – and Madonna would have to agree – it comes down to a way of seeing the world. "I just think about how, every day, if you got up in the morning and thanked the water and the trees for existing, for your own existence, how different your consciousness, your most mundane decisions, would be. Non-Aboriginal culture has basically drained the land of those qualities. But it's still there – if you know how to look." And listen.

Acknowledgment
A version of this chapter appeared in the *Georgia Straight,* 1 April 1999.

Note
1 A freely distributed, Vancouver-based weekly newspaper with a focus on the local arts scene, news, and entertainment.

37 Unsettling the West: First Nations Films in British Columbia
Michelle La Flamme

How to make an Indian movie. Buy 40 Indians. Totally humiliate and degrade an entire Indian nation. Make sure all Indians are savage, cruel and ignorant ... Import a Greek to be an Indian princess. Introduce a white man to become an "Indian" hero. Make the white man compassionate, brave and understanding ... Pocket the profits in Hollywood.
— From an American Indian Movement pamphlet

Cinematic representations inform and are informed by imperialist hegemonies. Consequently, understanding postcolonial identities involves interrogating the relationships between Eurocentrism, formations of national identity, and cinematic representations. The interdependence of these regimes of power is succinctly articulated in *Unthinking Eurocentrism* by Ella Shohat and Robert Stam. In their analysis, cinematic history is intimately connected with the legacy of imperialism in that the birth of cinema "coincided with the imperialist moment, when diverse colonial civilizations were already shaping their conflicting identities vis-a-vis their colonizers."[1] The emergence of a new First Nations cinema in British Columbia, with Native women at the forefront, has begun to unsettle the West.[2]

This chapter utilizes Shohat and Stam's analysis of the interdependence between nation, identity, and cinema to analyze some recent films and videos by First Nations women in British Columbia. The focus is on the work of three of the filmmakers in Vancouver, namely, Dana Claxton, Cleo Reece, and Thirza Cuthand, all of whom are members of Indigenous Media Arts Group (IMAG).[3] IMAG's mandate is to "organize aboriginal media events" and to "screen film and video works from across Turtle Island from emerging and established mediamakers."[4] These women work to challenge notions of First Nations identity through their own productions, film series, and educational programs and initiatives, in tune with IMAG's stated philosophy of "cultural autonomy in media production ... critical awareness and analysis of socio-political histories."[5] Its work establishes new representations of Fourth World[6] people's ontology and epistemology and challenges hegemonic notions of the West as "settled." The spatio-geographical dimension of the West is addressed in the first part of my analysis. I then look at the land as a metaphor and examine how it is linked to language and notions of gender and national identity, as represented in these women's films. Finally, I suggest that the usefulness of the term "postcolonial" must be questioned where First Nations identity is concerned.

Locatedness: Margins as Frontier

Emerging forms of cinema, as with emerging forms of all of the arts, are to be found in the margins. British Columbia is geographically in the margin of Canada, just as independent film and video productions are at the margins of mainstream cinema. BC Native Women's independent films represent a defiant affirmation of those marginal categories by asserting a vibrant and vocal presence that challenges the national myth of the disappearing Native.[7] Canadian foundational myths concerning the "settling" of the West are based on the fantasy that it was uninhabited and that the West was "won." Shohat and Stam refer to the legacy of imperialism that is encoded in language and illustrated by the use of the term "West," by which Europe is taken as the centre of the world. As an extension of this Eurocentrism, "Western cinema's geographical and historical constructs [are] symptomatic of the colonial imaginary,"[8] which positions the White, imperialist male as the central subject. IMAG challenges the temporality of Western cinema's geographical and historical constructs by placing the margins at the centre. It reconfigures the notion of a frontier by supporting the creation of films and videos that have the ability to push forth new boundaries and to express unconquered territories of First Nations peoples' imaginative spaces.

The Gendered West

The "colonial imaginary" is represented in American "Westerns"[9] that assert White, imperialist interests. Notions of "Indian savagery" are represented and normalized.[10] In such filmic constructions, the "racialized Other" appears in derogatory, racist terms.[11] In *Capturing Women,* Sarah Carter suggests that, "in the Canadian West, as in other settings, colonialism also functioned in a gendered way to develop powerfully negative images of indigenous women, who were projected as being a threat to the white community."[12] In fact, they were cast as the complete opposite of White women, as "agents of the destruction of the world and the cultural health of the community."[13] Carter refers to Rayna Green's concept of the "Pocahontas Complex" in American literature and "the squaw" as examples of two stereotypical images of Native women that have gained popularity. Carter also points out that Native women were assumed to be "immoral" and "accustomed to a great many partners,"[14] and she states that such images "not only prevailed but [were] deliberately propagated by officials of the state."[15]

The representation of Native women in the West is linked to representations of the postcolonial "other" through the genre of the Western. Shohat and Stam make this link and suggest that, whereas "the imperial adventure film conveyed the pleasures of the empire, the Western told the story of imperial-style adventure on the American frontier."[16] While this chapter does not attempt to provide a comprehensive account of representations of Native women in North America, it is important to note the relationship between the construction of Native women and national imperialist agendas and the fact that "there was a sharpening of racial boundaries and categories in the 1880s and an intensification of discrimination in the Canadian West."[17] It is necessary to consider this historical legacy in order to fully appreciate the presently emerging First Nations cinema in British Columbia as resistance to assimilation, as an assertion of cultural integrity, and as a reworking of these stereotypes.

Changing Images: Red Power Women

In *Celluloid Indians* Jacquelyn Kilpatrick divides the stereotypes of First Nations people in film into three categories: "mental, sexual and spiritual."[18] She suggests that the "noble savage" is the alter ego of the "bloodthirsty savage." Kilpatrick concludes that both stereotypes are manifestations of a broader "mythology of historical origin" that is a part of any national discourse.[19] She identifies a central American foundational myth in the classic

Western story of "How the West was Won," which is at the core of representations of First Nations people in filmic history. Initially, in cinematic history, "the noble image prevailed, whereas the bloodthirsty image became
more popular towards the end of the silent film era."[20] Like Shohat and Stam,
Kilpatrick and Carter note that these shifts in filmic stereotypes of indigeneity
corresponded to adjustments in imperialist and colonial strategies.

Although Canadian cinematic history differs from cinematic history in
the United States, the fact that Hollywood dominates the film industry and
controls much of North American distribution means that Canadians also
consume American distortions of First Nations people.[21] It is essential to
examine filmic representations made independently of the large studios,
with their hegemonic agendas of representation of the "other." IMAG actively encourages the creation of work that is not constrained by large
hegemonic distribution agendas. As a result, the work that IMAG produces,
circulates, and curates, can be less concerned with mainstream consumption, which ultimately allows for the possibility of challenging the status
quo through art.

The emergence of a newly constructed "urban savage" is in some ways a
reconfiguration of the "noble savage" that has been central to the Eurocentric
rendering of history. In many recent films, First Nations people have been
represented by depictions of the despair and addiction of the urban Native.
In contrast to this, Cleo Reece's film *Red Power Women* (1998) presents an
active urban community of Native women in Vancouver who formed a political coalition in the 1970s in order to educate and empower themselves while
becoming politically vocal.

Red Power Women is transcultural in its scope, representing connections
between First Nations communities in Canada and our neighbours to the
south.[22] Through interviews, the women state that they were inspired and
politicized by writings from the Black Panthers and the American Indian
Movement as well as by the writings of Mao and Lenin. These transcultural
writings on empowerment were essential to the emerging political voice
of these "red power" women. One of the women in the film, writer Lee
Maracle, notes that an inspirational element in her education during this
time period was the work of Frantz Fanon. This transcultural education
may be seen as an instance of what Yuval-Davis terms "transversal politics" in action.[23] In addition to philosophical and Marxist readings, the
women's education included meeting Native medicine people and tradi-
tionalists at Frank's Landing,[24] where they became further empowered in
their quest for justice.

The quest for justice for Native women has meant dealing with the dual
axes of race and gender oppression by countering the racialized and
sexualized notions of Indian women.[25] Yuval-Davis develops "a framework
for discussing and analyzing the different ways in which the discourse on

gender and that on nation tend to intersect and be constructed by each other."[26] In *Gender and Nation,* she quotes Mohanty's view that, "in the writings of feminists, Third World women are 'frozen' into archetypal victims in discussions of issues such as genital mutilation and various forms of male violence."[27]

In *Red Power Women,* Geri Amber's explanation of what led to the formation of the Red Power Alliance counters the notion of "frozen" victimization. In Vancouver in the 1970s a newspaper article featured a Native woman who had been tortured, murdered, and thrown into a garbage dump in Williams Lake. Two men were involved in the crime. One man was acquitted, while the other received a $200 fine. On the facing page in the same newspaper was a story about a man who shot a moose out of season and was also fined $200. Recognizing that inherent biases in the legal system devalued the life of Native women,[28] the women decided to protest and mobilize themselves. They formed the Native Alliance for Red Power in Vancouver in order to challenge assumptions about gender and race in Canada and to seek justice. Thus, the victimization of the Native woman who had been murdered did not lead to frozen vicitimization for these women but, rather, galvanized them to action. Such stories of Native women as powerful, politicized, and active agents are rarely in circulation. Fortunately, Reece's *Red Power Women* ensures that this particular story of Native women's empowerment is not lost.

Agency

Red Power Women concentrates on issues of violence against Native women and the resulting politicization of the Native Alliance for Red Power using the documentary form. Other filmmakers have challenged power and gender issues through comedic representations. Thirza Cuthand's film *Colonization: The Second Coming* (1996), playfully challenges issues of gender and race by reworking the theme of first contact.[29] In one scene, Cuthand herself is interrupted by an alien creature while masturbating with a dildo. It becomes clear that the alien being has been summoned by her dildo, which has functioned as a beacon. To divert this invader, Cuthand asserts, "I've already been colonized." After a brief discussion, the alien creature leaves and Cuthand is free to enjoy her toy. The title is trebly suggestive of Christian prophecies, the neocolonization of North America, and sexual allusions. This video ends with the woman's assertiveness and celebration of her identity and desire. In this way the video inverts "first contact" myths of frozen victimization by focusing on the woman's capacity to both ward off colonizing aliens and to give herself pleasure.

Issues of agency are central to First Nations film. Many of these filmmakers use autobiography or first-person narration to explain how they have come to understand central aspects of their identity as First Nations women.

Reece's *Red Power Women* is framed by her own arrival in 1967 in Vancouver, the "hippie capital," where she was "accepted and admired even as an Indian."[30] According to the video, in the 1960s Native people were associated with the ideals of the hippie movement. Daniel Francis refers to this phenomenon as "neo-noble savagism," attributing it to the "civil rights movement, the environmental movement, [and] the anti-materialism of the counter-culture," all of which combined to "bring Indians back in fashion" in the late 1960s and early 1970s.[31] Reece's own personal story and experience of her Native identity in Vancouver at that time literally frames her depiction of the politicization of a group of Native women in Vancouver, which is the central focus of the film's narrative.

The Political Personal

The coming-of-age story, found in many First Nations films, is often framed by elders who have guided a young person towards adulthood. The *Bildungsroman* for First Nations people is traditionally connected to intergenerational teaching. However, in Dana Claxton's video *I Want to Know Why* (1994), the intergenerational connection with grandmothers is not the usual passive and peaceful sharing of tradition seen in countless National Film Board films on indigeneity. Claxton inverts the stereotype of a positive integration of intergenerational traditional knowledge by exposing a legacy of inherited pain as well as an inheritance of the strength to survive that was passed to her through her maternal line.

Claxton's video, her great-grandmother's "story," and her maternal line evoke lessons of survival. In this video, images of Native people from the past dissolve into an image of a teepee inset with Indian heads. These images are looped and provide the continuity in the video. Claxton's voice-over begins: "My great-grandmother walked to Canada starving." She states, then yells, "And I wanna know why!" She refers to her grandmother, who "died of alcohol poisoning in skid row," and yells, "And I wanna know why!" In the third sequence of looped voice-overs Claxton says, "My mother died at thirty-seven of suicide," and then whispers, "And I wanna know why." Through the voice-over Claxton expresses rage because there is no official answer as to why generations of women in her family have been victims of oppression. The pain of her loss is conveyed in the third part of the voice-over, where the impact of intergenerational trauma is evident in the softness of her voice.

The language is looped and the still images are cut to upbeat music, making the piece disjointed and rhythmically continuous at the same time. Thus, the structure of the video, suggestive of fragmentation and continuity, represents First Nations experience of colonization in Canada. The video closes with an ironic montage of an image of Native women, a man, and the

Statue of Liberty. During this montage Claxton recites the names of her grandmother and mother, linking her personal story of fragmentation and loss with the continuity that her very presence in the film suggests, as it is she who has lived to tell a fragment of these women's and her own story. Ultimately, the viewer is left with the disembodied voice of the filmmaker who has learned valuable lessons about racism and survival, both of which give her a sense of entitlement to rage and pain.

This "Kookum film" runs counter to many films that depict the legacy of tradition being passed through the maternal line and the image of the "peaceful traditionalist Kookum" that is part of Native mythology (a European construction) and the lived experience of many Native people.[32] Elders are often depicted in films as apolitical or peaceful. In Claxton's film the grandmother is represented not as the "Imaginary Kookum"[33] represented countless times before but, rather, as a tragic figure who has given Claxton the vitality and power to resist oppression. Similarly, in *Red Power Women* Lee Maracle states that "the elders were political," undermining the notion of the "passive traditionalist" kookum. *Red Power Women* closes with an intergenerational ode, in which Reece gives thanks for those who came before and expresses hope for those who will come after. By tracing her own history as an activist in Vancouver, Reece herself becomes the Kookum whose political activism will inspire the next generations. In the final scene of *Red Power Women*, Reece's eldest daughter, Nitanis Desjarlais, is shown speaking at a huge political rally while her mother stands by and raises her fist in a gesture that suggests an intergenerational commitment to activism.

(Re)Productions of Identity(ies)

Much of the debate about "identitarian" politics[34] centres on the search for the "authentic" subaltern voice. Issues of authenticity and essentialism are represented through comedy by Thirza Cuthand in her film *Through the Looking Glass*, which introduces a Red Queen and a White Queen, representing Native and European essentialisms.[35] In the video, both queens are limited by their essentialist notions of race. These notions are challenged by Alice, who is the miscegenated subject that does not adhere to either ideology. In this comedic piece, Cuthand destabilizes notions of race essentialism(s). Through the use of humour, she playfully deconstructs both of the queens' ideologies and suggests that modern First Nations women, and especially the "racial hybrid," or "half-breed," do not fall into either of these camps.

Shohat and Stam distinguish between various forms of hybridity and make the important point that "hybridity preceded colonialism and will continue after it."[36] They also suggest that this term, while it may be in vogue in academia, is also ambiguous in that it "fails to discriminate between the diverse modalities of hybridity: colonial imposition, obligatory assimilation, political co-optation, cultural mimicry, and so forth."[37] The "cultural mixing"[38] that is a part of Third World cinema as identified by Shohat and Stam can be seen within the context of First Nations films as well.

Progressive cinema such as *Through the Looking Glass* can utilize inversions as an element of the "Aesthetic of Resistance" identified in Shohat and Stam's *Unthinking Eurocentrism*. One such inversion can be seen in Dana Claxton's film *The Red Paper* (1996).[39] Colonial binaries are inverted as the Natives are the "civilized" people dressed in European finery and the Europeans are the "savages" who appear on the coastline.[40] This comedic inversion is also a progressive realignment of power and the gaze, which is achieved by locating the subject position as First Nations and the object of the gaze as the Europeans. Only one European is represented and, bound in a straightjacket and gagged, he can only repeat "I did not know they tried to take your God/forced assimilation/relocation/blankets that kill/I did not know." In addition to this structural diversion, the colonizers are referred to as the "invaders." This linguistic shift in perspective places the hegemonic White colonizer on the margins.

The Red Paper is an abstract and surreal inversion of first contact from a Native perspective. It also represents the intergenerational links between First Nations people who participated in first contact with Europeans and their ancestors, suggesting that the histories are linked. Two of the characters recite the following lines: "blood of ancestors/ I felt your scream/ I hear your breath/ my eyes have seen your visions/ my memory holds your memory/ I felt your scream/ I felt the bullet." This transhistoric intergenerational link dislocates spatio-temporality and is juxtaposed with the cultural amnesia that the "invader" reveals in his rant of ignorance. Through multiple levels of inversion, Claxton's video questions the categories of savage and civilized and destabilizes binaries of the "colonial" and the "Indian," ultimately exposing the constructedness of race and identity.

Stuart Hall states that, instead of thinking of identity as an already accomplished fact, we should see it as a "production, which is never complete, always in process, and always constituted within, not outside, representation."[41] In Dorothy Christian's video *Indians and Who* (2000), the categories of "colonial" and "Indian" identity are unsettled. Cleo Reece and her family are shown arriving for a family portrait at an "old times" photo studio where they don the costumes of the pioneers. Throughout the video, Cleo's children speak about their sense of Native identity and why they choose to wear certain costumes for their family photo – that of a priest, a European pioneer, a gold miner, a saloon gal, a cowboy – while Reece herself dresses as a fur trapper's wife. All of the children express a self-conscious awareness of the gaze of the non-Native while retaining a solid identity of themselves as First Nations people, regardless of their conscious appropriation of racial "drag."[42]

Central to this video is the theme of Native people's agency as expressed in their ability to disrupt fixed concepts of indigeneity. By staging the "actors" as a real Native family posing as White colonial pioneers, the images of the Wild West are dislocated, reformed, and inverted. This visual inversion is suggestive of a political realignment of power.[43] The fact that this video is about a family photo also suggests that the members of the new urban Indian family are not constrained by notions of Nativeness and traditionalism or by colonial notions of "the noble savage" but, rather, that they can adopt those elements most suited to modern urban life and construct themselves according to their own notions of indigeneity and family.

Language, Land, and Nation

The reclamation of "pre-contact languages" is a part of First Nations resistance to assimilation and an assertion of pride in a cultural heritage. Language acquisition is one of the fundamental issues faced by First Nations communities today; unlike the mythical "disappearing Indian," the elders who speak First Nations languages are literally dying out. In Canada, preservation of pre-contact languages is a crucial concern, because "with the exception of Cree, Ojibway, Inuktitut, most of the fifty-three Aboriginal languages are perilously close to extinction."[44] The colonial agendas of both French and English Canada were aimed at eliminating indigenous languages by penalizing children who used their mother tongue in the residential schools. Thus, Cuthand's inclusion of Cree in the video *Word for Word* is suggestive of a reappropriation of indigenous language.

Cuthand's video explores the relationship between identity and nation as it is mediated by language. In this video Cuthand's mother, Ruth, is heard speaking French, with French subtitles. This is juxtaposed with an English voice accompanied by English subtitles and a third voice-over in Cree, with Cree subtitles. The French is grammatically incorrect, and the Cree is spelled phonetically. This video conveys the difficulty of knowing one's mother tongue without practice as well as the impact of colonization on language retention. It illustrates the intergenerational linguistic disjunction that is a frequent theme in indigenous society. However, it also suggests a renewed effort to "rescue" First Nations languages from obscurity. *Word for Word* presents an allegory of Canadian history in that three of the largest language groups are represented in their unsuccessful attempts to communicate with one another. The use of juxtaposition in the video suggests the fragmentation of intergenerational communication and the discontinuities in each person's "mother tongue" – discontinuities that result from a colonial legacy that creates "creolized languages." This video suggests that a transcultural identity results from the colonization of one's mother tongue.

For First Nations people, the mother tongue is often linked to the land, as Native language groups represent and codify cosmologies based upon traditional relationships with a specific territory. Across Canada, within traditional Native cosmologies, despite the specificities of language groups, the land is represented as the embodiment of the Great Spirit: the earth is flesh, the water is human emotion, fire is blood, and the air is breath. For some First Nations people, this cosmological framework is represented by the medicine wheel or in traditional prayers and ceremonies.[45]

Thirza Cuthand's two-minute video *Earth Flesh* must be understood within this framework and cosmology. *Earth Flesh* represents the traditional metaphor of earth as flesh by projecting images of the earth onto Thirza's own body. As the video ends, a voice-over asks a provocative and rhetorical question: "There has been a lot of talk about who owns the land, but nobody has asked the question, who does the land own?" This question echoes Native concepts of the people as the "guardians of the land" as well as a traditional ethic based on "balance, respect and reciprocity."[46] By conflating the images of the earth with Cuthand's female body, the video conveys a gendered view of the land. It may also be seen as a gendered statement steeped in irony in that Cuthand may also be questioning both Native and colonial images of the land as female.

The symbiotic relationship between the land and the people is also addressed in Claxton's video *Buffalo Bone China* (1997). In this video, the laws of balance, respect, and reciprocity are not followed, and the demise of the buffalo is visually linked to the demise of a traditional way of life. Through visual montage, Claxton layers images of the buffalo, a non-Native man with a gun, and a Native man who screams but whose voice is not heard. This montage conveys the convergence of themes being explored: the slaughter of the buffalo, the "silent genocide" of First Nations people, and the European imperialism that led to the demise of both. In the next sequence of images, fine bone china is shown, with long Native hair trailing over it as it is lovingly caressed by Native hands. A buffalo head is inset in the frame, conflating the precarious life of the Native man with the death of the buffalo. British imperialist interests are represented by the bone china. The video ends with a Native man opening gates and walking confidently towards the camera, asserting that First Nations people, unlike the buffalo, have survived the effects of colonization and are entering the "frame" of the future.

While there are enormous divisions within and between First Nations communities regarding land claims, there is a national interest, a Spivakian "strategic essentialism," in asserting Native identity, particularly with regard to redress for the effects of colonization.[47] First Nations' assertion of an inherent right to the land becomes a metaphor for sovereignty, and strategies for the implementation of that right range from a militant philosophy of armed resistance to negotiations to lease or sell land in exchange for "inherent rights." In between these positions is a whole range of responses and associations with the land.[48] The films *Buffalo Bone China* and *Earth Flesh* show the centrality of the land as the site of a political battle and also as a metaphor for First Nations people. This conflation of the land, human beings, religion, and government is in opposition to Eurocentric notions of distinct divisions between the environment, the individual, the Church, and the State.[49] In order to "read" First Nations films, one must understand some of the cosmological subtexts from which these metaphors spring.

Post What?

The separation of concepts into binaries such as "pure" and "mixed" or "Cowboys and Indians" is symptomatic of a belief in a mythical purity of identity. The same essentialism is manifest in the term "postcolonial," which implies that there can be a "post" to colonial occupation. This notion demands investigation because, as Stuart Hall and Shohat and Stam point out, there is no "after state" to colonial occupation. If existing economic structures, the governmental apparatus, language, and legal system are remnants of the colonial regime, then it is a misnomer to refer to any "postcolonial" state. Stuart Hall suggests that "colonization" refers to "direct colonial occupation and rule" and that the transition to "postcolonial" is "characterized by independence from direct colonial rule, the formation of new nation-states, forms of economic development, dominated by the growth of indigenous capital and ... the politics which arise from the emergence of powerful local elites managing the contradictory effects of underdevelopment."[50] This definition is particularly problematic for indigenous people who are still in fact "occupied" by the European settlers. In Canada, this issue is most relevant and urgent in British Columbia since the land was not ceded by treaty to the colonizers, and land claims, for the most part, remain unsettled by the courts. Many First Nations artists agree with the Gitxsan artist Doreen Jensen, who states that the term "land claims" "is really a misnomer: We're not really claiming land because it is our land."[51] Jensen suggests that it is more accurate to state that First Nations people are "redefining our boundaries." Within this framework, First Nations people in British Columbia are still living in a colonial regime, and it is incorrect to refer to the current state of affairs for First Nations people as "postcolonial."[52]

British Columbia was one of the last North American areas to be developed, and it has consequently come to symbolize the edge of the frontier. This spatio-geographical definition has resonance as a metaphor for the margins: it has been seen as the West of the West as constructed by the colonial gaze and imagination. The edges, or what Homi Bhabha refers to as the "interstitial state of survival,"[53] are the liminal borderlands from which unsettling ideas are generated. In British Columbia IMAG is challenging Western myths, asserting the vibrancy of creative expression, and meta-phorically pioneering new territory beyond the border of the West. In an-swer to the question posed by Gayatri Spivak, "Can the subaltern speak?"[54] I suggest that the voices of Native women filmmakers in British Columbia assure us that she does speak, that she speaks loudly when necessary, and that she also makes films and videos. In the Canadian West, IMAG is un-settling concepts of the West by challenging the notion that it was ever "won"[55] and by causing its audience to reflect upon the ways in which na-tional identity has been formed. Canadian history and a myriad of identi-ties will continue to be reworked, reconfigured, and informed by the representations of First Nations identities produced through the Indigenous Media Arts Group in its quest to unsettle the West.

Notes

1   Ella Shohat and Robert Stam, *Unthinking Eurocentrism: Multiculturalism and the Media* (Lon-don: Routledge, 1994), 51

2   I am using the terms "First Nations" and "Native" interchangeably throughout this chap-ter. At one point I used the term "Aboriginal." The word "Indian" is a misnomer with derogatory historical connotations and, for that reason, will not be used unless used by a First Nations person.

3   The IMAG collective members are: Marie Baker, Darryl Shawn Bird, Arlene Bowman, Thirza Cuthand, Dana Claxton, Allan W. Hopkins, Cleo Reece, Molly Morin Starlight, and Cease Wyss.

4   These objectives are taken from IMAG 2000, *Aboriginal Film and Video Festival Guide*, No-vember 1-5, Vancouver, British Columbia. Turtle Island is the name for the North Ameri-can continent according to traditional mythology.

5   Through festivals, training workshops, media residencies, and collaborative projects, IMAG seeks "to contribute to the cultural discourse in independent production and to dissemi-nate aboriginal production" (*IMAGeNATION 2000: Aboriginal Film and Video Festival Guide*, November 1-5, Vancouver, BC). The women of IMAG produced Vancouver's first Aborigi-nal Film Festival in 1998 and regularly hold meetings and workshops on television and film production at their office at Video In, Vancouver's largest independent video dis-tributor. Recently, they curated videos and films by First Nations artists that toured West-ern Canada, and they hosted the IMAG-Nations four-day film festival in November 2000, which featured panel discussions on the role of the media in (mis)representing First Nations people.

6   I am using this term, but I recognize the limitations and stagism implied in the hierarchy established by the Eurocentric First World. It is particularly problematic in reference to First Nations in Canada, which is a First World nation.

7   See Jacquelyn Kilpatrick's *Celluloid Indians: Native Americans and Film* (Lincoln and Lon-don: University of Nebraska Press, 1999).

8   Shohat and Stam, *Unthinking Eurocentrism*.

9   They suggest that the Western "inherited a complex intertext embracing classical epic, chivalric romance, Indianist novel, conquest fiction, the paintings of George Catlin and the drawings of Frederic Remington" (ibid., 115).

10 See Daniel Francis, *The Image of the Indian in Canadian Culture* (Vancouver: Arsenal Pulp Press, 1992); or Kilpatrick, *Celluloid Indians*.

11 I have chosen to focus on images of the Native woman in the West, but some of these terms were used to refer to men and non-Natives. Sarah Carter identifies the use of "squaw men," a term that began to have wide circulation in the late 1880s in the Canadian West denoting "men of the lowest social class." See Sarah Carter, "Categories and Terrains of Exclusion: Constructing the Indian Woman in the Early Settlement Era in Western Canada," in *Gender and History*, ed. Joy Parr and Mark Rosenfeld (Toronto: Copp Clark, 1996), 39.

12 Sarah Carter, *Capturing Women: The Manipulation of Cultural Imagery in Canada's Prairie West* (Montreal and Kingston: McGill-Queen's University Press, 1997), xvi.

13 Ibid.

14 Carter, "Categories and Terrains," 43.

15 Ibid., 31-2.

16 Shohat and Stam, *Unthinking Eurocentrism*, 114.

17 Carter, "Categories and Terrains," 31.

18 Kilpatrick, *Celluloid Indians*, xvii. According to Kilpatrick, the mental myth is of inferior intellectual capacity, the sexual is related to oversexualized capacities, and the spiritual stereotypes represent spiritual purity. See also Daniel Francis, *The Imaginary Indian: The Image of the Indian in Canadian Culture* (Vancouver: Arsenal Pulp Press, 1992), 5. Kilpatrick identifies James Fenimore Cooper's *The Leatherstocking Tales* and *The Last of the Mohicans*, as well as Robert Montgomery Bird's *Nick of the Woods* (1837) and various other dime novels of the 1860s, as works that represent Native people as killers.

19 Similarly, Yuval Davis, *Gender and Nation* (London: Sage, 1997), 21, refers to the "genealogical dimension which is constructed around the specific origin of a people," but she does not refer to the mythical origins that become the foundations of national identities.

20 Kilpatrick, *Celluloid Indians*, 22.

21 As Shohat and Stam point out, "Western cinema not only inherited and disseminated colonial discourse but also created a system of domination through monopolistic control of film distribution and exhibition in much of Asia, Africa and Latin America" (Ella Shohat, "Gender and Culture of Empire: Towards a Feminist Ethnography of Cinema," in *Film and Theory*, ed. Robert Stam and Toby Miller [New York: Blackwell, 2000], 669). Francis, *Imaginary Indian*, 79, suggests that, "as with popular fiction, the Americans simply produced Westerns with Mounties in the saddle instead of cowboys" and that "Canadian history was rewritten to satisfy the demands of Hollywood." Further research is needed on the intricate distinctions between the filmic representation of Canadian Mountie versus Native and the American Cowboy versus Indian, in order to determine whether or not Canadian colonial objectives were manifested differently than American objectives in cinematic representations of the Native Other.

22 I am strategically utilizing transnational links between the United States and Canada to draw attention to their difference and also to establish that First Nations are, in fact, nations; therefore their links to other groups may be referred to as nation-to-nation interaction.

23 Yuval-Davis, *Gender and Nation*, 4, describes transversal politics as "a model for feminist politics," which takes into account national as well as other forms of difference amongst women without falling into the trap of identity politics. One might also analyze "transversal links" between First Nations films and other films by Third World women filmmakers or other "Fourth World" peoples. The recent World Indigenous Youth Conferences imply that the youth of today are also intent on forging those transversal links while maintaining the specificity of their own struggles.

24 Frank's Landing, an area of six acres along the Nisqually River in Washington state, was the site of the "Fish Wars." It is named after the Nisqually tribal leader Billy Frank, and, in the 1960s, became a focal point for the assertion of tribal treaty rights central to the sovereignty movement. See Charles Wilkinson, *Messages from Frank's Landing: A Story of Salmon, Treaties and the Indian Way* (Seattle: University of Washington Press, 2000).

25 See Francis, *Imaginary Indian*, regarding depictions of First Nations women.

26 Yuval-Davis, *Gender and Nation*, 4.

27 Yuval-Davis also discusses feminists' representations of "sati" in India.

28 In terms of male violence towards Native women, there is also the case of Vancouver's "barbershop killer." This man was charged with the murder of eleven Native women but

has recently been released from jail. Local First Nations writer Marie Humber-Clements has written a play, entitled *The Unnatural and Accidental Women,* dealing with this tragedy.

29 Another video that Cuthand produced, entitled *Working Baby Dyke Theory: The Diasporic Impact of Cross-Generational Barriers* (1997), deals with lesbian identity in a comedic manner. See also the recent series of essays in Sue-Ellen Jacobs, Wesley Thomas, and Sabine Lang, eds., *Two Spirited People* (Chicago: University of Illinois, 1997).

30 Central to "fitting in" is the requirement that one fulfil essentialist notions of one's racial or ethnic group.

31 Francis, *Imaginary Indian,* 42, also suggests that the revival of interest in the photographs by Edward S. Curtis, which were published between 1907 and 1930 in a series of twenty books entitled *The North American Indian,* was due to people being "seduced by the nostalgic images of a spiritual people, innocent of the polluting machinery, existing in what appeared to be a pristine state." We know now that many of these photos were manipulated and did not represent First Nations people accurately, but the revival of interest in the photos during the hippie movement is what Francis is addressing here.

32 "Kookum" is Cree for "grandmother." Many representations of the kookum in film have presented the peaceful traditionalist. While these kookums do exist, I want to draw attention to the overrepresentation of this figure.

33 By this I mean the grandmother who lives in the imagination. Many Canadian "wanna-be Indians" refer to their great-great-grandmother who was an Indian princess. While Canadian history may attest to some of the imaginary kookum mythologies as being true, invocations of this type of pseudo-genealogy are a part of Canadian mythology and suggestive of an element of fear and envy regarding connectedness to First Nations genealogy.

34 These are my own terms. I am referring to the political debates of the 1980s and 1990s in which rigid and fixed notions formed the basis of beliefs about identity, itself considered to be a fixed, immutable, essentialist category. Much of that debate was undermined by ontological shifts theorized by postmodernists and postcolonial theorists. Yuval-Davis, *Gender and Nation,* refers to Bhabha and contrasts his notions of the hybrid with the model presented by Gloria Anzaldua, claiming that Bhabha's model is a "response-oriented model of hybridity," whereas Anzaldua's model focuses on the community of hybrids, suggesting that the "hybrid's refusal of individuation empowers them to agency as a community."

35 Using the same colour symbolism, Drew Hayden Taylor refers to himself as a "Pink man," or as an "Occasion," a cross between Ojibway and Caucasian. In "Pretty Like a White Boy," in *An Anthology of Canadian Literature in English,* ed. Daniel David Moses and Terry Goldie (Oxford: Oxford University Press, 1992), 330.

36 Shohat and Stam, *Unthinking Eurocentrism,* 42.

37 Ibid.

38 Ibid., 41.

39 One example is evident in the film *New Orleans Black Indians,* which focuses on the mixing of traditions and blood that has resulted in elaborate Mardi Gras costumes that are reconstructions of traditional First Nations regalia, synthesizing Cherokee, West African, and Haitian traditions. This film represents the "cross-appropriation" of specific traditions that are incorporated or understood within another nation and become a syncretic amalgamation of both worlds. As for *The Red Paper,* the title itself is an inversion of the controversial White Paper of Pierre Trudeau's 1969 government, which proposed to end Indian status, abolish the Department of Indian Affairs, and repeal the Indian Act. It was retracted in 1971 due, in part, to Native opposition.

40 This type of film can be understood within the context of recent work on the trope of the "cannibal" as identified in Francis Barker, Peter Hulme, and Margaret Iversen, eds., *Cannibalism and the Colonial World* (Cambridge: Cambridge University Press, 1998).

41 Stuart Hall, "Cultural Identity and Cinematic Representation," in *Film and Theory* (Cambridge: Blackwell, 2000), 711.

42 Judith Butler's notions of "drag" as a parody of gender identity suggests that Native identity, based upon cultural fabrications of "Indianness," is a double inversion with multiple encodings as the "original" itself is the construction of a European fantasy. As she speaks of

drag as gender parody, perhaps the conscious use of Indianness may also be seen as a form of "race parody" or racial drag.

43 More work is needed on notions of the "double consciousness" that is experienced in being Native and having to form awareness of the simulacra that are supposed to present your identity and the manner in which an authentic or real self is formed despite the hegemonic stereotypes of "Indianness."

44 Augie Fleras and Jean Leonard, eds., *The Nations Within: Aboriginal-State Relations in Canada, the United States and New* Zealand (Toronto: Oxford University Press, 1989), 22.

45 Sun Bear and Wabun, *The Medicine Wheel: Earth Astrology* (New York: Prentice Hall, 1980), 2-3.

46 See Harold Cardinal, "A Canadian What the Hell It's All About," in *An Anthology of Canadian Literature in English,* ed. Daniel David Moses and Terry Goldie (Oxford: Oxford University Press, 1992), 190. Cardinal suggests that First Nations relationships to the land are "a religious-cultural definition of being Canadian" and that the Cree word that expresses being from this land included the concept of guardianship and responsibilities towards the land.

47 Francis, *Imaginary Indian,* summarizes the fieldwork of Diamond Jenness in the 1920s (published in 1932 as *The Indians of Canada*) and concludes that "the contact experience was totally negative for almost all native groups in Canada." On the socio-cultural impact of colonization on Aboriginal nations within Canada, see also Fleras and Leonard, *Nations Within.*

48 More work needs to be done on representations of the land in First Nations narratives, both film and fiction.

49 In one of Claxton's early performances she represented the centrality of the land by constructing herself as a tree throughout the performance, which dealt with nature, epistemology, and ontological concerns literally framed by the conflation of the human (Claxton as actor) and the land (signified by the tree costume).

50 Stuart Hall, "When Was 'the-Post-Colonial'? Thinking at the Limit," in *The Postcolonial Question: Common Skies, Divided Horizons,* ed. Iain Chambers and Lydia Curti (London: Routledge, 1996), 247.

51 Linda Bell and Carol Williams, "Interview with Doreen Jensen," *BC Studies* 115/6 (Autumn/Winter 1997/8): 294.

52 Shohat and Stam, *Unthinking Eurocentrism,* 39, pose the question: "When exactly, then, does the postcolonial begin and what are the relationships between its diverse beginnings?" They suggest that the use of the term is problematic because it "collapses diverse chronologies."

53 Homi Bhabha interviews Trinh T. Minh-ha in Trinh T. Minh-ha, *Interval* (London: Routledge, 1999), 27.

54 Gayatri Spivak, *A Critique of Postcolonial Reason: Toward a History of a Vanishing Press* (Cambridge, MA: Harvard University Press, 1999), 269.

55 For an examination of the ideological manifestations of this belief, see Shohat and Stam, *Unthinking Eurocentrism.*

Filmography

(N.d.) *Earth Flesh.* Direction: Thirza Cuthand
(N.d.) *If Only I Were an Indian.* Direction: John Paskievich; production: NFB
(N.d.) *Word for Word.* Direction: Ruth Cuthand and Elizabeth Mackenzie with Thirza Cuthand
1983 *New Orleans Black Indians.* Faces of Culture Series, Province of British Columbia
1986 *Doctor, Lawyer, Indian Chief.* Direction: Carol Geddes; production: NFB
1987 *... and the Word was God.* Direction: Ruby Truly
1991 *Women in the Shadows.* Direction: Christine Walsh; production: NFB
1994 *I Want to Know Why.* Direction: Dana Claxton
1996 *The Red Paper.* Direction: Dana Claxton
1997 *Buffalo Bone China.* Direction: Dana Claxton

1996   *Colonization: The Second Coming.* Direction: Thirza Cuthand
1997   *Working Baby Dyke Theory: The Diasporic Impact of Cross-Generational Barriers.* Direction: Thirza Cuthand
1998   *Singing Our Stories.* Direction: Annie Frazier Henry
1998   *Keepers of the Fire.* Direction: Christine Walsh; production: NFB
1998   *Red Power Women.* Direction: Cleo Reece
2000   *Indians and Who.* Direction: Dorothy Christian

38   Leaving Gender Aside: The Legacy of Studio D?
Diane Burgess

Variously described as "a National Treasure" and "a kind of ghetto for women at the NFB," Studio D has received both praise for its "'tradition of passionate, provocative filmmaking'" and criticism for being "out of touch ... with the feminist film community."[1] These conflicting assessments reflect the challenges that confront the process of measuring the achievements of the women's studio, which combined the seemingly contradictory goals of creating a separate space for women filmmakers and increasing the participation of creative talent within the National Film Board's (NFB's) overall institutional structure. Established in 1974, Studio D became the first government-funded feminist film unit in the world and, over the course of two decades, "produced over 125 films and won more than 100 international awards, including three Academy Awards."[2] Encompassing a variety of forms and formats, such as documentary, multimedia, and short films, the studio's repertoire focuses on the expression of women's perspectives. In 1986, a restructuring program sought to integrate members of the permanent staff into other departments while, at the same time, opening up space for the articulation of a more diverse range of women's voices. Despite its achievements, Studio D was closed in 1996 as part of a move towards a leaner, more streamlined, NFB.

The challenge of assessing the legacy of Studio D arises in part from the difficulty of demarcating the boundaries of its practices within a national cultural institution. In particular, the desire to foster professional development within a segregated environment, accompanied by the goal of achieving equity within the film board as a whole, appears to generate a contradictory, even redundant, institutional structure. The process of balancing difference and equity raises questions concerning how resources should be allocated and how success should be measured. At the same time, the studio's philosophy centred on a liberal feminist perception of unity in difference that exerted a reductive pressure on the shifting definitions of feminism. Initially, with this chapter, I had intended to explore the influence of the NFB's feminist unit on current filmmaking practice. However, a question mark found its way onto the end of my title, and my research took a different turn. What does it mean when the legacy of Studio D becomes a question? Is it that the legacy is questionable? or is it, rather, that the legacy remains only partially understood? What emerges from further reflection is a consideration of the complexity of approaching the regulation of equity and diversity through cultural policy.

Feminism and Cultural Policy

Even though Studio D marks a key moment in the intersection of feminism and film policy, the sparseness of writing on this relationship, especially within the Canadian context, has left the terms of the debate unclear. Studio D was founded during a period when women's issues occupied a central position on both national and international policy agendas. For example, 1970 saw the tabling of the Report from the Royal Commission on the Status of Women, while in 1972 it was announced that 1975 would be International Women's Year. However, Chris Scherbarth cautions against attributing the studio's genesis solely to the federal government's "active endorsement of the United Nations' objectives."[3] In addition to the existence of a favourable political climate, Scherbarth cites the lobbying efforts of filmmakers such as Kathleen Shannon and notes that the idea for a women's studio had been discussed as early as 1971. The origins of the women's studio can also be traced to the NFB's Challenge for Change program, a grassroots project that sought to represent the unrepresented.[4]

During the early 1970s, as part of Challenge for Change, Kathleen Shannon produced and directed a series of documentaries entitled *Working Mothers*. Concurrently, in the francophone unit, Anne Claire Poirier produced a program of five one-hour films for a series entitled *En tant que femmes,* which was similarly designed to probe women's issues. The success of these series encouraged Shannon to lobby for the creation of a separate women's studio. In spite of the impossibility of securing a separate budget, Studio D was formed and Kathleen Shannon became the first woman to head an NFB film unit since the Second World War. Poirier, however, rejected the offer to head a francophone women's film unit. Scherbarth notes that Poirier's concern was that such meagre funding would marginalize women's work;[5] instead, Poirier continued to lobby for funding that would be equal to that of other French productions. As a result, there would be no French counterpart for Studio D until October 1986, when Studio B (Regards de femmes) was organised under Josée Beaudet.

As the executive producer of Studio D from its inception in 1974 until her resignation in 1986, Kathleen Shannon helped to shape the unit's mandate, and it is her feminist vision that informs its legacy. Shannon attributed being chosen to head the studio to the success of the *Working Mothers* series and the valuable insight that she gained during production. The research for the series included distributing a questionnaire to the NFB's female staff that "primarily concerned questions of salary, job satisfaction and perceived discrimination."[6] Discovering that she was not alone in her workplace experiences, Shannon continued to lobby the NFB's administration for the creation of a separate studio devoted to making films by, for, and about women. Since Shannon had watched men whom she had trained pass her on the corporate ladder, receiving salaries that exceeded her own,[7] she believed that a "'separationist' response"[8] comprised the best approach. The resulting collective environment would encourage the training of women filmmakers while also empowering them to take part in the decision-making process; in other words, a separate space would allow women's perspectives to thrive.

Thus, in many ways, approaching the complexity of Studio D's legacy involves looking at numerous interpretations of the idea of "leaving gender aside." Not only did the studio seek to create a separate space for women, but its practices were eventually left aside in favour of a more integrationist approach to equity. The concept of leaving difference aside was brought to my attention most forcefully at a roundtable discussion that accompanied the launch of Michael Dorland's book, *So Close to the State/s: The Emergence of Canadian Feature Film Policy,* at the 1998 Film Studies Association of Canada annual meeting. In response to a question concerning the positioning of gender in his study, Dorland remarked that he wanted to "leave gender aside." The next day the comment became fodder for the Martin Walsh Memorial Lecture, "Cinemas, Nations, Masculinities," as Thomas Waugh challenged "the traditional definition of the 'national' in terms of gender and cultural hegemonies."[9] Indeed, issues of gender are also notably left aside in Manjunath Pendakur's *Canadian Dreams and American Control* and in Ted Madger's *Canada's Hollywood.* As indispensable as these texts are to the study of Canadian film policy, difficulties arise from the extent to which they both conceal and maintain "silences around gender."[10]

Dorland employs Foucault's concept of "governmentality" in order to explore "the ways in which the conduct of an ensemble of individuals [finds] itself implicated in the exercise of power."[11] This methodology involves examining the limitative process – the shifting relationship between knowledge and policy that privileges certain aspects over others – through which the administrative state intersects with the emerging discourse of the Canadian feature film industry. For the purposes of Dorland's study, what emerges is a focus on economics, feature filmmaking, and the growth of the private sector. Yet, despite his interest in the "conceptual difficulties" that plague the "writing of the film history of Canada,"[12] Dorland does not explore all of the limiting boundaries of policy development; instead, he replicates the common critical agenda of privileging a focus on the economics of the development of cultural industries over a consideration of the diversity of cultural production, which would necessarily include addressing issues of difference. As a result, the question Alison Beale poses remains: "How well [can we] understand the practices that we study – the economy, politics, cultural policy, regulation – if we fail to question the artificial boundaries of these activities and the silences around gender in relation to them[?]"[13] Dorland's neo-Foucauldian analysis carries an implicit male perspective in that feminist film practice is not included as a term in the debate.

It is important to avoid over-simplification here, since a variety of factors contributed to the desire to foster a fiction feature film industry in Canada – a complex interaction of nationalist, economic, and cultural goals. However, the majority of the players involved in this convergence of factors were men. Hence, a distinction needs to be made between consciously writing women out of the history of cultural policy, as in the case of Dorland, Madger, and Pendakur's studies, and merely perpetuating a pre-existing discursive practice (although many would argue that both procedures generate a similar result).

Measuring Success

In "A Brief History of Women Filmmakers in Canada," Kay Armatage sums up Studio D not only as "a success story," but also as "a kind of ghetto for women at the NFB, left behind in the 1980's move into the production of more high-profile feature films."[14] Due to funding constraints and its community-driven focus, Studio D's productions often reflect an alternative to mainstream commercial fare. In response to a tiny budget for the 1974-5 fiscal year, which would not allow for the making of a film, funds were directed to a training project called *Just a Minute*, for which twenty-seven one-minute films were made by women from across the country.[15] Similarly, in 1989, for the studio's fifteenth anniversary, filmmakers from across Canada were invited to submit proposals for *Five Feminist Minutes*, a project designed to "open up the studio to a more diverse group of 'voices.'"[16]

Insufficient value would be placed upon these types of collaborative projects within the context of a critical and policy focus that emphasized gaining access to a theatrical audience. For example, a 1998 Department of Canadian Heritage publication entitled *Culture and Heritage: Making Room for Canada's Voices* focuses on cultural production in both national and economic terms by highlighting the "market share of [domestic] content ... in [each of] the cultural industries."[17] Problems associated with foreign dominance in the area of film distribution merit specific attention in a subsequent section, "Seldom Showing at a Theatre Near You," which notes that Canadian films take up less than 5 percent of screen time in Canadian cinemas.[18] It is interesting to note that, while the 1999 *Report of the Feature Film Advisory*

Committee cites the goal of increasing screen time to 10 percent by the year 2004,[19] the subsequent *From Script to Screen* policy document has switched to the goal of "captur[ing] 5% of the domestic box office in five years."[20] Despite the shift from screen time to domestic box office revenue, in each instance access to the mainstream theatrical audience serves as the official marker of the health of national culture.

In her assessment of Studio D's impact, Armatage notes that "women remain, 50 years after the founding of the NFB under Grierson, making short documentary and children's films which have lower budgets, smaller crews, and less opportunity for financial return."[21] This vision of the studio's legacy clearly draws its criteria of value from the realm of economics while also placing primary importance on the preoccupation with screen time. Similarly, two major articles reflecting upon the fiftieth anniversary of the NFB[22] focus almost exclusively on its involvement with feature filmmaking; in fact, neither article addresses the contributions of Studio D. While Armatage's comments do adequately reflect a measure of disappointment and frustration with the lack of involvement of the women's studio in the higher prestige projects that gain access to theatrical audiences, she overlooks the studio's key contributions to national culture. In fact, the perception of Studio D as a ghetto for women filmmakers may be more informative about the discourses surrounding Canadian cinema than about the value of a separatist cultural practice.

At the same time, there is the troubling implication that the film forms used by Studio D carry less value than do those of the feature film industry, almost suggesting a split between film with a social purpose and films with an entertainment purpose. While both of these categories provide authentication, only the latter carries the financial promise of mainstream success. Furthermore, there is a pejorative edge to Armatage's assessment that relegates the studio's productions to the lesser category of craft. The question remains, then, as to where exactly notions of artistic diversity, or alternative practice, find currency within this discursive economy. Although Armatage's desire to remove barriers to participation is laudable, invoking the dominant evaluation criteria works, conversely, to further marginalize the cultural work women have accomplished. In other words, negatively judging the studio's continued use of non-feature formats entails taking part in, rather than challenging, dominant critical paradigms.

Given that the shifting rationalities of governance constitute a "protracted, mobile negotiation between the limits of agenda and non-agenda,"[23] it would seem necessary to remain aware of the arbitrary nature of this positioning. As such, in addition to seeking equity for women in the feature film industry, the imbalance could be rectified through access to improved distribution for a wider range of formats. At the same time, the perceived value of this cultural work could be addressed by shifting the criteria of canonical value to encompass the actual diversity of filmmaking. To a certain extent, arguing for a shift in the criteria of value is significant only in the realm of the analysis and not for the production of films, since increased analysis of a variety of cultural forms is of little practical use to filmmakers unless it stimulates a shift in market value; but a sustained increase in critical interest could, potentially, encourage such a shift.

The study of cultural policy as it affects women should also benefit the questioning of definitional boundaries, particularly within the context of a multicultural country like Canada. As such, Studio D provides a case study for government intervention with regard to regulating diversity in cultural practice. Through a process that can be described in terms of "leaving gender aside," the studio provided a separate space for women, though tensions would arise between the objective of articulating difference and the overarching nationalist goals of a federal cultural institution.[24] However, the potential contribution of examining the studio as a case study for cultural policy is compromised by the reductive focus of existing explorations of Canadian cinema and their predisposition to marginalize the discussion of difference.

Issues of canonical value contribute to a segregation of knowledge that is most literally displayed by the library catalogue. Two research sources for this chapter – *Gendering the Nation: Canadian Women's Cinema* and *Changing Focus: The Future of Women in the Canadian Film and Television Industry* – are indexed, based on the Library of Congress system, under PN1995.9W, with books about women and film, rather than under PN1995.3C, with the other general books on Canadian film, thereby indicating that these books have more to do with the category of "women" than they do with the history of the national film industry. In his discussion of the writing of alternative canons, Thomas Waugh notes that "the practice of 'leaving' women's and even more marginal cinemas for 'non-national' categorization has hardly shifted ... [and] has been pointedly symptomatic of a desperate avoidance to acknowledge the shifting demographics and proliferating diversity of Canadian cinemas."[25]

The cataloguing of these texts separately from the remainder of the general books about the history of Canadian film exerts a limitative pressure on the discussion of national cinema. Given that one of the objectives of *Gendering the Nation* is to rethink "paradigms of relations between cinema, the nation, and gender,"[26] it would seem logical for the book to be located amongst the traditional approaches that the editors hope to challenge. Instead, the chances of a student or researcher stumbling upon this book, without specifically searching for it, are reduced. Similarly, following the closure of the women's studio, articles exploring its philosophy and achievements, while also protesting its loss, were published in feminist journals such as *Herizons* and *Kinesis* but not in journals with a general film or communications focus.

The former's readership would orient this debate within the realm of women's studies, whereas an article published in a journal such as the *Canadian Journal of Communication* is immediately integrated into the larger realm of cultural policy analysis. This point is not meant to belittle the academic achievements of gender studies but, rather, to indicate that the more conservative constituents, who would likely be most in need of rethinking their perspective (but least inclined to), will probably never encounter gender studies arguments in the first place. As a result, the process of shifting dominant paradigms becomes hampered and, to a certain extent, is relegated to the margins. Alison Beale invokes concepts of legitimacy and authority with her reminder that gender "operates not as a binary scheme of classification ... but as a hierarchy."[27] From this perspective, segregation of knowledge actually denies these texts a voice within the study of Canadian film history.

Measuring Difference

Over the course of twenty-two years, Studio D would produce more than 100 films in an environment shaped by the mandate "to address women's information needs and facilitate the framing of women's perspectives through the medium of film and to provide an environment of mutual support in which to do so."[28] Scherbarth explains that, in contrast to the NFB's other production units, Studio D's practices emerged from a particular philosophical positioning rather than from a focus on specific regional centres, forms, or genres. The other exception was Studio E, or the Challenge for Change unit, which was similarly "centred on a philosophy."[29] Studio D's philosophy focused on the concept of difference by stressing the "otherness" of the female voice; this means that the cinematic voice that addressed audiences stressed the idea that "'we' were the women and 'they' were the men."[30]

Although cultivated within a segregated collective environment, the studio's goals extended beyond the unit's boundaries with the intent of increasing the overall creative participation of women at the NFB. As such, these goals reflect a type of "separatism" alongside a desire for equity. The studio undertook training programs, hired apprentices, and contracted work out to freelance filmmakers in order to foster a strong base of creative talent. Shannon also built upon the legacy of the Challenge for Change program's interaction with the audience. Films were intended to be screened by a community audience rather than to have wide diffusion via television. Shannon explains that "many of our films did not just report on existing social movements but were part of their impetus."[31] For example, *Not a Love*

Story: A Film about Pornography (Klein 1982) not only "sensitised thousands of Canadians to the problem of the sexual exploitation of women," but also marked an important contribution to the anti-pornography debate.[32] In addition, Studio D was the only NFB unit to employ a full-time audience researcher. By maintaining direct participatory contact with the audience, as Scherbarth notes, "Studio D has served as a model for an alternate approach to determining filmmaking priorities."[33]

Probably the best known titles from the studio's repertoire are Bonnie Sherr Klein's *Not a Love Story* and Terri Nash's *If You Love This Planet,* both produced in 1982. With other popular titles, like *I'll Find a Way* (Shaffer 1978) and *Speaking Our Peace* (Klein and Nash 1985), Studio D films are "in greater demand than the average NFB film." "The forty English-language originals produced exclusively by the Studio as of March 1985 (discounting, therefore, co-productions and sponsored films) have been booked twice as frequently as a matched random sample of NFB fare."[34] And so begins the numbers game that dominates not only the limited amount of writing about Studio D, but also the more general discussion of the participation of women at the NFB. For example, to return momentarily to the decision finally to establish a women's studio in the French program in 1986, 1987 figures show that women made up one-third of the anglophone filmmakers but only one-fifth of the francophone filmmaking staff.[35]

In "Understanding the Numbers," Pat Armstrong argues that "these numbers hide some very real segregation within the Film Board."[36] Specifically, women occupy significantly fewer of the senior managerial positions than do men, and the women in senior positions are more likely to be on term contracts (i.e., they have less secure positions) than do their male counterparts.[37] Yet Armstrong also notes that closing Studio D resulted in the disappearance of "over half the female producers ... but almost all the men would stay."[38] This observation highlights the extent to which Studio D became a ghetto for women filmmakers. What emerges from a perusal of the statistics, which are often also accompanied by an array of graphs and charts showing how much of the pie belongs to women, is an overwhelming emphasis on a quantitatively measurable women's presence. Thus, notions of equity begin to overwhelm the less easily measured idea of difference.

In an interesting policy parallel, the guidelines for obtaining Canadian government funding measure Canadian content according to the nationality (in terms of both citizenship and country of residence) of the creative talent involved with the project, as though the cultural value of a film could be assessed by doing a Canadian head count. Similarly, what gets lost in the numbers game is a qualitative measure of the contribution of Studio D. This contribution includes the community focus of programming as well as the collective training environment fostered by Kathleen Shannon. According to the qualitative findings of the *Equality and Access* study, "women find

Dr. Helen Caldicott, in Terri Nash's *If You Love This Planet*
(1982), courtesy of NFB of Canada

'women only,' or at least 'majority women' situations to be preferable in
the initial stages of training."[39] Prepared by Bonnie Diamond and Francine
Fournier, in order to assist with the implementation of federal employment
equity legislation, this 1987 report recommends key roles for Studio D in
the areas of training and technical advice.

Leaving Difference Aside

One of the first steps towards the demise of Studio D occurred with a restructuring plan implemented in 1989 under the guidance of Executive Producer Rina Fraticelli. At that time, permanent staff were reassigned to other
studios, and the production budget became a source of funding for freelance filmmakers. The NFB's *Annual Report, 1988-1989*, describes the rationale for this restructuring in terms of a "move to integrate NFB women
filmmakers and their perspective [sic] into the drama and documentary studios."[40] As well, prior to these changes, access to government resources had
become increasingly difficult for independent producers and directors. Although a *Cinema Canada* article refers to the Studio as "another victim" of
"reduced government funding,"[41] the restructuring does demonstrate a return to a community-driven focus that had previously been a hallmark of
the studio's production practices: "all the films made before 1979, in fact,
were made by freelancers."[42]

As part of the repositioning of Studio D, Fraticelli also inaugurated the
New Initiatives in Film (NIF) program. Designed to address the diversity of

women's experiences, the five-year professional development program fostered the "increased participation of Aboriginal women and women of colour ... through internships, apprenticeships, and scholarships."[43] Thus, as a natural continuation of the studio's original mandate, institutional support would be offered to provide for a voicing of difference that would adequately reflect Canada's multicultural fabric. Fraticelli even made the following analogy: "'as Studio D to the NFB, so NIF to Studio D.'"[44] Her statement further evokes the connection of Studio D to Challenge for Change. Ironically, however, all three of these projects have generated quite similar results – results that constitute less than encouraging indications of entrenched systemic resistance to difference.

Initiated in 1967, the Challenge for Change program sought "to encourage experimental approaches to the use of film and television in the fostering of social change."[45] A key aspect of this documentary project entailed including the subjects in the production process so as to minimize "the possibility of distortion or exploitation."[46] However, it is important to note the actual limit of the subjects' involvement in the making of these films. Although the proposal for *You Are on Indian Land* (Ransen 1969) for example, originated within the Mohawk community and the production employed a First Nations crew,[47] both the producer and the director worked for the NFB. Issues of voice become complicated as a result, given that neither Mort Ransen nor George Stoney is First Nations. In other words, regardless of the participation of those directly involved with the conflict on the St. Regis reserve, overall control of the project remained outside the community. As a result, despite the goal of encouraging social change, the program comprised an incomplete attempt to give voice to disenfranchised groups by ultimately not allowing them to determine the final structure, or positioning, of their own perspective.

David Barker Jones notes an additional limiting pressure on the potential of the Challenge for Change project. Jones concludes that films could be "highly critical" as long as their subject matter did not comprise a "threat to the fabric of Canadian society."[48] As long as the focus remained on barriers and inequities encountered by minorities or disenfranchised groups, then there would be little threat to the functioning of the mainstream sectors of society. As a result, certain proposals, such as one about militant trade unions in Quebec, were rejected by the Interdepartmental Committee. Consisting of representatives from different federal government departments, the committee would meet to "generate jointly the parameters of a given story-line or idea,"[49] thereby further distancing production decisions from the minority groups in question. Even though the Challenge for Change process positioned the disenfranchised more as objects than subjects with regard to the decision-making aspects of production, the films did allow for the articulation of difference and the challenging of social barriers. Indeed, individual films contributed to improvements for specific groups. Nevertheless, contained occurrences reinforce the marginalization of minority groups by not extending their reach to the larger social infrastructure.

Similarly, Elizabeth Anderson finds that the NIF project did not lead to substantive structural changes within Studio D. Despite the valuable contribution of films such as *Sisters in the Struggle* (Brand and Stikeman 1991), which explores the experiences of Black Canadian women, there was no real power sharing with women of colour. Given that the permanent staff of filmmakers at Studio D was reassigned with the shift to a focus on freelance contracts, questions arise as to the potential for the staff recruitment that Anderson claims was lacking. If the majority of employment opportunities offered by Studio D consisted of contract positions for independent filmmakers, then it would appear that NIF allowed for the equitable distribution of these contracts. Yet transitory jobs do not alter the fundamental make-up of the NFB's production management structure.

Fraticelli's description of the relationship of NIF to Studio D carries more significant implications than she may have intended. Ultimately, NIF replicates the positioning of Studio D within the NFB, just as Studio D echoes the legacy of Challenge for Change. The complex, contradictory achievements of these three projects can be summed up in terms of the creation of *images* of diversity[50] or, in the earliest case, social change. Although a space was created for the articulation of difference, that space remained separate and, thereby, contained in relation to mainstream cultural practice. At the same time, as it secured its institutional standing, Studio D became resistant to the types of structural change that its founder initially sought. Anderson accurately interprets Studio D's project as "both interventionist and additive" in that, despite initially allowing for greater representation, it ultimately "reproduced the race- and class-based hierarchies present in the larger society."[51]

Additional criticisms focus on the continued reliance upon a conventional documentary approach, and a tendency to seek "unity in diversity,"[52] that created a growing distance between the women's studio and the activities of the feminist film community. Anderson links Studio D's liberal feminism to the NFB's liberal humanism and notes that both, in turn, contributed to a discourse of national identity that stresses the presence of shared elements regardless of diverse experiences. Jacqueline Levitin notes that the studio was not oriented towards "theoretical experimentation."[53] An exception to these tendencies can be found in films such as *Forbidden Love: The Unashamed Stories of Lesbian Lives* (Fernie/Weissman 1992), which contradicts the studio's "didactic aesthetics" and embraces diversity within the women's community.[54] Thus, it can be concluded that the potential did exist for shifts in Studio D's philosophy and practices and that the segregation of feminist filmmaking did not necessarily have to result in a limiting pressure on the articulation of diverse views.

Chris Scherbarth may have foreseen the fate of Studio D when, in 1987, she wrote that "the rhetoric of the present management has implicitly followed the line that an expanded Studio D would materialize only at the expense of the fuller integration of women throughout the NFB."[55] A 1989 review of the NFB noted that the number of films produced on women's issues disproportionately exceeded audience demand.[56] Unfortunately, the study does not clarify the distinction between a women's issue and a women's perspective on an issue. In fact, it is suggested that the NFB's own cataloguing of films may mirror the cataloguing of books mentioned earlier. For example, a documentary made by a woman director about environmental issues may have been counted as a woman's film rather than as an environmental film, thereby skewing the results. Nonetheless, in the face of increasing budget restrictions, the need for staff reductions, and the requirements of equity legislation, Studio D was closed in 1996 as part of the move towards a leaner, more streamlined, NFB.

The decision to abandon the studio system emerged from the findings of the Mandate Review Committee (Juneau Report) in combination with the NFB's concurrent drafting of a Year 2000 Action Plan. The Juneau Report cites "pervasive structural problems at the NFB," including uncertainty about its role and inefficient use of resources.[57] Taking into account the Juneau Report's recommendations, the NFB's strategic action plan requires increased reliance on freelance personnel, offers revised mission and vision statements, and restructures the program branches into program streams – documentary, animation, children, multimedia. A subsection concerning equity issues shares the responsibility for equity between all NFB producers and calls for special mandate teams to "monitor the progress."[58]

Leaving Gender Aside?

I do not offer a comprehensive critique of the legacy of either Studio D or of the NIF project; instead, rather than contributing to an endless listing of shortcomings, I have chosen to focus on particular aspects of Studio D's legacy that provide insight into the relationship between government regulation and feminist filmmaking. Kathleen Shannon readily admitted that Studio D could never satisfy the numerous possible visions of, and approaches to, feminist filmmaking. Reflecting upon her experiences as executive producer, she felt that detractors both inside and outside the studio "sometimes seemed bent on destroying it rather than building what they needed *in addition to* Studio D."[59] An exhaustive critique would resemble the "numbers game" by merely generating a series of distractions that inhibits, or overwhelms, attempts to discuss what can be learned from Studio D.

The NFB's strategic action plan for the new millennium offers a politically correct but somewhat soft-edged vision for approaching the articulation of difference. Specifically, the document states that "NFB productions should reflect through their content and personnel the diversity of Canadian society."[60] The legacy of Studio D – locating a feminist filmmaking collective within a federal cultural institution – demonstrates the effects of adopting an integrationist approach.[61] Christina Gabriel notes that one of the key limitations of the integrationist model lies in a "particular dynamic" that arises between the mainstream and minority group, involving cultural difference as constructed from the perspective of the latter.[62] The mainstream is positioned to be merely tolerant of the goals and achievements of the minority group, without having to engage in substantive change.

While Gabriel's discussion refers to issues surrounding multiculturalism, the founding of Studio D effectively amounted to segregating women's filmmaking as a minority enterprise within the NFB. Conversely, the assessment of Studio D's achievements carries significance for government funding of diversity in cultural practice. Since Studio D ultimately entrenched the pre-existing gender hierarchy at the NFB and proceeded to solidify an ethnic hierarchy through the NIF, the choices facing cultural policy become increasingly complicated. Although the NIF allowed for the professional development of women of colour, problems arise when one faces the reality that these contract positions would not necessarily lead to changes in the management structure at the NFB. However, with an increase in the number of qualified candidates, equity policy could assist with long-term structural change.

At the same time, as noted in the 1987 *Equality and Access* study, the initial training environment has an important qualitative impact on professional development.[63] Although the study recommends seeking the input of Studio D with regard to the creation of women's training programs, implementing its equity directives would create a level of institutional redundancy that is not addressed by the recommendations: issues would arise concerning the overlap between the training programs of Studio D and the NFB. Furthermore, the effects of the subsequent transition from the women's studio to integration within the board's other production units would need to be addressed in greater detail. As noted earlier, the study cites a greater percentage of both women directors and producers in the English programming branch than in the French programming branch. In 1985-6, for example, 29 percent of the films in the English branch were produced by women, whereas only 1 percent of the French branch's films had a women producer. This shows that, even though these women producers were concentrated in Studio D, numbers still point to the achievements of the "separationist" approach.[64] Rather than opting for the integration at the expense of separatism, the challenge may lie in achieving the correct balance between the two.

Perhaps the framing of my research by that accidental question mark was shrewdly appropriate. The legacy of Studio D remains difficult to assess in all of its complexity, especially when many necessary terms are either excluded or undervalued. Alison Beale argues for "new visions for cultural policy [that] can be created by advocating for alternative values."[65] A repositioning within the main/maelstrom of policy analysis could encompass the realities of Canadian cultural production as well as the challenges facing the articulation of diverse voices. In the meantime, what remains is the tentative phrasing of the aforementioned component of the NFB's new vision statement. The phrase "NFB productions should" admits its potential shortcomings in advance by avoiding the stronger "will." If the NFB is to (continue to) reflect the diversity of Canadian experience, then it will be interesting to see how difference manages to assert itself effectively within equity. Or will difference, like gender, continue to be left aside in the realm of governmentality?

Notes

1   National Film Board of Canada, *Annual Report, 1984-1985* (Montreal: Communication Services, NFB, 1985), 9; Kay Armatage, "A Brief History of Women Filmmakers in Canada," in Toronto Women in Film and Television (organization), *Changing Focus: The Future for Women in the Canadian Film and Television Industry* (Toronto: University of Toronto Press, 1991), 137; Chris Scherbarth, "Canada's Studio D: A Women's Room with an International Reputation," *Canadian Woman's Studies* 8, 1 (1987), 25; Elizabeth Anderson, "Studio D's Imagined Community: From Development (1974) to Realignment (1986-1990)," in *Gendering the Nation: Canadian Women's Cinema,* ed. Kay Armatage, Kass Banning, Brenda Longfellow, and Janine Marchessault (Toronto: University of Toronto Press, 1999), 48.
2   Cheryl Cornacchia, "Kathleen Shannon's Legacy," *Montreal Gazette,* 25 August 1997, E8.
3   Chris Scherbarth, "Studio D of the National Film Board of Canada: Seeing Ourselves through Women's Eyes," MA thesis (Ottawa: Carleton University, 1986), 10.
4   I have summarised the details in the next paragraph, as presented in Gary Evans, *In the National Interest: A Chronicle of the National Film Board of Canada from 1949 to 1989* (Toronto: University of Toronto Press, 1991), 210-2.
5   Scherbarth, "Studio D," 25.
6   Ibid., 17.
7   Jacqueline Levitin, "Contrechamp sur les démarches de quelques réalisatrices," in *Femmes et cinéma québécois,* ed. Louise Carrière (Montreal: Boréal Express, 1983), 226.
8   Scherbarth, "Studio D," 1.
9   Thomas Waugh, "Cinemas, Nations, Masculinities: The Martin Walsh Memorial Lecture, 1998," *Canadian Journal of Film Studies* 8, 1 (Spring 1999), 18.
10 Alison Beale, "Cultural Policy as a Technology of Gender," in *Ghosts in the Machine: Women and Cultural Policy in Canada and Australia,* ed. Alison Beale and Annette Van Den Bosch (Toronto: Garamond Press, 1998), 233.
11 Michael Dorland, *So Close to the State/s: The Emergence of Canadian Feature Film Policy* (Toronto: University of Toronto Press, 1998), 21.
12 Dorland, *So Close to the State/s,* 3.
13 Beale, "Cultural Policy," 232-3.
14 Armatage, "A Brief History," 137.

15   Kathleen Shannon, "'D' Is for Dilemma," *Herizons* 9, 2 (Summer 1995): 26.

16   Anderson, "Studio D's Imagined Community," 51.

17   Canadian Heritage, *Culture and Heritage: Making Room for Canada's Voices* (Hull: Minister of Public Works and Government Services Canada, 1998), 2-3.

18   Ibid., 8.

19   Department of Canadian Heritage, Cultural Industries Branch, *The Road to Success: Report of the Feature Film Advisory Committee* (Hull: Minister of Public Works and Government Services Canada, 1999), 5.

20   Department of Canadian Heritage, Cultural Industries Branch, *From Script to Screen: New Policy Directions for Canadian Feature Film* (Hull: Minister of Public Works and Government Services Canada, 2000), 2.

21   Armatage, "A Brief History," 137.

22   Gerald Pratley, "The Eyes of Canada: The National Film Board at Fifty," *Sight and Sound* 58, 4 (Autumn 1989): 229-36; and Bob Verrall, "Which Way to the Future?" *Cinema Canada* 160 (February/March 1989): 9-11. Verrall mentions the founding of Studio D "as feminism and regionalism were in ascendancy" (11). Both articles name *To a Safer Place* (Shaffer, 1987) but make no other mention of Studio D's productions or contributions to the NFB.

23   Dorland, *So Close to the State/s*, 58.

24   However, in addition to the potentially disruptive influence of the studio's mandate, Elizabeth Anderson finds striking similarities between the liberal feminism of Studio D and the dominant nationalist discourse of the NFB. See Anderson, "Studio D's Imagined Community," 41-2.

25   Waugh, "Cinemas, Nations, Masculinities," 18.

26   Kay Armatage, Kass Banning, Brenda Longfellow, and Janine Marchessault, "Gendering the Nation," in *Gendering the Nation: Canadian Women's Cinema*, ed. Kay Armatage, Kass Banning, Brenda Longfellow, and Janine Marchessault (Toronto: University of Toronto Press, 1999), 12.

27   Beale, "Cultural Policy," 233.

28   Scherbarth, "Canada's Studio D."

29   Scherbarth, "Studio D," 30.

30   Evans, *In the National Interest*, 211.

31   Shannon, "'D' Is for Dilemma," 27.

32   For a critique of Klein's film see B. Ruby Rich, "Anti-Porn: Soft Issue, Hard World," in Armatage et al., *Gendering the Nation*, 62-75.

33   Scherbarth, "Canada's Studio D," 26.

34   Ibid., 27.

35   Ibid., 26.

36   Pat Armstrong, "Understanding the Numbers: Women in the Film and Television Industry," in Toronto Women in Film and Television, *Changing Focus: The Future for Women in the Canadian Film and Television Industry* (Toronto: Women in Film and Television, 1991), 7.

37   Ibid., 8.

38   Ibid., 7.

39   Bonnie Diamond and Francine Fournier, *Equality and Access: A New Social Contract* (Montreal: National Film Board, 1987): 72.

40   National Film Board of Canada, *Annual Report, 1988-1989*, (Montreal: Communications Branch, 1989): 17.

41   "NFB: Studio D Shuffles Staff," *Cinema Canada* 160 (February/March 1989): 49.

42   Anderson, "Studio D's Imagined Community," 47.

43   E. Centime Zeleke, "Studio D Dumped," *Kinesis* (April 1996): 7.

44   Anderson, "Studio D's Imagined Community," 52.

45   David Barker Jones, "The National Film Board of Canada: The Development of Its Documentary Achievement," PhD diss. (Stanford University, 1976), 278.

46   Jones, *National Film Board of Canada*, 289.

47   Evans, *In the National Interest*, 169, seems to differ on this point, suggesting that a First Nations crew was unavailable.

48 Jones, *National Film Board of Canada,* 298.

49 Evans, *In the National Interest,* 160.

50 This is in response to Anderson's question as to whether "Studio D's images [are] just that – *images* that add up to an *image* of diversity." See Anderson, "Studio D's Imagined Community," 55.

51 Ibid., 56.

52 Ibid.

53 Levitin, "Contrechamp," 229.

54 Anderson, "Studio D's Imagined Community," 53, 56.

55 Scherbarth, "Canada's Studio D," 27.

56 *National Film Board Review: Integrated Analysis, Final Report* (Ottawa: Department of Communications, 1989).

57 Mandate Review Committee (CBC, NFB, Telefilm), *Making Our Voices Heard: Canadian Broadcasting and Film for the 21st Century* (Ottawa: Department of Canadian Heritage, 1996): 162-4.

58 "The National Film Board of Canada in the Year 2000: A Charter for a New Century," unpublished action plan, 18 March 1996, 4.

59 Shannon, "'D' Is for Dilemma," 29.

60 "The National Film Board in the Year 2000," 2.

61 This approach includes separatist aspects that are stressed by the Diamond and Fournier study, *Equality and Access,* which favours the designation of "separationist" (72). These qualities disappear with the dissolution of Studio D and the integration of its staff into the NFB's other units.

62 Christina Gabriel, "One or the Other? 'Race,' Gender and the Limits of Official Multiculturalism," in *Women and Canadian Public Policy,* ed. Janine Brodie (Toronto: Harcourt Brace and Company, 1996), 181.

63 Diamond and Fournier, *Equality and Access,* 72.

64 Ibid., 28-32, 37.

65 Beale, "Cultural Policy," 248.

39 The Gender of the Gaze in Cinematography: A Woman with a Movie Camera
Zoe Dirse

When I look at the movies, film theorists try to tell me that the gaze is male, the camera eye is masculine, and so my look is also not a woman's. But I don't believe them anymore, because now I think I know what it is to look at a film as a woman.

— Teresa de Lauretis, *Technologies of Gender*[1]

For the last twenty years, feminist film theory has explored gender in cinema through detailed analysis of filmic texts, focusing on elements such as modes of narrative address, structuring principles of vision, and patterns of identification. Beginning with Laura Mulvey's landmark essay, "Visual Pleasure and Narrative Cinema,"[2] the evolution of feminist film theory was grounded in a paradigm of sexual difference in which the gaze of spectorial pleasure was affiliated with masculinity, and the "female" within mainstream cinema was assigned the position of object and spectacle, connoting, as Mulvey put it, an exemplary "to be looked-at-ness." Now, a recent generation of feminist film theorists has critiqued this founding paradigm, and the axioms of psychoanalysis on which it was based, arguing that it does not allow for other forms of difference: sexual orientation, race, and ethnicity. These arguments were largely based in deconstructions of mainstream (i.e., Hollywood) films. The task of theorizing how sexual difference and spectorial patterns of pleasure and identification are produced in films authored by women is certainly a less developed part of feminist film theory.

I would like to examine whether or not there is a unique and distinguishable difference in the aesthetic perception of the female gaze and whether or not there is a concomitant difference in the audience's response to that gaze. For the purposes of this chapter, I will look at various excerpts from my own work in cinematography and attempt to analyze them within this context. How do we, as women filmmakers, theorize about experience in the world? What is the nature of the different experiences of women's vision on film? Perhaps my examples will shed light on how to theorize experience not as something that is unmediated or value free but, rather, as something that is culturally produced. For example, Teresa de Lauretis tries to devise a feminist approach to theorizing.[3] She examines the theoretical relations between the social and the subjective, experience and representation, the personal and the political. For her, meaning is produced in language, but language is the process and practice of mutually determining interactions between meaning, perception, and experience.

In shifting my methodology away from a purely textual-based analysis of Hollywood films, I look at sexual difference at the point of production (not reception), and I look at "perception" as the ground where sexual difference is played out. My role in the cinematic process is that of cinematographer. American filmmaker Morgan Wesson describes cinematography as the art of creating visual images and imagery unique to every motion picture. The cinematographer must take anything a writer or director can imagine, help find or create that image, and then record it for audiences. The influence of a cinematographer can be great or small, depending on the relationship with the director and scope of the film. The major body of my work has been in documentary film, where the cinematographer has the most licence and freedom. She must respond spontaneously to events happening around her and, thus, has little time to mediate the reality of any given situation. A documentary is a film authored by a director who chooses, or is given, a subject to document as a story or event that unfolds in real time: it is not reconstructed time, as in a narrative or fiction film. In documentary, there is a symbiotic relationship between the director and the cinematographer. They discuss the style, the philosophy, the ideas, the desired focus, the visual approach, and the overall look of the piece, and then it is up to the cinematographer to capture the images on film or tape that best conform to the director's wishes. Often, in documentary filmmaking, a collaborative relationship will develop where the approach and look of a piece will be arrived at by mutual agreement.

According to Judith Mayne, "All feminist inquiry is, in a sense, a reading against the grain of patriarchal institutions, an unearthing of contradiction and ambivalences at first invisible to the naked eye."[4] Historically, women's representation in film as cinematographers has hardly been documented. Ann Kaplan explains that "women are not linked to a specific historical context but to patterns in relation to marriage, sexuality and the family which transcend traditional historical categories, women are relegated to absence, silence and marginality and thus the outskirts of historical discourse, if not totally outside of history and culture which is defined by white middle-class man."[5]

Alice Guy Blaché, the first woman filmmaker, began her career working for Léon Gaumont in Paris in the late 1800s. She wrote, directed, and photographed most of her films. After working in France for several years, she married and moved to the United States, where she created her own production company, Solax Studios in New Jersey, and had great success. Moving to California in the 1930s and eventually selling her film rights to a shady distributor, she went bankrupt and moved back to France, where, to no avail, she tried to resurrect her career. In the 1960s, she attempted to locate some of the several hundred films that she had made but succeeded in finding only a few dozen. In frustration, she went on French television to try to gain some recognition for her work and began writing her memoirs. Like most women it has only been recently that she has found a place in cinema history (the National Film Board of Canada produced a documentary on Alice Guy Blaché in 1995). I found a remark she made in 1914 particularly inspiring: "There is nothing connected with the staging of a motion picture that a woman cannot do as easily as a man, and there is no reason why she cannot master every technicality of the art. The technique of the drama has been mastered by so many women that it is considered as much her field as a man's and its adaptation to picture work in no way removes it from her sphere. The technique of motion-picture photography, like the technique of the drama, is fitted to a woman's activities."[6]

In cinematography, women have traditionally been underrepresented. Although some women, such as Dorothy Dunn, Grace Davidson, and Margery Ordway, did emerge as successful cinematographers in the early days of cinema in the 1920s and 1930s, they were pushed out of the industry once it began to be considered glamorous, profitable, and powerful. Women briefly regained some ground during the Second World War, when there was a shortage in the workforce, but soon lost their foothold as the men returned and the social order was re-established. In North America today, women are vastly underrepresented in the technical areas of filmmaking and, in particular, in cinematography. IATSE 600, in Hollywood, the most powerful film union in North America, currently has only 11.24 percent female membership (this includes camera assistants). IATSE 649, in Toronto, has only three female cinematographers out of several hundred, and Montreal boasts four working female cinematographers.

Anne Ross Muir makes an interesting point when she says, "recent feminist debates have used psychoanalytic theory to explore why the 'male gaze' is dominant in mainstream cinema. But there may be a more concrete (if related) explanation: that the masculine point of view is prevalent simply because men control the industry."[7] I tend to agree with Muir's explanation as this is still true today, but I also believe that psychoanalytic theory is valid in that it spurred the beginnings of feminist film theory with Mulvey's argument on sexual difference. Mulvey describes visual pleasure in the cinema as rooted in a hierarchical system, whereby the male is the bearer of the look and the woman is the object of the look. What happens when the bearer of the look is female and the object is female? Mulvey was one of the first feminist film theorists of the 1970s. She used a Lacanian interpretation of the visual objectification of women to argue that, if the female image is iconicized, then this threatens the male (castration anxiety), and that classic Hollywood cinema has developed various devices and structures to give the male hero (and, by proxy, the male spectator), control over this enchanting and threatening image. Many feminist theorists have gone on to explain that the techniques of filming (such as lighting, camera angles, cutting between actors, and use of close shot versus long shot) are used to radically differentiate the presentation of men and women on the screen. Techniques that are normally used to depict women in films essentially produce a specularity in relation to the character in a way that places her role in the film as "iconic" (image) rather than as "diegetic" (storyteller), thus conveying the classical sexual objectification of women in films.

Ann Kaplan notes that, according to Mulvey, "this eroticization of women on the screen comes about through the way the cinema is structured around three explicitly male looks or gazes: there is the look of the camera in the situation being filmed (called the pro-filmic event); while technically neutral, this look, as we've seen, is inherently voyeuristic and usually 'male' in the sense that a man is generally doing the filming; there is the look of the men within the narrative, which is structured so as to make women objects of their gaze; and finally there is the look of the male spectator ... which imitates (or is necessarily in the same position as) the first two looks."[8] Eileen McGarry describes reality as being coded before the filmmaker arrives so that she, in fact, is dealing with the *pro-filmic event:* that which exists and happens in front of the camera.[9] In fiction film, the filmmakers exert a good deal of control over the pro-filmic event, through costumes, sets, and scripts. In traditional documentary, it is presumed that the filmmaker exerts no control over the pro-filmic event but that she/he makes certain decisions about reality: the choice of subject, the location, the preconceptions of the filmworkers, the presence of the crew and equipment all control and encode the pro-filmic event within the context of the technology of cinema and the dominant ideology. Given that the male gaze is predominant in our film and TV culture, it is only fair to assume that we are profoundly influenced by such a gaze. Not only is the gaze male, but it is also generally the gaze of a White middle-class male as those who enter the profession are usually from the wealthier classes, with access to education or contacts within the industry. The film industry is a very closed and guarded old boys' club because of its glamour, its mystique (illustrated by the Marlboro cigarette ads featuring two leather-clad men in cowboy hats straddling a camera dolly), and its high-wage potential. Those of any other ethnicity, class, or gender who dare to break into the ranks must either persevere in the face of rejection, abuse, and intolerance or search out like-minded directors and producers in order to progress in their field. Thus it is common to find women working on women's films, or minorities working with minorities (as is the case with Spike Lee, who works exclusively with his own Black cameraman). Once women or members of other groups enter the equation, then there needs to be a shift in the gaze to reflect their point of view.

Mulvey's ideas are based on difference theory, the premise being that there is an inherent difference between the sexes. Her concept of three looks, or gazes, helped to establish the debate. Now, in the 1990s, these three looks have been radically redefined as gender, race, and ethnicity enter the equation and new modes of interpretation are necessary in order to evaluate the gaze. Hélène Cixous[10] and Luce Irigaray[11] developed theories related to *écriture feminine,* a "feminine" writing whereby gender gains entry to culture through an embodied difference rather than a historical context. *Ecriture feminine* provided a link between theories of sexual difference and theories of deconstruction (Derrida's method of textual analysis based on the premise that there is no "reality" unmediated by discourse). Hence binary notions in language – such as man/woman and Black/White – are not immutable but constructed oppositional pairs. Rosemarie Buikema explains that "the consequence of deconstructive thought for feminist theory is that femininity is disconnected from a specific female identity. Femininity can be regarded as a discursive construction and not as exclusively related to a specific biological social group. An insight into the way in which positions of power are distributed in texts between masculine and feminine, and/or between white and black, can be a forceful instrument in the struggle against the one-sided and/or equivocal representation of femininity."[12] In exploring feminist film theory around the gaze, I will use Mulvey's three looks as a base and move on to deconstructive notions of the gaze, examining my own camera work within these theoretical contexts.

I will use methodology based on experience that comes from my own work in the field as a cinematographer. I have prepared a showreel of approximately twelve minutes, which illustrates various styles and approaches in documentary film. For the purposes of this book, several of the film excerpts are illustrated as still images. There are some dramatic sequences, but they are used within the documentary to contextualize the historical references. Often these films are called "docudramas" (which were pioneered by director John Smith in *Train of Dreams* [1987], a work in which I participated at the NFB). It took three weeks to prepare the showreel and two weeks to arrange the scheduling of my editor, myself, and the editing facilities as well as to track down professional master tapes of the selected films and to make preliminary selections of sequences. The third week involved the off-line editing (final sequence selection, assembling of the material, music, sound edit, and titles), the on-line editing process (information is taken from an EDL list on computer disk and transferred to high-quality digital tape in order to create a master tape), and, finally, the making of the multiple copies from the master tape. It cost approximately $1,000 to produce this showreel, and it is not uncommon for professional cinematographers to spend several thousands of dollars to produce similar reels to show prospective employers. I bring up the issue of cost only to further support an earlier argument in which I stated that women are shut out of the industry because of its profitability. For women to get jobs they need to be able to show examples of their work, but they need to be employed in order to create that work. Since there is no network for women (as there is for men) in the industry, this can be a real obstacle.

The showreel consists of twenty excerpts from nine films (see Filmography). I refer to them by number and visual reference. I chose not to identify each sequence on the tape because I wanted to utilize the editing process as a creative tool to illustrate the cinematography aesthetically and, in some transitions between sequences, politically. Teresa de Lauretis claims that the fact that "confrontation is itself discursive in nature – in the sense that language and metaphors are always embedded in practices, in real life, where meaning ultimately resides – is implicit in one of the metaphors of feminism: the personal is political."[13] Because my work is largely based in the area of documentary film and feminist subject matter, the political manifests itself in how I see and construct the images for a film, and I will point out where this becomes obvious in the excerpts.

The first excerpt is from the film *Forbidden Love*, which tells the stories of older lesbians coming out in the 1950s and how this experience came from reading drugstore pulp fiction with lesbian themes. In this sequence, which is a dramatic reenactment of a pulp novel scenario, two ex-lovers say good-bye while the boyfriend, Victor, watches in a classic patriarchal stance (see photo 1). The drama is played out in a standard narrative form, but the irony is portrayed by the era and the young women's quirky playfulness, reminiscent of classic male-directed B movies. In this film, almost all the gazes are female: the look of the camera, or *pro-filmic event*, the look of the narrator, and often the look of the spectator (lesbian audiences). Here the two feminist, lesbian directors are playing with the film genre and reconstructing their own versions of reality, which are supported by the testimonials in the documentary interviews. I bookended the reel with a love-making scene from *Forbidden Love*, which was very delicate to film because both actresses were heterosexual and had never appeared nude on camera before. The scene ultimately appears seamless due to the delicate direction and non-threatening female technical crew and camera eye. There were many factors that contributed to the success of this film, but I believe that when the gaze is so deliberately subverted from the male to the female, we finally have an opportunity to view ourselves as we really are – in the case of this film, not as objects of male desire but as objects of female desire.

As the first excerpt ends at a railway station, we cut to train tracks receding from the perspective of an observer on the back of a train (see photo 2). This scene is from *A Balkan Journey*, a documentary about women's resistance groups struggling against the violence in the Balkans during the civil war. A female narrator explains, over ominous images of dark, obscured men in Belgrade bars and cafés late at night, how incidences of violence against women have increased since the beginning of the war. In this particular instance, only the director, a terrified local driver, and I ventured out to film these scenes; my male camera assistant refused to accompany us, fearing for his safety. Because it truly was dangerous, I shot the scenes with high-speed film stock and zoom lenses, which gave a grainy, gritty feel to the images. It was also necessary to shoot from safe distances, so the shots are looking through doorways, windows, curtains (see photo 3), and they are taken from a moving vehicle, which give the sequence a sense of volatility and peril. Although the men in this sequence are unaware that I am filming them, it is curious to observe the way they look at the camera; it almost seems as though they knew a camera was watching them. In excerpt twenty, from *Shadow Maker*, a film on the poet Gwendolyn MacEwen, the gaze of the subject is very different. Here I am filming a Sufi parade in the bazaar in old Cairo (a potentially threatening environment to any woman). I throw myself into the crowd to try to capture some of the claustrophobia that Gwendolyn must have felt when she visited Cairo in the 1970s. At first,

1

2

3

4

5

6

7

Stills from cinematographer Zoe
Dirse's showreel of documentary
films. Courtesy of Zoe Dirse.

8

9

10

11

12

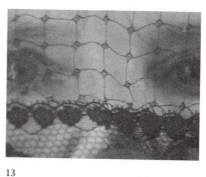

13

1 *Forbidden Love*; 2 and 3 *Balkan Journey*; 4, 5, 6, and 7 *Shadow Maker/Gwendolyn MacEwen, Poet*; 8 and 9 *Stolen Moments*; 10 *Baltic Fire*; 11 *A Tale of Two Sisters: The Dale Sisters*; 12, 13, and 14 *Erotica: A Journey into Female Sexuality*

14

the men seem curious, staring directly into my lens (curious at the camera or my gender) (see photo 5), and then suddenly the look changes and I feel danger as they start to push and shove (at which point I escape to safety). As a female cinematographer, I could feel the fear and instability that women living in such volatile environments must experience daily, and I could feel the urgency to tell of their plight through my eyes, look, and gaze. Not only was a female gaze crucial to understanding the situation of the Balkan women, but it also enabled me to be an unobtrusive observer, as in excerpt eight, where Rada, a resistance worker, comforts an older woman in a refugee camp. The two women seem totally oblivious to the camera (see photo 6). Is it because the gender of the bearer of the look is female and the subjects feel safe and not threatened? Later, in excerpt eleven (see photo 7), gypsies sing and perform to my hand-held camera with abandon and pleasure, their faces and gestures open to my inviting lens, allowing me to capture the sadness and joy in this ancient love song for Sarajevo. Is my gender an issue in relating to the subjects? or are all gypsies just natural performers?

In excerpt three, I cut away from threatening male images in the night to gay women dancing exuberantly in a Berkeley night club in the film *Stolen Moments* (see photo 8). Here women have taken back the night and their sexuality and have exiled men from their environs. My editing choice is now political, for I chose to show women who, in another part of the world, have made bold choices that defy the patriarchal social order. *Stolen Moments* is a historical testament to women who refused to be silenced by oppression – women who insist upon telling the stories of lesbians in Europe and North America. Excerpt nine shows a high-angle shot (filmed from a crane, nine stories high) of Amsterdam in the misty dawn. Next we see four female musicians dressed in black, travelling by boat on one of the canals to pay homage at the gay monument to all the homosexuals killed during the Second World War. I chose to shoot this scene with the women's backs to the camera. Notice how one of the women turns around and glances back, to one of the other musicians or to me (see photo 9)? The gaze of the camera is obscured by the backs, but the subject fearlessly takes control and returns the gaze or, in fact, subverts the gaze of the camera, which inadvertently adds thematically to the scene. Having the musicians turned away from the camera symbolizes the unknown identities of the dead, but the look back draws the spectators in and forces them to remember the past. This shot was not consciously constructed but, rather, evolved out of the relationship between the camera, the subject, and the moment.

The personal becomes political in my own directorial debut, *Baltic Fire*, where, after witnessing the murder of my friend and fellow cameraman, Andris Slapins, I decide to document the unfolding events in the Baltic states in January 1991. Eventually, these events led to the dissolution of the

Soviet Union, and I follow the story to 1993, positioning myself as eye-witness, narrator, and subject – hence two of the looks now become one. My decision to make the film came from my dissatisfaction with the mass media coverage of events, which I felt was biased, one-sided, and very male. Despite the difficult financial and moral obstacles, I managed to complete the film and received some acknowledgment and a tremendous sense of accomplishment. Hélène Cixous claims that women must "steal" in order to have a voice because they do not share in the dominant culture; and, in many ways, I felt that I too had to "steal" in order to produce *Baltic Fire*. Ultimately, my femaleness and feminist perceptions come into play through-out the film, as in excerpt seven, where my camera focuses on the faces of friends and family at Slapins's funeral. The lens is so intimate that it almost seems to feel the same sorrow as the mourners, and the flashback that I recreate over the corpse (see photo 10) is an attempt to breathe life back into my friend as he recalls his final moments on this earth. My own feel-ings of sadness are transmitted through the camera lens, and so, when the look of the camera and the narrator become one, and are both female, this radically changes the natural (or unnatural) order of the cinematic gaze and throws into question Mulvey's theory of the "three explicitly male looks or gazes" basic to cinema structure.

Excerpt sixteen is from the CBC biography, *A Tale of Two Sisters,* which concerns the Dale sisters (Cynthia and Jennifer), two Canadian television, film, and stage actresses. I chose the sequence where they are both prepar-ing themselves to go before the camera or audience. These two looks are generally male, especially for these actresses, but in the biography the gaze of the narrator and the camera is female, and something seems to shift in the scene on the couch where the two sisters relax in front of the camera and lose some of their self-conscious performing role (see photo 11).

Claire Johnston states that "myth has been the major means in which women have been used in the cinema: myth transmits and transforms the ideology of sexism and renders it invisible and therefore natural. Feminist or politically sensitive filmmakers can call the myth and its apparent natu-ralness into play."[14] Johnston and Mulvey both claim that, in order for a cinema to be feminist, it has to be a counter-cinema. In the case of the Dale sisters, the format is not necessarily counter-cinema; however, when femi-nist filmmakers engage in the process, then the film has feminist elements. The director, Maya Gallus, acknowledges a conscious attempt to subvert the material so as to reveal a truer version of the sisters, as distinct from their media personae (sibling rivalry, Cynthia as the bitch, Jennifer as the sex-goddess and bad mother, etc.). She accomplishes this best in the posi-tioning of the two sisters on the couch; my gaze further accentuates the situation through the framing, lighting, and placing of the sisters in the environment. Here we a have a potentially explosive situation, no one quite knowing what would come next. The subversion here lies in the fact that the sisters, who are so accustomed to performing in front of the camera, are now expected to reveal themselves, and they cannot manipulate the viewers' response. Through her editing, the director juxtaposes the sisters on several different levels: careers, relationships, hobbies, current work choices, and goals. Another subversion occurs in the use of a narrator – often a male approach to documentary, telling the audience what to think. Here, despite the narrator, you will notice that there is minimal narration and that the subjects are given a voice so that the audience is forced to draw its own conclusions.

I also began to think of the Dale sisters in terms of ideas around gender identity. When Mulvey describes visual pleasure in the cinema as rooted in a hierarchical system, whereby the male is the bearer of the look and the woman the object of the look, what happens when the bearer of the look is female and the object is female, as in the Dale sisters' biography? And then consider the impact of the male bearer of the look who created the images of these two actresses. Judith Butler proposes that "the very injunction to be given a certain gender takes place through discursive acts: to be a good mother, to be a heterosexually desirable object, to signify a multiplicity of guarantees in response to a variety of different demands at once."[15] The Dale sisters are constructs of their gender in a dominant White, middle-class male ideology, and this is even more accentuated by their roles as actresses in TV and cinema. Butler argues that gender is *performative;* that is, that it "constitut[es] the identity it is purported to be." To her, gender is "the repeated stylization of the body, a set of repeated acts within a highly rigid regulatory frame that congeal over time to produce the appearance of substance, of a natural sort of being. A political genealogy of gender ontologies ... will deconstruct the substantive appearance of gender into its constitutive acts and locate and account for those acts within the compulsory frames set by the various forces that police the social appearance of gender."[16] For Butler, who you are depends on your repeated performance, over time, of the acts that constitute a particular identity. Deborah Cameron explains that these acts are produced or resisted in relation to normative pressures and forces that "police" what is permissible.[17] Change occurs through repetition, and Butler concludes that, if identities are no longer fixed in binary notions of sex, then the possibilities of "cultural configurations of sex and gender might then proliferate [and] then become articulable within the discourses that establish intelligible cultural life."[18] I wonder if the Dale sisters, who are so accustomed to repetitive acts, have undergone any change since their early beginnings as child models and stage actresses, and whether performing for a female gaze affects their gender identity.

Finally, I now discuss excerpts from the film *Erotica: A Journey into Female Sexuality,* which shows women who use erotica to express themselves in their art, be it filmmaking, photography, fiction, music, or performance genres. Excerpt five begins in a Paris church near Saint Germain des Prés and cuts to Jean de Berg, a French dominatrix and author, in her Normandy château (see photo 12). The elegance of her surroundings and the use of extreme close-ups, especially the eyes behind the veil, add a sense of mystery and intrigue, which urges the spectator to keep watching (see photo 13). I found the return gaze of the subject to the camera very powerful and compelling, and at times disturbing, as she would challenge the female crew's attitudes to sexuality by inviting us to participate in her rituals. At times she would be the perfect heterosexual wife of author Alain Robbe-Grillet, and then she would become Jean de Berg, France's most famous veiled dominatrix, whose identity was only recently revealed. She challenges preconceived notions of sexuality and gender identity through acts of performativity by her dual selves. This poses some interesting questions, which consequently challenged my camera gaze, the narrator's gaze, and, ultimately, the spectators' gaze.

In excerpt twelve we see Lique, a young Black rap singer, who sings to audiences like herself about discovering sex and controlling one's own sexuality. The interview was shot in a series of extreme close-ups so that the camera eroticized the facial features of the character. There is a double play with the camera gaze in excerpt seventeen, where a lesbian photographer engages with three women in a dark alley during a photo shoot (see photo 14). The photographer is exploring her own sexuality through her lens, as she shoots the women playing to the camera and amongst themselves, while the cinema lens explores the dynamics of the scene. Here the gaze takes on another dimension, and one wonders how it shifts when the gender or sexual orientation of the camera gaze changes. In this film, women take control of their art through sexuality as expression. We, as the women filmmakers (director, producer, editor, sound-recordist, production manager, and cinematographer) take a direct view of the subjects and, ultimately, of ourselves. The bearer of the look is female, the subject is female, and the subject subverts the gaze and gazes at herself. The multiple layers of the female gaze in this particular film add some new and evocative dimensions to the context of feminist film theory and to questions concerning identity.

I believe it is crucial for women to take control of their art (and, in my case, of the cinematic images that show the world who we are) in order to subvert patriarchal assumptions concerning gender. If, in fact, the female gaze is almost absent from dominant culture, then the challenge is to change the patriarchal way of looking by imposing the female gaze on our cultural life, even if, as Hélène Cixous suggests, we must "steal" in or "fly" by.[19]

Notes

1 Teresa de Lauretis, *Technologies of Gender* (Bloomington: Indiana University Press, 1987), 11.
2 Laura Mulvey, "Visual Pleasure and Narrative Cinema," *Screen* 16, 3 (Autumn 1975), 6-18.
3 Teresa de Lauretis, *Alice Doesn't: Feminism, Semiotics, Cinema* (Bloomington: Indiana University Press, 1984).
4 Judith Mayne, "Woman at the Keyhole," in *Re-Vision: Essays in Feminist Criticism*, ed. Mary Ann Doane, Patricia Mellencamp, and Linda Williams (Los Angeles: American Film Institute, 1984), 63.
5 E. Ann Kaplan, *Women and Film: Both Sides of the Camera* (New York: Methuen, 1983), 2.
6 Alexis Krsilovsky, *Women behind the Camera* (Westport, CT: Praeger, 1997), xx.
7 Ann Ross Muir, "The Status of Women Working in Film and Television," in *The Female Gaze: Women as Viewers of Popular Culture*, ed. Lorraine Gamman and Margaret Marshment (Seattle: Real Comet Press, 1989), 143.
8 E. Ann Kaplan, *Women and Film: Both Sides of the Camera* (New York: Methuen, 1983), 30.
9 Eileen McGarry, "Documentary Realism and Women's Cinema," *Women and Film* 2, 7 (1975), 50-9.
10 Hélène Cixous, "The Laugh of the Medusa," in *New French Feminisms*, ed. Elaine Marks and Isabelle de Courtivron (New York: Schocken Books, 1981), 245-64.
11 Luce Irigaray, *This Sex Which Is Not One*, trans. Catherine Porter and Carolyn Burke (Ithaca: Cornell University Press, 1985); and *Speculum of the Other Woman*, trans. Gillian C. Gill (Ithaca: Cornell University Press, 1985).
12 Rosemarie Buikema, "Windows in a Round House: Feminist Theory," in *Women's Studies and Culture: A Feminist Introduction*, ed. Rosemarie Buikema and Anneke Smelik (London and New Jersey: Zed Books, 1993), 13.
13 de Lauretis, *Alice Doesn't*, 113.
14 Claire Johnston, "Women's Cinema as Counter-Cinema," in *Movies and Methods*, ed. Bill Nichols, vol. 1 (Berkeley: University of California Press, 1976), 208.
15 Judith Butler, *Gender Trouble: Feminism and the Subversion of Identity* (New York: Routledge, 1990), 145.
16 Ibid., 33.
17 Deborah Cameron, "The Language-gender Interface: Challenging Co-optation," in *Rethinking Language and Gender Research: Theory and Practice*, ed. V. Bergvall, J. Bing, and A. Freed (London: Longman, 1996), 31-53.
18 Butler, *Gender Trouble*, 149.
19 *Voler*, in French, means both "to steal" and "to fly."

Filmography (Showreel)

1989 *A Song for Quebec*. Direction: Dorothy Hénaut
1992 *Forbidden Love*. Direction: Lynne Fernie and Aerlyn Weissman
1993 *Baltic Fire*. Direction: Zoe Dirse
1994 *The Lucky Ones: Allied Airmen and Buchenwald*. Direction: Michael Allder
1996 *A Balkan Journey: Fragments from the Other Side War*. Direction: Brenda Longfellow
1997 *Erotica: A Journey into Female Sexuality*. Direction: Maya Gallus
1997 *Stolen Moments*. Direction: Margaret Wescott
1997 *A Tale of Two Sisters: The Dale Sisters*. Direction: Maya Gallus
1998 *Shadow Maker/Gwendolyn MacEwen, Poet*. Direction: Brenda Longfellow

Selected Film Sources

Useful Sites

<http://uk.imdb.com/>
<http://libweb.uoregon.edu/subjguid/women/femfilm.html>
<http://german.about.com/cs/germancinema/>
<http://www.imdb.com/>
<http://www.docos.com>
<http://www.moviem.co.uk/film>
<http://www.film.queensu.ca/links.html>
<http://halldirectors.com/>
<http://www.bifi.fr>
<http://www.library.yale.edu/humanities/film/internatl.html>
<http://www.allocine.com/>
<http://buyindies.com/>

Code	Distributor
AAA	Acteurs Auteurs Associés, Paris, France.
AAC	Alliance Atlantis Communications. Toronto, ON, Canada. Tel. 416-967-1174; fax. 416-960-0971. <www.allianceatlantis.com>
AGM	Anne G. Mungai. B.P. 47779, Nairobi, Kenya. Tel. 254-2-573138/254-2-562169; fax. 562136.
ALI	Alliance International. 920 Yonge Street, Suite #400, Toronto, ON, Canada M4W 3C7. Tel. 416-967-1174; fax. 416-960-0971.
ALR	Alliance Releasing. 5 Place Ville Marie, Suite #1435, Montreal, QC, Canada H3B 2G2. Tel. 514-878-2282; fax. 514-878-2419.
AML	AML. 10 rue Lincoln, 75008 Paris, France. Tel. 01 40 76 91 00; Fax. 01 42 25 12 89.
ARD	Ariane Distribution. 41, rue des Acacias, 75017 Paris, France. Tel. 01 58 05 25 00; fax. 01 58 05 25 25.
BFI	British Film Institute. E-mail: video.films@bfi.org.uk.
BIF	Birne Film. Mr. Kristov Brändli, Cranachstrasse 46, D 12157 Berlin, Germany, Tel. 49-30-8547125; fax. 49-30-8547378.
BOS	Bioskop Filmproduktion GmbH. Rosenheimer Str. 143d, 81671 Munich, Germany. <http://www.bioskop.de/>: Tel. 49-89-409092-0; fax. 49-89-409092-20; e-mail: info@bioskop.de
BTC	Buzz Taxi Communication. Toronto, ON, Canada. Tel. 416-920-3000
BVG	Basis-Film Verleih GmbH. Koenerstr. 59, Berlin 12169, Germany. Tel. 49 30 793 5171. World Sales: Kinowelt Lizenzverwertungs GmbH. Contact Jochen Hesse, Annegret Rönnpag Schwere-Reiter-Str. 35/Geb. 14, D-80797 Munich, Germany

<http://www.kinoweltworldsales.com>. Tel. +49-89-3 07 96 70 60; fax. +49-89-3 07 96 70 67; e-mail: worldsales@kinowelt.de.

CFI   Cori Film Distributors. 19 Albermarle Street, London W1X 3HA, UK.

CFM   CFMDC Canadian Filmmakers Distribution Centre. 37 Hanna Avenue, Suite 220, Toronto, ON, Canada M6K 1W8. <http://www.cfmdc.org/main.html> Tel. 416-588-0725; fax. 416-588-7956; e-mail: cmdc@interlog.com.

CFP   CFP Distribution Inc. Contact: Shane Kinnear, 2 Bloor St. West, Suite 1901, Toronto, ON, Canada M4W 3EL. Tel. 416-944-0104; fax. 416-944-2212.

CHF   Chrysalide Films, 7 Rue Casteja, F–92100 Annaud, France. Tel. 33 1 469 46500; fax. 33 1 469 46599.

CIL   Cinéma Libre. 460 St. Catherine Street West, Bureau 500 Montréal, QC, Canada H3B 1A7. <http://www.cinemalibre.com>. Tel. 514-861-9030; fax. 514-861-3634; e-mail: infocine@cinemalibre.com.

CIN   Cinenova. UK, <http://www.cinenova.org>.

CME   Unbound Films, Inc. 2303 Graveley Street, Vancouver, BC, Canada V5L 3C3. Tel. 604-255-6599; fax. 604-255-6549; e-mail: cmorgado7@shaw.ca.

DFL   Yale University (DEFA Film Library). <http://www.umass.edu/defa/>.

EWF   East-West Film Enterprises Ltd. 8058 Fraser St., Vancouver, BC, Canada V5X 3X4. Tel. 604-322-6146; fax. 604-322-6177; e-mail: yang@intouch.bc.ca.

FLP   First Look Pictures. 8800 Sunset Blvd., Los Angeles, CA 90089. Tel. 310-855-1199; fax. 1-800-855-0152; e-mail: firstlook@ofg.com.

FOX   20th Century Fox Home Entertainment. <http://www.foxhome.com>.

FRF   First Run Features. US, <http://www.firstrunfeatures.com>.

FRI   First Run/Icarus Films. <http://www.frif.com>.

FRU   Film Resource Unit, PO Box 11065, Johannesburg, 2000.

GFP   Gerda Film Productions, 120 Ivy Avenue, Toronto, Canada M4L 2H7. Tel. 416-466-5494; e-mail: Brenda Longfellow, brendal@yorku.ca.

GIV   Groupe Intervention Video (GIV). 5505 boul. Saint-Laurent, bureau 3015, Montreal, QC, Canada H2T 1S6, <http://www.givideo.org/ang/mainA.html>. Tel. 514-271-5506; fax. 514-271-6980; e-mail:giv@cam.org.

GMC   Groupe Multimédia du Canada. 5225 rue Berri, Montréal, QC, Canada H2J 2S4. Tel: 514-273-4251.

GTV   GTV, PO Box 1916, Parklands 2121, Gauteng, South Africa.

HMF   Helke Misselwitz Film, Albrechtstrasse 22, D-10117 Berlin Allemagne. Tel./fax. + 40 30 28384578; e-mail: h.misselwitz@hff-postdam.de

ICE   Icestorm International, Inc. World-wide distribution rights of East German DEFA (1946-1990) film stock on video and DVD, on both NTSC and PAL video format with English subtitles, plus 100 titles in PAL format in original German language. 78 Main Street, Northampton, MA, 01060, <http://www.icestorm-video.com>. Tel. (413) 587-9334; fax. (413) 587-9305; e-mail: info@icestorm-video.com.

ICM   ICE Media (PTY) Ltd., 2 Clamart Road, Richmond 2092, South Africa, Mrs. Heidi Meiring, Suite 62, Private Bag X9, Melville 2109, South Africa. Tel. (27 11) 482 8155; fax. (27 11) 726 5993; mobile: 27 83 6017 808; e-mail: hmeiring@icemedia.co.za.

IIL   Canal+ Image International. Paris, France. Tel. +33 1 46-10-12-00; fax. +33 1 46-10-12-20.

KIN   Kino International, 333 West 39 Street, Suite 503 New York, NY 10018, <http://www.kino.com>. Tel. 212-629-6880; fax. 212-714-0871.

KIW   Kinowelt Lizenzverwertungs GmbH, a division of Kinowelt Media Group. Contact: Jochen Hesse, Stelios Ziannis, Schwere-Reiter-Str. 35/Geb. 14 D-80797 Munich, <http://www.kinoweltworldsales.com>. Tel. +49-89-3 07 96 70 60; fax +49-89-3 07 96 70 67; e-mail: worldsales@kinowelt.de.

LAC   Les Acacias Ciné Audience. Simon Simsi, 122 rue La Boetie 75008 Paris (France). Tel. 33-(0)1 56 69 29 30; fax. 33-(0)1 42 56 08 65. Contact in France: Philippe Cosson, Tel. 33-(0)1 47 70 51 75; e-mail: acaciadi@club-internet.fr.

LGE	Lion's Gate Entertainment. 2 Bloor St. West, # 1901, Toronto ON, Canada, <http://www.lionsgatefilms.com/index_pic.html>. Tel. 416-944-0104; fax. 416-944-2212.
LNP	Light Night Production. SA Filature 22, CH–1227 Carouge, Switzerland, <http://www.lightnight.com>. Tel. 41 22 342 3131; fax. 41 22 300 1171.
MCA	Motion International Distribution. 33 Yonge Street, # 1020, Toronto, ON, Canada M5E 1S9, <http://www.motioninternational.com>. Tel. 416-956-2000; fax. 416-956-2020.
MDM	Mediamax. 387 St-Paul O., Montréal, QC, Canada H2Y 2A7, <http://www.lafete.com>. Tel. 514-848-0417; e-mail: ditribution@lafete.com.
MER	Connoisseur/Meridian Films Inc. <http://www.meridanvideo.com>.
MID	Moving Images Distribution. 402 West Pender St., Ste. 606, Vancouver, BC, Canada V6B 1T6, <http://www.movingimages.bc.ca>. Tel. 604 684 3014; fax. 604 684 7165; e-mail: mailbox@movingimages.ca.
MIR	Miramax. <http://www.miramax.com>.
MK2	MK2 DIFFUSION. <http://www.mk2.com>. E-mail: sales@mk2.com>.
NAA	National Asian American Telecommunications Association, distribution: <http://www.naatanet.org>.
NFB	National Film Board, PO Box 6100 Station Centre-Ville, Montreal, QC, Canada H3C 3H5, <http://www.nfb.ca>. Tel. 1-800-267-7710.
NYF	New Yorker Films. Jose Lopez, 16 West 61 Street, New York, NY 10023, <http://www.newyorkerfilms.com>. Tel. 212-247-6110; fax. 212-307-7855; e-mail: info@newyorkerfilms.com.
PAD	Pathe Distribution. E-mail: barbara.grousseau@pathe.com.
PAR	Parafrance. Paris, France. Tel. 01 45 63 06 12.
PGD	Pierre Grise Distribution. 21 Ave. du Maine, 75019 Paris, France. Tel. 01.45.44.20.45; fax. 01.45.44.00.40
PRG	Progress Filmverleih GmbH. Burgstraße 27, 10178 Berlin, Germany, <http://www.progress-film.de/high.htm>.
PYR	Pyramide. <http://www.pyramidefilms.com>. E-mail: infos@pyramidefilms.com
REI	Regent Entertainment International. 1401 Ocean Avenue, Suite 300, Santa Monica, CA 90401 USA. Tel. +3102603333; fax +3102603343; e-mail: jalambert@earthlink.net (John Lambert).
RMS	Remstar Distribution. <http://www.remstarcorp.com/>.
RMV	Raman Mann c/o Viewfinders. A4 House 8 DLF Qutab Enclave, DLF Phase 1, Gurgaon-122002, India. E-mail: rmann@giasdl01.vsnl.net.in (Raman Mann).
RZF	Rezo Films (Walid). E-mail: walid.zaiane@rezofilms.com.
SKH	Ster-Kinekor Home Entertainment (Pty) Ltd. PO Box 76378, Wendywood, 2144, Gauteng, South Africa.
SNS	Norstar Entertainment. 86 Bloor St. West, 4th Floor, Toronto, ON, Canada M5S 1M5. Tel. 416-961-6278; fax. 416-961-5608.
SPC	Sony Pictures Classics, US. <http://www.sonyclassics.com>.
SYT	Synercom Téléproductions Inc., 5179 rue St-Denis, Montréal, QC, Canada H2J 2M1. Tel. 514-273-4333.
TLF	Téléfiction Inc. 4446 Boul. St-Laurent, bur. 701, Montréal, QC, Canada H2W 1Z5. Tel. 514-499-0972.
TMU	Trimark Pictures (US). 2644 30th Street, Floor 2, Santa Monica, CA 90405-3009. Tel. 310-314-2000; fax. 310-399-1570.
TWF	Thomas Wilkening Film Gesellschaft. August-Bebel-Strasse 26-53, D-14482 Potsdam, Germany. Tel: 49-331 721-3046; fax. 49-331 721-3047; e-mail: thwfilmbbg@aol.com.
UBP	Unbound Films, Inc. Claudia Morgado Escanilla, 2303 Graveley Street, Vancouver, BC, Canada V5L 3C3. Tel. 604-255-6599; fax. 604-255-6549; e-mail: cmorgado7@shaw.ca.
UGC	L'Union Générale de Cinématographie. 24, ave. Charles de Gaulle, 92200 Neuilly, France, <http://www.ugc.fr>. Tel. 01.46.40.44.00.

VIF   Vidéo Femmes. 291, rue Saint-Vallier Est, bureau 104, Québec, QC, Canada G1K 3P5, <http://videofemmes.org/accueil/index.asp>. Tel. 418-529-9188; fax. 418-529-4891; e-mail: info@videofemmes.org>.

VIO   Video in distribution, Video Out. <http://www.video-in.com>.

VTP   V-tape, 401 Richmond St. West #452, Toronto, ON, Canada M5V 3A8, <http://www.vtape.org/>. Tel.(416)351.1317; fax.(416) 351-1509; e-mail: kimt@vtape.org.

WEG   West Glen, subsidised source for German films. 1430 Broadway, New York, NY 10018, <http://www.wgcn.com/feature.htm>. Tel. 212-921-0966.

WMM   Women Make Movies, Inc. 462 Broadway, Suite 500 Q New York, NY 10013 <http://www.wmm.com> Tel. 212-925-0606; fax. 212-925-2052.

ZGF   Zeitgeist Films. 247 Center Street, 2nd floor, New York, NY 10013. <http://www.zeitgeistfilm.com>. Tel. 212-274-1989; fax. 212-274-1644; e-mail: web@zeitgeistfilm.com.

Code   Video/DVD Purchase Outlets

AMZ   Amazon. <http://www.amazon.com>

CIP   Cipta Video. Sdn. Bhd., 338 1st floor WISMA SYS, Jalan Raja Laut, 50350 Kuala Lumpur, Malaysia.

CTH   Columbia TriStar Home Video. <http://www.cthv.com>

DVT   Discount Video Tapes Inc. <http://www.hollywoodsattic.com>

MUN   Movies Unlimited. <www.moviesunlimited.com>

OWF   One World Films. <http://1worldfilms.com>

THE   Turner Home Entertainment. <http://www.turner.com>

VRF   Version Française. <http://www.francevision.com/vf/videoclub/index.htm>

WAH   World Artists Home Video. <http://www.worldartists.com>

Code   Libraries

DEF   DEFA Film Library, University of Massachussetts, Amherst. <www.umass.edu/germanic/defa_film_library.htm>.

HFF   Hochschule fuer Film und Fernsehen, Konrad Wolf in Babelsberg. University for Film and Television, Marlene Dietrich Avenue 11 14482 Potsdam, Germany, <http://www.bibl.hff-potsdam.de>. Tel. + 49,331 6202 401; fax. + 49 331 6202 400.

MBC   Mary Baldwin College, Staunton, Virginia, US, <mbc.edu/library/audvis/languages.htm#anchori>.

MRC   Media Resource Center, Moffitt Library, UC Berkeley, <http://www.lib.berkeley.edu/MRC/level2.html>. Tel.510-642-8197.

NFV   National Film and Video Lending Service, Australia (available only in Australia), <www.cinemedia.net>.

Code   Other

GOE   Goethe Institute, UK. Holds 16 mm film. Please address all booking enquiries to British Film Institute, 21 Stephen Street, London W1P 1PL, <http://www.goethe.de/gr/lon/film/index.htm>. Tel. 020-7957 8938; fax. 020-7580 5830; e-mail: Andrew.Youdell@bfi.org.uk.

IMC   Instituto Mexicano de Cinematografia. Insurgentes Sur 674, Col. Del Valle, 03100, Mexico, <http://www.imcine.gob.mx>. Tel. 52 5544 5425; fax. 52 5549 2119; e-mail: promint@InstitutoMexicanodeCinematografia.gob.mx.

Akerman, Chantal
Je tu il elle/I You He She (1974) WAH; OWF
Jeanne Dielman, 23 quai du commerce, 1080 Bruxelles (1975) AMZ
Les Rendez-vous d'Anna/The Meetings of Anna (1978) AMZ
Golden Eighties (1986) AMZ
Nuit et jour/Night and Day (1991) AMZ
A Couch in New York (1996) AMZ

Arzner, Dorothy
Christopher Strong (1932) MUN; THE; NFV
Craig's Wife (1936) MUN; CTH
Dance, Girl, Dance (1940) MUN; THE; NFV

Baba, Shuhaimi
Layar Lara (1997) CIP

Bailey, Norma
Women in the Shadows (1991) NFB

Balasko, Josiane
Gazon maudit/French Twist (1995) AML; OWF

Bellon, Yannick
La Triche (1984) AAA; VRF

Bemberg, María Luisa
Camila (1984) MER; OWF
Miss Mary (1986) MUN
Yo, la peor de todas/I, the Worst of All (1990) FRF; OWF
I Don't Want to Talk About It (1993) CTH

Berto, Juliet
Neige (1981) UGC

Bigelow, Kathryn
Point Break (1991) FOX
Strange Days (1995) FOX

Bjornson, Michelle
A Round Peg (1997) MID

Brückner, Jutta
Ein Ganz und gar vemahrlosches Mädchen/A Thoroughly Demoralized Girl (1977) GOE
Hungerjahre/Years of Hunger (1979) GOE; WEG

Chadha, Gurinder
I'm British, But ... (1989) NAA
A Nice Arrangement (1991) NAA
Bhaji on the Beach (1993) FLP

Claxton, Dana
I Want to Know Why (1994) VIO
The Red Paper (1996) VIO
Buffalo Bone China (1997) VIO
Yuxweluptun, Man of Masks (1998) NFB
The People Dance (2001) VIO

Cranmer, Barb
Laxwesa Wa: Strength of the River (1995) NFB

Cuthand, Thirza
Colonization: The Second Coming (1996) VIO
Working Baby Dyke Theory: The Diasporic Impact of Cross-Generational Barriers (1997) VIO
Helpless Maiden Makes an "I" Statement (1999) VIO

Dash, Julie
Illusions (1983) WMM
Praise (1991) WMM
Daughters of the Dust (1991) BFI; KIN; NFV

Dörrie, Doris
Keiner liebt mich/Nobody Loves Me (1995) CFP

Ducharme, Carole
Straight from the Suburbs (1998) CIL

Dulac, Germaine
The Smiling Madame Beudet (1922) CIN
The Seashell and the Clergyman (1928) MRC; CIN; NFV

Duras, Marguerite
India Song (1975) NFV

Garcia, Nicole
Un weekend sur deux/Every Other Weekend (1990) MK2; OWF
Place Vendôme (1998) AML

Geddes, Carol
Doctor, Lawyer, Indian Chief (1986) NFB; WMM

Ghorab-Volta, Zaïda
Souviens-toi de moi/Remember Me (1996) PGD

Giguère, Nicole
C'est pas le pays des merveilles/It's not a Wonderland (1981) VIF
Histoire infâme (1988) VIF
L'Humeur à l'humour (1989) VIF
Arrêtons d'en demander/Enough Is Enough (1995) NFB

Aller simple pour Sirius/One-way Ticket to Sirius
(1997) GMC
Dépasser l'âge/The Age to Be (1998) MDM
Barbie la Venus de vinyle (1999) TLF
Québec en ondes (2001) SYT
Alice au pays des gros nez (2002) VIF

Gómez, Sara
De cierta manera/One Way or Another (1977)
NYF

Heyns, Katinka
Fiela se Kind (1987) GTV
Die Storie van Klara Viljee (1991) GTV
Paljas (1997) SKH

Holland, Agnieszka
Aktorzy prowincjonalni/Provincial Actors
(1978) OWF; NYF; AMZ
Kobieta samotna/A Woman Alone (1981) OWF
Bittere Ernte/Angry Harvest (1985) OWF
Zabić księdza/To Kill a Priest (1987) AMZ
Europa, Europa (1990) WEF; OWF
Washington Square (1997) AMZ
Trzeci cud/The Third Miracle (1999) AMZ

Huppert, Caroline
Signé Charlotte (1986) PAR

Jaoui, Agnès
Le Goût des autres (2000) PAD

Kędzierzawska, Dorota
Crows (1994) NYF
Nothing (1998)

Kermadec, Liliane de
La Piste du télégraphe (1994) LAC

Kinyanjui, Wanjiru
Battle of the Sacred Tree (1994) ICM; BIF

Lanoé, Annick
Les Nanas (1984) UGC

Lemercier, Valérie
Le Derrière/From Behind (1999) AML

Longfellow, Brenda
Our Marilyn (1987) GFP
Gerda (1992) GFP
*A Balkan Journey: Fragments from the Other
Side War* (1996) GFP
Shadow Maker (1998) GFP

Makhmalbaf, Samira
The Apple (1999) ZGF

Mallet, Marilú
Lentement (in *Il n'y a pas d'oubli*) (1975) NFB
Les Borges (1978) NFB
Journal inachevé (1982)/*Unfinished Diary*
(1986) WMM; CIL
Mémoires d'un enfant des Andes (1985) NFB
Child of the Andes (1988) NFB
Ma Chère Amérique (1989) NFB; CIL
2, rue de la mémoire/Suspended Memories
(1996) CIL
Double portrait (2001) CIL

Mann, Raman
For all Raman Mann's films see RMV

Marshall, Tonie
Pas très catholique (1994) ARD

Masson, Laetitia
A vendre (1997) PYR

Medina, Claudia
In Between the Middle/Entre el medio (2000)
MID

Mehta, Deepa
Camilla (1993) AMZ
Fire (1996) ZGF; OWF; NYF; AMZ
Earth (1998) ZGF; OWF; NYF; AMZ

Merlet, Agnès
Artemisia (1997) MUN

Misselwitz, Helke
The main distributor post-1989 for Misselwitz's films is Thomas Wilkening Film
(code TWF). Prior to that it was Progress
(code PRG). (See also ICE.)

Documentaries
TangoTraum/Tango Dream (1985)
Winter Adé/Winter Farewell (1988)
*Wer fuerchtet sich vorm schwarzen Mann/
Who's Afraid of the Black Man* (1989)
Sperrmüll/Trash (1990) DFL
Leben ein Traum/Living a Dream (1994)
Meine Liebe deine Liebe/My Love Your Love
(1995)

Features
Herzsprung/Heart Leap (1992) DFL
Fremde Oder/Obca Odra (2001) HMF

Moffatt, Tracey
Nice Colored Girls (1987) CIN; WMM; NFV
Moodeijt Yorgas (1990) CIN
Night Cries (1990) WMM; NFV
BeDevil (1993) WMM; NFV
Heaven (1997) WMM
Lip (with Gary Hillberg, 1999) WMM; NFV

Morgado Escanilla, Claudia
Oda a las Chilotas/Ode to the Chilotas (1990) UBP
Spit It Out (1992) UBP
Sin ataduras/Unbound (1995) WMM; UBP
Angustia (1996) WMM; UBP
Sabor a mí/Savour Me (1997) WMM; CFM; UBP
Martirio (2000) BTC; UBP
Bitten (2002) UBP

Mungai, Anne
Saikati (1992) AGM

Parmar, Pratibha
See Pratibha Parmar's Web site for links to her films: <http://www.tibha.demon.co.uk/index.html>

Emergence (1986) WMM; CIN; GIV; VTP
Sari Red (1988) WMM; CIN; GIV; VTP
Reframing AIDS (1987) GIV; VTP
Memory Pictures (1989) CIN; GIV; VTP
Bhangra Jig (1990) WMM, VTP
Flesh and Paper (1990) WMM; CIN; VTP
Khush (1991) WMM; CIN
A Place of Rage (1991) WMM; CIN
Double the Trouble, Twice the Fun (1992) WMM; CIN; VTP
Warrior Marks (1993) WMM; CIN
The Colour of Britain (1994) NAA
Memsahib Rita (1994) CIN
Jodie: An Icon (1996) WMM; CIN
Wavelengths (1997) WMM; CIN
Brimful of Asia (1998) VTP
The Righteous Babes (1998) WMM; CIN; VTP

Plattner, Patricia
Piano panier ou la recherche de l'équateur (1988-1989) LNP
Made in India (1998) WMM
Les Petites Couleurs (2002) LNP

Potter, Sally
Thriller (1979) WMM
The London Story (1979) WMM
The Gold Diggers (1983) not available at this time
Tears Laughter Fear and Rage (1986) made for TV, has never been distributed
Women Filmmakers in Russia (a.k.a. *I Am an Ox, I Am a Horse, I Am a Man, I Am a Woman*) (1988) WMM
Orlando (1993) SPC; NFV
The Tango Lesson (1997) SPC
The Man Who Cried (2000) Universal Focus

Proctor, Elaine
Friends (1993) CHF; FRI; OWF
Kin (1999) REI

Rainer, Yvonne
Journeys from Berlin (1971) ZGF; NFV
Film about a Woman Who ... (1974) ZGF; NFV
The Man Who Envied Women (1985) ZGF; CIN; NFV
Privilege (1990) ZGF; CIN
MURDER and murder (1997) ZGF

Reece, Cleo
Land Use (1993) VIO

Roüan, Brigitte
Overseas (1990) OWF
Post coitum animal triste/After Sex (1998) NYF; OWF

Sander, Helke
All-Around Reduced Personality: Redupers (1978) GOE; OWF

Sanders Brahms, Helma
Germany, Pale Mother (1979) BVG; KIW; WEG; OWF; NFV
Mein Herz – niemandem!/My Heart Is Mine Alone (1997) KIW

Sass, Barbara
Without Love (1980) OWF
Paradise Appletree (1985) OWF

Schmidt, Evelyn
Das Fahrrad/The Bicycle (1982) ICE

Schyfter, Guita
Novia que te vea/Like a Bride/Fiancée Who Sees You (1993) IMC
Las caras de la luna/The Faces of the Moon (2001) IMC

Serreau, Coline
Trois hommes et un couffin/Three Men and a Cradle (1985) AAA; OWF
Romuald et Juliette (1989) UGC; MIR

Tobing Rony, Fatimah
On Cannibalism (1994) WMM; NAA

Todd, Loretta
The Learning Path (1991) NFB; FRI
Hands of History (1994) NFB
Forgotten Warriors (1997) NFB
Colours of My Ancestors (2002) NFB

Trinh T. Minh-ha
Reassemblage (1982) WMM; CIN; NFV
Naked Spaces (1985) WMM; CIN; NFV
Surname Viet Given Name Nam (1989) WMM; CIN; NFV
Shoot for the Contents (1991) WMM; CIN; NFV
A Tale of Love (1995) WMM; NFV
The Fourth Dimension (2001) WMM

Trotta, Margarethe von
The Lost Honour of Katharina Blum (with Volker Schlöndorff, 1975) BOS; GOE; MBC
The Second Awakening of Christa Klages (1977) OWF
Schwestern, oder, die Balance des Glücks/Sisters, or The Balance of Happiness (1979) GOE; OWF
Die bleierne Zeit/Marianne and Juliane (1981) OWF; NYF
Rosa Luxemburg (1985) OWF; NYF
The Promise (1994) OWF

Varda, Agnès
Cléo de 5 à 7/Cléo From 5 to 7 (1961) ZGF
Le Bonheur/Happiness (1964) ZGF
Sans toit ni loi /Vagabond (1985) MK2; ZGF; MUN; OWF
Jacquot de Nantes/Jacquot (1990) ZGF
Les Cent et une nuits/One Hundred and One Nights (1994) ZGF

Vernoux, Marion
Personne ne m'aime (1994) RZF

Veysset, Sandrine
Y aura-t-il de la neige à Noël? /Will It Snow for Christmas? (1996) NYF

Walsh, Christine
Keepers of the Fire (1994) NFB

Weber, Lois
Suspense (1913) CIN
The Blot (1921) CIN; NFV; DVT

Weissman, Aerlyn
A Winter Tan (1987) KIN

Weissman, Aerlyn, and Lynne Fernie
Forbidden Love: The Unashamed Stories of Lesbian Lives (1992) WMM
Fiction and Other Truths: A Film About Jane Rule (1995) NFB

Wertmüller, Lina
Pasqualino Settebellezze/Seven Beauties (1976) OWF; AMZ

Wheeler, Anne
For a list of Anne Wheeler's episodic television, short dramas, and documentaries, see her Web site: <http://www.anne.wheeler.com>.

Loyalties (1985/86) SNS Simcom/Norstar Releasing
Bye Bye Blues (1988/89) CFP; IIL; Circle Films USA
Angel Square (1989/90) CFI; Festival Films (Canada)
Mother Trucker: The Diana Kilmury Story (1996) ALR
Better than Chocolate (1998) TMU, ALI, MCA
Marine Life (1999/2000) AAC
Suddenly Naked (2000/2001) RMS
Edge of Madness (2001) LGE

Wilson, Lindy
Last Supper at Horstley Street (1985) FRU

Yang, Yue-Qing
Nu Shu: A Hidden Language of Women in China (1999) EWE; WMM

Zauberman, Yolande
Lola/Clubbed to Death (1996) FPI

Select Bibliography

Note: This bibliography comprises two sections on general background ([1] film history, cultural studies, and postcolonial theory; [2] gender, feminist, and queer theory) and two sections on women in film ([1] feminist theory and studies of women filmmakers; [2] postcolonial theory and criticism, indigenous and non-Western perspectives).

Background: Film History, Cultural Studies, and Postcolonial Theory

Abdel-Malek, Kamal, and David C. Jacobson, eds. *Israeli and Palestinian Identities in History and Literature.* New York: St. Martin's Press, 1999.

Ahluwalia, Pal, and Paul Nursey-Bray, eds. *Post-colonialism: Culture and Identity in Africa.* Commack, NY: Nova Science Publishers, 1997.

Aitken, Ian. *European Film Theory and Cinema: A Critical Introduction.* Bloomington: Indiana University Press, 2001.

Allan, Seán, and John Sandford, eds. *DEFA: East German Cinema, 1946-1992.* New York: Berghahn Books, 1999.

Andrew, Dudley. *Concepts in Film Theory.* Oxford: Oxford University Press, 1984.

Appadurai, A., ed. *The Social Life of Things.* Cambridge: Cambridge University Press, 1986.

Appiah, Kwame Anthony, and Henry Louis Gates, Jr., eds. *Identities.* Chicago: University of Chicago Press, 1995.

Asby, Justine, and Andrew Higson. *British Cinema, Past and Present.* London: Routledge, 2000.

Atack, Margaret. *May 68 in French Fiction and Film: Rethinking Society, Rethinking Representation.* Oxford: Oxford University Press, 1999.

Aufderheide, Patricia. *The Daily Planet: A Critic on the Capitalist Culture Beat.* Minneapolis MN: Minnesota University Press, 2000.

Austin, Guy. *Contemporary French Cinema: An Introduction.* Manchester: Manchester University Press, 1996.

Bahri, Deepika, and Mary Vasudeva, eds. *Between the Lines: South Asians and Postcoloniality.* Philadelphia: Temple University Press, 1996.

Bakari, Imruh, and Mbye B. Cham, eds. *African Experiences of Cinema.* London: British Film Institute Pub., 1996.

Baker, Houston A., Jr., Manthia Diawara, and Ruth H. Lindeborg, eds. *Black British Cultural Studies: A Reader.* Chicago: University of Chicago Press, 1996.

Bakhtin, Mikhail Mikhailovich. *Rabelais and His World.* Cambridge: Massachusetts Institute of Technology Press, 1968.

–. *The Dialogic Imagination.* Trans. Carly Emerson and Michael Holquist. Austin: University of Texas Press, 1981.

Bal, M., with B. Gonzales, eds. *The Practice of Cultural Analysis: Exposing Interdisciplinary Interpretation.* Stanford, CA: Stanford University Press, 1999.

Barker, F., P. Hulme, M. Iverson, and D. Loxley, eds. *The Politics of Theory*. Colchester: University of Essex Press, 1983.

Barta, Tony, ed. *Screening the Past: Film and the Representation of History*. Westport, CT: Praeger, 1998.

Barthes, Roland. "The Death of the Author." In *Image, Music, Text*. Trans. Stephen Heath. 142-8. London: Fontana, 1977.

Berg, Cristian, Frank Durieux, and Geert Lemout, eds. *The Turn of the Century: Modernism and Modernity in Literature and the Arts*. Berlin: Walter de Gruyter, 1995.

Berger, John. *Ways of Seeing*. London: Penguin Books, 1972.

Bergstrom, Janet, ed. *Endless Night: Cinema and Psychoanalysis, Parallel Histories*. Berkeley and London: University of California Press, 1999.

Bernardi, Daniel, ed. *Classic Hollywood, Classic Whiteness*. Minneapolis, MN: Minnesota University Press, 2001.

Berry, Chris, ed. *Perspectives on Chinese Cinema*. London: BFI, 1991.

–. "These Nations Which are Not One: History, Identity and Postcoloniality in Recent Hong Kong and Taiwan Cinema." In *Span* 34-34 (October 1992 and May 1993): 37-49.

–. *A Bit on the Side: East-West Topographies of Desire*. Sydney: EmPress Publishing, 1994.

Berry, Ellen E., ed. *Postcommunism and the Body Politic*. New York: New York University Press, 1995.

Berry, Venise T., and Carmen L. Manning-Miller, eds. *Mediated Messages and African-American Culture: Contemporary Issues*. Thousand Oaks: Sage Publications, 1996.

Bhabha, Homi K. "The Other Question: The Stereotype and Colonial Discourse." *Screen* 24, 6 (November-December 1983): 18-35.

–. "Of Mimicry and Man: The Ambivalence of Colonial Discourse." *October* 28 (1984): 125-33.

–. "The Commitment to Theory." In *Questions of Third Cinema*, ed. Jim Pines and Paul Willemen. 111-32. London: British Film Institute, 1989.

–. *Nation and Narration*. London: Routledge, 1990.

Blignaut, Johan, and Martin Botha, eds. *Movies, Moguls and Mavericks: South Africa Cinema, 1979-1991*. Johannesburg: Showdata, 1992.

Braendlin, Bonnie, and Hans Braendlin, eds. *Authority and Transgression in Literature and Film*. Gainesville: University Press of Florida, 1996.

Brecht, Bertolt. *Brecht on Film and Radio*. Trans. and ed. Marc Silberman. London: Methuen, 2000.

Broderick, Mick, ed. *Hibakusha Cinema: Hiroshima, Nagasaki and the Nuclear Image in Japanese Film*. New York: Columbia University Press, 1996.

Bruzzi, Stella. *New Documentary: A Critical Introduction*. London: Routledge, 2000.

Burch, Noel. *Life to Those Shadows*. London: British Film Institute, 1990.

Burton, Julianne, ed. *Cinema and Social Change in Latin America: Conversations with Filmmakers*. Austin: University of Texas Press, 1986.

–, ed. *The Social Documentary in Latin America*. Pittsburgh: University of Pittsburgh Press, 1990.

–. "Film and Revolution in Cuba: The First Twenty-five Years." *New Latin American Cinema*. Vol. 2, *Studies of National Cinema*, ed. Michael T. Martin. Detroit: Wayne State University Press, 1997.

Canadian Heritage (Department of). *Making Our Voices Heard: Canadian Broadcasting and Film for the 21st Century (Mandate Review Committee: CBC, NFB, Telefilm)*. Ottawa: Department of Canadian Heritage, 1996.

Cartmell, Deborah, I.Q. Hunter, Heidi Kaye, and Imelda Whelehan, eds. *Alien Identities: Exploring Differences in Film and Fiction*. London and Sterling, VA: Pluto Press, 1999.

–. *Classics in Film and Fiction*. London and Sterling, VA: Pluto Press, 2000.

Caughie, John, ed. *Theories of Authorship: A Reader*. London/Boston: Routledge/Kegan Paul in association with the British Film Institute, 1981.

Centre for Contemporary Cultural Studies, University of Birmingham. *The Empire Strikes Back: Race and Racism in 70s Britain*. London: Hutchinson, 1982.

Chadwick, Kay, and Timothy Unwin, eds. *New Perspectives on the Fin de Siècle in Nineteenth-and Twentieth-century France*. New York: Edwin Mellen Press, 2000.

Cham, Mbye B., and Claire Andrade-Watkins, eds. *Blackframes: Critical Perspectives on Black Independent Cinema*. Cambridge, MA: MIT Press, 1988.

Chambers, Iain, and Lidia Curti, eds. *The Post-colonial Question: Common Skies, Divided Horizons*. London: Routledge, 1996.

Champagne, Duane, ed. *Contemporary Native American Cultural Issues*. Walnut Creek, CA: AltaMira Press, 1999.

Chanan, Michael. *The Cuban Image: Cinema and Cultural Politics in Cuba*. London/Bloomington: British Film Institute/Indiana University Press, 1985.

–. "Modernity, Masculinity and Imperfect Cinema in Cuba." *Screen* 38, 4 (Winter 1997): 245-59.

Chatman, Seymour. *Story and Discourse: Narrative Structure in Fiction and Film*. Ithaca and London: Cornell University Press, 1978.

Chatterjee, Partha, ed. *Wages of Freedom: Fifty Years of the Indian Nation-state*. Delhi and New York: Oxford University Press, 1998.

Chow, Rey. *Ethics after Idealism: Theory, Culture, Ethnicity, Reading*. Bloomington: Indiana University Press, 1998.

Chowdhry, Prem. *Colonial India and the Making of Empire Cinema: Image, Ideology and Identity*. Manchester: Manchester University Press, 2000.

Churchill, Ward. "Fantasies of the Master Race: Categories of Stereotyping of American Indians in Film." In *Film and Theory: An Anthology*, ed. Robert Stam and Toby Miller. 697-703. Malden, MA: Blackwell Publishing, 2000.

Clerc, Jeanne-Marie. *Littérature et cinéma*. Paris: Nathan, 1993.

Clifton, James A. *The Invented Indian: Cultural Fictions and Government Policies*. New Brunswick, NJ: Transaction Publishers, 1990.

Coetzee, J.M. *White Writing: On the Culture of Letters in South Africa*. Sandton, S. Africa: Radix, 1988.

Cohan, Steven, and Ina Rae Hark, eds. *Screening the Male: Exploring Masculinities in Hollywood Cinema*. London: Routledge, 1993.

Collier, Peter, and Helga Geyer-Ryan, eds. *Literary Theory Today*. Ithaca, NY: Cornell University Press, 1990.

Cook, Pam. *The Cinema Book*. London: British Film Institute, 1990.

Cornelius, Sheila. *New Chinese Cinema: Challenging Representations*. New York: Columbia University Press, 2002.

Corner, John. *The Art of Record: A Critical Introduction to Documentary*. Manchester: Manchester University Press, 1996.

Crawford, Peter Ian, and David Turton. *Film as Ethnography*. Manchester: Manchester University Press, 1992.

Danesi, Marcel. *Encyclopedia Dictionary of Semiotics: Media and Communications*. Toronto: University of Toronto Press.

Darby, Phillip, ed. *At the Edge of International Relations: Postcolonialism, Gender, and Dependency*. London/New York: Pinter, 1997.

Davidson, John E. *Deterritorializing the New German Cinema*. Minneapolis, MN: Minnesota University Press, 1999.

Davies, Catherine. "Modernity, Masculinity and Imperfect Cinema in Cuba." *Screen* 38, 4 (Winter 1997): 245-59.

–. "Reply to John Hess." *Screen* 40, 2 (Summer 1999): 208-11.

Davis, Peter. *In Darkest Hollywood: Exploring the Jungles of Cinema's South Africa*. Randburg, South Africa/Athens, OH: Ravan Press/Ohio University Press, 1996.

Delgado, Richard, and Jean Stefancic, eds. *Critical White Studies: Looking behind the Mirror*. Philadelphia: Temple University Press, 1997.

Desmond, Jane, ed. *Meaning in Motion: New Cultural Studies of Dance*. Durham: Duke University Press, 1997.

Department of Canadian Heritage. *Culture and Heritage: Making Room for Canada's Voices*. Hull: Minister of Public Works and Government Services Canada, 1998.

–. Cultural Industries Branch. *The Road to Success: Report of the Feature Film Advisory Committee*. Hull: Minister of Public Works and Government Services Canada, 1999.

Diawara, Manthia. *African Cinema: Politics and Culture*. Bloomington: Indiana University Press, 1992.

Dixon, Wheeler Winston. *The Films of Jean-Luc Godard*. New York: State University of New York Press, 1997.

Dorland, Michael. *So Close to the State/s: The Emergence of Canadian Feature Film Policy*. Toronto: University of Toronto Press, 1998.

Downing, John D.H., ed. *Film and Politics in the Third World*. New York: Autonomedia, 1987.

Dyer, Richard. *White*. London: Routledge, 1997.

Elliot, J.E. "What's 'Post' in Post-Colonial Theory?" In *Borderlands: Negotiating Boundaries in Post-colonial Writing*, ed. Monika Reif-Hülser. 43-53. Amsterdam; Atlanta, GA: Rodopi, 1999.

Elsaesser, Thomas. *New German Cinema: A History*. London: Macmillan, 1989.

Erhlich, Evelyn. *Cinema of Paradox: French Filmmaking under the German Occupation*. New York: Columbia University Press, 1985.

Evans, Gary. *In the National Interest: A Chronicle of the National Film Board of Canada from 1949 to 1989*. Toronto: University of Toronto Press, 1991.

Fabian, Johannes. *Time and the Other: How Anthropology Makes Its Other*. New York: Columbia University Press, 1983.

Fairservice, Don. *Film Editing: History: Theory and Practice – Looking at the Invisible*. Manchester: Manchester University Press, 2001.

Falkowska, Janina, and Marek Haltof, eds. *The New Polish Cinema: Industry, Genres, Auteurs*. Trowbridge, Wiltshire: Flick Books, 2000.

Fanon, Frantz. *The Wretched of the Earth*. Trans. Constance Farrington. New York: Grove Press, 1963.

Fleras, Augie, and Jean Leonard, eds. *The Nations Within: Aboriginal-State Relations in Canada, the United States and New Zealand*. Toronto: Oxford University Press, 1989.

Forbes, Jill. *The Cinema in France: After the New Wave*. Bloomington: Indiana University Press, 1994.

Foucault, Michel. *The Archeology of Knowledge*. Trans. A.M. Sheridan Smith. New York: Harper Colophon, 1972.

–. "What Is An Author?" *Screen* 20, 1 (1979).

Francis, Daniel. *The Imaginary Indian: The Image of the Indian in Canadian Culture*. Vancouver: Arsenal Pulp, 1992.

Franco, Jean. *Critical Passions: Selected Essays*. Edited and with an introduction by Mary Louise Pratt and Kathleen Newman. Durham, NC: Duke University Press, 1999.

Gabriel, Teshome H. *Third Cinema in the Third World: The Aesthetics of Liberation*. Ann Arbor, MI: UMI Research Press, 1982.

–. "Towards a Critical Theory of Third World Films." In *Film and Theory: An Anthology*, ed. Robert Stam and Toby Miller. 298-316. Malden, MA: Blackwell Publishing, 2000.

Gaines, Jane, and Michael Renov, eds. *Collecting Visible Evidence*. Minneapolis and London: Minnesota University Press, 1999.

Gazetas, Aristides, ed. *An Introduction to World Cinema*. Jefferson, NC: McFarland, 2000.

Givanni, June, ed. *Symbolic Narratives/African Cinema: Audiences, Theory and the Moving Image*. Bloomington: Indiana University Press, 2001.

Gillespie, David. *Early Soviet Cinema: Innovation, Ideology and Propaganda*. New York: Columbia University Press, 2001.

Gittings, Chris. *Canadian National Cinema: Ideology, Difference and Representation*. London: Routledge, 2002.

Glatzer, Robert. *Beyond Popcorn: A Critic's Guide to Looking at Films*. Vancouver: UBC Press, 2001.

Goldie, Terry. *Fear and Temptation: The Image of the Indigene in Canadian, Australian, and New Zealand Literature*. Montreal: McGill-Queen's University Press, 1989.

Gomes, Alberto, ed. *Modernity and Identity: Asian Illustrations*. Bundoora, Australia: La Trobe University Press, 1994.

Grant, Barry K., ed. *Film Genre: Theory and Criticism*. Metuchen, NJ: Scarecrow Press, 1977.

Greene, Naomi. "Artaud and Film: a Reconsideration." *Cinema Journal* 23, 4 (1984): 28-40.

Guha, Ranajit, ed. *A Subaltern Studies Reader, 1986-1995*. Delhi: Oxford University Press, 1998.

Hake, Sabine. *German National Cinema*. London: Routledge, 2001.

Hall, Stuart. "Who needs 'Identity'?" In *Questions of Cultural Identity*. ed. Stuart Hall and Paul du Gay. 1-17. London: Sage Publications, 1996.

–. "When Was 'The Post-Colonial'? Thinking at the Limit." In *The Post-colonial Question: Common Skies, Divided Horizons*, ed. Iain Chambers and Lidia Curti. 242-60. London: Routledge, 1996.

–. "Cultural Identity and Cinematic Representation." *Framework* 36 (1989): 68-81.

–, and Paul du Gay, eds. *Questions of Cultural Identity*. London: Sage Publications, 1996.

Hallam, Julia, with Margaret Marshment. *Realism and Popular Cinema*. Manchester: Manchester University Press, 2000.

Hamamoto, Darrell Y., and Sandra Liu, eds. *Countervisions: Asian American Film Criticism*. Philadelphia: Temple University Press, 2000.

Hansen, Miriam. *Babel and Babylon: Spectatorship in American Silent Film*. Cambridge, MA: Harvard University Press, 1995.

Hargreaves, Alec G., and Mark McKinney, eds. *Post-colonial Cultures in France*. London: Routledge, 1997.

Haynes, Jonathan, ed. *Nigerian Video Films*. Rev. ed. Athens: Ohio University Center for International Studies, 2000.

Hayward, Susan. "A History of French Cinema, 1895-1991: Pioneering Filmmakers (Guy, Dulac, Varda) and Their Heritage." *Paragraph* 15, 1 (1992): 19-37.

–. *Cinema Studies: The Key Concepts*. 2nd ed. London: Routledge, 2000.

–, and Ginette Vincendeau, eds. *French Film: Texts and Contexts*. London: Routledge, 2000.

Hess, John. "No mas Habermas, or ... rethinking Cuban Cinema in the 1990s." *Screen* 40, 2 (Summer 1999): 203-7.

Hight, Craig, and Jane Roscoe. *Faking It: Mock Documentary and the Subversion of Factuality*. Manchester: Manchester University Press, 2001.

Hill, John, and Pamela Church Gibson, eds. *The Oxford Guide to Film Studies*. Oxford: Oxford University Press, 1998.

Hjort, Mette, and Scott MacKenzie, eds. *Cinema and Nation*. London: Routledge, 2000.

Hogan, Patrick Colm. *Colonialism and Cultural Identity: Crises of Tradition in the Anglophone Literatures of India, Africa, and the Caribbean*. New York: State University of New York Press, 2000.

Hollows, Joanne, and Mark Jancovich, eds. *Approaches to Popular Film*. Manchester: Manchester University Press, 1995.

Hollows, Joanne, Peter Hutchings, and Mark Jancovich, eds. *The Film Studies Reader*. London/New York: Arnold/Oxford University Press, 2000.

Holmes, Diana, and Alison Smith, ed. *100 Years of European Cinema: Entertainment or Ideology?* Manchester: Manchester University Press, 2001.

Hsiao-peng Lu, Sheldon, ed. *Transnational Chinese Cinemas: Identity, Nationhood, Gender*. Honolulu, HI: University of Hawaii Press, 1997.

Innis, Harold A. *The Bias of Communication*. Toronto: University of Toronto Press, 1951.

Johnson, Randal, and Robert Stam. *Brazilian Cinema*. New York: Columbia University Press, 1995.

Jones, David Barker. "The National Film Board of Canada: The Development of Its Documentary Achievement." PhD diss., Stanford University, 1976.

Jordan, Barry, and Rikki Morgan-Tamosunas. *Contemporary Spanish Cinema*. Manchester: Manchester University Press, 1998.

Kahn, Joel S. "Subalternity and the Construction of Malay Identity." In *Modernity and Identity: Asian Illustrations*, ed. Alberto Gomes. 66-95. Bundoora, Australia: La Trobe University Press, 1994.

Khan, Hatta Azad. *The Malay Cinema*. Bangi, Selangor, Malaysia: Penerbitan Universiti Kebangsaan Malaysia, 1997.

Kilpatrick, Jacquelyn. *Celluloid Indians: Native Americans and Film*. Lincoln and London: University of Nebraska Press, 1999.

Kniesche, Thomas W., and Stephen Brockmann, eds. *Dancing on the Volcano: Essays on the Culture of the Weimar Republic*. Columbia, SC: Camden House, 1994.

Kolinsky, Eva, and Wilfried van der Will, eds. *The Cambridge Companion to Modern German Culture*. Cambridge: Cambridge University Press, 1998.

Konstantarakos, Myrto, ed. *Spaces in European Cinema*. Exeter, England, and Portland, OR: Intellect, 2000.

Kuenzli, Rudolf E., ed. *Dada and Surrealist Film*. New York: Willis Locker and Owens, 1987.

Kuhn, Annette, and Jackie Stacey, eds. *Screen Histories: A Screen Reader*. Oxford: Clarendon Press, 1998.

Lapsley, Robert, and Micheal Westlake. *Film Theory: An Introduction*. Manchester: Manchester University Press, 1989.

Leaman, Oliver, ed. *Companion Encyclopedia of Middle Eastern and North African Film*. London: Routledge, 2001.

Lee, Hyangjin. *Contemporary Korean Cinema: Identity, Culture and Politics*. Manchester: Manchester University Press, 2001.

Lerner, Loren R. *Canadian Film and Video: A Bibliography and Guide to the Literature*. Toronto: University of Toronto Press, 1997.

Levy, Emanuel. *Cinema of Outsiders: The Rise of American Independent Film*. New York: New York University Press, 1999.

Lewis, Alison. "Unity Begins Together: Analyzing the Trauma of German Unification." *New German Critique* 64 (Winter 1995): 135-59.

Linville, Susan E. "*Europa, Europa*: A Test Case for German National Cinema." *Wide Angle* 16, 3 (1997): 40-3.

Lotman, Jurij. *Semiotics of Cinema*. Trans. Mark E. Suino. Ann Arbor: Department of Slavic Languages and Literature, University of Michigan, 1976.

Ma, Sheng-mei. *The Deathly Embrace: Orientalism and Asian American Identity*. Minneapolis: University of Minnesota Press, 2000.

MacDonald, Kevin, and Mark Cousins, eds. *Imagining Reality: The Faber Book of the Documentary*. London and Boston: Faber and Faber, 1998.

Maitra, Prabodh, ed. *100 Years of Cinema*. Calcutta: Nandan, 1995.

Martin, Michael T., ed. *New Latin American Cinema*. Vol. 2, *Studies of National Cinema*. Detroit: Wayne State University Press, 1997.

Mazdon, Lucy, ed. *France on Film: Reflection on Popular French Cinema*. New York: Columbia University Press, 2001.

McLuhan, Marshall, and Eric McLuhan. *The Laws of Media: The New Science*. Toronto: University of Toronto Press, 1988.

Michalek, Boleslaw, and Frank Turaj. *The Modern Cinema of Poland*. Bloomington: Indiana University Press, 1988.

Mihesuah, Devon A., ed. *Natives and Academics: Research and Writing about American Indians*. Lincoln: University of Nebraska Press, 1998.

Mishra, Vijay. *Bollywood Cinema: Temples of Desire*. London: Routledge, 2001.

Mongia, Padmini, ed. *Contemporary Postcolonial Theory: A Reader*. London: Arnold, 1996.

Moran, Albert, ed. *Film Policy: International, National and Regional Perspectives*. London: Routledge, 1996.

Morgan, Jenny. *Film Researcher's Handbook: A Guide to Sources in Africa, Australasia, North and South America*. London: Routledge, 1996.

Moses, Daniel David, and Terry Goldie, eds. *An Anthology of Native Canadian Literature in English*. Toronto: Oxford University Press, 1992.

Mwaria, Cheryl B., Silvia Federici, and Joseph McLaren, eds. *African Visions: Literary Images, Political Change, and Social Struggle in Contemporary Africa*. Westport, CT: Greenwood Press, 2000.

Naficy, Hamid. *Otherness and the Media: The Ethnography of the Imagined and the Imaged*. Langhorne, PA: Harwood Academic Publishers, 1993.

National Film Board of Canada. *Annual Report, 1984-1985*. Montreal: Communication Services, NFB, 1985.

–. *Annual Report, 1988-1989*. Montreal: Communications Branch, 1989.

–. *National Film Board Review: Integrated Analysis, Final Report*. Ottawa: Department of Communications, 1989.

Nelmes, Jill, ed. *An Introduction to Film Studies*. 2nd ed. London: Routledge, 1999.

"NFB: Studio D Shuffles Staff." *Cinema Canada* 160 (February-March 1989): 49.

Ngugi, Wa Thiong'o. *Decolonising the Mind: The Politics of Language in African Literature*. London/Portsmouth, NH: Currey/Heinemann, 1986.

Nichols, Bill, ed. *Movies and Methods*. 2 vols. Berkeley: University of California Press, 1985.

Nixon, Rob. *Homelands, Harlem and Hollywood: South African Culture and the World Beyond*. New York: Routledge, 1994.

Noriega, Chon A., and Ana M. López, eds. *The Ethnic Eye: Latino Media Arts*. Minneapolis, MN: University of Minnesota Press, 1996.

Nowell-Smith, Geoffrey. *The Oxford History of World Cinema*. Oxford: Oxford University Press, 1996.

Osuri, Goldie. "Genealogies of the Body Politic: History and Resistance in the Cinema of Sembene." In *Post-colonialism: Culture and Identity in Africa*, ed. Pal Ahluwalia and Paul Nursey-Bray. 91-110. Commack, NY: Nova Science Publishers, 1997.

Patel, Niti Sampat. *Postcolonial Masquerades: Culture and Politics in Literature, Film, Video, and Photography*. London: Routledge, 2001.

Paul, David. "The Esthetics of Courage: The Political Climate for the Cinema in Poland and Hungary." *Cineaste* 14, 4 (1985): 16-20.

Perkins, V.F. "Film Authorship: The Premature Burial." *CineAction* 21/22 (1990): 57-64.

Pettitt, Lance. *Screening Ireland: Film and Television Representation*. Manchester: Manchester University Press, 2000.

Petty, Sheila, ed. *A Call to Action: The Films of Ousmane Sembène*. Trowbridge, Wiltshire, UK: Flick Books, 1996.

–. *Archeology of Origin: Transnational Visions of Africa in a Borderless Cinema*. Halifax, NS: Mount Saint Vincent University Art Gallery, 2000.

Pick, Zuzana. *The New Latin American Cinema: A Continental Project*. Austin: University of Texas Press, 1993.

Pines, Jim, and Paul Willemen, eds. *Questions of Third Cinema*. London: British Film Institute, 1989.

Pratley, Gerald. "The Eyes of Canada: The National Film Board at Fifty." *Sight and Sound* 58, 4 (1989): 229-36.

Rattansi, Ali, and Sallie Westwood, eds. *Racism, Modernity and Identity: On the Western Front*. Cambridge, UK, and Cambridge, MA: Polity Press, 1994.

Rayner, Jonathan. *Contemporary Australian Cinema: An Introduction*. Manchester: Manchester University Press, 2000.

Reif-Hülser, Monika, ed. *Borderlands: Negotiating Boundaries in Post-colonial Writing*. Amsterdam, GA: Rodopi, 1999.

Rich, B. Ruby. "An/Other View of New Latin American Cinema." *Iris: A Journal of Theory on Image and Sound* 13 (Summer 1991): 5-28.

Richards, Jeffrey. *Film and British National Identity: From Dickens to Dad's Army*. Manchester: Manchester University Press, 1997.

Rodriguez, Clemencia. *Fissures in the Mediascape: An International Study of Citizens' Media*. Cresskill, NJ: Hampton Press, 2001.

Rollins, Peter C., and John E. O'Connor, eds. *Hollywood's Indian: The Portrayal of the Native American in Film*. Lexington: University of Kentucky, 1989.

Rosen, Philip. *Change Mummified: Cinema, Historicity, Theory*. Minneapolis: University of Minnesota, 2001.

Rutherford, Jonathan, ed. *Identity, Community, Culture, Difference*. London: Lawrence and Wishart, 1990.

Salmane, Hala, Simon Hartog, and David Wilson, eds. *Algerian Cinema*. London: British Film Institute, 1976.

Screen. *The Sexual Subject: A Screen Reader in Sexuality*. London: Routledge, 1992.

Shapiro, Michael, J. "National Times and Other Times: Re-Thinking Citizenship." *Cultural Studies* 14, 1 (2000): 79-89.

Sherzer, Dina, ed. *Cinema, Colonialism, Postcolonialism: Perspectives from the French and Francophone World*. Austin, TX: University of Texas Press, 1996.

Shohat, Ella, and Robert Stam. *Unthinking Eurocentrism: Multiculturalism and the Media*. London: Routledge, 1994.

Smith, Paul Julian. *Vision Machines: Cinema, Literature and Sexuality in Spain and Cuba*. London: Verso, 1996.

Smith, Valerie, ed. *Representing Blackness: Issues in Film and Video*. New Brunswick, NJ: Rutgers University Press, 1997.

Solanas, Fernando, and Octavio Gettino. "Towards a Third Cinema," *Afterimage* 3 (Summer 1971): 16-35. Reprinted in Bill Nichols, ed. *Movies and Methods: An Anthology*. Berkeley, CA: University of California Press, 1976.

Spass, Lieve. *The Francophone Film: A Struggle for Identity*. Manchester: Manchester University Press, 2001.

Spivak, Gayatri C. *In Other Worlds: Essays in Cultural Politics*. New York: Methuen, 1987.

–. "Poststructuralism, Marginality, Postcoloniality and Value." In *Literary Theory Today*, ed. Peter Collier and Helga Geyer-Ryan. 219-44. Ithaca, NY: Cornell University Press, 1990.

–. *A Critique of Postcolonial Reason: Towards a History of the Vanishing Present*. Cambridge, MA: Harvard University Press, 1999.

Stam, Robert. *Film Theory: An Introduction*. Oxford: Blackwell, 2000.

–, and Toby Miller. *Film and Theory: An Anthology*. Malden, MA: Blackwell Publishing, 2000.

–, and L. Spence. "Colonialism, Racism and Representation: An Introduction." *Screen* 24, 2 (April 1983): 2-20.

Stevens, Donald, ed. *Based on a True Story: Latin American History at the Movies*. Wilmington: SR Books, 1997.

Stock, Ann Marie, ed. *Framing Latin American Cinema: Contemporary Critical Perspectives*. Minneapolis and London: University of Minnesota Press, 1997.

Stokes, Jane, and Anna Reading, eds. *The Media in Britain: Current Debates and Developments*. New York: St. Martin's Press, 1999.

Tang, Xiaobing, and Stephen Snyder, eds. *In Pursuit of Contemporary East Asian Culture*. Boulder, CO: Westview Press, 1996.

Tarr, Carrie. "French Cinema and Post-Colonial Minorities." In *Post-colonial Cultures in France*, ed. Alec G. Hargreaves and Mark McKinney. 59-83. London: Routledge, 1997.

Tasker, Yvonne, ed. *Fifty Contemporary Filmmakers*. London: Routledge, 2001.

Taylor, Drew Hayden. "Pretty Like a White Boy." In *An Anthology of Canadian Native Literature in English*, ed. Daniel David Moses and Terry Goldie. Toronto: Oxford University Press, 1992.

Taylor, Richard, Nancy Wood, Julian Graffy, and Dina Iordanova, eds. *The BFI Companion to Eastern European and Russian Cinema*. Bloomington and Indianapolis: Indiana University Press, 2001.

Thompson, Kristin, and David Bordwell. *Film History: An Introduction*. New York: McGraw-Hill, 1994.

Thomson, Philip. *The Grotesque*. London: Methuen, 1972.

Tinkcom, Matthew, and Amy Villarego, eds. *Keyframes: Popular Cinema and Cultural Studies*. London: Routledge, 2001.

Tomaselli, Keyan. *The Cinema of Apartheid: Race and Class in South African Film*. Sandton, South Africa: Radix, 1989.

Trinh T. Minh-ha, and Judith Mayne. "Critical Essay: 'From a Hybrid Place.'" In *An Introduction to World Cinema*, ed. Aristides Gazetas. 305-12. Jefferson, NC: McFarland and Co., 2000.

Verrall, Bob. "Which Way to the Future?" *Cinema Canada* 160 (February/March 1989): 9-11.

Vincendeau, Ginette. *The Companion to French Cinema*. London: Cassel and British Film Institute, 1996.

Waugh, Thomas, ed. *Show Us Life: Toward the History and Aesthetics of the Committed Documentary*. Metuchen, NJ, and London: Scarecrow Press, 1984.

Wayne, Mike. *Political Film: The Dialetics of Third Cinema*. London and Sterling, VA: Pluto Press, 2001.

Williamson, Judith. *Deadline at Dawn: Film Criticism, 1980-1990*. London: Marion Boyars, 1993.

Wollen, Peter. *Signs and Meaning in the Cinema*. London: Secker and Warburg, 1974.

Wood, Robin. *Sexual Politics and Narrative Film: Hollywood and Beyond*. New York: Columbia University Press, 1998.

Yau, Esther C.M., ed. *At Full Speed: Hong Kong Cinema in a Borderless World*. Minneapolis: Minnesota University Press, 2001.

Zhang, Yingjin, and Zhiwei Xiao. *Encyclopedia of Chinese Film*. London: Routledge, 1999.

Zimmerman, Patricia R. *States of Emergency: Documentaries, Wars, Democracies*. Minneapolis: University of Minnesota Press, 2000.

Zizek, Slavoj, ed. *Mapping Ideology*. New York: Verso, 1994.

Background: Gender, Feminist, and Queer Theory

Alderson, David, and Linda Anderson, eds. *Territories of Desire in Queer Culture: Refiguring Contemporary Boundaries*. Manchester: Manchester University Press, 2000.

Anthias, Floya, and Nira Yuval-Davis, in association with Harriet Cain. *Racialized Boundaries: Race, Nation, Gender, Colour and Class and the Anti-racist Struggle*. London: Routledge, 1992.

Aziz, R. "Feminism and the Challenge of Racism: Deviance or Difference?" In *Black British Feminism: A Reader*, ed. H.S. Mirza. London: Routledge, 1997.

Bad Object-Choices, eds. *How Do I Look: Queer Film and Video*. Seattle: Bay Press, 1991.

Balsamo, Anne Marie. *Technologies of the Gendered Body: Reading Cyborg Women*. Durham: Duke University Press, 1996.

Barrett, M., and A. Phillips, eds. *Destabilising Theory: Contemporary Feminist Debates*. Cambridge: Polity Press, 1993.

Beale, Alison. "Cultural Policy as a Technology of Gender." In *Ghosts in the Machine: Women and Cultural Policy in Canada and Australia*, ed. Alison Beale and Annette Van Den Bosch. Toronto: Garamond Press, 1998.

Benjamin, Jessica. *The Bonds of Love: Psychoanalysis, Feminism and the Problem of Domination*. New York: Random House, 1988.

Benshoff, Harry M. *Monsters in the Closet: Homosexuality and the Horror Film*. Manchester: Manchester University Press, 1997.

Bergvall, V., J. Bing, and A. Freed, eds. *Rethinking Language and Gender Research: Theory and Practice*. London: Longman, 1996.

Blackwell, Jeannine, and Susanne Zantop, eds. *Bitter Healing: German Women Writers from 1700 to 1830*. Lincoln: University of Nebraska Press, 1990.

Brandt, Beth. "From the Inside Looking at You." *Canadian Women's Studies* 14, 1 (1990): 16-17.

Brinker-Gabler, Gisela, and Sidonie Smith, eds. *Writing New Identities: Gender, Nation, and Immigration in Contemporary Europe*. Minneapolis and London: University of Minnesota Press, 1997.

Brodie, Janine, ed. *Women and Canadian Public Policy*. Toronto: Harcourt Brace and Company, 1996.

Buikema, Rosemarie, and Anneke Smelik, eds. *Women's Studies and Culture: A Feminist Introduction*. London and Atlantic Highlands NJ: Zed Books, 1993.

Burston, Paul, and Colin Richardson, eds. *A Queer Romance: Lesbians, Gay Men, and Popular Culture*. London: Routledge, 1995.

Burt, Sandra, Lorraine Code, and Kindsay Dorney, eds. *Changing Patterns: Women in Canada*. 2nd. ed. Toronto: McClelland and Stewart, 1993.

Butler, Judith. *Gender Trouble: Feminism and the Subversion of Identity*. London: Routledge, 1990.

–. *Bodies That Matter: On the Discursive Limits of Sex*. London: Routledge, 1993.

–, and J.W. Scott, eds. *Feminists Theorise the Political*. New York: Routledge, 1992.

Cameron, Deborah. "The Language-Gender Interface: Challenging Co-optation." In *Rethinking Language and Gender Research: Theory and Practice*, ed. V. Bergvall, J. Bing, and A. Freed. London: Longman, 1996.

Case, Sue-Ellen. *The Domain-Matrix: Performing Lesbian at the End of Print Culture*. Bloomington: Indiana University Press, 1996.

Darren, Alison. *Lesbian Film Guide*. London: Cassell, 2000.

Davidman, Lynn, and Shelly Tenenbaum, eds. *Feminist Perspectives on Jewish Studies*. New Haven: Yale University Press, 1994.

Diamond, Bonnie, and Francine Fournier. *Equality and Access: A New Social Contract*. Montreal: National Film Board, 1987.

Doty, Alexander. *Flaming Classics: Queering the Film Canon*. London: Routledge, 2000.

–, and Corey K. Creekmur, eds. *Out in Culture: Gay, Lesbian, and Queer Essays on Popular Culture*. Durham: Duke University Press, 1995.

Dyer, Richard. *Now You See It: Studies on Lesbian and Gay Film*. London: Routledge, 1990.

–. *Images: Essays on Representations*. London: Routledge, 1993.

Gabriel, Christina. "One or the Other? 'Race,' Gender and the Limits of Official Multiculturalism." In *Women and Canadian Public Policy*, ed. Janine Brodie. 173-98. Toronto: Harcourt Brace and Company, 1996.

Garber, M. *Vested Interests: Cross-Dressing and Cultural Anxiety*. New York: Routledge, 1992.

Gedalof, Irene. *Against Purity: Rethinking Identity with Indian and Western Feminisms*. London: Routledge, 1999.

Gever, Martha, Pratibha Parmar, and John Greyson, eds. *Queer Looks: Perspectives on Lesbian and Gay Film and Video*. London: Routledge, 1993.

Grewal, Inderpal, and Caren Kaplan, eds. *Scattered Hegemonies: Postmodernity and Transnational Feminist Practices*. Minneapolis: University of Minnesota Press, 1994.

Grossman, Andrew, ed. *Queer Asian Cinema: Shadows in the Shade*. New York: Harrington Park Press, 2000.

Grosz, Elizabeth. *Volatile Bodies: Towards a Corporeal Feminism*. Bloomington: Indiana University Press, 1994.

Hasan, Zoya, ed. *Forging Identities: Gender, Communities, and the State*. New Delhi: Kali for Women, 1994.

hooks, bell. *Ain't I a Woman: Black Women and Feminism*. London: Pluto Press, 1982.

Hoshino, Edith, Jeanette Clausen, Dagmar Schultz, and Naomi Stephan, eds. *German Feminism: Readings in Politics and Literature*. New York: State University of New York, 1984.

Jacobs, Sue-Ellen, Wesley Thomas, and Sabine Lang, eds. *Two-Spirit People: Native American Gender Identity, Sexuality and Spirituality*. Urbana: University of Illinois Press, 1997.

Jackson, Claire, and Peter Tapp, eds. *The Bent Lens: A World Guide to Gay and Lesbian Film*. St. Kilda, Australia: Australian Catalogue Company, 1997.

Jordan, Glenn, and Chris Weedon. *Cultural Politics: Class, Gender, Race and the Postmodern World*. Oxford, UK, and Cambridge, MA: Blackwell Publishers, 1995.

Kaplan, Caren, Norma Alarcón, and Minoo Moallem, eds. *Between Woman and Nation: Nationalisms, Transnational Feminisms, and the State*. Durham, NC: Duke University Press, 1999.

Kaplan, Carla. *The Erotics of Talk: Women's Writing and Feminist Paradigms*. New York: Oxford University Press, 1996.

Kerber, Linda K. *No Constitutional Right to Be Ladies: Women and the Obligations of Citizenship*. New York: Hill and Wang, 1998.

Kuzniar, Alice A. *The Queer German Cinema*. Stanford, CA: Stanford University Press, 2000.

Looser, Devoney, and E. Ann Kaplan, eds. *Generations: Academic Feminists in Dialogue*. Minneapolis: University of Minnesota Press, 1997.

Lutz, Helma, Ann Phoenix, and Nira Yuval-Davis, eds. *Crossfires: Nationalism, Racism, and Gender in Europe*. London and East Haven, CT: Pluto Press for the European Forum of Left Feminists, 1995.

Mirza, H.S., ed. *Black British Feminism: A Reader*. London: Routledge, 1997.

Mohanram, Radhika. *Black Body: Women, Colonialism and Space*. St. Leonards, NSW: Allen and Unwin, 1999.

Mohanty, Chandra Talpade, Ann Russo, and Lourdes Torres, eds. *Third World Women and the Politics of Feminism*. Bloomington: University of Indiana Press, 1991.

Moi, Toril. *Sexual/Textual Politics: Feminist Literary Theory*. London: Methuen, 1985.

Murray, Raymond. *Images in the Dark: An Encyclopedia of Gay and Lesbian Film and Video.* Philadelphia: TLA Publications, 1994.

Nair, Janaki, and Mary E. John, eds. *A Question of Silence: The Sexual Economies of Modern India.* New York: St. Martin's Press, 2000 (London: Zed Books, 1998).

Nfah-Abbenyi, Juliana Makuchi. *Gender in African Women's Writing: Identity, Sexuality, and Difference.* Bloomington: Indiana University Press, 1997.

–, with an introduction by Eloise A. Brière. *Your Madness Not Mine: Stories of Cameroon.* Athens: Ohio University Center for International Studies, 1999.

Nicholson, Linda J., ed. *Feminism/Postmodernism.* London: Routledge, 1990.

Nnaemeka, Obioma. "Feminism, Rebellious Women and Cultural Boundaries: Re-reading Flora Nwapa and her Compatriots." *Research in African Literature* 26, 2 (Summer 1995): 81-113.

–, ed. *The Politics of (M)othering: Womanhood, Identity, and Resistance in African Literature.* London: Routledge, 1997.

–, ed. *Sisterhood, Feminisms, and Power: From Africa to the Diaspora.* Trenton, NJ: Africa World Press, 1998.

Oyewumi, O. *The Invention of Women: Making Sense of Western Gender Discourses.* Minneapolis: University of Minnesota Press, 1997.

Parr, Joy, and Mark Rosenfelds, eds. *Gender and History in Canada.* Toronto: Copp Clark, 1996.

Pratt, Mary Louise. *Imperial Eyes: Travel Writing and Transculturation.* London: Routledge, 1992.

Ramazanoglu, C. *Feminism and the Contradictions of Oppression.* London: Routledge, 1989.

Rowe, Kathleen. *The Unruly Woman: Gender and the Genres of Laughter.* Austin: Texas University Press, 1995.

Russo, Mary. *The Female Grotesque: Risk, Excess and Modernity.* London: Routledge, 1994.

Siegel, Carol, and Ann Kibbey, eds. *Forming and Reforming Identity.* Genders 21. New York: New York University Press, 1995.

Skeggs, Beverley, ed. *Feminist Cultural Theory: Process and Production.* Manchester: Manchester University Press, 1995.

Spender, Dale. *Nattering on the Net: Women, Power and Cyberspace.* North Melbourne: Spinifex Press, 1995.

Stasiulis, Daiva, and Nira Yuval-Davis, eds. *Unsettling Settler Societies: Articulations of Gender, Race, Ethnicity and Class.* London and Thousand Oaks, CA: Sage Publications, 1995.

Straayer, Chris. *Deviant Eyes, Deviant Bodies: Sexual Re-orientations in Film and Video.* New York: Columbia University Press, 1996.

Thapan, Meenakshi, ed. *Embodiment: Essays on Gender and Identity.* Delhi and Oxford: Oxford University Press, 1997.

Tong, Rosemarie. *Feminist Thought: A Comprehensive Introduction.* London: Routledge, 1992.

Valdivia, Angharad N., ed. *Feminism, Multiculturalism, and the Media: Global Diversities.* Thousand Oaks, CA: Sage Publications, 1995.

Waugh, Thomas. *Hard to Imagine: Gay Male Eroticism in Photography and Film from Their Beginnings to Stonewall.* New York: Columbia University Press, 1996.

–. "Cinemas, Nations, Masculinities: The Martin Walsh Memorial Lecture (1998)." *Canadian Journal of Film Studies* 8, 1 (1999): 8-44.

–. *The Fruit Machine: Twenty Years of Writings on Queer Cinema.* Durham, NC: Duke University Press, 2000.

Waylen, Georgina. *Gender in Third World Politics.* Buckingham: Open University Press, 1996.

Wazir Jahan Karim. *Women between Adat and Islam.* Boulder, CO: Westview Press, 1992.

Weedon, Chris. *Feminist Practice and Poststructuralist Theory.* Oxford: Blackwell, 1987.

Wing, Adrien Katherine, ed. *Global Critical Race Feminism: An International Reader.* Foreword by Angela Y. Davis. New York: New York University Press, 2000.

Woodward, Kathleen, ed. *Figuring Age: Women, Bodies, Generations.* Bloomington: Indiana University Press, 1999.

Yuval-Davis, Nira. *Gender and Nation.* London and Thousand Oaks: Sage Publications, 1997.

Women in Film: Feminist Theory and Studies of Women Filmmakers

Acker, Ally. *Reel Women: Pioneers of the Cinema, 1896 to the Present.* New York, NY: Continuum, 1991.

Adler, Laure. *Marguerite Duras.* Paris: Gallimard, 1998.

Armatage, Kay, Kass Banning, Brenda Longfellow, and Janine Marchessault, eds. *Gendering the Nation: Canadian Women's Cinema.* Toronto: University of Toronto Press, 1999.

Attwood, Lynne, with Maya Turowskaya and Oksana Bulgakova. *Red Women on the Silver Screen: Soviet Women and Cinema from the Beginning to the End of the Communist Era.* Trans. Lynne Attwood and Kirsten Sams. London: Pandora, 1993.

Blonski, Annette, Barbara Creed, and Freda Freiberg, eds. *Don't Shoot Darling! A History of Independent Women's Filmmaking in Australia.* Richmond, Victoria: Greenhouse, 1987.

Bobo, Jacqueline. *Black Women as Cultural Readers.* NY: Columbia University Press, 1995.

–, ed. *Black Women Film and Video Artists.* London: Routledge, 1998.

Brooks, Louise. *Lulu in Hollywood: Expanded Edition.* Minnesota: Minnesota University Press, 2000.

Brückner, Jutta. "On Autobiographical Filmmaking." *Women in German Yearbook* 11 (1995): 1-12.

Brunsdon, Charlotte, ed. *Films for Women.* London: British Film Institute, 1986.

Carrière, Louise. *Femmes et cinéma québécois.* Montreal: Boréal Express, 1983.

Carson, Diane, Linda Dittmar, and Janice R. Welsch, eds. *Multiple Voices in Feminist Film Criticism.* Minneapolis: University of Minnesota Press, 1994.

Carter, Sarah. *Capturing Women: The Manipulation of Cultural Imagery in Canada's Prairie West.* Montreal: McGill-Queen's University Press, 1997.

Citron, Michelle. *Home Movies and Other Necessary Fictions.* Minneapolis, MN: Minnesota University Press, 1998.

Cole, Janis, and Holly Dale. *Calling the Shots: Profiles of Women Filmmakers.* Kingston, ON: Quarry Press, 1993.

Cook, Pam, and Philip Dodd, eds. *Women and Film: A Sight and Sound Reader.* London: Scarlet Press, 1993.

Cottenet-Hage, Madeleine, and Robert P. Kroller. "The Cinema of Duras in Search of an Ideal Image." *The French Review* 63, 1 (1989): 88-98.

Cowie, Elizabeth. *Representing the Woman: Cinema and Psychoanalysis.* Basingstoke: Macmillan, 1997.

Creed, Barbara. *The Monstrous-feminine: Film, Feminism, Psychoanalysis.* London: Routledge, 1993.

"'D' is for Dilemma." *Herizons* (Summer 1995): 24-9.

Dawson, Jan. "Shadows of Terrorism in the New German Cinema." *Sight and Sound* 48, 4 (1979): 242-5.

–. "A Labyrinth of Subsidies: The Origins of the New German Cinema." *Sight and Sound* 50, 1 (1980/1): 14-20.

Doane, Mary Ann. *The Desire to Desire.* London: Macmillan, 1987.

–. "Masquerade Reconsidered: Further Thoughts on the Female Spectator." *Discourse* 11 (1988-9): 42-54.

–, Patricia Mellencamp, and Linda Williams, eds. *RE-Vision: Essays in Feminist Criticism.* Los Angeles: American Film Institute, 1984.

Donougho, Martin. "Margarethe von Trotta: Gynemagoguery and the Dilemmas of a Filmmaker." *Literature/Film Quarterly* 16, 1 (1988): 149-60.

Duras, Marguerite. *India Song.* Paris: Albatros, 1979.

Elsaesser, Thomas. "Mother Courage and Divided Daughters." *Monthly Film Bulletin* 50, 594 (July 1983): 176-8.

Erens, Patricia, ed. *Issues in Feminist Film Criticism.* Bloomington: Indiana University Press, 1990.

Falkowska, Janina. "A Case of Mixed Identities: The Representation of Women in Post-Socialist Polish Films." *Canadian Woman Studies: Women in Central and Eastern Europe* 16, 1 (1995): 35-7.

Fieldman Miller, Lynn. *The Hand That Holds the Camera: Interviews with Women Film and Video Directors.* New York: Garland, 1988.

Fischer, Lucy. *Shot/Countershot: Film Tradition and Women's Cinema.* Princeton, NJ: Princeton University Press, 1989.

Flitterman-Lewis, Sandy. *To Desire Differently: Feminism and the French Cinema.* Urbana: University of Illinois Press, 1990.

Frieden, Sandra, Richard W. McCormick, Vibeke R. Petersen, and Laurie Melissa Vogelsang, eds. *Gender and German Cinema: Feminist Interventions.* 2 vols. Berg: Providence, 1993.

Gaines, Jane. "White Privilege and Looking Relations: Race and Gender in Feminist Film Theory." In *Film and Theory: An Anthology,* ed. Robert Stam and Toby Miller. 715-32. Malden, MA: Blackwell Publishing, 2000.

Gamman, Lorraine, and Margaret Marshment, eds. *The Female Gaze: Women as Viewers of Popular Culture.* London: Red Comet Press, 1989 (Seattle: Women's Press, 1988).

Hanley, JoAnn. *The First Generation: Women and Video, 1970-75: Essays by JoAnn Hanley and Ann-Sargent Wooster.* New York: Independent Curators Inc., 1993.

Harper, Sue. *Women in British Cinema: Mad, Bad and Dangerous to Know.* London: Continuum, 2000.

Haskell, Molly. *From Reverence to Rape: The Treatment of Women in the Movies.* 2nd ed. Chicago: University of Chicago Press, 1987.

Hehr, Renate. *Margarethe von Trotta: Filmmaking as Liberation.* Trans. Ilze Klavina. Stuttgart and London: Edition Axel Menges, 2000.

Higashi, Sumiko. *Virgins, Vamps, and Flappers: The American Silent Movie Heroine.* St. Albans, VT: Eden Press Women's Publications, 1978.

Hill, Leslie. *Marguerite Duras: Apocalyptic Desires.* London: Routledge, 1993.

Hollows, Joanne. *Feminism, Femininity and Popular Culture.* Manchester: Manchester University Press, 2000.

Holmlund, Chris. *Impossible Bodies: Femininity and Masculinity at the Movies.* London: Routledge, 2001.

hooks, bell. *Black Looks: Race and Representation.* London: Turnaround, 1992.

–. *Reel to Real: Race, Sex, and Class at the Movies.* London: Routledge, 1996.

–. "The Oppositional Gaze: Black Female Spectators." In *Film and Theory: An Anthology,* ed. Robert Stam and Toby Miller. 510-23. Malden, MA: Blackwell Publishing, 2000.

Humm, Maggie. *Feminism and Film.* Edinburgh/Indiana: Edinburgh University Press/ Indiana University Press, 1997.

Indiana, Gary. "Getting Ready for the Golden Eighties: A Conversation with Chantal Akerman." *Artforum* (Summer 1983): 55-61.

Jayamanne, Laleen. *Kiss Me Deadly: Feminism and Cinema for the Moment.* Sydney: Power Publications, 1995.

Jenny, Elisabeth, ed. *The Centenary of Cinema: Women's Path through European Film History.* Brussels: Information for Women, Directorate, 1996.

Johnston, Claire. "Women's Cinema as Counter Cinema." In *Movies and Methods: An Anthology,* ed. Bill Nichol. 208-17. Berkeley: University of California Press, 1976.

–, ed. *Notes on Women's Cinema.* London: Society for Education in Film and Television, 1973.

Juhasz, Alexandra. "Our Auto-bodies, Ourselves: Representing Real Women in Feminist Video." *Afterimage* (February 1994): 10-4.

–, ed. *Women of Vision: Histories in Feminist Film and Video.* Minneapolis: University of Minnesota Press, 2001.

Kaplan, E. Ann. "Aspects of British Feminist Film Theory." *Jump Cut* 12, 13 (1976): 52-5.

–. "Women's Happy Time Commune: New Departures in Women's Films." *Jump Cut* 12, 13 (1976).

–. *Women and Film: Both Sides of the Camera.* London: Routledge, 1988 (New York: Methuen, 1983).

–. *Rocking around the Clock: Television, Postmodernism and Consumer Culture.* London: Routledge, 1987.

–. *Motherhood and Representation: The Mother in Popular Culture and Melodrama.* London: Routledge, 1992.

–, ed. *Feminism and Film.* Oxford: Oxford University Press, 2000.

Kay, Karyn, and Gerald Peary, eds. *Women and the Cinema: A Critical Anthology.* New York: Dutton, 1977.

–. *Images of Women in the Cinema.* New York: Doubleday, 1980.

Knight, Julia. *Women and the New German Cinema.* London: Verso, 1992.

Kosta, Barbara. *Recasting Autobiography: Women's Counterfictions in Contemporary German Literature and Film.* Ithaca: Cornell University Press, 1994.

Krsilovsky, Alexis. *Women behind the Camera.* Westport, CT: Praeger, 1997.

Kuhn, Annette. *The Power of the Image: Essays in Representation and Sexuality.* London/Boston: Routledge/Kegan Paul, 1985.

–. *Women's Pictures: Feminism and Cinema.* 2nd ed. London: Verso, 1994.

Lane, Christina. "From *The Loveless* to *Point Break*: Kathryn Bigelow's Trajectory in Action." *Cinema Journal* 37,4 (1998): 59-81.

–. *Feminist Hollywood: from Born in Flames to Point Break.* Detroit: Wayne State University Press, 2000.

Lauretis, Teresa de. *Alice Doesn't: Feminism, Semiotics, Cinema.* Bloomington: Indiana University Press, 1984.

–. *Technologies of Gender: Essays on Theory, Film, and Fiction.* Bloomington: Indiana University Press, 1987.

–. *The Practice of Love: Lesbian Sexuality and Perverse Desire.* Bloomington: Indiana University Press, 1994.

–. "Rethinking Women's Cinema: Aesthetics and Feminist Theory." In *Film and Theory: An Anthology,* ed. Robert Stam and Toby Miller. 317-35. Malden, MA: Blackwell Publishing, 2000.

Lawrence, Amy. *Echo and Narcissus: Women's Voices in Classical Hollywood Cinema.* Berkeley: University of California Press, 1991.

Lejeune, Paule. *Le Cinéma des femmes.* Paris: Atlas Herminier, 1987.

Lesage, Julia. "*One Way or Another*: Dialectical, Revolutionary, Feminist." *Jump Cut* 20 (May 1979): 20-3.

MacDonald, Scott. "Interview with Sally Potter." *Camera Obscura* 35: (1995): 187-220.

Magretta, William R., and Joan Magretta. "Lina Wertmüller and the Tradition of Italian Carnivalesque Comedy." *Genre* 12 (1979): 25-43.

Marchessault, Janine, ed. *Mirror Machine: Video and Identity.* Toronto: YYZ Books, 1995.

Martin-Márquez, Susan. *Feminist Discourse and Spanish Cinema: Sight Unseen.* Oxford: Oxford University Press, 1999.

Matthews, Nicole. *Comic Politics: Gender in Hollywood Comedy after the New Right.* Manchester: Manchester University Press, 2001.

Mayne, Judith. *The Woman at the Keyhole: Feminism and Women's Cinema.* Bloomington: Indiana University Press, 1990.

–. *Cinema and Spectatorship.* London: Routledge, 1993.

–. *Directed by Dorothy Arzner.* Bloomington: Indiana University Press, 1994.

–. *Framed: Lesbians, Feminists and Media Culture.* Minneapolis: Minnesota University Press, 2000.

McGarry, Eileen. "Documentary Realism and Women's Cinema." *Women and Film* 2, 7 (1975): 50-9.

Mellencamp, Patricia. *A Fine Romance: Five Ages of Film Feminism.* Philadelphia: Temple University Press, 1995.

Meyers, Marian, ed. *Mediated Women: Representations in Popular Culture.* Cresskill, NJ: Hampton Press, 1999.

Modleski, Tania. *The Women Who Knew Too Much.* London: Methuen, 1988.

Moeller, H.B. "Women's Cinema: The Case of Margarethe von Trotta." *Film Criticism* 9 (1984-5): 111-26.

Mulvey, Laura. "Visual Pleasure and Narrative Cinema." *Screen* 16, 3 (1975): 6-18.

–. *Visual and Other Pleasures.* Basingstoke: Macmillan, 1989.

Negra, Diane. *Off-White Hollywood: American Culture and Ethnic Female Stardom.* London: Routledge, 2001.

O'Sickey, Ingeborg Majer, and Ingeborg von Zadow, eds. *Triangulated Visions: Women in Recent German Cinema.* Albany: State University of New York Press, 1998.

Pallister, Janis L. *French-speaking Women Film Directors: A Guide.* Madison, NJ: Fairleigh Dickinson University Press, 1997.

Paris, Barry. *Louise Brooks: A Biography.* Minneapolis: University of Minnesota Press, 2000.

Penley, Constance, ed. *Feminism and Film Theory.* New York/London: Routledge/BFI, 1988.

–. *The Future of an Illusion: Film, Feminism and Psychoanalysis.* London: Routledge, 1989.

Pietropaolo, Laura, and Ada Testaferri, eds. *Feminisms in the Cinema.* Bloomington: Indiana University Press, 1995.

Pomerance, Murray, ed. *Ladies and Gentlemen, Boys and Girls: Gender in Film at the End of the Twentieth Century.* Albany: State University of New York Press, 2001.

Portuges, Catherine. *Screen Memories: The Hungarian Cinema of Márta Mészáros.* Bloomington: Indiana University Press, 1993.

Potter, Sally. "Like Night and Day. Interview with Sheila Johnston." *Film Bulletin* 51, 604 (1984): 140-1.

Pribram, D., ed. *Female Spectators: Looking at Film and Television.* London: Verso, 1988.

Quart, Barbara Koenig. *Women Directors: The Emergence of a New Cinema.* NY: Praeger, 1988.

–. "Three Central European Women Directors Revisited." *Cineaste* 19, 4: 58-61.

Rabinovitz, Lauren. *Points of Resistance: Women, Power and Politics in the New York Avant-garde Cinema, 1943-71.* Urbana: University of Illinois Press, 1991.

Rainer, Yvonne. *The Films of Yvonne Rainer.* Bloomington: Indiana University Press, 1989.

Rascaroli, Laura. "Steel in the Gaze: on POV and the Discourse of Vision in Kathryn Bigelow's Cinema." *Screen* 38, 3 (1997): 232-46.

Read, Jacinda. *The New Avengers: Feminism, Femininity and the Rape-revenge Cycle.* Manchester: Manchester University Press, 2000.

Redding, Judith M., and Victoria A. Brownworth. *Film Fatales: Independent Women Directors.* Seattle: Seal Press, 1997.

Rich, B. Ruby. "In the Name of Feminist Film Criticism." In *Jump Cut: Hollywood, Politics and Counter-Cinema,* ed. Peter Steven. 208-30. Toronto: Between the Lines, 1985.

–. *Chick Flicks: Theories and Memories of the Feminist Film Movement.* Durham NC: Duke University Press, 1998.

Rinke, Andrea. "From Models to Misfits: Women in DEFA Films of the 1970s and 1980s." In *DEFA: East German Cinema, 1946-1992,* ed. Seán Allan and John Sandford. 183-203. New York: Berghahn Books, 1999.

Rollet, Brigitte. *Coline Serreau.* Manchester/New York: Manchester University Press/St. Martin's Press, 1998.

–. "Femmes cinéastes en France: l'après May '68." *Clio: Femmes, Histoire et Société* 10 (1999): 233-48.

Rose, Jacqueline. *Sexuality in the Field of Vision.* London: Verso, 1986.

Rosen, Marjorie. *Popcorn Venus: Women, Movies and the American Dream.* New York: Coward, McCann and Geohagen, 1973.

Roth, Nancy L., and Katie Hogan, eds. *Gendered Epidemic: Representations of Women in the Age of AIDS.* London: Routledge, 1998.

Russo Bullaro, Grace. "Gender, Role, and Sexual Identity in the Works of D.H. Lawrence, Lina Wertmüller, and Jean Genet." PhD diss., State University of New York, 1993.

Scherbarth, Chris. "Studio D of the National Film Board of Canada: Seeing Ourselves Through Women's Eyes." MA thesis, Carleton University, Ontario, 1986.

–. "Canada's Studio D: A Women's Room with an International Reputation." *Canadian Woman's Studies* 8, 1 (1987): 25.

Shohat, Ella. "Toward a Feminist Ethnography of the Cinema." In *Film and Theory: An Anthology,* ed. Robert Stam and Toby Miller. 669-96. Malden, MA: Blackwell Publishing, 2000.

Showalter, Elaine, ed. *The New Feminist Criticism: Essay on Women, Literature and Theory.* New York: Pantheon Books, 1985.

Silverman, Kaja. *The Acoustic Mirror: The Female Voice in Psychoanalysis and Cinema.* Bloomington: Indiana University Press, 1988.

Smelik, Anneke. *And the Mirror Cracked: Feminist Cinema and Film Theory.* Houndmills, Basingstoke, Hampshire/New York: Macmillan/St. Martin's Press, 1998.

Smith, Alison. *Agnès Varda.* Manchester/New York: Manchester University Press/St. Martin's Press, 1998.

Smith, Sharon. *Women Who Make Movies.* New York: Hopkinson and Blake, 1975.

Smith, Sidonie, and Julia Watson, eds. *Women, Autobiography, Theory: A Reader.* Madison: University of Wisconsin Press, 1998.

Staiger, Janet. *Bad Women: The Regulation of Female Sexuality in Early American Cinema.* Minneapolis: University of Minnesota Press, 1995.

Steven, Peter, ed. *Jump Cut: Hollywood, Politics and Counter-Cinema.* Toronto: Between The Lines, 1985.

Tasker, Yvonne. *Working Girls: Gender and Sexuality in Popular Cinema.* London: Routledge, 1998.

Tarr, Carrie. *Diane Kurys.* Manchester/New York: Manchester University Press/St. Martin's Press, 1999.

–, with Brigitte Rollet. *Cinema and the Second Sex: Women's Filmmaking in France in the 1980s and 1990s.* London: Continuum, 2001.

Thornham, Sue. *Passionate Detachments: An Introduction to Feminist Film Theory.* Oxford: Oxford University Press, 1997.

–, ed. *Feminist Film Theory: A Reader.* New York: New York University Press, 1999.

Thumim, Janet. *Celluloid Sisters: Women and Popular Cinema.* London: Macmillan, 1992.

Toronto Women in Film and Television. *Changing Focus: The Future for Women in the Canadian Film and Television Industry.* Toronto: Women in Film and Television, 1991.

Vincendeau, Ginette. "Women's Cinema, Film Theory and Feminism in France." *Screen* 28, 4 (1987): 4-18.

Waldman, Diane, and Janet Walker, eds. *Feminism and Documentary.* Minneapolis: University of Minnesota Press, 1999.

Walsh, Andrea S. *Women's Film and Female Experience, 1940-1950.* New York: Praeger, 1984.

Ward, Jennifer K. "Enacting the Different Voice: Christa Klages and Feminist History." *Women in German Yearbook* 11 (1995): 49-65.

Weiss, Andrea. *Vampires and Violets: Lesbians in the Cinema.* London: Jonathan Cape, 1992.

Wilkinson, Kathleen. "Filmmaker Deepa Mehta is on Fire." *Lesbian News* 23, 2 (September 1997): 38-9.

Williams, James S., with Janet Sayers. *Revisioning Duras: Film, Race, Sex.* Liverpool: Liverpool University Press, 2000.

Wilton, Tamsin, ed. *Immortal, Invisible: Lesbians and the Moving Image.* London: Routledge, 1995.

Young, Lola. *Fear of the Dark: "Race," Gender, and Sexuality in the Cinema.* London: Routledge, 1996.

Women in Film: Postcolonial Theory and Criticism, Indigenous and Non-Western Perspectives

Alexander, M. Jacqui, and Chandra Talpade Mohanty, eds. *Feminist Genealogies, Colonial Legacies, Democratic Futures.* New York: Routledge, 1997.

Berry, Chris. "Chinese 'Women's Cinema,' Introduction. Interviews with Zhang Nuanxin, Peng Xiaolian, Hu Mei." *Camera Obscura* 5, 18 (1989): 5-19.

Bloul, Rachel A.D. "Veiled Objects of (Post)-Colonial Desire: Forbidden Women Disrupt the Republican Fraternal Space." *Australian Journal of Anthropology* 51, 2 (1994): 113-23.

Cham, Mbye B. "African Women and Cinema: A Conversation with Anne Mungai." *Research in African Literature* 25 (Fall 1994): 93-104.

Creed, Barbara, and Jeanette Hoorn, eds. *Body Trade: Captivity, Cannibalism and Colonialism in the Pacific.* Sydney: Pluto Press, 2000.

Da Cunha, Uma, and Maithili Rao, eds. *Film India: The New Generation, 1960-1980: An Examination of India's New Cinema, Its Preoccupation with a Changing Society and the Status of Women, Highlighted in the Work of 19 Representative Directors*. New Delhi: Directorate of Film Festivals, 1981.

Dash, Julie, with Toni Cade Bambara and bell hooks. *Daughters of the Dust: The Making of an African American Woman's Film*. New York: New Press, 1992.

Davies, Carole Boyce. *Ngambika: Studies of Women in African Literature*. Trenton, NJ: Africa World Press, 1986.

Davies, Miranda, ed. *Third World, Second Sex*. Vol. 2. London and New Jersey: Zed Books, 1987.

–. *Women Filmmakers of the African and Asian Diaspora: Decolonizing the Gaze, Locating Subjectivity*. Carbondale, IL: Southern Illinois University Press, 1997.

Ghosh, Bishnupriya, and Brinda Bose, eds. *Interventions: Feminist Dialogues on Third World Women's Literature and Film*. New York: Garland, 1997.

Gopalan, Lalitha. "Avenging Women in Indian Cinema." *Screen* 38, 1 (Spring 1997): 42-59.

Green, Rayna. "The Pocahontas Perplex: The Image of Indian Women in American Culture." *Massachusetts Review* 16 (Autumn 1975): 698-714.

Harrow, Kenneth W., ed. *With Open Eyes: Women and African Cinema*. Amsterdam, AT: Rodopi, 1997.

–, ed. *African Cinema: Postcolonial and Feminist Readings*. Trenton, NJ: Africa World Press, 1999.

Hershfield, Joanne. *Mexican Cinema/Mexican Woman, 1940-1950*. Tucson: University of Arizona Press, 1996.

Jennings, Karen. "Ways of Seeing and Speaking about Aboriginal Women." *Hecate*, 13, 2 (1987/88): 113-33.

–. *Sites of Difference: Cinematic Representations of Aboriginality and Gender*. South Melbourne: Australian Film Institute Research and Information Centre, 1993.

Jinhua, Dai. "Invisible Women: Contemporary Chinese Cinema and Women's Film." *Positions* 3, 1 (Spring 1995): 255-80.

Kaplan, E. Ann. "Problematising Cross-cultural Analysis: The Case of Women in the Recent Chinese Cinema." In *Perspectives on Chinese Cinema*, ed. Chris Berry. 2nd ed. 141-54. London: BFI, 1991.

–. *Looking for the Other: Feminism, Film and the Imperial Gaze*. London: Routledge, 1997.

Khanna, Ranjana. "*The Battle of Algiers* and *The Nouba of the Women of Mont Chenoua*: From Third to Fourth Cinema." In *Third Text* 43 (Summer 1998): 13-32.

McClintock, Anne, Aamir Mufti, and Ella Shohat, eds. *Dangerous Liaisons: Gender, Nation, and Postcolonial Perspectives*. Minneapolis and London: University of Minnesota Press, 1997.

Mukora, Wanjiku Beatrice. "Disrupting Binary Divisions: Representation of Identity in *Saikati* and *Battle of the Sacred Tree*." MA thesis, McGill University, 1999.

Ngo-Nguidjol, Emilie. "Women in African Cinema: An Annotated Bibliography." In *African Cinema: Postcolonial and Feminist Readings*, ed. Kenneth W. Harrow. 305-37. Trenton, NJ: Africa World Press, 1999.

Parmar, Pratibha. "Strategies of Representation." In *Identity: Community, Culture, Difference*, ed. Jonathan Rutherford. London: Lawrence and Wishart, 1990.

–, and Alice Walker. *Warrior Marks: Female Genital Mutilation and the Sexual Blinding of Women*. New York: Harcourt Brace, 1993.

Petty, Sheila. "How an African Woman Can Be: African Women Filmmakers Construct Women." *Discourse* 18, 3 (Spring 1996): 72-88.

Rayns, Tony. "Position of Women in New Chinese Cinema." In *East-west Film Journal* 1, 2 (June 1987): 32-44.

Robin, D., and I. Jaffe, eds. *Redirecting the Gaze: Gender, Theory, and Cinema in the Third World*. Albany: State University of New York Press, 1999.

Rony, Fatimah Tobing. *The Third Eye: Race, Cinema and Ethnographic Spectacle*. Durham: Duke University Press, 1996.

Tarr, Carrie. "Ethnicity and Identity in Contemporary French Cinema: The Case of the Young Maghrebi-French Woman." *Iris* 24 (1997): 125-35.

Trinh T. Minh-ha. *Woman, Native, Other*. London: Routledge, 1985.

–. *When the Moon Waxes Red: Representation, Gender and Cultural Politics*. London: Routledge, 1991.

–. *Framer Framed: Film Scripts and Interviews*. London: Routledge, 1992.

–. *Cinema: Interval*. London: Routledge, 1999.

Notes on Contributors

Kass Banning teaches Cinema Studies at the University of Toronto. She co-founded and co-edited *CinéAction* and *Borderlines* for a decade and is co-editor of and contributor to *Gendering the Nation: Canadian Women's Cinema*. She has written extensively on Canadian and black diasporic cinema and was recently awarded a grant from the Department of Canadian Heritage to complete a study on configurations of race and nation in Canadian film.

Kathryn Barnwell teaches English and Women's Studies at Malaspina University-College, Nanaimo, British Columbia.

Suzanne Buchan, formerly a lecturer in Cinema Studies at the University of Zurich, Switzerland, is now Head of the Animation Research Centre at the Surrey Institute of Art and Design, UK. She is co-director of the FANTOCHE International Festival for Animation Film (Baden, Switzerland).

Penelope Buitenhuis, who lives in Toronto, has been writing and directing films since 1982. After making two "movies of the week" and three features, she won two Geminis in 2001 for *Tokyo Girls,* a documentary produced by the National Film Board of Canada.

Diane Burgess is a PhD student in the School of Communication at Simon Fraser University, Burnaby, BC. She is also a programmer for the Canadian Images component of the Vancouver International Film Festival.

Maria de los Angeles Carbonetti is a doctoral student in Hispanic Studies at the University of British Columbia working on gender representation in the cultural magazine *Plus Ultra* (Argentina, 1900-30).

Corinn Columpar is a doctoral student in the Institute for Women's Studies at Emory University in Atlanta, Georgia, and teaches Film Studies and Women's Studies at Keene State College in Keene, New Hampshire.

Josette Déléas has a doctorate in cinema from the Université Paul Valéry, Montpellier, France. She teaches film at Mount Saint Vincent University, Halifax, and is working on a book about the life and work of Italian director Lina Wertmüller.

Jocelyne Denault, who obtained her PhD from the Université de Montréal, has written a number of articles on women in film in Quebec, as well as a book, *Dans l'ombre des projecteurs: Les Québécoises et le cinéma* (1995). She has been teaching film for twenty years, is the former president of Cinéma Femmes, and helped organize the women's film festival "Silence elles tournent" for ten years. She is currently president of Création/ Femmes/Diffusion, an organization that promotes women's artistic expression, and teaches at the CEGEP de Saint-Laurent (Montreal).

Zoe Dirse is a documentary filmmaker and cinematographer who has worked for the National Film Board of Canada in the Camera Department for fifteen years. One of her many projects is a documentary entitled *Madame President*, about Vaira Vike-Freiberga, a former University of Montreal psychology professor who is now President of Latvia.

Caroline Eades teaches at Stendhal University, Grenoble, France, and at the University of Maryland, College Park, USA. She was previously French Cultural Attachée in Boston and in San Francisco, and worked in the commercial division of Unifrance Film International, Paris.

Ken Eisner edits the film section of the *Georgia Straight*, for which he has been writing since 1987. He has been a travelling film critic for *Variety* since 1991. Before that, he was an illustrator, photographer, and art director, working for publications in Northern California and Alberta. He is currently producing a first feature from his own script.

Mónica Escudero is a graduate student in the Latin American Studies Program at Simon Fraser University, Vancouver, BC.

Janina Falkowska teaches Film Studies in the Department of English at the University of Western Ontario, London, Ontario. Her publications include *The Political Films of Andrzej Wajda* (1996) and reflect her interest in post-socialist Eastern European cinema.

Elena Feder has a PhD in Comparative Literature from Stanford and is currently a SSHRC Research Fellow in the Humanities Department, Simon Fraser University, BC, working on a book on diasporic challenges to visual representation in the Americas.

Catherine Fowler is Reader and Course Leader of the MA program in Independent Film and Filmmaking at Southampton Institute of Higher Education, UK. She has published several articles on Chantal Akerman in edited collections and is currently working on a book about Belgian cinema.

Nicole Giguère is a Quebec writer, producer, and filmmaker who has been involved in film and television for twenty-five years. Her many films range from documentaries on Quebec history, women's humour, rock music, aging, and, most recently, the Barbie doll.

Rita de Grandis teaches contemporary Latin American Literature and Comparative Literature at the University of British Columbia, specializing in literary theory, cultural and postcolonial criticism, and gender issues.

Agnes Huang is a former editor of *Kinesis*, a national feminist newspaper in Canada, which was published from 1974 to 2000.

E. Ann Kaplan is Professor of English and Comparative Studies at SUNY Stony Brook, where she also founded and directs the Humanities Institute. Author of numerous film publications on feminism, psychoanalysis, postmodernism, and postcolonialism, her current project is on trauma, cinema, and witnessing.

Gaik Cheng Khoo graduated with a PhD from the Interdisciplinary Studies program at the University of British Columbia and has taught in Film, Asian Studies, Women's Studies, and English departments. Her research focus is on gender, modernity, and the nation in Malaysian literature and film. She now teaches Southeast Asian culture and literature at the University of Victoria, BC.

Michelle La Flamme is an independent filmmaker and a doctoral student in English at the University of British Columbia. As a mixed-race woman of colour, she has chosen to work on representations of racially hybrid characters in contemporary Canadian literature.

Larissa Lai was a regular contributor to *Kinesis* in the early to mid-1990s. Her first novel, *When Fox Is a Thousand* (1995), was nominated for the Chapters/Books in Canada First Novel Award, and a second novel, *Salt Fish Girl*, is forthcoming. She is currently working on a PhD at the University of Calgary.

Ute Lischke teaches in the Department of Languages and Literature, Wilfrid Laurier University, Waterloo. Her latest book is *Lily Braun, 1865-1916: German Writer, Feminist and Socialist*. She is currently working on a book on women filmmakers in the former German Democratic Republic.

Brenda Longfellow is a director, producer, and teacher of film at York University, Ontario. Her documentary on poet Gwendolyn MacEwen won the 1999 Genie Award for Best Short Documentary. She has written extensively on feminist and Canadian cinema and is the co-editor of an anthology on Canadian women's cinema, *Gendering the Nation*.

Susan Lord is Associate Professor of Film Studies at Queen's University in Kingston, Ontario, where she is also cross-appointed to Women's Studies. She has two co-edited collections in progress, *Fluid Screens: Time and Digital Cultures* and *Killing Women: Representations of Gender and Violence*, and is completing a manuscript on gender, indigeneity, and multiculturalism in the films of Anne Wheeler.

B. Amarilis Lugo de Fabritz obtained her PhD from the Department of Slavic Languages and Literatures at the University of Washington, Seattle, Washington. She is currently working as a Mellon Post-Doctoral Fellow in the Department of Russian and East Asian Languages and Cultures at Emory University, Atlanta, Georgia.

Raman Mann is an Indian filmmaker and recipient of the 1998-99 Media Fellowship Award from the Canadian International Development Agency (CIDA) and the Shastri Indo-Canadian Institute (SICI) to conduct media research on women in prisons.

Angela Martin teaches film studies and practice at Sheffield Hallam University, UK. Previously she was a book editor at the British Film Institute, and then a film and video editor. Her publications include *African Films: the Context of Production* (editor), and a contribution to *Women in Film Noir* (2nd edition).

Lesley Marx teaches in the Department of English at the University of Cape Town, South Africa, and is currently Deputy Dean in the Faculty of Humanities. She co-directs the Cape American Studies Association. Her publications focus on American literature and film, and South African theatre and film, and she is especially interested in the intersections of gender, genre, and region in verbal and visual texts.

Sharon McGowan is a producer of feature films, including *Better than Chocolate* (directed by Anne Wheeler), "movies of the week," and television series. She is also a director and writer of over twenty independent and National Film Board documentaries. She is currently the graduate advisor and an assistant professor in the Film Programme, Department of Theatre, Film and Creative Writing, at the University of British Columbia.

Jan Mennell is an associate professor in the Department of Spanish and Italian at Queen's University in Kingston, Ontario. She has worked on the dictator novel in Latin America and is currently writing a book on Jewish Argentine women's narrative. She has also written and published on Latin American film, especially on the work of María Luisa Bemberg, and has published several articles on both the novel and film versions of *Novia que te vea.*

Donia Mounsef, who completed her doctorate in French at the University of British Columbia, currently teaches French and Theatre Studies at Yale University, USA. She works on theories of the body in postmodern French theatre and film, feminist film theory, and the politics of gender and performance.

Beatrice Wanjiku Mukora holds a BA in Film Studies from Carleton University, Ottawa, and an MA in Communications from McGill University, Montreal. While working on her MA thesis, she began her exploration of postcolonial issues related to identity and gender as well as the developments of the Kenyan film industry. She currently works as a technical writer in the film and video industry in Montreal.

Siew Jin Ooi is a graduate student in the Department of Germanic Studies at the University of Sydney, Australia. She is writing her doctoral dissertation on Margarethe von Trotta.

Tracy Prince is Assistant Professor of Urban Studies and Planning at Portland State University in Oregon. Her teaching and journal publications focus on race relations, cultural studies, gender studies, postcolonial studies, and national identity as explored in literature and film.

Brigitte Rollet is a lecturer at the University of London/Institut Britannique de Paris. She is author of *Coline Serreau* and co-author, with Carrie Tarr, of *Cinema and the Second Sex: Women's Filmmaking in France in the 1980s and 1990s.*

Omar Rodríguez is a doctoral student in Hispanic Studies at the University of British Columbia, specializing in the relationship between cinema and literature, with a focus on Venezuela.

Marni Stanley teaches English and Women's Studies at Malaspina University-College, Nanaimo, BC.

Carrie Tarr is a research fellow at Kingston University, UK, and has published widely on gender and ethnicity in French cinema. Her latest book (with Brigitte Rollet) is *Cinema and the Second Sex: Women's Filmmaking in France in the 1980s and 1990s.*

Steven Taubeneck teaches German and is Chair of the Comparative Literature Department at the University of British Columbia. He has a strong interest in contemporary theory as it relates to European cinema.

Peggy Thompson teaches in the department of Theatre, Film and Creative Writing at the University of British Columbia. She wrote screenplays for *The Lotus Eaters,* for which she received a Genie Award for Best Screenplay, and *Better than Chocolate,* and produced and directed *Broken Images,* about photographer Michelle Normoyle. She is co-author of *Hardboiled: Great Lines from Film Noir.*

About the Editors

Jacqueline Levitin teaches in the Department of Women's Studies and the School for the Contemporary Arts (film program) at Simon Fraser University, and has made a number of films, both documentaries and fiction. She is currently working on a documentary about women and housing in the Downtown Eastside of Vancouver.

Judith Plessis is Director of Language Programs and Services at the University of British Columbia. Her research is on women writers who become filmmakers and she is currently working on a book on Margarethe von Trotta.

Valerie Raoul is Professor of French and Women's Studies, and former director of the Centre for Research in Women's Studies and Gender Relations at the University of British Columbia. Her research is on first-person narratives by women, including autobiographical films, with a focus on experiences of illness, trauma, and disability.

Left to right: Judith Plessis, Valerie Raoul, Jacqueline Levitin. Courtesy of Judith Plessis.

Index

Note: "(i)" after a page reference denotes an illustration

NFB *(see* Challenge for Change;
National Film Board; Studio D;
Studio E)
Regards de Femmes (Studio B, NFB),
374-5, 419
themes in films, 189
Vidéo Femmes, 373-4
See also Dirse, Zoe; First Nations
filmmakers; Latinø-Canadian
filmmakers; Longfellow, Brenda;
Mehta, Deepa; Quebec; Weissman,
Aerlyn; Wheeler, Anne; Yang,
Yue-Qing
Canadian (Roja 1978), 358
Carnivalesque
in *Europa, Europa* (Holland 1990),
105-6
in *Nobody Loves Me* (Dörrie 1995),
122-5
in *Seven Beauties* (Wertmüller 1976),
151-6
Carré, Louise, 378, 381
Carter, Sarah, 405
Chadha, Gurinder, 26
Challenge for Change (Studio E,
National Film Board), 424, 427-8
Cham, Mbye, 220, 223
Chanan, Michael, 251, 255, 256-7
Child of the Andes (Mallet 1988), 358-9
Chilean-Canadian films, 356-8, 358-60.
See also Mallet, Marilú
China
Nu Shu language, 264-70
sworn sisterhoods, 268
Yao culture, 268-9
See also Yang, Yue-Qing
Chinese Forest Frog, The (Yang), 265
Chopra, Joyce, 26
Chowdhry, Ranjit, 275, 281n5
Christian, Dorothy, 410-11
Christopher Strong (Arzner 1932), 17
Cinécriture ("filmic writing"), 35
Cinefeminism
cinematography, 434-6, 439-45
écriture féminine, 437-8
feminist theoretical positions, 18
filmmaking in Germany in 1970s, 86
French women filmmakers, 128
"male gaze," 16, 52-3, 434, 436-7
theory vs. practice (1980s), 56-7

See also Imaging of women; "Look-
ing" relations
Cinéma des copines (Switzerland), 191,
194
Cinéma vérité (in documentary films),
254-5
Cinematography, by females, 434-6,
439-45
Ciria, Alberto, 240, 242-3
Cixous, Hélène, 437, 443, 445
Clair, Jean, 46
Clarke, Shirley, 31
Claxton, Dana
Buffalo Bone China (1997), 412, 413
focus on neocolonialism, 398-9
I Want to Know Why (1994), 408-9
The Red Paper (1996), 399, 410
Yuxweluptun, Man of Masks (1998),
399
Clubbed to Death (Zauberman 1997),
323-5
Cohan, Steven, 112
Collier, Colin, 18
Colonization: The Second Coming
(Cuthand 1996), 407
Colour of Britain, The (Parmar 1994),
294-6, 304
*Coquille et le Clergyman, La (The Seashell
and the Clergyman)* (Dulac 1928),
38-9, 41(i), 43-5
Côté, Ghyslaine, 383
Cottenet-Hage, Madeleine, 45, 49
Craig's Wife (Arzner 1936), 17
Cranmer, Barb, 371, 399-401,
400(i)
Crofts, Stephen, 33
Crossroads (Crucero) (Puerta and
Verdecchia 1994), 365-6
Crows (Wrony) (Kędzierzawska 1994),
175-6, 175(i)
Crucero (Crossroads) (Puerta and
Verdecchia 1994), 365-6
C't'à ton tour, Laura Cadieux (Filiatrault
1990), 383
Cuba, 249-50, 255-9. *See also* Gómez,
Sara
Cultura Viva (Living Culture) (Lozano
and Rozo 1997), 362
*CUT: Women Film and Video Makers in
Switzerland* (Blöchlinger 1995), 193

popular vs. *auteur* cinema, 128-9
road movies, 129-30, 133-4, 138
Germany
autobiography and women (1970s on), 182-5
difficulties of filmmaking, 200-1
feminism and filmmaking in 1970s, 86
film industry in 1950s and 1960s, 65-6
films about Berlin Wall, 80-3, 185
Germany, Pale Mother (1979), 65, 66, 68-70, 69(i), 71-6, 183
New German Cinema (1970s on), 67, 68, 80, 180
reunification, 185-6, 200
See also Brückner, Jutta; Dörrie, Doris; Sander, Helke; Sanders Brahms, Helma; von Trotta, Margarethe
Germany, East. *See* East Germany
Germany, Pale Mother (Deutschland, bleiche Mutter) (Sanders Brahms 1979), 69(i)
comments by Sanders Brahms, 71-6
controversy, 68-70
shock post-war, 65, 183
use of "Deutschland," 66, 69
Ghorab-Volta, Zaïda, 323, 325-6
Gidal, Peter, 53
GIFTS (Gulf Islands Film and Television School), 215
Giguère, Nicole, 208-16, 209(i), 373-8
Gilliam, Terry, 205
Giménez, Martha E., 349
Girard, Hélène, 378, 381
Godard, Jean-Luc, 46
Göel, Véronique, 195
Gold Diggers (Potter 1983), 56, 57(i), 110
Gómez, Sara, 250(i)
contribution to Cuban film, 249-50, 256
documentary films, 251-2, 256
Mi aporte (1970), 253-5, 257
One Way or Another (De cierta manera, 1977), 218, 251
politics of time, 249-50, 257
themes of films, 253, 257-9, 260-1
treatment of time and identities, 252
González, Rodrigo, 358
Gorączka (Fever) (Holland 1980), 102
Goretta, Claude, 191

Governess, The (1998), 27
Grandis, Rita de, 342-7
Groulx, Sylvie, 378, 381
Gruben, Patricia, 18
Gulf Islands Film and Television School (GIFTS), 215
Gusner, Iris, 180
Gutierrez, Leopoldo, 358, 361

Hall, Stuart, 410, 413
Hamilton, David, 278
Hammer, Barbara, 18
Hands of History (Todd 1994), 209, 396
Harris, Leslie, 26
Hausheer, Cecilia, 193
Heart Leap (Herzsprung) (Misselwitz 1992), 180, 186
Heinrich, Jutta, 183
Herzsprung (Heart Leap) (Misselwitz 1992), 180, 186
Hesse, Isa, 191
Heyns, Katinka
background, 331-2
Die Storie van Klara Viljee (1991), 333(i), 337-40
Fiela se Kind (Fiela's Child) (1987), 334-7
filmography, 341
Palijas (1997), 332, 332(i), 333(i), 334, 338-40
themes of race, class, and gender, 336-7
Hirtz, Dagmar, 93
Hispanic. *See under* Latin America
Histoires d'amour finissent mal en général, Les (Fontaine 1993), 323-5
Hitchcock, Alfred, 17
Hivon, Julie, 379(i)
Holland, Agnieszka
Angry Harvest (Bittere Ernte) (1985), 171-2
Europa, Europa (1990), 97(i), 98, 102-7, 172-3
exile from Poland, 102-7
Fever (Gorączka) (1980), 102
filmography, 177-8
identity as cultural construct, 104
Olivier, Olivier (1991), 107
Provincial Actors (Aktorzy prowincjonalni) (1978), 97, 99-102, 106-7, 171-2

Printed and bound in Canada by Friesens

Set in Stone by Artegraphica Design Co. Ltd.

Copy editor: Joanne Richardson

Proofreader: Deborah Kerr

Indexer: Patricia Buchanan